COLLECTIVE BEHAVIOR

second edition

RALPH H. TURNER
University of California at Los Angeles

LEWIS M. KILLIAN
University of Massachusetts

PRENTICE-HALL, INC., ENGLEWOOD CLIFFS, NEW JERSEY

Herbert Blumer, Series Editor

ISBN: 0–13–140657–4

Library of Congress Catalog Card Number: 79–167632

PRINTED IN THE UNITED STATES OF AMERICA

10   9   8   7   6   5   4   3   2   1

PRENTICE-HALL INTERNATIONAL, INC., *London*
PRENTICE-HALL OF AUSTRALIA, PTY. LTD., *Sydney*
PRENTICE-HALL OF CANADA, LTD., *Toronto*
PRENTICE-HALL OF INDIA PRIVATE LIMITED, *New Delhi*
PRENTICE-HALL OF JAPAN, INC., *Tokyo*

1659358

165355

CONTENTS

part five
SOCIAL FUNCTIONS
OF COLLECTIVE BEHAVIOR

PREFACE

Our hope for the first edition of this book was that it might provide a baseline, however uneven, from which better maps of the field of collective behavior might be developed. In 1957 only Blumer's brief, though admirable, statement and LaPiere's interesting but unconventional work supplied comprehensive views of the field. Interest as measured by the number of courses offered in colleges and universities was slight. Since publication of our first edition, two other comprehensive statements, by the Langs and by Smelser, have appeared, and the vintage decade of the sixties has stimulated student interest as well as research and publication. Collective behavior is now one of the core fields for investigation and teaching in sociology.

We have retained the basic outline and approach to the field, but have completely rewritten the book. A major aim in the revision has been to incorporate what we have learned from the events of the tumultuous sixties. We have extended our own text relative to the readings, limiting the latter largely to case materials that make abstract principles concrete. We have elaborated and extended some of the distinctive features of our approach, especially the emergent norm framework, for understanding collective behavior. Finally, we have greatly increased the attention to conflict and violence as aspects of collective behavior and as normal features of social life. As before, our book is unique in offering the student a complete and continuous

text with readings carefully integrated into the text.

Since we have drawn upon many disciplines, our treatment may seem incomplete or quixotic to those who do not follow our conception of collective behavior. For example, we have selected excerpts from the vast literature on public opinion with a view to clarifying the public as a functioning collectivity. Consequently we have hardly noted the majority of literature in this field that concerns the psychological dynamics of individual attitudes and opinions. Similarly, our treatment of social movements omits the discussions of political parties that usually are included when movements are viewed from the standpoint of political sociology. At the same time our purpose requires us to seek generalizations applicable to phenomena frequently not viewed together. We look, for example, for principles common to political, religious, and minority movements, and for uniformities of crowd behavior in economic, political, religious, racial, and recreational contexts. In disregarding conventional groupings of materials from other standpoints, we hope we have made some beginning toward their organized treatment as collective behavior.

We are indebted to the many authors and publishers whose materials appear in our book. To our many friends who have steadily encouraged us to complete this work we extend our warmest appreciation. In many of the tasks of securing permissions and manuscript work, Christine Turner has assisted greatly.

The ideas in the book reflect most directly the tradition established by Robert E. Park and Ernest W. Burgess, and subsequently extended by Herbert Blumer. Chief among our teachers whose ideas appear unacknowledged throughout the text are E. S. Bogardus, Hans Gerth, Everett Hughes, and Melvin J. Vincent. The influence of our colleague, Muzafer Sherif, will be evident to any who know his work.

Our greatest debt is to Herbert Blumer. As our teacher, his contribution to our thought has received only token acknowledgment in footnotes. As our editor, he reviewed both this and our first edition with painstaking care. As author of the definitive statement on collective behavior, he has consistently encouraged us to retain in this book our disagreements and departures from his own analysis.

RALPH H. TURNER

LEWIS M. KILLIAN

part one

THE NATURE AND EMERGENCE
OF COLLECTIVE BEHAVIOR

I

THE FIELD OF
COLLECTIVE BEHAVIOR

In the year 1096, in the square before the cathedral at Clermont, Pope Urban II issued his call for a crusade to free the Holy Land. Within a short time the whole of Europe was in a state of unprecedented excitement and feverish activity.

The Crusades

For several months after the Council of Clermont, France and Germany presented a singular spectacle. The pious, the fanatic, the needy, the dissolute, the young and the old, even women and children, and the halt and lame, enrolled themselves by hundreds. In every village the clergy were busied in keeping up the excitement, promising eternal rewards to those who assumed the red cross, and fulminating the most awful denunciations against all the worldly-minded who refused or even hesitated . . . All those who had property of any description rushed to the mart to change it into hard cash. Lands and houses could be had for a quarter of their value, while arms and accoutrements of war rose in the same proportion . . . During the spring and summer of this year (1096) the roads teemed with crusaders, all hastening to the towns and villages appointed as the rendezvous of the district. Some were on horseback, some in carts, and some came down the rivers in boats and rafts, bringing their wives and children, all eager to go to Jerusalem. Very few knew where

From Charles MacKay, *Extraordinary Popular Delusions and the Madness of Crowds* (Boston: L. C. Page and Co., 1932; originally published in London by Richard Bentley, 1841), pp. 365–67.

Jerusalem was. Some thought it fifty miles away, and others imagined that it was but a month's journey; while at sight of every town or castle the children exclaimed, "Is that Jerusalem? Is that the city?"

Nearly a thousand years later, in the United States, hundreds of "crusaders" converged at the call of a modern spiritual leader, Martin Luther King, Jr., to march the fifty miles from Selma to Montgomery, Alabama.

The Selma March

In a growing stream, the marchers assembled in Selma. The men, women, and children who had followed King into the streets and into jail all through the campaign were ready to walk again. And outsiders flocked to his call; clerics and nuns, pert coeds and hot-eyed student rebels; VIP's like the U. N.'s Ralph Bunche and anonymous farmhands from the southwest Alabama cattle, corn and cotton country. A blind man came from Atlanta, a one-legged man from Saginaw, Michigan. An Episcopal minister from Minneapolis got plane fare from a parishioner and took the gift to be a sign from God that he should make the pilgrimage. And a little Selma Negro girl tagged along "for freedom and justice and so the troopers can't hit us no more."

From "The Selma March," copyright Newsweek, Inc., April 5, 1965, p. 25.

Both of these crusades, as far separated in history as they were, raised the same sorts of questions and doubts in the minds of observers. Were the goals as simple and noble as the leaders represented them to be? Were the leaders really devout men of God seeking to overcome the forces of evil, or were they cynical schemers seeking fame, treasure, or power? Were the rank and file of the crusaders, ancient and modern, motivated by sincere religious conviction, or were they, wittingly or unwittingly, really seeking adventure, loot, or publicity? What did these events, which social scientists call social movements, accomplish? After all the sacrifices made by the participants in a social movement, is the course of history significantly altered, and if it is, to what extent is the change in the direction envisioned by the leaders and followers?

The social movement is only one of the forms of human groupings that engages in what the sociologist calls *collective behavior*. The descriptions of the early crusaders gathering in appointed towns and of the modern crusaders converging on the small city of Selma for their march bring to mind the temporary, densely packed, very active assemblage known as the crowd. The relationship between the crowd and the scholars who are interested in collective behavior is a long and close one. During the French Revolution the group known as the *sans-culottes* made up most of the mobs that engaged in food riots and committed much of the violence in Paris, which has attracted the attention of novelists and historians. A modern historian, Bruce Mazlish, argues that one byproduct of the activities of the *sans-culottes* was the development of crowd psychology, which collective behavior is sometimes still called. He says:

It was specifically introduced into the study of the French Revolution by Gustave Le Bon in 1895, but it was already present in the work of Taine and others before that and even earlier as a fear in the minds of the European middle and upper classes. Even so penetrating an observer as Sigmund Freud, as a young man in Paris toward the end of the century, allowed his imagination to carry him away: "The town and the people are uncanny," he wrote, "they seem to be of another species from us. I believe they are all possessed of a thousand demons. ...I hear them screaming '*A la lanterne*' or '*A bas dieser and jener.*' They are the people of psychical epidemics, of historical mass convulsions." In short, the events of 1789 saw the *canaille* give way to the mass (as well as to the mob of the nineteenth and twentieth centuries), at least in the European imagination. To put it more strongly, the actual *sans-culottes* took on mythical shape in the "crowd." It is only recent scholarship that has removed this mask.[1]

This interpretation of the origins of crowd psychology suggests the kinds of questions that the actions of the crowd, particularly when it becomes violent, raise in the minds of observers. Like the young Freud, they wonder what possesses people to make them act in such a wild, extraordinary manner. Are they basically different from the quiet, well-behaved citizens that are usually encountered in daily life? The notion of crowd psychology or mob psychology suggests another explanation—that crowd members are perfectly normal people who react to some unusual type of influence while in the crowd situation. One popular theory is that crowds are made up of normally moral, law-abiding citizens whose "thin veneer of civilization" is stripped away temporarily. Similar questions are raised when large numbers of widely dispersed people seem to lose their usual cautions and inhibitions and take part in speculative crazes or silly fads.

Particularly in modern society, laymen are intrigued by another type of collectivity that the sociologist studies under the heading of collective behavior—the public. The layman does not have any clear conception of what the public is, but he believes in its importance. He is sensitive to how closely his own views correspond to public opinion, and he speculates on what causes changes in public opinion.

The crowd, fads, crazes, the public, and social movements are the subject matter of collective behavior. Some of the questions, which journalists, historians, casual observers, and even the participants themselves raise about these subjects, have been indicated. Because the behavior of people in such collectivities so often contrasts with their routine group activities, seems much more unpredictable, and frequently involves a great deal of excitement, it is not only fascinating but somewhat mysterious to the average person.

The sociologist, familiar as he may be with the many forms that the human group may take, also finds that such types of behavior stimulate novel questions for him. Accustomed to studying the regularities of group life made predictable by stable social structures and traditional norms, he too asks questions about the social and psychological forces that come into play in situations where the usual conventions cease to guide human activities. He has come to use the term collective behavior to distinguish this sort of activity from normal, traditional, or conventional behavior. The sociologist asks questions that are related primarily to the interaction between the individuals who make up a collectivity. How do individuals engaged in collective behavior influence each other? Are the processes of interpersonal influence and the operation of social control similar to those found in ordinary group behavior, or are different ones brought into play? To what extent are the actions of members coordinated with each other? If there is coordination, what is the relative importance of imitation, suggestion, role-taking,

[1] Bruce Mazlish, "The French Revolution in Comparative Perspective," *Political Science Quarterly,* 85 (June, 1970), 255.

and conformity to social norms in producing it? Can it be said that norms exist in a collectivity? If so, how do they develop, what is their relationship to the preexisting norms of the society, and what leads people to conform to them? A common view of collective behavior implies that it consists simply of the violation of usual norms by a large number of people at the same time—that it is disorganized, deviant behavior. The sociologist asks whether there may not be some sort of social organization present and conformity to some norms, no matter how deviant the behavior may seem as measured by ordinary standards.

Since a collectivity is made up of individuals, the sociologist is also concerned with the relationship of the characteristics that these people bring with them to the situation. How do such individual properties as age, education, and socioeconomic status affect the propensity of persons to become involved in collective behavior and the types they will engage in? How much does knowledge of the preexisting attitudes and the personality characteristics of participants help to predict and explain both the emergence and the nature of collective behavior?

It is the fact that people do, at times, collectively engage in behavior that seems to contrast with normal social and institutional behavior that leads the sociologist to define a special field of study. That this behavior appears to be not simply a large number of deviant acts by individuals that happen to occur at the same time, but rather seems to reflect some common influence on the participants or some interaction between them, leads the sociologist to look for the sources of coordination that make the behavior truly collective despite its contrast to conventional group behavior. Three general types of theory have emerged during this quest, each emphasizing a different possible source of coordination. *Convergence* theories focus on the characteristics and predispositions which individuals bring to the situation, suggesting that the simultaneous presence of people who are already similar in some way explains the emergence and the course of action of a collectivity. *Contagion* theories emphasize special psychological mechanisms whereby moods, attitudes, and behavior are communicated rapidly and accepted uncritically. *Emergent norm* theories suggest that collective behavior is regulated by a norm, but a norm that arises in a special situation.

Definition of Collective Behavior

Collective behavior, as a clearly delimited field of sociology, is still relatively new. Gustave Le Bon is often identified as the founder because of his emphasis on the crowd as the prototype of all group behavior.[2] He did not, however, use the term *collective behavior,* and his approach was more psychological than sociological. It was Robert E. Park and Ernest W. Burgess who, in 1921, introduced the term and defined the field as one of the major areas of sociological inquiry.[3] Their analysis was extended by Herbert Blumer, whose definition suggested that collective behavior should occupy a central position in the study of sociology. He stated, "The student of collective behavior seeks to understand the way in which a new social order arises, for the appearance of a new social order is equivalent to the emergence of new forms of collective behavior."[4]

As the field is understood at the present time, it is clearly a division of sociology, not of psychology or even social psychology. Collective behavior refers to the action of collectivities, not to a type of individual

[2] Gustave Le Bon, *The Crowd: A Study of the Popular Mind* (New York: The Viking Press, Inc., 1960; originally published in London by Ernest Benn, Ltd., 1896).
[3] Robert E. Park and Ernest W. Burgess, *Introduction to the Science of Sociology* (Chicago: The University of Chicago Press, 1921), p. 865.
[4] Herbert Blumer, "Collective Behavior," in A. M. Lee, ed., *Principles of Sociology* (New York: Barnes and Noble, Inc., 1951), pp. 168–69.

behavior. For example, an individual may be thrown into a state that would be diagnosed by a psychiatrist as panic, but only the panic of a number of interacting persons is an instance of collective behavior.

As a group, a collectivity is more than simply a number of individuals. A group always consists of people who are in interaction and whose interaction is affected by some sense that they constitute a unit. This latter sense is most universally expressed in the members' concern to define the group's opinions and what the group expects of its members. Thus, the operation of some kind of group norms is a crucial feature of interaction. When we say that collective behavior concerns groups we are referring to the study of individuals interacting in such a manner as to acknowledge and create social norms.

But collective behavior is not merely identical with the study of groups. A contrast is generally drawn between collective behavior and organizational behavior. Organizational behavior is the behavior of groups that are governed by established rules of procedure, which have the force of tradition behind them. Even in the case of a new organization, there is generally a concern to find operating rules that have sanction in the larger culture, such as Robert's *Rules of Order,* and any action once taken becomes an incipient tradition through the principle of observing precedent. Collectivities, or the groups within which collective behavior takes place, are not guided in a straightforward fashion by the culture of the society, however. Although a collectivity has members, it lacks defined procedures for selecting and identifying members. Although it has leaders, it lacks defined procedures for selecting and identifying them. The members are those who happen to be participating, and the leaders are those who are being followed by the members. The collectivity is oriented toward an object of attention and arrives at some shared objective, but

these are not defined in advance, and there are no formal procedures for reaching decisions.

There is coordination of at least an elementary sort between the individual members' actions. In some instances, such as panic flight, the behavior of each individual is similar and parallel to that of the others, and the behavior of all is directed toward the same objective. In other cases, a division of labor may be discerned in the collectivity, giving the impression of a more complex coordination of the members. Yet the coordination and direction do not seem amenable to explanation in terms of established norms, preexisting social organization, or primary-group integration. There exists, nevertheless, a sense of constraint that forces individuals into certain types of behavior and leads to punishment of nonconformity. The task of studying collective behavior involves identification of the sources of this coordination and exploration of the relationship to ordinary social behavior.

Collective behavior may be even more sharply contrasted with institutional behavior. Institutional behavior characterizes groups that are envisaged in and guided by the culture of the larger society. Accordingly, institutional behavior refers to activities that are necessary to the conduct of society's business, which support the norms of the larger society. Collective behavior, on the other hand, seems to be governed by norms that are not envisaged in the larger society and that may even modify or oppose these broader norms.

The relation of collective behavior or certain other areas—such as small groups, the study of informal groups in industry and other formal associations, and social psychology—is somewhat more complex. Groups may be classified by different criteria. The area of collective behavior is based upon a classification of groups according to the nature of the social norms that govern them. The field of small groups is based upon a classification of groups according to size. The two systems of classification overlap, so that collective behavior may be found in both small and large groups, and small groups may exhibit either collective or organizational behavior.

So-called informal groups may have certain features of collective behavior. Generally, however, they have a continuity of membership, leadership, and norms that limit the incidence of collective behavior. Furthermore, they are usually studied from the standpoint of their effect upon formally organized associations that they operate in. Thus interest is not concentrated upon the collective-behavior aspects of informal groups. However, it appears again that there is an overlapping between the study of collective behavior and informal groups because their isolation as areas of subject matter is based upon two somewhat different dimensions of classification.

Finally, collective behavior is to be distinguished from social psychology. In collective behavior the absence of tradition-imposed stability leaves more room for group patterns to be shaped by the attitudes of individual members than in regularly organized groups. Consequently collective behavior acknowledges that the group is composed of interacting individuals. The collectivity rather than the individual is the ultimate center of interest.

Recurring Issues in Collective Behavior

Collective behavior is not yet an area in which generalizations can be presented in precise form with the backing of experimental or quantitative evidence. There is no dearth of ideas derived from historical analysis and from the impressionistic examination of cases. But few steps have yet been taken toward the verification of these ideas through more rigorous procedures. Consequently, collective behavior abounds with, as yet, unresolved issues that must not be prejudged.

Among the issues, however, there are some that rest on semantic confusion, obvious oversimplification, or sheer dogmatism. These issues are used to assign students to "schools of thought" which can be dealt with by name-calling. Such issues impede communication that might lead to discovery of convergences of thought, and by requiring that each person "show his colors," they prevent each faction from modifying its viewpoint to take account of valid observations by the other. Likewise, these pseudoissues divert attention from many issues of real importance.

By eliminating certain major pseudoissues and by trying to state other issues in their essential terms, it may be possible to avoid some of the false leads found in the literature on collective behaviors. With this objective in mind, we shall briefly examine two groups of issues. First, we shall attempt to separate semantic from empirical questions in the so-called group mind problem. Second, we shall consider the justification for describing collective behavior in terms of irrationality or emotional behavior and for the use of such terms as *emotional contagion*.

THE GROUP MIND ISSUE. A great deal of heat has been generated as to whether there is a group mind, whether the group is something other than the sum of individual responses, and similar questions. These issues have received unusual attention in the area of collective behavior, where the studies of individual and group behavior tend to merge. Accusations of "group mind fallacy" and "individualistic fallacy" have been freely hurled. Some of the confusion lies in the fact that not one but several questions are actually involved. By looking at some of these questions separately, we may be able to eliminate spurious issues and clarify the legitimate points of disagreement.

The first question is how to describe group activity. A group is both many individuals and a totality. Groups tend to impress observers more strongly as wholes, with the result that descriptions usually are cast in terms of the group's acting and reacting, rather than the separate member's. We hear that "the mob attacked its victim" or "the public favored a particular course of action." There are dangers in this prevalent way of describing group behavior. In the first place, it is often a serious oversimplification. By thinking in these terms we may be blinded to any diversity of individual behavior or differing degree of individual conviction backing up the apparent behavior of the group.

In the second place, the description of group behavior as the actions of a total unit often leads us to think of the group through analogies derived from individual behavior. Here we find the tendency to attribute to the group a mind, a conscience, a sense of responsibility, a lack of self-control, or a sense of self-esteem. A shift in crowd behavior is the crowd "changing its mind," as if a group could change its mind in the same sense as an individual does. These tendencies to personify the group are accentuated in those spectacular instances of crowd behavior that arouse our indignation and make us seek something that can be an object of moral blame.

In order to escape these fallacies, some investigators insist that only the behavior of individuals can be described. But this solution is not without danger. In its most naive form it becomes a mere semantic sleight of hand whereby the action of the group is restated as though applying to each of its members. Thus we may be told that the members of the crowd attacked their victim. The same danger of overlooking complexity applies here as in group description. And the danger of thinking in terms of analogy between the individual and group remains but in changed form. The tendency is to impute to the individual members of the group the motives and attitudes that would explain the action of the total group—if it had been the action of an individual. Thus the explanation of

war is sought by attributing hostile attitudes to the members of the warring nations. Because individuals usually fight each other only when they feel hatred toward one another, it is assumed that war eventuates from the hatred that members of the warring nations feel toward one another. Modern research on war has demonstrated clearly that this is not so, but the pattern of thinking continues to be applied to group behavior in many ways.

Even when these fallacies are assiduously avoided, simple description of individual actions is likely to be both inefficient and incomplete. Where something more than an aggregation exists, some division of labor inevitably arises, and individual behavior is patterned into roles that in some way complement one another in furthering a group objective. In a lynching, the individuals who bring ropes are not necessarily interested in ropes per se; those who threaten the sheriff are not distinguished by their hatred of sheriffs. In each instance these are tasks that fall into place as part of the total objective of lynching, and what one man does is determined in part by what others have left to be done. Specifying the general end and pattern of behavior in the group may be more useful than detailed accounts of individual behavior, and they will most certainly provide the necessary orientation for interpreting the individual behavior.

There is a place for both group and individual types of description, when the respective sets of fallacies can be avoided. Neither the group nor the individual descriptive approach is inherently more error-free than the other. Each type of description completes the other. Which will be given priority depends on the purpose at hand. Groups as wholes have effects on society, and they tend to be perceived as wholes. To the degree to which we are interested in society, then individual description will be subordinated to group description. When groups are of interest only as contexts for the study of individual psychological processes, group description will be subordinated but not omitted.

A second question involved in the group-versus-individual issue concerns whether the individual in the group acts differently from the way he would act if not in the group. Answers have ranged from one extreme view—that the group suffuses its members with attitudes and motives that have no counterparts in their individual psyches—to the opposing view—that the group is no more than several individuals with common purposes doing what each as an individual would be doing anyway. Actually, neither extreme answer has often been given. The individualists have admitted that division of labor takes place and that the intensity of behavior may be heightened by the presence of like-minded persons, while contending that the behavior remains an expression of attitudes that were present in the individual originally. The group mind advocates have often meant only that there is a decision-making process, which takes place on a group basis, reaching conclusions that would not have eventuated from individual decision making.

Many of the discrepancies between these points of view vanish when certain observations are made. First, a person seldom has a single, clear-cut attitude on any given matter. The typical American is both for and against granting Negroes equality with whites; the typical laborer conceives of himself as both opposed to and identified with his employer. Not all attitudes on a given question are equally well recognized by the individual. In the extreme case of repression the actor possesses attitudes that affect his behavior but that he would vigorously disclaim. Consequently, any individual can find attitudinal support for a variety of actions regarding any particular object. In a group situation certain attitudes are elicited and reinforced, so that individuals act in accordance with attitudes that would not necessarily have become

dominant had they been acting as individuals.

Second, action is a consequence not merely of attitudes toward the object in question but of attitudes toward the group, toward the self, and toward many others. A man who fears a crowd may conform to a course of action that is not in accordance with any of his attitudes toward the object in question. A man who conceives of himself as a leader may sense the direction in which the group decision is going and actively espouse it in order to retain leadership. His private attitudes toward that course of action may be different.

For these reasons it is entirely appropriate and not in the least mystical to speak of collective decision making. Group decisions and group actions could never have been predicted simply by the summing up of individual attitudes. At the same time, the attitudes of the individuals, both toward the object in question and toward matters that become indirectly involved, do make decisions in certain directions easier to obtain than decisions in other directions, and will render other potential decisions impossible. Thus both the processes of group decision making and individual attitudes must be taken into account. The individual in the group does indeed act differently from the way in which he would if alone, though not without some basis for this action in his own attitudes.

Answers to these two questions indicate the answer to the final question. Some have argued that since the only real actions are the actions of individuals, there can be no special set of principles governing group action but merely the application of the psychology of individual behavior to action in a group context. Experience has demonstrated that at the group level regularities can be observed and generalizations formulated quite apart from the understanding of individual psychological principles underlying them. Best documented are the regularities of economic behavior. Study of the individual processes, which culminate in these observed regularities of economic functioning, is a useful type of investigation but does not take the place of generalizations at the collective level. Animals and plants are made of chemicals, but generalizations at the chemical level do not take the place of generalizations about the characteristics of plants or animals. Similarly, generalizations at the group level are needed and can be made, whether the individual psychological processes underlying the group are understood or not. Each level of investigation can benefit by cues from the other, so investigators at one level keep informed of developments at the other. Each benefits from advances at the other level, but each level has its own generalizations to develop.

IRRATIONALITY AND EMOTIONALITY. Another recurring problem in collective behavior is the tendency to single out for study only those collective phenomena of which the observer disapproves and to depict the processes of collective behavior in value-laden terms. Alarm about destructive mobs, panics, and revolutionary or totalitarian social movements is reflected in this tendency. On this basis collective behavior is often erroneously contrasted to rational behavior by being designated irrational or emotional. There are two important errors involved in approaching collective behavior in this way.

In the first place, the terms *irrational* and *emotional* have reference to individual behavior. In accordance with our discussion of the group mind problems, the application of these terms to the group means one of two things. Either it is a shorthand way of saying that each of the members in the collectivity is acting irrationally, or it is reasoning by analogy that a group, like an individual, can be emotional or irrational. The latter procedure we recognize as fallacious, and the former assumption of homogeneity among members of collec-

tivities is not supported by our knowledge.

In the second place, the very distinctions themselves are difficult to make. Emotion and reason are not today regarded as irreconcilables. Emotion may accompany the execution of a well-reasoned plan, and the execution of an inadequately reasoned plan may be accompanied by no arousal of emotions.

The rational-irrational dichotomy seems to have two distinct kinds of meanings. Based on external criteria, behavior can be called rational when it is an efficient way of achieving some goal. By this definition much institutional behavior is irrational and much collective behavior is rational. In the light of the widespread and increasing use of marijuana among young people in the United States, one might argue that the passage of existing drug-control laws constituted irrational action, even though it was done within the institutional framework. In contrast, the destructive ghetto insurrections of the 1960s might be viewed as rational because they did serve to focus attention on certain problems and to evoke relief measures, which more deliberative and institutionalized approaches had not secured.

Using internal criteria, behavior is irrational when the individual does not weigh all the possible alternatives of which he can be aware in deciding his course of action. By this definition most institutional behavior is irrational, since social norms narrow the range of alternatives that the individual or the group can effectively consider. For example, the famous court-martial of General Billy Mitchell was almost certain to result in a conviction, since he made no attempt to prove that he had not publicly criticized the policies of his superior officers in defiance of orders. Although history would soon prove that his criticisms were well grounded, the norms of the military system did not provide for excusing deliberate defiance of official policy on the grounds that the dissenter might be right. Thus collective behavior is not different from other types of behavior in regard to restricting attention within the range of potential alternatives. When people, attempting to escape from a burning building, pile up at a single exit, their behavior appears highly irrational to someone who learns after the panic that other exits were available. To the actor in the situation, who does not recognize the existence of these alternatives, attempting to fight his way to the only exit available may seem a very logical choice as opposed to burning to death. Indeed, a large proportion of human behavior appears irrational when it is subjected to after-the-fact analysis.

The basis for these errors lies in the fact that in folk-usage we tend to confuse rationality with behavior in conformity with the dictates of culture. When an individual uncritically follows the courses of action that are sanctioned in his society, we think of him as a reasonable person, largely because he is (1) like us and (2) predictable and therefore easy to deal with. When a person challenges the established dictates or is forced to act when cultural dictates are nonexistent, vague, or contradictory, his behavior becomes unpredictable to others about him, making him hard to deal with, and his fellows may find it difficult to understand his behavior. Hence he is said to be acting emotionally or irrationally. This discussion brings us back to our definition of collective behavior: the action of groups that operate without clear-cut direction from their culture. To refer to this behavior as irrational or emotional is either fallacious or tautological.

ORGANIZATION OF THE BOOK. Collective behavior encompasses the activities of many kinds of collectivities, from the short-lived, compact crowd to the enduring, dispersed social movement. But the same principles underlie the development of the various forms of collective behavior, and the same

elementary processes are involved in all forms. Historically, since the early writings of Le Bon, the crowd has been regarded as the form of collectivity in which the operation of the basic mechanisms could best be observed. As Robert Merton observes of Le Bon's writing:

> But in devoting much attention to the short-lived aggregations that form political mobs as well as to longer-lived publics and even more enduring social classes, Le Bon in effect seized upon strategic occasions for studying processes of collective behavior by studying them where they were highly visible.[5]

In this spirit the balance of Part One will employ the crowd principally as a model for examining the elementary forms and processes that characterize a wide range of collective behavior. The main theoretical approaches to collective behavior, briefly mentioned above, will be examined at length in Chapter 2. The communication most characteristic of collective behavior, with emphasis on rumor, is the subject of Chapter 3. Whether characteristic forms of communication develop and whether they eventuate in fully developed forms of collective behavior depends on the presence of conditions that are conducive to the emergence of collective behavior, and these will be explored next.

In Part Two our attention shifts toward fully developed crowd forms, though the processes continue to have broader applicability than to crowds alone. Chapters 5 and 6 compare the types of behavioral coordination that lead to either individualistic or solidaristic tendencies in the crowd and the forms of symbolization that give the crowd either expressive or active modes of behavior. Next the principles governing compact crowds are extended and supplemented to explain diffuse crowd forms, in-

[5] Robert Merton, "Introduction" to Compass Edition, Gustave Le Bon, *The Crowd: A Study of the Popular Mind* (New York: The Viking Press, Inc., 1960), p. xii.

cluding fads and crazes. In Chapters 8 and 9 manipulation, control, and conventionalization of collective behavior will be examined as they appear in the crowd.

Publics constitute a form of collective behavior in many respects similar to crowds but in crucial respects quite different. Since publics and public opinion occupy a pivotal location in all theories of democracy, an adequate understanding of their processes is of more than merely academic concern. In Part Three, the distinctive nature of publics is explored, and the manner in which public opinion forms and changes is outlined in general terms. In Chapter 11 this simple conception of the public and its processes is refined to take account of the intimate relationship between publics and established community structure. Finally, in Chapter 12, the impact of conflict on the processes of public opinion formation is reviewed.

The most extensive, continuous, and well-organized form of collectivity is the social movement. It is most likely to have broad and enduring effects on the social order, and other forms of collectivities achieve their greatest significance when they are related to social movements. Part Four is devoted to the processes and forms of social movements. The nature of social movements and the elements of an approach to their study occupy Chapter 13. Some of the preconditions to the development of a major social movement, organized about a pervasive public redefinition of what constitutes an injustice, are enumerated in Chapter 14. The characteristics and sources of the goals and ideologies of social movements are the subject of Chapter 15. Strategies in the exercise of power and tendencies for power considerations to subvert goals and ideology are examined in Chapter 16. Next we note the transformations effected in social movements when conflict comes to dominate their relations, as in the case of revolutionary movements, and when their immediate goals are separation from a parent community. A movement ceases to exist without a loyal and enthusiastic membership. Hence in Chapters 18 and 19 we examine the determinants of member commitment, the mechanisms by which movements control members, the sources of defection, and the effects of the members' satisfaction in a movement on the course followed by the movement. Finally, Chapter 20 describes varied types of organization and leadership and their effects on social movements.

The last section, Part Five, seeks to relate collective behavior to the ongoing life of the larger society. Drawing upon the answers supplied in the earlier sections, we examine the part that collective behavior plays in the maintenance of stability and the promotion of change in society. Were collective behavior merely an inconsequential byproduct of underlying historical forces that causes social change, it would constitute only sound and fury deserving little sociological study. But it is the position of this book that collective behavior is the form of human action through which social change is effected and that the institutionalization of collective behavior is one of the important ways in which social stability is maintained.

2

APPROACHES
TO THE CROWD

One of the salient characteristics of all collective behavior is the appearance of unanimity that it creates. To the casual observer, the numerous members of a crowd may appear to act in an identical fashion, dominated by a common impulse. So strong is this illusion of unanimity that it is easy to speak of the crowd in the singular, as if it were a real being—"the crowd roars," "the angry mob surges forward." Countless laymen who have never heard of Gustave Le Bon and "the mental unity of crowds" speak glibly of "the mob mind" and "mob psychology." Similarly, characterizations of crowd behavior formulated by sociologists and psychologists have resulted in a picture of a homogeneous mass of individuals, all thinking, feeling, and acting alike.

Yet another widespread conception of the crowd is the notion that the members are almost always individuals of low social status, with little education, who are personally insecure and unstable. While specific exceptions, particularly in crowd leaders, are often noted, the stereotype of the crowd as an undifferentiated rabble of poorly educated, low-status, highly suggestible individuals persists.

Thus many existing formulations of crowd behavior seem to present a picture of a mass of people who are, in one way or another, identical. At one extreme is the popular stereotype of the crowd as composed of people who are identical in social position, in motives, and in behavior. Approaching most closely the usual, empirical crowd phenomena is a conception of a collection of individuals who may be heterogeneous in many ways, particularly in initial motivation, but who go through an identical process as crowd action develops. It is this latter conception that suggests such familiar explanations as the operation of suggestion, hysteria or emotional contagion. Most sociological study of collective behavior, from the early work of Le Bon through modern American treatments, has emphasized some form of contagion whereby unanimous, intense feelings and behavior, at variance with usual predispositions, are induced among the members of a collectivity.

Contagion Theory

A form of crowd behavior that readily suggests the operation of some sort of contagion is that in which a form of highly visible, unusual, bodily behavior spreads rapidly through people assembled in one place. The panic flight of a crowd seems to constitute one such form. Historically, epidemics of bizarre behavior, such as the "Dancing Mania" of the Middle Ages, have seemed to represent the operation of social contagion in its purest form. The description of the following contemporary case, labeled an epidemic, shows that such bizarre instances of behavioral contagion have lost neither their fascination nor their mystery for observers.

Epidemic Hysteria

In the generations that have passed since such occurrences at the "dancing mania" or fits en masse in a nunnery, epidemic hysteria has seemed to disappear. Or has it? A recent instance, affecting nearly a third of the 550 pupils of a Church of England girls' school in Blackburn, Lancashire, has now been reported to the *British Medical Journal* by Peter D. Moss, a pediatrician at the local hospital, and Colin P. McEvedy, a London psychiatrist. An intensive survey of faculty and students revealed that on the first day of the epidemic, a Thursday, 141 girls complained of dizziness, fainting, shivering, tooth-chattering, headache, nausea, and similar symptoms. Eighty-five of the girls were hospitalized and school was dismissed for a long weekend. When classes resumed on Monday, 79 girls made similar complaints and 54 were hospitalized; school was then dismissed for the rest of the week. The next Monday, 11 days after the initial outbreak, 58 girls made the same complaints; none were hospitalized and that day's episode was the final event in the waning epidemic.

Noting that the girls were not malingering and the school staff was not being deceived, Moss and McEvedy report that in spite of intensive studies no possible physical basis for the incident could be discovered. The investigators learned, however, that on the day before the initial outbreak the student body had constituted the audience at a ceremony under royal patronage performed at the Anglican cathedral in Blackburn. The ceremony was notable for a three-hour delay during which

20 of the schoolgirls had to break ranks and lie down because of faintness. On at least one school bus the next morning an air of excitement prevailed and there was much discussion about who had fainted and how often. "The stage," Moss and McEvedy write, "was set."

During the first two morning periods that day 10 girls complained of faintness. They were sent to sit on chairs in the school's central corridor, but a teacher who feared they might hurt themselves should they actually faint and fall had them lie on the corridor floor instead. The 10 girls were thus seen in this position by the rest of the student body at morning recess; the hysteria became epidemic and soon reached a rate of one collapse per minute.

The ceremony at the cathedral was almost certainly the trigger; all 20 of the girls affected on that occasion collapsed again on the first day of the school epidemic, whereas not one of nine girls who had been absent was affected. A pattern of repeaters was also evident; 95 of the girls stricken on the first day of the school epidemic were present the following Monday and 51 of them succumbed for a second time. Moreover, of the 58 girls stricken on the last day of the epidemic, 52 had been victims in either the first or the second outbreak.

Pointing out that abnormally rapid breathing, a common result of panic, can produce all the symptoms of which the girls complained, the investigators conclude that whatever the triggering effect of the cathedral incident the victim's emotional vulnerability probably arose from a general anxiety existing in Blackburn because of a recent outbreak of poliomyelitis.

When the term *epidemic*, borrowed from the language of medicine, is used, the question arises, What is the mechanism for the spread of the infection? No germ theory is implied, despite the suggestiveness of the term *contagion*. Instead, powerful psychological mechanisms have been invoked to explain the rapid spread of emotional states and behavior. Walter Bagehot and Gabriel Tarde argued that the universal and elemental tendency of men to imitate was the explanation not only of collective behavior but also of traditional forms of social behavior. Thus Tarde undertook to build a whole theory of society on the basis of the laws of imitation. The herd instinct or gregariousness postulated by Wilfred Trotter[1] was similar to the tendency toward imitation proposed by Tarde. To Trotter, as to Tarde, crowd behavior and other forms of social behavior were to be explained by psychological mechanisms that maximized the homogeneity of the collectivity. When applied to crowd behavior, this view suggests a simplistic model of the crowd as an undifferentiated collection of persons imitating each other or a leader uniformly and impulsively.

The mechanism of contagion most widely relied on is *suggestion*. Whereas reliance on the concept of imitation suggests continuity between crowd behavior and organized group behavior, the notion of suggestion leads to a search for special circumstances under which individuals become unusually suggestible and therefore subject to what Le Bon called "the law of the mental unity of crowds." Le Bon advanced the prototype of the most common explanation of the suggestibility of people in a crowd. This explanation rests, first, on the effect of numbers. In Le Bon's words:

> ...The individual forming part of a crowd acquires, solely from numerical considerations, a sentiment of invincible power which allows him to yield to instincts which had he been alone, he would have perforce kept under restraint. He will be the less disposed to check himself from the consideration that, a crowd being anonymous, and in consequence irresponsible, the sentiment of responsibility which always controls individuals disappears entirely.[2]

But in addition to the sense of invincibility and anonymity that numbers engender, Le Bon postulated another essential mechanism: the operation of unconscious, instinctual forces, which are released by the crowd situation. This corresponds to the popular notion of man as a creature possessing a thin veneer of civilization, which may easily be stripped away. There is the implication that social control ceases to operate in the crowd and that the influence of social norms is replaced by the operation of an individual, psychological mechanism. However, it may be explained, this mechanism consists of interindividual influence, not of social influence operating through norms and sanctions. The crowd leader and the crowd itself are often described as being analagous to a hypnotist. The suggestible individual is viewed as becoming selectively and uncritically responsive to suggestions emanating from this source.

Rather than relying on the concept of suggestion, Herbert Blumer proposed another mechanism to account for the condition of unanimity and emotional intensity that seems to prevail in the crowd.[3] This was *circular reaction,* which he contrasted with *interpretative reaction.*

Interpretative interaction is what we see in behavior such as a calm conversation between two people. One states a proposition. The other evaluates it, tries to understand what the first speaker means, and answers with a response of his own which may agree with, modify, or contradict the initial statement. This process of interaction, interpretation, and adjustment goes on as each partner attempts to take the role of the other. If the discussion becomes heated, circular reaction may be observed. As one participant in the debate speaks in a loud, angry tone, the other may answer in an even louder voice. As the in-

---

[1] Wilfred Trotter, *Instincts of the Herd in Peace and War: 1916–1919,* 2nd ed. (London: Oxford University Press, 1919).

[2] Gustave Le Bon, *The Crowd,* 1st ed. 1895 (New York: The Viking Press, Inc., 1960), p. 30.

[3] Herbert Blumer, "Collective Behavior," in A. M. Lee, ed., *Principles of Sociology* (New York: Barnes and Noble, Inc., 1953).

teraction proceeds, the loudness of each speaker increases until the debate reaches the shouting stage. As the two become angrier, each may pay less and less attention to the meaning of the other's words. The conversation degenerates into an exchange of accusations or insults rather than a reciprocal exploration of points of view.

The interpretative interaction, the response of one actor to the behavior of another is mediated through the meaning attached to the behavior. The response to the stimulus of another's act is a delayed, critical response. It is typically different from the stimulus behavior, being an adjustment to it. This, according to the theory of symbolic interaction, is characteristic of behavior in normal, structured groups. In circular reaction, which is characteristic of the crowd, the response follows directly upon the stimulus behavior and reproduces it. The response becomes, in turn, the stimulus to call forth a repetition of the same behavior in the first actor.

Feelings, and behavior which reflects these feelings, are central to Blumer's theory of both the causes and the effects of circular reaction. A state of unrest, caused by disturbance of the ordinary routine of group life and reflected in feelings of inner tension, interferes with the interpretative interaction and sets the stage for circular reaction. Since individual unrest is basically an emotional state, it is essentially feelings or emotions that are communicated through circular reaction. As excitement spreads and is intensified, the self-consciousness of individuals and their ability to interpret the behavior of others is lowered, and the prevailing mood and form of behavior spread rapidly and irresistibly. The usual forms of social control cease to operate. There is, in effect, an absence of social norms for the time being.

Instead of suggestibility, Sigmund Freud proposed *identification* as the mechanism that explains the development of unanimity in the crowd. This proposal emphasizes the importance of the leader, for identification is held to develop out of love of a leader.[4] Yet there appear to be many instances in which leadership in a crowd shifts. Often, too, the leader emerges only after a great deal of crowd development has already taken place. Again, the notion of identification emphasizes the importance of a common feeling or mood as the factor that makes individuals susceptible to social contagion.

Ladd Wheeler, a psychologist, has suggested two processes, *social facilitation* and *behavioral contagion,* to explain some instances of the spread of behavior.[5] Explanation in terms of either process assumes that the action which the actor initiates already exists in his repertoire of responses but is not exhibited initially. In the case of social facilitation, the action of the model, the person who is imitated, simply reminds the imitator of this form of behavior, and he then engages in it. Wheeler cites as an example how when one person lights a cigarette, a number of other habitual smokers in his presence may light up. This occurs, he suggests, even when they have not been previously prohibited from smoking, and some may not even be aware that they have engaged in the behavior.

Wheeler reserves the term *behavioral contagion* for a process in which the act of the model reduces restraints that have been keeping his imitators from engaging in the same type of activity. The restraints may be external, as when a forbidding authority figure is present, or they may be internal in the form of fear that guilt and regret will follow the action. The model's behavior may remove the external restraints by demonstrating that one can get away with the behavior. Internal restraints may be

4 Sigmund Freud, *Group Psychology and the Analysis of the Ego,* trans. J. Strachey (London: The Hogarth Press Ltd., 1922).
5 Ladd Wheeler, "Toward a Theory of Behavioral Contagion," *Psychological Review,* 73 (March, 1966), 179–92.

removed if the model is the kind of person who makes his imitators feel that the behavior must be all right, not immoral or improper, if he engages in it. This effect is contingent upon the absence of overt disapproval of the model's behavior by other group members. Wheeler describes the cumulative effect of this kind of behavioral contagion in his statement, "In general, when the restraints are group derived and a group member performs the forbidden act, the behavior should spread quickly throughout the group. Every member that performs the act reduces the restraints further."[6]

Wheeler's analysis suggests that the contagion theory is useful in explaining the rapid dissemination of a type of behavior among people who are already inclined to act in that particular manner. With its emphasis on the removal of restraints, the concept of behavioral contagion differs from that of social pressure. The latter, as Wheeler points out, forces a person to engage in behavior that goes against his inclinations.

The notion that collective behavior develops primarily through some form of contagion assumes a degree of uniformity in the collectivity that may be exceptional rather than typical. Even in the case of epidemic hysteria described earlier, only a minority of the girls exposed to the hysterical behavior reproduced it themselves. In other cases of collective behavior, even crowd participants who engage in what seem to be similar forms of behavior may not be experiencing the same feelings. Not all those who flee in panic flight necessarily do so because of wild, uncontrollable terror. There may be varying degrees of fear, and for some, the action may be quite deliberate. Most important, it may be that the development in the crowd of a dominant mode of behavior, which is not contradicted even by those members who do not participate in it, reflects the imposition of a new norm, not the dissolution of all norms and the abrogation of social control. The introspective account of a participant in a highly emotional crowd situation reveals individual differences in responses to behavior, which to an outside observer, might well have appeared to be contagious.

---

[6] Ibid., p. 188.

Weekend Retreat

Robert W. Hamilton

The occasion was a weekend religious retreat up in the mountains of Southern California near Big Bear Lake. It was a conference composed largely of about forty university students and a few working people, most of whom were of college age. The retreat was under the direction of the Presbyterian Church and the participants were mainly of the denomination although there was a scattered representation from other churches as well.

Throughout Friday and during the day on Saturday, things progressed smoothly and according to plan. There was recreation, group Bible study, short sermons, singing, etc. On Saturday night, however, there occurred a phenomenon known as the "fellowship of the burning heart." This procedure is a fairly well-established practice within the Presbyterian Church for Sunday evening gatherings of youth groups and Christian Endeavor societies. It is a fairly routinized affair, with the same people arising to speak and to give testimonies regarding answers to prayer for some relative or friend, the benefits that one has obtained from studying a particular portion of scripture, etc. It is a very business-like arrangement with relatively little emotion involved. It was

Student paper, U.C.L.A., reprinted by permission.

against this background that the activities of this Saturday night took place.

At first everything proceeded along the familiar pattern. The church extrovert led a chorus of songs just as he had for years. An assistant pastor spoke briefly on the difficulties of keeping the faith and leading a Christian life in modern times, particularly in the University environment. The only variation from the established Sunday evening pattern at the church was the physical surroundings. Logs had been laid out in a semi-circle amid a clearing in the trees on a hillside, in a type of amphitheatre arrangement. Down where the speaker stood was a small bonfire.

The assistant pastor closed his message with a prayer and asked if "anyone felt led to give a brief testimony." The first few testimonies were of the orthodox variety. One girl, a perennial testimony-giver since her high school days, said how much the retreat had benefitted her and advocated that they become regular monthly affairs. There were several others in a similar vein. Then there arose a girl who had long been a member of the church, who was considered one of the most attractive and popular girls, and who very rarely said anything at any of these meetings. She asserted that during her individual meditation period down by the stream that afternoon, and again while she had been sitting in the meeting praying that night, the Lord had spoken to her "in a very real way," and that she trusted that God would give her the strength to say what was upon her heart. She then went on to relate, amidst sobs, that although she had been a member of the Church for a long time and had always considered herself a Christian, she never really knew Christ, and that through her own selfish will and because of the hardness of her heart, she had prevented Christ from actually coming into her life. She then said that now, in front of her friends, she would like to "confess Christ as my personal savior for I know now for the first time in my life what it really means to be born again." The atmosphere of the meeting changed sharply, from one of mere token reverence to absolute silence. When this girl had arisen to speak, everyone had turned his head to look at her, but as she spoke and sobbed people either stared at the ground or buried their heads in their hands. The silence was broken only

by the words of the assistant pastor who at the conclusion of the testimony commented, "The Lord bless you." Another girl then got up and said that she had been violating all of the principles of Christian love—that she had been envious of two other girls present because of their popularity with the group and because of their fine clothes. Another arose and said that she had been guilty of spreading false rumors about another girl's behavior, called her by name, and asked forgiveness of the Lord and of the girl she had offended. All of these confessions were accompanied by tears. A fellow (a long-time personal friend of mine) stood up and said that what he was about to do was the hardest thing in his life. He then proceeded to relate that when he was in the army overseas he had been living in sin with a German girl. (The girl to whom he was presently engaged was also present that night.) One girl arose and claimed that her mind had been deteriorating for some time and that she didn't *think,* she *knew* that she was going insane, but felt that the Lord was still with her. The testimonies then reverted to the confessional pattern again. One after another individuals would arise, confessing everything from cheating on exams to fornication, each apparently outdoing the preceding in describing the intensity of his sinfulness.

While all this was taking place, individuals at different intervals would slip to their knees, turn around and place their heads on the logs in prayer. This procedure was eventually followed by about three-quarters of those present. It should be mentioned here that, unlike Roman Catholics and Episcopalians, Presbyterians and other evangelical Protestants never kneel when they pray, but merely bow their heads while sitting or even standing. Presbyterians like to think that in this manner they are placing a more proper emphasis on attitude and spirit than upon form and ritual, so that this kneeling represented a considerable deviation from the usual Calvinistic simplicity. The testimonies continued on for about an hour and a half although they usually last no more than ten or fifteen minutes.

Finally, one young man whom I knew, who was studying for the ministry, arose and made the following statement: "I have been examining my heart to determine whether there was something wrong in my life which was preventing me from obtaining the same sort of spiritual blessings which others have evidently been receiving here tonight. Rather I believe the nature of these activities here tonight are in conflict with our Protestant heritage and hinder rather than encourage our Christian development. One of the primary benefits of the reformation was the recognition of an individual's right to immediate access to his God without the necessary mediation of a priest or anyone else. I think that many of the things which have been said here tonight might better have been said in private prayer to our Lord rather than through public confession." After this there was a long period of silence as no one seemed inclined to speak, and all remained absolutely stationary. Finally the assistant pastor said, "Let us pray." In his prayer he spoke of the varieties of religious experience in Protestantism and how "the Lord speaks to his children in diverse ways." Following his prayer, the meeting began to break up. Slowly the individuals would arise, dust themselves off, and make their way down the hill back to their quarters. In the main individuals walked alone and even among those who were in pairs or groups, there was no conversation. I heard only one comment which was, "Well, the Lord's presence was certainly felt tonight."

During the confessions there were not any conversations, but the sobbing, choked voices giving testimonies, and the bowing of heads, with individuals kneeling all about, could not help but convey attitudes and sentiments throughout the group and develop a common mood. As one person after the other got up to confess the most personal of sins, individuals began to examine their own consciences, and felt compelled to "get it off their chest." As a member of the crowd, I know that I myself experienced similar feelings. At first I felt extremely uncomfortable in that environment and eagerly awaited the end of these proceedings. I had enjoyed the activities of the weekend, and was happy to have had the opportunity to renew old friendships, but this mass unburdening of the soul was more than I had bargained for. But as I saw many of my friends who I had thought had long since abandoned the outmoded theology of a personal, anthropomorphic type of deity, and whom I considered as intelligent and sophisticated as I liked to think I was—as I saw them arise to confess their errant ways, I could not help but feel some pangs of guilt myself, for there they were, engaged in sincere repentance, exposing their intimate past, while I remained stolid, with a superior attitude, looking on disdainfully at the entire affair.

An observer of this episode might have seen many participants who, it would appear, had been caught up in the contagion of religious excitement and guilt triggered by the confession of the first, popular girl. Yet not all of those present engaged in the same type of behavior. Some participated actively in the confessional. Others participated only by engaging in what was, for them, an unusual type of silent prayer. Yet some, like the reporter, did not imitate the behavior of the others. What is most significant is his report that he felt uncomfortable and even guilty because he did not participate. The young man who finally interrupted the crowd trend also revealed that he felt social pressure, which caused him to "examine his heart to see if there was something wrong in his life" that prevented him

from conforming to the dominant mode of behavior. This may be interpreted as evidence of the rapid formation of a norm that defined a certain type of behavior as appropriate to the situation. This norm might be similar to a norm that was familiar to some through participation in other groups or situations, such as the church services or revivals. Moreover, contagion might be an adequate explanation of the actions of some who imitated the original model, the popular and attractive but ordinarily reserved girl.

Convergence Theory

But could it not be that those members of the crowd who did engage in what was, for them, unorthodox religious behavior, were without knowing it, using this opportunity to get rid of guilt feelings? Perhaps those individuals who did not participate did not share this need. Another approach to the crowd, which we shall call *convergence theory,* accounts for collective behavior on the basis of the simultaneous release of already existing predispositions, which a number of people share as latent tendencies. According to this theory, people merely reveal their true selves in a crowd, the crowd serving only as an excuse or a trigger. The problem is not to explain how heterogenous individuals come to act in a uniform fashion. It is, rather, to identify the latent tendencies in people that will cause them to act alike, the circumstances that will bring people with such tendencies together, and the kinds of events that will cause these tendencies to be released.

One such theory relies on the notion that all members of the human species possess unconscious, primitive tendencies, which are ordinarily held in check by organized society. Prominent among such tendencies are sexual desire, aggression, and defensive reactions against danger. Theories that find the explanation of collective behavior in the release of instinctual tendencies reflect the psychoanalytic concept of the unconscious. An important corollary of this is the notion that it is pathological and socially undesirable.

Joost A. Meerloo, a psychiatrist, seeks to explain a wide variety of behavior, from the apathetic reaction of silent panic, through wild flight, to riots and festive panics, in terms of man's "sudden consciousness of biological defenselessness against danger," of being "an animal without claws and fangs."[7] To him, the tendency of civilized man to panic is "an instinctual remnant of the reaction to danger in prehistoric days." Under primitive conditions, wild flight was an adaptive reaction to danger. In civilized society, with more varied and complex perils, it becomes

an archaic, maladaptive form of behavior. Nevertheless, this instinctive tendency remains imbedded in man's emotions, ready to burst out under threatening circumstances. These "sleeping fears and drives" are found in individuals, but the reaction is also highly contagious. It is, however, the common individual proclivity to panic that makes this contagious.

Frustration is another psychological state that has been suggested as the basis of a common predispositon to collective behavior. The general proposition is that frustration universally generates aggression in proportion to the extent of frustration. A corollary is that where aggression toward a perceived source of frustration is blocked, aggression is redirected toward objects that are both safe and available. Dollard, Doob, Miller, Mowrer, and Sears felt that they had found empirical verification of this proposition in the correlation between economic indices in southern states and the incidence of lynchings of Negroes.[8] They concluded that the amount of frustration experienced by southern poor whites because of the decline of cotton prices was connected with the redirection of aggression against an available and safe object, the Negro. Similarly, race riots during the period of economic readjustment following World War I, during World War II, and during the "long, hot summers" of 1964–67 have been attributed to accumulated frustrations growing out of both absolute and relative deprivation. The important thing to note about such explanations is that the object of crowd behavior need have nothing to do directly with the source of frustration. Deprivation can be shown to exist without there being an accompanying outburst of aggressive collective behavior.

Not all the variations on convergence theory are derived from a psychoanalytic approach, however. Psychologists working

[7] Joost A. Meerloo, *Patterns of Panic* (New York: International Universities Press, 1950), p. 14.

[8] John Dollard, L. W. Doob, N. E. Miller, O. H. Mowrer, and R. R. Sears, *Frustration and Aggression* (New Haven: Yale University Press, 1939).

in the tradition of learning theory, notably Floyd Allport, Neal Miller, and John Dollard, have developed a highly individualistic theory of collective behavior epitomized by Allport's declaration, "The individual in the crowd behaves just as he would behave alone, *only more so*."[9] Thus crowd behavior is viewed as the sum of individual reactions. Uniformity of reaction means that all crowd members are exposed to the same stimulus and that all, through similar past experiences, are predisposed to react to this stimulus in the same way. The crowd influences the behavior of the individual only by intensifying his behavior. This results from what Allport labeled "social facilitation"; the reaction of each individual is intensified by seeing other people respond in the same way.

The assumptions of this convergence theory are reflected in a great deal of sociological research devoted to identifying the common characteristics of participants in collective behavior. Some research has a definite psychological orientation. The key variables examined are such traits as authoritarianism, anomie, or alienation. Other research implies that similarity in social position predisposes individuals to uniformity of response, such as joining a particular type of social movement. The salient variables thus become social class, income, education, downward mobility, relative deprivation, or other sociological background characteristics.

In a report reviewing research on the characteristics of National Farmers' Organization members, participants in a social movement, Denton E. Morrison and Allan D. Steeves conclude that a high degree of homogeneity in relative deprivation was the chief factor influencing the composition of the movement.[10] They found that,

compared to other farmers, NFO members were as well or better off in their economic and social situations, but that they also had higher aspirations and were therefore more discontented. Thus, Morrison and Steeves argued, "Although we would not discount the importance of attitude and belief changes which are consequences of movement participation, we submit that attitudes existing prior to membership will strongly influence the very fact of individual membership and, ultimately, whether, when, and where a movement will emerge."[11]

On the other hand, Clark McPhail performed extensive statistical analysis on the data reported in a large number of studies of the characteristics of participants in civil disorders between 1965 and 1969 and found only limited evidence that riot participation could be predicted from background characteristics. Out of 288 associations between independent variables and measures of participation, he found only 20 that could be classified as moderate and only 2 that were high. He concluded, "There is little systematic empirical evidence to support explanations of crowd behavior or civil disorder participation in terms of individual attributes.... Our traditional preoccupation with determining what attributes [people] carry, and the "tendencies to behave" which we believe those attributes indicate, has preempted our attention to behavior sequences themselves. Perhaps it is time to give serious attention to the possibility that behavior is the product of behavior."[12]

Reliance on percentages and probability statistics to determine if people with the focal characteristics are overrepresented among the participants can create an illusion of homogeneity, which does not reflect the actual composition of the collectivity.

9 Floyd H. Allport, *Social Psychology* (Boston: Houghton Mifflin Company, 1924).
10 Denton E. Morrison and Allan D. Steeves, "Deprivation, Discontent, and Social Movement Participation: Evidence on a Contemporary Farmers' Movement, the NFO," *Rural Sociology,* 32 (December, 1967), 414–34.

11 Ibid., p. 432.
12 Clark McPhail, "Civil Disorder Participation Studies and the Analysis of Crowd Behavior: A Critical Examination of the Research Literature," unpublished paper delivered at 1969 annual meeting of the American Sociological Association.

Through these statistical artifacts, a picture of the typical crowd member can be drawn that is nothing more than a stereotype reflecting statistically defined tendencies, not the variety of participants in the crowd. Such an oversimplification reveals nothing about the interaction that takes place between individuals, whether they be of the same or different type. A quite atypical member may, for example, play a key role in defining the direction that collective behavior takes.

The major limitation of convergence theory is its neglect of the complexity of man's psychological makeup. It is important, however, to recognize that men do have latent tendencies that they do not ordinarily express. Convergence theory reminds us that because men behave in an extraordinary manner does not signify that some entirely novel mode of behavior has been induced by imitation, suggestion, or some other form of contagion. It has become clear that people may have several latent tendencies that are relevant to a given situation. After a particular mode of behavior has appeared in a crowd, it is appealingly simple to theorize that this course of behavior is a manifestation of a single predispositon that was appropriate to the situation. By this reasoning, the shared predisposition explains the crowd behavior. Recognition of multiple latencies renders such a simple explanation inadequate. Some other factor must be postulated to explain why this latency, rather than another, is selected as appropriate to the situation. A convergence approach leads to formulations that take for granted that the crowd behavior is an automatic response to the nature of the situation which, in turn, is assumed to be self-evident to each individual. A situation may be perceived by individuals as ambiguous, however. Then the collective definition of the situation, developed through interaction, may be the crucial factor in determining the course of action.

At the same time, convergence theory underscores an important principle that

may be overlooked in approaches that emphasize group influence over the individual. Whatever the nature of group influence may be, individuals are not uniformly amenable to it. Personal characteristics act as a selective factor in the recruitment of individuals to a crowd and in determining the degree and the nature of their participation in it. A highly trained scientist is not likely to be caught up in the religious fervor of a crowd that witnesses a miracle. A sedate, middle-class businessman is not as likely to join in the physical violence of a crowd as is a lower-class laborer. Yet exceptions may be found even to these generalizations. More important, the scientist may be disturbed or fascinated by the excitement of the religious crowd even though he does not share its imagery, as was the case with the ministerial student during the retreat described earlier. The businessman may encourage the laborer in his violence by shouts of approval, thus remaining an active participant in the crowd, although he fits into a different division of labor. Indeed, it may be his verbal aggression that initially inspires the laborer to physical aggression! Another theory is needed to take into account this sort of differential participation in collective behavior.

The Emergent Norm Approach

The contagion and the convergence approaches accept the unanimity of the crowd as its most salient feature. The key problem is to explain how this unanimity in the feelings, imagery, and action of the participants develops. To the extent that some members do behave similarly because of the possession of common predispositions or because of susceptibility to suggestion along the same lines, these approaches are valuable in attacking this problem. Yet it may be seen in the case of "Weekend Retreat" that neither accounts fully for what was going on. Not all the members of this deeply moved religious gathering acted in the same way, nor can it be assumed that all those who engaged in the confessional did so because of the same preexisting attitudes. In particular, although the reporter and the ministerial student were affected by the dramatically changed mood of the crowd, their feelings about what was going on were different from those of some other members, and they did not join in the overt behavior. Yet they were part of the crowd and, by their silence, assented to the actions of other members until the ministerial student finally dispelled the mood that prevailed.

An emergent norm approach reflects the empirical observation that the crowd is characterized not by unanimity but by differential expression, with different individuals in the crowd feeling differently, participating because of diverse motives, and even acting differently. The illusion of unanimity arises because the behavior of part of the crowd is perceived both by observers and by crowd members as being the sentiment of the whole crowd. Variant views and divergent forms of behavior go unrecognized or are dismissed as unimportant. If, however, complete similarity of the crowd members is regarded as an illusion, another key problem arises. This is explaining the development and imposition of a pattern of differential expression that is perceived as unanimity.

The concept of the development of a norm, a common understanding as to what sort of behavior is expected in the situation, seems to provide an explanation of a pattern of differential expression. Such a shared understanding encourages behavior consistent with the norm, inhibits behavior contrary to it, and justifies restraining action against individuals who dissent. Since the norm is to some degree specific to the situation, differing in degree or in kind from the norms governing noncrowd situations, it is an emergent norm.

The operation of a norm in a laboratory situation is described in the classic experiment in group influence on judgment con-ducted by S. E. Asch.[13] It should be recognized that the norm—the incorrect judgments—did not develop spontaneously, as in a crowd situation, but was imposed as part of the experiment. Since the naive subjects were not aware of this, they responded to the behavior of the experimenter's confederates as if it were the manifestation of an emergent norm.

In his basic investigation Asch placed a subject performing a judgmental task in the position of being a minority of one facing the pressure of a unanimous majority. The task was that of judging which of three vertical black lines of varying length was equal to a standard line shown simultaneously on a separate white card. The task appeared simple, for the unequal comparison lines, the wrong choices, were clearly longer or shorter than the standard line. In each trial the critical subject was one of a group of seven to nine students who, in each other's presence, called out the number of the comparison line each chose as equal to the standard line. There were twelve trials, each with a different set of lines, for each experimental group. During the first two trials each individual would call out the same judgment, confirming the impression that the discriminations were simple to make. But in the third, all but one of the group would choose one of the wrong lines. In most of the trials thereafter this one subject was faced with the dilemma of being a minority of one, when he chose what appeared to be the correct line, or of going along with the majority in making what seemed to be an incorrect choice.

The naive or critical subject did not know until the experiment was concluded that all the other members of the group were confederates of the experimenter. In most of the trials after the first two, these confederates deliberately made incorrect judgments. In response to the pressure of

[13] Solomon E. Asch, *Social Psychology* (Englewood Cliffs, N.J.: Prentice-Hall Inc., 1952), p. 461.

the unanimous majority, and in spite of the apparent validity of their own initial judgments, some naive subjects gave the same incorrect responses that they heard their fellows give. After thirty-one naive subjects had each gone through the twelve trials, it was found that one-third of their responses were identical with the erroneous judgments of the majority. Subjects ranged, however, from one-fifth who remained completely independent to some who always went along with the majority.

A superficial interpretation of the results of the experiment might be that a single mechanism such as suggestion or imitation was operating, with some subjects being more susceptible to contagion than others. An important part of the investigation was discussion with the naive subjects of their reactions to the situation—before they were enlightened as to the nature of the experiment. These discussions showed that the subjects felt themselves constrained by group pressure: to remain independent seemed to be to violate a norm, or the consensus, of the group. According to Asch, most of the subjects felt that they, not the majority, were the center of the trouble. In his words, "No subject disregards the group judgments. . . . [The subject] notes immediately the convergence of the group responses, his divergence from them, and the contradiction between them."[14] Moreover, Asch's analysis of the reactions of individuals according to whether they had given submissive or independent responses showed that subjects who behaved overtly in the same manner might do so with different feelings and for different reasons. Only one submissive subject imitated the majority to the extent of perceiving the lines in the same way that they reported. Most of the submissive subjects indicated that they still saw the lines in a way which contradicted the judgments of the majority, but that they became confused and doubted their own judgments.

They felt that there was pressure on them from the majority and were afraid of exposing themselves to ridicule. Thus, despite their doubts, they went along. A third type of submissive subject seemed to experience no doubt. They remained convinced that the majority was wrong but still acted as if they agreed with them. In Asch's words, ". . . They lose sight of the task and become relatively unconcerned with the question of their correctness. Instead they experience one imperious need: not to appear different."[15]

Not all subjects who were independent in their judgments felt the same way as each other. Some were confident and determined. Their outstanding quality was "a staunch firmness and vigor in opposing the majority and defending their position."[16] Some other subjects remained independent but did not feel such confidence. They reported feeling the pressure of the majority and experiencing doubts about their own judgment; they even wondered if the majority might not be right. Unlike the yielders, however, they did not go along with the crowd.

This experiment illustrates an important difference between the spontaneous induction of feeling, imagery, or behavior under contagion and the imposition of conformity under a norm. Under a norm, people experience social pressure against nonconformity but do not necessarily share the emotion or belief themselves. In a crowd setting, in contrast to the laboratory situation, some members who feel the pressure but do not share the sentiments demanded by the norm may simply remain silent. In the laboratory experiment this option was not open to the subjects. In the crowd, even the silence of dissenters may provide a form of passive support for the emergent norm and contribute to the illusion of unanimity.

The significance of a norm, experienced as group pressure, in contrast to the stimu-

---

14 Ibid., p. 461.

15 Ibid., p. 471.
16 Ibid., pp. 465–66.

lus value of the responses of other individuals is also shown in subsequent investigations that vary the experimental conditions. In these later experiments Asch found that it is not the size of the opposing majority so much as the unanimity of the opposition that produces conformity in the individual. The presence of a single supporting partner, or even of another dissenter whose judgments were nevertheless inaccurate, sharply reduced the influence of the majority. Going along with the crowd is not just a matter of imitating the behavior of the majority; it is, instead, a matter of responding to a norm that appears to have been accepted by the crowd collectively. In the words of Muzafer Sherif, the norm is a "group property," not the mere sum of the properties of the individuals who make up the group.

There is yet another important difference between contagion and normative theory. The former implies that contagion is a function of arousal and excitement. The notion of the imposition of a norm, however, can be used to explain both quiet and excited states. This is illustrated in the following accounts of the reactions of two college classes to an earth tremor that shook central Oklahoma in 1952. The two students giving the accounts were in different classes but were on the same floor in the same building.

A fear reaction emerged in the first classroom, culminating in the flight of the class from the building:

One of the girls said loudly, "What's happening?" Immediately the room began buzzing. Everyone started talking about it. It seemed as though the room was still shaking. We heard a commotion in the halls so we jumped up and looked out the window. People were filing out like flies, so we immediately began to talk about leaving. The poor teacher said that if it would make us feel any better we could leave. We left!

The second class, in almost the same physical setting, was exposed to the same threatening stimulus. After a brief period, however, they defined the situation in a different way:

The class went to the window and looked out. We couldn't see anything. The professor went out in the hall to see the reaction of others. The class members started joking about it and saying that the quotation the professor had just read probably caused the earth to tremble! Nobody seemed terribly interested and the class continued after a very few minutes.

Here there were two norms that might be applicable in the classroom situation. One was the usual academic norm that, unless the professor is absent or dismisses the class, class should go on. The other was the norm that would come into play were the fire alarm sounded, signifying that classes should be terminated and the building evacuated. The symbolic exchange that went on in each of the classrooms may be viewed as more than just the communication of a dominant mood and suggestions for action in accordance with the mood. In another situation in which classes were terminated, students cutting classes for a victory celebration were heard seeking assurance from each other that enough students would be absent to prevent professors from attempting to hold classes. Thus a conspicuous part of the interaction involved in the development of collective behavior is the seeking or supplying of justifications for the course of action of the collectivity. This interaction serves to define the facts that are specifically necessary to determine the applicability of a particular norm. So, in contrast to the suggestion of contagion theory that communication serves primarily to express and diffuse the dominant emotion of the crowd, emergent norm theory emphasizes communications that serve to indicate the applicability of a particular norm, thus justifying the actions of the crowd.

Normative theory gives rise to another hypothesis that could not be derived from either contagion or convergence theory. If it is the operation of an emergent norm that makes it possible for the crowd to engage in behavior that is not usually acceptable, the norm may also define limits to this behavior. As a corollary it may be postulated that many forms of crowd behavior are rendered possible as much by the conviction that behavior will not go beyond certain bounds as by the interstimulation of like-minded participants. It often happens in conventional crowds, such as a crowd engaged in revelrous behavior at a party, that the person whose behavior goes too far serves to dampen the crowd mood rather than to facilitate its further development. It may be that popular imagery of crowds has given insufficient attention to limits on crowd behavior.

Finally, emergent norm theory suggests a reexamination of the significance of anonymity for crowd behavior. This is a factor that is strongly emphasized in contagion and convergence approaches. If crowd behavior results from the absence of social control or the release of repressed tendencies, then anonymity would indeed be of primary importance in accounting for the elimination of controls that ordinarily keep impulses in check. If, however, crowd behavior is subject to social control under an emergent norm, it is important that the individual in the crowd have an identity so that the control of the crowd can be effective. Thus evidence should be sought to test the hypothesis that the control of the crowd is greatest among persons who are known to one another rather than among anonymous persons.

Crowd Participants: Differences in Motives

Approaches that assume the existence of unanimity in the crowd suggest that, either because of the release of common predispositions or the communication of a mood, crowd participants act on the basis of the same motives. The illusion of unanimity that impresses both crowd members and observers lends strength to this conclusion. Yet many people who are engaging in quite similar forms of behavior and contributing to the development of a common line of action may be acting from a variety of motives. The unity of the crowd is actually produced through the interaction of participants who act from different motives and in somewhat different fashions.

Types in Disaster Situations

A common instance of crowd behavior in disaster situations has been called "convergence behavior" by Charles E. Fritz and J. H. Mathewson.[17] By this they mean the informal, spontaneous movement of people, information, and materiel toward the scene of a disaster—a type of behavior that is widely recognized as a serious problem in time of disaster. (This is not the sort of psychological convergence implied by convergence theory.) They point out that the people who engage in convergence behavior are commonly lumped together under the heading of *sightseers*. Through an intensive review of studies of specific disasters, however, they were able to identify not one but five major types of convergers.

They first identify the returnees:

Under this heading, we classify the disaster survivors who have left or who have been evacuated from the disaster area, but who, for various reasons, wish to return to the homesite. The category also includes residents of the disaster area who were temporarily absent from the community when the disaster struck and non-resident property owners who return to assess the nature of the damage and loss; and "substitute" returnees—relatives and friends of disaster victims who enter the disaster area to assess the victims' losses, and to retrieve, guard, and salvage their property.

[17] Charles E. Fritz and J. H. Mathewson, *Convergence Behavior in Disasters* (Washington: National Academy of Sciences—National Research Council, Pub. 476, 1957). Selections reprinted by permission.

There appear to be two basic motivations for the convergence of these returnees: (1) the immediate goals of locating and helping other persons, and assessing damage to and protecting private property, and (2) the *longer range* goals of returning to familiar surroundings, and re-establishing pre-existent social relationships.[18]

Differing from the returnees are the anxious. They have not been in the area of the disaster but in the area indirectly affected.

The separation of primary and extended family members and friendship groups is perhaps the most significant single fact to comprehend in understanding the large amount of anxiety-motivated convergence that occurs in disasters. A word-of-mouth announcement, radio or television broadcast, or newspaper story that conveys, for example, the information: "City X has been struck by disaster; N number of persons are reported killed and injured," becomes an immediate anxiety-arousing stimulus for all persons who have family members, relatives, close friends, or other significant identifications in the disaster-struck community. This anxiety-stimulating news usually starts a complete "chain reaction" of information-seeking behavior that places great strains or overloads on existing communication and transportation facilities. Persons in zones contiguous or proximate to the disaster area usually attempt to phone their homes or drive to the area. Persons in distant cities phone newspaper offices, broadcasting studios, and other information centers to get further information, or attempt to communicate directly with persons or agencies in or near the disaster area by long distance telephone or telegraph. Thus the communication networks and roadways leading toward the disaster area often become seriously overloaded almost immediately after news of the disaster becomes disseminated.

A study of 231 evacuee families in the Farmington-Unionville, Connecticut, flood of August 1955, showed that 163 families, or 70 percent of the total sample, had out-of-town relatives and friends visit them during the first month following the flood. Each of these families had an average of about six visitors during the month; thus the total number of

external personal convergers for this sample alone was nearly 1,000 persons. Anxiety over the whereabouts, safety, and welfare of the victim families was the most frequently cited reason for these visits. The desire to help the victim family by direct physical assistance (e.g., aid in moving belongings, clearing debris, taking care of children, bringing supplies of food, clothing, bedding, etc.) was the next most frequent motivation for the convergence. Over 60 percent of the sample families also received long distance telephone calls or telegrams during the first month following the flood and, like the personal visits, the most frequently ascribed reasons for the communications related to anxiety or concern over the victim families. Although the majority of external visitors and communicators were residents of the State of Connecticut (80 percent of the visitors and 61 percent of those who phoned or telegraphed), approximately 25 different states and five countries or areas outside the continental United States were represented by both types of convergers.[19]

The third type of converger, the helper, is similar to the anxious, but he need not be concerned about a loved one in the disaster area. He may simply be a volunteer who offers his aid when he hears of the disaster. The helpers tend to come in successive waves from areas increasingly remote from the area of impact.

The speed and volume of external help convergence is determined essentially by personal identification with victims in the area and spatial proximity to the disaster area. The early volunteer arrivals are most likely to be those from the contiguous zone who have directly perceived some of the effects of the disaster or who are suddenly confronted with requests for aid from the victims who are leaving the area. This contiguous-zone group constitutes the first wave of informal helpers arriving at the scene.

Successive waves of external personal convergers will occur as the news spreads to the proximate zone. Being somewhat removed from the disaster site, but still within, say, an hour to two hours travel time from the area, those most intensely concerned with potential victims will drive to the area to assess the condition of loved ones and render whatever assistance they

---

18 Ibid., p. 30.

19 Ibid., pp. 37–39.

can. Residents of proximate zones who have less concern for particular individuals tend to volunteer their assistance to hospitals, relief centers, and communication centers that operate in the proximate communities. In the White County, Arkansas, tornado, for example, over 25 percent of the total adult population of Searcy, Arkansas, a community of about 6,000 persons located a few miles from the tornado-struck area, volunteered or rendered some form of medical assistance during the first night following the tornado. Numerically, this meant that over 1,000 adults out of a total adult population of about 3,800 engaged in some type of help convergence on four medical centers.[20]

The fourth type identified by Fritz and Mathewson corresponds to the sort of converger so often emphasized in accounts of disasters—the sightseers or the curious. The prominence of the fifth and last type also tends to be exaggerated. This type Fritz and Mathewson call the exploiters; they include looters, souvenir hunters, relief stealers, and profiteers.

Thus the hundreds or thousands of individuals who converge on the scene of a disaster are heterogeneous in motivation despite the similarity of their behavior. To ascribe their reactions to a single mechanism, such as imitation, or to the arousal of a common psychological impulse, such as fear or morbid curiosity, would not be faithful to the empirical evidence gathered in numerous studies of disaster. Nor should it be assumed that the participants in other types of collective behavior are homogeneous in motivation. Analysis of the motives of the members of a destructive mob would no doubt produce a comparable heterogeneity.

A General Classification of Participants

A more general classification of types of participants in the collectivity may serve as a framework for the analysis of types in specific crowds or social movements. The

type of participant who most readily comes to mind is the one who is in some way ego-involved in the situation that gives rise to collective behavior. A crowd arises because of some incident that is outside the normal pattern of expectations, what Blumer has called "the exciting event." There are some people who are incensed, or frightened, or perhaps elated over this event. Because of their relationship to it, they define the situation as demanding immediate action. This type of participant we will call the committed. This type of person may not have a clear picture of what should be done, but he feels that he must do something. If he does visualize some line of action, he may not see how he alone can carry it out. His feelings about the situation go beyond mere anxiety or curiosity.

The second type of participant may be described as the concerned. It cannot be assumed that everyone who is concerned about an incident feels committed to take some immediate action. Some people, who share the intense ego-involvement of the committed participant, may feel that action should be left up to the authorities and that whatever action is taken should be congruent with the norms of the group. Such people are not as likely to suggest lines of action as are the committed, yet they become part of the crowd as it gathers. Furthermore, because of their concern, they are likely to be highly responsive to emergent norms that define appropriate action.

In situations where intergroup conflict is involved, the orientation of the concerned is such that they feel the issue must be made to go in one direction—the side with which they identify must win. Ordinary group loyalty contributes to this sort of attitude. When an individual's group is committed to action in one direction, particularly against an out-group, he often feels that he must support his group even if it is wrong. Such an attitude is reflected in the historic slogan, "My country, right or wrong."

Some people seem to be brought into the collectivity by a third type of motivation. These are people who derive direct satisfaction from participation in collective behavior, regardless of the circumstances. It does not matter to them what the issue is —they get certain gratifications out of participating in the collectivity itself. It is frequently observed, for instance, that adolescents make up a disproportionate element of those people who are in the active core of a crowd. Studies of youth culture in the United States suggest that, in our society, many young people would derive gratification from any activity that represents rebellion against the ordinary controls of society. Other types of people, such as the poor, may also occupy a marginal and therefore insecure status in society.

Two features of collective behavior may be particularly appealing to the insecure person. In the first place, there is a terrific sense of power in the collectivity, be it a relatively small crowd or a vast social movement. The individual in the crowd has a sense of unanimity. The crowd seems all-powerful. Hence the individual who, in his day-to-day existence, finds himself constantly blocked by his superiors and other people now finds himself in a situation where there are no obstacles. He personally partakes of this sense of power.

The other element is that of the righteousness of the crowd or the social movement. William Graham Sumner long ago pointed out the social origin of our conventional ideas of right and wrong, of the mores. The norms of our identification groups become our own standards of right and wrong. Our idea that something is morally incontestable is essentially a conversion of our experience: nobody in the groups that mean anything to us, nobody whose opinion we consider worth listening to, contradicts this idea. The sense of absolute righteousness of an idea is derived from the unanimity with which it is held.

In a crowd situation the range of attention of the individual is narrowed. In the extreme case, the individual's orientation is determined solely in terms of the members of the present crowd. The influence of his usual identification groups and their norms is attenuated, and the individual's sense of moral rightness is determined by the compelling presence of other crowd members. The appearance of unanimity in the crowd, even though it may be illusory, gives the same kind of basis for believing that the position of the crowd is morally incontestable that the individual gets from groups with which he identifies outside the crowd situation.

A fourth category of people that has often been noted in crowds is the group of spectators. They must be regarded as part of the crowd, even though they may be relatively inactive. The gathering of a crowd in the vicinity of the precipitating event, if not the incident itself, draws many people who are motivated chiefly by curiosity. They may be quite unaware of the nature of the occurrence that has created the crowd situation, or they may be quite disinterested in the outcome of the crowd process. However, such spectators, motivated initially by curiosity, may be absorbed into the more active core of the crowd.

The curiosity that attracts spectators to the scene of an exciting event need not be regarded as evidence of ghoulishness, although it is often interpreted this way. As Fritz and Mathewson observe:

Curiosity, by its very nature, is excited by unusual circumstances, by events which cannot readily be fitted into or explained by previous experience. Disasters are events which are inherently unusual and dramatic; they excite attention and require investigative activity if they are to be coped with and understood. Viewed in this fashion, the curiosity manifested in disasters is simply an example of the normal human tendency to be attracted by and to inquire into any phenomenon which is strange. Curiosity provides the stimulus to investigate and "structure the field"—to explain and assimilate unusual happenings.[21]

A fifth and very important type of participant will be characterized as the exploiter, borrowing from the typology of convergers in disaster. Whatever his particular motive may be, such a participant differs from others by having ego-detachment rather than ego-involvement. It may be hypothesized that even the curious spectators have an involvement in the situation, even though it may involve no personal relationship to the others. As Fritz and Mathewson suggest, however, an exploitative attitude requires a "depersonalized" perspective: viewing other people as means or instruments for securing goals rather than ends or values in themselves. Such people may be the looters in a disaster situation; they may be instigators who, in an area of racial tension, callously attempt to precipitate violence to advance their own political ends. They may be ordinary criminals or members of delinquent gangs who see in a crowd situation a cover for their criminal acts. They may be drunks or psychopaths who are only dimly aware of what the excitement is all about but are free of the ordinary inhibitions that restrain many people in the early stages of crowd development. They may be racketeers who enter social movements because they perceive opportunities for personal profit or glory.

It is not suggested that such people create the collectivity or collective behavior. They do not create the incidents that give rise to the crowd situation, and they may not even be present when an incident occurs and a crowd assembles. Nor would their irresponsible actions set off crowd behavior if the other crowd members were not present. They do serve, however, as facilitating agents, furnishing models of deviant behavior for the initially more inhibited members.

[21] Fritz and Mathewson, *Convergence Behavior,* p. 46.

Heterogeneity and Differential Expression in the Crowd

The notion that a crowd is composed of people who are heterogeneous in motivation stands in contrast to both contagion and convergence approaches. These assume that a common impulse to action, arising either through contagion or through the release of common predispositions, gives the crowd its dominant mood and its direction. If, however, the crowd is initially heterogeneous in composition and remains so during a large part of its existence, then the unity it achieves must result from the interaction of these different elements. In the course of this interaction, norms emerge that are specific to the situation. These emergent norms define those acts that, out of many sorts of behavior that might be possible in the situation, are expected or permitted in this particular crowd. Tendencies to behave in a different fashion are then restrained, and individuals who remain a part of the crowd experience pressure to behave in the manner that has been defined as appropriate. Not an absence of social control but the operation of emergent norms thus characterizes collective behavior. Calling these *emergent* norms does not imply that they must be completely new. They may be norms that ordinarily would come into play in some other situation but are now defined as appropriate in the present setting.

The key to the emergence of such situationally specific norms is differential expression. It is not simply the preponderance of participants sharing a particular motivation that determines the mood and actions of a crowd. Those views and sentiments that are expressed as representing the sentiments of the entire crowd give the appearance of unanimity and impose organization and coherence upon its actions. The central process in crowd development or any other collectivity, therefore, is not unwilling imitation nor the simultaneous release of common predispositions but symbolic communication.

3

COMMUNICATION
IN COLLECTIVE BEHAVIOR:
RUMOR

Collective behavior, it has been suggested, is not the random, disorganized activity of a gathering of individuals free of the influence of social control. Collective behavior occurs when the established organization ceases to afford direction and supply channels for action. The occurrence of events that are inadequately defined in the culture of the group or for which no traditional organization exists confronts the group and the individuals in it with an ambiguous, critical situation. In such a critical situation new norms may emerge to give direction to the collective behavior that follows. These norms make the coordination of the individuals' actions possible by supplying a shared definition of the situation.

Rumor and Established Channels of Communication

Any sort of coordinated human behavior rests on a substratum of communication. The communication that provides direction for traditional social behavior flows through established channels. These include formal channels, which are accepted as authoritative because of their official nature or their supposedly superior access to sources of information. They also include informal channels, the word-of-mouth network through which the traditional norms, the folkways and mores, are transmitted and reaffirmed. This network carries those items of folk knowledge that are taken for granted by all in the group except new-comers and the young. The consensus that seems to prevail in society, not just in the temporary assemblage, gives this type of communication its validity.

One of the crucial characteristics of a critical situation is that information and directives for action cannot be validated through these normal channels of communication. The formal channels may be closed by mechanical failure, may be overloaded, or may have their usual sources of information severely restricted. In some situations, people may find official communications so hard to believe or to assimilate that they refuse to rely on them. This often happens in flood-threatened communities; official warnings are given varying degrees of credence by citizens who would flee from their homes if they believed the warnings.

Official channels may seems to be closed even though they are still functioning. Thus, Scott and Homans explained the wildcat strikes of the forties as resulting primarily from faulty communication.[1] During World War II the companies for which the strikers worked and the unions to which they belonged expanded rapidly, lengthening the chain of communication between the workers and officials of both management and the union. In addition, many decisions affecting union locals were made in Washington by representatives of

[1] Jerome F. Scott and George C. Homans, "Reflections on the Wildcat Strikes," *American Sociological Review*, 12 (June, 1947), 278–87.

the companies and central officers of the union in conjunction with the War Labor Board. With decisions vital to their welfare being made at a point so remote from them, many workers felt that they were being given the run around by both management and their own union officers. Scott and Homans concluded:

> In short, the feeling of the working man that he was at last in a position to insist on being heard became strong at a time when the actual avenues of communication, both for the company and the union, became weaker and more indirect than they had been in the past.[2]

Informal modes of communication may become inadequate because the traditional norms transmitted through them seem inappropriate to the critical situation. J. Prasad says of the situation in a province of India following a great earthquake:

> Earthquakes in the region concerned were certainly not uncommon. But so severe a shock, lasting for so long a time, and followed by terrible disasters, was certainly a strange and uncommon phenomenon. The uncommon and strange are by themselves apt to call forth highly toned affective reactions, probably because a ready and adequate response to them is not available. In such situations, imaginative responses arise, to compensate for, or fill up, the gap left by a sense of the lack of ready response or its inadequacy.[3]

A critical situation may create a demand for explanations that are simply not available in the culture because they have never been needed before. Thus Prasad observes:

> ...The causes of earthquakes were not known to these people, and so long as no such event occurs, the popular mind has no interest in knowing or inquiring about its causes. But once the phenomenon has happened and led

to serious practical consequences, the popular mind, knowing but little about it, attempts to find an explanation of it. So long as a change in the environment remains unaccounted for, it leaves a distracting sense of incompleteness.... What is wanting in the given situation, viz., a knowledge of the causes of the change, must be supplied in some way or other so that the tension of incomplete apprehension may be relieved. Nor can the popular mind postpone its judgments on the phenomenon until a thorough and scientific investigation has provided a rational account of it. The gap must be filled up immediately, the tension must be relieved quickly, and to do this explanations must be promptly invented.[4]

Under such circumstances communication takes on characteristics different from those of normal times. More reliance is placed on informal and unconventional channels. Even though news may be available through formal channels, such as radio or television, individuals seek to confirm and supplement it by exchanging information with other listeners. In a critical situation, a common opening to a conversation is, "Did you hear...?" Thus the speaker both conveys the news, seeks confirmation that he heard it right, and invites the person to whom he speaks to share additional information that he may possess.

THE PARTICIPANTS IN RUMOR. The network of informal communication may become quantitatively and qualitatively different from what it is in normal times. Shibutani notes of one type of critical situation, "Communication among disaster victims is facilitated by the disappearance of conventional social barriers."[5] Individuals may become part of a communication network that extends beyond and cuts across ordinary group boundaries. Strangers who know little about each other, except that they share an interest in the ambiguous situation, interact and become part of an emergent collectivity.

It is from the collectivity, the people in

2 Ibid., p. 287.
3 J. Prasad, "The Psychology of Rumor: A Study Relating to the Great India Earthquake of 1934," *British Journal of Psychology,* 26 (July, 1935), 6–7. Reprinted by permission of the publishers.

4 Ibid., p. 7.
5 Tamotsu Shibutani, *Improvised News* (Indianapolis, Ind.: The Bobbs-Merrill Co., Inc., 1966), p. 34.

current interaction, that verification and validation are sought rather than from sources external to the temporary assemblage. The usual standards of judgment and morality, which people derive from their reference groups, may be suspended as this novel, but immediately available and quite visible, source provides new norms. But because of the temporary and unstable nature of the collectivity, congnition takes on a spontaneous, tentative, and emergent character. "That is what everybody is saying!" constitutes the measure of truth, and "Everybody else is doing it!" becomes the standard of morality. This may be the reaction among people closely gathered, as in a crowd, or widely dispersed, as when participating in a fad or social movement.

DIFFERENTIAL RESPONSIVENESS. This does not mean that individuals are indiscriminately responsive to anyone who happens to be present without regard to preexisting relations. Confronted with a novel and ambiguous situation, however, people do turn to others confronted by the same situation for cues on how to respond. An unusual opportunity to observe the operation of this tendency was provided in 1960, when false air raid warnings were sounded by accident in three American cities. Studying the responses of people who heard the sirens, Mack and Baker concluded:

> Probably the most conclusive general finding from the research experience in the three cities is that hearing the warning siren alone is totally inadequate to stimulate people to immediate protective action. What people do, in fact, upon hearing the siren, is to seek additional information either to validate or to refute their own initial interpretation of the meaning of the signal.[6]

Seeking cues in the behavior and interpretations of others was a general reaction.

[6] Raymond W. Mack and George W. Baker, *The Occasion Instant*, Disaster Study No. 15 (Washington, D.C.: National Academy of Sciences—National Research Council, 1961), p. 39.

There were differences, however, in who the others were. In Washington:

> Proportionately more non-civil defense personnel looked out the window as a means of validating the warning signal. Agency civil defense personnel were more likely to check out the signal by going to another civil defense member, a supervisor, or other office personnel.[7]

Rumor and Collective Behavior

The type of communication described above is what is usually called rumor. *Rumor is the characteristic mode of communication in collective behavior.* It is the process through which emergent norms develop to give direction to the activities of the collectivity. This implies a conception of rumor as a collective problem-solving procedure. Shibutani provides such a conception when he defines rumor as "communication through which men caught together in an ambiguous situation attempt to construct a meaningful interpretation of it by pooling their intellectual resources."[8]

RUMOR, SUGGESTIBILITY, AND GROUP NORMS. As has been shown earlier, the concepts of suggestion and suggestibility have played a prominent part in explanations of interpersonal influence in collective behavior. Contagion theory implies that suggestibility designates an excited state in which an individual is likely to uncritically imitate the models of behavior provided by others. When the interaction of men in an ambiguous situation is regarded as collective problem solving, suggestibility takes on a different connotation. It refers to the heightened responsiveness of the individual to cues provided by others when situational anchorages are inadequate.

Muzafer Sherif and O. J. Harvey have demonstrated this kind of suggestibility through experiments. A critical situation was created for laboratory subjects by giving them a task involving judgment of an

[7] Ibid., p. 22.
[8] Shibutani, *Improvised News*, p. 17.

ambiguous stimulus and by manipulating the conditions under which this task was performed. The anxiety and feelings of insecurity, the need to find a meaningful interpretation of the situation, and the increased reliance on the actions of others, which are found in rumor-inducing situations, were produced in the subjects and reported in their study. Sherif and Harvey show that the model for their experiment was found in life situations in which stable anchorages are minimal.

Implications of Observations from Life Situations

Muzafer Sherif and O. J. Harvey

Experimental study must ring true to the characteristics of situations and behavior in the run of things in men's lives. For our problem we are specifically concerned with life situations of little structure, that is, situations with few stable anchorages. An example is the battlefield in modern, mechanized war. In his description of the modern battlefield, Marshall[1] wrote, "The harshest thing about the field is that it is *empty*. No people stir about. There are little or no signs of action. Over all there is a great quiet which seems more ominous than the occasional tempest of fire." This is in contrast to the recruit's expectations after being trained in the presence of great numbers of men and massive mechanical power all around him. But "he finds himself suddenly almost alone in his hour of greatest danger, and he can feel the danger, but there is nothing out there, nothing to contend against."[2] "There is nothing to be seen. The fire comes out of nowhere. But that is all that he knows for certain."[3] As the men scatter under fire, they may even be out of sight of one another. And, as Vilfroy's account of the early days of the war in France (1940) puts it, he feels utterly alone, "forward and isolate."[4]

.   .   .

The individual, in a situation having few or no anchorages to guide him, caught in the throes of anxiety, tries to establish some level of stability. He seeks to find some standard and is susceptible to accepting a standard from another source. Take, for example, the pilots preparing to take off from a ship before day-break. On a completely dark deck, they must find their ships. "Old hands get used to memorizing the *relative positions* of all the planes the afternoon before the next morning, which helps."[5] It is a common enough observation that some conclusion to awaiting an indefinite future, even finally entering combat, may bring intense relief and stabilization, in spite of objective dangers in the certainty.[6]

Marshall investigated the problem of why enemy fire against an advancing infantry line invariably caused a delay of from 45–60 minutes.[7] His observations (of 11 infantry companies and one reconnaissance troop) led him to conclude that the line did not proceed until *effective communication* was restored. This might be simply one bold individual standing up and shouting "Follow me! We're going on!"[8] If withdrawal becomes necessary, but is not coupled with some brief explanation (e.g. "Get the hell out of here and follow me to that tree line on the far side of the creek."), panic is likely to result.

In such stress situations, where the individual

From Muzafer Sherif and O. J. Harvey, "A Study in Ego-Functioning: Elimination of Stable Anchorages in Individual and Group Situations," *Sociometry,* 15 (1952), 272–305. Reprinted in part by permission of the authors and the editor.
[1] S. L. A. Marshall, *Men Against Fire.* New York: Morrow, 1947, p. 44.
[2] Ibid., p. 45.
[3] Ibid., p. 47.
[4] D. Vilfroy, *War in the West.* Harrisburg: Military Service Publishing Co., 1942, p. 105.

[5] M. L. Wordell and E. N. Seiler, *Wildcats Over Casablanca.* Boston: Little, Brown, 1943, p. 26.
[6] W. Simpon, *One of Our Pilots is Safe.* New York: Harper, 1943, p. 4.
[7] Op. cit.
[8] Ibid., p. 130.

perceives only confusion, he may long for something or someone to provide standards of conduct. Thus soldiers caught in a hasty withdrawal of British forces after the breakthrough by Rommel's army in Libya, completely surrounded by confusion, "bewilderment and fear and ignorance," *wanted* to receive orders.[9] Here is the statement of a veteran wounded in the North Africa campaign: "One time we begged our lieutenants to give orders. They were afraid to act because they didn't have the rank. We took a beating while they were waiting for orders—how did they know the commander hadn't been knocked off?"[10]

In the absence of other anchors or standards for anticipating the future, men put their faith in the wisdom and experience of the captain of their vessel or the pilot of their plane.[11] In such situations, the individual becomes increasingly depen-

dent upon his own group for feelings of security.[12]

In short, the effect of extreme stress, uncertainty, lack of stable anchorages may be to increase suggestibility—in the sense of increasing the likelihood of accepting a standard for behavior from a source other than the individual's own. When shared with others, this increasing desire for some stable anchorage leads in group process to the rise and spread of *rumors,* as the study and reports of rumor have amply shown.

Rumor may, of course, be based on some specific event or action which is not defined for those watching. Marshall who investigated the sources of panic which occurred in battle during World War II concluded that *in every case the "common denominator" was that "somebody failed to tell other men what he was doing."*[13] Thus, in one case, a sergeant wounded during battle dashed back to a first aid station without telling his squad why. They took after him, and the rumor spread through the whole line, "The order is to withdraw."

[9] A. Moorehead, *Don't Blame the Generals.* New York: Harper, 1942, pp. 69–71.

[10] Stouffer, op. cit. p. 117.

[11] E.g., Pyle, op. cit., p. 4, and R. Rehm, "Fifty Missions over Europe," in D. G. Wright (edit.), *Observations on Combat Personnel.* New York: Josiah Macy Foundation, 1945.

[12] E.g., Stouffer, op. cit., p. 144, and Marshall, op. cit., pp. 129–30.

[13] Op. cit., p. 146.

In their experiment, these two psychologists are concerned with the effects of the elimination of stable anchorages upon the individual and his self-feelings. Their general hypothesis is that in such an unstable situation the individual will experience insecurity and that his behavior will fluctuate greatly:

When, under critical circumstances, the stability of our physical and social bearings are disrupted with the subsequent experience of not being anywhere definitely, of being torn from social ties of belongingness, or when nothing but a future of uncertainty or blockages is experienced as our lot, the by-product is the experience of insecurity. The individual tossing in such a state of anxiety or insecurity flounders all over in his craze to establish for himself some stable anchorages. The fluctuations of his experience and behavior are greatly increased.

In our opinion great fluctuations or variability in experience and behavior occur *first,* even in cases of persons who may *eventually* turn into themselves to build internally paranoid anchorages which are completely out of line with the facts of reality surrounding them.

The consequences of the ego-tensions, anxiety or insecurity are a state of restlessness, floundering all over to find some stable anchorages, heightened fluctuations of behavior. If these states of anxiety or insecurity are widespread among the individuals of a group, the result is an increased degree of suggestibility, the increased credulity for events that are bizarre and unexpected, a greater degree of susceptibility to the spread of wild rumors, the greater likelihood of panics.[9]

[9] Muzafer Sherif and O. J. Harvey, "A Study in Ego-Functioning: Elimination of Stable Anchorages in Individual and Group Situations," *Sociometry,* 15 (1952), 280–81.

In this experiment Sherif and Harvey used the "autokinetic phenomenon." The autokinetic phenomenon is the apparent movement of a pinpoint of light viewed by the subject as it is exposed against an otherwise totally dark background. While the light does not actually move, it appears to move because of the absence of any stable anchorages in the background. In previous experiments Sherif had found that, in repeated judgments of the movement of the light, individuals established persistent ranges and norms for their estimates of the distance the light moved. Furthermore, it was found that when subjects made repeated judgments as members of groups, *group* norms were established reflecting the reciprocal effects of the judgments of the individuals composing the groups.

In the present experiment, Sherif and Harvey repeated the earlier experiments, using individuals as subjects both alone and in groups, but under three different conditions. Under "Condition A" the experimenter was as friendly and encouraging as he could be, the room in which the experiment took place was small, and the subjects had a brief glimpse of the interior of the room before it was darkened. Thus the subject in Condition A had some opportunity to orient himself in relation to definite anchorages, such as walls and furniture.

Condition B differed from Condition A in that a much larger room was used and the subject never saw the space relations inside the experimental hall. He was led to his chair in the dark. In group sessions under Condition B the subjects held hands and were led to their seats. Returning to the reading from Sherif and Harvey, Condition C is here described in detail.

1659358

PROCEDURE: CONDITION C

This was intended to be the situation in which spatial anchorages were eliminated as much as possible, hence the most difficult. *The experimenter made no attempt to establish rapport with the subjects, being matter of fact instead of warm and cordial, and engaging in only the necessary minimum of conversation throughout the sessions. More significant than the changed air of the experimenter was the increased difficulty in the experimental conditions.* The experimental room was the same one used for Condition B, but several factors were introduced which made it much more difficult.

At a distance of 12 feet from the entrance, stairs were placed containing 4 steps in the front and 3 steps down in the back. The area of the room was marked off with ropes so that the only way the subject could reach his chair was by passing over the stairs (unless he crawled through the ropes, which none did). The ropes were introduced after preliminary work showed that the subjects in search of their chairs usually ended up at the right or left wall. They tended to stick by the wall despite instructions from the experimenter on how to find their goal. Therefore, in order to eliminate vertical anchorages as much as possible, rope barriers at hip level were used. It should be pointed out, however, that when subjects lost their way and came to the ropes, the ropes did not provide any definite anchorage as to their exact location.

After finding the stairs and passing over them, it was necessary for the subject to turn exactly 45 degrees to his left and proceed straight for 39 feet before reaching his goal (chair). There was nothing between the stairs and the chair but space.

Certain landmarks in simple relation to the subject's chair were set up in order that the experimenter could direct him to his seat when he became completely lost.

Individual session. Before going to the dark room the subject was instructed:

You are to enter a dark room. (The subject had been shown the entrance he was to use previously.) After you have gone through the door, you are to pull it tight behind you and pull the curtains closed, too.

(The curtains were used to insure against light leakage.) Then, place your back to the door which you have just entered and walk straight ahead. You will come to some stairs. When you have passed over the stairs, stop and turn left 45 degrees, and walk straight in the direction you are then facing. You will come to your chair and a table in front of it. After you find your chair, sit down and face directly forward.

Is there anything that is not clear?

The subject was then left in an office, several doors from the experimental room, while the experimenter made his way to his chair in the experimental room. He then called the subject, who could not tell from where in the experimental room the sound had come. As soon as the subject had closed the door of the experimental room, the experimenter started recording by stop clock the time it took for him to reach his chair, as well as all pertinent remarks of the subject. The experimenter maintained complete silence despite frequent attempts of the subjects to establish contact by asking for direction and aid. The experimenter's silence was broken only after the subject had wandered for 3 minutes without finding his chair, had expressed the fact twice that he was lost and had given up, or had reached his chair. When the subject became lost the experimenter directed him to his chair by explaining the relationship of certain landmarks to the subject's table.

After the subject had reached his chair, either through his own ability or by directional aid, he was instructed:

There is a table in front of you. On this table there is a box with a button on it. You will be shown a point of light like this. (Light was shown.) It shall always appear in this place. Several seconds before it is to appear I shall tap like this. (Experimenter tapped the table with a pencil.)

The tapping was substituted for saying "ready" to reduce further the contact between experimenter and subject.

The rest of the procedure was the same as that for the individual sessions in Conditions A and B.

Group session. Here the subjects sought their seats in pairs. Before entering the dark room, the same instructions as for the individual session of Condition C were given. After the subjects had reached their chairs, the same procedure as for the other group sessions was followed except that instead of saying "ready" before the appearance of the light, the experimenter tapped his pencil. [After the second, or group, session under each condition, each subject filled out a questionnaire. Among the items on it was an open general question concerning the subject's reactions to the individual session, and also questions about his feeling of certainty accompanying the judgments in the group session, and on the positive or negative effect of another person's presence and estimates upon his own judgments.

Responses to the questionnaire and comments made by the subjects during the experiment reveal that feelings of insecurity were actually produced in the subjects by these uncertain, though clearly not dangerous, situations.]

RESPONSES AND COMMENTS REVEALING INSECURITY

One questionnaire item concerned the subject's difficulty in making judgments. Under Condition A (relatively easy), 14 or 70% of the subjects indicated that "estimates were easy" or "no major difficulty in any estimates." In contrast, 90% of subjects in Condition C (with fewest anchorages) reported difficulty in half, the majority, or most of their estimates, only 2 subjects indicating that their "estimates were easy."

Content analysis of answers to an open general question asking for the subject's reactions to the individual session revealed increasing uncertainty and confusion from Condition A to Condition C. In Condition A, 5 (25%) subjects indicated uncertainty as contrasted to 9 (45%) in Condition B and 13 (65%) in Condition C. Typical comments of subjects in each condition reveal qualitative differences even in this experienced uncertainty, among those who spontaneously included it in their responses:

Condition A: "I felt ill at ease, but curious."
Condition B: "Bewildered. I don't ever remember even being in such complete darkness. And it was a little nerve-wracking."
"Very unsure and a little afraid, not of anything in particular, just of a strange and totally unexplained situation."
Condition C: "Felt helpless and ill at ease—was very puzzled."
"Completely confused. Lost as heck."

Further spontaneous remarks of the subjects substantiated this supposition that uncertainty and instability were not only experienced more frequently under Condition B and especially C, but that such uncertainty was more intense in the latter conditions. For example, one subject in Condition B remarked: "The first time when I was there by myself, it sometimes seemed as if the room was moving with me. Sometimes it seemed like my chair was turning over to one side. When I would move my feet away from a spot and replace them, it seemed like the floor was laying at an angle."[1]

[1] Sherif and Harvey, "A Study in Ego-Functioning," pp. 272–305.

Statistical analysis of the fluctuations of the judgments of the subjects, in both individual and group sessions, and under the three different conditions, led to the following conclusions:

(1) The more uncertain the situation, the greater the scale within which judgmental reactions are scattered.

(2) The more uncertain the situation, the greater the magnitude of the norm or standard around which judgments are distributed.

(3) The more uncertain the situation, the larger the differences between the scales and norms of judgment of different individuals.

(4) The more uncertain the situation, the greater the tendency, on the whole, toward convergence in group situations.[10]

These conclusions confirm the general hypothesis that, with increasing situational uncertainty, the greater will be the fluctuations in the judgmental behavior of the individual. The last conclusion (4) suggests, furthermore, that increasing the uncertainty of the situation increases the susceptibility of the individual to the suggestions of others. In this and other studies utilizing the autokinetic phenomenon, Sherif has emphasized that judgments are not developed through a simple process of follow the leader. Instead a collective solution is developed which all the subjects contribute to, and a group norm emerges.

MILLING. Also noted in this experiment was the random, erratic behavior of individuals in response to situational uncertainty, as shown by conclusions (1), (2), and (3). Such searching behavior is commonly observed in life. In these situations a great deal of bodily movement as well as purely verbal activity is involved particularly if the individuals are excited. An individual caught in the throes of uncertainty and blocked in his activity may act in such a restless fashion. The behavior of an assemblage of people all engaging in a random, restless, excited circling is like that of cattle. Thus the milling of human beings has often been compared to that of animals.

Physical activity and manifestations of emotion are only of incidental importance in the development of collective behavior. Reliance on the analogy to the milling of animals overemphasizes the rapid dissemination of a feeling state and of forms of agitated physical behavior. It obscures the fact that with human beings milling becomes a form of symbolic communication, or rumor. Even though individuals may not be conscious of their own restless activity, they interpret the activity of others through role taking. Therefore milling can involve a minimum of verbal and physical activity, rather than the wild, excited behavior that contagion theory suggests. An example of such calm, quiet milling is found in the following personal experience of one of the authors:

One day in church, in the middle of the sermon, we heard a fire engine drive into the church parking lot, next to the sanctuary.

[10] Ibid., p. 303.

There was an uncertain feeling—were we in danger? The obvious impulse to get out of the place was countered by the obviously inappropriate character of any such behavior in the sacred setting of the church. I found myself looking to left and to right to see whether other people looked frightened, to see whether anyone was doing anything about the situation. I looked at the minister to catch any gestures which might indicate his feelings. What I saw was a lot of other people also looking about, presumably in the same way I was!

Other situations permit a greater range of activity. There may be more room to move about and fewer normative restrictions on exploratory activity. When an unusual event occurs in such a setting, very active milling may begin. Milling of this sort may be seen in a crowd waiting eagerly, but impatiently, for a parade to start. People move about from one vantage point to another, trying to see what has happened so far. More important, milling becomes primarily a verbal process. People ask each other questions about what they have seen and heard and answer similar questions and others with bits of information, guesses, and theories. In this communication they move about, talking first to one person, then to another. Excited talking in one knot of people or the movement of a few individuals to a new point of observation may cause a sudden, brief gravitation of a large portion of the crowd to the new point of interest. All the time, communication is going on as scraps of information, guesses, and predictions are passed from one person to another.

Milling may take place over a still larger area, particularly where automobiles and telephones are part of the culture. An automobile accident, a plane crash, or an explosion occurs in some part of a city. Typically, many people who hear the sound, see smoke rising, or hear the scream of sirens will rush toward that location to see what has happened. Their movement attracts the attention of others, who ask questions and often join in the movement.

Some people pick up their telephones to call friends, the police, or newspaper offices, to ask questions, or to repeat their own versions of what has happened. In what often seems an incredibly short time, interest may be aroused and reports spread far beyond the immediate vicinity of the unexpected incident. Such convergence behavior constitutes a form of milling.

Milling and Sensitization

It may be seen that milling is simply the physical activity incidental to the rumor process. This physical activity does, however, have an important function in the development of collective behavior. It serves to sensitize individuals to each other. Human beings spend a great deal of time in each other's presence without being aware of one another or influenced by each other's activities. Each individual may be preoccupied with his own interests and activities, only vaguely noticing people around him except when they intrude upon his activities. Such is often the situation on a crowded street, in a busy store, or in a classroom where students are taking an examination. People gathered under such circumstances constitute hardly more than an aggregate of psychologically isolated individuals.

The stir of physical movement and the murmur of conversation, which accompany the beginning of milling, serve to draw attention to the people and their actions. The emerging crowd is itself an important stimulus, arousing curiosity and focusing attention upon the novelty and the ambiguity of the situation. The milling of a few distracts the attention of others from their own preoccupations and focuses it upon the collectivity and the object of its attention. These others, too, may then enter the milling process.

As milling continues, with an increase of physical and verbal activity, it becomes a more compelling stimulus. The individual finds it increasingly difficult to disregard the activity about him. Numerous individuals become acutely aware of the exciting aspects of the situation and of each other's reactions to them. Because of this spread of interest in a common object of attention, the term *social contagion* is appropriate.

Presensitization. Sensitization is not entirely dependent on milling, however. Even before the occurrence of an event that creates a critical situation people may be differentially responsive to one another because of group ties. Thus, prior sensitization may exist. J. R. P. French conducted an experiment in which the reactions to situations designed to evoke frustration and fear of organized and unorganized groups were compared. The results of the experiment showed that communication was freer, emotion more intense, and group action quicker to develop in groups characterized by prior sensitization because of preexisting group ties.

Organized and Unorganized Groups Under Fear and Frustration

John R. P. French, Jr.

In addition to the general attempt to study the total behavior of groups in emotional situations, the more specific purpose of the present experiment was to discover whether there is any characteristic difference between two types of groups, organized vs. unorganized, in two specific situations: one producing frustration, the other producing fear. An organized group with a recognized leader, for example, might make decisions more quickly, cooperate better, and show less interpersonal aggression when frustrated than an unorganized group. Conversely an organized group might be expected to be less afraid in a danger situation than a group of strangers gathered together for the first time.

Sixteen groups were used, eight of them unorganized and eight organized groups.

The first five organized groups were members of basketball or football teams from the upper-class Houses at Harvard. Each team had a manager through whom the experimental session was scheduled. Usually the same man was also the captain of the team, though some teams had a different man for captain and one team rotated captains at each game. Many of the members within each group had played together for more than a year. In addition to being organized as an athletic team, the members of each group lived together in the same House, often ate together, and were to some degree a friendship group. The remaining three organized groups were clubs from a neighborhood house in the Italian section of East Boston. They, too, were organized for athletics as well as being friendship groups.

Each group was put in two separate situations: (a) a frustration situation produced by working on insoluble problems; (b) a fear situation in which smoke poured into the locked rooms. The purpose of the experiment was carefully concealed from the subjects. They were told that it was an experiment in group problem solving and led to believe that all the problems were soluble. When the problem-solving session was over, the experimenter announced that the experiment was finished, dismissed the observers from the room but asked the subjects to stay a few minutes to fill out a questionnaire. The experimenter then left the room on a pretext, locking the door as he went out. Thus the group was alone in a locked room, in an apparently 'nonexperimental' situation, when the smoke started to come in. To the subjects, therefore, the two situations appeared quite

From J. R. P. French, Jr., "Organized and Unorganized Groups Under Fear and Frustration," in Kurt Lewin *et al.*, eds., *Authority and Frustration* (Iowa City: University of Iowa Press, 1944), pp. 229–308. Reprinted in part by permission of the publishers and the author.

different even though they were contiguous in time.

The results of the ratings give the most valid measurement of the motivation, frustration, we-feeling, and interdependence in the groups.

The striking differences between the two types of groups are clear. The organized groups rank higher than the unorganized on each of the four variables. As measured by Fisher's "t" test, the significance of the difference between the means for the two types of groups is above the 1 per cent point for frustration and we-feeling, above the 2 per cent point for interdependence, and slightly above the 10 per cent point for motivation. The results [of questionnaires administered to the subjects] confirm the ratings. Again the organized groups are definitely higher on both motivation and frustration.

The running comments of the observers, though not quantifiable, definitely confirmed the results of the ratings. They showed that the organized groups were more highly motivated, more frustrated, more interdependent, and had more we-feeling.

The most noticeable and probably the greatest difference between the two types of groups could not be quantified. This difference was in the degree of social freedom or social restraint in the experimental situation. Almost immediately the observers could distinguish between the organized and the unorganized groups on this basis. The running accounts of social freedom showed clearly that the organized groups were very free and uninhibited among themselves, whereas the unorganized groups were restrained, shy, and socially ill at ease at the beginning of the experiment.

Closely related to the differences in social freedom, were the differences between the two types of groups in the degree to which the members participated in the group activity. Early in the session it was particularly evident that a number of individuals in the unorganized groups were contributing practically nothing to the solution of the problem although later they participated more in the group activity. In the organized groups, on the other hand, there was markedly more equal participation at the start, but frequently one or two individuals subsequently took over more of the activity. The check list results indicated that on the whole there was more equality of participation in the organized groups.

THE FEAR SITUATION

The descriptive protocols indicate that there was considerable consistency in the behavior of individuals in the two experimental situations. The group members who were leaders in the frustration situation were usually leaders in the fear situation also. Likewise, those who were shy and restrained in the first situation tended to maintain the same role in the group during the second situation.

The reactions of the thirteen groups subjected to the fear situation varied all the way from fairly complete skepticism to genuine panic. Some groups almost immediately diagnosed the smoke as a hoax and consequently were not frightened. Three of the groups, on the contrary, apparently accepted the situation as a real fire without considering the possibility that it might be a hoax.

From the qualitative observations and from a consideration of certain imperfectly controlled factors in the situation it was clear that the production of fear was dependent on a complex of experimental factors—smoke, locked doors, sound effects, no knowledge of the situation, etc.—each one of which was important in determining the atmosphere. The organized groups showed markedly more fear than the unorganized groups. Not only were the organized groups more frightened, but it seemed to be true in general that they reacted more quickly once they were alarmed. Certainly they acted more vigorously and overtly as indicated by the fact that six out of eight organized groups attacked the door—usually with immediate results.

SUMMARY OF QUANTITATIVE RESULTS

The organized groups showed greater social freedom, we-feeling, equality of member participation in the group activity, interdependence, motivation, frustration, aggression, initial leadership, and fear. There was a statistically demonstrable effect of the social atmosphere of a group on the behavior of its members in respect to aggression, praise and encouragement, and fear.

RUMOR AND MILLING. Approaches to collective behavior relying on contagion theory have placed heavy emphasis on milling and certain related concepts. Social unrest, the incorporation of individual restlessness into a collective activity through circular reaction, has been regarded as a prelude to milling. Milling, in turn, leads to collective excitement, which then becomes the basis for the final stage of social contagion. Each of these stages apparently involves increasing suggestibility and declining critical facility. The milling process and its sequels thus provide the basis for the coordination of crowd behavior.

To view what goes on in the development of a crowd as essentially rumor rather than milling places emphasis on the development of a collective definition through symbolic interaction. This contrasts with emphasis on the development of a common pattern of behavior through suggestion. Such a conception requires, however, that rumor be regarded as a genuine group activity.

Rumor: Interaction vs. Serial Transmission

What is probably the best known and most highly elaborated theory of rumor portrays it as a type of behavior that has little resemblance either to milling or to a group activity. This is the formulation of Allport and Postman, based on laboratory studies of the serial transmission of the content of rumor.[11] This theory implies that an essential characteristic of rumor is the progressive distortion of an originally accurate statement. Shibutani comments:

The assumption is that the first speaker in the chain is an eyewitness whose report is accurate and that distortions are subsequently introduced in the relay. The account becomes

distorted as each person in the chain of transmitters drops some items and adds his own interpretation.[12]

Allport and Postman conceptualized this distortion in terms of *sharpening*, selecting and accentuating a limited number of details from a larger context, and *leveling*, making the account more concise and more easily told. Both of these processes are governed by the process of *assimilation*, "the powerful attractive force exerted upon rumor by the intellectual and emotional context existing in the listener's mind."[13]

While the processes of assimilation and sharpening have been generally recognized by students of rumor, there has been extensive debate as to whether leveling occurs in life situations. For example, Peterson and Gist challenged the existence of the economizing process of memory implied by leveling, as a result of their study of rumors that circulated in a community following the rape-murder of a babysitter.[14] They found that new themes were added to the rumor at various times, so a great deal of detail came and went. While the many themes were all related to the basic theme of the rumor, there were many details that were divergent and even contradictory. These details were not part of a series of independent rumors; they were part of the general speculation and discussion.

Gist and Peterson point out one of the important distinctions between rumor in real situations and the serial trasmission that takes place in laboratory experiments. There is a give and take in discussion, not just a unidirectional chain of communication. The hearer of a rumor is not a passive listener; he interacts with the teller, thus influencing what is transmitted to him. In

12 Shibutani, *Improvised News*, p. 14.
13 Allport and Postman, *Psychology of Rumor*, p. 100.
14 Warren A. Peterson and Noel P. Gist, "Rumor and Public Opinion," *American Journal of Sociology*, 57 (September, 1951), 159–67.

11 Gordon W. Allport and Leo Postman, *The Psychology of Rumor* (New York: Holt, Rinehart and Winston, Inc., 1947).

turn he, as a transmitter, may relay somewhat different versions to other persons because of differences in their relationships and in their reactions to his story.

ASSIMILATION. Assimilation still seems important as an explanation of how personal orientations affect the content of rumor. A person who dislikes the victim of a rumor is likely to accept and transmit a damaging report about him in a very different way than will a friend of the victim. Firth, in a study of rumors in Tikopea, suggested that certain types of rumors may serve as a social instrument in the hands of individuals or groups to improve their status.[15]

The most important function of rumor, however, is producing what Festinger and his associates have called "cognitive clarity"[16] or in Cantril's terms, "the pursuit of meaning."[17] Everyone has had the experience of being confronted with an unusual event that needed some explanation. In some circumstances, action seems desirable, but cognitive clarity is needed to guide and justify this action. When a family was mysteriously murdered in their own living room in a southern town, rumors about the identity of the murderer and the motive swept through the community. Numerous householders were wondering if the same thing might happen to them, but as long as the crime was unsolved, they did not know whom to fear. There was also a feeling that someone should be punished for such a heinous crime, but who? After a time, one theme of the rumors was that the police knew the identity of the murderer but could not arrest him because of his family's influence.

Prasad has argued that the content of

rumor may serve another function even if no action seems to be required.[18] After an unusual, highly dramatic event, rumor may serve to justify the emotions people feel by presenting imagery consistent with the feelings, whether they be of exhilaration, fear, suspicion, or grief. Thus the rumors that follow a disaster, such as the earthquakes Prasad studied, usually exaggerate the carnage.

THE SOCIAL DEFINITION OF REALITY. The pursuit of meaning is not an individual activity, nor is meaning something that the individual attains alone. In Shibutani's words, "what is called 'reality' is a social process; it is an orientation that is continuously supported by others."[19] He asked, "How does one differentiate between a hallucination and reality?" His answer:

A hallucination is a genuine sensory experience, but it is questioned precisely because it lacks social confirmation. One who sees an apparition or a flying saucer turns to his companions expecting a reaction of amazement; his faith in his own senses is badly shaken if the others act as if nothing had happened. In this sense, all knowledge is social.[20]

THE RUMOR GROUP. Rumor must be understood as a form of group interaction that involves a network of communicators who engage in a collective decision-making process, not as the chain-like transmission of a story that becomes progressively distorted. That rumor is not a constant process is explained through the validation of many experiences by culture. *Culture* constitutes a group framework for experience, and the individual is taught to master the culture so that he may comprehend his experiences without constantly referring to the immediate group for validation. When cultural explanations are not adequate, however, individuals refer to the immediate group, that is, to each other, for a verified conception of the situation.

15 Raymond Firth, "Rumor in a Primitive Society," *Journal of Abnormal and Social Psychology,* 53 (1956), 122–32.
16 Leon Festinger et al., "A Study of Rumor: Its Origin and Spread," *Human Relations,* 1 (1948), 464–86.
17 Hadley Cantril, *The Psychology of Social Movements* (New York: John Wiley and Sons, Inc., 1941), pp. 53–77.

18 Prasad, "Psychology of Rumor," p. 10.
19 Shibutani, *Improvised News,* p. 170.
20 Ibid., pp. 170–71.

It is appropriate, then, to think of rumor as occurring in a collectivity that may be called the rumor group. This is an ephemeral, emergent group—the people engaged in the rumor process. This group has a rudimentary structure and some norms. Since the rumor group is defined by only a common concern for the subject of the rumors, the norms and structure are tentative, and they are validated in the rumor process itself. Hence, in contrast to the norms and structure of more permanent, stable groups, they shift and are re-formed quickly and easily until interest in the subject subsides or some standardized, collectively sanctioned imagery has developed.

The reading, "Corpus Delicti" shows in detail the process through which a crowd arrives at such a collectively sanctioned version of an event. While a generally accepted definition of what had happened developed quickly, the complexity of the rumor process and the essentially tentative character of rumors are evident in the early stages. Initially a variety of tentative explanations was advanced. Some suggestions were accepted and others were rejected. Gradually the version that was finally accepted by the crowd became dominant, taking on a normative character. As this version received more general acceptance, group pressure was applied to individuals who advanced incompatible definitions.

Also evident in this case are the heterogeneity of the crowd and the emergence of a structure. A prestige structure developed, based not upon ordinary criteria of status but upon the relationship of different elements of the crowd to the object of interest in this particular situation.

Corpus Delicti

Eileen J. Irvin

Shortly before 9:45 a.m. one morning a woman left the room she shared with her husband in a small hotel in a suburb of Los Angeles and went downstairs. She approached their car, which was parked in a parking lot on the property of a small venetian blind factory next door to the hotel. When she opened the door, she discovered the dead body of a man wedged tightly on the floor of the back seat. The woman, suffering from heart trouble, collapsed and was taken to her room.

Her husband told police that he had been working the previous night until two o'clock and had left the car, unlocked, in a parking lot outside a local theater. He admitted that the body might have been in the back seat when he drove home, since he had not looked in the back of the car. He denied knowing the man.

The man was a stranger. Police found on the body only a social security card, a Salvation Army meal ticket, and a crude burglar's tool. He had less than one dollar in change in his pockets.

After questioning the residents of the Salvation Army hotel in Los Angeles, where the victim had been staying, the police announced that a friend of the victim had identified the owner of the car as the man with whom he and the victim had gone on a drinking spree the night before. Police arrested both men on suspicion of murder.

The car owner then changed his story. He claimed his memories of the night before had been unclear until his identification by the other man, but he was now able to reconstruct some of the events. He admitted having met the two men the previous evening and visiting several bars with them, and with an unidentified fourth man. He said that he remembered someone (presumably the "fourth man," since the other man left the party early) putting a "drunken buddy" in the

Student paper, University of California, Los Angeles. Published by permission.

back seat of the car. He claimed that the person then left to get some cigarettes and never returned. He forgot about the "drunk," and drove home, he said. His story aroused considerable skepticism. Both men were released the following day, however, when an autopsy revealed the cause of death to be acute alcoholism.

I was fortunate enough to be present shortly after the body was discovered. It was not yet ten o'clock when my mother phoned to tell me that a body had been discovered in the parking lot across the street from the store where she is employed.

Residents and employees of a factory, stores, and apartments facing the parking lot made up the initial crowd. Most of them were gathered in the parking lot when I arrived. Some of the residents of a hotel were standing on the steps, which afforded a clear view of the parking lot, or leaning from the windows.

The most striking thing about the crowd, from the very beginning, was the profusion of rumor. It is most interesting to note that, in the three days that the affair was a matter of public concern, I heard not one rumor which was not present in some form in the first hour after the discovery of the body. Even with the new information, no new rumors arose. I heard none about the unidentified "fourth man," probably because no one believed he existed.

It was less than twenty minutes since the discovery of the body and already rumors, misconceptions and speculations had arisen. It was, indeed, a rumor which had sent me to the scene. My mother relayed to me the information which she had received from some of the employees of the store who had crossed the street to the parking lot to see what the excitement was. Seeing that the car was parked in the factory parking lot, and hearing only fragments of the story, they assumed that the car belonged to the owner of the factory. They said that he had left it in the lot all night and that his wife had discovered the body after they arrived at the factory that morning. When I talked to them on my arrival they were still under this impression. It was corrected shortly, however, when the real story began to circulate more widely.

About this time, the other residents of the apartments and hotels in the neighborhood began to arrive. These were the people whose apartments were situated on the wrong side of the building, so that they were unable to see the lot. They had either heard the excitement or been told the story by their neighbors.

Up to this point I had not noticed much milling. The people were excited and curious, but they tended to stay in little groups of factory employees, store employees, or hotel residents. With the arrival of the other residents and some passers-by who had been attracted by the crowd, milling began, however. Movement had been restricted largely to getting up close to the car, taking a quick and cautious look at the corpse, and retreating hurriedly to one's own group to remark how horrible it all was. (Most people, of course, had no idea of how horrible the body actually looked, since only those with strong stomachs examined the body. They did what I confess to doing—took a quick look and ran, but not so far that they were out of range of the excitement.) Now, however, the newcomers, of whom I was one, began to move about from group to group. I will assume that my own explanation serves for the others, also. Those who had not been on the scene originally circulated from group to group trying to get the full account of what had happened. This movement on the part of the newcomers facilitated more general movement, and the milling process started, slowly at first, then becoming more intense.

I began to circulate among the factory employees. They had been the first on the scene, since they had answered the woman's screams for help when she discovered the body. From these people came the most factual account, and the most authoritative statements about the case—whether these statements were factual or not. They enjoyed considerable prestige in the crowd as a result of being first. In fact, before it was over, they were recognized authorities on the "murder." The rumors beginning here had considerable circulation.

Considered only slightly less important were the residents of the hotel where the couple resided. They could supply important background material on the personalities involved. Most of them seemed quite sure that the owner of the car was the murderer. It seemed that they could all remember "something queer" about him in the light of the murder. This view was shared by most of the members of the crowd. With only two exceptions, they were convinced that it was a murder, and the majority felt that the owner of the car was involved. Everyone, of course, had a solution to the murder even before the police arrived.

It is valuable here to note the types of rumors which arose. One timid voice was raised suggesting suicide, but this was scornfully overruled for the logical reasoh that the body had obviously been jammed into the back seat by another person, as well as because of the fact that it was contrary to the symbol of a murder which the crowd had built up.

The rest of the crowd was divided as to whether it was an accident or the result of a drunken brawl which someone had attempted to cover up by hiding the body in the car, or whether it was actually "foul play." Since those who had examined the body declared that the cuts on the face could not have been sufficient to cause death (how they knew, I cannot imagine, but it was accepted) those who believed it to be murder gave creative imagination free rein in determining the cause of death. There were probably as many causes as there were people!

Among those who believed the owner of the car to be the guilty party, reasoning was pretty much the same. They asserted that he killed the man, accidentally or otherwise, and hid the body in the car. Opinion was divided again as to the purpose of this. Some argued that he intended to find the body and act surprised, while others maintained that he intended to get rid of the body, but his wife discovered it before he could.

No rumors arose about the wife's participation in the crime. Those few suggestions which arose (usually offered by those who had not seen the woman) were vehemently rejected by the two groups with the highest prestige in the crowd—the factory employees and the hotel residents. They felt that her shock on finding the body had been too real for her to have known of its existence. Some of the hotel residents even suggested that she had collapsed not so much from the shock of finding the body, but of realizing that her husband was the murderer. There seemed to be general sympathy for the wife. She was never under police suspicion, either.

The crowd was steadily growing now. The people had spread from the parking lot to the sidewalks and the curb. They were now visible to those whose view was blocked by the front of the building, and more people stopped to inquire as to the cause of the excitement. With each repetition of the story, the excitement was heightened.

Even though the police station was a scant two blocks away, the police had not yet arrived. It was sarcastically suggested that they needed time to read up on investigating murders. This is a small town and, outside of a few robberies and waterfront brawls, the police do not have much opportunity to display their skill as investigators. A murder was an exciting event, and when the police did arrive they were as excited as the crowd.

Several cars pulled up, sirens screaming, and police piled out, all exhibiting a fine and hitherto unexpected sense of drama. They moved to the car and to the door of the hotel, clearing a path and shouting, "Get back there! Don't touch anything!" Since everyone was making way with alacrity and no one had shown any inclination to touch the car, this was rather useless, but we all decided it was part of the ritual.

By this time the crowd was really excited. This was the highest pitch of excitement and the highest phase of crowd development that the crowd attained.

Several policemen stayed outside to guard the car, while several others went inside to question the owner. Some of his story had already circulated through the crowd—spread by the hotel residents—and this was repeated for the benefit of the curious newcomers.

With the removal of the body, the first really serious opposition to the crowd image of murder was voiced. This proved later to be the correct solution! A man helping the police to move the body looked at it carefully, and then remarked scornfully and loudly, "Oh, hell! This is no murder. The guy's a lush!"

This was considered briefly, but the crowd rejected it. I rejected it myself. It was much more exciting the other way.

After the body was removed the crowd began to break up. People stayed for a while repeating the story and speculating, but the main impetus was gone. Little by little, people broke up into groups. Some went back to their work—reluctantly. Others drifted away to discuss the event over coffee or a beer. Only a few lingered on the scene, hoping for more excitement.

As this account shows, the rumor process creates an organization, with at least the beginnings of differentiation into roles. In one important aspect this organization is a prestige structure. Since prestige is established by laying claim to a rumor element that is accepted and attracts interest, another motive for participating is present. When a rumor is a subject of group preoccupation, appearing to be in the know enhances the prestige of an individual. This factor may also affect the content of the rumor, for maintaining one's prestige depends upon discrediting dissenting versions. So, in "Corpus Delicti," the continued prestige of firstcomers on the scene was dependent upon the discrediting of interpretations advanced later. LaPiere has observed that rumor creates a division between leader and audience, but the leader is in constant danger of losing his audience.[21]

DIFFERENTIAL PARTICIPATION. This should not be taken to signify that participation in a rumor group is based simply on the contemporary factors of proximity, in time and space, to the event. While this may be so in some instances, rumor does not typically take place in a collection of strangers with no preexisting interrelationship but all related in the same way to the subject of the rumor. Because of preexisting orientations and relationships, there is differential participation in the rumor process, reflected in differences in hearing, believing and relaying rumors.

As Allport and Postman have suggested in their analysis of the process of sharpening, there is selective perception, retention, and reporting of the details of a rumor

because of the preexisting wishes or fears in the mind of the listener. Simply stated, whether a person repeats a rumor and how he distorts what he does repeat is partly a function of what he wants or expects to be true. Leon Festinger and his associates, in their study of a rumor concerning alleged communist influence in an action-research project in a housing project, found that the rumor served an identifiable purpose for those who were most active in passing it on.[22] In addition they concluded that the preexisting social structure affected the spread of the rumor. Intimacy between individuals lessened the restraint against telling the rumor—more people with close friends heard it than did those with only acquaintances.

While many people may be involved in the transmission of a rumor, some participate more actively in the rumor group than do others. Not all individuals merely hear a rumor from one person and pass it on to another in a chain of communication. Instead, the interaction is transactional—many of the same people are involved over and over in the building up of the dominant imagery. The rumor passes back and forth. One person may hear, discuss, and shape not one but many versions. Thus the imagery that finally emerges as dominant is shaped by collective interaction, not simply by a series of individual distortions.

Selective Definition

The concepts of differential participation and assimilation account only partially for how a group comes to accept one definition out of all those offered in an ambiguous situation. A process of selective defini-

21 Richard T. LaPiere, *Collective Behavior* (New York: McGraw-Hill Book Company, 1938).

22 Festinger, "Study of Rumor," p. 485.

tion takes place, with the group choosing between alternative and competing interpretations, attending to some features of the situation and ignoring others. The mechanisms of keynoting, symbolization, and coordination help to complete the picture of selective definition.

KEYNOTING. When an unusual, difficult-to-assimilate event occurs, an undecided, ambivalent audience is created. Individuals entertain a variety of interpretations of the event. They may engage in a brief period of covert restructuring activity, turning over in their minds various possible explanations of what the situation is and what action may be appropriate. A gesture or symbolic utterance made to such an audience may be characterized as *keynote*. If it embodies one of the competing images held by members of the crowd, it encourages those members to express themselves. The keynote and these supporting expressions shift the balance in support of the keynoted image. Of course, if such expressions of support are not forthcoming, the effect of the utterance is lost. Thus the notion of keynoting presupposes the existence of latent support, which has not been expressed because of doubt or timidity.

Sometimes events have their own keynoting effect. Not every interpretation is equally congruent with what appears to be the situation. The nature of the event, such as finding the body in the car in "Corpus Delicti," strengthens one image at the expense of others and silences the dissenter, whose representation may sound weak and unexciting—"He's just a lush!"

The crowd's preexisting frame of reference may also give a competitive advantage to certain images. Shibutani speaks of situations of "sustained collective tension" in which responses have already begun to be mobilized.[23] In periods of racial tension, such as those in the U. S. during the long, hot summers of the 1960s, many people

were prepared to interpret the most inconsequential events as the signal for a race riot. Thus many Negroes were not ready to accept the incidents that triggered some riots as merely the manhandling of obstreperous drunks by policemen. The cry "police brutality" was a keynote that has a competitive advantage because so many Negroes anticipated mistreatment of members of their race.

Whatever the factors that cause a particular utterance to become the keynote in a crowd, the important thing is that this theme soon takes on a normative character. As more people resolve or suppress their ambivalent feelings and vocally assent to the keynote proposal, the stronger the impression grows that this is the feeling of the majority. Other crowd members find it more difficult to weigh various alternatives, particularly those that run counter to the line of action that is developing.

SYMBOLIZATION. An essential part of the preparation of a crowd for action is the development of a shared image of the object. In crowd situations, no less than at other times, man lives and acts in a symbolic environment. Symbols are the material and the product of rumor. Blumer has called this product the "object," on which "the impulses, feelings, and imagery of the people become focused." "It is," he says, "an image which has been built up and fixed through the talking and acting of people as they mill."[24] Smelser refers to "a generalized belief, which identifies the source of strain, attributes certain characteristics to this source, and specifies certain responses to the strain as possible or appropriate."[25]

The symbol functions to indicate the implementation of the situation, or what is to be done about it, and to clarify the claim to legitimacy for this line of action.

---

[23] Shibutani, *Improvised News*, p. 49.

[24] Herbert Blumer, "Collective Behavior," in A. M. Lee, ed., *Principles of Sociology* (New York: Barnes and Noble, Inc., 1951), p. 179.

[25] Neil J. Smelser, *Theory of Collective Behavior* (New York: The Free Press, 1963), p. 16.

Thus symbolization simplifies the situation. As Smelser put it, "Generalized beliefs restructure an ambiguous situation in a short-circuited way...Short-circuiting involves the jump from extremely high levels of generality to specific, concrete situations."[26] Drabek and Quarantelli have found, for example, that following a disaster that involves a complex set of causes, such as a fire in a public building, the public tends to symbolize the responsibility by blaming the occurrence on the dereliction of duty of a few public officials who can be fired or otherwise penalized.[27] The individual official constitutes an accessible symbol.

A southern college community, like many others, experienced social disruption in 1960 because of sit-ins staged at lunch counters by students from white and Negro colleges in the town. The sit-ins were planned in great secrecy by a CORE chapter, which had no official standing with the administration of either college. A rumor soon developed among outraged townsmen to the effect that certain professors at the white university were behind the plot. While these professors had been outspoken in their criticism of segregation, they had no connection with, or even prior knowledge of, the sit-ins. Yet a segment of the citizenry united in a program of action designed to have them dismissed from their jobs and to run them out of town.

A classic example of the function of a symbol in directing and facilitating crowd action was the destruction of the Bastille by the Paris mob in 1789. Lightly garrisoned, containing only a few prisoners, this fortress was no longer a bulwark of the oppressive Old Regime. It was, however, a visible and accessible symbol of oppression. The example of the Bastille shows that the object is not simply a stimulus that, because of its intrinsic or objective character, evokes a particular response from the crowd. It is, rather, an object that symbolizes the cause of the situation and that stirs the demands for action. It has the additional characteristic of being accessible. It enables the crowd to act quickly and forcefully, permitting the expression of aroused feelings. Logical analysis may show that the action does not accomplish what the crowd thinks it will. It may change the situation little or not at all. Yet a symbol is necessary before the crowd will act, so the crowd evolves some symbol that will permit action.

In the instance of the college professors in the southern town, an important element of the rumor was the inflammatory label "integrationist." In the prevailing context, this label served to legitimatize the action proposed. This constituted a mystical type of symbol, which Levy-Bruhl distinguished from a cognitive symbol.[28] The referent for the cognitive symbol, according to the French sociologist, is sharply separable from the feelings that the object arouses in the user. The object of a mystical symbol, however, tends to be identified primarily by the emotional response that it arouses. The symbols most likely to gain currency in collective behavior are mystical rather than cognitive. They invest the object of the crowd action with an aura of infamy, of tragedy, or of nobility. Symbols may also arise to characterize the crowd itself. Members of a mob bent on some type of vigilante action may refer to themselves as patriotic, red-blooded Americans.

The development of an unambiguous, mystical symbol also serves to neutralize norms that might inhibit the crowd from unrestrained action toward its object. Such a symbol serves to eliminate connotations that arouse ambivalence. The operation of this process over a long period of time is illustrated in the following study.

---

26 Ibid., p. 82.
27 Thomas E. Drabek and Enrico L. Quarantelli, "Scapegoats, Villains, and Disasters," *Trans-Action,* 4 (March, 1967), 12–17.

28 L. Levy-Bruhl, *Les Fonctions Mentales dans les Societes Inferieurs* (Paris: Librairie Felix Alcan, 1910).

Zoot-Suiters and Mexicans: Symbols in Crowd Behavior

Ralph H. Turner and Samuel J. Surace

In this paper we shall report the test of an hypothesis concerning the symbols with which a hostile crowd designates the object of its action. Our hypothesis is that hostile crowd behavior requires an unambiguously unfavorable symbol, which serves to divert crowd attention from any of the usual favorable or mitigating connotations surrounding the object being attacked. The hypothesis has been tested by a content analysis of references to the symbol, "Mexican," during the ten and one half year period leading up to the 1943 "Zoot-Suit" riots in Los Angeles and vicinity. We shall begin by discussing the theory from which the hypothesis is derived, followed by a statement of findings and their interpretation in light of the hypothesis.

Theory and Hypothesis. The hypothesis under examination is related to two important characteristics of crowd behavior. Based on these two characteristics, certain conditions are indicated as necessary to the development of hostile acting crowd behavior. These necessary conditions can, in turn, be related to the connotations surrounding the symbols by which the crowd designates the object of its hostile attack.

First, crowd behavior is *uniform* behavior in a broad sense. By contrast, much noncrowd behavior exposes the infinitely varied attitudes of diverse individuals. Many attitudes and gradations of feeling can be evidenced in a group's actions toward any particular object. However, the crowd is a group expressing *one* attitude, with individual variations largely concealed. Many people are acting in accordance with a single dominant definition of the situation.

In noncrowd situations uniform behavior may be achieved in a group by a process of majority

From Ralph H. Turner and Samuel J. Surace, "Zoot-Suiters and Mexicans: Symbols in Crowd Behavior," *The American Journal of Sociology*, 62 (1956), 14–20. Reprinted in part by permission of the University of Chicago Press.

decision, acceptance of authority, or compromise of some sort. But the uniformity of crowd behavior is not mediated by such slow and deliberate procedures for reaching agreement. Within the crowd there is a readiness to act uniformly in response to varied suggestions. Until such readiness to act *uniformly* has spread throughout the crowd's recruitment group, fully developed and widespread acting crowd behavior is not possible.

The response in the community to shared symbols is crucial to this uniformity of action. Ordinarily any particular symbol has varied connotations for different individuals and groups in the community. These varied connotations prevent uniform community-wide action, or at least delay such action until extended processes of group decision-making have been carried out. But when a given symbol has relatively uniform connotations in all parts of the community, uniform group action can be taken rather readily if the occasion seems to demand it. *To the degree, then, to which any symbol evokes only one consistent set of connotations throughout the community, only one general course of action with respect to that object will be indicated, and the union of diverse members of the community into an acting crowd will be facilitated.*

Second, the crowd follows a course of action which is at least partially sanctioned in the culture, but which is normally inhibited by other aspects of that culture. Mob action is frequently nothing more than culturally sanctioned punishment carried out by unauthorized persons without "due process." The fact that such behavior has support in everyday life is attested to in many ways. Organizations such as the Ku Klux Klan and other vigilante groups act as self-appointed "custodians of patriotism," and are fairly widely accepted as such. The lynching of two "confessed" kidnappers in California in 1933 was given public sanction by the then governor of the state on the grounds of its therapeutic effect on other would-be criminals. The legal system in America implicitly recognizes these supports by including laws in the statute books designed to counteract such actions.

Hostile acting crowd behavior can take place only when these inhibiting aspects of the culture cease to operate. In a sense there is cultural conflict between the norms sanctioning the crowd's action and the norms inhibiting it. For the crowd to blossom into full-scale action the conflict must be resolved by neutralization of the inhibiting norms.

The connotations surrounding the symbol which designates the object of a crowd's hostile actions are crucial in this connection also. There is normally some ambiguity in the connotations of any symbol, so that both favorable and unfavorable sentiments are aroused. For example, even the most prejudiced person is likely to respond to the symbol, "Negro," with images of both the feared invader of white prerogatives and the lovable, loyal Negro lackey and "mammy." The symbol, "bank robber," is likely to evoke a picture of admirable daring along with its generally unfavorable image. It is our contention that these ambiguities of connotation, which evoke ambivalent feelings in persons using the symbols, play an important part in inhibiting consummatory or extreme hostile behavior against the object represented by the symbol.

The diverse connotations of any symbol normally inhibit extreme behavior in two interrelated ways. First, the symbol evokes feelings which resist any extreme course of action. A parent, for example, is normally inhibited from punishing his child to excess no matter what the child's offense may be because feelings of affection are also aroused which limit the development of anger. Sentiments of pity and admiration for courage or resolute action, or sympathy for a course of action which many of us might like to engage in ourselves, or charity toward human weakness, usually moderate feelings of hostility toward violators of the mores. So long as the individual's feelings are mixed his actions are likely to be moderate.

Second, the mixed connotations of the symbol place the object *within the normative order,* so that the mores of fair play, due process, giving a fair hearing, etc., apply. Any indication that the individual under attack respects any of the social norms or has any of the characteristics of the in-group invokes these mores which block extreme action.

On the other hand, symbols which are unambiguous in their connotations permit immoderate behavior toward the object in question. In the absence of ambivalence toward an object there is no internal conflict to restrict action. Furthermore, a symbol which evokes a pure image of a person outside the normative order provides no justification for applying the ingroup norms of fair play and due process. The principle that "we must fight fire with fire," or that a person devoid of human decency is not himself entitled to be treated with decency and respect, rules out these inhibiting norms.

In summary, then, we have observed that crowd behavior consists of (a) action reflecting a uniform sentiment throughout the group involved in crowd behavior and (b) behavior which is not moderated by the usually inhibiting social norms and sentiments. *A necessary condition for both uniform group action and unrestricted hostile behavior is the presence of a symbol which arouses uniformly and exclusively unfavorable feelings in the group toward the object under attack.*

Two qualifications must be added before we discuss the empirical test of the hypothesis. First, our discussion of the connotations of the symbol refers to the manner in which the symbol is presented to the mass or partially developed crowd. Changes in the connotations of a symbol *to the mass or crowd* do not necessarily imply a generality of closely corresponding changes *within individuals.* The symbol as presented in the group context mediates the *overt expression* of attitudes in terms of *sanction* and the focus of *attention.* (a) The individual in whom a particular symbol evokes exclusively unfavorable feelings may nevertheless be inhibited from acting according to his feelings by the awareness that other connotations are *sanctioned* in the group. Or the individual in whom ambivalent feelings are evoked may conceal his favorable sentiments because he sees that only the unfavorable sentiments are sanctioned. He thereby facilitates crowd use of the symbol. (b) Furthermore, of all the possible connotations attached to a symbol, the individual at any given moment acts principally in terms of those on which his *attention* is focussed. By shielding individuals from attending to some of the possible connotations of a symbol, the unambiguous public symbol prevents the evocation of attitudes which are normally present. Thus, without necessarily undergoing change, favorable individual attitudes toward the object of crowd attack may simply remain latent because of the uniform connotations of the symbol before the crowd. This process is one of the aspects of the so-called "restriction of attention" which characterizes the crowd.

Second, while the emergence of unambiguous symbols is a necessary condition to full-fledged crowd behavior, it may also be a *product* of the earlier stages of crowd development. In some cases a rather sudden crowd development is probably facilitated by the pre-existing linkage of an already unambiguous symbol to the object upon which events focus collective attention. But more commonly we suspect that the emergence of such a symbol or the stripping away of alternative connotations from an established symbol takes place cumulatively through interaction centered on that object. Over a period of time, community-wide interaction about an object takes on increasingly crowd-like characteristics, as there is a gradual preparation for the final consummatory crowd action.

With this latter qualification in mind we shall hypothesize that *a period of overt hostile crowd behavior is usually preceded by a period in which the key symbol is stripped of its favorable connotations until it comes to evoke unambiguously unfavorable feelings.*

The "Zoot-Suit Riots." Beginning on June 3, 1943, Los Angeles, California was the scene of sporadic acts of violence involving principally United States Naval personnel with the support of a sympathetic anglo community and members of the Mexican community. This period of crowd violence has come to be known as the "zoot-suit riots." The designation "zooter" referred mainly to two characteristics. First, the zoot suit was a style of clothing featuring long suit-coats and trousers which were extremely pegged at the cuff, draping fully around the knees and terminating in deep pleats at the waist. Second, the zooters wore their hair long, full, and well greased.

We shall not describe the action in detail. It is sufficient to state that many attacks and injuries were sustained by both sides. Groups of sailors were frequently reported to be assisted or accompanied by civilian mobs who "egged" them on as they roamed through downtown streets in search of victims. "Zooters" discovered on city streets were assaulted and forced to disrobe amidst the jibes and molestations of the crowd. Streetcars and buses were stopped and searched. "Zooters" found therein were carried off into the streets and subjected to beatings. Cavalcades of hired taxicabs filled with sailors ranged the east-side districts of Los Angeles seeking, finding and attacking "zooters." Civilian gangs of east-side adolescents organized similar attacks against unwary naval personnel, inflicting injury and swelling the cries of "outrage."

It is, of course, impossible to isolate a single incident or event and hold it responsible for the riots. Local, State, and Federal authorities, and numerous civic and national groups were ultimately involved in the attempt to assess blame and prevent further violence. The most prominently reported *claim* of both antagonists referred to the other as molesting "our girls." For example, it was reported that sailors became enraged over learning that zoot-suiters were responsible for "assaults on female relatives of servicemen." Similarly, the claim against sailors was that they persisted in molesting and insulting girls belonging to the Mexican community. While many other charges were reported in the newspapers, including unsubstantiated suggestions of sabotage with respect to the war effort, the *precipitating* context was dominated by implications of acute and improper sexual competition.

Method. In the absence of any direct sampling of community sentiment in the period preceding the riots we have assumed that the use of the symbol, "Mexican," by the media of mass communication can be taken as an indication of the connotations prevalent in the community. In making this assumption we beg all questions of moral responsibility for the riot and of direction of influence between community sentiment and the mass media. Whether the mass media passively reflect community sentiment or whether they actively mold it, or whether, as we suppose, some combination of the two processes occurs, we should still be justified in using the content of mass media to indicate community feeling. Ideally we should have sampled a variety of mass media to correct for biases in each. However, with the limited human resources at our disposal we chose one newspaper, the *Los Angeles Times*. The *Times* has the largest circulation of the four major newspapers in the Los Angeles area. It is conservative in emphasis, and tends away from the sensational treatment of minority issues. In the past a foremost romanticizer of old Mexico had been a prominent member of the *Times* editorial staff and Board of Directors.

In order to uncover trends in the connotations of the symbol under study, one newspaper per month was read for the ten and one half year period from January, 1933, until June 20, 1943. These monthly newspapers were selected by assigning consecutive days of the week to each month. For example, for January, 1933, the paper printed on the first Monday was read; for February, the paper printed on the first Tuesday was read. After the seven day cycle was completed the following months were assigned, respectively, the *second* Monday, the *second* Tuesday, etc. To avoid loading the sample with days that fell early in the first half of the month, the procedure was reversed for the last half of the period under consideration.

In order to secure an intensive picture of the critical period, consecutive daily editions were read for one month starting with May 20, 1943, through June 20, 1943. This covered approximately ten days before and after the period of violence. Data gathered from this group of newspapers will receive separate analysis.

Any editorial, story, report, or letter which had reference to the Mexican community or population was summarized, recorded, and classified. The articles were placed in five basic categories: favorable themes, unfavorable themes, neutral mention, negative-favorable mention, and "zooter" theme.

If the hypothesis of this paper is to be supported, we should expect a decline in the favorable contexts of the symbol "Mexican," as it manifests itself in the newspaper content throughout the indicated time span. The change should serve to produce the type of symbol suggested by the hypothesis, a symbol dominated by unambiguously unfavorable elements.

Findings. The favorable and unfavorable themes are reported alone in Table 1 for the ten and one half year period. The table by itself appears to negate our hypothesis, since there is no appreciable decline in the percent of favorable themes during the period. Indeed, even during the last period the mentions appear predominantly favorable, featuring the romanticized Mexican. However, there is a striking decline in the total number of articles mentioning the Mexican between the second and third periods. Treating the articles listed as a fraction of all articles in the newspapers sampled and using a sub-minimal estimate of the total number of all articles, the "t" test reveals that such a drop in the total number of articles mentioning Mexicans could have occurred by chance less than twice in one hundred times. We conclude, then, that the decline in total favorable and unfavorable mentions of Mexican is statistically significant.

TABLE 1 Favorable and Unfavorable Mention of "Mexican" during Three Periods

Period	Favorable Themes	Unfavorable Themes	Percent Favorable
Jan., 1933– June, 1936	27	3	90
July, 1936– Dec., 1939	23	5	82
Jan., 1940– June, 1943	10	2	83
Total	60	10	86

While the hypothesis in its simplest form is unsubstantiated, the drop in both favorable and unfavorable themes suggests a shift away from *all* of the traditional references to Mexicans during the period prior to the riots. If it can be shown that an actual *substitution* of symbols was taking place, our hypothesis may still be substantiated, but in a somewhat different light than anticipated.

From the distribution of all five themes reported in Table 2 it is immediately evident that there has been no decline of interest in the "Mexican," but rather a clear-cut shift of attention away from

TABLE 2 Distribution of All Themes by Three Periods

	Percent Favorable	Percent Unfavorable	Percent Neutral	Percent Negative-Favorable	Percent Zooter	Total Percent	Total Number
Jan., 1933–June, 1936	80	9	11	0	0	100	34
July, 1936–Dec., 1939	61	13	23	3	0	100	38
Jan., 1940–June, 1943	25	5	32	8	30	100	40

traditional references. The straightforward favorable and unfavorable themes account for eighty-nine percent, seventy-four percent, and thirty percent of all references respectively during the three periods. This drop and the drop from sixty-one to twenty-five percent favorable mentions are significant below the one percent level. To determine whether this evidence confirms our hypothesis, we must make careful examination of the three emerging themes.

The *neutral* theme shows a steady increase throughout the three periods. While we have cautiously designated this "neutral," it actually consists chiefly of unfavorable presentations of the object, "Mexican," without overt use of the symbol, "Mexican." Thus it incorporates the unfavorable representation of Mexican, which we assume was quite generally recognized throughout the community, without explicit use of the symbol.

The *negative-favorable* theme, though small in total numbers, also shows an increase throughout the period examined. At first we were inclined to treat these as favorable themes. However, in contrast to the other favorable themes, this one gives recognition to the extent of negative connotation which is accumulating about the symbol, "Mexican." By arguing openly against the negative connotations these articles acknowledge to the reader that there is widespread community sanction for such negative connotations. When the implicitly favorable themes of romantic Mexico and California's historic past give way to defensive assertions that all Mexicans are not bad, such a shift can only reasonably be interpreted as a rise in unfavorable connotations.

The most interesting shift, however, is the rise of the *Zoot-suit* theme, which did not appear at all until the third period when it accounts for thirty percent of the references. Here we have the

emergence of a new symbol which has no past favorable connotations to lose. Unlike the symbol, "Mexican," the "Zoot-suiter" symbol evokes no ambivalent sentiments but appears in exclusively unfavorable contexts. While in fact Mexicans were attacked indiscriminately in spite of apparel, the symbol *Zoot-suiter* could become a basis for unambivalent community sentiment supporting hostile crowd behavior more easily than could "Mexican."

It is interesting to note that when we consider only the fifteen mentions which appear in the first six months of 1943, ten are to *zooters,* three are *negative-favorable,* two are *neutral,* and none are the traditional favorable or unfavorable themes.

In Table 3 we report the results of the day-by-day analysis of the period immediately prior, during, and after the riots. Here we see the culmination of a trend faintly suggested as long as seven years before the riots and clearly indicated two or three years in advance. The traditional favorable and unfavorable themes have vanished completely and three-quarters of the references center about the *zooter* theme.

Discussion. From the foregoing evidence we conclude that our basic hypothesis and theory receive confirmation, but not in exactly the manner

TABLE 3 Distribution of All Themes from May 20 to June 20, 1943

Theme	Percent of All Mentions
Favorable	0
Unfavorable	0
Neutral	3
Negative-favorable	23
Zooter	74
Total	100
Total (number)	(61)

envisaged in advance. The simple expectation that there would be a shift in the relative preponderance of favorable and unfavorable contexts for the symbol "Mexican" was not borne out. But the basic hypothesis that an unambiguously unfavorable symbol is required as the rallying point for hostile crowd behavior is supported through evidence that the symbol "Mexican" tended to be displaced by the symbol *Zoot-suiter* as the period of actual crowd behavior was approached.

It should be recalled that the conception of the romantic Mexican and the Mexican heritage are deeply ingrained in Southern California tradition. The Plaza and Olvera Street in downtown Los Angeles, the Ramona tradition, the popularity of Mexican food, and many other features serve to perpetuate this tradition. It seems quite probable that the force of this tradition was too strong to be eradicated entirely from community awareness, even though it ceased to be an acceptable matter of public presentation. In spite, then, of a progressive decline in public presentation of the symbol in its traditional favorable contexts, a certain ambivalence remained which prevented a simple replacement with predominantly unfavorable connotations.

Rather, two techniques emerged for circumventing the ambivalence. One was the technique of presenting the object in an obvious manner without explicit use of the symbol. Thus an obviously Mexican name, a picture, or reference to "East side hoodlums" was presented in an unfavorable context. But a far more effective device was uncovered with the emergence of a new symbol whose connotations at the time were exclusively unfavorable. This symbol provided the public sanction and restriction of attention essential to the development of overt hostile crowd behavior. The symbol, *Zoot-suiter*, evoked none of the imagery of the romantic past. It evoked only the picture of a breed of persons outside of the normative order, devoid of morals themselves and consequently not entitled to fair play and due process. Indeed, the zoot-suiter came to be regarded as such an exclusively fearful threat to the community that at the height of rioting the Los Angeles City Council seriously debated an ordinance making the wearing of zoot-suits a prison offence.

The *zooter* symbol had a crisis character which simply unfavorable reference to the familiar *Mexican* symbol could never approach in effectiveness. And the zooter was an omnibus symbol drawing together the most reprehensible elements in the old unfavorable themes, namely, sex crimes, delinquency, gang attacks, draft dodgers, etc. Any one of these elements by itself lacked the wide applicability possessed by the *zooter* symbol.

The *zooter* symbol also supplies an objective tag with which to identify the object of attack. It could be used, when the old attitudes toward Mexicans were evoked, to differentiate Mexicans along both moral and tangible physical lines. While the active minority were attacking Mexicans indiscriminately, and frequently including Negroes, the great sanctioning majority heard only of attacks on *zoot-suiters*.

Once established the zooter theme assured its own magnification. What previously would have been reported as an adolescent gang attack would now be presented as a zoot-suit attack. Weapons found on apprehended youths were now interpreted as the building up of arms collections in preparation for zoot-suit violence. In short, the *zooter* symbol had absorbed many of the elements formerly present and sometimes associated with Mexicans along with the objective accoutrements of the zoot-suiter into a new unity. This new unity relieved the community of ambivalence and moral obligations toward the objects who could then become the sanctioned victims of widespread hostile crowd behavior.

APPENDIX

The following themes and sub-themes were found to recur in the data. The subthemes were not used separately in the report.

(1) *Favorable*
   (a) Old California Theme
       This is devoted to extolling the traditions and history of the old rancheros as the earliest California settlers.
   (b) Mexican Temperament Theme
       This describes the Mexican character in terms of dashing romance, bravery, gaiety, etc.
   (c) Religious Theme
       This has reference to the devout religious values of the Mexican community.

(d) Mexican Culture Theme

This pays homage to Mexican art, dance, crafts, music, fifth of May festivities, etc.

(2) *Unfavorable*

(a) Delinquency and Crime Theme

This theme includes the specific mention of a law violator as "Mexican," associating him with marihuana, sex crimes, knife wielding, gang violence, etc.

(b) Public Burden Theme

This attempts to show that Mexicans constitute a drain on relief funds and on the budgets of correctional institutions.

(3) *Neutral*

This is a category of miscellaneous items including reports of crimes committed by individuals possessing obvious Mexican names but without designation of ethnic affiliation.

(4) *Negative-Favorable*

This category consists of appeals which counter or deny the validity of accusations against Mexicans as a group. For example, ". . . not all zoot-suiters are delinquents; their adoption by many was a bid for social recognition . . ."; or ". . . at the outset zoot-suiters were limited to no specific race . . . The fact that later on their numbers seemed to be predominantly Latin was in itself no indication of that race . . ."

(5) *Zooter Theme*

This theme identifies the zooter costume as "a badge of delinquency." Typical references were, "reat pleat boys," "long coated gentry," coupled with mention of "unprovoked attacks by zoot-suited youths," "zoot-suit orgy," etc. Crime, sex-violence, and gang attacks were the dominant elements in this theme. Almost invariably, the "zooter" was identified as a Mexican by such clues as "Eastside hoodlum," a Mexican name, or specific ethnic designation.

COORDINATION. A third function of the symbol for the crowd is the coordination of disparate elements. A symbol that calls attention to the separate interests of the collectivity does not permit unified action. The effective coordinating symbol must emphasize those features that a wide range of people may respond to in a uniform manner. In illustration, Leighton found that two unifying symbols, which facilitated collective action by Japanese-Americans in the Relocation Center at Poston during World War II, were those of the dog (informer) and the martyr.[29] The Japanese-Americans were divided into numerous factions, the major cleavage being between American-born and Japanese-born internees. All could respond uniformly, however, to those symbols that were rooted in Japanese tradition and emphasized the hostility that all factions felt toward the Caucasian camp managers. The unity of the Japanese-Americans was disrupted, on the other hand, when the Japanese-born

[29] S. H. Leighton, *The Governing of Men* (Princeton, N.J.: Princeton University Press, 1946).

internees invoked symbols of Japanese nationalism.

RUMOR AND CROWD ACTION. It has been emphasized that collective behavior does not take place in a normless situation; it occurs under the influence of emergent norms that define the crowd action as right. Furthermore, norms that seem to legitimatize the action of the crowd also enhance the sense of power. The sense of righteousness and the illusion of invincibility grow together, each reinforcing the other. Symbols that simplify the situation, eliminate ambiguous and conflicting connotations of the object, and provide a basis for uniform response to the object constitute the fundamentals of crowd action. It is through the communicative process identified as rumor that such symbols and the norms congruent with them develop.

THE TERMINATION OF RUMOR. It is a popular misconception that when the truth about a situation is announced, rumor ceases. While this may be true in some cases, this belief is a great oversimplification of the conditions under which rumor terminates. As was shown in "Corpus Delicti," the true story may be advanced during the course of rumor without being accepted by the rumor group. In other cases, versions that are subsequently proven false may be accepted and become the basis of crowd action. This was one of the tragic elements of many lynchings. Not only were they savage acts of extralegal punishment, but in many cases, the victim was not even the criminal. In other cases, no crime had even been committed—except by the crowd that believed a rumor!

Shibutani proposes that "the process of *rumor construction is terminated when the situation in which it arose is no longer problematic.*"[30] In line with the proposition that reality is a social process, a situation ceases to be problematic when consensus about its meaning is reached. Sometimes effective consensus flies in the face of official pronouncements or logico-empirical tests of truth. Festinger has observed:

> *If more and more people can be persuaded that the system of belief is correct, then clearly it must, after all, be correct.* Consider the extreme case: if everyone in the whole world believed something there would be no question at all as to the validity of this belief.[31]

As a keynote elicits increasing expressions of support, the crowd becomes the whole world for the members. Those who are ambivalent find their doubts resolved in favor of the developing definition. Those who are still inclined to dissent experience a growing sense of pressure to hide their disagreement by remaining silent or withdrawing.

[30] Shibutani, *Improvised News*, p. 139.
[31] Leon Festinger et al., *When Prophecy Fails* (Minneapolis: The University of Minnesota Press, 1956), p. 28.

In a crowd situation the individual's range of attention is narrowed. In the extreme case, the individual's orientation is determined solely in terms of the present crowd members. The influence of his usual identification groups and their norms is attenuated, and the individual's sense of moral rightness is determined by the compelling presence of other crowd members. The appearance of unanimity in the crowd, even though it may be illusory, gives the same kind of basis for believing that the crowd's position is morally incontestable that the individual gets from groups that he identifies with outside the crowd situation.

THE DEVELOPMENT OF CROWD ACTION. It is obvious that the termination of the rumor process does not always result in crowd action of a particular kind. At times the crowd's curiosity is satisfied. The crowd has constituted nothing more than an audience that disperses when the show is over. Even if externally-oriented action—to do something about the situation—is not defined as appropriate, the crowd may engage in expressive behavior, giving vent to feelings of amusement, exhilaration, or grief. In some situations, however, the definition is such that normative pressure develops for the crowd to do something, and a line of behavior develops that is active, not merely expressive.

In this chapter we have concentrated on the communication process that goes on within the collectivity, compact or diffuse, in the development of unified crowd action. A broader question is, "When does collective behavior take place?" The emergence of collective behavior must be considered in the context of those societal conditions under which the established organization and culture cease to afford direction and supply channels for action.

4

THE EMERGENCE
OF COLLECTIVE BEHAVIOR

Episodes of collective behavior contrast, sometimes quite dramatically, with what appears to be the routine, smooth-flowing course of social life. People who usually follow their accustomed, day-to-day schedule of working, playing, sleeping, and eating with others whose patterns of behavior seem almost as predictable suddenly become part of a crowd. They forsake their normal patterns for a few minutes, for hours, or even for days, to gather at the scene of an accident, to linger in abnormally long bull sessions speculating about the outcome of a political crisis, or to become part of a mob burning and looting a section of a city. The agencies that are ordinarily relied upon to manage the complex affairs of society according to accepted principles are challenged by new constellations of people. These social movements question the principles by which the agencies operate and sometimes the legitimacy of their authority. In most cases the shift of people from their usual pattern of activity is related to some exciting event that disrupts the smooth flow of life and, in this sense, seems to cause the collective behavior.

The analysis of rumor as the characteristic form of communication in the collectivity reveals that events do not simply trigger the transition from normal to collective behavior. Instead, the latter develops through a search for meaning and a process of collective redefinition of the situation. To understand the emergence of collective behavior, we must examine the conditions and forces that lead men to engage in such a process. This involves a consideration of the sources of social stability in an established social order and the circumstances under which men are impelled to construct a new social order.

Sources of Social Stability

Terms such as *stable social order* and *social system* suggest that in its normal state, a society operates smoothly, like a well-oiled machine. Individuals and groups, the components of the system, play their parts correctly and comfortably, guided by universally understood and accepted values and norms. There would seem to be no need for the construction of a new social order unless the machine broke down and failed to function normally. Strain, conflict, and social change would be regarded as abnormal phenomena, signifying the existence of a state of social disorganization.

Actually social life is never such a smooth, orderly, day-to-day routine. In spite of the presence of many regularities, there are always stresses, conflicts, unfulfilled aspirations, and unexpected disruptions. At the same time the strains and the exciting events are not always critical, in the sense of being incidents that precipitate collective behavior. It has often been pointed out, for example, that many of the conditions of stress and deprivation, which have been invoked to account for the urban riots of the 1960s, were present for many years without uprisings. While these conditions may have contributed over the years to many acts of individual deviant behavior, they did not lead to collective behavior of the sort witnessed later.

THE TAKEN-FOR-GRANTED BASIS OF EVERYDAY LIFE. People do act much of the time as if they did operate within a stable, well-ordered social system. Any teacher of introductory sociology will testify that while his beginning students are quick to challenge the proposal that human social behavior can be predicted, they act as if they live in a highly predictable world. Even in a highly complex, mechanized culture, the average man proceeds through each day of his life by taking a tremendous number of things about the system for granted. He assumes that skyscrapers will remain firm on their foundations; that the elevators will take him safely to his floor; that the intricate and delicate telephone net will keep him in touch with the world while he perches in the lofty cell that is his office. He takes for granted the existence and performance of a whole army of functionaries who direct traffic, extinguish fires, keep the stores filled with merchandise, process the food he eats, and perform other tasks that would take up most of his waking hours if he had to do them himself. He does not carry a gun or a knife because he assumes that there is a structure of authority that regulates his relationships with his fellow citizens and protects him from his enemies. It is obvious that his predictions are not always correct. His perplexity, frustration, and anger when any of his assumptions prove, even temporarily, unfounded testify to the strength of his belief in the orderliness of his world.

Of course social life, even in the best of times, is not nearly so orderly as this conception of reality implies. As Shibutani observes, "Although some societies may give a superficial appearance of stability, some kind of change is inevitable. New events are continually taking place, and nothing hap-

pens twice in exactly the same way. Each situation must successively be defined as action develops in it, for the activity itself modifies the situation."[1] When a sizable proportion of society ceases to take for granted the orderliness and predictability of everyday life, collective behavior will increase. Some observers have suggested that an underlying condition for the social unrest and collective behavior which is so prevalent among young people who have grown up in the nuclear age, is their feeling that they cannot take the future for granted.

THE NORMATIVE ORDER AND SOCIAL STRUCTURE. One of the major contributions of sociology to mankind's fund of knowledge is the theory that while there is a degree of order and regularity in man's social life, this regularity is not imposed by man's biological nature but by society. This does not mean that society is a metaphysical force that mysteriously guides the affairs of men. It means that as men, in their interaction, develop groups with properties of their own—social structure, values, and norms—these group properties become part of man's environment. This is what Emile Durkheim alluded to when he said that "collective representations" were characterized by exteriority, priority, and constraint. Although men lack the natural adaptive mechanisms that instinct would provide, the human individual does not experience life as a constant succession of crises in which he must decide for himself what to do next. Instead, as he is cared for and taught by the older members of his group, he acquires guidelines and directions that structure his encounters with his environment. He learns classifications for the many objects in his world, including himself and other persons. He learns what things it is good to strive for—values. He acquires norms—rules on how to behave. He learns standardized patterns for regulat-

---

[1] Tamotsu Shibutani, *Improvised News* (Indianapolis: The Bobbs-Merrill Co., Inc., 1966), p. 167.

ing his own interaction with other people—roles. Thus we may identify two of the major sources of social stability as the normative order and social structure.

The normative order refers to agreement on values, the goals of social action, and norms, formal or informal rules defining the behavior expected of group members. To the extent that there is such agreement or consensus, the behavior of the individuals in a society should mesh together in a smooth, predictable manner.

The social structure refers to a division of labor in the society—the relating of the tasks or activities of individual members to each other and to group purposes. Out of this division arises a structure of interdependent roles, consisting of stabilized expectations for the behavior of each member in relation to other members. Again, to the extent that each role is filled and each occupant plays his role in the expected manner, the group should function smoothly in achieving its goals.

Sources of Conformity and of Change

Much of the orderliness and predictability of human behavior may be explained by individual internalization of values, norms, and roles. One outcome of the socialization process is that the individual learns what the group expects of him. Then those norms and values become his own. He does not question them or disagree with them; he conforms to them. Were compliance with social norms based solely on this sort of acquiescence, then the regularity of social behavior would have a much less tenuous and labile character than it does. Although the individual may internalize norms in the sense of knowing them, this does not mean that he always agrees or that he is never tempted to violate them.

CONFORMITY AND FEAR OF PUNISHMENT. As Dennis Wrong has suggested in a critique of the notion of internalization as simple acquiescence, some of man's ob-servance of social norms is rooted in fear of punishment for violation of these norms.[2] The sanctions that might be imposed range from illegal violence, through legally imposed punishments, to the withdrawal of acceptance by other people. Obviously, reduction of the fear that deviations from the norms will be punished increases the likelihood that new patterns of behavior will be followed. This is the process suggested by Ladd Wheeler in his analysis of behavioral contagion.[3]

The internalization of norms may result in another kind of fear—fear that violations will lead to feelings of guilt or remorse. Such fear of self-punishment does not necessarily eliminate the temptation to act, however. Psychologists have conceptualized this sort of internal conflict as the balance between approach and avoidance tendencies. Here again it is obvious that reduction of the likelihood that intropunitive responses will follow increases the probability that normally inhibited behavioral tendencies may be acted out.

AMBIVALENCE. This sort of internal conflict is a specific instance of the more general ambivalence that characterizes the attitudes of individuals. As has been pointed out before, people may simultaneously hold not just one or two but several orientations toward an object, and these different attitudes may come into play in different situations. Influences that inhibit the expression of certain attitudes in a situation increase the likelihood that others will be expressed, even though the latter may be ones that are usually restrained. Thus, a private citizen may ordinarily regard a policeman as a protector who should be respected and as an underpaid public servant who must perform unpleasant and dangerous tasks. As a member of a crowd

2 Dennis Wrong, "The Oversocialized Conception of Man," *American Sociological Review*, 26 (April, 1961), 183–93.
3 Ladd Wheeler, "Toward a Theory of Behavioral Contagion," *Psychological Review*, 73 (March, 1966), 179–92.

whose activities the policeman is opposing, this same citizen may think of the officer as an oppressor who enforces unjust laws.

CONFORMITY AS ADAPTATION. To portray conformity to norms as the result of fear of punishment is as inaccurate as regarding it as simple acquiescence. Another source of conformity is adaptation. An important part of growing up in a society is learning how to get along, or better yet, how to play the game. As individuals grow older and reflect on the norms of their groups, they may conclude that there is no inherent virtue in many norms but that it is easier to follow these norms because that's the way people do things. Jean Piaget has shown that as children grow older they come to recognize the conventional nature of rules, including the fact that they can be changed by mutual agreement. Thus while some norms may be regarded as sacred in the sense that William Graham Sumner spoke of the mores, many are recognized as simply instrumental. The restraints against deviation are weak; all that is necessary to lead to their abandonment is the recognition that people cannot or will not observe them.

PLURALISTIC IGNORANCE. Even while the vast majority of people may conform to existing norms, agreement on these norms may be much less extensive than the behavior of the group would indicate. There may be a state of pluralistic ignorance, creating what might be called a false consensus.[4] If for some reason individuals do not communicate their private opinions to one another, each may think that his attitude of dissent is shared by no one else or by only a small minority. Actually, a majority of the group may privately disagree with a norm without knowing that there is extensive support for their position. If a small but powerful segment of the group is dedicated to suppressing and punishing expressions of dissent, their attitudes may be perceived as almost universally held, even though this apparent consensus is mythical.

Role-Playing as Role-Making. Modification of a model of stable and well-ordered society is also suggested by a view of role-playing as something more than conformity to internalized prescriptions for conduct. In analyses of social structure that have little concern for the individual performance, it is useful to view roles as sets of preexisting norms applicable to any actor playing a part in a group. Thus role-playing might be regarded as simple conformity to these norms and any deviation from them as a source of social disorganization.

Role-playing may, however, be regarded as an adaptation to the expectations of others—which guides social interaction. While roles may sometimes become highly standardized, as in a bureaucratic system, they typically are tentative in character. "The actor is not the occupant of a position for which there is a neat set of rules —a culture or set of norms—but a person who must act in the perspective supplied in part by his relationship to others whose actions reflect roles that he must identify."[5] The notion that in playing roles people are typically engaged in making these roles, sometimes modifying them, sometimes creating new ones, takes into account the ever-changing character of social structure. It also suggests that when role-conflict is encountered the individual may do more than simply choose "which set of expectations to honor in the face of an urgent desire to adhere to two or more incompatible sets."[6] He may also create a third role that encompasses the requirements of both. This notion also implies that in situations of collective behavior, indi-

---

[4] See Thomas J. Scheff, "Toward a Sociological Model of Consensus," *American Sociological Review,* 32 (February, 1967), 32–46.

[5] Ralph H. Turner, "Role-Taking: Process versus Conformity," in Arnold M. Rose, ed., *Human Behavior and Social Process* (Boston: Houghton Mifflin Co., 1962), p. 23.

[6] Ibid., p. 37.

viduals may generate a whole new division of labor with new roles specific to the situation.

THE NORMALITY OF SOCIAL CHANGE. This alternative view of the relationship of the individual to the normative order and social structure suggests why sociocultural change is possible at all. Human actors are not puppets responding automatically and uncritically to strings pulled by a mystical, self-determining culture. While responding to and using preexisting cultural forms, they are constantly engaged in modifying and creating culture. According to this conception, collective behavior contrasts with normal social behavior in terms of the speed with which new norms emerge and the manner in which social control operates, not in the absence of social control or the presence of totally different forms.

This analysis of the individual's relationship to the group and its norms and structure indicates why change is as much a constant feature of social life as is stability. The task of the student of collective behavior is not, however, to explain why new events are continually occurring and requiring modifications of the definition of the situation. It is, rather, to identify the conditions under which men collectively develop new definitions of social reality and to examine the process through which such new definitions emerge.

Questions for Collective Behavior

There are three questions implied here. The first concerns the conditions which make possible or facilitate the questioning of normal expectations. Neil Smelser calls these "conditions of structural conduciveness," asking, "Do certain structural characteristics of a social system permit or encourage episodes of collective behavior?"[7]

Closely related is the question as to what situations or events are likely to lead to a collective questioning of the existing norms, given a condition of structural conduciveness. Smelser subsumes such conditions under the concept of "structural strain." Kurt and Gladys Lang speak of a condition of "disequilibrium" resulting "when new elements are being assimilated" into a system of norms.[8] Muzafer and Carolyn Sherif postulate that under conditions conducive to collective behavior, such behavior is centered around a "focal issue," some sort of problematic or critical situation.[9] All these writers emphasize that the situations under which the collective behavior emerges must be distinguished from a state of conduciveness and from the precipitating event or series of events that mark the transition of the collective behavior from its earlier stages to its later, more specific forms.

The third question or level of analysis concerns the process through which collective behavior develops. As was indicated in Chapter 3, this is essentially a process of communication. Analysis on this level also includes the study of the differentiation of collectivities into specific forms, including various types of crowds, the public, and social movements.

Conditions Conducive to Collective Behavior

CONDUCIVENESS: ECOLOGICAL FACTORS. Since collective behavior develops through a communication process and culminates in people's acting together in relatively large collectivities, conditions that facilitate communication and mobilization are essential to conduciveness. Hence, like all forms of human interaction, collective behavior rests on an ecological base—the mere arrangement of people in space.

While men, as social animals, are always

[7] Neil J. Smelser, *Theory of Collective Behavior* (New York: The Free Press, 1963), p. 15.

[8] Kurt Lang and Gladys Engel Land, *Collective Dynamics* (New York: Thomas Y. Crowell Company, 1961), p. 42.

[9] Muzafer Sherif and Carolyn W. Sherif, *An Outline of Social Psychology* (New York: Harper and Row, Publishers, 1956), p. 715.

together in some sense, they also experience various degrees of isolation from each other. It is a common experience for faculty members of a university who move from crowded quarters into a building with sumptuous private offices to complain that communication within the department has been destroyed. They experience a sense of being fragmented and isolated. Communication does continue between them, but it loses much of its spontaneous and casual character. Since each professor must now deliberately invade the privacy of a colleague's office and perhaps interrupt his work in order to talk, communication takes on a more planned and purposive nature. Random, perhaps far-fetched, thoughts are not as likely to be given expression as readily as they are when one may simply turn in his chair to speak to his colleague. Thus communication tends to be more controlled than when there are ample opportunities for small talk.

Any arrangement of people that increases the opportunities for spontaneous, uncritical communication increases conduciveness for collective behavior. Malls on which students may lounge between classes, mess halls and dayrooms in which soldiers gather while off duty, sidewalks and stoops onto which people escape from hot, crowded city apartments are examples of such arrangements.

Physical proximity is not necessary, of course, for spontaneous communication. The telephone and the automobile have preserved opportunities for gossip even as the disappearance of the village square and the back fence over which housewives used to chatter threatened to decrease the opportunities. Even though communication through the media of television and radio is highly controlled, the development of call-in radio programs, in which listeners interact in a highly unstructured fashion with argumentative, somewhat reckless commentators or disc jockeys, has contributed directly to the emergence or accentuation of collective behavior in some cities.

Conditions that increase the possibility of spontaneous communication also facilitate mobilization—the rapid convergence of people for collective behavior. The mere physical presence of large numbers of people in a condition of high density enhances the individual's feeling that collective action is possible. Prison administrators have long recognized that the danger of riots is greatest when prisoners are massed in the mess hall or the yard. The crowding together of Negro Americans in the black ghettoes is a type of mobilization that has contributed to urban insurrections. The prevalence of privately owned automobiles and the rapidity with which news is communicated by television and radio increases the opportunities for mobilization through convergence behavior when a disaster occurs. For many people the increasing density of traffic as they approach the scene of an unusual event makes the event even more interesting—"It must be something big if so many people are going to see what happened."

SOCIAL CONTROL AND CONDUCIVENESS. Opportunities for spontaneous communication and physical mobilization are influenced by another factor that has an important effect on conduciveness. This is the type of social control that exists in the group. Fragmentation of a group into isolated individuals or small groups who find that some special effort is required to communicate or to come together can result from an unplanned ecological order, such as the dispersion of English workers in cottage industries before the rise of the factory system. Such fragmentation can also be the result of the deliberate imposition of social controls designed to reduce communication and mobilization. A restrictive system of social control that minimizes freedom of speech and of assembly has this effect. A system that imposes harsh, swift, and certain punishment on individuals who become involved in collective behavior also reduces conduciveness. By the same token, a permissive attitude by the authorities increases conduciveness. Thus, in the southern states during the years following the school desegregation decision of 1954, the obvious reluctance of public officials to impose sanctions on white people who assaulted integrationists created a situation conducive to active crowd behavior and to social movements advocating defiance of the law. A relaxation of harsh measures of social control may also increase conduciveness. Historians who have studied revolutions have concluded that, paradoxically, when a government begins to make concessions to a revolutionary movement, the aggressiveness of the movement is most likely to increase.

Government control of every channel of communication, constant propaganda, and a network of informers and police agents who report any expressions of criticism or dissatisfaction constitute the means of what is called thought control. After studying this sort of social control as it operated in Communist North Korea, Wilbur Schramm and John W. Riley, Jr., reported " 'Wherever there were more than two people gathered,' said a North Korean, 'there was sure to be one spy.' The Koreans were careful to whom they talked, what they said, where they were seen. Insecurity and inhibitions were built into life in Korea."[10]

A system that makes inhibition of criticism a built-in aspect of daily life maximizes ignorance and minimizes conduciveness to collective behavior. Any change that reduces the monolithic control of communication and makes possible a freer exchange of information and attitudes increases the likelihood that collective behavior will develop.

An ecological order and a system of social control that facilitate communication and mobilization are not the only factors that contribute to conduciveness, however.

The people who make up the potential collectivity may vary in certain attitudes that influence conduciveness to collective behavior.

CONDUCIVENESS: ATTITUDINAL FACTORS. In the discussion of rumor it was indicated that pre-sensitization increases the responsiveness of individuals to one another. It may be postulated that the more heterogeneous an aggregate is, the less conducive the situation is for collective behavior. At least a minimum of cultural homogeneity and a certain "we-feeling" are necessary as a basis for the communication between individuals that is essential to the development of collective behavior. A device used by slaveholders in the United States to prevent slave uprisings was to break up tribal groups so that the slaves on any one plantation would have only their African ancestry and their slave status in common, not a common culture and an established group identity.

People's perception of the nature of the social system in which they operate also affects conduciveness. Social change takes place through institutionalized mechanisms of adjustment as well as through collective behavior. Some governments provide for petitions and referendums; a military organization may have an inspector-general to whom the lowliest soldier may complain; a factory may have employee suggestion boxes or a union "griever" in every department; a store may have a complaint window. When such mechanisms exist in a system and are perceived as functioning effectively to produce adjustments, individuals may have little disposition to engage in collective behavior to bring about change.

Smelser points out that certain kinds of conduciveness can themselves be institutionalized.[11] Such a condition exists in a social system in which activities are structurally differentiated (for example, economic action as opposed to the demands of kinship ties); rationality rather than

---

[10] Wilbur Schramm and John W. Riley, Jr., "Communication in the Sovietized State, as Demonstrated in Korea," *American Sociological Review*, 16 (December, 1951), 759.

[11] Smelser, *Collective Behavior*, p. 175.

sentiment is expected to govern action; resources can be committed and withdrawn with freedom; and a medium exists that can be stored, exchanged, and extended to future commitments. In short, a condition that permits freedom to engage in a variety of actions not prescribed by traditional group loyalties, that entails, thereby, a certain degree of risk, and that demands choices of the individual increases conduciveness for collective behavior. Smelser points to a differentiated market economy, a democratized political system, and a Protestant religious tradition as types of situations in which conduciveness has been institutionalized.

A final factor that may be identified as contributing to conduciveness may be summed up in the single word, *hope*. It is a commonplace observation, borne out by many historical examples, that revolutions do not originate in the most oppressed and depressed classes of people. An essential psychological condition for conduciveness is the existence of some shared image of a better state of affairs that can be attained by collective action—a hope for things to come and a belief that they can be made to come. Quite obviously these factors that militate against the sharing of dreams of a better world, such as an ecological order that fragments the group or a system of social control that produces pluralistic ignorance, reduce the possibility that hope will constitute a source of conduciveness.

Situations Giving Rise to Collective Behavior

Conditions of conduciveness do not give rise to collective behavior. They only make possible the questioning and the exchange of views that are necessary for its development. There are specific kinds of situations that, given a relatively high state of conduciveness, set off the rumor process and thereby give rise to various forms of collective behavior.

THE UNANTICIPATED EVENT. It has been argued that men live in a world in which

social reality consists of things taken for granted. Nevertheless, unanticipated events do occur. The simplest and most frequent situation in which collective behavior arises is one where an event, or a series of events, occurs for which the culture offers insufficient directives or means for actions. On rare occasions such events are so novel as to be inconceivable, as in the case of the first use of a new and secret weapon in warfare. The people in Hiroshima did not even have a word for *atom bomb* and called the event that devastated their city the *pikadon,* meaning "flash-boom."[12] More often, unexpected events fall into some category of phenomena known to be possible but still unanticipated. Hence, their culture and social organization do not provide adequate directives for coping with the situation. What is an emergency for one group may be routine for another. For example, a collision between two racing cars on the speedway at Daytona Beach gives rise to no collective behavior among the track attendants; they possess a social organization and a standardized set of procedures for dealing with an event that they know is likely to occur during any race. A similar collision on a quiet, suburban street is likely to give rise to very intense collective behavior. Even though the householders in the vicinity may know the meaning of the event and know that they should call the police, they have no organization or set of norms for dealing with such an event. It is routine for the staff of a mental hospital to cope with the psychotic behavior of patients. If a university professor were suddenly to go into a psychotic state in the classroom, collective behavior would likely arise among the students!

CUES SOUGHT IN UNSTRUCTURED SITUATIONS. People confronted with unanticipated events are primarily concerned with three types of cues as they engage in searching, questioning behavior. Unless the definition of what has happened is self-evident,

[12] Michihiko Hachiya, *Hiroshima Diary* (Chapel Hill: University of North Carolina Press, 1955), p. 37.

there are attempts to define the situation. Is the professor drunk, is he putting on an act for pedagogical purposes, or is he "off his rocker"? Even when the event is partially defined, as when a tornado strikes a town, there is a need for additional definition—the extent of the damage or whether the danger had passed.

People are concerned with rules—what people are supposed to do in such situations. Should a person with no medical training attempt to give first aid to a victim who appears to be bleeding to death? Should students violate the usual norms governing student-faculty interaction by physically restraining a professor who seems about to injure himself or someone else?

In some instances the search for cues to help define the situation takes the form of assigning blame or of absolving actors of blame. When the rule governing how to act seems to become clear-cut, such considerations as these become dominant. A satisfactory definition of who is to blame may become essential to action. That the person on whom the burden of guilt comes to rest may be innocent may thus be forgotten. If the rule is, "Someone must pay for this," the effort to identify the "someone" becomes more important than considerations of due process of law.

The fact that the collectivity arrives at a rule and a definition of the direction that action should take does not mean that further groping is not necessary. There usually remains the question, "Who will act first?" In a problematic situation many members of the collectivity may contemplate an action but still hesitate to initiate it because they are not certain how much support they will receive from other members of the group. Thus, there is a search for leadership. The person who acts first becomes a leader; he, by his behavior, legitimates the emergent norm and assumes the onus of initiating action under it. One of the principles of crowd control is to maximize the risks for such emergent leaders, so that no member of the crowd will dare to place himself in such an exposed position.

The questions that are aroused by an unanticipated event are illustrated in the following account of a crime in a quiet neighborhood near a state university. Although the crime of rape occurs every day in some part of American society, most citizens conceive of it as something that could not happen in their neighborhood. The readiness of these peaceful citizens to abandon the usual and lawful procedures for apprehending criminals may be seen. After debating with himself whether he should join a manhunt or leave action to the police, the writer of the account picked up his pistol because he definitely wanted to be in the gathering posse! But punishing the criminals was not the only kind of action that was suggested. Things previously taken for granted, such as the existence of a heavily wooded area in a family neighborhood, were brought into question. (The woods were cleared out shortly after the incident.) Despite the presence of law enforcement officers, the potential for a lynching would have been great had the two men, or any two strange men, been found when the crowd was armed and ready for action. The fact that subsequent investigation proved that one of the men was not guilty of rape would have been of no value to him had he been discovered by the mob. The crowd had quickly arrived at its definition of the situation and was looking for the persons to blame.

Rape at High Noon

Jack R. Blough

This is a shocking title, isn't it? So too, are the thoughts that such an act was done almost in my backyard on Sunday, the 25th of October, 1959, at approximately 12:30 noon. Sunday is a sort of lazy day; most of us reserve it for rest and the usual attendance at church. Then the balance of the day is for reading or what have you.

I was sitting at the table working on some school papers when my wife came running in the front door, out of breath, and gasped, "Do you know what has happened?" Not being in the mood for guessing games I said, "No what has happened?" After a short pause, and with a troubled expression, she distinctly said, "You know Carol, the little girl who lives behind us? Well, some men just raped her." Those words were the equivalent of telling me that Russia had just dropped an H-bomb on an American city; I couldn't believe I had understood her correctly. Those were sinister, crude and violent words to me. I sat there for a moment, speechless; I didn't know what to say, or do, for that matter. What should one do when his friends and neighbors are threatened by a mad dog? Should he go hunt it down and dispose of it, or sit back and leave that to the law enforcement officers?

Maybe he should grab his firearms and join the manhunt like my next door neighbor did. Just prior to my wife's telling me what had taken place, I noticed more activity than is usual for the neighborhood on a Sunday afternoon. I recalled my neighbor's saying to her husband, "Now Fred, you be careful." He replied, "I'll shoot if I see them." Since he is an avid sportsman I thought he was kidding about the game he was possibly going out to hunt. I just didn't pay any further attention after hearing his reply; I did chuckle a little though. The words sounded familiar but of course I didn't know what he was talking about at the time.

Student paper, Florida State University. Published by permission.

Carol, the victim, is a ten-year-old girl. She is a well-behaved youngster and tends toward being on the quiet, conservative side in temperament. My daughter plays with her frequently and the two of them apparently play together fine. For that matter the whole group in the neighborhood played together with no real problems among them. Behind our houses is a large vacant lot bounded on three sides by roads and on the fourth side by a thickly wooded area. Our daughter had strict instructions to never go near this wooded area and to the best of my knowledge she never did. Carol too, had been given the same instructions, as had all the rest of the young ones around there. This particular Sunday she had apparently forgotten about what she had been told and had gone to the far side of the lot to play with her brother and a neighbor boy. This was the day when she definitely should not have been there.

Two transient men, one of them nineteen and the other about twenty-five, were traveling through the Southern states looking for work at a carnival which was due in Tallahassee in a few days. Somehow, through fate or whatever you want to call it, they chose to drive down one of the roads bordering this vacant lot and they spotted the small ones playing in this area. This is apparently the time when their minds started plotting. By searching the local area, they discovered the road which circles this particular area of houses and the vacant lot. Eventually they came upon the desired place and parked their vehicle, an old model Ford automobile on one side of the lot and walked down into the woods. Later interrogation revealed that the older of the two men assaulted Carol, while the younger forced the two small boys to remain at the point of an ice pick as well as disrobe in the presence of the group. The younger fellow did not assault the girl. However, he did act as a lookout for the other man during the unlawful act. After the assault, the two men fled from the scene in their car, and here is where all the confusion started.

At the time I was told, the men had been gone for possibly as much as thirty to forty-five minutes. However, when they parked their car on the road next to the lot, two teen-age girls living in the vicinity observed the car and also saw them running from the woods. This did cause them to be on the suspicious side, and as a result the girls were able to furnish the police with some limited amount of information. They were able to recall the color combination of the license plates, but no numbers. They knew the paint colors but not the combination, and they knew the kind of car it was, but not the year model.

In the meantime a crowd had gathered in front of Carol's house. As I looked out the window and saw this group, I also saw a bunch of the men with guns. I figured they were going to start a manhunt and I definitely wanted to be in on it, so I picked up my pistol and proceeded to walk over to the group. There was a police car on the spot and one up at the place where the two men had parked their car. At first the consensus was that the two men were in the woods, and a posse was being formed to help in apprehending them. Before any actual search was started through the woods, the Sheriff brought in some bloodhounds in hope they could trace the suspects. This proved to be useless because after the word got out as to what had happened, many curiosity seekers proceeded to the scene and as a result the dogs were unable to pick up any one scent. While the dogs were trying to get a scent, the police concluded from the information the two teen-age girls gave that the suspects had definitely fled the scene. After the two police cars conversed by radio, the one in our group told us we could go home because they were sure that the two men had fled and they were going to take the search out onto the highways to see if they could possibly locate the car from the description they had to work with. This was about three o'clock in the afternoon, and it

was shortly after this when the Florida Highway Patrol was given as much information as possible about the suspect car, and the two men in it.

By now, there were at least twenty-five to thirty people in the crowd, which does not include those parked over on the various roads which bounded the field and woods. Most of the group were residents of the local area and some of them had plenty to say. The ladies on the whole were quite upset; one stated that she was going to start a campaign to get all the weeds and foliage cut down because that area in discussion was too densely wooded, especially with so many young ones around, and she wanted more police protection. The word really went out that day to the little ones that they had better not ever get caught out of their yards if they knew what was good for them. It was impossible to tell the little ones what had really taken place that afternoon, and even if we had they wouldn't have understood, so something was made up to leave a lasting impression on their little minds. The men were very irate and powerfully threatening. There is no doubt in my mind, had those two been caught that afternoon, I wouldn't have bet a plugged nickel on their chances of not getting a rope tied around their necks and stretched from the nearest handy tree. I will not reprint here the words used that day because they would be too obscene for all to read, but you can take it from me, and I would have no other motive than to tell you anything but what happened, they were powerful words. All of us had children out in the area playing that day and it could just as well have been any one of them. That was pretty much the attitude the men took that day, Sunday, the 25th of October, 1959. Many words were spoken that afternoon, and I didn't hear any kind ones. There was one individual who was so upset he wanted to go to the jail if the suspects were caught and take them to a tree.

DISRUPTION OF THE SOCIAL STRUCTURE. Unanticipated events are frequently accompanied by a disruption of the social structure. The usual occupants of roles in the existing organization have been killed or injured, have abdicated their positions, or are unable to function effectively. The situation becomes more complex because of the need, not only to develop norms to cope with the unanticipated event but also to reconstitute the social structure, to care for essential social functions. Such a condition arises in the typical disaster situation when police, fire fighting, medical, and communications agencies are disrupted or overloaded. Over a longer period of time, the social structure may be ineffective because of the inefficiency, corruptness, or self-imposed isolation of officials who have the authority to deal with social problems. When leaders are defined as unresponsive or hostile, members of the group may seek ways of coping with their problems that bypass or oppose the usual social structure.

How people respond to a breakdown of the social structure is seen most clearly in the case of precipitous and massive disruptions, such as the rare police strike. On October 7, 1969, almost the entire police force of Montreal went on strike. This had happened once before in a major North American city, Boston, in 1919. Half a century later citizens of Montreal could no more believe that the guardians of law and order would actually walk off their jobs than had Bostonians in their time of crisis. The consequences were similar: anarchy seemed to reign in both instances.

An account of what happened during the one-day strike of Montreal policemen reveals that the complete disorganization suggested by the term *anarchy* did not really prevail. When awareness dawned that the city was without police protection, the majority of people remained calm, at least for a time. They did not rush to give expression to repressed antisocial impulses. It was professional criminals, for whom violating the law was no novelty, who first took advantage of the opportunity to stage robberies with relative impunity. Then

groups which did not ordinarily behave in an illegal way but had long-standing grievances began to change their manner of expressing their dissatisfaction and hostility. The state that had limited interaction to a verbal level was broken as the external restraint of law enforcement remained absent. Taxi drivers, French-Canadian separatists, and anti-Americans gave expression to old sentiments in a newly violent fashion. The change in the social structure indicated that a new set of norms, governing economic and political controversy, was possible and acceptable in this situation.

It was not until the violation of the usual norms became widespread that some respectable, middle-class people began to join in the disorder, looting stores that stood open and unprotected. The onset of darkness seems to have contributed to their participation; perhaps curiosity replaced their initial uncertainty and drew more of them to the business district. More important, however, was the development of what Gerald Clark calls "a carnival atmosphere." By the end of the long day the abnormal had become normal. Actions that would have seemed dangerous and immoral the day before appeared commonplace.

At the same time, it should be kept in mind that the majority of the city's people did not join the mob. They remained in their homes, uncertain and fearful. Some of them participated in the collective behavior, not by breaking the law but by taking unaccustomed precautions to insure their own safety. One of the two deaths that could be charged to the disorders resulted when a psychologist, sleeping with a pistol by his bed, awoke and shot a burglar.

What Happens When the Police Strike

Gerald Clark

On the day Montreal became a city without policemen, Gilles Madore unsuspectingly left his home as usual at 9:30 A.M. to drive to work. Madore, a 32-year-old bank inspector, had been filling in for the past few months as manager of the City & District Savings Bank branch at the corner of St. Denis Street and St. Joseph Boulevard, almost entirely a French-speaking residential area with only a splash of English and Italian. It was a perfect October day—clear and crisp—and during the 15-minute drive Madore noted that the trees were at their peak of gold and crimson. He was listening to the car radio, but since it was an FM all-music station, he caught no bulletins. Madore, in fact, did not know the police had walked off the job until he arrived at the bank and a nervous teller greeted him with the news that the city was wide open to criminals. "Don't worry," Madore said reassuringly. "We're a small branch. Holdup men won't come here." Besides, this was a Tuesday, by experience the quietest day in the week for bank robberies.

Madore was not alone in his ignorance of the strike. Most Montrealers were only now beginning to hear of it, for there had been no forewarning, no build-up. The morning newscasts had carried, as a routine item, the report that police were to meet in the Paul Sauvé Arena at 9 A.M. to hear the results of an arbitration board's findings on wages and other issues that had remained unsettled for almost a year. But no one had anticipated a walk-out; it was illegal for policemen and firefighters to strike.

Thus, on Oct. 7, the largest city in Canada, and one of the most civilized cities in the world, found what it was like to be without police protection during a day and night. Before the ordeal was over, a psychologist would shoot and kill a burglar; another man—a provincial police corporal —would be slain, and 49 persons would be wound-

Reprinted in part from the *New York Times Magazine* (November, 1969), p. 45. © 1969 by The New York Times Company. Reprinted by permission.

ed or injured in rioting. Nine bank holdups, almost a tenth of the total for the whole of last year, would be committed, along with 17 other robberies at gunpoint. Ordinarily disciplined, peaceful citizens would go wild; smashing 1,000 plate glass windows in the heart of the city and looting shop displays. The losses and damage would exceed $1-million.

But the gray statistics alone would not be very meaningful. It was on the social and psychological levels that the story held its horror. For the real message was about the "thin blue line"—the phrase used by Sgt. Guy Marcil, president of the Policemen's Brotherhood—that separates civilization from chaos and anarchy.

Essentially, it was not the rise in professional crime—12 times the normal—that counted. It was the way political grievances, and private and group frustrations, shot to the surface when no one was around to enforce the law. These included: an attack by taxi drivers on a company holding an exclusive franchise to provide limousine service at Montreal's International Airport; an attack by French-Canadian separatists on symbols of the "English Establishment"; an attack on the Mayor's property by social agitators who contend that not enough is being done for the poor; an attack on the United States Consulate by anti-Americans, and then, simply, an attack on a code of ethics and behavior by conventional men and women who chose to join a mob.

Most people appeared relaxed, even if some behaved irrationally. Metropolitan Montreal numbers 2.5 million inhabitants, but only half live in the city proper, where the strike was taking place. The others live in separate municipalities—some of them, like Westmount and Outremont, enclaves surrounded by the City of Montreal—with their own police and fire services. None of these was on strike. However, a Westmount resident, arriving home at 7 P.M. from work, found his way barred by the door chain, a device never before used by his wife. "What's the idea?" he asked her. She replied that Saulnier had told people to be on guard. Another man returned from work to find that every light in his home in Outremont had been switched on; his wife was certain this would ward off intruders.

As it happened, the population, at the start, did heed Saulnier. It kept away from the downtown areas. A visitor driving along Ste. Catherine, the biggest shopping and entertainment street, would have thought it a Sunday rather than Tuesday evening. Theaters, cinemas and restaurants functioned. It was just that the traffic was light and shushed. But not everywhere. Around City Hall, in the old quarter of Montreal, several taxis started hooting their horns before forming a procession and driving west to Barré and Mountain Streets. At that point, approximately 7:30 P.M., began the buildup for a night of havoc.

Other cabs headed downtown to join the cavalcade, and by the time it reached its objective, the garage of Murray Hill Limousine Service Ltd., it numbered 75 vehicles—carrying not only cabbies but political extremists. An alliance had been formed between the Mouvement de Libération du Taxi, which could claim a membership of no more than 100 of Montreal's 10,000 cab drivers, and the Front de Libération Populaire, a small group of Maoists and student radicals who charged that a "fascist Drapeau-Saulnier administration had sold out taxi drivers' interest to the capitalists." In fact, it was a Federal concession that had given Murray Hill the sole right to pick up passengers at Montreal's airport, in return for guaranteed service. But the grievance was an old one among drivers of city taxi associations.

For separatists and terrorists, with no riot squad to restrain them, this was obviously a night to make political gain in the wider goal of removing Quebec from "English domination." Murray Hill, as an example, was owned by an English-speaking Montrealer, Charles Hershorn, whose home had been bombed a year ago.

At 8:03 P.M. a Q.P.P. radio dispatcher sent four cars to Murray Hill. They fumbled through unfamiliar back streets flanked on the north by railway yards and on the south by the waterfront. At 8:08 P.M. another four cars were told to get there in a hurry. By now demonstrators were chanting, "Québec aux Québécois," and throwing

rocks and Molotov cocktails. The targets of the fire bombs were four Murray Hill buses and four cars in the parking lot, and quickly they were aflame. Demonstrators pushed one of the burning buses down an incline to crash into the barred garage doors. The tactics were terrifying to the Murray Hill employes inside; they were sitting above underground storage tanks containing 18,000 gallons of gasoline. Firemen, forced back by the rioters, were compelled to set up hoses at a distance. Then a guard on the roof of the two-story building opened fire on the crowd with a 12-gauge shotgun. "How big is the crowd?" a Q.P.P. dispatcher asked over the radio. "Over 200," replied a cruiser, "and impossible to control." A city police striker, using a hijacked car transmitter, cut in—and a Q.P.P. man cursed him.

By now a second guard was shooting from the garage roof, and there was return fire from a tenement roof across the road. It was the first time that street war of this type had ever struck Montreal, and when it was ended, a provincial plainclothesman, Cpl. Robert Dumas, 35, was its chief victim. Dumas, a member of the Q.P.P. anti-subversive squad, had been one of the first police on the site. He entered the Murray Hill garage to phone for reinforcements; then, racing out to try to halt rioters tossing Molotov cocktails, he was fatally wounded by a shotgun blast. Another 19 persons—some cabbies, some youths—were taken to hospitals with buckshot wounds. Thirty more suffered injuries at Murray Hill and in the subsequent bouts that took place as the crowd began moving, around 10:30 P.M., up the hill.

The next destination was the Queen Elizabeth Hotel, chosen because Murray Hill had a concession there; thus it deserved to have its storefront windows smashed. From here it was a short and logical step to the Sheraton-Mount Royal Hotel, for the same reason. But on the way, the demonstrators paused at the Windsor Hotel, where Mayor Drapeau's restaurant was located in the basement level. Drapes were ripped down, glassware smashed and small fires set. By now Drapeau, having landed from St. Louis an hour and a half earlier, was in City Hall receiving reports of the growing violence.

The streets in Drapeau's beloved heart of the city—the complex around Place Ville Marie and the Ste. Catherine Street area—were beginning to fill with more than the original couple of hundred separatists and agitators who had started out with an organized line of attack. Arriving from all directions, looters and vandals were hitting out indiscriminately. A provincial police officer radioed headquarters: "Send help to the corner of Peel and Ste. Catherine. People are breaking windows at the Bank of Nova Scota." Minutes later: "We need more help. We are 25 against 500."

For two uninterrupted, chaotic hours the plunderers went to work, barely touched by the undermanned and bewildered Q.P.P. At one point young people surrounded a parked cruiser, rocking it and blocking the doors so the occupants could not escape. All along central Ste. Catherine Street, for a stretch of 21 blocks, the shattering of $300,000 worth of plate glass windows was hardly heard above the roar of the mob and the incessant ringing of unanswered alarm bells. In the distance sirens sounded. Their screech receded, however, as a new touch was added. Provincial police were receiving more and more calls about other riots in widely scattered parts of the city, only to find them fictitious. Later, Q.P.P. Director Maurice St. Pierre was to suggest the calls came from strikers.

In all, something like 156 shops had windows smashed and display contents hauled away— stereo units, radios, fur coats, dresses, an assortment of goods. The major department stores— Eaton's, Simpson's, Morgan's—were hit, along with lesser ones. Pink Poodle, a medium-priced women's specialty shop, caught it from two directions. While the ordinary looters were content to strip Pink Poodle's window mannequins of $3,000 worth of garments, professional burglars entered the premises through a back door and made off with 150 fur and cloth coats valued at $20,000.

There were riffraff out that night and maybe some poor people; but also there were so-called respectable, middle-class people. A well-dressed man, with a fur coat over each arm, scampered down Ste. Catherine Street shouting, "One for my wife, one for my girl friend." There were some orderly people, too. A middle-aged man, seeing a young man reaching for a fur coat, tried to talk him out of it—whereupon he was set upon by

two other looters for interfering. At Seltzer Drugs, where the window offered transistor sets, hair dryers and other fairly expensive items, a woman reached for a yellow box of Kleenex, ripped away the wrapping and stuffed the tissue into her hand-bag. She laughed aloud, for no one in particular to hear, as though to proclaim that suddenly she had a license to break the rules.

Or maybe she simply needed to blow her nose, and in spirit of gaiety took the Kleenex. For in a sense there was also a carnival atmosphere, a pre-Christmas festivity about the street. There was nothing furtive in the stealing. Many of the people who now descended on Ste. Catherine Street, drawn by radio and television accounts, were content to stand by as spectators; but some, when they saw windows smashed, helped themselves to what was inside. Often they seemed to wait for just the right window to be smashed. But with no bothersome police around—at one stage a busload of Q.P.P., arriving from out of town, drove along Ste. Catherine Street without any pause in the looting—a sense of fear was absent.

At the Paul Sauvé Arena, René St. Martin heard the Brotherhood president, Guy Marcil, announce that the Quebec Legislature had ordered the strikers back to work by one minute past midnight, or they would face severe fines and loss of accreditation as a trade union. Some men hissed. "We must obey," said Marcil. St. Martin was glad that the decision was, at last, made for him. But he felt it was not the Government's threat alone that got the men back on the beat. "It was," he said, "the way the rioters and looters were tearing our city to ribbons."

At 12:57 A.M. Montreal city police calls returned to the air. The 17-hour trial was over, and people cheered the first familiar blue-and-white cruisers that arrived at the corner of Peel and Ste. Catherine Streets. The police grinned back and began the business of chasing off the remaining looters and, along with the Q.P.P., making 104 arrests.

Many angles were left for later examination. Political extremists, after leaving the Sheraton-Mount Royal Hotel, shattered windows at nearby McGill University. But this was predictable, since separatists consider McGill a bastion of the English Establishment. Equally foreseeable was the small routine march on McGregor Avenue, where demonstrators threw stones through the windows of the United States Consulate while they left untouched in the same block consulates of Israel, West Germany, Switzerland and Italy. Nor was there any special significance to the other crimes—except, as might be expected, that there were more than usual.

For instance, 456 burglaries were reported for 17 hours, compared with the normal 350 for a whole week. The pattern and timetable suggested that professionals, rather than amateurs, were at work. From 9 A.M. to 11 A.M., before criminals could be assured a police strike was indeed underway, no major incidents were logged. Then the signals began to come in from banks. After the banks closed, four jewelry stores in succession were held up. When jewelers shut down, at 6 P.M., the drug stores and food stores raised the alarm. The police, in making their analysis, did not believe that a single, massive gang was involved. Rather, several compact groups were thought to be operating, independently but with a common and logical program of attack based on known schedules of business establishments.

It was the behavior of ordinary people at night that caused the most perplexity and anxiety. No special denominator tied together the shops they looted; some were owned by Catholics, some by Protestants, some by Jews; some represented "English" interests, others "French" interests. Men and women of every kind and variety flocked to the Ste. Catherine Street area because it was here that the action, set off initially by organized extremists, was taking place. And then they abandoned inhibitions.

It was only in retrospect that Montrealers sensed how close a grim experience had come to gross tragedy. During the rioting and looting many people, sitting in suburban homes and watching television, thought it must be happening to a city in a foreign country. The awakening the next morning was acute when they traveled to downtown offices and saw the debris and damage. But the awful part was the realization that terrorists had selected relatively few targets, and that by and large the mob that later emerged was a good-natured one rather than vicious. No explosive bombs were thrown, no one cried out in a crusade of personal vendetta or racial or religious war. But if there is a next time with more targets and objectives, the thin blue line might indeed prove thin.

Although it proved inadequate, a social structure was emerging in Montreal to replace the police force. It consisted of provincial police forces assigned to take over unfamiliar duties in the city and of private citizens who began to act like vigilantes. Allen H. Barton has called the structure that develops following a breakdown of social structure an "emergency social system."[13] Such a system is made up of *ephemeral roles*, a term suggested by Louis A. Zurcher. Zurcher studied the three-day career of a volunteer work crew that, with the aid of a Civil Defense power wagon, cleared away debris and rescued

[13] Allen H. Barton, *Social Organization Under Stress* (Washington, D.C.: National Academy of Sciences-National Research Council, Publication 1032, 1963), pp. 19–20.

persons following the Topeka, Kansas tornado of June 1966. This was not a preformed, trained group but a crew that was organized after the tornado had passed. The ten members included two psychologists, five other white-collar workers, a heavy equipment operator, and two house painters; yet the crew became quite expert at their unfamiliar task. Zurcher's analysis of the nature of the ephemeral role shows how it differs from the roles people play in normal, enduring social structures:

Seven characteristics can be identified for the ephemeral role as postulated at this point.

1. The actor has experienced (a) disruption to the good order of a significant part of his social world, and (b) a feeling of doubt concerning his ability to cope

with components of his environment. He is thus impelled toward behavior (the ephemeral role) which will help him to restructure that social world and reaffirm his sense of mastery.

2. The social structure of which the ephemeral role is part is initially quite "primitive" in that status and role definitions are unrefined, norms and sanctions are undeveloped, and group cohesion is provided primarily by a vague, mutual need for some kind of restructuring activity, leading to a "definition of the situation."

3. The behaviors which comprise the role are also quite "primitive" in being physical rather than intellectual, in emphasizing *doing* rather than planning, and in their cathartic and "acting out" nature.

4. Both the behaviors comprising the ephemeral role and the social structure underpinning it can therefore be considered an adaptive return to earlier behavioral forms and more elementary social organization which allow the individual to test his threatened capacities and to experience again socialization processes that reaffirm the dependability of social roles and social structure.

5. The ephemeral role, during its brief existence, evolves constantly and rapidly from diffuse, vague behavioral expectations around an undefined position in an isolated *ad hoc* group to crisp role definitions around specific positions in that group as the group becomes similar in structure to previously known groups and interacts more clearly with the community, thus allowing the actor to make the transition from his ephemeral role back to the social world he temporarily doubted.

6. Where the position defines the role in more formalized social organizations, the ephemeral role evolves and defines the position. The searching and cathartic behaviors come first, and the position evolves from within the group formed by a number of other searching and reacting individuals.

7. The actor, more or less explicitly,

knows that the ephemeral role is short-lived and (for him) unique.[14]

As this analysis suggests, the disruption of the familiar social world and the breakdown of the normal social structures place severe strain on many individuals. What results is not a prolonged state of total social disorganization manifest in uncoordinated individual actions. Instead, men act collectively to create new, even though temporary, social structures that will restore meaning and order to the situation. These structures, or groups, rapidly develop emergent norms that guide the interaction of the members with each other and with outsiders.

CONFLICTS OF VALUES. It is not necessary to have a breakdown of the existing social structure for collective behavior to arise. A functioning social system may not satisfy all the important values of the members of the society. Large numbers of individuals may cherish diverse and conflicting values, some of which remain unfulfilled. Different population segments may hold values that are opposed, so that satisfaction of the demands of one segment denies the needs of another. In such a situation, collective behavior involves actively opposing the established organization and attempting to set it aside, if only temporarily. Persistent value-conflicts, growing in the gravity of their consequences, may lead to the development of social movements.

Since the school desegregation decision of 1954, there have been many episodes in which white Americans have engaged in collective behavior opposing the established order. This social order has been reflected in court rulings and administrative orders requiring desegregation of public schools. Opposition to "the law of the land" has occurred in every region, rang-

14 Reprinted in part by permission of the publishers from Louis A. Zurcher, "Social-Psychological Functions of Ephemeral Roles: A Disaster Work Crew," *Human Organization*, 27 (Winter, 1968), 283–84.

ing from assaults on Negro school children to the picketing of schools. The situation that gave rise to such episodes involved both conflicts of the values of separate population segments and value-conflicts within the minds of individuals.

Obviously many white people with traditional, explicit attitudes of white supremacy saw the new legal definition as threatening deeply cherished values. Many prominent and influential white southerners denounced the decision of the United States Supreme Court as part of a communist plot, and the day of the decision was called Black Monday. Organizations dedicated to resisting school desegregation arose, and white citizens were assured that they did not have to obey the federal law. With this sort of encouragement, some of it coming from public officials, many people joined mobs and attempted to prevent, by physical force, the entrance of Negro children into white schools.

There were other white Americans for whom the issue did not constitute a clear-cut conflict of the rights of white men and the aspirations of Negroes. In the North some members of groups with traditionally liberal attitudes, such as Jews, also opposed official proposals for school desegregation in their neighborhoods. Kurt and Gladys Lang studied the participants in a controversy over a neighborhood school in a predominantly Jewish section of New York City.[15] They found that despite the greater liberalism expressed on a "social distance" test, Jews showed no greater readiness to accept a school "pairing" proposal than did their non-Jewish neighbors. It was people who were relatively low in education and economic standing and strongly bound to the neighborhood by both financial and social ties who were most likely to be active opponents of the plan. The value-conflict

experienced by such people was characterized as follows:

Thus, insisting that they were not "prejudiced," opponents repeatedly proclaimed their welcome of any Negro who enrolled "naturally" as a bona fide resident within the school zone as redrawn before the pairing. "If they want to go to our school, let them move into our neighborhood" came to be a familiar cat call at turbulent meetings as soon as any speaker rose to support the plan. But the queries of our interviewers revealed that the number who "minded living in a neighborhood where a good many of your neighbors" were Negroes was actually more than twice as great as those who "minded having their child go to a school where about half the children were Negroes" (52 per cent compared with 24 per cent). Negroes in small numbers could evidently be assimilated; in large numbers they are a threat to the character of the neighborhood.[16]

The neighborhood which seemed to be threatened was perceived thusly:

For many of the Jews against the plan, the neighborhood was in certain respects an upgraded version of the familiarly comfortable but shabby and rundown ghetto from which they had escaped. Many respondents stressed the fact that they (and others) had worked hard to get here; it was a good neighborhood and they wanted nothing to spoil it.[17]

Commenting on similar opposition to school desegregation observed among white parents in many cities, John F. Scott and Lois Heyman Scott suggest, "They are not so much anti-Negro as pro-middle class."[18] The crisis over school desegregation does not persist simply because of bigotry. Instead, the now widely approved but ab-

16 Ibid., p. 104.
17 Ibid., p. 103.
18 John F. Scott and Lois Heyman Scott, "They Are Not So Much Anti-Negro as Pro-Middle Class," in Raymond W. Mack, ed., *Prejudice and Race Relations* (Chicago: Quadrangle Books, Inc., 1970), pp. 56–70.

15 Kurt Lang and Gladys Engel Lang, "Resistance to School Desegregation: A Case Study of Backlash Among Jews, *Sociological Inquiry*, 35 (Winter, 1965), 94–106.

stract value of racial democracy conflicts with another highly respectable value. As the Scotts express it, "The problem is that the evil of *de facto* segregation is sustained by a number of factors, at least one of which—parents' concern for what they judge to be the welfare of their children—is conventionally regarded as an important social good."[19]

In the course of the prolonged racial crisis, some black Americans have concluded that it is not the failure of whites to live up to the ideals of American democracy that blocks their progress; it is the values of American society itself. They have begun to rediscover their African past and to proclaim that "black is beautiful." The competition for a higher status, one symbolized by material possessions, cherished by many Americans as the outcome of an open society has come to be defined as a fatal flaw in a sick society. Eldridge Cleaver, a self-proclaimed black revolutionary leader, has declared that the black protest movement must set itself in opposition to some basic American values: "The goal must be to make possible a more equitable distribution of goods and services—but also to have a different set of values, so that things themselves don't become a substitute for life itself."[20]

Sources of Legitimation of Collective Behavior

Collective acts defying the established order and attempting to set it aside must not be regarded as random, mindless, hostile outbursts comparable to the temper tantrums of a child. No matter how unconventional by previous standards, all forms of collective behavior are governed by norms. What is involved, however, is the discovery of a special norm to legitimize the action and the development of a

19 Ibid., p. 57.
20 Eldridge Cleaver, *Post-Prison Writings and Speeches* (New York: Random House, Inc., Ramparts Book, 1967), p. 207.

conception of the situation, which defines this rule as the appropriate guide.

THE VALUES OF THE EXISTING ORDER. This is true even when the situation is near the complex end of the continuum, involving the setting aside or overthrowing of the established order. Paradoxically, even in antiorganization behavior, justification is derived from the existing order. White segregationists who defied the interpretation handed down by the Supreme Court did so in the name of a return to constitutional government. On the other side of the racial controversy, delegates to a black nationalist convention held in Newark in 1968 adhered, at least, to the forms of the old order, drawing up a "declaration of independence" and drafting a "constitution" just as white Americans had done when they founded the republic that was now to be repudiated. H. Rap Brown, when calling for violence in defense of Negro rights, proclaimed that "violence is as American as cherry pie." So strong is the impact of the established order upon the normative conceptions of its members that ideological justifications and legitimating rituals are borrowed from it to give the collective behavior legitimacy.

REPUDIATION OF THE ESTABLISHED ORDER. At the same time there must be justification for repudiating the established order. Such justification is frequently found in incidents that are interpreted as repudiations of legitimate appeals for redress of grievances and as signs of bad faith on the part of the established order. A breakdown of communication is generally alleged to have occurred. Thus, most of the ghetto riots of the 1960s were triggered by instances of alleged police brutality. Usually these instances were viewed against the background of repeated and unsatisfied demands by Negroes for civilian review boards to investigate charges of police misconduct.

THE SENSE OF RIGHTNESS. A third source of legitimation of collective behavior is a conviction of in-group rightness and effectiveness. This conviction is supplied in part by the mechanical solidarity, the sense of cohesiveness, that develops in the collectivity. The crowd itself becomes the salient reference group for its members; doubts that might be raised by reflection on the norms of usual reference groups are blocked out by the sense of unity with the collectivity. In more diffuse and long-lasting collectivities, such as a social movement, there may be a prior development of an ideology that supplies the necessary definition of the situation and the significance of the collectivity's action. For example, the seeds of defiance of the federal government, in the violent phase of "the Negro Revolution," were sown years earlier in the civil rights movement when King and other leaders began to justify peaceful resistance to local laws through an appeal to the higher law of God. While a different, nonviolent form was advocated in those early days, civil disobedience to the laws of an oppressive social order were given ideological justification.

THE SENSE OF POWER. Some events may, by their nature, facilitate the development of collective behavior by generating a sense of confidence and power in the potential participants. Precipitating events do not always represent new misfortunes or added insults that push people to a point of unbearable dissatisfaction. They may be a source of joy, triumph, and hope. An illustration of such an event and its effect is seen in the rioting of a crowd in Russian-occupied Czechoslovakia. After several months of frustration and hopelessness following the Soviet invasion of their country, an invasion that they had been unable to defeat, these people suddenly perceived themselves as winners. They felt empowered to engage in a revolution of good feeling during which they expressed both their joy and their feelings of hostility toward the Russians.

Czechs Wreck Prague's Russian Airline Office

PRAGUE (UPI)—Thousands of Czechoslovaks burst into the streets of Prague Friday night in a frenzy of celebration for the nation's 4–3 victory over the Soviet Union in the semifinals of the world hockey championships.

Most of the celebrants converged on Wenceslas Square, where they waved burning brooms and newspapers, chanted "For August! For August! For August!" and demolished the offices of the Soviet airline Aeroflot.

The Soviet-led invasion of Czechoslovakia took place last August, and Soviet occupation troops are still stationed in the country.

A pall or smoke hung over the square from the burning brooms and newspapers. Taxis and other autos were trapped by crowds in streets approaching the square, and they added the sound of their horns to the general din.

Rockets burst into the sky above the square. Firecrackers exploded among the cheering multitude.

The Czechoslovakian national hockey team defeated the defending champion Soviet Union for the second time in the tournament at Stockholm Friday and next will play Sweden for the title. The game was broadcast and telecast live throughout Czechoslovakia.

Within seconds after the game ended, crowds began to converge upon the city's principal square where last August Soviet tanks and troops maintained positions. The square, whose official capacity is 200,000 persons, was jammed with yelling celebrants.

The crowd singled out the Aeroflot offices,

the only Soviet office on the square, for destruction and had virtually demolished it before police fought through to set up a protective cordon. The office's windows and signs were smashed, its files scattered and burned and its furniture pitched into the street.

"It is a revolution of good feeling," cried one man. But another shouted, "Russian beasts, go home."

There were no immediate reports of injuries.

The celebration was considerably larger than the one a week ago in honor of Czechoslovakia's first victory over the Russians in the hockey tournament.

Changes in Communication

The relative degree of stability created by the normative order and social structure depends upon another factor, the state of communication in society. On the one hand, a free flow of communication provides the feedback that makes adjustments possible in the system and forestalls the development of intense value-conflicts and breakdowns in the social structure. Moreover, the free flow of communication between various levels of the social system helps sustain the belief that access to the legitimate order does exist. On the other hand, severe restrictions on communication —strict censorship and prohibition of free discussion—may perpetuate a state of pluralistic ignorance that is in itself a basis of social stability.

Hence, changes in the state of communication may give rise to collective behavior. The closing of channels of communication, particularly vertical channels, may lead to an accentuation of value-conflicts or to inefficiency of key functionaries. Inadequacy of communication leads to uncertainty and lack of confidence in the predictability of social life. These, in turn, give rise to rumor and the emergence of new norms.

The opening of communication channels may also give rise to collective behavior by disrupting a state of pluralistic ignorance. The sudden disclosure of corruption in a high government office may shake the confidence of people in the legitimacy and effectiveness of the entire political structure. An increase of communication between people who have been afraid of disclosing their individual dissatisfaction to one another may open up a vision of possibilities of change that had previously been unimaginable.

THE COMPLEXITY OF CONDITIONS GIVING RISE TO COLLECTIVE BEHAVIOR. It is evident that the division of labor, the normative order, and communication are interdependent and interacting features of social order. Changes in one are likely to be accompanied by changes in the others. By the same token, collective behavior arises out of a complex of societal roots and not from a single condition. In different instances one factor may be of greater weight than others, but some change in all these basic features of a social system is likely to be present.

These are the conditions that, given a state of conduciveness, give rise to collective behavior. As was pointed out in Chapter 3, it is through the process of rumor that collective behavior develops and assumes different forms. These forms may be analyzed in terms of two organizing principles. One is the sort of coordination that develops in the collectivity, leading either to individualistic or to solidaristic forms. The other is the type of symbolization that emerges in the rumor process, giving rise to expressive tendencies or to acting forms of crowd behavior. These organizing principles are subjects for the first two chapters in Part Two, beginning our more direct treatment of the organization and processes of crowds.

ORGANIZATION AND FUNCTIONING

OF CROWDS

5

COORDINATION IN THE CROWD

Of the many forms of collective behavior, the crowd is the one of which people are most aware. Crowd behavior is frequent, often spectacular, and greatly varied in its specific manifestations. The mob, murderous or destructive; the rioting crowd, angry or triumphant; crowds engaged in orgies of joy, grief, or religious fervor; audiences that "go wild"; groups in panic; clusters of gawking spectators—all these are manifestations of the crowd. The initial stages of crowd behavior have been discussed in connection with rumor. The elements common to all crowds and the features that distinguish subtypes of this form of collectivity may now be examined.

Common Characteristics of Crowds

The conditions for the development of collective behavior indicate some of the features that characterize the crowd and the individuals who compose it. The situa-

tion is ambiguous or unstructured; the participants do not share clear-cut, pre-existing expectations as to how they should behave; the outcome of the situation appears uncertain. Yet these conditions are not sufficient for the emergence of crowd behavior unless another factor is present— a sense of urgency, a feeling that something can and must be done *now*. It is this sort of definition that Smelser calls "a generalized belief, which identifies the source of strain, attributes certain characteristics to this source, and specifies certain responses to the strain as possible or appropriate."[1]

This is also the "meaningful interpretation" or "the social definitions of reality" that according to Shibutani, develops in the rumor process. As was pointed out in Chapter 3, symbols constitute the material and the product of rumor. These symbols, emerging out of the rumor process, serve

[1] Neil J. Smelser, *Theory of Collective Behavior* (New York: The Free Press, 1963), p. 16.

to indicate the implementation of the situation—what sort of action is appropriate—and they carry with them implications for the kind of coordination of the crowd members' actions that is required.

The notion of a conception of appropriate action should not be understood to imply a specific plan of action. Although in some crowds a precise pattern of action may quickly be defined as appropriate, there usually exists only a sense that certain kinds of action are appropriate and that other kinds are not.

The mood, imagery, and conception of appropriate action are not only communicated in the crowd; they take on a definitely normative character. As more and more people come to think and feel in the same way, or appear to do so, there is a growing sense that everyone should share these feelings and definitions. There is increasing pressure on individuals to conform; a sense of constraint develops in the crowd.

Thus, on the group level, there is the emergence of a norm. On the individual level there is heightened suggestibility, but this suggestibility is not of an unfocused, indiscriminate nature. It amounts to a tendency to respond uncritically to suggestions that are consistent with the mood, imagery, and conception of appropriate action that have developed and assumed a normative character.

Finally, the crowd is permissive; attitudes may be expressed and actions taken that would normally be inhibited. Usually it is possible for the individual to reconcile normative conflicts by techniques of avoidance and rationalization, inhibiting certain acts inconsistent with others in which he is motivated to engage. He is aided in this by cultural sanctions that inhibit, modify, or limit the expression of some attitudes as against others, while still permitting the inhibited attitudes to exist. It is rare, for example, for the majority of an audience to walk out on a speaker in the middle of his discourse, although after the speech many of them may express the opinion that "he wasn't worth going to hear."

The attitudes that are expressed in the crowd are those which, while being sanctioned in the culture of the crowd members, are ordinarily limited in their expression. But situations arise in which conflicting attitudes can no longer be reconciled, and attitudes that have previously received only limited expression are more fully expressed. Thus it may be said that the basic condition out of which crowd behavior arises is one of cultural conflict, or a breakdown of normative integration; it is not a condition of absence of culture. Crowd members may also evolve new attitudes and ways of acting in the process of resolving the dilemma of conflicting cultural demands. New forms of behavior, not previously existing in the culture of the group from which the crowd is drawn, may emerge.

These elements, then, are common to all crowds: (1) uncertainty; (2) a sense of urgency; (3) communication of mood and imagery; (4) constraint; (5) selective individual suggestibility; and (6) permissiveness. A collectivity that does not develop sufficiently to engage in a distinct, differentiated type of crowd behavior but that has these basic characteristics may be called an *elemental crowd*. As crowds develop further, they may differ markedly from each other, as is suggested by the many schemes of crowd classification that have been proposed by different writers. One of the important dimensions in which crowds differ is the type of coordination in the behavior of the members.

The Individualistic Crowd

In some crowds the definition of reality suggests an objective that the individual could not accomplish alone. Such an objective demands that the members of the crowd integrate their behavior in a cooperative but differentiated fashion. Such a crowd may be characterized as *solidaristic*.

In other situations the nature of the crowd objective is such that, except for cultural inhibitions, it could be accomplished as well by the individual acting alone as by his acting as a member of the crowd. The actions of the crowd members are parallel and similar rather than differentiated and cooperative; they are even competitive. This type of crowd behavior may be described as *individualistic*. The example that immediately suggests itself is panic, in which each member of the crowd seems willing to fight the other members in pursuit of the common objective, safety.

THE NATURE OF PANIC. Typical treatments of panic tend to emphasize two features, fear and disorganization. Thus Meerloo defines panic by saying, "One speaks of panic when a dangerous occurrence causes a spontaneous, disorganizing reaction in the individual or the community...The socially important factor is the sudden reaction, the decomposing effect, the disintegration of the social formation or the individuality which results."[2] Lang and Lang stress this element in panic when they refer to extreme panic as "a collective retreat from group goals into a state of extreme privatization." They observe, "Acts cease to be oriented toward the collectivity. Each person's concern is with his own safety and personal security, whether the danger is physical, psychological, social or financial."[3]

There are well-documented cases of individual or solo panic in which lone individuals react to terrifying stimuli with the sort of headlong, heedless flight that may be observed in collective panic. When individuals simultaneously exposed to the same danger react with similar feelings of fear and attempts to escape, convergence theory alone would account for collective panic. There would seem to be no need to invoke either contagion or norm formation to account for the simultaneity and intensity of the flight behavior. Yet collective panic displays characteristics that clearly indicate that interaction between the crowd members, not merely the convergence of individual acts which "have a private, even autistic orientation,"[4] plays a significant part.

Even when the solitary individual is confronted by a stimulus that produces severe fear reactions, there is a social factor involved. His interpretation of the stimulus as a symbol of danger is a product of his earlier social experiences in which it has acquired this meaning for him. Foreman suggests that something resembling convergence may take place when a group is confronted by a situation that has previously been linguistically defined as "acutely terrifying and unmanageable". Such a stimulus "may induce immediate terror and guide action directly to flight."[5] The traditional caution that one should not shout "fire" in a crowded theater reflects recognition of this principle.

Panic may also emerge after a period of milling in which the crowd itself evolves a definition of the situation as dangerous and indicates that the response of flight is appropriate. As the failure of many people to become frightened at false air raid alerts indicates, even though a signal has been officially designated as warning of danger, the operation of the rumor process may make it seem innocuous. Even when the situation is defined as dangerous, social pressures and definitions often determine whether people translate their fear into flight behavior or conceal their fear behind heroic behavior. In some ship disasters loss of life is minimized because "abandon ship" procedures are followed calmly, and lifeboats are fully and efficiently utilized. In others, lives are lost because lifeboats are

2 Joost A.M. Meerloo, *Patterns of Panic* (New York: International Universities Press, 1950), p. 11.

3 Kurt Lang and Gladys Engel Lang, *Collective Dynamics* (New York: Thomas Y. Crowell Company, 1961), p. 83.

4 Ibid.

5 Paul B. Foreman, "Panic Theory," *Sociology and Social Research*, 37 (May-June, 1953), 302.

overloaded or lowered too fast and smashed as a result of panic.

That there is a normative element in the development of fear and the adoption of a flight response is revealed by the following introspective analysis of an individual's feelings when in a situation that other people, but not he, defined as dangerous. In spite of his own accurate interpretation of the situation, as one that held no danger, this man experienced a sense of social pressure not only to respond as other people did but also to reevaluate his own diagnosis.

Why Can't I Be Afraid?

Ralph H. Turner

In early afternoon I was taking my son (age 7½) and my daughter (age 5) for one last look at Christmas toys, while my wife attended to other pre-Christmas chores. My daughter and I were looking at toys near the west wall of the large basement toy room. My son was somewhere on the opposite side of the room, looking at boys' toys. The two wide exits, leading to stairways up to the first floor were at the southwest and southeast corners of the room.

Suddenly there was a loud and continuous hissing noise from the center of the room, a few cries of fear, and in an instant the entire basement room was cleared of shoppers and clerks alike. I was astonished and even amused at the panicky flight of women shoppers and clerks. I felt no fear—it sounded to me as if one of the automatic sprinkler heads had been broken, which was nothing to be afraid of. I looked down at my daughter, who was holding my hand and looking rather wide-eyed, but giving no sign of fear. I looked across the room for my son, but could see no one in the room. I felt quite concerned lest he be hurt or frightened, being alone in the crowd. I looked for the broken sprinkler so that I could cross the room to find him without getting drenched. There was no sign of water, so I walked with my daughter toward the center of the room where the hissing was still coming from. Then I saw the gas escaping from the hydrogen container used to inflate toy balloons. My first impulse was to go over and try to

From *The Sociological Quarterly,* 5 (Spring, 1964), 130–31. Reprinted by permission of the Midwest Sociological Association.

shut it off, but I immediately felt that I should find my son first. So I started walking, with my daughter, across the room to the opposite exit, where my son must have gone out with the crowd.

As I started to walk out across the room, I felt a sudden strangeness—was there something wrong with me? Why did I feel no fear when a hundred or so people had run in panic from the room. Still I felt no fear, but I began to reexamine the situation. No, the amount of gas in the one container could not possibly be dangerous in a room so large, with a high ceiling. Furthermore, both doors leading upstairs were wide open, and they were wide doors. There would be plenty of natural air circulation. And yet, there I was, with my daughter who simply mirrored my confidence, the only ones left in the basement. Could my reasoning really be right—could everyone else's fear be unjustified? I could find no flaw in my reasoning —but I began to wish that I did feel some fear. Then I felt the responsibility for my daughter. There was no danger—but if anything *did* happen to hurt my daughter, all these other people would be around to say that I brazenly carried her into danger.

I turned back, walked quickly to the nearest exit, told my daughter to walk to the first landing (half a flight up), wait right there while I went and found her brother. Then I hurried across the room toward the other exit, feeling immensely relieved. When I was halfway across the room the hissing stopped; and then I saw Santa Claus, who had also not left the room. Suddenly I felt normal again —someone else had seen the situation the same way I had. As men in American culture, we were better equipped than women shoppers and clerks to define the situation correctly. The violence of my sense of relief at this moment has been paralleled by few other experiences in my lifetime. As people began filing back in, I met my son at the door, listened to him assure me spontaneously that he just ran because everyone else did, as we walked back to the other exit, where my daughter waited obediently. I took the children over to the empty hydrogen container, explained just what had happened, and in a minute we were back looking at Christmas toys as before.

CONDITIONS FOR PANIC. Extensive research on instances of panic has shown that it is not simply the intensity of fear that accounts for panic flight. Accounts by combat soldiers, firemen, and members of other dangerous occupations demonstrate that highly disciplined, heroic actions may be performed even though the members of a group are experiencing intense fear. Indeed, heroes generally scoff at the assertion of an individual that he was unafraid in the face of danger. Flyers have a saying, "There are old pilots and bold pilots, but not old, bold pilots!" People may also react to a dangerous situation with resignation, apathetically awaiting what seems to be an inevitable outcome. In their discussion of "The Problem of Panic," the Committee on Disaster Studies of the National Research Council pointed out that while the presence of a severe and imminent threat is necessary for the development of panic, it is not a sufficient condition. Panic occurs when, in the presence of severe threat, the collective definition indicates that escape is possible but that the means of escape are limited. The situation becomes essentially individualistic and competitive; a number of people are each trying to gain an objective whose attainment is problematic for each of them. The situation may become a competitive one not because of its objective features but because of the crowd members' definition of it. This happens when they overlook escape routes or think that a route that is actually blocked is still open.

The Problem of Panic

Panic is undoubtedly a dramatic term, but it is an ambiguous one. It has been used to refer to so many different kinds of behavior—ranging from a wild outburst of flight to paralysis of action—that its meaning has become vague. Often the word is employed merely as a vivid term to refer to any kind of behavior that occurs when people feel afraid or worried. To give the word a specific meaning, it is desirable to apply it to highly emotional behavior which is excited by the presence of an immediate severe threat, and *which results in increasing the danger for the self and for others*

From "The Problem of Panic," Civil Defense Technical Bulletin, TB-19-2 (June, 1955), pp. 1–2. Reprinted in part by permission of the Federal Civil Defense Administration.

rather than in reducing it. This concept of panic recognizes the negative connotation that the term usually carries. Thus, we avoid referring to all instances of excited behavior as panic. In these terms for example, flight is not necessarily panic, for flight may result in *reducing* the danger.

The current hunches and guesses seem to go far beyond the known facts in emphasizing the likelihood of its occurrence in this country. Many of the forecasts and discussions concerning panic which have received wide publicity assume that it will not be too difficult for an enemy nation to strike terror into the hearts of Americans—especially through the use of atomic and thermonuclear bombs. To the enormous loss of life and property—so runs the theme—panic or mass hysteria will add devastating disorganization and paralysis, a weapon more horrible in its effects than any known to man.

MASS PANIC OCCURS RARELY

An assessment of the facts shows that the existing evidence falls far short of supporting such a vivid and dramatic prediction. The authenticated instances of mass panic known to have occurred in the last 50 years have been few in number and have been very restricted in their effect. Although there has been war somewhere in the world almost continuously during this time, it is a significant and somewhat astonishing fact that there have been few instances of mass panic directly connected with enemy attack on a civilian population. Moreover, studies of terrified people who have been stunned by an overwhelming disaster indicate that panic states are usually of short duration, and that excited and irrational behavior can usually be prevented or quickly brought to a stop if effective leadership and realistic information is provided. A striking finding that emerges from observations in large scale disasters, including the A-bomb attack against Japan and the massive bombing assaults against England and Germany, is that the people who are most frightened and most upset very soon become extremely docile and can easily be induced to conform to the rules and regulations of the local authorities.

The logical conclusion from the evidence, then, is that mass panic is a rare event which arises only under highly specialized circumstances. We do know something about the conditions which give rise to panic behavior—though not as much as we would like.

There are four main factors which are characteristic of the panic-producing situation.

1. *Partial entrapment.* There is only one, or, at best an extremely limited number of escape routes from a situation dominated by (2).

2. *A perceived threat.* The threat may be physical, or psychological, or a combination of both, and it is usually regarded as being so imminent that there is no time to do anything except to try to escape.

3. *Partial or complete breakdown of the escape route.* The escape route becomes blocked off, or jammed, or it is overlooked.

4. *Front to rear communication failure.* The false assumption that the exit is still open leads the people at the rear of the mass to exert strong physical or psychological pressure to advance toward it. It is this *pressure from the rear* that causes those at the front to be smothered, crushed, or trampled. In instances where people are trampled to death, as in the Coconut Grove fire, this is usually the single, most important factor.

When a mass panic occurs, it usually happens that people do not actually see the "escape hatch," whatever its nature may be, but infer its existence from the fact that other people are moving in a specific direction. This inference made by the individual is reinforced by statements of people in the immediate vicinity. None of these communications, however, is based on realistic information about the actual conditions at the "escape hatch." The people at the rear of the mass, especially, are too far away from the exit to be able to obtain accurate information about its actual state. Thus, when the exit becomes blocked or jammed, the people at the rear behave as if it were still open.

There is some evidence to support the conclusion that when people know that the escape route is actually blocked, and that no escape is possible, they are likely to remain fatalistically hopeful or else become apathetic and depressed—but the likelihood of panic behavior is actually very slight.

This analysis suggests that the failure of communication is the condition that lends ambiguity and lack of direction to the urgent situation. The possibility of escape is the basis for action, but the probability that only the first will escape makes the situation competitive. Yet this same probability translates panic into a reasonable effort of self-preservation in the situation as it has been defined by the collectivity. Characterizations of panic as behavior that is essentially irrational, hysterical, and marked by lack of self-control overlook its origin as a response to a particular kind of collective definition of a situation. That an observer, analyzing the situation after the fact, may see that it could have been defined differently, with less destructive consequences, does not change the fact each crowd member's behavior may have seemed to him highly appropriate in the situation as he perceived it.

COMPETITION IN THE INDIVIDUALISTIC CROWD. In describing the situation in which mass panic occurs as competitive, we acknowledge one of the most familiar and dramatic features of such behavior. This is the lack of cooperation among the members of the collectivity, with the result that each person's behavior becomes highly selfish and aggressive. Such actions may be observed in crowds that are faced not with danger from which escape seems urgent but with opportunity that must be seized at once. If there is an element of fear, it is merely the fear of each individual that he may be unable to avail himself of the opportunity. The threat to his hopes, the factor that lends urgency to the situation, is the presence of other people with the same goal. It is in this aspect of the individualistic crowd that the social influence of the collectivity is most clearly evident. Were he not hampered by the presence of so many other people seeking the same goal, the individual's chances of success— whether in escaping or in taking advantage of a rare opportunity—would be enhanced. The collectivity, however, increases the ambiguity of the situation, makes the situation a competitive one, and thereby changes the behavior of the individual. This type of individualistic crowd, showing the same disregard for the usual norms of courtesy as a crowd in panic flight, is described below.

15,000 Women Storm Loeser's

Meyer Berger

The hell-hath-no-fury element in some 15,000 Brooklyn housewives broke out violently yesterday at the bargain sales in Loeser's department store in Fulton Street. The sales mark the requiem for the 83-year-old store.

It looked for a while, when the store opened at noon, that the sales might spell requiem for the bargain hunters, too. They smashed glass store panels, all but routed the finest and brought motor traffic to a dead halt.

Policemen, perspiring though the temperature was five degrees below freezing, gaspingly summoned support, squeezed the broken doors shut again, and temporarily imprisoned a few thousand triumphant women who had broken through.

Then, outside, mounted policemen used their horses to back the flushed hordes from the door-

The New York Times Friday, February 15, 1952. © 1952 by The New York Times Company, Reprinted by permission.

ways. Police sound trucks hoarsely blared: "This store is jammed beyond fire regulation capacity. Come back another time."

Frozen motor traffic wailed and tooted in Fulton Street, in Bond Street, in Elm Place and in Livingston Street, tight as mid-winter ice. A few shoppers moved out of the crush, mainly easily intimidated males.

The distaff bargain-seekers stood their ground. They eddied around the cops and their horses like rough water around a storm-beset reef. Three hours after the initial break-through they gained their objective—and still more came.

The widely-publicized sale had seemed, at 10 A.M., to have fallen a little flat. But at 11 A.M. the crowds converged. Shortly before noon they seemed to come up through the pavement. They streamed from nearby Loeser competitors, where they had gone to keep warm.

Then the rush started. Bond Street filled from

building line to building line. Traffic ground to immobility in Fulton Street. Additional waves moved in and took Livingston Street—and the police took panic.

Albee Square filled with shoppers from remote Boro Park, Canarsie, Greenpoint and Dyker Heights. Frightened—or henpecked—husbands balked at hitting such a line. A little man with a large spouse trembled at the curb in front of the Dime Savings Bank of Brooklyn.

He said: "This is stupid; let's go home, Ida."

Ida's eyes blazed—the glare of the bargain fanatic. She retorted: "Everybody's stupid but you. All those people wanting to save money are stupid. Not my Mr. Rockefeller."

The little man winced and turtled into his coat collar. "It's a rat race," he persisted. "A man could be killed."

Ida curled her lip at such poltroonery. She forced the man off the curb with her impressive bulk and herded him into the violent human tide.

Another woman said to a neighbor: "I wouldn't do that to my man. Why a person can't even turn around in that mob." And a person couldn't.

The thousands who had made the indoor beachhead were heady with shopper delirium, but only for a little while. They snatched at bargains with utter disregard of their needs, used their elbows and strident speech, made like huskies trying out for a Notre Dame backfield.

By 3 P.M. the worst was over and a quivering calm prevailed. They still snatched, but with surer eye and a bit more judgment. The sad-eyed salesgirls, and other help—some 1,400 all told—grew armweary wrapping what was thrust at them.

Individualistic crowd behavior as a general class is thus distinguished by the competitive relation that exists between the members, contrasting with the solidaristic crowd in which the presence of other people governed by the same impulse is an aid to each person's pursuit of his goal. Alexander Mintz has produced in the laboratory the type of situation that gives rise to individualistic crowd action.[6] The subjects in his experiment, working in groups of from 15 to 21, had the task of pulling cones through the neck of a glass bottle. Each subject held a piece of string to which a cone was attached. Since only one cone could come out at a time, cooperation between the subjects was necessary in order for any of them to perform the task successfully. Otherwise "traffic jams" of the cones developed. In some experimental conditions subjects were given rewards or were fined for success or failure in withdrawing their cones within announced time limits. In other conditions no rewards or fines were involved but accomplices of the experimenter made noise and

attempted to stir up excitement in the group.

Mintz found that it was the existence of a reward structure that produced traffic jams or nonadaptive group behavior. Emotional excitement produced by the accomplices had little effect on the efficiency of group behavior. Noting that the threat to the subjects was no more serious than the loss of ten cents, at most, and a feeling of failure, Mintz concluded that intense fear was not an essential condition of chaotic, competitive behavior analogous to that occurring in panics.

PERMISSIVENESS IN THE INDIVIDUALISTIC CROWD. It has been pointed out that the individualistic crowd displays a normative aspect in creating social pressure on the individual to experience the same impulses as those seemingly experienced by the other members. The father in the toy store wonders if perhaps he should not be afraid; Ida sneers at her husband for not agreeing with the bargain hunters that the savings are worth the battle. A second essential normative aspect of this type of crowd is the moral neutralization of usual norms because of dramatic evidence that conventional reciprocities are not being observed.

[6] Alexander Mintz, "Non-Adaptive Group Behavior," *Journal of Abnormal and Social Psychology*, 46 (April, 1951), 150–59.

The crowd is in this sense permissive. The norms that permit people to live together in a relatively peaceful, harmonious state require that the individual forego some of his own gratifications. He does so with faith that others are also adhering to these norms and making their own sacrifices. Evidence that other members of the collectivity are disregarding these norms and, instead of being punished as deviants, are gaining an advantage in the pursuit of a scarce object releases the individual from the moral obligation to observe the norms. A new norm arises, collective support for untrammeled pursuit of individual survival or gain, and the behavior of the crowd becomes individualistic and competitive.

The Solidaristic Crowd

In the individualistic crowd the objectives of the members may be viewed as individual as well as crowd objectives. They constitute a crowd objective only in the sense that they are identical and parallel. The generalized belief under which the crowd acts is of a nature to suggest that each individual could achieve the objective alone. The presence of other crowd members makes the situation a competitive one.

Another definition of the situation may arise, one that suggests a common crowd objective that the individual could not attain alone. It is an objective that he might attain with the cooperation and support of other members of the crowd. Hence the kind of relationship that develops between the crowd members is one of cooperation. For example, an armed policeman whom no lone individual in the crowd might dare attack may appear vulnerable if a unified attack by a multitude is anticipated. An individual who would be terrified at the thought of singing a solo, no matter how joyful he might feel, may not hesitate to voice a loud, though tuneless, song as part of a crowd. To the ordinarily inhibited person, singing or cheering in a crowd is like singing in the shower!

A crowd in which this sort of coopera-

tive, mutually supportive relationship exists may be characterized as *solidaristic*. The feature that distinguishes it most sharply from the individualistic crowd is that in it a division of labor develops. Instead of being parallel and identical, the actions of the crowd members are differentiated, and they supplement each other. Although there is differential participation by the members, the crowd acts in unison.

Unifying and Empowering Symbols. The unity of the solidaristic crowd depends upon the process and the products of symbolization. First of all, an objective must be defined that unifies the crowd; it arouses a common image and mood in the members. If the objective is to be action on some tangible object external to the crowd, then this object must be symbolized in a manner that will evoke at least a minimum of sentiment among the potential crowd members. Turner and Surace showed how the symbol "Mexican," which could arouse both positive and negative responses among Californians, was replaced by the symbol "zoot-suiter," as a prelude to the riots of 1943. Unified, hostile crowd action toward political partisans can be aroused by the emergence of such symbols as "communist" or "peacenik."

If the objective is to be the evoking of some subjective experience in the crowd members, then the situation may be symbolized as one in which strong feelings are appropriate. The many dramatic, collective expressions of grief following the assassination of President Kennedy were facilitated by the emphasis of the mass media on his youth, his devotion to his children, and his courage in combat. That he was a highly controversial political figure, elected to office in a close race, and despised by many Americans was not allowed to detract from the aura of profound tragedy. On Armistice Day in 1918 and V-J Day in 1945, objective appraisal of the fact that not all the troops would come home immediately and of the difficulties to be encountered in winning the peace would not have provided a stage setting appropriate to the victory celebrations that followed.

Symbols that emphasize the unity and the power of the crowd must also emerge. Such symbols tend to draw a contrast between the crowd members, the object toward which they act, and other persons who might not become members of the crowd. Such phrases as "all red-blooded Americans," "any decent person," and "everybody but the kooks" imply that the crowd members have a vast if invisible reserve of supporters. The object of the crowd's hostility is, by implication, part of a small and weak minority, easily overwhelmed. Crowd members may even derive a sense of power from such a vague saying as, "Everybody is indignant about this!" That "everybody" may consist only of the crowd members who share the sentiments of the speaker does not diminish the effectiveness of the crowd as a reference group.

THE SENSE OF RIGHTEOUSNESS. Closely related to the symbolization that emphasizes the power and unity of the crowd are those symbols that contribute to the development of a sense of righteousness. Power and right are not sharply separated in practice. Whatever affords an impression of legitimacy to the group enhances its sense of power, and whatever conveys a sense of strength reinforces the sense of rightness. Symbols may also serve to legitimize action by linking the definition of the present situation to other situations, tying the developing course of action to already sanctioned courses of action. Belin-Milleron, in the analysis of political tracts that appeared in connection with successive political disturbances in France during the nineteenth century, shows that each succeeding disturbance borrowed symbols from the earlier movements.[7] The meanings and contexts of the symbols were altered, but the

current activities were symbolically associated with favorably evaluated efforts of the past. Similarly, during anti-integration disturbances in the South after 1954, the symbols of the Confederacy, the highly romanticized Lost Cause of the region, were regularly employed—the Confederate battle flag and "Dixie."

Obviously the same symbolic expressions may have unifying, legitimizing, and empowering effects. As these symbolic expressions are picked up and repeated by the crowd members, they grow in strength. Our idea that something is morally incontestable is essentially a conversion of our experience that nobody in the groups that mean anything to us, nobody whose opinion we consider worth listening to, contradicts this idea. The sense of absolute righteousness and invincibility of an idea is derived from the unanimity with which it seems to be held. In a crowd situation the range of the individual's attention is narrowed. In the extreme case, the individual's orientation is determined solely in terms of the present crowd members. The influence of his usual identification groups and their norms is attenuated, and the individual's sense of moral rightness is determined by the compelling presence of other crowd members. The appearance of unanimity in the crowd, even though it may be illusory, gives the same basis for believing that the position of the crowd is morally incontestable and that the crowd is invincible that the individual gets from groups with which he identifies outside the crowd.

THE DIVISION OF LABOR IN THE CROWD. Although the solidaristic crowd acts under the influence of unifying symbols, not all the members behave in the same way. Some members act as leaders, exerting marked influence in the defining of the situation. Others are very active and vigorous in carrying out the suggestions of the leaders. Yet others may appear to be mere spectators, limiting their activity to shouting, cheering, or clapping. There is differential

7 Jean Belin-Milleron, "Les Expressions Symbolique dans la Psychologie Collective des Crises Politiques," *Cahiers Internationaux de Sociologie*, 10 (1951), 158–67.

participation and an emergent division of labor. The differentiated actions all contribute to the unified action of the crowd.

LEADERSHIP AND KEYNOTING. The most obvious and familiar differentiation is between leaders and followers. In the individualistic crowd, leadership is manifested primarily in the provision of a behavioral model, which is imitated by other crowd members. In the solidaristic crowd the leader's behavior is more likely to have a directing and coordinating function. Although he may play a prominent part in defining the situation and suggesting an appropriate line of action, he may play a relatively minor role in carrying out this line of action. He is important primarily as a keynoter. He advances suggestions that help to resolve the feelings of ambivalence experienced by many crowd members. Many people approach the crowd situation feeling that something should be done but not knowing what. They may have grave doubts as to the desirability of any action that deviates sharply from the usual social norms.

The person who feels no such uncertainty is capable of proposing definite action tersely and forcibly. A positive, unqualified statement may have additional power because most of the crowd members are tentatively thinking along the same line, considering this as a possible line of action without yet being committed to it. The presentation of a positive suggestion in an ambivalent frame of reference may be called keynoting.

Obviously the effect of a keynote depends upon a number of factors. The preexisting status of the speaker, if he is known to some members of the crowd, may lend weight to his suggestions. Visible symbols of status may have the same effect. It has been noted that in train wrecks, many people look to passengers in military uniforms for leadership. Mere temporal primacy—speaking first and loudest—may give a speaker an advantage in becoming the keynoter. Acclaim received from even a small portion of the crowd may create fear in those who disagree that they hold an unpopular, minority viewpoint. Observers of the keynoting process have reported, however, that often there is a succession of potential keynoters who offer a variety of alternatives from which the crowd selects.[8] Those suggestions that do not have some significant latent support are likely to go unheeded or even be hooted down.

The important effect of keynoting is that for some people the uncertainty and ambivalence is resolved by the keynote statement. One position is reinforced for them, and they now find it easier to express themselves, agreeing with a proposal that someone else has enunciated. As more people resolve or suppress their feelings of ambivalence, one viewpoint is expressed with greater frequency, to the exclusion of other proposals. The illusion of unanimity grows until extraordinary courage is required for an individual to express a dissenting viewpoint. The emergent definition of the situation and of a proposed line of action begins to take on a normative character. Permissiveness still characterizes the crowd, but it is a permissiveness that is congruent with the developing mood and definition. Thus, as a crowd develops a mood of hostility toward a public figure, members feel free to condemn him in language that would ordinarily be regarded as being in bad taste. By the same token, the crowd may now feel empowered to undertake drastic actions that the individual members would have considered too dangerous or too cruel.

The importance of the leader as a keynoter has been emphasized up to this point. The keynoter is not necessarily the person who physically carries out the line of action that develops in the milling process. Al-

[8] James Hundley, Jr., "The Dynamics of Recent Ghetto Riots," in Richard A. Chikota and Michael C. Moran eds., *Riot in the Cities* (Rutherford, N.J.: Fairleigh Dickinson University Press, 1970), p. 143.

though he may do so, the fact that there is a division of labor in the crowd signifies that other leaders may arise to implement his suggestions. Whereas one leader may provide the validating symbols for crowd action, others may direct the coordinated action, and yet others may perform the crucial physical feats necessary for attaining the objective.

The following account of the action of a hostile, solidaristic crowd, in driving two speakers from a public platform, illustrates the emergence of validating symbols, the development of a line of action (silencing the two speakers), and the division of labor in the crowd. Although the veterans were the active nucleus of the crowd, it was the shouts of the "pachucos" that goaded them into aggressive action and suggested the form that this action should take. But it was not the keynoters, the "pachucos," who surged toward the platform, shouting taunts and threatening physical harm to the speakers.

Freedom of Speech—But for Whom?

Paul H. Moeller

Saturday morning I went into town to do some shopping. I first went to the post office and then up the street to the stores. I was shopping for thirty to forty-five minutes when I walked out of Penney's and was confronted by a friend who told me a "Communist" was speaking on the lawn in front of the Post Office. Being curious about what Auburn's idea of a communist was, I walked down to where the speech was taking place. At this time, about twelve to seventeen people were listening to the speaker. One local college boy was there and I asked him who was speaking. He said that two members of VDC-SDS from Sacramento State College had come to speak against the U.S. position in Vietnam. He also said this was the first speech of this kind by such a group since 1967. At this moment, I was struck by the fact that here was possible crowd action about to develop. I decided to act very unknowing of all events in Auburn because of my being away at school. This was to prove useful in asking questions and getting answers without people being hesitant to answer because of suspicion. I began to ask questions. Most of this small group disagreed with the speakers but had come to hear them because of "wanting to be informed."

At this time, the speakers were rather modest in their speech pattern and exhortations. A few more

Student paper, University of California, Los Angeles. Published by permission of the author.

people stopped and listened within the first fifteen minutes. This was surprising because Auburn seemed to be more crowded with people than I could remember on a weekend in February (outside of December when Christmas shopping is prominent). I thought more people would stop and listen than the now twenty people. I continued asking questions. John M. said he was here to see "what was going to happen." When I quizzed him further, he told me that the Veterans of Foreign Wars had heard about this speech at a gathering they had had on Thursday night commemorizing three local boys who had been killed in Viet Nam. John M's. father, a member, had told John that they were going to show up at this speech and disrupt it with opposition speeches and shouts. John M. then said he hoped the veterans drove these "traitors" out of town. Here was the first instance of hate and prejudice that reared its head to me that morning.

Five minutes later, I noticed a crowd gathering across the street. This crowd was a conglomerate of people. I went across the street to question these people. Upon talking to seven or eight people here I gathered that they also anticipated that the veterans would show up, and they wanted to be far enough away from "any possible trouble" but close enough to see what would happen. More people started to gather on the fringes of this group. I talked to five of them including one relative. They were just curious as to why this group had formed across the street from the speakers. Now you had one group listening to the speakers and another group across the street curious and anticipating "some type" of spectacle. Believe me, I was stunned. Auburn usually ignored nor wished to foster trouble of this type. My experiences had told me that Auburn's residents get more excited over a drunk driving charge against a local citizen than over two VDC-SDS speakers. The part of the crowd across the street anticipating trouble, of course, sensed the mood of Auburn, being a part of that mood.

At this moment, someone shouted, "Oh boy, here come the veterans." I looked up the street and saw about thirty to forty people dressed in their Veterans' uniforms and a few carrying American flags. I also now anticipated trouble. These veterans looked all over forty years of age. There were few of the Ladies' Auxiliary present. Most of the group were men. To me, they marched down as if they had a purpose in mind. Now both previous crowds grew bigger as the clash between veterans and speakers loomed. At this point, two policemen walked up to the speaker's platform and stationed themselves on each side. (Important is the fact that most Auburnites know the police and the police know them.) When the veterans came close to the speaker's platform, they first merely seemed content to listen as good citizens. In the meantime, I had recrossed the street to be close to the action. The post office crowd at this instant was joined by about one dozen seventeen-year olds who had been congregating at Foster's Freeze (a drive-in restaurant) down the street. These boys for the most part were boys that good Auburnites in previous years would have called "pachucos." These boys (I knew half of them) were those who had been in and out of trouble with local authorities and who usually congregated at Foster's on Saturdays to discuss cars, girls, and booze parties.

The quiet, anticipating crowds on both sides of the street would no longer be so silent when these twelve boys came. Two of these boys were important keynoters. One shouted to the Veterans, "Are you going to do anything, or are you going to let these murderers of Randy S. and Jack B. (the two marines killed in Vietnam) talk like traitors."

I thought this statement extreme and that the crowds would laugh it off, but to my shock they were silent. The veterans seemed to take this statement as a reason for action. They began to demand that the two VDC-SDS speakers leave the platform and let the spokesmen for the veterans speak. The two speakers refused and said they had gotten permission from the city-manager to speak. (I verified this later for myself as true. I asked the city-manager myself.) Some of the veterans became furious and asked the police to take the speakers off the platform. The police refused. The second Foster's patron shouted that the veterans themselves should "take over the platform." At this moment, the bulk of the crowd across the street came over to the post office side (several of them told me they wanted to get a better look). This was a cue to the "pachucos" and veterans that their ideas were being strengthened by like minded people. Now, I became truly scared that something very ugly might happen that Auburn might regret. I began to circulate among the crowd while it, so far, just continued its shouting. I kept asking people if we might set up a debate that very night between these two speakers and local concerned citizens. The most frequent answer I got was that debates only help the "communists." I quit this gambit. Now it seemed as if the Korean affair and Vietnam deaths preying on the minds of many of the crowd's members was an excuse to lose control and prevent these two speakers from exercising a cherished American right of free speech.

The crowd now was getting increasingly ugly. The speakers could no longer talk above a torrent of shouts and invectives. One policeman now left to call for help (he went to his nearby police car and got on the radio). With only one policeman left, a couple of eggs were thrown (who threw these eggs I never found out). I could see now that the two speakers were becoming increasingly afraid for themselves. But instead of leaving now, they began to shout back at the crowd. I could hear them call the crowd "prejudice, small town hicks" and "backwater jerks." The hysteria of the crowd turned two cool speakers (at least at the beginning) into shouters just like the crowd. This action by the VDC-SDS speakers seemed to give license to the crowd for further action. The veterans, prodded by the crowd (as I saw it), began to surge forward with shouts of "we'll take you off the platform ourselves" and "our boys in Auburn are patriots." I feared for the two speakers now but I felt so helpless among my fellow Auburnites. At precisely this moment, about eight or nine police came and hustled the boys off of the back of the platform (nobody had gathered there) and began to take them to the police cars to get them away. This was the signal for the crowd to stop surging toward the platform and merely hurl taunts at the two young men but not the police (remember the policemen were either well known or of local origin). Now that the crowd had vented their frustrations and stopped the speech, they seemed to cool off and dissipate. The police drove off behind the post office and sped away down a back street leaving nothing for the crowd to yell at. I heard comments like "we showed those college punks" and "filthy protestors." With this the veterans walked back up the street, the local "pachucos" back to Foster's, and the remaining crowd back to its shopping, etc. Violence didn't get a chance to develop but a delay of five minutes by the police, and I might be telling a different story.

SHIFTS IN LEADERSHIP. In the relatively short-lived crowd described above, leadership was diffuse and shifting. In all crowds leadership roles, like other roles, are ephemeral for they are not based on formal authority or stabilized patterns of influence. In some crowds the leaders may be more clearly defined and more visible than in others. Even in such cases, however, the leadership may shift. Events that occur during the career of the crowd may provide the basis for a new definition of the situation. New lines of action may be proposed and accepted by the crowd. At this point the old leaders must change their tactics or give way to new leaders, who find the newly proposed actions more congenial.

During a political riot in Panama City in 1957 such a shift in leadership was seen. The original leaders were students who, because of their preexisting status in student organizations, had been the organizers of a march on the Presidential Palace. As the march progressed, the composition of the crowd changed. Elements joined who were not parties to a compromise worked out before the demonstration between the moderate and the radical students. Their presence strengthened the position of those students who were in favor of drastic action. Then, when the National Guard introduced the element of physical force into the situation by firing tear gas at the crowd, the violent faction was able to seize the leadership. An observer described the shift in leadership and the accompanying change in the mood and behavior of the crowd:

This initial act of forceful resistance on the part of the National Guard was a very serious mistake as it provided the bridge that was needed by the agitators to cause a shift in the mood of the crowd from one of mild aggressiveness to a high pitch of hostility. The students who had first advocated violence began bringing out rocks which they had concealed on their persons and pressed them upon some of the student leaders, while others pointed out the location of rocks which had been cached in alleyways and garbage cans. Thus the students were armed with missiles without a thought as to the source of supply. Several of the student leaders, evidently fearing loss of leadership and prestige, complied with the wishes of the subversive element of the crowd and began stoning the Guard. Almost instantly most of the students in the vicinity followed suit. The Guardsmen replied with tear gas and automatic weapons fire over the heads of the crowd, followed by deployment in a predetermined maneuver to force the crowd back down the street.[9]

DIFFERENTIAL PARTICIPATION. Not all the members of a crowd are equally active, particularly if the crowd action takes the

9 From student paper, Florida State University. Author's name withheld by request.

form of overt, physical movement or assault. Even if the action is confined to the verbal level, some members shout more loudly than others, and some may remain silent. The influence of the crowd leaders touches all members of the crowd, but its effect is most clearly reflected in the behavior of the active nucleus. In a crowd that develops a hostile mood and an aggressive line of action, some members may physically attack the object. Others may confine their action to shouting, and yet others may be mere spectators. In a fervent religious crowd some members sing more loudly and shout "hallelujah" more often than do others; some dance while others merely clap their hands.

Even the relatively more active members, behaving in essentially the same manner as one another, may do so on the basis of different motives. As was pointed out in Chapter 2, some members may be defined as committed. Because of preexisting orientations they perceive the situation from the outset as one in which certain attitudes and actions are appropriate. Thus in the case of the anti-Vietnam speakers, the members of the veterans' organization marched to the Post Office lawn with an already formed conviction, derived from their ordinary reference groups, that the speakers were traitors and should be opposed.

Other participants, whom we have described as the concerned, may come to the crowd situation with less clearly defined attitudes based on different aspects of the situation. Thus while some crowd members are definitely hostile to a speaker because of the views he expresses, others feel a vague, general hostility toward him because of his physical appearance or his manner of speaking. Others have no well-formulated basis for disagreeing with him but recognize that people with whom they ordinarily identify are opposed to him. They may even take part in the crowd action without ever knowing what the issue is.

The "pachucos" involved in the hostile action against the antiwar speakers seem to illustrate a third type of participant, the one who derives direct satisfaction from participation in a crowd regardless of the circumstances. The description of their previous relationship to the "respectable citizens," represented by the veterans, suggests that the committed members of the veterans' organization did not represent an important reference group for them. Like a small boy who goads two other boys into fighting each other, the "pachucos" saw in the confrontation between the veterans and the speakers an opportunity for some excitement. Hence they urged the veterans to even more aggressive action than had been originally contemplated.

THE PERFORMER-AUDIENCE RELATION. An element of the crowd that is not part of the active nucleus but is nevertheless important is the *spectators*. Their activity is slight and may be limited to watching the behavior of the more active members. They may be present at the crowd scene because they approve of what the crowd is doing or simply because they are curious. Some may even disagree with the crowd definition of the situation but remain to see what the outcome will be.

Sometime the spectators make up the majority of crowd members. They play a relatively passive role and are like an audience to the active nucleus. Their relative passivity does not mean, however, that the audience portion is unimportant in the development of the solidaristic crowd's action.

First, to the extent that individuals in the audience category engage in vocal activity, they contribute to the process that builds up the impression of unanimity. This encourages the members who are disposed to be physically more active. Furthermore, some members of the audience or spectator element may become identified with the active nucleus and enter into the performer group.

But crowd members who only look, even those who may covertly disapprove of what the active performers are doing, are important in crowd interaction. They make the crowd larger numerically, increasing the impression of strength and of support for what is being done. The Southern Commission on the Study of Lynchings noted that sometimes spectators constituted a source of protection for the very elements of which they might disapprove.

The onlookers play an important part in another process, which we will call the process of commitment. In this process, the active element of the crowd becomes committed to a line of action once begun because of the presence of a large group of observers. It is a general characteristic of human relations that an opinion formed or a resolution made in private can be changed more easily than can one to which the person has publicly committed himself. To embark upon a line of action and then to fail to pursue it is to back down and, if done in the presence of observers, is to lose face. That this process of commitment operates in crowd situations may be seen in the following episode in the Chicago riot of 1919.

The Influence of the Audience in the Chicago Riot

Among the spectators of mob violence were men, women, and children of all ages; they included tradesmen, craftsmen, salesmen, laborers. Though the spectators did not commit the crimes, they must share the moral responsibility. Without the spectators mob violence would probably have stopped short of murder in many cases. An example of the behavior of the active nucleus when out of sight of the spectators bears this out. George Carr, Negro, was chased from a street car. He out-

stripped all but the vanguard of the mob by climbing fences and hiding in a back yard. This concealed him from the rest of the crowd, who by that time were chasing other Negroes. The young men who followed Carr left him without striking a blow, upon his mere request for clemency. In regard to the large non-active elements in the crowds, the coroner said during the inquest, "It is just the swelling of crowds of that kind that urges them on, because they naturally feel that they are backed up by the balance of the crowd, which may not be true, but they feel that way." Juror Ware said, "If sightseers were lending their aid and assistance—" Juror Dillon interrupted and finished, "they ought to be punished."

From The Chicago Commission on Race Relations, *The Negro in Chicago* (Chicago: University of Chicago Press, 1922), pp. 22–23. Reprinted by permission of the University of Chicago Press.

APPLICATION OF THEORETICAL APPROACHES. Convergence, contagion, and emergent norm approaches all contribute to the explanation of both individualistic and solidaristic forms of crowd behavior. It has been pointed out that convergence theory has its greatest utility in accounting for the emergence of a simultaneous and parallel definition of the situation that leads to individualistic tendencies in the crowd. A contagion approach focuses attention on the heightened sensitivity of crowd members to one another in a situation perceived as competitive. This heightened sensitivity, combined with the similarity in the mood and imagery experienced by individuals, makes each one more likely to imitate the behavioral models offered by others. Yet these approaches are not adequate, separately or together, to account for all that takes place in an individualistic crowd. The eagerness to escape or to gain a scarce reward is not merely an individual need but takes on a normative character. As the behavior of an increasing number of crowd members reflects the emergent definition of the situation, it becomes increasingly difficult for the individual to cling to a conflicting conception. Moreover, emergent norm theory helps to explain the breakdown of usual norms of reciprocity and the development of an every-man-for-himself spirit.

Emphasis on the division of labor and differential participation in the solidaristic crowd might suggest that convergence and contagion approaches have little to offer in explanation of this form. It must be remembered, however, that collective behavior does not develop in a completely heterogeneous aggregate. Preexisting, latent tendencies, common to many members of a crowd, facilitate the development of a common mood and imagery. Which of several potential keynotes becomes dominant may reflect the convergence of predispositions shared by a significant portion, but not all, of the crowd. Similarities in background, such as ethnic or class identity and loyalties, may contribute to the power of the crowd as a reference group, even though the members may not know each other personally.

It has been argued that a condition of ambiguity increases the suggestibility of individuals to the actions of others. Keeping in mind the evidence from the Asch experiment that individuals vary in the degree of suggestibility, contagion may still account for some of the spread of mood, imagery, and overt behavior in members of a solidaristic crowd. In the excitement of a crowd, unwitting imitation through social facilitation may be increased as individuals become less self-conscious and less inhibited.

The excited, intense individual may unwittingly imitate the nervous movements, the loud tones, and the extravagant language of other crowd members, adding to the air of crisis. Or, eager to act but uncertain as to what he may do, the crowd member may deliberately imitate the actions of others when restraints are removed through behavioral contagion, as hypothesized by Wheeler.

Empirical crowd observations reveal that even though the solidaristic crowd acts as a unit, differences in the motives and the behavior of the members still remain. Not all the crowd members immediately perceive the situation as calling for a particular line of action, as convergence theory would suggest. Symbols and norms that override divergent interpretations must be developed. Even when a norm defining an appropriate line of action has emerged, individuals may comply externally without agreeing internally. The concept of differential expression suggests that the emergence of a norm not only sanctions behavior consistent with this norm but also inhibits behavior contrary to it and restrains those who dissent. Thus contagion—the spread of a common mood and image—is not necessary to account for the unified and coordinated action of the crowd. Moreover, individuals acting under the influence of a norm may participate in different ways and yet contribute to the accomplishment of a common objective.

What the crowd objective is may vary in both individualistic and solidaristic crowd forms. On the basis of the nature of the objective, crowds may display acting or expressive tendencies. This distinction provides a second major dimension along which crowds may be classified.

6

CROWD SYMBOLIZATION: ACTING AND EXPRESSIVE TENDENCIES

Examination of the forms of coordination in the crowd, solidaristic or individualistic, has suggested how the members of a collectivity are able to act together without the guidance of preexisting, traditional norms and organization. What a crowd may be doing, what its objective may be, has been incidental to this analysis. Whether solidaristic or individualistic tendencies predominate, a crowd may engage in a wide variety of activities.

Some crowds are aggressive and destructive, injuring people or destroying material. Such a collectivity is brought to mind by the value-laden term, *the mob*. Yet other crowds seem to have no visible object towards which their actions are directed; they are turned inward. Their actions affect only the crowd members themselves, producing or accentuating intense emotions which are often accompanied by unusual behavior. Such crowds are usually regarded as bizarre but harmless.

ACTING AND EXPRESSIVE CROWDS. A distinction has long been made, by laymen and sociologists, between crowds which change their external environment and those which seem only to give expression to the members' feelings. Since the latter type are often linked to religious fervor, they have been regarded as possessing great social significance. In an early classification of types of crowds, Herbert Blumer suggested the terms *acting crowd* and *expressive crowd* to distinguish between these two major forms. To Blumer, the acting crowd

is marked by the presence of an aim or an objective toward which the activity is directed. The distinguishing trait of the expressive crowd is "that excitement is expressed in physical movement merely as a form of release instead of being directed toward some objective."[1]

Blumer's language obscures the fact that both types of crowds may be said to have an objective or goal, but that the objective of the acting crowd involves action affecting an *object* which is external to the crowd. Guy E. Swanson has refined Blumer's concept by saying that members of an acting crowd attempt to manipulate the environment external to themselves, while expressive crowd members have the aim of manipulating self-images and norms of participation.[2]

The Acting Crowd

THE CROWD OBJECT. Both individualistic and solidaristic acting crowds have as their objective action on some object external to them. The nature of their actions or how they manipulate the external environment, may take many forms. For the members of a crowd in panic, the object is a limited avenue of escape, a part of the

[1] Herbert Blumer, "Collective Behavior," in A. M. Lee, ed., *Principles of Sociology* (New York: Barnes and Noble, Inc., 1951).
[2] Guy E. Swanson, "A Preliminary Stury of the Acting Crowd," *American Sociological Review*, 18 (October, 1953), 523.

external environment which each member of the crowd wishes to attain. Although the participants in a collective panic may experience intense fear, their behavior is not merely an aimless release of emotion. It is competitive behavior directed toward gaining the reward of placing themselves in a safe place.

How an individualistic acting crowd may engage in aggressive, destructive behavior toward an object or a class of objects is illustrated in the account by a participant in one of the earliest property riots in a black ghetto in the United States, the Harlem riot of August 1 and 2, 1943. The object of the crowd's action consisted of white-owned stores and the commodities in them. According to the interview below, the mob was not solidaristic but consisted of numerous individuals and small groups pursuing parallel individual objectives in a competitive fashion. The crowd provided a permissive atmosphere for various types of aggressive behavior toward objects which were ordinarily safe from such action.

A Participant in the Harlem Riot

Kenneth B. Clark and James Barker

R. is a dark-brown-skinned Negro, 18 years old. He was born in New York City. For the past two years he has lived alone in a roominghouse in the center of Harlem. When the interviewer saw him for the first time on the evening of the interview he was engaged in animated conversation with two other members of his CD messenger unit.

During the course of this conversation, R., *unprompted by the interviewer began to discuss the 1943 Harlem riot and his role in it.* The riot had taken place about a month before this. After he finished his account to the group, the interviewer casually said to R., "You ought to write a book." He replied (probably because he knew that the interviewer was a college student), "Why don't you,—are you going to write a book?" This gave the interviewer an opportunity to tell him that he would like a record of his account of his experiences in the riot. He readily agreed to cooperate and the interviewer immediately made arrangements to interview him in a private office.

[The following paragraphs are excerpts from

this private interview, as recorded by Clark and Barker.]

Before the riot starts I was in the Harlem Dump theater. Some two-by-four runs in there and says that: "Harlem is on fire!" The "niggers" jump up half full of juice and running for the door, me leading of course. By this time the "niggers" have tored-off half of Harlem.

The riot started when a colored man got shot. About half hour later the riot was going full blast, and the people was going 'round stores. They messed up 25th St. badly. They hit shoe stores, beat up a cop standing there unmercifully.

The party that you're writin' about goes in a store and helps himself to the man's cash register. The store next to the A & P—goes in there. There was nothin' there. While I goes in there a lady was stealin' a man's big half-a-cow.

One boy broke into Busch, located 125th Street and 7th Avenue. A flatfoot with a sawed-off rifle watches the boy when he enters the store, wait 'til the boy comes out, draw a bead on the boy an' begins to fire. A colored lady jumps in front of the cop, turns her black—up the cop and tells him: "Why don't you shoot me in the back?" The cop gets excited when the rest of the crowd begins to walk over, puts the rifle down, lowered it rather, and walks away.

Walkin' a little ways, they caught a 'fay (*white*),

Adapted by permission of the authors, from Kenneth B. Clark and James Barker, The Zoot Effect in Personality: A Race Riot Participant," *Journal of Abnormal and Social Psychology,* 40 (1945), pp. 143–148. Reprinted by permission of the American Psychological Association.

beatin' hell outa him half ta death. The man starts throwing money into the air and runnin' like hell. The boys was fightin' left and right for a two dollar bill, tearin' it in half; one of the boys say:

"You gimme your half!" the other one says: "You gimme your half!" Stubborn as they was, neither one of them gave in. As tired as I was I was scuffling, I gets myself $50.

The solidaristic acting crowd acts in an organized fashion toward its object, with a division of labor emerging. The old-fashioned lynch mob provided a clear example of this type of coordination. The acting crowd need not physically harm its object, however. In recent years crowds of student demonstrators have, on occasion, succeeded in driving speakers from public platforms by concerted jeering and other nonviolent manifestations of their hostility, such as throwing miniature marshmallows. It should not be inferred, either, that the acting crowd is always a hostile collectivity. A crowd may cheer a speaker rather than jeer him. In a disaster a crowd may become an impromptu rescue force.

SYMBOLISM IN THE ACTING CROWD. Even when the objects of the acting crowd have been identified, the question remains as to why the crowd *acts* on these objects rather than engaging only in expressive behavior. Why do people who are in a state of grief and anger because a tragedy has befallen one of their number seek to find a scapegoat who can be held responsible? Why not collectively give vent to their emotions and leave the search for the offender up to the police? Why don't people who are threatened by hunger or some other form of deprivation engage in some escapist, expressive behavior rather than looting or setting fire to stores where they feel they have been exploited? In recent years many Americans have wondered why blacks have ceased to spend so much time lamenting their plight in otherworldly religious services and have begun to take violent action.

Much more research is needed to identify the circumstances which lead crowd de-

velopment to take an acting rather than an expressive direction. It may be postulated that acting crowd behavior is likely to arise when the circumstances and the emergent definition of the situation suggest that manipulation of the external environment may be both effective and legitimate. An outlook on life and a conception of their own status that picture the population segments from which the crowd is drawn as powerless to change their conditions are not conducive to such a definition. Thus the increase in demonstrations, involving strong acting tendencies by college students in the United States, may be ascribed, in part, to an increased sense of power and importance felt by a burgeoning student population. The shift of black crowd behavior from almost exclusively expressive forms to property riots was preceded by an increased conviction of power, growing out of favorable federal court decisions and the successes of the civil rights movement. It has been pointed out before that panic is unlikely to occur when no avenue of escape is perceived as available. After a natural disaster, such as a tornado, the members of a community are not as likely to seek a villain or a scapegoat as they are after a disaster which is defined as man-made.

The concept of the scapegoat suggests, however, that the relationship between an acting crowd and its object is not simple or logical to the uninvolved observer. The object is always a symbol. Its symbolism is a matter of crowd definition. The symbolic importance, which the crowd attaches to it, may correspond closely to the definitions of people outside the crowd. Political scientists may agree that a public official who is the victim of hostile crowd action is indeed responsible for the conditions which angered the members. A door or a barricade may be a real barrier to the physical movement of people; its relationship to their action may be quite easily understood. On the other hand, the symbolism of some objects may be more obscure. Observing that in civil disturbances, crowds often direct destructive attacks against symbols of authority, Russell Dynes and E. L. Quarantelli tell of an incident in which a crowd of students spent more than an hour trying to destroy an overhead traffic light.[3] During antigovernment riots in Panama City in 1957, parking meters as well as traffic lights were objects of attack.

In "Two Patterns of Looting" Dynes and Quarantelli suggest a second important aspect of symbolization in the acting crowd. In addition to defining objects as appropriate targets for action, emergent norms serve to legitimize the crowd's action toward them. Dynes and Quarantelli show that the kinds of looting which occur in disasters and civil disturbances are accompanied by redefinitions of property and the relationship of people to it. Rescue parties and first-aid workers often appropriate tools and supplies for use in aiding survivors of a disaster. The definition which

[3] Russell Dynes and E. L. Quarantelli, "What Looting in Civil Disturbances Really Means," *Trans-action*, 5 (May, 1968), 13.

legitimizes appropriation of this sort of property is that of saving lives and relieving hardship by whatever means are necessary. There is the implication that most of the people who engage in this sort of looting actually use their loot to relieve suffering. Therefore the definition of looting is narrowed to include only appropriation of property for personal gain, usually by "outsiders."

While the goods that are appropriated during civil disturbances—liquor, clothing, furniture—may be used to satisfy physical needs, Dynes and Quarantelli suggest that the objects have the greatest significance as symbols of white exploitation. The norm that legitimizes this sort of theft involves a redefinition of the dominant societal conception of property. As an acting crowd, the rioters have as their object not only the stolen property itself but the persons who exercise power in the larger society.

The distinction between acting behavior and expressive behavior becomes finely drawn at this point, however. Much of the looting constitutes a symbolic act of defiance. Thus it may be said that the crowd members are magnifying and releasing their feelings of anger at the same time that they are doing something to change their situation. There may be a strong expressive component, a carnival spirit, in what must be classified as predominantly acting crowd behavior.

Two Patterns of Looting

E. L. Quarantelli and Russell R. Dynes

There are two major types of community crises, some reflecting consensus, others mirroring dissensus. The best examples of these two types of crises are, respectively, natural disasters and civil disturbances. Contrary to the image presented in

From "Property Norms and Looting: Their Patterns in Community Crises," *Phylon*, 31 (Summer, 1970), pp. 168–82. Reprinted by permission.

most news accounts as well as in fictional stories of emergencies, there is not total social chaos and anarchy in such situations. Behavior in both kinds of crises shows definite patterns which are neither random nor idiosyncratic for each specific case. Furthermore, while there is a pattern to the behavior, it differs in the two kinds of crises. This is as true of looting behavior as it is of many other emergency behaviors.

There are at least three major differences between the looting in civil disorders and the looting in natural disasters.

1. In civil disorders looting is very widespread whereas in natural disasters actual looting incidents are quite rare. It is widespread in at least three senses. One, it occurs in almost all major disorders and many of the less serious ones. Two, looters come from all segments of the population, females as well as males, oldsters as well as youngsters, middle-class as well as lower-class persons, and so on. Looting is not the behavior solely of a delimited or distinctive part of black communities. Three, if we extrapolate figures from some studies made by other researchers, in at least the major disturbances it seems possible that as many as a fifth of the total ghetto residents may participate in the activity.[1] This contrasts sharply with natural disaster situations. In those, looting often does not occur at all, and in the infrequent cases where it does take place, it is apparently undertaken by a handful of individuals in the general population.

Furthermore, looting in civil disorders is almost always, if not exclusively, engaged in by local residents, whereas in natural disasters it is undertaken by "outsiders." It is local ghetto dwellers who participate in urban civil disturbances. Arrest records for all offenses show that those involved overwhelmingly reside in the city experiencing the disorder.[2] There is in fact reason to suspect, when the high percentage of women who engage in massive looting is taken into account, that the great majority of looters are from the local neighborhoods around the places looted. In contrast, in natural disasters such looting as there is, in general, is done by non-local persons who venture into the impacted community. Sometimes they are part of the very security forces often sent in from outside the area to prevent such behavior (as was recently reported to be the case regarding some National Guardsmen dispached to the Gulf coast of Mississippi after Hurricane Camille).

2. One of the most striking aspects of looting

in civil disturbances is its collective character. This is dramatically depicted in many television and movie films of such incidents. Looters often work together in pairs, as family units, or in small groups. This is a marked contrast to looting in natural disasters, where it is carried out by solitary individuals. In civil disturbances, the collective nature of the act sometimes reaches the point where the availability of potential loot is called to the attention of bystanders, or where in extreme instances spectators are handed goods by looters coming out of stores.

The collective nature of massive looting is also manifest in its selective nature in civil disorders compared with its situational nature in disasters. Press reports to the contrary, ghetto dwellers have been far from indiscriminate in their looting. Grocery, furniture, apparel and liquor stores have been the prime objects of attack. In Newark they made up 49 percent of those attacked; in Watts they made up the majority. Many other kinds of establishments such as plants, offices, schools and private residences have been generally ignored. Furthermore, within the general category of stores and places selected for attack, there has been even finer discrimination. One chain store in Washington, D. C., had 19 of its 50 stores looted while supermarkets of other companies located in the same neighborhoods were left untouched. Such massive action obviously is not a matter of individual but of collective definition of "good" and "bad" stores from the viewpoint of ghetto dwellers. In contrast to this focus in civil disorders on commercial enterprises, in natural disasters such early looting as there is often seems to center on personal effects and goods. It likewise appears to depend on the opportunity presented by the availability of discarded clothing of victims, open doors into residences, spilled items on sidewalks from storefronts and the like. In other words, the looting in natural disasters is highly influenced by situational factors that present themselves to looters rather than any conscious selection and choice of places to loot, as is the case in civil disturbances. (However, even in natural disasters, there are far more situational opportunities for looting than are taken advantage of.)

3. The public nature of the looting behavior in civil disorders is also striking. Looting is not a private act, as it is in natural disasters. Goods are

---

[1] Robert Fogelson and Robert Hall, "Who Riots? A Study of Participation in the 1967 Riots." in *Supplemental Studies for the National Advisory Commission on Civil Disorders,* pp. 229–31.

[2] *Ibid,* p. 235.

taken openly and in full view of others, bystanders as well as co-participants, and often even policemen. In natural disasters, such looting as occurs is covert and secret, with looters taking care not to be observed by others. The open dashing into stores or the carrying of stolen goods through the streets in broad daylight as is common in the urban disturbances does not occur in the wake of such catastrophes as hurricanes and earthquakes.

Furthermore, in natural disaster, acts which are defined as looting are condemned severely. In civil disturbances, in contrast, both during and after the event there is little local community sanction against such behavior. In fact, while the disturbances are going on, and looting is at its peak, there is actually strong local social support for the activity. The so-called carnival spirit observed in the major civil disturbances, rather than being a manifestation of anarchy, is actually an indication of the local open collective support for looting. Even after the disturbances are over, as different studies and surveys show, the disorders are justified by most blacks and are judged as helpful in bringing about change.[3] In contrast, looting is considered a very serious crime in natural disasters, spoken of in highly condemnatory tones by the residents of an area, and is never seen as justifiable behavior.

To summarize: looting in civil disorders is widespread, collective and public, and is undertaken by local people who are selective in their activity and who receive community support for their actions. In contrast, looting in natural disasters is limited, individual and private, and is engaged in by outsiders to the community who take advantage of the emergency situation and who are strongly condemned for their actions.

EMERGENT PROPERTY NORMS

In order to explain the looting patterns in the two kinds of community crises just considered, it is necessary to examine the nature of property. In this we may be misled by the term *looting*. In the military context from which it is derived, looting implies the taking of goods and possessions.

However, property has reference not to any concrete thing or material object, but to a right. "Property consists of the *rights* held by an individual . . . to certain valuable things, whether material or intangible."[4] But if we talk of rights we are talking of shared expectations about what can or cannot be done. Property can therefore be viewed as a set of cultural norms that regulate the relation of persons to items with economic value. In effect, property is a shared understanding about who can do what with the valued resources within a community.

Normally, these understandings or expectations are widely shared and accepted. There are all kinds of norms, the legal ones in particular, which specify the legitimate forms of use, control, and disposal of economically valued resources within a community. It is these expectations which change in both kinds of community crises we are talking about.

In natural disasters, in American society at least, there quickly develops a consensus that all private property rights are suspended temporarily for the common good. In one way, all goods become "community property" and can be used as needed for the general welfare. Thus, warehouses can be broken into without the owner's permission to obtain generators necessary to keep hospitals functioning; and the act is seen as legitimate if undertaken for this purpose even though the participants might agree that it was technically an act of burglary. However, the parties involved, the local legal authorities and the general public in the area at the time of the crisis do not define such actions as looting and would react negatively to attempts to impose such a definition.

On the other hand, there is very powerful social pressure against the purely personal use of goods while major community emergency needs exist. In a way, the individual who uses anything for himself alone is seen as taking from the common

---

[3] Joseph Boskin, "The Revolt of the Urban Ghettos, 1964–1967," *Annals of the American Academy of Political and Social Science,* CCCLXXXII (March, 1969), 1–14.

[4] Alvin and Helen Gouldner, *Modern Sociology* (New York, 1963), p. 218. A more comprehensive statement is that "property is the name for a concept that refers to the rights and obligations and the privileges and restrictions that govern the behavior of man in any society toward the scarce objects of value in that society." This definition and a general discussion of property is presented in David Sills (ed.), *International Encyclopedia of the Social Sciences,* Vol. XII (New York, 1968), p. 590.

store. The new norm as to property is that the affected group, as long as it has emergency needs, has priority.

It is this community expectation or consensus that develops which explains the characteristic pattern of looting in natural disasters outlined earlier. Thus, it is understandable why such looting as occurs is undertaken typically by someone from outside the impacted area. Such persons not having undergone the experience are not part of the new although temporary community consensus regarding property. They can act as individuals toward strangers, pursuing highly personal goals and appropriating whatever resources opportunities provide them.

In civil disturbances, there is also a redefinition of property rights. The looting undertaken is likewise a temporary manifestation of a new group norm, in which the right to use of available resources becomes problematical. If property is thought of as the shared understanding of who can do what with the valued resources within a community, in civil disorders we see a breakdown in that understanding. What was previously taken for granted and widely shared becomes a matter of dispute among certain segments of the general population.

Viewed in this way, much of the pattern of looting in civil disturbances discussed earlier also makes sense. At the height of such situations, plundering becomes the normative, the socially accepted thing to do. Far from being deviant, it becomes the conforming behavior in the situation. As in natural disasters, the legal right does not change; but there is local group consensus on the massive use and appropriation of certain public and private goods, be these police cars or items on grocery store shelves. In many ways, a new property norm has emerged.

As most sociologists have argued, social behavior is always guided by norms, traditional or emergent.[5] Looting does not constitute actions in the absence of norms. Even situations of civil disorder are not that unstructured. The cases observed of looters continuing to pay attention to traffic lights should be seen as more than humorous anecdotes; they are simple indications of the continuous operations of traditional norms even in situations that seem highly confused. The parties involved in massive looting are simply acting on the basis of new, emergent norms in the ghetto group with regard to some categories of property. They are not behaving in a situation devoid of social structuring.

---

[5] See Ralph Turner, "Collective Behavior," in Robert E. Faris (ed.), *Handbook of Modern Sociology* (Chicago, 1964); Russell R. Dynes and E. L. Quarantelli, "Group Behavior Under Stress: A Required Convergence of Organizational and Collective Behavior Perspectives," *Sociology and Social Research,* LII (July, 1968), 416–29, and E. L. Quarantelli and Russell R. Dynes, "Looting in Civil Disorders: An Index of Social Change," *The American Behavioral Scientist,* II (March–April, 1968), 7–10.

The Expressive Crowd

THE CROWD OBJECTIVE. The expressive crowd does not have an object. Its objective is not to change the relationship of the crowd members to some feature of the external environment—an object—but to change the mood, the imagery, and the behavior of the members themselves. More than a mere release of already existing feelings is involved. A religiously oriented person may go to church with an attitude of reverence but without the feeling of religious ecstasy which he may later experience as the service progresses and "the spirit moves the congregation." A young man may go to a dance hoping that he will have a good time, but he counts on the music, the crowd, and perhaps a bit of alcohol to help him get in the mood so that he can say later, "I really let myself go!" The emergent definition in the expressive crowd is one which makes behavior sensible that would normally be regarded as eccentric or immoral. It gives significance to subjective sensations which would otherwise be meaningless or disturbing.

Attention is directed away from outsiders in the expressive crowd rather than toward an outside object, as in the acting crowd.

If the expressive crowd has any kind of imagined audience, it is a remote and intangible one—a god, the spirits of the ancestors, or the nation conceived of as a mystical entity. The measure of achievement of the crowd's objective is to be found in the experience of the crowd members, not in any observable effect on an external object. If the activity consists of secular, revelrous behavior the relevant question is, Did the participants let themselves go so that they lived temporarily in a different and exciting world, contrasting to the routine of everyday life? If the occasion is an outburst of patriotic feeling, the crowd members should come away with a heightened sense of loyalty and *esprit de corps.* If the expressive behavior is religious, then the members should be able to meet various tests of the validity of their religious experience, such as the conviction of "being saved," feelings of closeness to God and their fellow-worshippers, or engaging in overt behavior signifying possession by spirits. This sort of experience has been called sanctification. In some types of religious services the setting and the interaction among the members enable the individual to attain this subjective state. This attainment, which is the crowd objective, is symbolized by certain expressive acts.

The dancing which is often a feature of this type of religious behavior, reflects an important effect of the expressive crowd—the lowering of inhibitions. The religious dance has posed a problem for church leaders for centuries. The dancers, in their abandon, have sometimes gone beyond the limits of ordinary decency and morality. As early as the fourth or fifth century, St. Chrysostom and St. Augustine condemned "wild, abandoned dances, performed to the accompaniment of indecent songs," even while granting the propriety of dancing as a part of Christian worship.[4] Expressive

crowd behavior, whether religious or secular, characteristically consists of bypassing, to some extent, the normal procedures of established social organizations. The crowd creates a permissive setting in which the individual can express his feelings more freely and with less regard for conventional formality than is permitted in an institutionalized setting. For example, religious revivals have both supplemented and competed with the routine activities of established denominations by seeming to offer the worshipper a more direct, less complicated approach to God. The individual, supported by the crowd definition, feels that he has validated his own salvation. The possibility exists, therefore, that the forms which this validation takes may violate the ordinary religious norms.

SOLIDARISTIC AND INDIVIDUALISTIC TENDENCIES. The expressive crowd behavior described above may be regarded as solidaristic. There is a careful staging of the crowd setting, and there is a definite division of labor between the worshippers, the minister, and the musicians. Anyone who has ever attended such a service is aware that a norm of participation quickly develops. A member of the congregation who does not show some external signs of getting the spirit soon feels out of place. The rhythmic nature of the expressive behavior, the feature which led Blumer to call the expressive crowd the dancing crowd, adds to the discomfort of the individual who fails to dance, sing, or at least clap his hands in unison with the crowd.

Individualistic expressive crowds arise when many individuals are exposed to some situation which gives rise to strong emotional reactions—happiness, relief, or grief. Although there is differential participation, there is no clear division of labor. But the unabashed expression of strong emotions by some crowd members facilitates similar expressions by others. The permissiveness of the crowd makes behavior sensible which might otherwise seem disturbingly excessive. For many people, unrestrained expres-

---

[4] E. Louis Backman, *Religious Dances* (London: George Allen and Unwin, Ltd., 1952), pp. 323–33.

sions of enthusiasm require the participation of others to protect them against being labeled unsophisticated. The person who would ordinarily be inhibited from dancing in the streets, shouting his joy, and embracing strangers may feel free to do so when he sees others disregarding the usual norms of restraint and dignity. A spirit of competition develops in the expressive crowd, although it is a friendly competition. The extravagant expressions by some members seem to encourage others to outdo them in their outbursts. The competitiveness of expressive behavior is well illustrated in the highly individualized "jam sessions" of jazz musicians in which each performer attempts to excel in virtuosity.

THE LIMITING EFFECT OF EMERGENT NORMS. In the expressive crowd, the principle that emergent norms serve to limit and encourage the development of crowd emotion and behavior may also be seen. Were expressive crowd behavior to be explained solely in terms of contagion theory, then there would be no limit to the expressions of fervor and the abandonment of conventional restraints. Yet observations indicate that the person whose abandonment of conventional mores goes too far serves to dampen the mood rather than to facilitate its further development. Thus normative theory suggests the hypothesis that many instances of crowd behavior are made possible as much by the conviction that behavior will not exceed certain limits as by the interstimulation of like-minded participants.

ACTING TENDENCIES IN THE EXPRESSIVE CROWD. Although we may speak of acting and expressive crowds as contrasting types, all crowds display both acting and expressive tendencies in differing degrees. Since man lives in a symbolic environment, his own actions and the objects in his external environment have meanings which extend beyond their properties as physical stimuli.

While the expressive crowd does not have the manipulation of the external environment as its objective, it may use phys-

ical objects as well as the behavior of its members to symbolize the feelings which it produces. Blumer observes:

> When an expressive crowd reaches the height of...collective ecstacy, the tendency is for this feeling to be projected upon objects which are sensed as having some intimate connection with it...These objects may vary; they may include persons (such as a religious prophet), the dance, a song, or physical objects which are felt to be linked with the ecstatic experience.[5]

It is important to keep in mind that such objects have a purely symbolic significance to the crowd; they are outward, visible signs of the mood and imagery which the members experience. It is not the physical idol that the religious devotee worships but the invisible god for whom the idol stands. People who engage in glossalalia, or "speaking with tongues," do not think that they have merely acquired another language; their babbling is interpreted as a sign that the Holy Spirit is speaking through them. Thus expressive crowd behavior is marked by a highly symbolic quality. To the observer who is an unbeliever, it may appear that it is the sacred objects, not the supernatural phenomena believed to lie behind them, which the crowd attempts to influence.

The most enduring types of expressive behavior rest on the illusion that the actions of the crowd will influence powerful but invisible forces. The history of millennial movements shows that faith in the responsiveness of these forces may persist in the face of repeated disappointments. The rites performed by participants in South Sea island "Cargo Cults" are justified as techniques to acquire cargo, the material wealth possessed primarily by Europeans. Although the magic of the ritual never produces the miracle of cargo, the rites are repeated and modified. The production of appropriate symbolic behavior by the crowd members becomes the objective of the crowd and the evidence of the effectiveness of the crowd

5 Blumer, "Collective Behavior," p. 184.

action. Part of the symbolic behavior in one such cult has been described as follows:

One man, the individual, was encouraged into a coma or symbolic death by the joint activities of the others. When he had "died" the others, society, brought him back to life: to a new kind of life in which he said things which could not be understood by Kanakas as they are. Turn by turn each participant, each individual, attempted his death and rebirth into a new environment.[6]

The production of such a dramatic and mystical experience, convincing the participants that it was possible to escape the hardships of the real world, was rewarding enough to make the expressive crowd behavior worthwhile as well as to sustain faith in the ultimate efficacy of the rites.

Shifts in Crowd Behavior

Some explanations of crowd behavior imply that the expressive crowd is an incomplete development of an acting crowd. This idea rests on the conception that the expressive crowd does not develop an objective until it identifies an object, at which point it is transformed into an acting crowd. Acceptance of the proposition that the expressive crowd develops an objective which does not include acting on an object contradicts the notion that it will become an acting crowd if only it endures long enough.

It is true that expressive crowds often develop into acting crowds. Two factors contributing to such development are the establishment of an emergent morality and a sense of power, which legitimize actions which the members could not envision earlier. Interference with the activities of an expressive crowd may cause it to change into an acting crowd and bring about a major transformation of mood. Representatives of the structure outside the crowd

force themselves into its sphere of attention if they fear it and treat it as an acting crowd. They may then become the objects of acting crowd behavior.

Such an increase in acting tendencies has often developed as a result of interference by the police with revelrous crowds of college students. During the 1960s Fort Lauderdale, Florida, became a well-known example of the type of community which crowds of students converged on during spring vacations. A participant in one of these pilgrimages described the attitudes that the students brought with them:

The college students arrive at Fort Lauderdale with the hope of having an immense amount of fun. Many of these students have become acquainted with Fort Lauderdale through television and motion pictures and think of it as almost a modern tropical paradise in which there are beautiful women running around in bikinis, lots of beer to drink, and where a "hell of a good time" can be had.[7]

The following incident, culminating in a battle between the students and more than a hundred riot police, illustrates how quickly a crowd can change from a mood of joyous revelry to one of active hostility. To the crowd of students, the activity around the palm tree was an enjoyable game and an outlet for their high spirits. To the police, it was an illegal and dangerous impediment to traffic on heavily traveled Highway A1A. Soon the merrymakers changed from a happy, expressive crowd to a hostile mob with the police as its object:

Around two o'clock in the afternoon one of the college students started climbing one of the coconut trees along the beach across from the Elbo Room. He tried to climb high enough to pull down a fresh coconut but could not reach one. He jumped down and another young person took his place. As he was trying to descend from the tree several people began "goosing"

---

[6] K. O. L. Burridge, *Mambu: A Melanesian Millennium* (New York:: Humanities Press, Inc., 1960), p. 220.

[7] Selected from student paper, Florida State University, by John Clinton Murphy. Published by permission.

him, poking him in the rear with palm fronds. A crowd gathered around to watch and began laughing at the event. Suddenly police arrived from different directions to put a stop to the incident. About fifty motorcycle police arrived and blocked AIA adjacent to the Elbo Room.

Word of the police action quickly spread among the students lying on the beach. Before long a crowd had gathered to watch the traffic jam created by the hasty action of the police. The kids started chanting, "Cops eat shit!" This chant lasted about two minutes. The crowd was laughing as they watched the inability of the police to handle the situation. The crowd next began shouting, "Cops *are* shit!" Then the police moved across AIA to disperse the crowd. At the sight of the police coming toward them the kids began running in all directions. The police then returned to their positions across the highway.

The crowd, filling the beach across from the Elbo Room, felt that the police had unjustly ruined their fun. To seek retaliation they began doing whatever they could think of to annoy the police. Students took blankets and began bouncing girls up and down on them. The police again came across the highway on to the beach to disperse the crowd. There was loud booing then, and a host of derogatory names called at the police. The chants of "Cops are shit!" began again but with even more people joining in. Suddenly all the police raced toward the beach and began swinging their billy clubs to break up the crowd. The kids retreated into the water and the police withdrew to their former position. Before long, however, the crowd emerged from the water and began throwing empty soft drink bottles, beer cans and sand at the police. The police managed to dodge most of the flying objects but the cars parked along the beach received much damage. Soon riot police with helmets and armed with clubs and guns arrived.[8]

A change in the symbolic value of an object toward which a crowd acts may lead to a shift in both the mood and the behavior of the collectivity. A dramatic shift of this sort is described in "Sendoff for Devil's Island."

[8] Ibid.

Sendoff for Devil's Island

W. A. S. Douglas

For 28 years now—ever since the end of the first World War—France has been talking about cleaning up its private hellhole to the south of us, the convict settlement of French Guiana. Matter of fact, the movement began after it was learned that Maj. Alfred Dreyfus was not a traitor to his country—as were those who had sent him there. All that was done at that time was to clean up the place a little—a very little.

We once watched the loading of the prison ship which, before the German occupation of France, used to make a twice-a-year journey to the penal colony. The march of the doomed over the cobble-

From W. A. S. Douglas, "The Sun Beam," Chicago Sun, May 3, 1946. Reprinted by permission of Field Enterprises, Inc.

stones of Marseilles was the most disgusting sight we have ever witnessed—and we have had our full share of disgusting sights. The prisoners tramped along between long lines of guards, old men, middle-aged men and boys; their crimes ranged from murder through treason to petty thievery; some were in the lineup through the machinations of political enemies.

A THROWBACK

Here was a throwback to France at her 18th-century worst. While weeping men and women walked outside the line of guards seeking a last glimpse of someone who, no matter how hated by others, was loved by them, other men and women —yes, and children, too—howled and cursed at the convicts. Outside the thin line of family mourners, outside the packed mass of men without hope, the people were on cruel holiday.

In the front row of the sentenced were two notorious murderers who had managed to cheat the guillotine—if it was cheating to trade an easy if gory death for a lifetime in the nearest place on earth to the popular conception of purgatory. The pair was singled out for special attention—but they gave back as good as they got, at any rate in filthy vituperation, though they were hampered by a lack of rotten vegetables. The audience had plenty, however.

As well as we can remember there were between 200 and 300 convicts in that shipment. The general attitude on their part was one of bravado. The really tough ones cursed, spat, howled and laughed at their tormenters; and those who were not so tough but pretended to be followed suit. In the lost column that tramped past us we saw only two in tears—a very old man and a boy who appeared to be no more than sixteen.

THE CROWD RELENTS

But at the quayside an extraordinary change came over the watching, hitherto howling populace —one of those mass switches of the mind which make the people of France so ununderstandable to the rest of us. The first of the launches had been loaded with the unfortunates, what was left of the column was moving to another launch. The convicts sat jammed together, hugging their pitiful belongings, still cursing, their misery masked by the forced grins of the toughs as well as the would-be toughs.

A woman, seemingly as hard-boiled in appearance as any of the men in the launch, threw a carton of cigarettes at random into the boat. It was caught by a shackled convict who rose as well as he was able and bowed his thanks in the approved fashion of French upper-crust society. The tossing of the carton seemed a signal to others on the quayside. More cigarettes followed, flowers followed, boxes of food went through the air, some to break in transit, others to land more or less whole in the laps of the prisoners. Before the launch pulled out for the convict ship, about every man aboard, including the guards, had a flower or food or cigarettes or all three.

A public denunciation had changed in a twinkling to a public ovation. Curses had changed to almost affectionate farewells. You would have thought—if you had not viewed the preliminaries —that these were soldiers of France off to do battle for their motherland.

Now we are assured that the tropical prison colony is to be liquidated. Twenty eight hundred "libérés"—men who have completed their sentence but who were doomed to live out their miserable lives in the jungle—are to be brought home. Twenty three hundred others—the balance of the convict population—are to be either pardoned or sent to serve the balance of their terms in more healthful places. Marseilles will miss its twice a year parade.

Several characteristics of the crowd and the imagery which it develops may account for such a change in symbolization. First, it is evident that ambivalence within a crowd and within its individual members may persist even after it seems to have been resolved. Differential expression may conceal differences of attitude on the part of the silent participants, creating the illusion of unanimity. Ambivalence may also continue to exist in some individuals, although they act on one set of attitudes. Yet even a slight change in the situation may lead to overt expression by members who previously dissented silently. A new keynote may be struck, suppressed feelings may be aroused again, and a new and different crowd mood may develop.

One such change in the situation may be some development which renders the crowd image of the object incongruous. The gentlemanly gesture of the convict who bowed his thanks for a carton of cigarettes seems to have caused such a shift in objective. The crowd now perceived the thinly masked misery of the prisoners, and the mood changed to one of compassion. Perhaps the weeping boy and the old man came to dominate the crowd's conception rather than the tough, recalcitrant murderers.

Another change may be a redefinition of

the situation in which the crowd action occurs, here exemplified by a change in locale. It was at the quayside that the shift in crowd mood and the first friendly gesture towards the prisoners came. Now the convicts no longer marched through the streets under guard but sat jammed together, hugging their pitiful belongings. As the launches pulled away from the shores of France, the finality of the prisoners' departure and the horror of their destiny became figure rather than ground in the crowd's perceptual field. Sentiments of compassion, fair play, and "not kicking a man when he is down," seem to have asserted themselves and been reflected in a transformation of the crowd's mood and actions.

THE RELATIONSHIP OF ACTING AND EX-PRESSIVE TENDENCIES. The acting and the expressive crowd are not empirical types which appear separately in pure form, nor are they successive stages in a universal sequence of crowd development. They are best regarded as ideal types used to reflect tendencies which appear simultaneously

but may alternate in predominance during the existence of the crowd. Changes in a crowd are the rule, not the exception. Attempts to identify stages in crowd development should not be allowed to obscure the fact that, at any time, further development may take any of several directions.

Ralph W. Conant, after reviewing numerous studies of riots by blacks in American cities, has proposed a tentative formulation of the phases of a riot. In his scheme the notion is emphasized that until a final state of polarization has been reached, the temper of the crowd may either cool off or heat up. The ambivalence and instability of the participants are also stressed. Describing Phase three as a "Roman Holiday," Conant reflects the observation that acting and expressive tendencies develop simultaneously and interact with each other. At the same time that milling and keynoting terminate and are replaced by violent action, the carnival climate emerges. The expressive tendencies serve to sustain the acting tendencies, while the action itself has a highly symbolic character.

The Phases of a Riot

Ralph W. Conant

A riot is a dynamic process which goes through different stages of development. If the preconditions described above exist, if a value conflict intensifies, hostile beliefs flourish, an incident that exemplifies the hostile beliefs occurs, communications are inadequate and rumor inflames feelings of resentment to a fever pitch, the process will get started. How far it will go depends upon a further process of interaction between the local authorities and an aroused community.

There are four stages within the riot process. Not all local civil disturbances go through all four stages; in fact, the majority do not reach stage three. It is still not certain at what point in the process it is appropriate to use the word "riot" to describe the event. In fact more information is needed about the process and better reporting of the phase structure itself.

Phase I. The Precipitating Incident. All riots begin with a precipitating event, which is usually a gesture, act or event by the adversary that is seen by the aggrieved community as concrete evidence of the injustice or relative deprivation that is the substance of the hostility and rage felt by the aggrieved. The incident is inflammatory because it is typical of the adversary's behavior toward the aggrieved and responsible for the conditions suffered by the aggrieved. The incident is also taken as an excuse for striking back with "justified" violence in behavior akin to rage. The event may be distorted by rumor and made to seem more inflammatory than it actually is. In communities where the level of grievances is high, a seemingly minor incident may set off a riot; conversely, when the grievance level is low, a more dramatic event may be required to touch off the trouble.

A significant aspect of the precipitating event, besides its inflammatory nature, is the fact that it draws together a large number of people. Hundley explains that some come out of curiosity; others because they have heard rumors about the precipitating event; still others because they happen to be in the vicinity. Some of the converging crowd are instigators or agitators who are attempting to get a riot started; others come to exploit the situation and use the crowd as a cover for deviant activities. Local officials, church and civic leaders come because they see it as their duty to try to control the violent outburst.

Phase 2. Confrontation. Following the instigating incident, the local population swarms to the scene. A process of "keynoting" begins to take place. Potential riot promoters begin to articulate the rage accumulating in the crowd and they vie with each other in suggesting violent courses of action. Others, frequently recognized ghetto leaders, suggest that the crowd disband to let tempers cool and to allow time for a more considered course of action. Law enforcement officers appear and try to disrupt the "keynoting" process by ordering and forcing the crowd to disperse. More often than not, their behavior, which will be discussed below, serves to elevate one or another hostile "keynoter" to a position of dominance, thus flipping the riot process into the next phase.

The outcome of phase 2 is clearly of crucial importance. The temper of the crowd may dissipate spontaneously, or escalate explosively. The response of civil authorities at this point is also crucial. If representatives of local authority appear, listen to complaints and suggest some responsive method for dealing with them, the agitation tends to subside; a "let's wait and see" attitude takes

over. If they fail to show up and are represented only by the police, the level of agitation tends to rise.

How the news media handle phase 2 has a critical effect on the course of the riot. During the "sensationalizing" era of a few years ago in the United States, almost any street confrontation was likely to be reported as a "riot." In the current policy of "restraint," a street confrontation may not be reported at all. Neither policy is appropriate. A policy of "adequate communication" is needed. The grievances stemming from the precipitating incident and agitating the crowd should be identified. The response of local authorities should be described. The adversary relations and their possible resolutions, violent or nonviolent, should be laid out insofar as possible.

Phase 3. Roman Holiday. If hostile "keynoting" reaches a sufficient crescendo in urban ghetto riots, a quantum jump in the riot process occurs and the threshold of phase 3 is crossed. Usually the crowd leaves the scene of the street confrontation and reassembles elsewhere. Older persons drop out for the time being and young people take over the action. They display an angry intoxication indistinguishable from glee. They hurl rocks and bricks and bottles at white-owned stores and at cars containing whites or police, wildly cheering every "hit." They taunt law-enforcement personnel, risk capture, and generally act out routine scenarios featuring the sortie, the ambush and the escape—the classic triad of violent action that they have seen whites go through endlessly on TV. They set the stage for looting, but are usually too involved in "the chase" and are too excited for systematic plunder. That action comes later in phase 3, when first younger, then older, adults, caught up in the Roman Holiday, and angered by tales of police brutality toward the kids, join in the spirit of righting ancient wrongs.

Phase 3 has a game structure. It is like a sport somehow gone astray but still subject to correction. Partly this openness derives from the "King-for-a-Day" carnival climate. Partly it is based on the intense ambivalence of black people toward the white system and its symbolic representatives; its hated stores and their beloved contents, its despised police and their admired weaponry, its unregenerate bigots and its exemplary civil rights advocates, now increasingly under suspicion. Because of the ambivalence, action and motive are unstable. Middle-class or upwardly mobile Negroes become militants overnight. Youths on the rampage one day put on white hats and arm-bands to "cool the neighborhood" the next. It is because of the ambivalence felt by Negroes, not only toward whites but toward violence itself, that so few phase 3 disturbances pass over into phase 4.

Phase 4. Siege. If a city's value conflict continues to be expressed by admonishment from local authorities and violent suppression of the Roman Holiday behavior in the ghetto, the riot process will be kicked over into phase 4. The adversary relations between ghetto dwellers and local and City Hall whites reach such a degree of polarization that no direct communications of any kind can be established. Communications, such as they are, consist of symbolic, warlike acts. State and federal military assistance is summoned for even more violent repression. A curfew is declared. The ghetto is subjected to a state of siege. Citizens can no longer move freely into and out of their neighborhoods. Forces within the ghetto, now increasingly composed of adults, throw fire bombs at white-owned establishments, and disrupt fire fighting. Snipers attack invading paramilitary forces. The siege runs its course, like a Greek tragedy, until both sides tire of this fruitless and devastating way of solving a conflict.

7

THE DIFFUSE CROWD

The term *crowd* usually brings to mind a group of people in close physical contact, within earshot of one another. Since much crowd behavior takes place within a limited area, we will refer to this type of collectivity as the *compact* crowd. Most of the illustrations, which we have used in describing the generic characteristics of collective behavior, have been drawn from compact crowds. But already in our discussions of the crowd we have dealt with instances in which not all persons are in immediate contact with all others. For example, rumor can travel among persons who are not all in direct or simultaneous contact with each other.

Observers have long noted that the characteristics found in the compact crowd —uncertainty, urgency, communication of mood and imagery, constraint, individual suggestibility, and permissiveness—may be manifest in the behavior of dispersed individuals. Students of collective behavior have never limited their attention to the compact crowd; the field has included the public and various types of social movements as well.

The public and the social movement differ from the compact crowd; they constitute diffuse collectivities. In addition, the public is divided about the issue which is its common object and is engaged in discussion about it. The social movement displays continuity and stability of structure and norms not found in the ephemeral compact crowd.

Dispersed individuals may show, over a relatively short period of time, the same sort of restriction of attention found in the compact crowd, without developing the debate characteristic of the public or the stability of the social movement. They may act as a collectivity which sanctions only one type of sentiment and the exploration of only a few interpertations and courses of action. We shall refer to such a collective as a *diffuse* crowd.

From widely dispersed sources within a diffuse crowd, the individual encounters expressions of the same sentiments, witnesses the same behavioral models, and quickly acquires the sense that he is part of a collectivity, sharing uniform sentiments and encompassing a large number of people. With this sense, he is able to act, in many respects, like the member of a compact crowd, to speak with minimum reflection and without qualification, to express feelings or engage in behavior that would place him in a bad light under more typical circumstances, and to disregard many of the more routine demands of everyday living.

Even more than in the case of the compact crowd, it is clear that the central problem—how collective behavior takes place in a diffuse collectivity—is one of communication. Much of the research which has been done on the spread of common mood, imagery, and behavior among dispersed individuals has been done in the name of mass communications research. This relatively new but fast-growing field of study has attracted specialists from political science, psychology, speech, and journalism, as well as from sociology.

Mass Society and the Diffuse Crowd

COMMUNICATION AND MASS SOCIETY. The very name of the field, mass communications, suggests that the phenomena studied are strongly related to, if not dependent on, the existence of mass society and the mass media. Certainly the latter —books, newspapers, magazines, radio, and television—along with the development of rapid means of transportation has facilitated the development of diffuse collectivities as well as making possible the mass society. As Louis Wirth pointed out, the great social aggregations of ancient times, such as the Roman Empire, were not truly societies but were little more than administrative areas containing many small societies tied together by the military and economic dominance of a very remote center of power.[1] The people dwelling in the various parts of such an area knew little and needed to know little about the people in other parts. While the modern mass society involves many more individuals, physically just as remote from one another, these people know vastly more about each other than did their ancient forebears, and they attach importance to the attitudes and behavior of countless individuals whom they do not know personally. They do not know each other, but they are aware of each other's existence and of their interdependence.

THE MASS: AN IDEAL TYPE. Yet the people who make up the mass in a mass society do not constitute a group despite their awareness of being part of a vast collectivity. Herbert Blumer suggested four distinguishable features of the mass.[2] It is

heterogeneous, its members coming from many diverse groups with their own distinctive cultures. It is composed of anonymous individuals, since any one member knows only a miniscule proportion of the total in any personal way. Because the members are physically separated, there is little interaction or exchange of experience between them. Finally, the mass has no definite leadership and only a loose organization.

While this characterization is useful in highlighting the essential features of the relationship among the many people who make up the mass society, the mass itself is best viewed as an ideal type. In its pure form, it would consist of a number of separate individuals, each responding independently to the same stimulus in the same way. A society whose members act in such a fashion, with interaction between them being limited to the most inconsequential aspects of living, was imagined by George Orwell in his famous novel, *1984*.[3] Some critics of mass communications research have charged that much of this research, done in real societies, has implied an image of the mass media's audience which corresponds too closely to the ideal construct of the mass:

> Their image, first of all, was of an atomistic mass of millions of readers, listeners and movie-goers prepared to receive the Message; and secondly, they pictured every Message as a direct and powerful stimulus to action which would elicit immediate response.[4]

The collective behavior that takes place among the dispersed members of a mass society does not consist of this sort of highly individualized, atomistic response, although on occasions it may approximate it. There is uniformity of response to a common object of attention. It will be shown that,

[1] Louis Wirth, "Consensus and Mass Communication," *American Sociological Review*, 13 (February, 1948), 1.
[2] Herbert Blumer, "Collective Behavior," in A. M. Lee, ed., *Principles of Sociology* (New York: Barnes and Noble, Inc., 1951), pp. 185–86.

[3] New York: Harcourt Brace Jovanovich, Inc., 1949.
[4] Elihu Katz and Paul F. Lazarsfeld, *Personal Influence* (New York: The Free Press, 1955), p. 16.

in addition, this uniformity of response occurs among individuals who are *acting in awareness of membership in a collectivity*. Uniformities based merely on learned cultural prescriptions do not constitute collective behavior. The role played in the individual's behavior by the sense that he is a member of a collectivity is the crucial determinant. If a person feels that he is a member of a nationwide audience, for example, and if he has some image of how the rest of this audience is acting and lets this influence his attitudes and behavior, we may justifiably speak of collective behavior, even though the individuals are not in direct contact and do not constitute a group.

THEORETICAL PROBLEMS. The concept of the diffuse crowd and the recognition that there are other types of diffuse collectivities raise theoretical questions not posed by the compact crowd nor by the ideal type of the mass. How does the type of communication which gives collective behavior its distinctive character take place among dispersed individuals? How can there be such a rapid spread of intense feeling, as is suggested by contagion theory, among people who are not exposed to the noise and physical movement of the compact crowd? Convergence theory suggests the hypothesis that if some mechanism exists for the rapid dissemination of a compelling stimulus, the intensity of the latent predispositions shared by a large number of scattered individuals could account for the uniformity and the novelty of their behavior. An emergent norm approach raises the question of how the collective decision-making process, through which new norms arise, can take place among individuals who do not have direct interaction with one another. How can a sense of social pressure develop in a collectivity which is both short-lived and dispersed?

The answers to such questions will be relevant not only to the diffuse crowd but also to other forms of diffuse collectivities. Problems of communication are common to all these forms, including the public and the social movement. Attention must be given to the relationship between the diffuse crowd and the compact crowd, for the two are not only similar but are also dynamically interrelated. Finally, consideration must be given to the relationship between the diffuse crowd and more enduring, organized groups.

Communication in the Diffuse Collectivity

Everyday impressions as well as systematic research on mass communications suggest a picture much more complex than that suggested by some of this research. Typically, people who respond to the messages of the mass media have some sense of being part of a larger audience rather than of acting alone. Some of the content of the mass media is devoted to enhancing this sense. In addition, a number of studies of the behavior of people who make up the mass audience show that this behavior is influenced by interaction with other people. As Eliot Friedson has observed, "Much of audience behavior takes place in a complex network of local social activity."[5] It is evident, also, that not all the individuals exposed to a message respond in the same way. No one takes literally the familiar declaration, "Everybody's doing it!" for it is only too clear that not even the most popular fad is adopted by everyone in a society.

Even before the development of the mass media, diffuse crowd behavior spread rapidly through large populations. With amusing hyperbole, Charles Mackay said of the Council of Clermont, which gave rise to the Crusades in the year 1095:

The news of this council spread to the remotest part of Europe in an incredibly short space of time. Long before the fleetest horse-

[5] Eliot Friedson, "Communications Research and the Concept of the Mass," *American Sociological Review*, 18 (June, 1953), 315.

man could have brought the intelligence, it was known by the people in distant provinces; a fact which was considered as nothing less than supernatural.[6]

In a chapter which has a distinctly modern tone but was written in 1841, long before the invention of radio and the rise of the disc jockey, Mackay described fads in slang which swept through London, such as "There he goes with his eye out!" and the jibe, "Does your mother know you're out?" Yet the significance of the rapidity with which a message can be disseminated to a large audience by electronic means cannot be minimized because of such early examples of communication in diffuse collectivities. Paul B. Sheatsley and Jacob J. Feldman concluded, on the basis of interviews with a national sample, that 99.8 percent of adult Americans had heard of President John F. Kennedy's death within five and one-half hours of the time he was shot.[7]

Sheatsley and Feldman present an equally significant finding with a different import, however. Only half of the subjects in their sample heard the news from radio or television. As many heard it through face-to-face communication or through telephone calls as heard it through the mass media. Regardless of how various individuals received it, the news did not impinge on an atomized mass of isolated individuals; only 32 percent of the subjects were alone when they first heard of the assassination.

The members of the national audience who are potential recruits to the diffuse crowd are at the same time members of local groups or, sometimes, of compact crowds, which constitute local audiences. Friedson, who proposed this distinction, suggests the relationship between the two

and the limited utility of the concept of the mass:

Members of one local audience are anonymous, heterogeneous, spatially separate and unorganized in relation to those of another local audience. . . . It is their experience as members of local audiences that determines how they act, not the fact that there happen to be members of other local audiences whom they do not know, who are not necessarily similar to them, do not interact with them and do not have well-organized relations with them.[8]

Although Friedson's observations overstate the influence of those people with whom individuals are in direct interaction, his comments do lend support to the proposition that two types of communication operate within the diffuse collectivity. This idea is also implicit in the "two-step flow of communication hypothesis" advanced by Lazarsfeld, Berelson and Gaudet.[9]

We have pointed out that if we speak of collective behavior among dispersed individuals, the sense that the individual is acting as part of a larger collectivity is a crucial determinant of his behavior. Within the collectivity, this sense may be created by communication from individual to individual and from small group to small group. This mechanism we will refer to as the *interaction net*. The second means through which the sense of membership in a collectivity is created, *mass communication*, refers to the virtually simultaneous exposure of a large number of people to identical communication emanating from a limited number of sources.

THE INTERACTION NET. In many cases the information which serves as the stimulus to diffuse crowd behavior is received by individuals who are not alone but are already gathered together in groups. Research on movie and television audiences shows that many people attend movies with

6 Charles Mackay, *Extraordinary Delusions and the Madness of Crowds* (Boston: L. C. Page, 1932), p. 365.
7 Paul B. Sheatsley and Jacob J. Feldman, "The Assassination of President Kennedy," *Public Opinion Quarterly,* 28 (Summer, 1964), 189–215.

8 Friedson, "Communications Research," p. 317.
9 Paul Lazarsfeld, Bernard Berelson, and Hazel Gaudet, *The People's Choice* (New York: Columbia University Press, 1948).

companions and watch television in family groups. In such cases the interpersonal influence, which flows in the interaction net, can begin to operate as soon as the message is received.

In those instances when the individual receives the message in isolation, it might be expected that his preexisting frame of reference, his predispositions, will be the first factor through which the impact of the mass media will be filtered. The influence of discussion with other persons will follow later.

Convergence theory directs attention to such individual predispositions as a variable intervening between the stimulus and the overt behavior. Much excellent research on the effects of communication, particularly mass communication, has contributed to the development of propositions which explain how unrelated individuals may respond in a similar fashion to a stimulus because of similarities in their frames of reference. To stop with these variables as the explanation for diffuse crowd behavior implies an atomistic conception of the audience, however, as if it were literally a mass. Kurt and Gladys Lang have observed:

The majority of social science propositions about the impact of mass communication have been generated by research designed to meet the operational needs of communicators and propagandists. In the latter's image of the communication process, the individual occupies a terminal point on which a whole series of inflluences converges.[10]

The concept of the interaction net suggests that the individual does not develop his interpretation of the message alone; he is not a "terminal point" but a link in a network.

A case in which the message was extremely vague and yet of great significance to the members of a number of local audi-

ences illustrates how, through discussion, members of these audiences may collectively construct the very content of the message itself. Frantz Fanon, the late Algerian revolutionist, described how news transmitted by the underground radio network, Voice of Fighting Algeria, was received and interpreted by listeners in scattered villages in spite of the limited number of radios and the jamming by French authorities. When the existence of the "Voice" was announced in printed tracts, giving the broadcast schedules, every remote village tried to acquire at least one radio. For the first time, the scattered members of the diffuse collectivity, the revolutionary movement, could learn quickly about the struggle's progress. The communication process was not a simple one, and the message was not clear, as Fanon shows:

Very often only the operator, his ear glued to the receiver, had the unhoped-for opportunity of hearing the *Voice*. The other Algerians present in the room would receive the echo of this voice through the privileged interpreter who, at the end of the broadcast, was literally beseiged. Specific questions would then be asked of this incarnated voice. Those present wanted to know about a particular battle mentioned by the French press in the last twenty-four hours, and the interpreter, embarrassed, feeling guilty, would sometimes have to admit that the *Voice* had not mentioned it.

But by common consent, after an exchange of views, it would be decided that the *Voice* had in fact spoken of these events, but that the interpreter had not caught the transmitted information. A real task of reconstruction would then begin. Everyone would participate, and the battles of yesterday and the day before would be re-fought in accordance with the deep aspirations and the unshakable faith of the group. The listener would compensate for the fragmentary nature of the news by an autonomous creation of information.

. . .

Because of a silence on this or that fact which, if prolonged, might prove upsetting and dangerous for the people's unity, the whole nation would snatch fragments of sentences in the course of a broadcast and attach to them

10 Kurt and Gladys Lang, *Collective Dynamics* (New York: Thomas Y. Crowell Company, 1961), p. 425.

a decisive meaning. Imperfectly heard, obscured by an incessant jamming, forced to change wave lengths two or three times in the course of a broadcast, the *Voice of Fighting Algeria* could hardly ever be heard from beginning to end. It was a choppy, broken voice. From one village to the next, from one shack to the next, the *Voice of Algeria* would recount new things, tell of more and more glorious battles, picture vividly the collapse of the occupying power.[11]

In this account there is far more than the mere dissemination of mood and imagery from opinion leaders to a suggestible mass or the distortion of a clear message through serial transmission. Interaction takes place within a communication network; a definition of reality is constructed and validated in the give and take of discussion. Certain of the characteristics of the crowd, compact or diffuse, are highlighted. The mood and imagery which have been created take on a normative character; individual suggestibility is along lines consistent with this mood and imagery; uncertainty and a sense of urgency combine to make the members of the collectivity create a definition of the situation which goes beyond the fragmented version received through the mass media.

As Fanon's account shows, communication through the interaction net is not limited by the boundaries of compact, local audiences. The news traveled from village to village. In more technologically advanced societies the telephone, the automobile, and the airliner extend the network of interpersonal communication over vast distances. Studies of disasters in the United States have shown that the long-distance telephone traffic to and from a disaster-stricken community increases manyfold during the emergency.[12] The accounts received

in distant communities via the mass media are supplemented by versions received from someone who was there.

The modern, sprawling, densely populated metropolis has become a symbol of the impersonality of mass society. The intimate neighborhood, with housewives gossiping over back fences, is assumed to have been replaced by the aggregation of "nigh-dwellers" who are strangers to each other. How can the social contagion that contributes to the spread of fad and fashion operate in such populations unless it is through the mass media? In a study of the spread of what was in 1954 a new buying habit, William H. Whyte, Jr., has described "the web of word of mouth," which is a form of the interaction net.[13] He found that in Philadelphia there were marked differentials in the purchasing of air conditioners, not only between neighborhoods but within them. One factor which accounted for the clustering of purchasers within certain blocks was what Whyte called the pattern of social traffic. The pattern of movement within and between blocks by housewives and children facilitated social contagion, causing some people to be exposed more often than were others to the behavioral model of neighbors who had already purchased the new item.

Yet differential response to such models was apparent. Some families held out longer than others. Moreover, the concentration of air conditioners in middle-class neighborhoods suggested that social background and individual predispositions were variables affecting who adopted the new mode. Neither a contagion nor a convergence model is sufficient to account for the pattern of diffuse crowd behavior in this case, however. The emergence of a norm and of constraint which brought individuals

11 Frantz Fanon, *A Dying Colonialism,* tr. by Haakon Chevalier (New York: Grove Press, Inc., 1967), pp. 85–86. Reprinted by permission of Monthly Review Press, Copyright ©️ 1959 by Francois Maspero. English translation Copyright ©️ 1965 by Monthly Review Press.
12 Charles E. Fritz and J. H. Mathewson, *Con-*

vergence Behavior in Disasters, Publication 476 (Washington D.C.: National Academy of Sciences—National Research Council, 1957), pp. 15–22.
13 William H. Whyte, Jr., "The Web of Word of Mouth," *Fortune,* 50 (November, 1954), 140–43, 202–12.

who initially resisted imitating their friends into conformity is suggested by Whyte's observation:

It is the group that determines when a luxury becomes a necessity. This takes place when there comes together a sort of critical mass. In the early stages, when only seven, say, of the fifty-four housewives in a block have a certain item, the word of mouth is restricted. But then, as time goes on and the adjacent housewives follow suit, in a mounting ratio others are exposed to more and more talk about the benefits of this item. People must rationalize their purchases, and soon the nonpossession of the item becomes an almost unsocial act—an unspoken aspersion on the others' judgment or taste. At this point only the most resolute individualists can hold out, for just as the group punishes its members for buying prematurely, so it punishes them for not buying....[14]

Some findings in a study of the adoption of a new drug by physicians lend support to the proposition that the interaction net is more than just a network through which individuals are exposed to new behavioral models, which they may or may not imitate.[15] It is also a mechanism for creating social support for the adoption of the new pattern. In this study it was found that while the drug was adopted as early by physicians who practiced alone as by those who shared offices with other doctors, its use spread much more rapidly among the latter. This, plus the finding that adoption spread more rapidly among doctors who attended many out-of-town specialty meetings and conscientiously attended conferences in their own hospitals than among those who did not, suggests the information-giving function of the interaction net. The authors point, however, to the second function, that of social support:

...It is only in the early months after a drug's appearance that a doctor needs the sup-

port and judgment of his colleagues. It is chiefly when the drug is new that the doctor who is to adopt it needs his colleagues to confirm his judgment and to share the feeling of responsibility in case the decision to adopt the drug should be wrong. At this time, familiarity with the new drug is minimal and the doctor is in an uncertain situation. Several socio-psychological experiments have shown that it is precisely in situations which are objectively unclear, situations in which the individual's own sense and other objective resources cannot tell him what is right and what is wrong, that he needs and uses social validation of his judgments most fully.[16]

The above, it should be recognized, is a graphic description of the cognitive situation of an individual in the early stages of a crowd's development. Through the interaction net the diffuse collectivity creates a sense of permissiveness and of constraint, which aids the individual in resolving the uncertainty that deters him from acting solely on the basis of his own judgment.

MASS COMMUNICATION. Emphasis on the function of the interaction net in the diffuse collectivity does not mean that mass communication is any less important. In reviewing studies of interpersonal influence, as a process extending and modifying the influence of the mass media, Elihu Katz found consistent evidence to show that opinion leaders are typically more exposed to mass media than are those whom they influence.[17]

Like the interaction net, mass communication can serve to create, in the individual, a sense of membership in a collectivity and of social support for his actions. Some of the messages transmitted are designed as powerful stimuli, intended to call forth an

---

14 Ibid., p. 212.
15 James Coleman, Herbert Menzel, and Elihu Katz, "Social Processes in Physicians' Adoption of a New Drug," *The Journal of Chronic Diseases,* 9 (1959), 1–19.

16 Ibid., p. 14. Reprinted by permission of Pergamon Press, Inc.
17 Elihu Katz, "The Two-Step Flow of Communication: An Up-to-Date Report on the Hypothesis," in H. Proshansky and B. Seidenberg, eds., *Basic Studies in Social Psychology* (New York: Holt, Rinehart and Winston, Inc., 1965), pp. 196–209.

uncritical response from the individual because of his previous conditioning. An extreme example of the use of such stimuli was the experiment conducted by some advertising agencies with the flashing of subliminal stimuli on television and movie screens. More typically, the operators of the mass media include suggestions to the listener or reader that he is not the only one who is responding and that he will be out of step if he does not succumb to their suggestions. For example, while some commercials may appeal to the individual to give a separate response, unmindful of the imagined actions of others, the mere addition of such a line as, "Buy now—the supply is limited!" suggests that he is part of a competitive, individualistic crowd. The development of symbols which are meaningful only to the regular audience of a particular program, the use of studio audiences, and the printing of letters to the editor help to create the impression of shared participation. At the same time, past experience tells the listener that many share his experience, and in the communication which occurs in interaction nets, he receives confirmation of this hunch.

THE DIFFUSE COLLECTIVITY AS A FRAME OF REFERENCE. Mass communication, it has been seen, does not merely convey powerful stimuli to which people respond as members of an atomized mass. The media may even convey to individuals who listen in isolation a sense of being part of a larger social world. Similarly, as communication spreads from small group to small group in the interaction net, the sense of a universe of persons much larger than those immediately present is created. The diffuse collectivity, too large and dispersed for any member to interact directly with more than a few of his fellow members, lacking the structure and continuity of a group, nevertheless constitutes a source of social influence.

Tamotsu Shibutani suggests a theoretical framework for relating this kind of collective influence to other types of social influence in his concept of "reference groups as perspectives." In modern mass societies, he points out, "men sometimes use the standards of groups in which they are not recognized members, sometimes of groups in which they have never participated directly, and sometimes of groups that do not exist at all."[18] In such societies the perspective of the individual is no longer derived primarily from geographically limited culture areas. Today "culture areas are coterminous with communication channels."[19] The magazines and newspapers a person reads, the radio programs he hears, and the television programs he views can each give rise to a different "structure of expectations imputed to some audience for whom one organizes his conduct."[20] Thus the diffuse collectivity, even unorganized, anonymous, and hence not truly a group, constitutes an imagined audience from which the individual derives a perspective or frame of reference.

Principal Forms of Diffuse Crowds

Four principal forms of diffuse crowds may be identified. The first, the crisis crowd, arises in response to a specific event and tends to be relatively brief in duration. Fads and a variant, crazes, tend to go through a somewhat longer cycle of development and disappearance. The third type, the deviant epidemic, closely resembles the fad in its course but consists of behavior that is classified as deviant in the sense of being antisocial. The mass movement, resembling a social movement because of its sustained activity, may still be classified as a form of the diffuse crowd because of its predominantly individualistic character and in spite of the presence of some solidaristic tendencies.

THE CRISIS CROWD. A diffuse crowd may develop like other crowds, as a sudden

18 Tamotsu Shibutani, "Reference Groups as Perspectives," *The American Journal of Sociology*, 60 (May, 1955), p. 565.
19 Ibid., p. 566.
20 Ibid., p. 565.

response to an unanticipated crisis or through an abruptly accelerating process of intercommunication. The national response to the Japanese attack on Pearl Harbor, on December 7, 1941, is an instance of precipitous crowd behavior. Radio reports were conveying completely unfounded rumors about fleet engagements thousands of miles away from Pearl Harbor, and the populace demanded more such accounts. Public officials rushed to outdo one another in declaring that they stood unqualifiedly for immediate retaliation. Even many who had previously doubted that our interests would be served by defending the Philippines and other Asiatic locations gave their support to the new sentiment.

A joyous, too-good-to-believe event as well as a catastrophe may give rise to a crisis crowd. V-J Day, marking the capitulation of the Japanese and the end of World War II, saw crowds literally dancing in the streets in towns and cities all over the United States; the content of the mass media was devoted almost exclusively to the event; the fact that the long-awaited end to the war had finally come was the main topic of conversation in interaction nets.

Mass communication transmits not only a point of view but also a sense that the voice of thousands of persons is being expressed. The result is frequently a merging of mass behavior and crowd behavior to the extent that they are indistinguishable. Such merging is exemplified in a famous instance of mass panic. On October 30, 1938, Orson Welles produced a radio program based upon H. G. Wells' story, "The War of the Worlds." It was handled as a series of special news bulletins, including on-the-scenes reports, concerning a successful invasion by mechanical monsters from outer space. Landing at various places in northeastern United States, the monsters crushed all resistance. Thousands of people are estimated to have fled from the area in panic upon hearing the radio reports.

While most of these people were acting as individuals responding to a common stimulus, they were acting in the belief that there was already a great crowd of fleeing persons whom they were joining. The sense of being part of the crowd, effectively conveyed through the radio presentation, undoubtedly was part of the cause of the resulting mass panic.[21]

Incidents that outrage the mores, such as certain sex crimes, create diffuse crowds, which are fed in large part through mass communication. The power of some diffuse crowds is such that a judge will fear to give any sex offender probation while a crowd is active. Efforts to extend treatment rather than punishment programs for such offenses will be suspended or kept behind the scenes.

Helene Veltfort and George Lee have prepared an informative description of a diffuse crowd which followed a panic and catastrophe in a nightclub fire, which killed several hundred people. Two among the many interesting features of this account should be noted. First, the diffuse-crowd mood was structured from the standpoint of those who were in the nightclub disaster. In the search for an explanation and an object of antagonism, only those suggestions consistent with this orientation were acceptable. Second, the paper shows well the function of the mass media as tentative keynoters. The newspapers offered a succession of objects to the diffuse crowd. But reflecting and responding to the crowd pattern themselves, the writers continued to offer new keynotes until those most acceptable to the diffuse crowd were found. Thus the tentative process through which the crowd defined the object of its pre-existing mood consisted of keynote, response, and modified keynote between the mass media and the crowd.

---

[21] Hadley Cantril, Hazel Gaudet, and Herta Herzog, *Invasion from Mars* (Princeton: Princeton University Press, 1940).

The Cocoanut Grove Fire: A Study in Scapegoating

Helene Rank Veltfort and George E. Lee

The word "scapegoat" is part of our everyday language, yet the term is not easily defined. The following definition of the process whereby individuals become scapegoats will serve our present purposes:

Scapegoating is a phenomenon wherein some of the aggressive energies of a person or group are focused upon another individual, group, or object; the amount of aggression released is greater than that usually released by similar provocation; the fixing of blame and the release of aggression are either partially or wholly unwarranted.

Scapegoating as a means of fixing blame and relieving guilt is age old; its practice was ritualized in Biblical times. In those days, however, so long as the scapegoat was only a *goat* no harm came of this convenient practice. But in our society today scapegoating is harmful. Particularly is this true in wartime. Scapegoating of our allies, of government officials, of minority groups not only misdirects our aggression away from the common enemy; it also impedes the war effort by causing internal dissension and thus prevents us from attaining maximum production and cooperation within the nation and with our allies.

The Cocoanut Grove fire provides an object lesson in scapegoating, perhaps not typical of all cases of scapegoating, but undoubtedly revealing some of its basic mechanisms. The writers were residing in Boston when the disaster took place and were able to follow the day-to-day attempts of the newspapers and of the public to fix the responsibility for the catastrophe. The complexity of the case, as evidenced by the many scapegoats that emerged in the aftermath of the tragedy, held the

From Helene Rank Veltfort and George E. Lee, "The Cocoanut Grove Fire: A Study in Scapegoating," *The Journal of Abnormal and Social Psychology*, 38, Clinical Supplement (April, 1943), 138–54. Reprinted by permission of The American Psychological Association, Inc.

promise of a fertile ground for testing certain hypotheses concerning the dynamics of scapegoating. Further, although the background of Boston's political life cannot be completely overlooked in this analysis, the scapegoating in the Cocoanut Grove fire was relatively free from the entanglements of the complex social, political, and economic forces of the past and present which make it so difficult to analyze completely the scapegoating of the Jews, of the British, or of our government officials. Had the Cocoanut Grove tragedy occurred in any other metropolitan city of the United States, the scapegoating might well have taken a similar form.

THE FACTS OF THE FIRE

Before proceeding with the study of the scapegoating which took place in connection with the disaster, we shall give a summary of the facts pertaining to the tragedy up to and including the return of indictments by the Grand Jury on December 31, 1942.

On Saturday night, November 28, 1942, a violent fire swept the Cocoanut Grove, a popular Boston night club, causing the death of nearly 500 people. The fire started when Stanley Tomaszewski, a 16-year-old busboy, lit a match in order to replace a light bulb which a patron of the club had removed. An artificial palm tree, one of the many used for decorative purposes, immediately caught fire and from there the flames spread swiftly through the several rooms of the club. The cause of the rapid spread of the fire has not been exactly determined, but it is assumed to have spread so rapidly because the ceilings and walls of the club were covered with various highly inflammable materials. Firemen arrived within a few minutes and the flames were quickly brought under control. Yet the death toll that first evening was about 450 victims. Subsequent deaths at the hospitals brought the total to 488.

This tremendous loss of life for a fire which lasted only twenty minutes was attributed in great part to the insufficient number of exits and to the panic which the sight of the flames created. Although the Grove had at least five exits (a number later admitted to be legally sufficient), one of these was locked, the "panic lock" on another was not functioning, and a third was a revolving door. The latter was the main entrance, and it is when this door jammed because of the pressure of the panicky crowd that many people became trapped inside the night club and died not only of burns but also of suffocation.

The investigation also brought out the following facts:

Although in its application for a license the Grove management specified it had 460 seats, it was the general consensus of all witnesses that there were about 1,000 people in the club that night.

The physicians attending the victims, many of whom died subsequently, felt that in most cases these deaths were caused by the inhalation of noxious fumes. Testimony of witnesses who survived coupled with that of experts, suggested that these fumes were probably nitrous oxide. It is generally accepted that these fumes were given off by the materials used in the club decorations.

Fire Inspector Frank Linney had inspected the Grove a week earlier and recorded the condition of the club as "good."

The inflammability of the materials used in the club was never clearly agreed on. The decorators declared that they bought the material as fire- or flameproof. There is also a record of the delivery to the club of several cans of a well-known flame-proofing compound. Further, Fire Inspector Linney testified that he put a match to one of the palm trees when he inspected the club and found that the tree did not burn. On the other hand all the tests made on the materials after the fire showed that they burned like tinder.

The Cocoanut Grove had recently been enlarged and the wiring in the new section was done by a nonlicensed electrician. The owner of the club received several notices from the city threatening the cutting-off of electricity unless the club employed a licensed electrician.

After more than a month of investigation by Attorney General Bushnell, ten men were indicted by the Suffolk County Grand Jury. The list of the defendants and the charges against them follow:

Mooney, James H., Boston Building Commissioner. Failure to enforce law prohibiting use of place of public assembly until a certificate had been issued by a Building Department inspector.

Welansky, Barnett, principal owner of the Grove. Manslaughter and conspiracy to violate the building laws.

Welansky, James, brother of Barnett and in charge of the club the night of the fire. Manslaughter and conspiracy to violate the building laws.

Goldfine, Jacob, manager of the night club. Manslaughter.

Linney, Lieut. Frank J., Fire Department Inspector. Accessory after the fact of manslaughter and willful neglect of duty.

Buccigross, Capt. Joseph, Night Captain of Division 4. Wilfully and corruptly failed, neglected, and omitted to enforce the fire laws.

Bodenhorn, Reuben, designer of the night club; Rudnick, Samuel, contractor; Gilbert, David, foreman for Rudnick. Conspiracy to violate the building laws.

Eldracher, Theodore, Boston City Building Inspector. Failure to report violations of the building laws and to report insufficient exits at the Grove.

All the defendants pleaded "not guilty." They are expecting trial in February.

The above facts as well as the evidence presented subsequently in this study were taken from several Boston newspapers, especially the *Boston Traveler* (an evening paper) and the *Boston Globe* (morning edition). The *Boston American,* the *Boston Post* and the *Boston Herald* were also consulted. These papers have of course quite divergent political tendencies, but the similarity of their approach to the Grove fire by far outweighs their differences.

In addition to the analysis of the news stories and editorials, our study relies heavily on the *letters to the editor,* especially those published in the *Traveler,* which seemed to feature more than any other paper the public's reaction to the fire.

FIXING THE BLAME

The immediate reaction to the fire was one of horror. The early edition of the *Herald* the morning after the fire spent pages describing the tragedy and the mutilation of the victims, with photographs as supporting evidence. The horror thus aroused gave rise to an outcry for avenging the victims; those resposible must be found and punished. This intense desire for "fixing the blame" is the predominant feature of the Cocoanut Grove case and is the subject of the present study. Many of the accusations made by the papers and the public were no doubt well founded; some of the persons involved in the case seem to be actually guilty of violation of safety ordinances. Yet whether these violations were the cause of the fire and of the terrific death toll is far from established. From the beginning, however, the papers and the public assumed that such violations, if not actually deliberate, were certainly among the *causes* of the catastrophe. The people felt some person or persons must be held responsible; attaching responsibility to mere laws or to the *panic* provided neither sufficient outlet for their emotions nor opportunity for punishment. Whenever Boston's lax and insufficient laws were blamed, the matter was personalized by blaming the *City Council* or *public officials* for failure to pass or to enforce laws; or more rarely by the public's blaming the *people* for failure to demand better laws. This personalization is the rule in scapegoating.

Significantly, newspapers and public alike overlooked the fact that the panic created by the fire must have been largely responsible for the great loss of life. In spite of statements by officials immediately after the fire, the people were not ready to accept the fact that "the Boston tragedy was due in part to a psychological collapse." To the extent that they ignored this fact, the blame that the newspapers and public placed on various persons involved in the fire was disproportionate to their responsibility.

An important contributing factor in the campaign to fix the blame was the recall in editorials and news stories of two similar catastrophes some years earlier: the Iroquois fire, Chicago, 1903, and the Pickwick Club disaster, Boston, 1925. In both these cases indictments were returned against several persons but none was found legally guilty and thus all escaped punishment. Editiorials and letters alike demanded that such should not happen again.

In the course of this analysis of scapegoating, we shall examine several aspects of the case. The most prominent feature was the number of diverse persons who were chosen as scapegoats by the newspapers and public alike. We shall try to show why these particular scapegoats were chosen, how they were scapegoated and how they responded to the accusations leveled against them. Another important contribution this study can make to an understanding of scapegoating is the exposition of the motivations involved.

THE SCAPEGOATS

The Busboy. As soon as a city dumbfounded with horror and shock had regained itself sufficiently to speak, Boston echoed the universal question: "Who started it?" The Boston press answered a few hours later: on their front pages for November 30 the newspapers featured prominently the story of "The Busboy," and his full confession; of how in striking a match to replace a light bulb removed by some prankster he had accidentally set fire to one of the decorative palm trees. The ordinarily conservative *Globe* declared in two-and-a-half-inch headlines: "Busboy Blamed" and ran a three-column picture of the 16-year-old "offender" on its front page. The busboy was Stanley Tomaszewski, Dorchester high-school student, who was employed by the Grove during week-end rushes. Thus emerged the first "scapegoat" of the Cocoanut Grove case.

To exactly what extent Stanley was acceptable to the public as the *immediate* scapegoat is difficult to ascertain. To some people at least he may have been a satisfactory object of blame during the first period of emotional upheaval, when little else was known factually about the disaster besides his admission. This admission was the determining factor in the selection of Stanley as the first scapegoat.

Just as quickly and decisively as had the press pointed the accusing finger at the youth, just as quickly did the majority of the public force the press to withdraw it. By Wednesday, December 2, the *letter to the editor* sections were flooded with letters protesting vehemently against this "persecution." On December 3, every letter printed in the *Globe* contained some agitation for the boy's exoneration. Most of these letters seemed to be from persons who had never blamed Stanley; others may have been from persons who had been inclined to scapegoat him originally but had since changed their views. At any rate the "Busboy Movement" passed the stage of full exoneration and soon reached one approaching near adulation. Proposals were forthcoming that he be appointed to West Point, and he received a substantial number of "fan letters," in one of which was included a check for $25.

What accounted for this sudden rise to the defense of Stanley? Quite a number of facts were in his favor. First of all, the admiration of the public was aroused by his straightforward, voluntary admission of having started the fire, and by his teachers' and friends' testimony that he was a model young man. Secondly, discovery that his family was impoverished and that his mother was seriously ill aroused general public sympathy. Thirdly, his youthfulness seemed to convince that he could not be held as responsible as could an adult. Finally, and perhaps most significantly, further acquaintance with the facts of the case revealed to the public the possibility of more satisfying scapegoats.

It was acknowledged that Stanley *started* the fire; but the public set out to discover who was *responsible* for it and for the staggering loss of life.

The Prankster. Sharing the spotlight of press blame in the early returns following the fire, though to a lesser degree, was the prankster who had removed the light bulb which Stanley had sought to replace. The *Globe* on November 30, the same day that the "Busboy Blamed" headline appeared, ran an article on page one headlined "Prankishness Real Cause of Club Tragedy."

Immediate acceptance of the prankster as the scapegoat instead of Stanley no doubt occurred among some people. The majority who pointed to the former seemed to do so as a protest against the publicizing of the busboy as the "cause of the disaster." There was not, however, any wholesale or continued blaming of the prankster. His exact identity was never discovered, whether it be because he perished in the fire or because he never came forward to admit his part in the disaster. Also, in itself, his action in removing the bulb was not sufficient to make him legally culpable; indeed the connection between his act and the starting of

the fire was not sufficiently direct for even logical condemnation. As in the case of the busboy, psychologically more satisfying scapegoats soon emerged as the investigation proceeded.

The Public Officials. The public had not long to wait for detailed reports on the circumstances of the disaster and the emergence of eagerly awaited successors to the exonerated busboy and the soon-forgotten prankster. The *Globe* sounded the kenote blast typical of the entire press on Tuesday morning, December 1, with its terse headline: "O.K.'d Grove—Fire Department Approved Club Week Ago." Thus an entire scapegoat group, the public officials, took over the unwelcome spotlight, and, unlike their two predecessors, held it.

Although it was the Fire Department that bore the brunt of the initial attack, it was followed by others, department by department, official by official. Press indictments were strongly phrased and in some instances inflammatory against Lieutenant Frank Linney, Fire Inspector. The text of his latest inspection report on the Grove, made just eight days previous to the fire, was printed in each of the papers with special emphasis placed upon sections of the report which labeled the exits and extinguishers "sufficient" in number and the general condition of the club as "good." His testimony at the inquest that he had tested the inflammability of the decorative palm trees and found them "treated (with flame-proofing liquid) to my satisfaction" was also relentlessly and unfavorably publicized. The *Boston American* seized upon an ill-chosen statement by Linney to the effect that he had taken fire-proofing of certain of the club's furnishings "for granted" and ran the following headline on December 1: "Inspector Took Grove's Safety for Granted!" The Fire Commissioner, William A. Reilly, took his share of journalistic flailing, although the accusations leveled against him were not as specific as were those against Linney. The accusation seemed to be that, as commissioner, he was responsible for his subordinate's performance of duty.

Shifting momentarily to the Police Department, the press lashed Captain Joseph Buccigross, who, the papers pointed out, was inside the club at the time of the fire, allegedly engaged in routine inspection duties. Much was made of the fact that he had been dressed in plain-clothes, the general implication being that perhaps his presence was more social than professional in nature. Furthermore, the papers revealed that while there he had made no effort to enforce the laws against overcrowding or the employment of under-age workers. No mention was made of any effort on his part to quell the panic that broke out at the first sign of fire. Police Commissioner Frank J. Timilty was portrayed either directly or by implication as being lax, negligent, and incompetent in not checking to see that his subordinate rigidly enforced the laws. The inference to be drawn was that his entire department was similarly ill-managed and undisciplined.

Surging onward and upward, the wave of journalistic censure inundated even the ultimate governing agencies of the city, namely the City Council and Mayor Tobin. On December 1, the *Globe* revealed that a building code, similar to those effective in some other cities, had been in the hands of the City Council for the past four years. The paper scored this body for having taken no action upon it.

The press had also opened fire indirectly upon the mayor. At first, though his name was not actually mentioned in this connection, the constant references to the negligence and laxness of certain heads of departments, along with their subordinates, brought to mind the fact that the mayor had appointed these same heads of departments; such associative thought could hardly reflect credit upon the mayor's administration, his exercise of discretion, or even his personal integrity. Secondly, in regard to the building code, it appeared that the mayor had exercised neither pressure nor influence upon the City Council to speed the code's adoption. Finally, and most significantly, the press gave reams of publicity to a statement allegedly made, some time before the fire, by Barnett Welansky, owner of the Cocoanut Grove, to the effect that "The mayor and I fit"; the immediate response of many readers was undoubtedly to picture the mayor as something other than the upright, honest servant of the people.

Through its news reports and featured articles, the press had directed its wrath against the public officials individually. The latter had been selected one by one for headlined denunciations; but throughout each had been scored as an individual official separately and uniquely culpable. It was almost as if the press had lined them up and said to the public: "Here you are; take your choice." Under these circumstances it would appear likely that different readers would either select different individual scapegoats or that there would occur a focusing of condemnation upon one or two individuals. Significantly, however, such was not the case; the reaction of the public was essentially against the public officials *as a group or class*. Since the time of the fire, of the letters to the editor printed by the *Traveler,* over 90 per cent which blamed any of the public officials refer to their *collective* negligence, laxness, and incompetence.

Just why this "blanket scapegoating" occurred is not immediately evident; perhaps desire for a simplification of the issues involved may partially account for it. Certainly the picture would be clearer if blame were focused on a minimum of persons; yet for some reason a blanket condemnation of officials was more satisfying. Why? The acknowledged complexity of the building laws with the consequent confusion as to the function of various city officials made blaming them collectively much simpler than blaming them as individuals. So complex was the issue and so equally was responsibility distributed among officials accused that it was simpler to select all than logically and rationally to select one.

Furthermore, the public officials were not normally separate in the public eye; they were a symbol of interacting function, a symbol of the city government; and often a symbol is as simple a mental concept as is an individual. Collectively they were "the rascals," for among certain elements of the public there is a deep-rooted, perhaps unrecognized latent hostility toward all political authority, toward those "higher up." Expression of this latent hostility is usually suppressed because such expression is not ordinarily in keeping with social convention. But, whenever the situation changes so that self-expression formerly frowned upon becomes socially approved and even encouraged, the latent hostility will become active and find immediate aggressive outlets. These circumstances probably help to account for the collective rather than individual nature of the scapegoating. People *preferred* to attack the entire administrative set-up rather than certain specific individuals.

The Owners. While engaged in wholesale denunciation of the city officials, the press was at the same time heaping abuse upon the owners and operators of the ill-fated Grove—an abuse calculated not only to emphasize their responsibility but also to disparage their personal characters. Thus in its editorial columns on December 10, the *Traveler* referred openly to the "greed and cupidity of the owners"; similar attacks by this and other papers, though usually more subtle, were nevertheless as damaging.

Significantly, indictment was almost invariably against "the owners" and seldom by name against Barnett Welansky, the acknowledged owner of the establishment. A number of factors may have accounted for this. First, at the time of the fire and during the investigation that followed, Welansky was confined to the hospital with a serious illness. Thus the press may have forsaken any direct charges against his name since he was unable to answer them personally. Another consideration was the attempt of the press to imply that actual control of the Grove was in the hands of some secret and probably subversive syndicate for which Welansky was a mere "front." This last explanation is partially substantiated by the editorial, appearing on December 7 in the *Traveler,* asking: "Who really owns the Cocoanut Grove?"

The means employed by the press to fix the responsibility of the owners and at the same time to disparage them personally were quite ingenious. One of these techniques was to give the impression that the owners were cheap, money-hoarding profiteers and that their so-called avarice had contributed to the huge death toll. Subtly colored words and phrases were frequently resorted to. Upon testimony of an expert that the lethal fumes might have come from the imitation leather covering the chairs, the *Globe*, among other papers, announced: "Cheap Leather Cause of Fumes." In like manner much was made of the "flimsy, tinsellike" decorations.

Disproportionate space was alloted to the revelation that the reserve supply of liquor, stored in a fire-proof vault, remained intact: implication—the Grove protected its liquor but not its patrons.

The testimony of an amateur electrician that he had been employed for a nominal wage to do the wiring in the club, despite the fact that he had no license, was prominently featured. Similarly, emphasis upon the employment of the "under-age busboy" implied that the owners were not willing to pay a "man's wage."

The press also tried to create the impression that the owners operated the club in direct, wilful disregard of the law. The emphasis upon the unlicensed electrician and the under-age busboy are also applicable here. The fact that a revolving door was used at one of the exits and that the decorations were not adequately fireproofed received enormous attention despite the fact that the existence of laws covering the use of either was never proved.

Further, the public was given the impression that the owners were "shady" in their dealings, that their pasts were somewhat soiled. The *Boston American* ran a serial feature entitled "The Rise and Fall of the Cocoanut Grove," in which the club was described as having been historically a base for racketeers and bootleggers. All the papers mentioned Welansky's association, as his lawyer, with the late Charles "King" Solomon, notorious lord of the underworld. James Welansky, brother of Barnett and in charge of the club the night of the fire, was "casually" mentioned by the *American* as a witness in a murder case some years before.

A consideration which must not be overlooked in accounting for "the owners" phraseology is the latent hostility that certain elements of the public maintain against those highly successful financially. They regard the latter as a class of profiteers with their hands in the pockets of the poor. As in the case of hostility against public officials, this latent hostility is usually suppressed but may become socially approved under certain circumstances. For the public Welansky as an individual object of wrath was not as satisfying as was the class he symbolized; and in this case the class could be most nearly represented by the term "the owners."

There is no doubt that the public was solidly behind the press in its scapegoating of the owners. The *Traveler's* editorial on "greed and cupidity" was taken up as a battle-cry by its readers, several of whom congratulated the paper for its "crusading spirit." Likewise the character disparagement of the owners which the paper often only implied was accepted as fact by irate readers.

Tie-up between Public Officials and Owners. While simultaneously flailing public officials and owners, the press was constantly seeking and playing up the slightest thread that might link the two in political intrigue. Mention has already been made of the "Mayor and I fit" statement attributed to Welansky. The papers immediately implied the existence of a Tobin-Welansky coalition involving the exchange of legal indulgence for political patronage. The mayor vigorously denied having made the statement; but such damage had already been done. Subsequently there were discovered in the ruins of the club a collection of unpaid checks; the *Traveler* headlined: "Grove Took Good Care of 'Right People.'" The *American* asserted that on these checks were "names you won't have to ask how to spell." Perusal of the tax-assessment records indicated that in 1942 the Grove had paid less taxes than in 1941; the implication was that city officials had secretly "taken care of" the Grove. When the Grove's account books were found the papers promised "startling developments" upon revelation of their contents.

In all these instances nothing even nearly conclusive was ever proved by the papers. But the public nevertheless went all-out for reform. "Corruption," "vice," "rotten mess," "crooked politics" were standard terms to be found in the correspondence. The press had failed to establish the link between officials and owners; the public readily supplied the connection.

MOTIVATIONS

The frustrations and fears aroused by the tragedy underlay much of the scapegoating that followed. During the initial period of shock and confusion there was a need for the release of emotional tensions created by the *frustrating* situation. Nearly five hundred lives had been lost and nothing could be done to restore them, no constructive action was possible; some outlet was required for the feelings of aggression aroused; the busboy and the prankster were the first scapegoats available. However, as the facts in the case developed more clearly, the actual selection of the scapegoat became gradually a more rational process. The frustrations still existed but other motivations played an increasingly important part.

Another important factor in the early stages was *fear*. Fear arose because people imagined themselves as being trapped in the flaming night club and they also feared the occurrence of similar tragedies, this time involving themselves or their loved ones. This fear might be alleviated by attacking some immediately responsible person—at first either the busboy or the prankster. By the time the public officials and the owners became objects of blame, these fears had been greatly diminished through the passage of time and the increase in rational control.

"Tabloid Thinking," expressing the desire for simplification of the issue, was from the outset conducive to scapegoating. The very confusion engendered by conflicting reports and lack of knowledge created within the people a desire for clarification, for establishment of some cause-and-effect relationship. By choosing definite scapegoats some simplification was achieved.

How *latent hostilities* led to the choice of public officials and owners as scapegoats has already been discussed. This aggression was most strongly expressed when owners and officials were linked in joint accusations, for then all the hostilities the people had accumulated against "political bigwigs" and "money czars" could be focused on this relationship. There is also evidence in some letters to the editor that peoples' prohibitionist sentiments and their grievances against both low wages for public employes and high taxes were responsible in part for the scapegoating of owners and officials.

It also seems probable that through debasing of officials and owners certain elements of the public may have found opportunity to *enhance* their own self-conceived prestige; they could, by scapegoating, feel, at least momentarily, superior to these so-called "higher ups."

Finally, it cannot be overlooked that the people themselves felt in some way responsible for the tragedy. For most this feeling of *guilt* was unconscious, and was eased by pointing out the culpability of some more directly involved. However a small minority did realize their responsibility for having elected the city administration. In their letters they said that "the public is responsible," and in these letters there was no evidence of scapegoating.

The above discussion does not attempt to trace the intricate patterning of motivations for individual scapegoats and for individual scapegoaters. We have merely indicated some general motivational trends which seem to be basic to the scapegoating.

THE INDICTMENTS

The immediate and desired objective of the scapegoaters was to relieve their feelings of frustration, of fear, of hostility, of guilt, by legally fixing the responsibility on the guilty so that they might be punished. Ten indictments were returned on December 31, and according to Attorney General Bushnell more were to come. But even in the drawing-up of the indictments there are indications of scapegoating. On January 13, the *Globe* reported a violent exchange of words between Bushnell and defense lawyer John C. Johnston. The latter was asking for a quashing of the indictments on the allegation that they were improperly drawn, for they do not specify the acts of the accused. In fairness to the allegation advanced, the generalized nature of the official charges does smack of scapegoating tactics, an impression strengthened by what followed. After Johnston presented argument for his petition, Bushnell is reported to have shouted: "Hair-splitting technicalities have no place here. . . . The voiceless public is not interested in a lot of words. We're dealing with a case where the death toll amounted to nearly five hundred—half a hundred of them our men in uniform. . . ." To which Johnston replied: ". . . The defendants should be tried by law and not by public clamor. The defendants should be tried by law and not by lynch law, which is the apparent tendency from the argument I have just listened to." No, scapegoating has not yet ceased in the Cocoanut Grove case.

CONSEQUENCES

The Government. During the past year, the *Traveler* has conducted several vigorous campaigns against state and federal officials; at the time of the fire, Oil Coordinator Ickes and Price Administrator Henderson were the targets of its attacks. In this atmosphere of resentment against federal officials, antagonism against city officials involved in the Cocoanut Grove case was easily aroused. In turn, the expose of alleged corruptibility and ineffi-

ciency of the latter can hardly fail to undermine even more the already shaken confidence in government officials generally.

Anti-Semitism. Another possible consequence of the scapegoating in the Cocoanut Grove case is the fanning of the anti-Semitism which Father Coughlin's followers have spread in Boston. To people who have learned to make the words "jews" and "cupidity" or "greed" synonymous, the editorial of the *Traveler* of December 10, declaring that "Human greed and human negligence cost human lives," strengthens the implication: "The Jews were responsible for the loss of lives." There is evidence that this implication was caught by many, in reported conversations blaming the "Jew Welansky" and "those dirty Jews." Some admit that their prejudices against the Jews have increased because of the Grove fire. We are not claiming that anti-Semitism was deliberately raised as an issue, but are simply pointing out that the scapegoating of the Grove owners furnishes ammunition to the "merchants of hate."

PRESS COVERAGE

Figure 1 shows the number of column-inches of news-space which the *Boston Traveler*, an evening paper, devoted to the fire over a period of approximately a month. News stories, editorials, letters to the editor, and photographs were all considered in the day-by-day accountings. However, the number of column-inches devoted to the photographs, lists of victims, obituaries, and accounts of funerals is reduced by half in the graphical representation. If we consider that over a period of a week the average daily amount of space devoted to news is 1350 column-inches (exclusive of 14 pages of sports, financial, social, women's, and entertainment features), we see that the ratio of Grove news to other news was rather staggering, especially during the first few days following the tragedy. At the peak of interest, stories and features about the Grove case constituted almost 50 per cent of the total news. Also significant is the length of time that the case was continually publicized, even late in January hardly a day passed without some reference to it. Although some of these articles were brief, they assumed front-page importance from November 29 to December 19, and took the limelight again from December 29 to January 1, the period of indictment. Banner headlines about

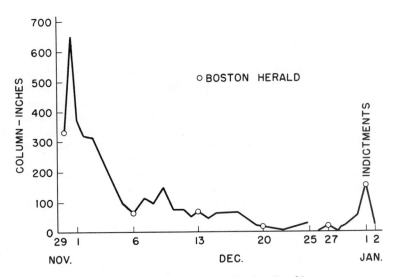

FIGURE 1 Amount of space devoted to the fire in the Boston Traveler, Nov. 29, 1942 to Jan. 2, 1943.[1]

the fire and the investigation that followed over-shadowed war news throughout the first week and part of the second.

The importance of the entire case was further indicated by the number of editorials and letters to the editor devoted to the subject. Altogether,

during this period thirteen editorials touched upon at least one aspect of the case, during the first week and part of the second week, this was the *lead editorial*. Most of these editorials were intent upon fixing the blame on one scapegoat or another.

Figure 2 shows the number of column-inches

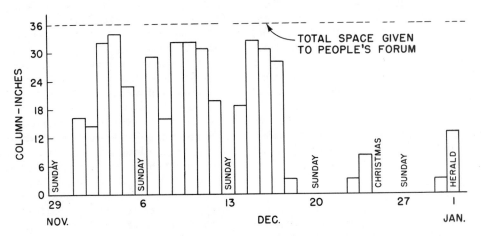

FIGURE 2 Proportion of all letters devoted to the fire in the Boston Traveler, Nov. 29, 1942 to Jan. 2, 1943.[2]

---

[1] The *Traveler* does not publish on Sundays or holidays, hence figures for Nov. 29, Dec. 6, 13, 20, 27, and Jan. 1 were taken from the *Boston Herald*, the *Traveler's* morning edition.

[2] See footnote 1.

devoted to the letters alone. It is especially significant that the letters about the Grove took up almost all the space of the *People's Forum* (two full columns devoted to letters to the Editor), at least for the first three weeks. The great majority of these letters demanded the punishment of the guilty and named one or more scapegoats. These letters were particularly useful in ascertaining the motivations for scapegoating.

SUMMARY

Frustrations and fears aroused by the Cocoanut Grove holocaust created a desperate desire on the part of the people of Boston to fix the blame and punish those responsible for the catastrophe.

There resulted violent accusations, if not unwarranted, at least out of proportion to the possible guilt of the accused. The scapegoating was most intense against the owners of the Grove and against the public officials responsible for the safety of Boston's citizens. Officials and owners were especially satisfying scapegoats since the tragedy permitted the releasing of much latent aggression. It is when such latent hostility is present that scapegoating is most dangerous. Because in Boston hostility against the Jews and hostility against our federal officials has been smoldering for months, the Cocoanut Grove fire may well have serious consequences beyond the loss of five hundred lives.

FADS AND CRAZES. The crisis crowd arises in response to a provocative situation, event, or series of events which becomes the focus of attention for dispersed individuals. The emotions—indignation, fear, grief, joy, and the like—which the precipitating event arouses are clearly connected to the actions of this type of diffuse crowd. The crowd searches for a collective definition of the event and validates the mood aroused by it.

Other types of collective obsessions lack this clear relationship to an emotionally charged situation and are episodic even though unpredictable. These include fads and crazes, particularly financial crazes with boom and bust phases. Deviant epidemics and mass movements have several features in common with fads and crazes. The feature which signals the existence of a diffuse crowd is the remarkable increase in the prevalence and intensity with which people, scattered over a fairly wide area, engage in a type of behavior or assert a belief. This widespread behavior may involve a new idea, such as belief in flying saucers, or an increase of interest in an old one, such as the surge of interest in astrology in the United States during the late 1960s. A second feature is that the behavior, or the excessive indulgence in it, appears ridiculous, dangerous, or immoral

to persons who are not caught up in the collective obsession. When the raucous noise of snowmobiles began to disrupt the quiet of snow-covered northern woodlands, it was easy for nonfaddists to point out how dangerous the machines were to the riders and to plant life, how annoying they were to people whose rest they interrupted, and how they constituted another source of air pollution. Third, after the behavior reaches a peak, it drops off abruptly and is followed by a counterobsession, even though a few devotees may persist in it in spite of now appearing old-fashioned. Some people continued to play gin rummy for recreation even after the game ceased to be a fad. It is more costly, of course, for the speculator not to respond to the counterobsession—the panic—which follows a financial boom.

Whereas the crisis crowd is commonly a response to a critical, well-publicized event, the fad is thought of as arising rather unpredictably. The sudden popularity of miniature golf during the 1930s, with many courses being built only for the majority to go bankrupt shortly, as interest declined, was not in any direct sense a collective response to a group crisis. Careful quantitative studies of fads over a long period might reveal that they are especially numerous in periods of group crisis, suggesting that recreational fads divert attention from the problems at hand. However, the fads are not created as a recognized effort to cope with any particular crisis.

Popular depictions of fads and crazes tend to overdramatize them and to equate them more closely with compact crowd behavior than is justified. In the true compact crowd, the mood and attention are sustained without interruption, and the excesses of crowd behavior are often attributable to the fact that participants have no chance to relax and survey their own behavior. The fad or craze, however, is sustained with constant interruptions. In spite of the interruptions, the attention of the faddist is severely restricted—to the point that alternatives pass unnoticed. Consequently, money may be invested in highly improbable schemes or exaggerated fears may be maintained, when the evidence against both is clear to the nonfaddist. Or people may undergo privation by paying inflated prices and waiting in long lines in order to participate in the current fad, when other recreational opportunities lie neglected close at hand.

Phenomena of this sort cover a wide range, from recreational to serious activities. Fads in amusements, such as discotheques, light shows, and rock festivals, fads in adolescent language, in music, and the like may have little significance for the participant beyond identifying him with an in-group and giving him a type of prestige. Fad participants develop strong in-group feelings, with special terms for the outgroup, such as *squares*. More serious activities involving financial speculation sometimes show similar characteristics. In the famous Holland Tulip Mania during which the value of tulip bulbs exceeded their weight in gold, in the South Sea Island Bubble, the Florida Land Boom, and many other such episodes, the worth of some object became inflated because of its speculative value. Tulip bulbs were not used but bought and sold among speculators. Florida lands were sold and resold at ever higher prices without even being seen. As soon as the speculative market declined and the objects had to be valued in terms of use, the entire structure crumbled quickly.

Fears, belief in special formulas, and moods may also have this faddish character. The greatly enlarged image of the Black Panthers among many white Americans, the "red scares" of the 1920s and the McCarthy era, and confidence in simple formulas to achieve the good life, such as the power of positive thinking, or eating only organic foods are examples of this. The fad may also exist as a permission to act contrary to folkways and mores, as in college panty raids. Finally, the fad may exist simply as a direction given to an activity which it does not create. At various times, motion picture heroes or comic strip figures have been emulated by juvenile delinquents on a wide scale. There is no clear evidence that delinquency was increased by these activities, but the pattern of the activity was adopted and widely spread.

A fad does not consist of simple, unimaginative imitation. It has collective enthusiasm for a wide range of individual innovation around a common theme, in behavior that is performed in association with others. When skateboards were popular, it was not enough for young people to learn to use them; there was competition to demonstrate how daring and ingenuous one's performance could be. It may be postulated that one factor differentiating inventions which become the object of fads from those that do not is the possibility for variations around the central theme, which the former offer.

In the case of a recreational fad, the game may become boring or the jokes stale when it is difficult to find new variations on the theme. In more serious fads, as those found in art or science, the creative spurt may subside when the full range of possibilities have been exhausted. The resulting curve of activity and interest resembles that of a fad. There is a tendency to emphasize the spread of fads among adolescents and other persons who are somewhat detached from the stable aspects of society. On the basis of such emphasis, theories are spun which attribute fad susceptibility to value-conflict, social detachment, and personal insecurity. Undoubtedly, some kinds of social isolation foster susceptibility in some persons and heighten fad resistance in others. But by examining a fad in an area not usually included in such discussions, we may demonstrate that no abnormal degree of isolation or insecurity is necessary to faddish behavior. At the same time, we can see how a key invention opens up heretofore unrecognized possibilities, leading to a rush to apply it in as many ways as possible, followed by a decline in interest.

A focus of attention on newly uncovered possibilities is not a fad, however, unless it includes diversion of attention away from what the participants might otherwise regard as unpleasant features of their behavior. L. S. Penrose has shown how restriction of attention sometimes characterizes the rising period of such a preoccupation, while the declining period shows an increased awareness of limitations. As his example he cites a scientific fad.

Analysis of Crazes

L. S. Penrose

A new idea which suddenly becomes important in the life of a community and which nevertheless does not appreciably disturb the pre-existing order can be called a craze. Examples are easy to find. A new game or pastime becomes popular almost overnight. The cult of a toy, Yo-yo, Bifbat, the crossword puzzle or a comic strip character, arises in an apparently unpredictable manner and vanishes again. Fashions in food and novelties in male and, especially, in female attire often show the same type of capricious advent. There can also be periodicity dependent upon the seasons of the year. Some crazes are merely magnifications of activities which are part of the normal life of members of the community, that is, endemic. Quite frequently, after the disappearance of a craze, the activity remains as part of the stock of possible pastimes without commanding any special attention when it occurs. When they hear an old-fashioned popular tune, people only remember vaguely that at one time everybody was expected to react to it with considerable emotion. The characteristic features of the craze, though they may seem trivial at first glance, are of great importance in the study of crowd psychology because, in the craze, we are able to examine in its purest form the behavior of a crowd under the influence of an infectious idea.

Judged from the psychopathological point of view, a craze is a crowd disorder so mild that it can be compared with an outburst of enthusiasm, excitement or anger which occurs in the ordinary daily life of an individual whose mind ranks as entirely normal. An idea which can infect the community, moreover, is not necessarily harmful or unreasonable because it is infectious. The only justification for including such activities under the heading of crowd mental illness would be that, during a craze, an abnormal amount of energy is discharged in one direction, and that, as a result, matters more vital to the welfare of the group may be neglected.

The course of any craze is marked by certain phases, which sometimes can be very clearly distinguished and which follow closely the pattern shown in an epidemic physical disease. First there is a latent period, during which the idea, though present in the minds of a few, shows little sign of spreading. Next comes the phase during which

From L. S. Penrose, *On the Objective Study of Crowd Behavior* (London: H. K. Lewis and Co., Ltd., 1952), pp. 18–22. Reprinted in part by permission of H. K. Lewis and Co., Ltd., and the author.

time the idea spreads rapidly. The number of people who accept the new idea mounts with an increasing velocity which may develop an almost explosive character. As the market of susceptible minds becomes saturated, the velocity of the wave as shown by the number of articles bought in a given time, for instance—begins to slacken. This is the third phase. The fourth phase is marked by the development of mental resistance against the idea which resembles immunity to infection in the sphere of physical disease. During this period, the mental infection wanes; in those already infected, the enthusiasm becomes weaker and there are few new cases. In the fifth or final phase, if the idea still persists, it remains stagnant; either it is incorporated into the occasional habits of many or kept alive in the minds of a few enthusiasts. In favourable circumstances, it may remain latent to blossom again at some future time, when the immunity has disappeared.

If any person should doubt the reality of mental resistance to an idea which has recently been the virus of a craze he should enquire into the experience of commercial firms which manufacture or sell material involved in these mental epidemics. The immunity has two important characteristics. In the first place, once started, it develops rapidly— probably the degree of rapidity depends directlty upon the degree of explosiveness of the outbreak, though this needs to be fully investigated. Secondly, the immunity is highly specific. There is resistance to exactly that form of the idea which caused the craze, but another idea, in many respects similar, may produce another craze soon after the first.

In spite of the great prevalence of crazes in human communities, precise data for the numerical analysis of their development are difficult to obtain. The type of data which would be valuable from this point of view could be obtained from a study of the actual sales of craze pastimes during the critical periods. The demand rather than the supply would perhaps furnish the best index of the crowd's state of mind but there are complicating factors which make the investigator pause before embarking upon the arduous task of collecting the data. Commercial reticence is also a serious obstacle. The example chosen here for analysis is imperfect in many respects, as an instance of a

craze, but it has the advantage that the data were easy to obtain. It concerns the development of a fashion in medical therapy. Crazes of this kind are common among physicians and they are, to some extent, the inevitable result of natural enthusiasm over fresh discoveries in medical science. As will be seen, however, there can be more than one side to the picture.

The use of thallium in the treatment of skin diseases, as a preliminary measure to remove the hair, was first advocated in 1914 both in Germany and in Mexico. The pioneers who drew attention to the possible therapeutic use of the metal were careful to issue the warning that poisonous effects of a most dangerous character might arise if an overdose were given. A survey of medical literature between the years 1914 and 1925, charted in Figure 1, reveals the fact that the drug was, in fact, very little used during this period, which corresponded to the first phase or latent stage of mental epidemic under discussion. In the next two years, however, use of the drug became rapidly fashionable. Thousands of children were treated in centres widely distributed over the globe. During this second period of the infection of the medical profession with the new idea, a large body of literature sprang into existence in which the results of treatment were described and commented upon, for the most part very favourably. The saturation of all possible clinics for skin diseases with the new idea would inevitably have slowed down the craze and produced the third phase about 1927. This effect, however, was masked by the rapid growth of the realization of the dangers attached to the treatment. Several fatalities resulted from overdoses. Some medical authorities proclaimed that the treatment was far more hazardous than the diseases which it was intended to cure. The fourth phase, which coincided with increasing immunity to the idea of this treatment, was reflected in the medical literature by a preponderance of writings which described experiments on laboratory animals and emphasized the poisonous nature of thallium compounds. At the same time, the total number of writings on the subject declined. From 1928 until 1940, this decline in interest was fairly continuous and recent scientific publications on the use of thallium have, for the most part, been confined to

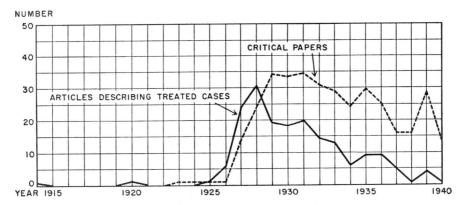

FIGURE 1 Literature on thallium therapy (from *Index Medicus*)
——————— Articles describing treated cases
- - - - - - - - Critical papers

experimental studies, to warning against proprietary preparations, which might poison unsuspecting lay people, and to descriptions of instances where thallium had been used for attempted murder or suicide. Notwithstanding, medical textbooks now accept that the treatment has value in selected cases under very carefully controlled conditions. The fifth phase has been reached and the craze is over.

Meteorologists have more knowledge of the origins of cyclones than of local storms. Similarly, it is more difficult to identify the predisposing causes of crazes than those of more disruptive mental epidemics. In the example which has just been analysed, there were elements which are commonly found in all types of crowd infection. The new idea gave a pleasurable feeling of superior power, and was probably welcomed by physicians as a visible proof of omnipotence which they might wish to possess. Furthermore, the factor of relative isolation from the general public, which the medical profession enjoys, possibly favours the development of crowd mental aberration among its numbers. Such epidemics as that described in the example might be even more frequent or significant among medical workers than is actually the case were it not for the lengthy and humiliating training in scientific caution which physicians undergo before qualification. A comparison of metal epidemiology between members of the medical profession with members of other groups, whose training is much less intensive from this point of view, such as osteopaths and chiropractors, might be instructive.

Indifference or opposition to a fad is not treated with toleration. In spite of the fact that some of these phenomena are distinctly competitive in nature (e.g., real estate booms), they are accompanied by both active proselyting and penalties for those who resist.

This proselyting attitude is more than a byproduct. It is actually essential for maintaining the fad and justifying the behavior of the faddist. In cases where the prestige of participating in the latest fad is important in motivating the faddist, prestige will only be accorded if enough people follow the fad. In speculation booms the amount of money each person makes will be determined by how many others join the speculation. In cases in which the mores or conventional inhibitions are challenged, as in contagious mass-religious confessions, membership in a large group similarly preoccupied is effective protection against self-criticism. The rewards, which the individual receives from participation in the fad require that other persons be constantly adopting the fad, and these rewards cease when adherence to the fad starts to decline.

Intolerance toward the nonfaddist serves to bring more people into the fad and to protect the member from seeing his behavior through the eyes of nonfaddists. By placing the outsider in the category of a person who is not important, the faddist is shielded from the need to respond to his judgments. An essential mechanism of the fad, then, as of the crowd in general, is the formation of a sharp in–group-out–group dichotomy, which insulates the participant against the impact of any reference groups except the faddists themselves.

ECONOMIC CRAZES. The economic craze, often called the boom, requires special attention, for it involves a risk which other fads do not. People may gamble their entire fortunes because of the belief, derived from the diffuse crowd definition, that they will get rich quickly if they will only seize the opportunity. The typical course which such crazes follow is well known, but over and over again the speculative mania convinces people that this time will be different. The Florida land boom of 1925–26 should have been a warning of the dangers of speculation, but it did not serve to frighten investors from repeating the same kind of behavior in the bull stock market which preceded the crash of 1929.

The tropical southern part of Florida, relatively isolated and thinly populated at the turn of the century, entered a period of steady growth as new rail lines and automobiles brought more people. The growth accelerated during the early 1920s —the city of Miami grew from a population of 30,000 to an estimated 75,000 between 1920 and 1925. In the latter year, in the midst of the national prosperity, which made the United States seem a land where every man could become rich, a number of financiers announced plans for grandiose real estate developments, and they offered lots for sale. One, D. P. Davis,

proposed to build a settlement on land dredged up from Tampa Bay. He sold $3 million worth of lots the first day—before dredging operations had even started! With such optimism about the future of these developments rampant, the belief that an investor couldn't lose on land in Florida gained wide acceptance. Rumors of tremendous profits, made in a single day by the purchase and resale of binders on lots, served as self-fulfilling prophecies, pushing prices up. The demand for lots, not to live on but to resell, became so great that realtors could sell land that was still under water simply on the basis of maps projecting future development, plus the buyer's belief that he could quickly sell his option to buy and do so at an easy profit. Thousands of people went to Florida to participate in the trading, but the lots were also being bought and sold in cities all over the nation by people who never expected to see the Sunshine State. During the summer and autumn of 1925, a mad race was on to get in the market before prices went even higher; eager buyers were easy to find.

But by January 1926, confidence in the Florida boom began to falter. Some shrewd investors reminded themselves that such an inflation would have to end sometime. The caution of a few, who took their profits and got out of the market, served as a self-fulfilling prophecy just as the initial optimism of the early investors had. Binders become harder to sell, and prices began to decline. Stories began to circulate of people who, unable to sell their binders, had been forced to default on their promises to actually buy the land, leaving the seller holding the bag.

In many booms a period of declining confidence, such as prevailed in the Florida land market during the spring and summer of 1926, ends with a crash as the belief becomes widespread that the market is not going to recover. There is a crisis of confidence, as even the most desperate investors can no longer reassure themselves that the boom is not yet ended. In Florida, nature intervened to precipitate the panic. In September 1926, a hurricane hit the Miami area, leaving over 400 people dead. Now the rush to unload land began in earnest; buyers defaulted on their binders, and developers and realtors went bankrupt. There was an exodus of forlorn speculators from the state, most of them with scarcely enough money to get home. Promoters who, a few months previously, had been regarded as public servants, showing small investors the route to Eldorado were now denounced as charlatans. Investors who had been envied by their neighbors as bold, shrewd adventurers were now pitied as gullible fools who had been fleeced.

Neil Smelser suggests certain preconditions for the development of economic crazes.[22] There must be market system in which economic exchange is free of external restraint by noneconomic elements, such as reciprocal obligations between buyer and seller based on status. Thus such crazes have been characteristic of modern capitalistic societies, not of tribal or feudalistic societies. In such an economic system, ambiguity as to the level of rewards to be expected from the current allocation of resources, plus the ready availability of excess capital for investment, make people susceptible to the spread of a wish-fulfillment belief, which defines the particular craze as a way to solve a desperate need for income or to derive an unusually high return from the investment of funds. The basis of this belief may have an enduring existence as an element of culture—the get-rich quick mentality does not have to be generated anew for each speculative craze. The appearance of a new opportunity for investment, plus the activities and assurances of the promoters and a few early investors, may be all that are needed to set the craze in motion.

As the craze continues, with speculation becoming rife, anxiety about the risk involved is bound to grow, even among those

who continue to invest. The condition for panic—a need to escape from what is perceived as a dangerous situation and to do so before other people—arises. A seemingly insignificant incident, such as a rumor, may be sufficient to set in motion the bust—the terminal phase of the craze.

Both the craze and the fad, representing what initially seems to be a vast, new realm of opportunity for gain in wealth or personal prestige, require that a distorted perception of the situation be maintained. When the diffuse crowd no longer sustains such a definition of the situation, the individual's perception quickly changes, and he seeks to dissociate himself quickly from a form of behavior that now seems dangerous or ridiculous.

DEVIANT EPIDEMICS. While all diffuse crowds involve somewhat novel behavior, some engage in what is defined as deviant behavior: that which is regarded as immoral by the larger society. In some instances, a fad spreads primarily among groups that are deviant in the sense of experiencing chronic tension and periodic conflict in their relationship to the established social order. During the 1960s college students and black youths constituted such classes in the United States. Fads comprising deviant epidemics may also spread among classes of unorganized persons who are generally at odds with society, such as juvenile delinquents. Edward G. Robinson's portrayal of a gangster in the motion picture, *The Little Tough Guy,* was imitated by numerous rebellious youngsters as well as by actual juvenile delinquents.

In 1959 and 1960 there was a rash of incidents in the United States in which swastikas were painted on Jewish synagogues—as had happened shortly before in Cologne, Germany. Anti-Semitic slogans were also painted on the walls of schoolrooms and other public places, and in some cases, bricks were hurled through the windows of synagogues. The fact that the first

[22] Neil J. Smelser, *Theory of Collective Behavior* (New York: The Free Press, 1963), p. 276.

outbreak in the United States occurred on December 26, 1959, two days after the widely reported incident in Germany, suggests that the latter provided the behavior model for the epidemic. The incidents occurred over a period of nine weeks, and there were 643 reported depredations. The findings of a research report by David Caplovitz and Candance Rogers show that the epidemic went through a cycle of three periods, with the incidents reaching a peak in the third week and with small communities lagging a little behind the large cities.[23] In the early and late weeks, the first and third phases, Jewish properties, such as synagogues and the homes of Jews, were the overwhelming targets. In the middle phase, anti-Semitic symbols appeared more frequently on non-Jewish targets. This, plus analysis of the motives of the small number of perpetrators who could be identified, led the investigators to infer that during the peak period, many participants were drawn in who were not specifically anti-Semitic but who were generally antisocial. Both individual rebels and members of deviant groups were identified as participants.

Thus a dramatic well-publicized incident keynotes an epidemic of this sort. There follows a rash of incidents in which socially disapproved feelings are expressed. At first, the participants are chiefly people who have been holding back a specific feeling for some time and now find encouragement to express it. The epidemic then builds up until persons with other types of suppressed feelings join, but as it recedes these secondary participants drop out first.

MASS MOVEMENTS. The Florida land boom included, in addition to the buying craze, the actual movement of a large number of crowd participants to the state.

This feature of the boom reflects another type of diffuse crowd which provides insight into the operation of contagion and an emergent definition of the situation in a dispersed collectivity. The term *mass movement* is applied to phenomena that fall somewhere between the ideal type of the mass and a true social movement. In a mass migration, such as a gold rush or a rush to settle newly opened territory, there is a certain amount of social contagion and we-feeling, even though in the final analysis, the activity remains primarily individualistic. The pioneers, journeying to Oregon in the 1840s to stake out individual claims, reflected a sense of collective endeavor in support of the nation in its boundary dispute with Canada by the slogan, "54–40 or fight!"

Students of population are generally agreed that in any migration, mass or gradual, there is both a push and a pull factor at work. The push results from hardships at home, leading to social unrest and individual willingness to seek new opportunities elsewhere. Since economic hardships or persecution for religious or political beliefs impinge more harshly on some population segments than others, migration tends to be selective, particularly in the early stages, as convergence theory would suggest. Thus in the great exodus from Ireland during the potato famine, the first wave during the peak year of 1847 "consisted mainly of the poorest cottiers, who were in no position to delay even a few weeks."[24] The effects of contagion as well as the emergence of a definition of the situation as competitive are reflected in what happened next, after this first wave. Emigration became less selective as the number participating increased and the prospects in Ireland came to be defined as frightening for a wider variety of people.

23 David Caplovitz and Candace Rogers, *Swastika, 1960: The Epidemic of Anti-Semitic Vandalism in America* (New York: Anti-Defamation League of B'nai B'rith, 1961).

24 See "Emigration During the Great Famine," p. 137.

Emigration During the Great Famine

Oliver MacDonagh

For the very first month of 1847 had brought a rush of Irish emigrants to Liverpool: in January, 6,000 had embarked. This first wave consisted mainly of the poorest cottiers, who were in no position to delay even a few weeks. But it was immediately followed by an outrush of smallholders of every sort. The current comments in pamphlets and parliamentary papers, and, more particularly, the reports and advertisements in the local press, establish that thousands of farms were being thrown upon the market in the south and west; that the internal transportation systems—canal and long-car—were completely overtaxed; that the demand on shipping rapidly outstripped the usual supply; and that epidemics of typhus and famine fever were sweeping through the embarkation ports where hundreds of disappointed emigrants had congregated. Almost every circumstance indicated that the existing machinery could not cope with the vast increase in numbers, or with the unprecedented disease, poverty and improvidence of the departing. No longer was the season confined to spring or summer; no longer was the movement held within a long established pattern of ports and trans-Atlantic shipping; no longer were decisions taken slowly and with care, or laborious months spent in preparation. On the contrary, the spring emigration bore all the marks of panic and hysteria, from the fights for contract tickets at the embarkation points to an outbreak of deliberate felonies, committed in the hope of transportation. Newspapers were filled with stories of men who had not dreamed of going a few weeks before, but were now feverishly arranging their departures. They proceeded from no settled calculation—'all we want', as one group put it, 'is to get out of

Ireland . . . we must be better anywhere than here'—but from the impulse of the moment and the example of their neighbours.

This element of hysteria explains why the movement took especially heavy toll upon particular communities. The returns for the diocese of Elphin, for instance, show that, in many parishes, between 10% and 17% of the total Catholic population left for North America during the spring, while from others the loss was relatively small. Similarly, it was said that some Galway villages lost almost one third of their people during March and April. In the light of such evidence, it seems reasonable to conjecture that the prevailing want and misery had left the peasantry in an unstable condition, ready to be swept by some mass sentiment; and that, in such a situation, the sight of one neighbour after another throwing up his holding had a powerful psychological effect upon the survivors. Thus, we would find (though as yet in pockets rather than generally) something which was more a headlong scrambling from a stricken area, more a flight of refugees, than an emigration as ordinarily understood.

To some extent, this is borne out by the relatively high proportion of 'snug' farmers and urban bourgeoisie amongst the emigrants of 1847; for, of all classes, these were the least likely to surrender so long as hope remained. Three of the most competent observers of the time, Fr Mathew, Monsell of Limerick and John Robert Godley, believed that it was the small farmer, if not indeed the class above him, who formed the backbone of the 1847 movement; and, all through the year, newspapers drew attention to the numbers of the 'well-to-do' amongst the current emigrants: to 10 or 20 acre men who felt they could not face another season of disaster; to merchants whose businesses were ruined once the famine destroyed the bacon and provision trades; and to holders of over 20 acres, and even landed men, who were frightened by the accumulated burdens of the labour rate and the proposed system of outdoor relief. Other evidence

From Oliver MacDonagh, "Irish Emigration to the United States of America and the British Colonies During the Famines," in R. Dudley Edwards and T. Desmond Williams, eds., *The Great Famine* (New York: New York University Press, 1957), pp. 320–22. Reprinted in part by permission of New York University Press. © 1957 by New York University Press, Inc.

and factors, amongst them colonial and American reports, the unsatisfactory nature of casual contemporary observations as a source for such conclusions, and the considerable extent of landlord assisted, pauper and cottier emigration during the year, all incline us to reduce the proportion of better class emigrants to 25% or thereabouts. But the surrender of even 50,000 of those who passed for 'well-to-do' in famine Ireland would be sufficient to establish an ominous weakening of spirit for so early a stage in the process of disintegration; and therefore to reinforce the conclusion that the unsettling of society had gone far already.

When the 1847 season ended, it was found that, apart from the tens of thousands who had settled in Great Britain, some 230,000 persons had emigrated to the new world and Australia. If the figures for 1846, 116,000, had caused astonishment and dismay, those for 1847 almost passed belief: so much so that popular tradition still dates the great migrations from that year. As we have seen, the tradition is not altogether wrong. 1847 was indeed a year of wonders, producing the first mass movement upon a grand scale, and containing the first considerable emigration of the more stable classes. The gnarled conservatism which had restrained the flood for decades was now broken, and the general morale perceptibly diminished.

The pull involved in a mass movement, the belief in the existence of opportunities at the other end of the trail, interacts with the push to set the movement in motion. In some cases, such as a gold rush or the defense migration to industrial centers in the United States at the end of the Depression, the opening up of unprecedented opportunities is the circumstance that sets off the movement. In others, accentuation of the hardships at home leads to a reevaluation of the comparative risks involved in clinging to the old rather than taking advantage of an opportunity which had not seemed attractive before. Oliver McDonagh points out that there had been migration from Ireland to North America, particularly to the United States, for some years before 1845. Part of it had been facilitated by a general belief among the Irish that the United States was a land of liberty where a degraded people might regain its dignity. The potato famine changed the balance between the push and the pull, however:

One might almost say that the potato blights of 1845–9 caused a *volte face* in the general attitude to emigration. Broadly speaking, by relaxing the peasant's desperate hold upon his land and home, they destroyed the psychological barrier which had forbidden his going for so long. Something of the same sort may have happened, under special circumstances and in particular districts during 1815 to '45. But it was now group rather than individual, universal rather than local. For in one sense, at least, the dreadful seasons of 1845 to 1849 broke the back of Irish farming. I do not mean, of course, that the tenant ceased to struggle fiercely to maintain his holding, but that these catastrophes, following upon decades of a hand-to-mouth existence, broke his exclusive passion for survival at home, and forced him to recognise that there was a *deus ex machina* at hand, a practicable, if unpalatable, alternative to be considered. Perhaps it may be put like this: where previously the average holder had regarded emigration as a most exceptional course of action, something that another might consider seriously rather than himself, he was now compelled to look upon it as a 'personal' possibility, a genuine alternative to maintaining the struggle against such fearful odds.[25]

In such movements, communication spans great distances as it sustains the emerging definition. A grapevine functions between the destination and the departure area. Letters and reports from travelers who have been there supplement newspaper stories in providing the material for rumors, magnifying the richness of gold strikes in California and Alaska. Telephone calls and quick automobile trips back home make available seemingly unimpeachable reports

25 MacDonagh, "Emigration During the Great Famine," p. 331.

about jobs and high wages offered in developing industrial centers. Early migrants have their own self-esteem at stake in the kinds of reports they send back to erstwhile neighbors and relatives, who might be induced to join them. Promoters—agents for transportation lines, real estate salesmen, labor recruiters and the like—have a vested interest in painting a rosy picture to potential clients. Once these clients have committed themselves psychologically to moving, their perception becomes selective; they pay special attention to clues which would justify the decision. The content of rumor is assimilated to the theme, "You can't lose!" These reports are fed into communities, so preexisting group ties add to the normative pressure to accept them as valid. The reestablishment of these ties in immigrant communities at the destination serve to make the move seem more attractive, as reports of a new life among old friends filter back.

The same mechanisms operate to bring about the demise of mass movements. Improvement of conditions in the home environment, sometimes resulting partly from the migration itself, may reduce the push. The decline of opportunities at the destination, such as the disappearance of easily garnered free gold, or disillusionment with living conditions in the slums of industrial cities becomes the basis of new, discouraging reports transmitted by the grapevine. The same community networks which helped to sustain an optimistic definition serve to put a damper on enthusiasm. The optimism, which discouraged questioning, is replaced by sober appraisal and discussion of the risks, and the mass movement comes to an end.

Diffuse Crowds in Larger Contexts

DIFFUSE AND COMPACT CROWD. The diffuse crowd is not merely similar to the compact crowd; the two are dynamically interrelated. The course of a compact crowd of any considerable duration is not fully comprehensible without attention to the diffuse crowd. At least five such interrelations deserve attention.

First and most obvious, the diffuse crowd is the major *mechanism through which new members are recruited into the compact crowd*. The diffuse crowd instills the essential imagery, sentiments, and conviction of group unanimity in advance of contact with the compact crowd. When persons thus prepared join the compact crowd, they are likely to intensify its tempo, since they do not need to pass through a gradual period of induction into the crowd mood.

A plausible hypothesis is that a considerable portion of the most extreme crowd participants are recruited in this way. Just as a child, talking about what he is going to do to that bully next time he sees him, can more easily build up a misconception of his own prowess and the bully's weakness when not in the bully's presence, so the members of diffuse crowds may develop a less ambivalent image of their object and be less restrained by the dangers involved because they are removed from the scene of action. Thus, newcomers recruited from the diffuse crowd may enter with less inhibitions than those who have been members of the compact crowd from the start.

Second, the diffuse crowd *precipitates new compact crowds* in other locations, crowds which are concerned with the same objects as the original crowd. Thus, in the southern California Zoot Suit riots of 1943, the initial major crowd action in downtown Los Angeles was reflected in a widespread diffuse crowd. Newspaper headlines and person-to-person communication reiterated the phobia, the hatred toward the Mexican-American youth, and the determination that things had now reached the point where something had to be done. Newspapers of the next few days reported a whole series of attacks on Mexican-Americans similar to the original attack, though smaller in scope, throughout Los Angeles county and as far away as San Bernardino

(50 miles) and San Diego (100 miles). People who discovered a unanimity of sentiment through reading newspaper accounts, listening to radio reports, and engaging in informal communication were either provoked to action by the sight of a Mexican-American, or they assembled and hunted out a suitable object. The widespread sentiment also provoked counterattack by Mexican-Americans against Anglos in several dispersed locations.

The diffuse crowd operates in a third way *to maintain the continuity of the interrupted compact crowd.* The famous Chicago race riots of 1919 consisted of a series of daily riots, beginning each day after noon and continuing into the early hours of the morning. The crowd spirit was maintained in the interim through the diffuse crowd, which dominated discussion at work, in the neighborhoods, and throughout the community.

Fourth, the diffuse crowd often *maintains an effective crowd situation for a considerable period after the compact crowd has dispersed.* The long-range effects of crowd behavior depend upon the character of the diffuse crowd. In many instances, especially those involving an acting crowd that has been controlled by force, the original crowd atmosphere persists long enough to create enduring attitudes which leave their impress on the mass. In other instances the diffuse postcrowd may convey attitudes that are a reaction against the excesses of the compact crowd. If we may judge from contemporary news reports, a diffuse crowd must have developed in the case of the 1921 anti-Negro riot in Tulsa. The riot was followed by a marshaling of community energies to rebuild the Negro neighborhood and demonstrate that "the real citizenship of Tulsa weeps at the unspeakable crime and will make good the damage, as far as it can be done, to the last penny."[26]

26 "The Tulsa Race Riots," *The Independent,* 105 (June 18, 1921), 647.

Finally, a diffuse crowd may develop prior to the compact crowd and *constitute the situation out of which the latter develops.* Typically, those crowds which revolve about a long-standing aggravation and are community-wide in scope develop first as diffuse crowds. This situation is often referred to as a state of community tension or unrest.

DIFFUSE CROWD AS AN ORGANIZATIONAL ADJUNCT. We have noted already that fads and crazes may appear as aspects of such organizational behavior as economic pursuits (land booms, for example) and scientific investigations. A margin of diffuse crowd behavior may also be an enduring aspect of organizational behavior. This margin appears when the rules and traditions governing organized behavior are in some respect incomplete. Phases of group behavior not fully governed by established rules and traditions may be governed by crowd mechanisms.

Whenever a group is involved in some unusual venture or in a conflict situation, the outcome is not wholly predictable. This indeterminacy provides room for the establishment of a group sense of confidence or hopelessness in the venture. A shared conviction concerning the worth of the group goal and a confidence in the eventual success of the group constitute *morale.* Morale may be simply a common, reasonable response to the facts of the situation. Thus, troops that are winning battles have higher morale than those who are losing. The crowd element cannot be said to enter until the group sense becomes vital enough to maintain a degree of high or low morale in the face of apparently inappropriate circumstances. A college with a losing football team may sustain high morale in spite of continued defeat. Or a school with a winning team may still share a communicated sense of dread of each game. The diffuse crowd processes fill the gap of uncertainty by establishing a collective mood.

Numerous illustrations of the utilization of the diffuse crowd by established organizations may be found. A popular advertising technique is to promulgate songs, slogans, and other symbols—such as "put a tiger in your tank"—which customers or supporters of a business may display or repeat. That many of the people who spread the symbol may not even be customers does not keep the product from the public eye, generating an impression of its popularity. The publicity directors for athletic teams, amateur and professional, seek to stimulate diffuse pep rallies prior to crucial contests. Symbols of the team are widely distributed and slogans expressing assurance of victory are formulated, not only to increase gate-receipts but to build up a collective mood of confidence shared even by the players. Governmental and religious organizations use similar techniques to promote morale, particularly during times of crisis. The Blue Eagle was used as a symbol of the National Recovery Administration and of national confidence when Franklin D. Roosevelt began his war against the depression.

Diffuse crowd behavior may precede the development of a social movement. During of 1960s many student demonstrations and disorders, which generated fears of nationwide conspiracies, were largely local in character, with little coordination between them. Much of the similarity between the scattered outbursts—similarities in issues, tactics, and rhetoric—could be explained by similarities in the situations of the protestors, the possession of common frames of reference, and the dissemination of behavioral models through mass communication and interaction nets. After a movement with a stable, comprehensive structure does develop, diffuse crowd behavior continues to be an important adjunct for it, just as it is for even more enduring associations. The variety of influences which

may be involved in the spread of a fad is well illustrated in the case of the peace cross. When this symbol first began to appear in the United States, sometimes appearing mysteriously on public buildings as if it were the mark of an underground organization, it was specifically connected with a few organizations that constituted the nucleus of the ban-the-bomb movement. As widespread opposition to the United States' involvement in Vietnam came to overshadow even the threat of nuclear war, the peace symbol took on a different significance and was seen more frequently. By the time a peace movement had emerged which was capable of staging massive marches on Washington, the symbol was available in forms ranging from inexpensive decals and plastic buttons to costly items of jewelry. Manufacturers had obviously recognized the opportunity for profit in what had become a fad. Wearing of the cross could signify for the wearer a philosophy of opposition to all wars, selective objective to the Vietnam War, a vague preference for peace rather than war, or the temporary enjoyment of a currently popular piece of jewelry! Of much greater significance, of course, was the fact that the spread of the fad, for whatever reason, increased the appearance of support for the peace movement. A counterfad, the display of the American flag, sprang up as an adjunct of a countermovement. Decals of this symbol were widely distributed by the publishers of a popular magazine and by an oil company.

The continuity which characterizes a social movement is based primarily on its degree of organization and its development of enduring values and norms. Diffuse crowd behavior serves as a useful adjunct for enhancing the sense of numbers and power felt by the widely dispersed members. Thus it, too, helps to sustain the continuity of the movement.

8

CROWD CONVENTIONALIZATION
AND MANIPULATION

Spontaneity and novelty are emphasized in differentiating collective behavior from organizational behavior. In its extreme form the crowd is unplanned, unanticipated, and ephemeral. Decisions made during its brief existence are based on the emergent definition of the situation; they do not seem to reflect preexisting conceptions of what the course or the outcome of the crowd behavior should be. The behavior consists, in essence, of deviations from the traditional norms of the society.

It is not surprising, therefore, that collective behavior is often regarded as antithetical to social order. As we have noted earlier, a number of theorists have regarded collective behavior as irrational, pathological, and socially undesirable. To the authorities in a social system, the crowd has an aura of danger about it. One of the most important phases of police planning and operations, even in democratic societies, is crowd control. The traditional admonition of the police officer at the scene of some incident, "Break it up—move along!" appears to symbolize an intrinsic conflict between established society and the crowd.

But the foregoing account caricatures the crowd and gives a one-sided view of the relationship between collective behavior and the social order. Just as common as the image of spontaneous crowd behavior is the concept of the agitator, reflecting a recognition of the element of manipulation. Often the critics of the behavior of a particular crowd, such as a rioting mob, will charge that the episode of collective behavior was not at all spontaneous but was deliberately planned and instigated by highly disciplined conspirators. In actuality, both spontaneity and manipulation can be involved at any stage in the development of a crowd. Individuals and organizations do find the behavior of crowds useful in the pursuit of preconceived ends. Hence they often deliberately set out to create situations which will give rise to collective behavior, or they take advantage of situations, which they had no part in creating, by systematically but covertly intervening to influence the direction that the crowd's behavior takes. Such deliberate, planned activities to instigate or direct collective behavior, we will call *manipulation*.

Charges that a crowd has been manipulated by agitators or conspirators suggest that collective behavior is useful only to the enemies of the established social order. On the contrary, collective behavior is a regular, recurrent aspect of social life as well as a source of exciting, unanticipated diversions. After commenting on the strength of the emotions that are aroused in a crowd, Kingsley Davis observes, "But it would be amazing if such a potent force were not socially utilized in some way. In fact it requires but little reflection to realize that the crowd situation is constantly being planned for and utilized by every type of social system."[1] In illustration he points out:

1 Kingsley Davis, *Human Society* (New York: The Macmillan Company, 1949), p. 351.

Religion has always included the crowd situation among its most important devices for maintaining its hold upon the people. . . . Similarly, political parties thrive on crowd-like conventions; governments rely upon public displays and enthusiastic assemblages; and colleges whip up college spirit with pep rallies, shirt-tail parades, and goal-post demolition squads. The excited, yelling, sometimes hysterical throng is a perennial asset of large organized groups from the community to the nation.[2]

Thus even while retaining a significant measure of its excitement and spontaneity, some collective behavior becomes conventionalized; it is anticipated and countenanced by the social system. In suggesting the concept of the conventionalized crowd, Herbert Blumer pointed to another feature of collective behavior, namely "that it is expressed in established and regularized ways."[3] These two features of crowd conventionalization—its anticipated nature and its regularized patterns—suggest its close relationship to crowd manipulation. Before analyzing techniques of crowd manipulation, however, we will consider the question, How can the element of spontaneity that characterizes collective behavior arise in a situation that has been anticipated or planned?

The Conventionalized Crowd

The sense of unity and group power generated in a crowd experience may be useful to an existing organization in reinforcing the solidarity of its members. Leaders may recognize this potential and seek to create situations in which collective behavior will arise. Individuals in a group also find the crowd experience satisfying and worth repeating, even though they may not be thinking of its value for the group. Giving free play to his feelings, without designating to himself all the consequences of his acts, and escaping for a time from

2 Ibid., p. 352.
3 Herbert Blumer, "Collective Behavior," in A. M. Lee, ed., *Principles of Sociology* (New York: Barnes and Noble, Inc., 1951), p. 178.

the bonds of convention can be an enjoyable experience for an individual. Because it serves these functions for groups and individuals, much of conventionalized crowd behavior is religious in nature, and much of it is essentially recreational or revelrous.

The distinguishing feature of the conventionalized crowd is that it arises when the participants gather with the hope that their assemblage will be transformed into a crowd. Although the term *crowd* is often used to denote any large number of people gathered in one place, this popular usage does not correspond to the concept of crowd employed by students of collective behavior. Le Bon pointed this out when he differentiated the psychological crowd from casual aggregations of people and from traditionally organized groups. He sought to describe the circumstances under which the individuals in such assemblages were transformed into a crowd.

Since the members of a conventionalized crowd gather with the expectation that collective behavior will develop, it is likely that at least a portion of them have experienced similar situations before. Sports fans may have attended many athletic contests before; members of churches may repeat their religious experience every Sunday; partygoers may celebrate every New Year's Eve with the same group of friends or in the same type of night club. Furthermore, the people who gather in a setting conducive to conventionalized crowd behavior are likely to share a common cultural background. Because of these prior experiences, the collective behavior which does take place may be regularized by becoming repetitive from one occasion to another, even though it represents a deviation from the usual norms.

SOURCES OF CONVENTIONALIZATION. Thus one source of the conventionalization of collective behavior is the repetitive nature of the occasion. Religious or secular festivals, conventions, and athletic contests between bitter rivals are examples of annual occasions in which there is a buildup, to a peak of excitement, along with a high degree of conventionalization of the forms of collective behavior. The situation need not become a traditional one for repetition and conventionalization to take place, however. In areas where hurricanes strike fairly frequently, conventionalized responses develop. In some Florida cities a storm warning is followed by a rush on food and liquor stores, as residents prepare for hurricane parties. Rather than fleeing before the storm, many people board up their houses and enjoy a break from the routine of daily life while the storm blows over.

The fact that there is usually two or three days' warning of a hurricane points to another source of the response. Conventionalization increases as the opportunity to prepare for crowd behavior becomes greater. While excitement is stimulated by uncertainty—how bad the hurricane will be or who will win the big game,—anticipation of the event makes possible not only a buildup of the excited mood but also some standardization of behavior. The merrymaking of the crowd in a night club goes through a period of preparation under the skillful guidance of the master-of-ceremonies. Even though the audience is composed of different people each night, their behavior is highly similar.

Some conventionalized crowd behavior has a ritualistic quality, as in "holiness" religious services. When expressive crowd behavior is expected to produce some sort of mystical effect, repetition of actions which have been associated with the experience on previous occasions is likely. Frequently this takes the form of rhythmic bodily movement.

A circumstance which promotes conventionalization of some crowds' behavior is that the participants, despite the unorthodox nature of their behavior, retain some sense of concern over public reactions to it. Thus vigilance committees, in the early days of the western United States, typically went through some form of a trial, even though the outcome was almost certain.

The lynching of a Negro in the South was almost always accompanied by rumors describing the bestiality and depravity of the man, even though he might not be accused of rape. Conventionalized forms and explanations of collective behavior thus emerge to justify the behavior of acting crowds.

Keeping in mind the anticipation and the repetitive nature which are salient features of conventionalized crowd behavior, we may now examine the process through which a gathering is transformed into a crowd. Two examples of recreational crowds will be examined—the party and the audience.

THE PARTY. In United States society, the party is an important aspect of the middle classes' culture. Willard Waller and Reuben Hill suggest that this pattern developed during the twenties. They characterize it in these words; "Party behavior, sometimes called partying, combines alcoholism with a partial relaxation of the rule of sexual exclusiveness in marriage."[4] These sociologists report that they obtained descriptions of many variations of party behavior involving the young married set in widely separated regions of the United States.

A party is planned; guests are invited to gather in the host's home at a particular time. Yet no more entertainment may be promised than the provision of food, liquor, and pleasant company. Such a gathering can and often does constitute an instance of informal, small-group behavior governed by traditional norms. The party may prove to be very dull and stiff or, at the most, pleasant but unexciting.

When party behavior develops, the event is wild or swinging, not merely pleasant. This sort of party results when the group is transformed into a crowd. The host and hostess can never be sure that a particular

4 Willard Waller and Reuben Hill, *The Family: A Dynamic Interpretation* (New York: The Dryden Press, 1951), p. 584.

party will be good in this sense. Loosening of ordinary restraints, letting oneself go, and a feeling of psychological closeness to other participants are the hallmarks of success. That such a crowd spirit is most likely to develop between people who already know each other does not mean that the feeling of intimacy is something ordinary. Various degrees of deviation from the usual sexual mores, either in language or in behavior, symbolize the heightened sense of intimacy.

Central to the development of collective behavior in a planned, conventional situation, such as a party, is the introduction of an element of uncertainty. The urgency which characterizes a crowd situation arises from the potential participants' being gathered together, hoping that the evening will not prove dull. A crucial incident in the production of the crowd spirit is any action which suggests an atmosphere of permissiveness. So simple a thing as the telling of an unusually risqué joke may create uncertainty as to whether this is going to be just another party or whether a Saturnalian mood will develop. Testing the limits of permissible behavior follows. Unless someone in the group serves as a wet blanket by showing strong disapproval, the permissiveness of the emerging crowd is confirmed. Communication of a mood of gaiety and abandon may be facilitated by various actions—laughter, singing, dancing, and games. Alcohol is, of course, an essential factor contributing to the relaxation of ordinary inhibitions.

Signifying most clearly the emergence of the crowd is the fate of the person who would prefer a sedate, conventional social atmosphere but who fails to interrupt the growing permissiveness during the testing stage. He finds himself confronted with constraints along the line of the norm that has emerged. The man who cannot contribute his own dirty joke or the wife who will not enter into the sexual games may now be defined as a party pooper.

As Waller and Hill point out, however, there are limits to the extent of deviation from ordinary norms even after the crowd develops. The emergent norm itself sets limits to the behavior that is permissible. The person whose actions get too far out may dampen or even destroy the party mood.

THE AUDIENCE. The audience resembles a compact crowd because it typically consists of large numbers of people gathered in a limited space. Blumer included audiences or spectator crowds in his category of conventionalized crowds. The audience is not always a crowd, although it frequently provides the raw material out of which a conventionalized crowd develops.

A typical audience consists of a group gathered to hear a speech or musical performance or to watch a theatrical or athletic performance. A religious congregation may also be classified as an audience, although the members' participation in the performance is more obvious than in other types. All audiences play some part in the performance, even as spectators. They applaud, they cheer, they may boo or hiss; in various ways they give an overt response to the behavior of the on-stage performers, thereby interacting with them.

Much audience behavior is not collective behavior at all, however. During some parts of a performance, they may be passive spectators responding on a one-to-one basis to the object of common attention and almost forgetting the presence of other spectators. Even when they applaud, they may engage in what is a highly ritualistic, traditional behavior. The clearest illustration of this may be seen in the behavior of audiences at symphony concerts or operas. The experienced aficionados know when it is proper to applaud—when the conductor appears, for example. Even at the conclusion of a performance it may be difficult to distinguish polite applause from a genuine outpouring of unusual approval. Moreover, even a poor performance receives its ritualistic round of applause. For such an audience to boo the performers or even to withhold perfunctory applause is a rare violation of the well-established norms of theater behavior.

Although somewhat less dignified, the behavior of audiences at athletic contests may be equally ritualized. Experienced football fans share a number of well-established norms: standing up for the kickoff is expected; booing a member of one's own team is taboo; applauding at the injury of an opponent is a sign of poor sportsmanship; indeed, if he must be carried from the field, he can expect a round of applause from the entire audience. The members may play their part as spectators in conformity with such norms, but the audience at a very one-sided athletic contest may, after a few minutes, be far more apathetic than excited. A disturbance in the stands may easily arouse more interest than the events on the playing field. Even the cheerleaders, supposedly expert in crowd manipulation, may abandon their efforts to stir up the spectators.

It is obvious that audience behavior which is so highly ritualized, so lacking in enthusiasm, is not exciting for the spectators no matter how great their enjoyment of the aesthetic or technical quality of the performance. The audience must be transformed into a crowd for the excitement and release of collective behavior to be experienced. When the audience becomes a crowd, the norms of audience behavior are modified; the one-to-one relationship of the individual spectator and the performer is replaced by interaction between the members of the audience. The self-consciousness of the individual is diminished, and he experiences a sense of unity and the sharing of emotion with his fellows.

It may be assumed that most of the spectators who gather for an event hope that it will be exciting, not routine and dull—that the time will fly, not drag, during its course. The stage is set for the emergence of a crowd from the audience, but this development is never assured.

Again, some element of novelty and uncertainty must be present. In the field of sports, a close contest with the outcome uncertain for most of the game almost always produces a crowd mood. Not only the general norms of courtesy and kindness but the norms specific to sportsmanship may be violated. Strangers may embrace or pound each other on the shoulders as they rejoice at the success of their team. Fans of the side which seems to be loosing may weep or curse without inhibition. They may even forget about good sportsmanship and act as if the game were a real conflict, not a make-believe one.

An unusually brilliant musical or theatrical performance may produce a sense of the unexpected and the exciting in an audience. Applause may burst forth at times when it is not traditionally expected, and it may last longer than politeness requires.

Both of the salient features of the conventionalization of crowd behavior may be seen in the comparison of various types of audience-crowds. Not only does the audience assemble with the desire that a festive crowd spirit may develop; no matter how strong the sense of permissiveness may become, there are still recurrent regularities in the crowd behavior. The crowd of music lovers which has just been enthralled by the premiere of a new singer still behaves quite differently from a sports audience which sees a stunning upset in the making. A football crowd, frustrated by the prospect of defeat, expresses its despair in forms different from those standardized among baseball fans. Even the imprecations directed at the officials differ! Yet the standardization or conventionalization of these terms does not lessen the frequency or the vigor with which they are shouted when the audience becomes a crowd.

Such occurrences as these provide a satisfying, yet legitimate, escape from the restrictions of the usual social norms. The conventionalized crowd, which may emerge in theater audiences, at sports events, festivals, and parties provides a socially sanctioned setting in which members of a society may enjoy the excitement, the loss of self-consciousness, and the relaxation that crowd participation engenders.

THE CONVENTIONALIZED CROWD AND THE SOCIAL ORDER. It has been pointed out that conventionalized collective behavior may not only provide release for the individual but may also serve to sustain and to strengthen the solidarity of social organizations. As Kingsley Davis noted, religious bodies, political parties, and governments rely on conventionalized crowd behavior for maintaining their hold upon the people. Skillful staging, utilizing music and rhythm, and building up suspense are some of the techniques which generate an air of excitement and transform a deliberate, contrived gathering into a crowd.

The services of some churches, repeated weekly, are conducted in such a manner as to induce strong religious emotion and excited behavior. Liston Pope studied the significance of such churches and their style of worship for cotton-mill workers in southern company towns during the 1930s. He concluded:

Religious services also help the mill worker to transcend his daily life through providing excitement. All ministers acknowledge that mill workers need a strong emotional outlet because of the damming up of self-expression by the conditions amid which they live. The company-village system preempts nearly all their fundamental choices, and jobs in the mills are highly mechanical and routine in character. When his day in the mill is over, the worker frequently feels the need of a vigorous emotional massage; he finds it in hair-raising movies and emotional religious services, among other outlets.[5]

It is not surprising that Pope found that the mill owners subsidized these churches heavily and exerted control to insure that

[5] Liston Pope, *Millhands and Preachers* (New Haven: Yale University Press, 1942), p. 90.

they maintained an otherworldly orientation. They were viewed as supporting rather than threatening the social and economic status quo in the mill villages.

Not all conventionalized crowd behavior supports the established social order. Behavior which was primarily expressive but was neither religious nor patriotic by usual standards could be seen in the rock festivals which attracted thousands of American youths during 1969. The first and most famous was the Woodstock Music and Art Fair held in the Catskill Mountains in August 1969.

This event proved to be remarkable in many respects, even to the men who planned and promoted it. The size of the aggregation—over 300,000 people—so far surpassed their expectations that they had to abandon their efforts to charge admission, even though thousands of tickets had already been sold. The behavior of the participants, although essentially peaceful, constituted a massive symbolic protest against the conventional morality of the society. Observers of the event are agreed that had the police attempted to interfere with the unconventional and often illegal behavior of the crowd, it would have become active and violent; it would not have remained expressive. Yet, as the following excerpts from an interview with some of the participants indicate, emergent norms were operating in this prolonged and intense crowd situation. The interview also shows that the young people gathered for a novel and exciting experience; they were to be the audience for a fantastic lineup of stars. The experience proved to be different from what they expected; it surpassed their fondest hopes. Most notable, it appears, was the sense that the crowd constituted a special community during its brief existence. Since most of the participants came from a specific stratum of society with its own subculture, and many had experienced a similar sense of community in demonstrations, was the development of the crowd mood and culture facilitated? As the young people who were interviewed pointed out, it would be inaccurate to view this collectivity as normless or promiscuous, despite the fact that the deviant norms of the crowd were an open affront to the norms of the older generation in the society.

Woodstock: Like It Was

In the minds of millions of adults who weren't there and who still imagine that popular music means Perry Como and Dinah Shore, it started out as a disaster, the kind of thing that makes governors call out their National Guards, a man-made—or rather youth-made—Hurricane Camille.

News bulletins told of the horrendous traffic jams, shortages of food, limited sanitary facilities, dangers of epidemics and "bad trips" on drugs. Most of the adult world concluded that clearly it was all an inevitable consequence of the mindlessness and rootlessness of today's youth.

But many soon found their first judgments inadequate as they learned more about the Woodstock Music and Art Fair, the most ambitious rock music festival ever held, which a week ago drew 300,000 young men and women to a farm in the Catskills.

For it gradually became apparent that the young people were not only oblivious to discomfort, but they also were surprisingly well-behaved for so great a crowd, at peace with themselves almost to the point of ecstacy. American culture, it seemed, had produced a new kind of mass phenomenon.

To discover what the festival meant to those who were there, and to answer questions in the minds of many adults, The New York Times last week invited five young men and one young woman to sit down with members of its staff for an open, spontaneous discussion of the weekend in all its aspects: the rock music that drew them to what they invariably called Woodstock (but actually was Bethel, N. Y.), their experiences there and what they felt about their hopes for the future.

The discussion began with the reasons they

went, the preparations they made for going and their first impressions when they reached "the scene."

MOTIVES ARE EXPLORED

Q. Why did you want to go?

Lindsey. It was the music. I wanted to go because of the music. That was the only reason.

Judy. They had the most fantastic line-up of stars that I've ever heard about, more than any place I've ever heard of, better than Newport.

Q. Did you have any idea where you'd sleep or what there would be to eat?

Judy. Well, we drove down in a caravan of two cars—there were four girls and two guys—but we were supposed to meet 20 or 30 other people who were driving down from New Hampshire and they were supposed to bring a tent, but we never met each other. We just scattered.

Q. What about food?

Judy. We brought a bag of carrots. And some soda.

Q. Did you expect to be able to buy more there?

Judy. We never really thought about it.

Q. At any point did your interest and excitement go beyond the music to just being there, being at the scene?

Lindsey: When we got up there and saw the people—the way they were dressed and talking. Everything was just so great—the attitudes, the atmosphere.

Judy: I just had a feeling that, wow, there are so many of us, we really have power. I'd always felt like such a minority. But I thought, wow, we're a majority—it felt like that. I felt, here's the answer to anyone who calls us deviates.

Q. Was that before you heard any music?

Judy: I never made it to the concert. I never heard any music at all.

Q. The whole weekend?

Judy: Yeh. The whole weekend.

Q. Were you sorry then that you went?

Judy: Oh, definitely not.

GROUP IS DESCRIBED

Q. Could you describe the group that was up there?

Steve: It was very, very representative of the age group involved.

All the participants stressed a sense of what they called "community." The question of whether this feeling had been spontaneously generated touched off debate.

Steve. Everyone came there to be together—not that everyone would cease to be an individual—but everyone came there to be able to express their life style.

Several voices. No, no, no.

Jimmy. Everyone came to listen to the music. Nobody knew everybody was going to be up there and feel all together and have that feeling.

Q. Have you experienced that feeling before?

Bill. I went to the peace march in Chicago and I found the same thing happening. You'd pass someone young or someone with long hair and you'd smile at each other. Or you'd give each other the peace sign, or know that he was thinking the same way you were thinking. And like the blacks go by each other and say "brother." It gave you the type of unity.

Steve. I think it's wrong maybe to compare what happened at Woodstock to a peace march.

Lindsey. I was at the Chicago convention and the whole difference was that there you were demonstrating against something and here you were for something.

SHARING WAS COMMON

Q. Was there a lot of sharing?

A voice: Everything was shared.

Lindsey: You'd walk along and see a guy with soda and you'd say, "Hey can I have a drop? Can I give some of the rest some soda?"

Steve: We went to sleep Friday night, just me and my girl friend. When I woke up there were a dozen people under our canopy. We all woke up together and we stayed together for the rest of the time up there. We shared food, we shared tents.

Lindsey: I was sleeping and when I woke up,

someone had rolled a joint and put it in my mouth.

Q. Did you finish it?

Lindsey: Yeh. Of course.

Bill. The first thing Saturday morning, they came around and started asking kids to step forward to help with bad trips. And they wanted kids to help with the garbage. And for a second you kind of waited to see if the kids stood up and did it. And they did it! The garbage bags came out and they were filled. And the kids went off and manned the first-aid trucks. And the girls went up to help with the bad trips. And the responsive people of the community rose to the need and accepted the need and carried out what they had to do.

All the panel participants carried some kind of drug to the festival—mostly marijuana known as "grass" or "pot."] But there was also hashish abbreviated as "hash," barbiturates "downs" and LSD called "acid" after its chemical name, lysergic acid diethylamide.)

On the way to Bethel, the participants worried about being searched by the police. One concealed drugs in a hollowed-out arm rest of a car; another hid his on the floor, ready to ram it through a hole if a search began. A third said he was prepared to hide his in his underwear and demand that the officers produce a warrant made out in his name. None was searched.

Once they reached the festival their caution evaporated in air made sweetish by thousands of burning "joints," cigarettes handfilled with marijuana. Anything they didn't bring seemed to be readily available, even heroin called "skag" though none of the participants actually sought or saw any.

Not infrequently drugs were given away by young people eager to share. What couldn't be had free could be bought from dealers roaming freely through the crowd, or others who stayed back in the woods on what they took to calling "High Street."

Most of the particpants regarded the drugs as an essential part of the scene—like flags at a Fourth of July celebration.

DRUG USE FREQUENT

Q. How much of the time were you people up there stoned?

Lindsey. About 102 per cent. [Laughter.]

Steve. Every minute of the waking hours. We would eat and in between eggs we would pass around the hash pipe.

Dan. Where the hell did you get eggs?

Q. Were you smoking openly from the start or were you a little apprehensive?

Lindsey. We started in the parking lot. We didn't stay in the cars, but we looked. You know, we kept an eye open.

Jimmy. When I walked into the concert on Saturday afternoon, I think, or Sunday afternoon, there was a guy sitting there selling acid as if it was hot dogs. I mean like just doing it, like, "Hey, get your drugs here!" or you know, "Last stop before the concert! Really good acid!"

Q. Is there anybody here who did not take anything the entire weekend?

[Silence.]

The search for new experiences—exemplified in the widespread use of drugs—gives the youth scene an aura of promiscuity in the minds of many adults. The participants in the discussion *were quick to point to the new standards of sexual conduct that their generation accepted.*

SEX PART OF SCENE

Q. Was sex an important part of the scene?

Dan. It was just a part. I don't know if it was an important part or not.

Steve. In any society of 500,000 people over the course of three days you're going to have sex—let's face it.

Jimmy. All you have to think about is that people right now, people of our generation are just a lot freer, a lot more free with themselves than people of previous generations. Woodstock was no different. They were no more free or less free in Woodstock than they are any other place.

Dan. There was some society to what people did. I mean, they waited until night.

Q. You mean there were certain standards of decorum?

Dan. I think there were, yes. People still have some reservations. Some. Not as many.

ACTING TENDENCIES IN THE CONVENTIONALIZED CROWD. Up to this point the examples of conventionalized crowd behavior presented have been predominantly expressive in nature. Even in such cases the potential for acting tendencies to become manifest is great. As has been suggested, police interference with the activities of the crowd at Woodstock almost certainly would have changed it into a violent acting crowd, resisting the officers of the Establishment physically as well as symbolically. This sort of crowd change has come about many times when authorities have sought to limit or terminate the expressive behavior of a revelrous crowd.

The conventionalization of acting crowd behavior at times serves an important function in facilitating the resolution of conflicting cultural values, permitting the social order to endure in spite of such conflicts. An organized society, with laws and officials, provides legitimate procedures for punishing violators of the norms, for obtaining redress for grievances, and for bringing about changes in the laws. Adherence to these procedural norms, symbolized in the United States by such concepts as due process, fair trial, and legal channels may become an important value in itself. Yet this respect for law may periodically conflict with other values, which demand quick and sure retribution for certain crimes and speedy adjustment of obvious injustices. The vigilante tradition constitutes a conventionalized collective response to secure quick and sure "justice" in the absence of effective law and order.

In *Their Majesties the Mob* John W. Caughey examines the argument that vigilante action arose in the early west to supplement or to substitute for regular justice.[6] From his analysis it is evident that while the absence or the inadequacy of duly con

6 Chicago: The University of Chicago Press, 1960.

stituted courts was advanced as a conventional justification of vigilante justice, this form of trial and punishment fell far short of providing due process for the accused. The absence of legal mechanisms to safeguard his rights, the sense of indignation and urgency which brought the vigilantes together, and the characteristic presumption of guilt all marked it as crowd action, not the action of an institutionalized, deliberative tribunal. The conventionalization of these acting crowds, through repetition and in self-justification, served to give them respectability in their own eyes but it did not cancel out the angry mood and the biased imagery of the crowd.

Vigilante action in the United States did not disappear with the passing of the Old West and the decline of lynching in the South. During the Civil Rights Movement of the 1960s, nonviolent demonstrators were often attacked by angry crowds, while police officers looked the other way. Because the activities of demonstrators, such as freedom-riders, were protected by federal law, officers were inhibited from upholding local laws and customs prescribing racial segregation. They could, however, desist from interfering with the development of crowd action by citizens who quickly learned that the enforcement of unconstitutional laws was being left up to them.

CONVENTIONALIZATION IN THE DIFFUSE CROWD. The existence of the mass media and interaction chains obviously makes possible the conventionalization of much of the behavior that takes place in diffuse collectivities. In modern, technological societies the mass audience is constantly exposed to the entertainment, the news, and the propaganda which are the content of television, radio, and newspapers. As in the case of the compact audience, the mass audience is not always engaged in collective behavior.

The elements of uncertainty and novelty, which can transform a compact audience into a conventionalized crowd, may also be introduced into the milieu of a diffuse collectivity, sometimes recurrently. The assassination of a president generates diffuse crowd activity, but this activity is not conventionalized. The drama of the nomination of presidential candidates and the election of a president is repeated every four years, however. The election night party is not an event confined to the national headquarters. It has its counterparts in hundreds of local party headquarters, taverns, clubs and, private homes throughout the nation.

Sports events, particularly crucial contests such as a world series, provide excitement and escape for far more people than those who witness the event from the stands. Even before the advent of radio and television in the United States, crowds used to gather outside newspaper offices across the land to await announcements of scores, received by teletype. Today television and radio, plus the highly organized interaction chain involved in betting pools, make such an annual event as the football Superbowl game the occasion for conventionalized diffuse crowd behavior. Cultural influences, specific to the societies in which these celebrations take place, are reflected in the collective behavior. The manner in which a victory is celebrated in a particular society becomes conventionalized through repetition and broad cultural influences which are manifest even in the midst of what seems to be madness, as the following account shows.

A Special Madness

World Cup soccer is a special kind of madness that descends regularly every four years on almost every nation on earth except the U.S. The passions evoked by the World Cup matches have produced examples of most of the varieties of violence and mayhem that man is master of, from international border clashes to murders, suicides and a host of lesser crimes. But to Americans, the intensity of these passions is something of a puzzlement, and the comparisons that spring to mind are usually wide of the mark. Thus the giddy reaction of New Yorkers to the Met's improbable triumph in last year's World Series was a pallid performance indeed by soccer standards—rather like the buzz afforded by a glass of 3.2 beer as compared with that provided by a double Martini.

It was against this background that the 1970 World Cup matches unfolded in Mexico. During the past two years, the battle to enter the finals had reduced the number of competing teams from 71 to 16. And when cup play finally began, some 700 million television viewers, from Moscow to Montevideo, watched its progress by satellite relay. The matches lasted for nearly three weeks as one team after another was eliminated—until at last Brazil and Italy faced each other for the final playoff. Brazil won, 4 to 1, and then the madness set in.

Thunder: No sooner had the final whistle blown than all of Brazil erupted in an orgy of cele-

brations. To Brazilians, the joy of victory was made all the more sweet because it meant they had won permanent possession of the Jules Rimet Cup—a golden statuette symbolic of world soccer supremacy—for being the first country to win three championships since the cup was established in 1930. The city of Rio de Janeiro trembled with the thunder of fireworks. Waves of screeching, intoxicated humanity poured onto the streets singing, dancing and chanting "Bra-sil! Bra-sil!" in an ear-splitting cadence that rolled on deep into the night. Other thousands squeezed into cars plastered with green-and-yellow national flags and blared their horns endlessly. Gaily costumed samba bands appeared as if from nowhere. Brazilian Navy helicopters showered colored streamers and confetti on the screaming throngs. The host city of Mexico, bursting with fraternal Latin American pride, also exploded into a night of frenetic bliss, and thousands paraded in the rain shouting "Me-hi-co! Bra-sil!"

But there was also a tragic side to the celebrations. By the end of last week, more than 100 persons had died and thousands more had been injured by fireworks, in traffic accidents, and by gunshot wounds, and the toll continued to rise. But the fact remains that these depressing statistics are considered an acceptable part of the madness by fanatical soccer enthusiasts and there seems no end in sight to Brazil's present joy over the victory. "I can assure you," predicted Brazilian coach Mario Zagallo, "there will be carnival in Brazil for quite a while."

FASHION. The fad has been described as a prominent example of diffuse crowd behavior. Although the terms *fad* and *fashion* are frequently linked and both are instances of this type of behavior, it is important to note that fashion occurs in a conventionalized crowd setting. Unlike fads, which arise frequently but quite unpredictably, fashion is a continuous process. Herbert Blumer points out the intrinsic relationship of two common expressions to the concept of fashion—*in fashion* and *outmoded.* He observes, "These terms signify a continuing pattern of change in which certain social forms enjoy temporary acceptance and respectability only to be replaced by others more abreast of the times."[7]

Blumer also postulates that fashion, like other forms of collective behavior, has the function of sustaining social solidarity. "Fashion should be seen as a process of reaching out for new, congenial forms in an area that is part of a continually changing world."[8]

A distinction usually made between fashion and fads is that fashion is introduced by the highest status levels in the society and spreads downward, while fads are lacking in prestige value. The findings of Katz and Lazarsfeld suggest some modification of this theory, for in their study of personal influence in fashion behavior, they found as many fashion leaders in their middle-status level of women as in their high-status level. Only the low-status women were underrepresented in fashion leadership.[9]

With this caution in mind, it may be postulated that the spread of fashion supports the established status structure in the society, while fads do not. New styles are available to those at the upper-status levels first, and persons at the lower levels emulate them. The reward for adopting a new style early is the prestige of possessing a high-status symbol. The penalty for adopting the style too early is the judgment that one is trying to act above his station in life. Rapidly changing fashion, therefore, depends upon a society in which upward mobility and prestige striving are favorably valued. The rapid succession of styles becomes necessary when the higher social strata are not able to maintain a monopoly of the high-status symbols.

While fashion tends to reinforce established status distinctions, fads may establish prestige at variance with the conventional scale. The pacesetters of a fad may come from any stratum, and the fad may be adopted more quickly within the lower levels of the society. Based upon priority of adoption and intensity of activity for the fad, the prestige accorded may be a substitute for established prestige. Thus fashion is conservatizing with regard to the social structure, while fads may promote change.

The cyclical character of style changes in fashion is often stressed but with a false impression of fixed repetition of styles. Of necessity the variation of some specific elements of style—such as dress length and width—will be cyclical within the limits of practicality and mores. However, style consists of the total effect rather than single elements. A. L. Kroeber's studies of fashion have shown that the periodicity of cycles in dress styles during recent centuries is different for different dimensions of the dress.[10] Furthermore, specific embellishments are added or eliminated in irregular sequence. While there is a tendency to put together items which are regarded as harmonious, there is seldom a total repetition of style. The cycles of recurrence which have been noted are fairly irregular, showing constant minor variation within the larger cycle. Thus, in the sense that a particular culture makes possible only variations of style within certain limits (e.g., restrictions imposed by canons of decency), there must necessarily be some alternation and recapitulation of styles. But the conception of any precise, total, predictable recurrence of identical styles is not justified by evidence at hand.

The important question in deciding whether collective behavior concepts can be applied to fashion concerns the relative

---

7 Herbert Blumer, "Fashion," in *The International Encyclopedia of the Social Sciences* (New York: The Macmillan Company and The Free Press, 1968), pp. 341–42.
8 Ibid., p. 343.
9 Elihu Katz and Paul F. Lazarsfeld, *Personal Influence* (New York: The Free Press, 1955), pp. 247–70.

10 A. L. Kroeber, "On the Principle of Order in Civilization as Exemplified by Changes of Fashion," *American Anthropologist*, n.s.21 (1919), 235–63.

determinacy and spontaneity of fashion behavior. Vigorous adherents to the cyclical theory of fashion have argued that individual choice does not enter into the selection of styles. It is possible to overlook the evidence against such complete predetermination and still grant the intervention of crowd mechanisms. So long as the ordinary participant in fashion behavior cannot predict the direction of style changes, the diffuse crowd can serve as the means through which consensus regarding new styles is established, even though that consensus reflects a principle of regularity.

It is sometimes contended that fashion is entirely rigged by the leaders of the industry involved. Industries have geared their production to an artificially high demand that can be maintained only by the regular obsolescence of goods on account of style before their intrinsic useful life has been exhausted. Consequently, there is much fashion planning and deliberate acceleration of normal rates of style change. But a large part of fashion planning is not the creation of fashion so much as the careful study of fashion trends in order to anticipate changes which will take place regardless of who assumes the style leadership.

Neither the cultural determinacy nor the organizational control of fashion change seems to be complete. Typically, the mass has several styles presented to it by competing style planners. Selection of the dominant style is made with the help of style leaders, persons of prestige who have personal followings and whose selections among available styles are watched by bodies of style followers. The style planners often have a showing for select groups of known fashion leaders for trial reactions, and after a style is fully launched the style planners watch carefully the general reactions. Thus there is abundant opportunity for popular selection and for establishment of a partially spontaneous consensus through crowd mechanisms, operating within the channels of the established status system.

At times of more radical style change, or of reversal in direction of style change, there is often an aroused collective opposition. Such aroused opposition developed at the close of World War II when the "new look" was abruptly introduced following wartime interruptions of normal style fluctuation. The opposition was unsuccessful, however. The "new look" was accepted and had its day. The same sort of opposition developed in 1970 when fashion designers proposed to replace the miniskirt with the midiskirt. In this case the resistance seemed to be more effective, partly because another new fashion item, the pants-suit, offered a third alternative to women who wished to be in fashion but did not like the midi. The little-understood transformations, whereby the reluctant and the violently opposed imperceptibly sometimes come to acquire the very tastes which they initially resisted, offer one of the most potentially fruitful subjects for research on the operation of the diffuse crowd within the institutional structure of fashion.

Crowd Manipulation

The members of a conventionalized crowd gather with the expectation that collective behavior may develop. The members of a spontaneous crowd suddenly find themselves in an unstructured situation, and quite unexpectedly engage in collective behavior. In either instance, one or more individuals may be present who consciously desire to see a crowd emerge and, whether they instigated the collective behavior or not, to influence its course. Sometimes they make no effort to conceal their efforts at manipulation, serving openly as the leaders. In other instances the manipulator may wish to operate covertly, not calling attention to his own activities and allowing other leaders to carry out the line of action which he has suggested in the guise of being just another member of a spontaneous crowd.

In order for there to be crowd manipulation, there must be a crowd. Rumors may be planted or an incident may be staged so as to draw a large number of concerned individuals together at a selected site. Other techniques of manipulation serve chiefly to transform the casual, mildly excited crowd into a fully developed collectivity.

TECHNIQUES OF MANIPULATION. In its early stages the potential crowd has relatively mild curiosity and only a vague sense of urgency. It has little unity and exerts only weak holding power and constraint on individuals. At this point manipulation involves enhancing the sense of uncertainty, making the situation more problematic. The skillful manipulator intervenes in the milling process, raising questions as to whether things are as they seem or expressing doubts as to whether anything is going to be done about a situation that demands action. If expressive behavior is the goal, then he attempts to create expectations that something rare and dramatic is about to happen. Like an expert master-of-ceremonies, the manipulator attempts to build up the suspense of the developing crowd. The activities of the preacher in revivals or holiness religious services illustrate the gradual building-up of suspense and excitement in an expressive crowd.

The use of symbols is particularly important in crowd manipulation. Introduction into the rumor process of terms which denigrate the potential opponents or victims —*pigs, Rotcee Nazis, Commie rats* and so on—prepare the way for acting crowd behavior. Some symbols serve to generate a sense of pressure on individuals to go along with the crowd. They portray the crowd members as good people—patriots, right-thinking people, etc.—and label individuals who do not support the crowd's line of action as traitors or defectors—finks.

Long recognized as contributing to the development of the crowd mood is rhythmic activity. Crowds often spontaneously develop rhythmic slogans which may be repeated as chants, but, like cheerleaders, crowd manipulators can deliberately introduce them. The importance of music in facilitating crowd development is repeatedly illustrated by its use in certain types of highly expressive religious services.

For a crowd to reach the stage of acting on some external object—rushing a police line, charging into a building, assaulting a victim—a precipitating incident, which is a signal for action, may be necessary. This provides another opportunity for intervention by the manipulator. By striking the first blow or merely giving what seems to be a signal for "Go!" he may trigger the release of the fury that the crowd has built up. In some situations an even more effective variant of this technique may be employed. This involves goading an opponent into striking the first blow so that he (usually the police) may be charged with having provoked the crowd action. For members of the crowd who have been reluctant to initiate violence in spite of their heightened indignation, the sense that they are acting in self-defense removes the last inhibitions against using force.

Some police authorities have concluded, on the basis of their experience, that some acting crowds are thoroughly manipulated by a cadre of skilled manipulators. Raymond M. Momboisse, deputy attorney general of California, has coined the term *professional mob* to characterize such a crowd. He describes the wide variety of techniques of manipulation that might be used in the ideal type of manipulated acting crowd.

Structure and Tactics of the Professional Mob

Raymond M. Momboisse

STRUCTURE OF THE MOB

1. *Introduction*

It must be realized that at times a mob will be led by professional agitators. In such cases the mob will be well organized and extremely dangerous. It is essential to be able to recognize such a mob, know its organization and its tactics.

2. *Mob Organization*

a. External Command

This is composed of demonstration commanders well removed from the activity, stationed where the entire "battlefield" can be observed. In a moving demonstration, it remains apart from the mass. It consists of the professional agitators who are trained and experienced in fomenting disturbances. It directs the entire operation by the use of radio and messengers.

b. Internal Command

This is a cadre of professional agitators within the mob. They are responsible for directing the demonstration, pursuant to the external command's orders. Once they have set the wheels in motion, whipped up the frenzy, they stand back and let the younger, more impulsive, persons do the actual fighting, for they are too valuable to be sacrificed. Great importance is attached to protecting the leaders of this group.

c. Bravadoes

This group acts as a loose bodyguard surrounding the internal command, protecting the leader from police, and screening his escape if necessary.

From Raymond M. Momboisse, *Confrontations, Riots, Urban Warfare* (Sacramento, Calif.: MSM Enterprises, 1969), pp. 12–14. Reprinted by permission of the author and publisher.

d. Messengers

They stay close to leaders, for whom they carry orders between internal and external commands.

e. Shock Guards

These individuals accompany mobs but march along the sidewalk where they are screened by spectators. They dash into the mainstream of mob action only as reinforcements. Their sudden and violent descent on the battle is designed to provide sufficient diversion to enable an orderly retreat of the main body of professional agitators who, upon signal from the external command, melt quickly into the ranks of spectators, leaving the milling bystanders and unwitting excitement seekers to the police.

f. Banner Carriers

The slogans used by this group and the cheering section are adapted to suit the prevailing mood. In such demonstrations key agitators will often be found close to certain conspicuous banners. In this way the command knows their location at all times and can dispatch messengers to them with instructions for stepping up the tempo, shifting slogans, or inciting violence.

g. Cheering Section

Specially briefed demonstrators are carefully rehearsed on the slogans they are to chant, and the order in which the cries are to be raised.

h. Police Baiters

Specially trained women scream hysterically, faint at policemen's feet or claw at their faces. Other pawns are instructed to roll marbles under the hoofs of policemen's horses, attack them with razor blades on the end of poles, or jab them with pins, causing them to rear and charge through the crowd and thus provide photographers with "proof" of "police brutality."

i. Snipers

This unit occupies key positions, such as roof tops, from which advancing police units are attacked with weapons, rocks and firebombs.

j. Sheep

This is the mass of people who make up the bulk of the mob. They are the expendables maneuvered into the actual conflict. They are the innocent martyrs whose blood will convert the issue into a crusade. They will make the leaders heroes, while they will be forgotten and pass back into obscurity or be so permanently scarred that they will be forever committed to rebellion.

TACTICS OF THE MOB

1. *Introduction*

The tactics employed by the mob indicate the caliber of its leaders. They will vary from maneuvers to embarrass the police to the application of the methods of guerrilla warfare.

2. *Embarrass the Police*

The mob leaders will try to embarrass the police and gain the sympathy of the public. To achieve this, mob leaders may place women, children, wounded war veterans, ministers, priests and nuns in the forefront. Obviously any encounter between such individuals and the police will reflect adversely on the police. The police will often be verbally and physically assaulted in order to force violent reaction which will make the police appear brutal and supply photographic "proof" of such brutality.

3. *Weaken Police Line*

The agitator will do everything possible to weaken the police line. One of the basic methods employed against police is the "baiting tactic." The purpose of this tactic is to "bait" the officer into leaving the formation, to entice him into premature action or an individual encounter so as to weaken the police unit and undermine the

respect of the mob for the discipline and efficiency of police units. The well-organized and well-led mob may appear to disperse so as to cause the police to break or be drawn out of formation or to actually withdraw from the scene. Once that has been accomplished, the mob reforms and proceeds towards its objective. The resourceful mob leader will utilize various diversionary tactics, such as disorders, destroying property, setting fire, feinting an attack on some objective, in order to divert the attention of the police from the true target. His true purpose is to divide or weaken the police force blocking the path to the actual objective.

4. *Disrupt Police Supply Lines*

To damage tires, large tacks are scattered in the streets along routes police vehicles will use to approach the mob. Trucks, buses, and similar vehicles are stalled, or accidents created that block off streets and prevent police elements from entering areas or leaving their headquarters.

5. *Disrupt Communications*

Cutting off electric power and telephone facilities is one of the first moves to be expected in support of any organized mob action. The intentional jamming or overloading of telephone, telegraph communications to police and fire departments can also be expected.

6. *Looting*

It is a standard tactic to organize or to encourage looting. In this manner, the uneducated, non-dedicated elements are attracted. Promises of easily acquired wealth, either in the form of material goods or money, is always a sure way to attract mob members.

7. *Outflank and Envelop*

The basic tactic of a mob is to outflank and envelop the police units, destroying their maneuverability and effectiveness.

8. *Seizing and Holding Buildings*

This tactic is particularly effective in college riots when the building seized is vital to the continued operation of the institution. In conjunction with such seizure there has been the tendency to destroy property. When top secret research is conducted on a college there is the added threat of theft of valuable records and material.

Whether such a highly manipulated and organized mob as that postulated above has ever actually existed is questionable. While putting them all together in a description of a crowd that would be a policeman's nightmare, the author does identify a variety of tactics that have been used piecemeal in many manipulated crowds. This account focuses on the actions of the leaders or manipulators. It should be kept in mind that the manipulated crowd is much broader in composition than this implies, including persons who are not privy to the tactics of the leaders but are the objects of their efforts. Skillful manipulation, including the chanting of slogans, the exploitation of legitimizing symbols, and the provocation of the police to violence, creates an illusion of spontaneity and enlarges and strengthens the crowd by drawing concerned spectators into its active ranks.

9. Ambushing

The newest technique of rioters is to lure a police unit into a prearranged ambush, inflict substantial causualties and then quickly flee.

9

SOCIAL CONTROL AND COLLECTIVE BEHAVIOR

From the standpoint of the agitator or crowd instigator who regards the existing social order as unjust and oppressive, collective behavior that overcomes the restraints imposed by the society and brings about social change is highly desirable. He may attempt to manipulate the crowd because it is his desire that social control reflect the emergent norms of the collectivity, not the preexisting norms of the larger society.

The concept of conventionalization suggests that the agents of social control may permit or even favor some types of collective behavior, so long as these forms remain within the bounds that have become regularized in repeated episodes and do not seriously threaten traditional values and the established pattern of authority. Vigillantism may even serve as a means of social control for powerful groups that find the formal procedures inadequate at times.

There is an inherent tension between collective behavior and any established social order. The crowd or the social movement always contains the seeds of social change. Le Bon reflected the typical mistrust of collective behavior felt by the establishment when he declared, "Crowds are only powerful for destruction."[1] As the concept of emergent norms implies, collectivities impose new constraints on their members which may conflict with the usual norms. The emergence of collective behavior may in itself signify a weakening of social control. Thus Morris Janowitz said of race riots in the United States, "In the language of the sociologist, a key element in the outbreak of riots is a weakness in the system of social control."[2]

The social control of collective behavior, including crowd control, will be taken to signify the efforts of social control agents in a society to prevent, limit, or terminate the development and the activities of collectivities. The efforts may range from the enduring, comprehensive measures taken by a national government to forestall the growth of dissident social movements to the immediate actions of a police force to disperse a compact crowd. The perception by authorities that the crowd is always potentially dangerous is well illustrated in the following statement by the United States Federal Bureau of Investigation on crowd control:

When a crowd is orderly and violating no laws and poses no danger to life or property, it is of little concern to police agencies except for possible circulation control. However, experienced police realize that problems often arise when groups are formed and an incident may occur which excites or inflames human emotions. A crowd, although innocent in its

---

1 Gustave Le Bon, *The Crowd* (New York: The Viking Press, Inc., Compass Books, 1960), p. 18.

2 Morris R. Janowitz, *Social Control of Escalated Riots* (Chicago: University of Chicago, Center for Policy Study, 1968), p. 7.

origin, nature, or purpose, can become a mob; a mob, in turn, can generate rioting.[3]

It is in the control of compact crowds, particularly those violently acting ones to which the term *mob* is usually attached, that the policies and procedures of social control agents are most visible. The major part of our analysis of social control and collective behavior will therefore be concerned with crowd control.

Crowd Control

THE LIMITS OF CROWD CONTROL. Were there no limits to measures which authorities might employ in controlling crowds, the principles would be simply a matter of military tactics. In fact, however, the measures which are required and which may be used to control a crowd are influenced by the relationship between the authorities, as conceived by each.

An extreme case where there would be no limits to the ability of authorities to control a crowd would be one in which neither side felt any normative restraints on its actions towards the other. In such a case, the effectiveness of social control would rest on the balance of physical force between the two sides. If the authorities regard the crowd members as people who have no rights that they are bound to respect, then they may attack the crowd with whatever means they have at their disposal. If these means include automatic weapons, a massacre may be the result. In such a case the only limit to crowd control would be the ability of the crowd to resist.

A condition where there are no limits to crowd control may be approached under a political regime that denies the citizenry, or certain people, the right to dissent. The gathering of a large number of people without government sponsorship may evoke

[3] Federal Bureau of Investigation, U.S. Department of Justice, *Prevention and Control of Mobs and Riots* (Washington D.C., 1967), p. 48.

efforts by the authorities to disperse the crowd by any means deemed necessary. Even within such a totalitarian system, certain limits to social control may operate, however. One is that not all of the control agents—the policemen or soldiers—may have been so brutalized that they feel no sense of sympathy for their victims as fellow human beings. Thus they may allow at least some members of the crowd to escape. The other restraint comes not from the crowd situation but from the larger political context. A government may be deterred from a policy of systematic extermination of hostile crowds because it fears sanctions, which might be imposed by other governments. For example, it is likely that the death toll of civil rights demonstrators in some southern communities during the 1960s would have been considerably higher had not local law officers and public officials been aware that they might have to account for their actions to federal officials and to potential investors from other states.

Minimization of restraint in crowd control is also likely to be present when deeply felt, longstanding antagonisms exist between the control agents and the crowd members. These antagonisms may reflect racial, ethnic, religious, or class differences within the society. Even an official policy of freedom of assembly and dissent may not deter control agents from attacking a crowd with all the force at their disposal. In effect, the police become one part of a factional crowd, comprised of two segments fighting each other, rather than disciplined, impersonal agents of social control. Not even the use of nonviolent tactics by the crowd will protect them when such antagonisms are present. Thus in 1960, white South African police killed 69 unarmed native demonstrators and wounded 180 in what came to be known as the Sharpeville Massacre. During the "troubles" of 1969 in northern Ireland, Catholics protesting against governmental policies feared that a similar fate might befall them if the B-Specials were not disarmed. The "B-Specials" were an auxiliary police force composed of Protestant men, traditional enemies of the Catholics they were organized to control. The conviction that during the Democratic national convention in 1968 at least a minority of Chicago policemen broke discipline and wildly attacked the crowds that confronted them led some critics to label the event a police riot. There is a growing danger in the United States that a sense of class conflict is developing between the police and the youthful demonstrators who make up many of the crowds which the police are called upon to control. The policemen, many of them from working-class backgrounds and still relatively poorly paid, know that many of the young people who confront them are from affluent upper or upper-middle class families. This may make the abuse heaped on them by the crowd harder for the policemen to take, even when it is only verbal.

If the crowd feels no obligation to respect the authorities, denying their legitimacy, then the restraints on the crowd's actions tend to be reduced to what the members sense they can get away with. Rarely, however, does a crowd have at its disposal the physical force sufficient for successfully combating the authorities. The very fact that the use of violence by control agents is legitimized means that they are likely to have more weapons at their disposal than any assemblage of private citizens. A rioting crowd may, nevertheless, have enough instruments of violence—rocks, bottles, sticks, improvised bombs, and even guns—to provoke the authorities into the use of their weapons. This leads, in turn, to the legitimization of even more violent behavior in the crowd norms and pushes the limits of crowd control to a point at which the conflict is almost unrestrained. In commenting on the urban riots of 1967, Lee Rainwater observed:

The riots elicit from the official world exactly the kind of behavior that confirms the ghetto's estimate of white justice. The trigger-happy behavior of the National Guard and the police and the haphazard way in which arrests are or are not made deepens the conviction that being accorded justice depends more on luck than on the rule of law. The rising hysteria of the fatigued and frightened men in uniform seems to relase all of their latent hostility to Negroes.[4]

THE ESCALATION OF FORCE. Rainwater suggests that once a riot gets under way, a process is started which makes likely an increasingly massive and forceful response from control agencies unless they withdraw entirely. Even the fact that a crowd develops a mood of hostility to the police puts the latter in a precarious situation which increases the likelihood of an escalation of force. This is particularly true in the United States, where the control of hostile crowds has been traditionally treated as a secondary, emergency mission for law enforcement agents.

Despite the long history of conflict between crowds and agents of social control, the major portion of the training and experience of the police prepares them to deal with other types of situations. On the one hand, much of their experience is with law-abiding citizens who look to them to perform a regulating function and who respond to directions with a minimum of opposition. On the other hand, the people from whom the police expect to encounter resistance are individual criminals deliberately violating the law. When a large number of people cease to comply readily with ostensibly legal orders, it is easy for the officers to put them collectively into the category of criminals. Unlike burglars or muggers, however, crowd members do not define their own actions as criminal. In the United States after 1960, the chances seemed to increase that some portions of any crowd engaged in a political demon-

---

[4] Lee Rainwater, "Open Letter on White Justice and the Riots," *Transaction*, 4 (September, 1967), 26.

stration would already be politically alienated, questioning the legitimacy of the established order which the agents of social control represent. When the police respond to such crowd members as if they were ordinary criminals, the negative imagery of the crowd is reinforced. The mood of opposition and rejection of authority spreads, particularly when individuals who are not engaged in aggressive behavior are arrested, manhandled, or clubbed.

The fact that the mission of the police is to maintain order puts them at a disadvantage. Only a minimum of noncooperation on the part of the crowd, such as failure to disperse when ordered to do so, confronts the officers with the dilemma of accepting this defiance or of creating disorder by use of aggressive tactics. If the objective of the crowd, or some elements of it, is to create disorder, then offensive behavior by the police plays into their hands. The crowd has the advantage of the initiative; the role of the law-enforcement agents is primarily that of reacting to what the crowd does. During student demonstrations, a period when agents of social control stand immobile while members of the crowd explore a variety of actions to express their grievances, often precedes violent action by the law-enforcement agents. When one of these grievances is the contention that the established political regime is oppressive, one course of action is to attempt to provoke the police into behavior which will confirm this definition.

Here an apparent advantage, the possession of superior weaponry, may prove to be a disadvantage for social control agencies. Public debate about the killing of four students at Kent State University by national guardsmen, in May 1970, suggested that many people viewed the weapons of the crowd—rocks and bottles—as virtually harmless in comparison with the rifles of the guardsmen. When the soldiers, outnumbered by the crowd and sensing themselves under attack, used the weapons at

their disposal with tragic effect, they dispersed the students but brought a storm of protest on themselves. More disorders followed on other college campuses, as the "overkill" in Ohio was perceived by many people as evidence that the United States government has become fascistic as well as imperialistic.

Although the social control agents almost invariably have superior firepower at their disposal, crowds sometimes do include members armed with genuine, not makeshift, weapons. In contrasting recent *commodity riots* (ghetto residents burn and loot within their own neighborhoods) with the older *communal riots* (factional crowds of whites and blacks clash in contested areas), Morris Janowitz suggests the term *escalated riot*. To him the central feature of the escalated riot is the use of weaponry:

The stark reality of the new type commodity riot is in the use of weaponry. It is truly an escalated riot. In the old fashioned communal riot, the police were armed with pistols and an occasional rifle. The national guard or federal units carried rifles tipped with bayonets, plus limited amounts of heavy infantry weapons. The bulk of the fighting by civilians was with brickbats of a variety of types plus a sprikling of small arms. The central fact about the commodity riots is the wide dispersal of small arms and rifles among the rioters.[5]

The crescendo of gunfire is the outward manifestation of the escalation of a riot. The firing comes not only from the rioters, however. Shotguns, rifles, and even heavy machine guns have been employed by policemen and national guardsmen; some city streets and college campuses sound like battlefields.

In societies which purport to be democratic, escalation of unrestrained violence in crowd control is not supposed to happen. Janowitz suggests the limits to crowd control which should ideally prevail in a democratic society:

5 Janowitz, *Social Control,* p. 11.

The constabulary function as applied to urban violence emphasizes a fully alert force *committed to a minimum resort to force and concerned with the development and maintenance of conditions for viable democratic political institutions.*[6]

PRINCIPLES OF CROWD CONTROL. Because such limits are supposed to exist (even though they are often violated), the principles of crowd control, which have been formulated by various agencies in the United States for the guidance of police and military forces, consist primarily of suggestions on how to control or terminate collective behavior with a minimum of force. These principles incorporate the premise that the control agents operate within a political system where crowd members have rights which must be respected and where the majority of individuals who make up a crowd respect the legitimacy of these agents. The use of maximum rather than minimum force is regarded as a last resort, one which techniques of crowd control are designed to make unnecessary.

Many assemblages, where police officers are routinely on duty, do not develop into crowds, or they only go through the early stages of crowd development before dispersing. They may be audiences or expressive crowds. Such assemblages include participants in political rallies and religious gatherings; spectators at athletic events or parades; merrymakers at picnics or festivals; and sightseers who gather at the scene of an accident, a fire, or a crime. Special problems are presented by certain activities which involve large numbers of people—strikes and peaceful demonstrations. The strikers or the demonstrators may, at least at the outset, constitute an organized, disciplined group rather than a crowd. The presence of sightseers, some of whom may be opposed to the purposes of the demonstrators, creates the potential for the de-

velopment of a factional crowd which may become involved in violent conflict.

In such cases the task of the control agents consists of protecting individuals from injury, preventing interference with legitimate public activities such as firefighting, and interrupting the development of violent crowd behavior or panic. Some specific activities are preventing overcrowding, particularly in buildings, preventing traffic congestion, and keeping individuals out of the parade's line of march or off the playing field at an athletic event. Another common activity is removing unruly individuals who may create incidents and precipitate crowd development. At times the police must serve as a barrier, isolating potentially conflicting segments of an assemblage from each other, or break up small fights before large numbers of people become involved.

Control may be said to be effective when such activities as these do not divert the crowd or audience from its primary ongoing activity. There is always a danger that interference with the crowd's activities may cause a major transformation of mood, with the result that the police become the objects of aggressive mob action. For example, at the height of the 1955 Mardi Gras festivities in New Orleans, the attempted arrest of one of the merrymakers changed the happy mood of the crowd to one of anger. Officers who came to the assistance of their fellows were beaten and pummeled. Even after the original disturbance was quelled, the aggressive, destructive mood continued to prevail and there were repeated riot calls, as the crowd expressed its aggressive mood by hurling rocks at cars and buses. The danger that the crowd may shift from expressive to acting behavior, with the police as their target, is particularly great when hostility towards the police is endemic among the crowd's population, as it is among the residents of many black ghettoes. Thus, for example, in 1964 a street dance in Rochester, New York turned into a riot which lasted for two

6 Ibid., p. 8.

days and was eventually quelled by the National Guard. The precipitating incident was the attempt of the police to arrest an intoxicated black youth.

Obviously it is the violent, acting crowd that presents the greatest challenge to agents of social control. The title of a manual issued by the Department of Justice of California, "Crowd Control and Riot Prevention," reflects the understandable preoccupation of police agencies with the rioting mob. In 1967, following several urban riots, during what came to be called the long, hot summers, the Federal Bureau of Investigation issued a manual for the use of police departments entitled *Prevention and Control of Mobs and Riots*. The gist of its recommendations for preventing riots is expressed in three words: *contain, isolate, disperse*. The elaboration of these principles is given in the following excerpt from the manual.

Organization for Riot Control

The vast majority of literature pertaining to riot control operations is based, in varying degrees, on the military concept, military tactics, and military formations. The military concept, tactics, and formations are sound for a military unit. They are not, however, necessarily sound or readily adaptable to the police role in riot control operations. The military possesses the basic ingredients which make its concept and operation sound: manpower and equipment.

How, then, should the police agency organize? Basically, the organization will be that which is required to accomplish the three missions assigned.

First, the police must CONTAIN the riot; that is, it must be held back and not permitted to expand its boundaries. Emphasis here is placed on the rapid dispatch of patrol cars and police officers to designated checkpoints on the perimeter. This is strictly a defensive tactic, employed to prevent any ingress or regress to the riot area. Because of the necessity for prompt action, a suggested method of organization would be to designate specific individuals or units for each shift of the day.

Second, the police must ISOLATE the riot. This is accomplished by establishing a special zone completely surrounding the critical area from which all unauthorized traffic is diverted by directing it elsewhere at checkpoints on the perimeter of the special zone. The special zone is considerably larger than the critical (CONTAINED) area, and its purpose is to provide a place where responding personnel and equipment may function in preparation for whatever tactical movements are necessary. Within the special zone should be staging or assembly areas, detention facilities, first-aid stations, the field command center, parking areas, and food and shelter areas for police officers. Only authorized personnel are permitted in the special zone, thereby preventing the curious from joining the disorderly, and affording an area for assembling forces and conducting the suppression operation. This mission of controlling ingress and regress to the special zone could well be assigned to forces from an adjacent law enforcement agency.

Finally, DISPERSE the mob and suppress the riot. This is the offensive action aimed at destroying the mob's organization, breaking its will to resist, and restoring law and order. Speed and decisiveness, coupled with an impressive show of force, should pervade this tactical situation. The force is composed of the riot squad (if one is available) and/or units organized on a reserve basis, with each member previously assigned a particular function or position on the riot unit which corresponds to his regular work shift. In the special zone, these individuals receive their riot equipment, assemble into unit organization, and prepare to go into action. All of this is accom-

From Prevention and Control of Mobs and Riots (Washington, D.C.: Federal Bureau of Investigation, United States Department of Justice, 1967), pp. 69–70.

plished out of sight of the mob. Once organized, they are moved quickly to the critical area; the first impression given the mob is of a well-organized, adequately equipped, highly disciplined force advancing in formation with a resolute purpose.

In a manual prepared twenty years earlier for the Chicago Park District Police, a sociologist, Joseph D. Lohman, emphasized the principle of isolating the crowd and suggested techniques for interrupting the development of collective violence. He proposed five techniques:

1. Removal or isolation of the individuals involved in the precipitating incident before the crowd has begun to achieve substantial unity.
2. Interruption of communication during the milling process by dividing the crowd into small units.
3. Removal of the crowd leaders, if it can be done without use of force.
4. Distracting the attention of the crowd from its focal point by creating diversions at other points.
5. Preventing the spread and reinforcement of the crowd by isolating it.

Lohman also made an important distinction between the use of force and the show of force by control agents. He declared, "The mere presence of sufficient numbers of men in uniform is what is meant by a *show of force*. This awes the crowd so that it becomes unnecessary to *use* force in removing key persons."[7] He also warned of the danger that the police incur through an inadequate show of force, one which fails to overawe the crowd and instead invites resistance.

An important limitation on the effectiveness of the show of force is the fact that the crowd may include members who want to be arrested or are willing to suffer physical violence in order to make the authorities appear brutal and to precipitate further crowd action. They may call the bluff of the police when a show of force is made. In doing so they may succeed in radicalizing other members of the crowd, including some of the audience segment. Indignation at violence employed by social control agents, particularly if it is directed against unarmed persons, may help resolve the ambivalence of such people and transform them into fully committed, active participants.

In an analysis of ghetto and college campus riots which occurred between 1963 and 1966, James R. Hundley, Jr. concludes that the principles suggested by Lohman are still not generally followed by police officers. He also suggests another source of crowd control. This is the influence of in-group leaders. Handley gives as an example the legitimate leaders of the ghetto community.[8]

The in-group members enlisted to aid in social control are not always legitimate leaders in the sense of having been accorded recognition by the authorities prior to the crowd action. Riots in urban black communities have often cast serious doubt on the assumptions of white officials about Negro leadership. In some cases the crisis created by a riot has brought to the forefront leaders whose influence had previously received little recognition or had been dismissed as undesirable. During a commodity riot in Tampa, Florida, in 1967, the executive of a city-sponsored human relations agency persuaded the sheriff to deputize a number of young black men known to him as having great influence among black youth because of their militant attitudes. Some of them had been partici-

[7] Joseph D. Lohman, *The Police and Minority Groups* (Chicago: Chicago Park District, 1947), p. 83.

[8] See "Interaction Between the Crowd and Social Control Agencies, pp. 166–67.

pating in the riot the day before! This group, known as the white hats because of distinctive headgear issued to them, proved effective in cooling the riot. The strategy of legitimizing a hitherto concealed or discredited stratum of leadership was subsequently followed in a number of other cities. As Hundley indicates, the utilization of in-group members as agents of social

control requires that the authorities enter into a bargaining relationship with them. Making concessions to the community from which the crowd is drawn becomes a technique of crowd control. The concessions may even include the withdrawal of official agents from the area of the riot, entrusting the task of peacemaking to the in-group leaders.

Interaction between the Crowd and Social Control Agencies

James R. Hundley, Jr.

In the beginning stages of crowd formation, the presence or absence of police officers can have various effects. In most instances, the very presence of the police creates an event, provides a point of focus, and draws people together among whom rumor can be easily transmitted. In other cases, sending too few officers to a scene results in actions being uncontrolled because not enough policemen are available to break the developing crowd structure. We suggest that if the police activity is seen by the rioters as legitimate, then the presence of small quantities of police will not precipitate a riot. However, even if the original police activity is viewed as legitimate, but the policemen are observed as being rude, impolite, unfair, or brutal, then these activities can precipitate a riot. It appears that the police officers, in their attempt to enforce a higher authority, are perceived by ghetto residents more as a causal factor than a deterrent of riot behavior.

One of the puzzles of recent ghetto riots is why, in some cases, the total withdrawal of police simply enhances riot activity. The success of police withdrawal is contingent upon officers or officials contacting the legitimate leaders of the ghetto community and in allowing them to exert

social control. Legitimate leaders will not attempt to exert this control unless police or city officials make immediate concessions or promises. The failure to make immediate concessions reinforces the ghettoites perceptions of the white structure's reluctance to respond, and creates a situation of social suicide for any Negro leader who attempts to approach the crowd with promises of a better tomorrow.

Particularly in the early stages of a riot, police forces are incapable of controlling the situation and resort to observation of riot activities. The very presence of the police, who do not exert control, further promotes the emergence of norms which allow deviant activity. In fact, we have reports of policemen weakly chasing looters, chiding observers, or driving back and forth among looters shouting verbal insults. These non-control activities encourage and promote still more hostile behavior.

Lohman outlines five ways to prevent and control crowds. These recommendations are to isolate the crowd, divide it into small units, create diversions, remove individuals involved in the precipitating event, and remove crowd leaders without force. These basic principles are generally not heeded by police departments. For example, policemen tend to stay around even when a crowd starts to form, and do not quickly remove or isolate individuals involved in the precipitating incident. Police do not take into account the communication process in a crowd and fail to divide it into small units. Instead,

From James R. Hundley, Jr., "The Dynamics of Recent Ghetto Riots," in Richard A. Chikota and Michael C. Moran, eds., *Riot in the Cities* (Rutherford, N.J.: Fairleigh Dickinson University Press, 1968), pp. 147–48. Reprinted in part by permission of the publisher.

they attack along a frontal line much like a military operation.

Other factors determine the length of recent ghetto riots besides the activities of the police. The sooner help comes from outside control agencies, the sooner a riot stops. Prior to Detroit, the national guard had been amazingly successful in controlling crowd behavior immediately upon their arrival. Apart from the sheer force of numbers, calling in the national guard indicates the success of rioters, since they have beaten the "boys in blue." The sooner the larger community seeks out real ghetto leaders and satisfies their grievances, the sooner a riot stops. The more exploiters and instigators in a ghetto, the more likely a riot is to occur and of long duration. Finally, the greater degree of normalcy that is maintained within the ghetto community, the more likely a riot will remain small or cease.

SUCESSFUL CROWD CONTROL: A CASE STUDY. As Hundley shows, many of the ghetto riots of the 1960s were terminated only when the military, with massive force at their disposal, supplanted the civilian police agencies. In some subsequent riots, particularly the Detroit uprising of 1967, not even national guard troops proved to be effective. Only highly trained, well-disciplined regular army units proved capable of terminating the riot, while still adhering to the principle of using only the minimum force necessary. Janowitz points out that this has long been the case, observing, "As in the case of labor disputes, the historical record reveals that federal troops were more effective in restoring order than state guard units. In particular they were more sensitive to the position of the unions and the Negroes, and were less likely to take sides."[9] In the decade from 1960 to 1970, evidence that in many instances police and national guardsmen displayed partisanship, acted like members of a factional crowd, and employed excessive force against rioters and bystanders alike makes the task of social control increasingly difficult. Growing mistrust of these forces among blacks and college students, exacerbated by the faddish diffusion of the epithet *pig*, increases the probability that in new situations they will encounter crowds which from the outset deny their legitimacy.

The record is not entirely dismal, however. In an unusual case during the summer of 1965, two psychologists were able to act as participant-observers in the preparation made by a police department for a weekend which might well have resulted in a riot. The following account by Robert Shellow and Derek V. Roemer suggests that some of the principles of crowd control are efficacious when used as the basis for planning riot prevention. A show of force proved effective several times when fighting had broken out but had not spread. The rapid removal of key individuals, with a minimum of force and without antagonizing the crowd, proved effective in the episode at the Old Tavern. Certainly one of the most significant preparations for the weekend was the "education" of the police to view the anticipated crowd as a heterogeneous collection of human beings, with the rights of citizens, rather than as an undifferentiated mob of outlaws. What could have been a police riot with the law officers behaving as one segment of a factional crowd was avoided. The polarization of the crowd and social control agents which pushes crowd control methods past the limits implied in a democratic system did not develop.

[9] Janowitz, *Social Control*, p. 14.

No Heaven for 'Hell's Angels'

Robert Shellow and Derek V. Roemer

Ever since Marlon Brando portrayed the leather-jacketed leader of a motorcycle gang in "The Wild Ones," a squadron of free-wheeling, anti-social highway roamers has loomed as a symbol of menace to many small communities across the country. In recent summers major riots have broken out at resort towns when unruly crowds have disrupted a schedule of motorcycle races and forced the police or National Guard into action.

As social scientists and police consultants we became involved in the summer of 1965 in a motorcycle riot that never happened. The experience we shared with a police department may be instructive in coping with riot conditions that confront communities in the future, not only with motorcycle gangs, but in the public arena of social protest.

A national motorcycle race was scheduled for Labor Day weekend at Upper Marlboro, the county seat of Prince George's Country, Maryland. The county, with a population of 500,000, is adjacent to Washington, D.C., and is partly suburban, partly rural. Upper Marlboro is a rural sector, but is only about 15 miles from well-populated suburbs.

The news media had reported all the gory details of the Weir's Beach riot on the Fourth of July which followed the National Championship motorcycle race near Laconia, New Hampshire. A police lieutenant reported that shortly after the Weir's Beach episode three motorcyclists, proclaiming themselves members of the notorious "Hell's Angels" of California, were arrested and jailed for disorderly conduct by town policemen in Prince George's County. Angered by being forced to bathe for a court appearance, they threatened to return over Labor Day to "tear up the county."

Learning of these events in a casual conversation with the lieutenant, and wishing to keep posted on the local situation, we spoke to the police inspector responsible for police action over Labor Day. He wasn't sure how seriously he ought to take these threats and rumors. Precious little was known about the Hell's Angels and how they were likely to behave among several thousand motorcyclists amassed for a big race. We offered to chase down the rumors, and bring the results of our inquiries back to the police. But two weeks of search failed to turn up so much as one Hell's Angel, though the rumors of invasion and destruction were persistent and proliferating.

When we reviewed accounts of several recent riots and disturbances in connection with recreational or sporting events, we noted several common factors that seemed significant in all of them:

An influx of outsiders into a small town or circumscribed amusement area, where the number of outsiders was large relative to the number of local inhabitants and police.

The outsiders were distinguished from "locals" by some common feature—an intense interest (such as motorcycling), an age group (college youth), race, etc.

The distinction between "locals" and "outsiders" was often made more visible by differences in dress, argot, and other expressive behavior.

The specific conditions under which exuberance and rowdiness exploded into rioting seemed to be the following:

Recreational, service, and control facilities were "flooded" by overwhelming numbers of visitors who were left at loose ends. They were ready for any kind of "action."

Ineffectual, often provocative attempts at control and expression of authority were made by police or civic officials.

A sense of group solidarity developed among members of the crowd.

Often the locals, including the authorities, contributed to the developing cohesion of outsiders by viewing the visitors as all of a kind; attributing negative class characteristics to them (dirty, rowdy, etc.); labelling them as "hoodlums" or "young punks"; and then treating them accordingly. The effect of opposition or attack in solidifying group cohesion is well documented. If the opposition is ineffectual as well, many members of the developing mob begin to sense their own potential power. (Several reports mentioned careful preplanning by a small cadre of dedicated instigators, who allegedly circulated rumors before the event and selected targets on the scene. Actual proof of "planning," as opposed to repetition of rumors, is difficult to obtain.)

In order to prepare for the special Labor Day situation ahead, we needed information about the organization of motorcycling both as a sport and as a way of life. Moving from one enthusiast to another, and interviewing at the local Harley-Davidson dealer, we made a number of discoveries. Motorcyclists come from all walks of life. The majority are employed, and need to be, since as much as $3,000 may be tied up in a "motor." The devotees insist that the size of the machine separates the men from the boys. Those who own enormous Harley-Davidsons and the large Triumphs or BSA's and who engage in competitive events such as races, "field events," and "hill climbs," see themselves as a breed apart from the "candy ass" owners of Hondas and the light-weights. For the former group, the motorcycle often serves as the fulcrum of social and even family life. They enjoy being able to take off any evening at a moment's notice and ride, say from Washington, D.C., to Atlantic City, returning as the sun rises. They travel regularly to field meets and races, usually camping overnight on the scene.

Like many hobby-sports, motorcycling has its formal organization, the American Motorcycle Association (AMA), and its "sanctioned" members. AMA clubs have tight rules and tolerate little deviance. Some non-AMA clubs are similar and may aspire to sanctioned status. Other clubs are available to those who enjoy a more relaxed and casual organization; these may require only that members not seriously embarrass the club in public. They tend to be more tolerant in their attitudes regarding noisy mufflers and styling, and less regimented during group expeditions. All get classified by the AMA as "outlaws."

Aside from these more or less conforming clubs, the "outlaw" class also includes groups of dedicated rowdies who pride themselves on their ability to intimidate and destroy. The Hell's Angels

Motorcycle Club of California is such a group, as are the Gooses, from New York and New Jersey, or the Pagans, from the Washington area.

Spokesmen for the motorcycling "establishment" often attribute the sport's bad image to the "1 percent who cause all the trouble." The rowdies have proudly accepted "1-percenter" as an honorific epithet, and often have it emblazoned on their costume as a badge of commitment. The 1-percenter personifies the motorcycle hoodlum stereotype.

Regardless of their organization or status within the sport, motorcyclists agree on one thing—they all complain of police persecution. They also report being victimized on the roads by car drivers. Many respectable motorcyclists sympathize with the view the "rowdy outlaws" have of themselves as a persecuted minority.

ON THE ROAD IN MARYLAND

With regard to the Labor Day weekend itself, we learned that the schedule of events was more complex than we or the police had thought. Aside from the big race on Sunday, the "Ninth Annual Tobacco Trail Classic" (for the first time a National Championship event) at the Upper Marlboro track, there were lesser races at the same track on Saturday. At the Vista track, 14 miles away but within the same police jurisdiction, there were to be "field events" such as drag races and "riding the plank" on Saturday and Sunday and an AMA-sanctioned race meet on Monday. The sponsors of the Upper Marlboro races had also scheduled a Saturday night race at a track 30 miles away in the Baltimore suburbs, "to give people something to do and keep them out of trouble."

The Vista track had in the past operated as an "outlaw" track without AMA sanction, and most or all of the competitors and spectators had been Negroes. However, in 1965 it had just achieved sanctioned status, and its events were listed in the national calendar. A dance hall, popular with Washington area Negroes, was located in the track infield and would be operating every night of the weekend, so it appeared that a large proportion of those attending the motorcycle events at Vista would be Negroes. The crowd at the Marlboro track was expected to be between 3,000 and 6,000; a much smaller croud was expected at Vista.

Most motorcyclists we spoke to throught there would be a great deal of migration during the weekend from one track to another and among the various camping areas (assuming there were more than one), the taverns, and other recreation spots. Easy mobility is the essence of motorcycling.

Concluding that we enjoyed a special and privileged relationship with motorcyclists, the police asked us whether or not the race should be called off. We did not feel justified in taking responsibility for the decision, but joined in the deliberations. To cancel a public event on the basis of thin rumor alone—the Hell's Angels threat—was a dangerous precedent to set, yet to jeopardize the safety of innocent people was unthinkable. The police decided to permit the race as scheduled, while making every effort to avert violence. (Our shift in role from outside consultant to partnership with the police at this point tied us much closer to the action and events of the weekend than would ordinarily be the case in the role of scientist-observer.)

Once the decision to permit the race was made, we developed a set of goals which we felt should guide planning, basing our thinking on the analysis of recent riots mentioned above and on a hurried and therefore unsystematic study of the social science literature. *Collective Behavior,* by Ralph Turner and Lewis Killian (1957) was particularly useful and supported our inferences from the riot accounts.

First, we encouraged sober planning for all the events of the long weekend. Naturally, advance planning was not new to the police department. Nonetheless we were grateful that the unsettled state of the "Hell's Angels" rumors, plus our refusal to make pseudo-authoritative pronouncements on the probable course of events, helped maintain some controlled anxiety among police officials. This limited anxiety went far to prevent a premature resolution of the planning process, either through panicky reliance on harshness on the one hand, or complacent relaxation on the other. Our goal was a plan with three major objectives:

anticipation of the kinds, numbers, and distribution of motorcyclists and spectators; the activities they would engage in; and the amount of localized roving to be expected;

the disposition of police officers and their instructions, both as to general attitude and specific actions to meet various contingencies;

coordination of the several police departments concerned, including the state police, and the local police of nearby towns and counties to which the motorcyclists might travel in search of recreation.

Our second goal was to avoid a polarization of relations between the authorities and the motorcyclists. We directed our efforts to both groups. As we explored the "culture" of motorcycling, we tried to keep the police informed and interested in what we learned. We arranged a meetng between some local motorcyclists and police officials at which films of sport motorcycling were shown; afterward each group expressed its gripes concerning the other. Our educational goals with the police were:

to show that motorcyclists are not essentially different from other citizens, and need not be treated as a breed apart;

to inform them that in point of fact motorcyclists are not a homogeneous class but come in a variety of shapes and sizes, some innocuous, some potentially troublesome;

to impress upon them that indiscriminate harsh treatment of all motorcyclists would confirm the latter's sense of persecution, increase group solidarity among them, and go far toward creating the very polarization we wished to avoid.

In working with local motorcyclists, our objectives were:

to involve the organized groups in the control effort, asking them not only to refrain from participating in observing as passive audience to rowdiness, but to help actively in identifying potential trouble areas and keeping police informed of large group movements;

to weaken the respectable motorcyclists' sense of solidarity with the "1-percenters" by reinforcing their concern for the deteriorating "image" of motorcycling and pointing out their vested interest in running peaceful races.

Our third major goal was to ensure that adequate facilities were provided for the visiting motorcyclists, with an eye to both containment and entertainment. Our objective was to inhibit the milling behavior that usually precedes crowd disturbances. Specifically, we suggested that adequate and convenient camping facilities were customary and essential at motorcycle meets. Also certain informal and rather dangerous recreations (such as drag racing and stunt riding in the camp grounds), which do not impinge on the non-motorcycling citizenry, are also customary and ought to be permitted. We had noted in the New Hampshire riots that the only camping area was 40 to 50 miles from the track. The campers were reluctant to make the long return trip after each day's racing, and some preferred simply to stay up all night. Thus they remained in the town of Weir's Beach long past the time when they might ordinarily have returned to secluded camping areas for an evening of drag racing, motor-revving and beer drinking—in mutually acceptable segregation from the resort citizenry.

Our fourth major objective was to monitor the events of the weekend and keep a continuous flow of intelligence coming into police command headquarters, so that the senior officer could make effective decisions. Here we served in something of a combined research and undercover capacity, checking out rumors, keeping current with the temper of various groups, clubs, and gangs among the motorcyclists, and observing fights or accidents as they occurred. We made a point of spending time in places where the county police could not routinely go.

HELL'S ANGELS IN THE WINGS

Rumors of the arrival *en masse* of the Hell's Angels of California persisted through Saturday of the three-day weekend and were *never* clearly proved or disproved. We learned that Hell's Angels were anticipated in resorts all the way from Ocean City, Maryland, 140 miles away, to the Pacific coast. Rumors circulated mostly among youth and motorcyclists that three scattered locations (a tavern, the race track, and a whole town) in Prince George's County were to be wrecked. We began to see that the Hell's Angels were assuming a mythical character. They had become folk heroes—vicarious exemplars of behavior most youth could only fantasy (unless swept away in mob activity), and legendary champions who would come to the rescue of the oppressed and persecuted. An older motorcyclist, witnessing police harassment of his fellows at a town outside Prince George's County, was heard to remark, "Just wait 'til the Angels hear about this when they come in tomorrow. They'll come tear this place apart."

The police never did accept the idea of actively involving local motorcycle clubs in the control effort, even though we offered to do all the leg work in getting club representatives together for a meeting. An exception was the large club that sponsored the Marlboro races. The inspector warned them severely that any trouble this weekend would greatly reduce the likelihood of the race being permitted next year. However, he emphasized that the department did not intend to discriminate in any way against motorcyclists. The inspector convinced the sponsoring club to hire uniformed guards for the race track. The club also assured us that camping facilities would be provided.

There was little advance coordination among the various police departments in the area. The state police announced a policy of "keep them moving," and said they would "get tough" with any rowdy-looking types they encountered. The detailed cooperation between departments we had envisioned, like involvement of the motorcycle clubs in police planning, was probably considered too far outside normal practice to be warranted by the situation.

Despite these largely negative circumstances, one particularly positive development stood out. At each police roll call prior to the Labor Day weekend, all the uniformed men were instructed to treat motorcyclists just as they would any motorist visiting the county. They were told that only a very small minority of motorcyclists were troublemakers, and that only the behavior, not the style of dress, haircut, or bodily cleanliness was a matter of police concern.

On Saturday morning of the race weekend, we and the police were dismayed to learn that the sponsoring AMA club had reneged on its promise to provide public camping facilities. Apparently they wished to avoid the expense of renting portable outhouses, which were likely to be broken up for firewood in the course of the weekend. We were further disturbed to learn that early arrivals, some of whom were pretty ragged and rough looking, had already set up a squatters' camp in the large field usually rented for that purpose.

This created a tricky problem for the police. They could not legitimately enter the field, which was private property, unless the owner complained or a violation of law occurred which was visible from the public highway. If the police officially notified the owner, he would be bound to ask that the trespassers be removed, because of his liability for damages incurred by people who were on his property with his implicit permission. Eviction of the growing crowd of squatters would have meant removing a noisy, potentially troublesome group from a location remote from residences and businesses where the amount of property they could damage was limited. Furthermore, they were not, at that time, visibly violating laws. There was no way to predict where they would go if evicted, but obviously they would not go home so early in the weekend. The problem might simply have been scattered all over the county, aggravating the difficulties of control while at the same time provoking resentment, which could have been turned against innocent citizens.

It was decided that notification of the owner of the field was not warranted and that there were tactical advantages in keeping the field open, since it seemed to be attracting and holding the rowdier element. So long as they were all in one place, surveillance would be simple and response to trouble could be quick.

The activities on the field were kept under continuous but unobtrusive observation. Police cars were continually passing the field, occasionally pausing near the entrance; the people on the field were thus kept aware of the police presence in the general area, but not so heavily as to arouse feelings of persecution. The 45-man Civil Disturbance Unit (CDU), trained in riot control but lacking experience in full riot conditions, had been mobilized and sent out on the road the night before (Friday). Only a few motorcyclists were seen in the county and the CDU was dismissed around midnight. The usual dance at the Vista track was held without incident.

A HARD LABOR DAY'S NIGHT

From Saturday through Monday the entire force, including the CDU, was ordered on 12-hour shifts. The men were kept on the road except when responding to trouble calls, thus providing extra control for the normally heavy holiday beach traffic. We felt that the men would be able to respond more quickly to large-scale trouble if they had been concentrated in two or three central standby locations rather than dispersed over the county's 486 square miles. However, police officials judged that the disadvantage of a possible delay in such emergency mobilization was offset by the double payoff from the same investment in overtime pay— more extensive traffic control *and* riot prevention.

An elaborate communications system was set up, employing not only the police radio (monitored by newspapers and wire services) but also a civil defense band, which permitted more detailed discussion and open references to likely trouble spots. This privacy greatly facilitated unobtrusive surveillance. A special radio code was established so that squad cars using the police band could notify headquarters briefly and in confidence of the presence of groups of motorcyclists.

On Saturday, only a few hundred spectators attended the scheduled lightweight and novice races at Marlboro. Across the highway those squatters, dusty out-of-towners, and locals who preferred the role of contestant to that of passive onlooker conducted their own impromptu field games. The entire center of the squatters' field, despite its ruts and hummocks, became a drag strip. Groups, clubs, even families had set up camp sites around the periphery of the field in a broken crescent.

Groups and couples who settled on the extreme ends of the crescent appeared to have expensive camping equipment and rather conventional dress. Dead center at the head of the drag strip, the most ragged troop of squatters set up headquarters in a large army tent, its center pole flying a red flag. Sullen young men and girls milled around this command post drinking beer and making menacing noises at curiosity seekers. Clusters of jackets marked"Hell's Angels,"''Pagans,'' or ''The Gooses,'' were seen. Some individuals sported a nose ring, a swastika, a Halloween wig, or gold cross earrings; many men wore their hair in shoulder-length manes.

A group of mostly short-haired locals, more or less neat in T-shirts and jeans, tried to introduce some order into the drag races. One tried to control racing by flagging each pair of racers to a start.

He was successful for several hours but finally the enormous quantities of beer, hard liquor, and green wine consumed by participants undermined the authority he had established. Racers roared past him without waiting for the flag. He shouted for order, but few responded. Non-racers crisscrossed the drag strip, narrowly escaping collision.

The proximity of the self-appointed track superintendents to the encampment of rowdy long-haired outsiders and locals became abrasive. Accidents began to occur. Finally a fight broke out between a very wobbly Pagan and a helmeted, short-haired local. After punching the Pagan unconscious, the short-haired hero was successfully defended by his associates from being pummelled by the rest of the Pagans. The victor had the poor taste and bad judgment to sit triumphantly astride the hood of a truck, waving his beer can in a bravado challenge for all to see. Now all the rowdy groups joined in a confederation and charged *en masse* toward the short-haired locals. Just at that moment a drunken cyclist lost his machine to a rut in the track. His mishap was noted by police on the highway who dispatched an ambulance along with five police cruisers. The vehicles poured onto the field and fanned out in a half-circle around the casualty, thus coincidentally presenting the crowd with an array of flashing red lights. The unexpected show of power was so sudden and instantaneous that the would-be warriors at the head of the strip broke ranks and returned to their staging area. Unknowingly the police had put a stop to what might have been a bloody war, since the local motorcycle enthusiasts were far outnumbered by the combined force of Pagans, "Hell's Angels," and Gooses. (We put "Hell's Angels" in quotes wherever the reference is to participants in local events, because we have serious doubts that any *bona fide* members were ever present in our area.)

Following the withdrawal of police, 20 "Hell's Angels" and Gooses set out to replenish their beer supply at the Old Tavern nearby. Just as they started to throw their weight around in the bar and threaten the owner, a police sergeant and another officer entered the room. The group quieted down and waited for the action. Three cyclists moved to the window to assess the size of the sergeant's force; four cruisers were visible. The sergeant opened with, "I hope you all are behaving yourselves." He remembered from a conversation with us that motorcycle chains worn loosely over the hips rather than through belt loops should be considered weapons, so he asked, "What's that chain for?" "Hey, man, I lock up my motor with it." "Well, aren't you afraid someone'll steal your motor, not being locked up and all? You better come with me while we put that chain on right, son." The group tensed, then relaxed as the young man elected to go quietly and do as the sergeant suggested. Shortly after this low-key encounter the group roared back to the field and the Old Tavern was prematurely closed for the weekend.

At 11 p.m. about 75 cyclists were seen by one of our staff at a rock'n roll beach resort in a neighboring county. The chief of police there had already advised the press of his intention to lock up any rowdy motorcyclists who showed up. He arranged for the state police to back him up. Twenty state troopers in riot dress and five dogs were lined up on the main street across from the crowd of motorcycle riders while six local policemen pushed and poked with night sticks, arresting several who took exception to their tactics. By 1 : 30 Sunday morning most of the motorcyclists had left town. Statements to the press by the chief greatly exaggerated the numbers present and arrested, thus giving an unwarranted notoriety to the evening.

By Sunday morning 300 motorcyclists had settled on the field at Marlboro. Those who had been driven from the beach resort were in a mean mood. Under the direction of the unofficial starter drag racing resumed at a more frantic tempo than on the day before. Across the highway a steady stream of spectators poured onto the track for the afternoon race. Few took notice of the accidents that were beginning to occur on the field.

At 2 p.m. a fire was set in a railroad caboose on a siding behind the field. Fire equipment and police responded quickly; no attempt was made to find the arsonists. At 3 p.m. a crane was started on an adjacent construction site and tools were stolen from its cab. At 4 : 30, coinciding with the "Tobacco Trail Classic" across the road, a man removed the license plates from his dilapidated old car and set it afire. With another sportsman straddling the hood, the owner drove onto the drag strip and jumped free. The car rammed an accelerating motorcycle. Both hood rider and motorcyclist were thrown on impact, both suffering broken legs. A fire truck arrived to put out the fire amid jeers from spectators. A police lieutenant supervised aid to the injured, making humorous asides to cool the excited crowd and enable the ambulance to remove the casualties to the hospital.

About 6 p.m. the long-haired groups demanded that locals turn over the starting flag to a "Hell's Angel" who appeared to be one of their leaders. Fighting broke out but subsided immediately when one squad of the CDU (10 men) drove onto the field. This time the police had riot equipment visible—helmets, clubs, shotguns, gas masks. The crowd dispersed; the squad withdrew. Since tension on the field seemed to be building, command officers set up an observation post on a cloverleaf approach overlooking the field. At 6:30 the flagman and a delegation from his club came up to plead with command officers to clear the field of hoodlums; they threatened to bring in their own weapons if police didn't protect them. Since the delegation could not agree on who should be charged with what, action was delayed.

At 7 p.m. several men broke away from the milling crowd at the center of the field and ran to their machines. From the observation post, it was clear they were returning with bars, chains, and other weapons. The entire CDU was sent on to the field where they quickly assembled in riot formation. The inspector drawled out over the bull-horn, "All right men, you've had your fun, now it's time to go home." Before he finished his sentence motorcycles began to move out of the field. Within 20 minutes the area was clear.

Up to this time, the importance of containing trouble makers on the field was dominant in the minds of commanding officers. But if the crowd were allowed to remain overnight, fighting probably would continue, under the cover of darkness. Dispersing all the squatters while it was still light would, hopefully, send them on their way home. The alternative—isolating and removing the instigators and mob leaders—was complicated because the police could not remain on the field

and because cyclists were unable or unwilling to serve as complainants.

Fifteen minutes after the field was vacated, 10 men and a girl were arrested outside the Old Tavern, where they had started to break windows. Within minutes, another 10, including the leading "Hell's Angel," were arrested as trespassers at a filling station where they refused to make way for customers. There was no further trouble in the county, at the Vista track, or at the beach resort, though an anxious lookout was maintained until early the next morning. By Monday it was obvious that the danger had passed.

REACTIONS TO THE WEEKEND

Both the command officers and the county commissioner responsible for police matters were satisfied that the police had conducted themselves effectively and the the control effort had been a success. They felt, however, that the situation had not warranted the extra expense and trouble. Estimates of cost ranged from $6,000 to $10,000, but certainly some of the overtime pay would have been necessary for a Labor Day weekend even without motorcyclists. The commissioner announced that he couldn't see why the county had "to put up with the influx of motorcycle tramps who camp out, drink and fight among themselves.'

Like the commissioner, most of the police leadership was opposed to permitting the race next year. We refrained from offering unsolicited and premature advice on the issue of future races. The club sponsoring the Marlboro races was considering cutting the meet down to a one-day event and preventing camping altogether, in the hope that this would make the event more acceptable to authorities.

Since we were unable to maintain contact among Pagans, Gooses, or "Hell's Angels," we could not ascertain their reactions to police policy and procedure. We did talk to our acquaintance at the local Harley-Davidson dealership, which provides service and parts for many out-of-town motorcycles. He reported that for the first time in nine years of races he had heard none of the usual atrocity stories of police mistreatment of motorcyclists. The local short-haired motorcyclists who had been in the fighting on the field felt that police had exercised entirely too much restraint in dealing with that situation. They did not know, until we told them, that the field had not been rented this year.

Was all the concern, planning, and extra police activity justified? We think so. Would the Gooses, Pagans and alleged "Hell's Angels" have been just as peaceful anyway, despite their frightening appearance? We think not. Consider the forays against the Old Tavern, the crane, and the caboose, the incinerated car, and the brawling which broke out repeatedly on the field. If unhindered and undaunted, the hoodlum element sooner or later would have left the camping area and sought glory and reputation in new arenas, before new audiences. These seem to be people who need and seek the stimulation of collective action, excitement, and violence. Without it they become depressed and demoralized. They have an affinity for the romantic role of outlaw, which is perhaps the only status in which they feel they can stand out as individuals.

STRATEGY AND LUCK

Four factors were critical in preventing the spread of violence:

Most important was the general police policy of strength, fairness, and neutrality, which influenced all the tactics employed. Law violations were dealt with immediately and firmly, but motorcyclists were not harassed or deliberately antagonized. The availability of overwhelming force, literally on a moment's notice, was demonstrated but not overdramatized. Thus potential mob leaders were deprived of the rallying point of "police brutality," and potential followers never developed the sense of mob power that results from evidence of police weakness.

The decision not to interfere with the motorcyclists who camped and drag raced on private property, until extreme violence impended, was also of critical importance, for several reasons. In the field the potential troublemakers were all contained in an open area where all their activities could be easily observed. They were segregated by the broad highway and differentiated from the much larger mass of spectators at the track, and thus deprived of both victims and audience. The amount of property vulnerable to damage was relatively small. Finally, they were allowed to occupy their time with activities which were both customary and satisfying (drinking, dragging, showing off, etc.) while not annoying other citizens. This business of "keeping them occupied" is not trivial. Mob action, except in a catastrophe, is usually preceded by a period of "milling," exchange of fact and rumor, and movement toward consensus. During such periods mob leaders can seize the initiative in directing the crowd toward specific objectives.

Another important factor was the continuous flow of intelligence both during the weekend and over the preceding weeks, important for helping break down police stereotypes as well as for its operational utility.

Plain and simple good luck favored us on several occasions. Undoubtedly there was an element of luck in the fact that the "hoodlum element" chose to remain at the campground rather than roam the county. The factional dispute between the short-haired locals and the "1-percenters" may have been fortunate in that it kept the warlike elements busy and precluded any alliance between the two groups. It was especially fortunate that when it finally became necessary to clear the field, most of the rowdier motorcyclists left the county entirely.

As it turned out we successfully avoided a general polarization of motorcyclists against police and the citizenry. We tried to apply in this situation the specialized knowledge and theory of our field, and found it useful. The police, logically, focus on the apprehension of persons who violate laws, protection of citizens from the acts of such persons, prevention of specifically violative behavior, and the deployment of strength in accordance with those goals. As social scientists we focused on the collection of data, the analysis of differences and similarities, the understanding of group and individual behavior, and the communication and exchange of fact and opinion. (The clarity with which these distinctions are drawn is not meant to deny that there are policemen who think like social scientists, and *vice versa*.)

Though the events of Labor Day, 1965, in Prince George's County were of little national or long-term import in themselves, we consider the principles applied and the lessons learned to have far broader relevance—a significant practice for things to come.

Social Control in a Broader Context

The relationship of social control to collective behavior is by no means limited to crowd control and riot prevention. Social control agencies are equally concerned with diffuse, more enduring forms. Controlling or terminating a compact crowd is a short-term, emergency operation. The protection of freedom of assembly and public discussion, the prevention of the spread and recurrence of riots, and the decision on how best to deal with social movements are matters of constant concern to governments. If a political regime strives to implement the principles of political democracy, its control efforts will be primarily directed towards protecting the freedom of public discussion and regulating, but not suppressing, social movements which seek to promote change through what are defined as legitimate means. As authoritarian tendencies increase, social control is directed more and more toward preventing any kind of collective behavior except conventional forms approved by the government.

As has been suggested before, the emergence of widespread collective behavior, reflecting hostility to the existing social order, such as a wave of riots, may be in part an indication that there is a weakening in the system of social control. The spread of such a general impression may lead to collective behavior by two types of people. On the one hand, those who are dissatisfied with their circumstances and are hostile to the authorities may be encouraged to express their discontent and to develop social movements which might threaten the existing regime. Concessions made to dissatisfied groups lead to even more demands, according to one theory, the theory of the "revolution of rising expectations."

On the other hand, people who feel threatened by the protests and the demands of the dissatisfied may engage in various forms of collective behavior. The editors of the report to the National Commission on the Causes and Prevention of Violence conclude:

Protective resistance to undesirable change has been a more common source of collective violence in America than "revolutions of rising expectations," however. For example, most ethnic and religious violence in American history has been retaliatory violence by groups farther up the socioeconomic ladder who felt threatened by the prospect of the "new immigrant" and the Negro getting both "too big" and "too close."[10]

Population segments which feel threatened by the prospect of social change may lose confidence in the ability or the willingness of the incumbent authorities to protect them. As a result they may become a source of recruits for social movements that promise to maintain order and preserve the status quo even at the cost of freedom. Threatened from two sides, the authorities may respond by strengthening the social control agencies. Many observers believe that the decline in frequency and magnitude of protest riots by blacks in the United States after 1968 resulted primarily from such an official response.

An alternative response is for the authorities to attempt to alleviate the conditions which contribute to riots and dissident social movements. Such positive control of collective behavior, by reform rather than repression, is a high goal, not easily attained. At the conclusion of its study of the ghetto riots of 1967, the National Advisory Commission on Civil Disorders advanced as its central recommendations reforms that would eliminate racial segregation and discrimination, re-

[10] Hugh D. Graham and Ted R. Gurr, *The History of Violence in America: A Report to the National Commission on the Causes and Prevention of Violence* (New York: Bantam Books, Inc., 1969), p. 805.

move feelings of powerlessness among disadvantaged groups, and improve communication across racial lines. Anticipating the opposition that their proposals would evoke, they described the dilemma which confronts the government of a democratic society and the middle course which they hoped the government night follow:

There are those who oppose these aims as "rewarding the rioters." They are wrong. A great nation is not so easily intimidated. We propose these aims to fulfil our pledge of equality and to meet the fundamental needs of a democratic civilized society—domestic peace, social justice, and urban centers that are citadels of the human spirit.

There are others who say that violence is necessary—that fear alone can prod the nation to act decisively on behalf of racial minorities. They too are wrong. Violence and disorder compound injustice; they must be ended and they will be ended.

Our strategy is neither blind repression nor capitulation to lawlessness. Rather it is the affirmation of common possibilities, for all, within a single society.[11]

11 *Report of the National Advisory Commission on Civil Disorders* (New York: Bantam Books, Inc., 1968), p. 413.

part three

IO

NATURE OF THE PUBLIC
AND PUBLIC OPINION

In the course of examining crowd behavior, we observed that many crowd processes can occur among widely dispersed individuals almost as effectively as among people in physical contact with each other. Collective behavior occurs in diffuse as well as compact collectivities. Chapter 7 was devoted to such diffuse crowd phenomena as fads, crazes, and deviant collective epidemics. Besides the diffuse crowd, there is another important form of diffuse collectivity—namely, the public. Publics incorporate the same elementary processes, such as milling and rumor, as crowds do. They also depend upon the mass media of communication and interaction nets. But publics are sufficiently different from other forms of collective behavior and sufficiently important in social stability and change for us to devote the next three chapters to their consideration.

The public, as a diffuse collectivity, should not be confused with the general public, referring to everybody. In our sense the public is much more specific. There are normally many distinct publics in any community or nation at a given time, and there are also many citizens who do not participate in any of these publics.

The public, as a diffuse collectivity, consists of persons in interaction and consequently must be something more than a mere audience or mass. *A public is a dispersed group of people interested in and divided about an issue, engaged in a discussion of the issue, with a view to registering a collective opinion which is expected to affect the course of action of some group or individual.*

As a basis for distinguishing the crowd from the public, Dawson and Gettys divide collective behavior into two types, "collective-emotional" and "collective-rational."[1] Such a distinction is difficult to apply, however, for at least three reasons. First, the rational can hardly be differentiated from irrational behavior without some judgment from the investigator concerning that which is logically correct, a definition which is prone to reflect cultural orientation. Second, rational and emotional are not polar concepts, since a person may become emotionally aroused when pursuing a rational course of action. Finally, rational forms of expression are used so extensively in the crowd, and emotional appeals are so much a part of the public, that the distinction does not seem to be the critical one.

A useful distinction can be found in the idea that the public is built about an issue. An issue is not merely a matter on which people disagree. It is a matter over which people acknowledge a *right* to disagree. The public, then, is distinguished from the crowd by the fact that interaction within it is governed by the assumption that disagreement, argument, and counterargument are legitimate. This does not mean that the other side is necessarily thought to have any worthwhile points, nor that members of the public will listen to the other side with any intention of testing their own position, nor that the appeals need even follow principally rational forms. But conceding the other man's "right to be wrong if he wants to be" keeps discussion open, restricts the public to registering an opinion rather than taking consummatory action, and makes the ascertainment of public opinion important to those concerned with the issue.

Definitions of public opinion used by students who are not chiefly concerned with collective behavior often stress the word *opinion,* leaving the term *public* as a rather unimportant modifier. In this sense public

opinion refers to opinion (1) as verbalization rather than action, (2) regarding a matter of concern to many persons, (3) about a controversial matter. Most students would further restrict the term to opinions which the individual is willing to give overt expression to. Under this general approach the fundamental unit for observation and measurement of public opinion is the individual expression. The group enters only implicitly with the assumption that interaction is an element in the formation of public opinion. Some writers speak of opinion toward a public object and can discuss the formation of public opinion as a process within a single individual. But public opinion more often refers to a summation of individual opinions. Thus public opinion becomes majority or preponderant opinion, or the distribution of support for alternative positions. A third group defines public opinion as statements that are actually made overtly in the presence of others as distinct from private opinion, which remains unspoken except to one's most intimate associates.

None of these conceptions introduces a collectivity as a necessary component. Only the existence of a mass is required in the first of these definitions. A bounded aggregate, i.e., a definite universe of persons not necessarily in interaction, is required in the second case, but no collectivity need be assumed. In the third instance some person-to-audience relation is assumed, but still there need be no collectivity.

Such definitions place public opinion within the study of the formation and expression of individual attitudes. For those primarily interested in group characteristics and processes, however, a different conception is necessary. For our purposes there is no public opinion without a public. We shall define public opinion as *that which is communicated to decision makers as a consequence of the functioning of a public.* Whether it consists of majority or diverse opinions, key individuals' opinions, or some

[1] C. A. Dawson and W. E. Gettys, *An Introduction to Sociology* (New York: The Ronald Press Company, 1948), p. 605.

other kind of summation depends on the organization of the public and the nature of the decision-making structure toward which it is directed.

ASPECTS OF THE PUBLIC. Nelson N. Foote and Clyde W. Hart have proposed that the processes within the public be viewed according to an idealized series of phases.[2] In the first or *problem phase* a group of people recognize their common situation as problematical and experience discontent. In the second or *proposal phase* a dominating sense that something has to be done leads to the advancement of many plans of action; some are rejected and others are accepted. During these first two phases the communication is only partially verbalized. There are vague feelings and gestures that are hardly recognized consciously by the participants themselves. During the third or *policy phase* there is explicit discussion revolving about the plans for action that have been selected in the preceding phase and culminating in group decision and responsible commitment. This phase prepares the way for the final or *program phase,* when the decision is converted into action. In a sense, with this phase the public as a collectivity is supplanted by an organized group—"a self-conscious organization of functionally differentiated persons cooperatively pursuing common objectives."[3] The authors suggest that there may also be a transitional phase that links the completed cycle to the beginning of a new cycle. This they call the *appraisal phase,*—new problems are defined covering the discrepancy between what was sought and what was attained.

In some situations these phases follow one another, but many publics exist about enduring problems that are in a continuous state of redefinition, with group decisions being registered and affecting programs continuously. Thus the phases are better labeled *aspects*; they occur simultaneously and continuously rather than cyclically, as in the usual public opinion situation.

EMPIRICAL PUBLIC AND DEMOCRATIC IDEAL. The reason for stressing the nature of the public as a collectivity is not to argue for one favored definition against others. The purpose is to offset a tendency to mistake our democratic ideal of public participation in policy determination for empirical reality. Publics do bring into operation some of the prevalent American ideals, and regulation and conventionalization of publics are often directed toward increasing the approximation to democratic procedure. But we must work with a conception of the public that is grounded in what we see happening rather than on what we wish to see happening.

Four values, incorporated in traditional democratic ideals, often shape the conception of how public opinion is formed. These values are *individualism, egalitarianism, persuasion,* and *objectivism.* Because Americans have traditionally been concerned with protecting the individual's integrity against the loss of his independence under group pressure and the loss of his separate identity in the group, we are inclined to think of public opinion as a simple sum of individual opinions, and of opinion change as the sum of individuals changing their minds. Egalitarianism often leads us to overlook the immensely unequal influence of some individuals at every stage of the public opinion process. The preference for persuasion over other methods for influencing others finds expression in the view of a public as people seriously arguing a substantive issue, each trying to convince others by intellectual discussion. This view overlooks the extent to which bargaining and coercion come into the public opinion process and the extent to which fear and the

[2] Nelson N. Foote and Clyde W. Hart, "Public Opinion and Collective Behavior," in Muzafer Sherif and M. O. Wilson, eds., *Group Relations at the Crossroads* (New York: Harper and Row, Publishers, 1953), pp. 308–31.
[3] Ibid., p. 316.

prospect of personal and group gain play a part. It also overlooks the extent to which alignments reflect conflict polarizations, the concern for peace and order, and other matters that are only fortuitously linked to the issue. Objectivism is an assumption that the real world of events produces the issues that publics debate. Objectivism keeps the student from seeing that the process *creates* the issue that is then debated. The issue is related to objective events, but it is characteristically only one of many different issues that might have been formulated to give meaning to the events.

Individuals are persuaded and do change their minds, and these changes do contribute to shifts in public opinion—though often these are merely compensating changes that cancel each other out. But the formation of public opinion as collective behavior focuses our attention on other ways in which it changes. Public opinion changes when (1) the issue is redefined and people discover themselves in different alignments without having changed their opinions on the first issue; (2) the alternative positions change and when the public expands or contracts; (3) the avenue for registering opinions changes, as between election and postelection periods; (4) the implications for group loyalties or for peace and order change; (5) group sanctions change so as to encourage or discourage the expression of certain private opinions; and (6) the legitimacy of the procedures by which public opinion was formed are evaluated. In the chapters on the public we shall examine several of these ways in which public opinion changes.

The Issue

The public is formed around an issue, and one of the fundamental processes within the public is the definition and change of the issue. Occasionally it is fixed in advance, but usually the public defines and redefines the issue in the course of its deliberations. Not all issues formulated by individuals are necessarily the subject of public opinion. The public rejects or ignores certain of them. When this happens an atmosphere is created where those who define the issue in a manner acceptable to the public can communicate intelligibly, and those who define it in other ways are thought to be confused, dealing with irrelevancies, and the like. *The issue, then, consists of those points about which people agree to disagree.*

From this point of view a major task in studying public opinion is to ascertain how the public defines the issue. When people are polled on a synthetic issue, i.e., an issue created in the laboratory, they are likely to provide misleading answers or answers that seem to shift rapidly and fortuitously.

When the public must register its opinion by electing a public official, the issues may not even be indicated. Errors arise in predicting the outcome of elections from incorrectly defining the issue. The accurate prediction by Louis Bean of the unexpected outcome of the 1948 presidential election, when Harry S. Truman was returned to office, led some persons to predict mistakenly a similar outcome in 1952. The error in prediction was probably caused by a shift in the predominance of particular issues. Thus people who had not changed their judgment of the economic issues may have felt that, in 1952, the Korean War and international issues were more important and hence shifted their vote to the Republican candidate.

Evidence of the constant shift in definition of issues is provided in a study of public opinion during the period leading up to American entry into World War II. Hadley Cantril has effectively pointed out that public opinion shifted in the direction of war not so much by the conversion of individuals from the antiwar to the prowar position as through a succession of issues, each of which aligned people progressively closer to war participation. This approach has at least two important implications. First, *many and perhaps most changes in public opinion consist of redefinitions of issues which group people differ-* ently. *And second, public opinion may change without equivalent change in the attitudes and opinions of individuals.*

Public Opinion in Flux

Hadley Cantril

John Adams once wrote that "public information cannot keep pace with facts." What was true in the early nineteenth century is not so true today. Our country is for the first time in a war during a period when the development of reporting and communicational facilities makes it possible for nearly everyone to keep pace with the facts. At least 90 per cent of us either have radios or read daily newspapers.

This familiar situation is more revolutionary than we may realize. Among other things, it means that public opinion in our democracy has become sensitized to events. We take it for granted that we shall be widely and instantaneously informed. And we take it for granted that the opinions we hold or evolve are important—for us and for the country of which we are a part. We, the people, feel and know that we have become more significant than ever before, with the narrowing of the barrier that separates "us" and our range of experiences from our elected representatives and their range of experiences.

This is also the first critical period in our Nation's history when it has been possible to determine rapidly what opinion is—a possibility Lincoln craved when he said just before the Civil War, "What I want is to get done what the people desire to have done, and the question for me is how to find that out exactly." The social scientist is, therefore, at last able to examine systematically the effect of events on a sensitive public. At the present time, data are being gathered more rapidly

From *The Annals of the American Academy of Political and Social Science,* 220 (March, 1942), 136–50. Reprinted in part by permission of The American Academy of Political and Social Science.

than they can be exhaustively analyzed. But the flux of American opinion since the outbreak of the war in Europe can at least be outlined.

THE ISSUES CHANGE

Under present conditions it is even more difficult than usual for us to look at the recent past with any perspective. Issues have changed with the march of events. We can recapture some impression of the war issues we faced at different stages of the conflict if we sample the answers to questions asked at six scattered intervals.

1. *Just before the outbreak of hostilities in Europe.* In the fall of 1938 most of us thought England and France had made a mistake when they gave in to Germany's Sudeten demands. We also thought at that time that the Munich agreement had increased the likelihood of a general European war. But in the bright summer of 1939 we refused to believe that the squabble over the Polish Corridor would cause a war, almost two-thirds of us saying there would be no major war in Europe during the next year. At the same time, however, the overwhelming majority of us who had opinions thought Hitler's claims to the Corridor were not justified.

The chief issue at that time was *whether or not we should sell war materials to England and France.* When we were asked what we *should* do if war broke out between England and France on one side and Germany and Italy on the other, we were about evenly divided on the question of selling food and war supplies to the democracies. Two-thirds of us believed that if we did sell war materials to England and France there would be little or no chance of our staying out of the war. When asked what we probably *would* do if a war broke out, about one-third of us thought we would remain neutral, one-fourth of us believed we would send troops to Europe, and almost half of us thought we would send war materials but no troops. When asked what side we wanted to see win if war should break out, 14 per cent of us had no opinion, 84 per cent of us voted for England and France, 2 per cent for Germany.

2. *The first two weeks after the outbreak of the European war.* During this period we harbored a complacent optimism. We wanted to watch and wait. The issue was still whether or not to help England and France by selling supplies. The great majority of us expected England and France to win the war; half of us believed the war would last one year or less. Slightly over half of us thought this country should sell supplies to the democracies, but if we did sell supplies, over 90 per cent of us thought we should be paid in cash. Almost half of us with opinions said at that time that if it looked as though England and France would be defeated in the next few months, we should declare war on Germany and send our troops abroad. But as further events showed, this opinion seemed based more on a remote sense of duty than on any sense of probable urgency.

3. *Month following French armistice.* We were aroused from our complacency with a horrified shock by the lightning successes of the German Army in the spring of 1940. Whereas fewer than half of us had thought we would be personally affected by a German victory before the conquest of France, by now two-thirds of us thought we would be affected. Our reaction was to turn our attention to our own defense. Approximately three-fourths of us were now saying that all able-bodied men should serve one year in the Army and that the National Guard should be called up for training. Most of us thought our defense production was inadequate.

Things looked dark on the Continent. We were not so sure of a British victory. The majority of us said it was more important for us to stay out of war than to help Britain. A majority of us were not in favor of sending food to Britain in our own ships. A majority of us felt we should try to have friendly trade and diplomatic relations with Germany if she won the war. The issue *now was*

whether or not we should give up our neutrality to help the British.

4. *Mid-fall 1940.* By late October, after the British demonstrated their capacity for resistance and after it became clear that the foreign policy of the Roosevelt Administration remained firmly set against appeasement and withdrawal, the question facing most people was *whether or not we should resist Hitler by aid to Britain short of war.* The emphasis shifted from a program of passive aid to Britain to a program of more active resistance to Nazi Germany. About half of us were now willing to let England borrow money to buy food and war supplies form this country. Over half of us were willing to send more planes to England, even though this might delay our own national defense program. Forty per cent of us with opinions were in favor of changing the Neutrality Law to permit American ships to carry war supplies to England.

5. *Late spring 1941.* After the Balkan invasion the issue was *whether or not to resist Hitler at any cost.* . . . Over half of us with opinions favored convoying ships to Britain. Over two-thirds of us approved the recent passage of the Lend-Lease Act.

. . . opinion varies when questions are stated under different contingencies, interventionist opinion vacillating from 78 to 8 per cent. . . . insofar as general objectives were concerned, two-thirds of us seemed definitely agreed that we should follow through with our aim of defeating Nazi Germany, even though this program seemed likely to involve us in war.

6. *Just before declaration of war.* By late November 1941 the question seemed to be *when will we fight?* Over 80 per cent of us thought we would get into the war in Europe; over two-thirds of us with opinions thought we would soon be at war with Japan. Seventy per cent of us said that if our present leaders and military advisers believed the only way to defeat Germany was for this country to go into the war, then we would go in. Approximately the same number thought it was more important to defeat Germany than to stay out of war. Almost a third of us now said we would vote to go to war against Germany if we had a chance to vote. Furthermore, we had a growing confidence

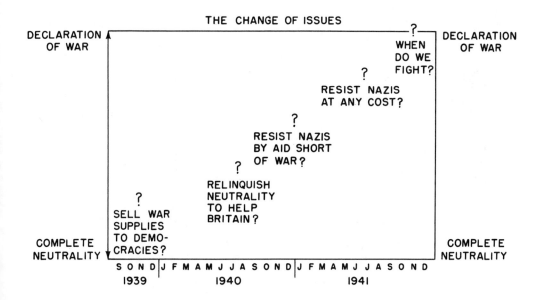

THE CHANGE OF ISSUES

DECLARATION OF WAR

?
WHEN
DO WE
FIGHT?

?
RESIST NAZIS
AT ANY COST?

?
RESIST NAZIS
BY AID SHORT
? OF WAR?

RELINQUISH
? NEUTRALITY
TO HELP
SELL WAR BRITAIN?
SUPPLIES
COMPLETE TO DEMO-
NEUTRALITY CRACIES?

DECLARATION
OF WAR

COMPLETE
NEUTRALITY

S O N D | J F M A M J J A S O N D | J F M A M J J A S O N D
1939   1940   1941

FIGURE 1   How public opinion stepped to war

in the armed forces of our side. Over four-fifths of us said Germany would lose the war. Only 5 per cent thought Germany would win. Of the great majority of us who thought Germany would lose the war, over two-thirds believed Germany would be brought to her knees only after our own Army, Navy, and air force had joined the fight. We were practically unanimous in saying that we could beat Japan. Eighty per cent of us were sure our Navy could beat the Japanese Navy.

This change of issues through time, leading step by step from complete neutrality to a declaration of war, is diagrammed roughly in Figure 1.

TRENDS OF OPINION

Since the social context changes so rapidly with events, questions that make sense one week may be meaningless the next. It is therefore difficult to frame many questions which can be repeated over a considerable period of time for trend purposes.

But some questions have been appropriate since the beginning of the war in Europe, and others have been repeated for shorter intervals. Some of these trends of opinion are shown in Figures 2, 3, and 4.

In general, these diagrams tell their own dramatic story. However, a few observations are noteworthy.

1. The ups and downs in the diagrams, especially Figure 2, show beyond any shadow of doubt that public opinion is sensitive to events.

2. The curve most sensitive to the course of events is that indicating which side people think will win the war. Here wishes are most closely related to opinion. Also, the average man has little solid and long-time strategic information on which to base his judgments. When separate trend curves of expectation are made by economic class, there is clear indication that persons of the upper income groups are more vacillating in their opininons than persons in the low income group The relationship

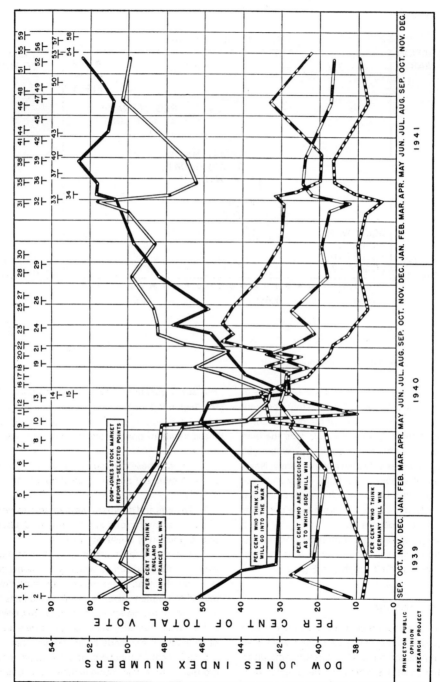

FIGURE 2

186

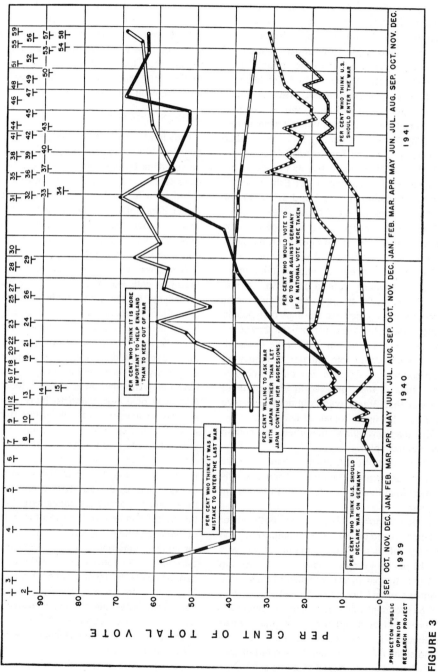

PER CENT OF TOTAL VOTE

PER CENT WHO THINK IT IS MORE
IMPORTANT TO HELP ENGLAND
THAN TO KEEP OUT OF WAR

PER CENT WHO THINK IT WAS A
MISTAKE TO ENTER THE LAST WAR

PER CENT WILLING TO ASK WAR
WITH JAPAN RATHER THAN LET
JAPAN CONTINUE HER AGGRESSIONS

PER CENT WHO WOULD VOTE TO
GO TO WAR AGAINST GERMANY
IF A NATIONAL VOTE WERE TAKEN

PER CENT WHO THINK U.S.
SHOULD ENTER THE WAR

PER CENT WHO THINK U.S. SHOULD
DECLARE WAR ON GERMANY

SEP. OCT. NOV. DEC. JAN. FEB. MAR. APR. MAY JUN. JUL. AUG. SEP. OCT. NOV. DEC. JAN. FEB. MAR. APR. MAY JUN. JUL. AUG. SEP. OCT. NOV. DEC.

1939   1940   1941

PRINCETON PUBLIC
OPINION
RESEARCH PROJECT

FIGURE 3

between the curve representing those who think England will win and the unadjusted Dow-Jones Stock Index is close but not surprising. Again if their upper income people are separated out, expectations are found to approximate more closely the trends in the Dow-Jones Index.

3. During the early period of the "phony" war, most Americans felt that we would not become involved. When hostilities began, however, more people thought we would be drawn in, but this expectation suddenly dropped when it seemed too late to help. Since late summer 1940, the number predicting our entrance has steadily risen.

4. A close relationship between our desire to help Britain and our expectation of a British victory is seen by comparing Figures 2 and 3. We do not like to bet on a loser, even if he is a friend.

5. The American people easily decided to resist Japanese aggressions. There have been no signs of appeasement on the part of public opinion.

6. The higher number of people (shown in Figure 3) who would "vote to go to war against Germany" than who thought we "should enter the war" was due chiefly to the fact that people were more willing to go to war if they felt they could personally play some part in making the decision.

7. The American people did not change their opinion concerning Britain's war aims. Approximately a third of them believed at the beginning of the war that Britain was fighting to preserve democracy. This figure remained constant.

8. The diagrams show the effect of certain events. For example:

a) The signing of the German-Italian-Japanese Pact of late September 1940 did not scare Americans away from their policy of aid to Britain at the risk of war.

b) During October 1940, when both major Presidential candidates were minimizing the probability of actual intervention, there was over a 10 per cent drop of those who favored aid to Britain at the risk of war and also of those who thought we would become involved in the war.

c) The President's fireside talk of December 29, 1940 increased by about 8 per cent the number who thought it was more important to help England at the risk of war than to keep out of war. If this talk had been sustained by some action, the rise in opinion might easily have held.

d) The effect of Russia's entrance into the war was to lift American optimism concerning the war's outcome and to decrease slightly the number of people who thought we would enter the war. After Russia was invaded, there was a slight increase of those who thought it was more important to aid Britain than to stay out of war. Hitler's talk of his Holy War against Communism made no impression on the American people.

OPINION AND POLICY

Early in May 1941 the Gallup poll first asked the question "So far as you personally are concerned, do you think President Roosevelt has gone too far in his policies of helping Britain, or not far enough?" ... In spite of the fact that United States aid to Britain constantly increased after May, the proportion of people who thought the President had gone too far, about right, and not far enough remained fairly constant.

This does not mean, however, that even a President with Roosevelt's popularity could have carried the 50 per cent middle-of-roaders as he did with any radically different policies than those he actually pursued. It seems almost certain that the majority of the American people, with access to news telling them of totalitarian aggressions and of our own state of preparedness, would never have followed either an appeasing Roosevelt or a Roosevelt obviously trying to hurry us into war. A close examination of poll results does show, however, that since the late spring of 1941 the public has been considerably ahead of the President's official stated policy. For example, if instead of using the President's name in the question above, the question is changed to "So far as you personally are concerned, do you think the United States has gone too far in its policies of helping Britain, or not far enough," the "not far enough" alternative generally draws about 32 per cent of the vote, instead of the usual 20 per cent when the President's name is mentioned. If the President had chosen to "get us into war" somewhat faster, there is every evidence that he could easily have done so. The public was half waiting for a push from its leader. The reverse may also have been true.

Anyone who has followed public opinion through the polls or any other systematic device

TABLE 1 Comparison of Public Opinion and Congressional Legislation

	Public Opinion		
	Per Cent of Those with Opinions Who Voted "Yes"	Date	When Passed by Congress
Repeal arms embargo	50	8–17–39	11– 3–39
Make war supplies available to democracies on noncash basis	52	5–14–40	3–11–41
Conscript man power	50	5–14–40	8–28–40
Use U.S. Navy to convoy supplies	53	4–25–41	11–13–41
Use American ships and crews to carry supplies	55	10– 1–41	11–13–41

knows that since the outbreak of World War II, the common man in this country has been ahead of his Congressman in urging more aid to Britain and her Allies. The complete record cannot be given here; but in Table 1 are listed at random some of the more important issues that have come before Congress, together with the dates on which at least 50 per cent of the people who had opinions voted for implementation of the interventionist program indicated. In every case it will be seen that Congress lagged behind the people—sometimes ten months, sometimes only one month, an average of about four months on our small sample. The figures err, of course, on the conservative side, since the polls did not tap opinion each week during the period when people were making up their minds.

With respect to Japan, the record shows that by late March 1941, 60 per cent of the total population wanted to stop Japanese aggressions at the risk of war, and as early as June 1938, over three-fourths of the total population favored an embargo on all war supplies to Japan—an embargo finally put into effect by the President more than three years later.

SOME CHARACTERISTICS OF OPINION

The trend charts and the national averages reported refer only to the *direction* of opinion. As we have already noted, the general orientation of opinion was set before the war began—only 2 per cent of us said we wanted Germany to win. To learn how we got more specific directives and to appreciate the dramatic climax of opinion with our entrance into World War II, it is therefore

necessary to see what other dimensions of opinion were operative.

Intensity. Changes of opinion depend in part upon how strongly people hold their opinions—how convinced they are of their beliefs. For a number of reasons, this dimension of intensity is difficult to measure in large population. What measures we have made are at least consistent with one another, and show that by and large, the ratio of "strongly" held to "mildly" held opinion was greater among interventionists than among noninterventionists (Figure 4). They also show a progressive increase in the intensity of interventionist opinion. With the possible exception of the brief critical period in midsummer 1940, it would have been consistently more difficult for interventionists than for noninterventionists to reverse their opinions.

Stability. The stability of opinion is essentially a measure of both the direction and the intensity of opinion at different times and under different circumstances. It is readily tested with polling devices by the use of split but comparable samples of the population, each of which receives questions biased in various directions. The results of many such tests indicate that opinion concerning war aims and objectives has been stable since the spring of 1941—the majority of us were convinced that the Nazis had to be defeated; however, opinion concerning the instrumentation of these aims, or opinion on topics which the common man knew little about or had little interest in, has been relatively unstable. Two examples of the stability of opinion concerning war aims may be cited. In both these instances, biased wordings produced no differences in results.

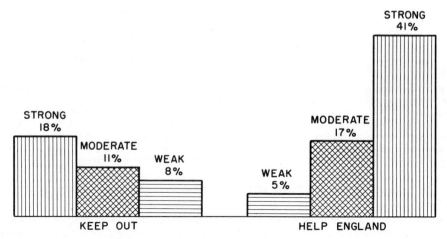

FIGURE 4 Intensity of opinion

Question: "Which of these two things do you think is the more important for the United States to try to do—to keep out of the war ourselves, or to help England win, even at the risk of getting into the war?"

	April 25, 1941:	Keep out	37%
		Help England	63%

In April 1941 the Fortune poll reported results on a number of questions deliberately biased in opposite directions when asked of two populations (A and B below) but asked in a straightforward way of a third comparable population (C below).

Population A:

Hitler will never be satisfied unless he dominates the U.S. because it is the richest country in the world.

Agree	68.3 per cent
Disagree	22.8 per cent
Don't know	8.9 per cent

Population B:

Hitler is only interested in making Germany a powerful nation in Europe, and talk about his wanting to dominate this country is just British propaganda.

Disagree	68.0 per cent
Agree	21.3 per cent
Don't know	10.7 per cent

Population C:

Do you think that Hitler wants to dominate the U.S.?

Yes	69.3 per cent
No	23.0 per cent
Don't know	7.7 per cent

July 1941 the Office of Public Opinion Research asked the following questions of comparable sample populations:

Population A:

Some people say that since Germany is now fighting Russia, as well as Britain, it is not as necessary for this country to help Britain.

Agree	20.2 per cent
Disagree	72.4 per cent
No Opinion	7.4 per cent

Population B:

Some people say that since Germany will probably defeat Russia within a few weeks and then turn her full strength against Britain, it is more important than ever that we help Britain.

Agree	71.0 per cent
Disagree	18.9 per cent
No Opinion	10.1 per cent

Breadth. A third dimension of opinion is its inclusiveness, or generality. We want to know if a person's attitude toward one problem has any bearing on his attitude toward another problem. Is one opinion merely something to which a person has become conditioned, or is it something related to a larger mental context? By and large, as we should expect, opinions concerning the war form consistent patterns, indicating that the various opinions in a common pattern trace back to the same roots or standards of judgment.

The way opinions hang together is illustrated in Table 2. If the opinion pattern of the "Keep Out" group is compared to the pattern of the "Help England" group, the significance of each becomes more apparent. Particularly noteworthy in this table is the fact that interventionist or noninterventionist opinion appears entirely unrelated to the presence or absence in the family of men of military age.

Depth. For the psychologist concerned with motivation, the most fascinating chapters in the story of public opinion during the war are those which trace different opinions of different people back to their basic determinants. From what comprehensive frames of reference are opinions derived? What are the bases of these frames of reference? How are opinions related to the ego? Each psychologist will explore the dimensions of depth according to his own conceptual framework.

We cannot describe this search for determinants here, but it is vital for us to record in the story of opinion flux the rationale behind opinions before this country became a partner in the shooting war. . . . Three conclusions stand out especially from [a classification of] the chief reasons people gave in June 1941 for thinking it was more im-

TABLE 2 Relationship of Opinions

Other Opinions		"Which of these two things do you think is more important for the United States to try to do: To keep out of war ourselves, or To help England win, even at the risk of getting into the war?" (3–12–41)	
		Keep Out (Per Cent)	*Help England* (Per Cent)
National Total		32	68
Any men in family between 16 and 36?	Yes	66	66
	No	34	34
Willing to fight or have family member fight?	Yes	33	75
	No	62	20
	No Opinion	5	5
If Germany defeats England will she attack U. S. in next ten years?	Yes	33	75
	No	54	19
	No Opinion	13	6
If England falls, will Germany control trade?	Yes	32	73
	No	53	21
	No Opinion	15	6
Was it a mistake for U. S. to enter last war?	Yes	66	26
	No	17	58
	No Opinion	17	16
Which side will win?	England	44	75
	Germany	20	12
	Neither	11	3
	Undecided	25	10
If Germany wins, will you be as free to do what you want as you are now?	Yes	52	24
	No	38	72
	No Opinion	10	4
If Germany wins, will we have to pay for strong defense and be poorer than we are now?	Yes	54	78
	No	35	16
	No Opinion	11	6

portant to try to keep out of war or to help England at the risk of war. . . . First, the great majority of people who favored an aid-to-Britain policy did so for hard-headed, realistic, selfish reasons. Second, noninterventionist attitudes were based primarily on traditional pacifist appeals, applicable to any war at any time. Third, the character of Britain's war aims was quite incidental in determining opinion.

In view of the nature of opinion as revealed by these dimensions, the increasingly belligerent interventionist answer of the American people to the course of world events is easily understood. Most of us were simply convinced that it was to our own self-interest to defeat the Nazis; this determination was so deeply rooted that it could not be sidetracked; our extensive news services and mass media of communication won our confidence and kept us so well informed that we became increasingly alert to the implications events and courses of action had for our self-interest. . . .

MATRIX OF ISSUES. Often it is an over-simplification to speak of a public as divided about an issue. Rather, the public is frequently organized about a matrix of issues that are conceived by the public as belonging together. In some instances there is a clearly defined hierarchy of issues; in others people are uncertain what they are supposed to be deciding; and sometimes there are factional definitions of issues.

Even when there is only slight disagreement over matters of substance, public opinion may be divided among sharply opposed groups because of differing definitions of the issue. The public which was concerned about the activities of Senator Joseph McCarthy and his investigations of un-American activities represented such a polarity, more in terms of issue definition than in terms of individual opinions. The anti-McCarthy group tended to define the issue as the preservation of free speech and thought against totalitarian inroads; consequently they defined the opposition as fascistically inclined. The pro-McCarthy group defined the issue as the protection of America from the fifth-column activities of an enemy power; hence, they regarded the opposition as being soft toward communism or unwilling to protect their nation from danger. On each side, those who saw the opposing arguments more clearly admitted some of the opponents' charges, but insisted that they did not bear on the most important issue. Thus, on one side a defender of freedom from "thought control" spoke of the necessary "calculated risk" of subversives in certain types of organizations. On the opposing side a pro-McCarthy speaker declared:

I was six months in the State Department, and I know how dirty they can play. It takes a dirty fighter to fight a dirty fighter. The junior Senator from Wisconsin has made a lot of mistakes but he has been pointing at the right thing.[4]

Alternative positions. Through discussion, the initially varied points of view concerning the issues are consolidated into a limited number of alternatives. Once this takes place it is difficult for an individual within the public to communicate any view other than one of those predefined. Each participant is assigned to one of the accepted divisions, and those who resist such classification are said to be confused and inconsistent. By such an attitude the public resists modification of its preestablished divisions.

The number of different positions that are recognized may be intrinsic to the issue or, more often, a function of the intensity of interest, the sense of urgency, and the type of action indicated. Within a public not marked by a sense of urgency, there are

4 From the files of R. H. Turner.

likely to be many positions which can be taken, but as a greater sense of urgency prevails, there is a tendency toward the consolidation of positions ultimately into only two opposing views. The public then treats all expressions as indicative of adherence to one of these two positions. A person who refuses to adopt either point of view completely is told to stop hedging, to come out in the open and reveal his true colors. This principle can be illustrated by contrasting the diversity of viewpoints regarding the toleration and recognition of Communist activity in the United States during the early 1930s to the polarization during the cold war period of the early 1950s.

Expansion and Contraction of the Public

Public opinion and deliberations within the public may change without alteration of existing alignments through the addition or new members or the withdrawal of old members. The public expands as more people become interested and enter into discussion of the issue. The public contracts as persons lose interest and cease to participate in the interaction.

The boundary of a public exists more as a theoretical construct than as an empirical reality. Mere interest and attention to communication do not necessarily constitute membership in a public. Studies indicate that many persons listened to enemy radio propaganda during World War II for amusement and because it provided interesting material for conversation but without ever taking the material seriously. On the other hand, these listeners included a proportionately large group who were inclined to be discontented with policies of their own government, suggesting that in some vague sense they may have exploring issues which they did not verbalize even to themselves.[5]

Nonvoting in elections can indicate lack of interest and hence noninvolvement in the public, or it can be an important way of registering a protest, expressing a desire to restructure the public. But nonvoting can also mean a defensive withdrawal from the public in response to cross pressures. Martin Kriesberg studied a labor union with Communist leadership and predominantly Catholic membership to see how cross pressures affected their attitudes toward Soviet-American relations. He found that union members who were most intensely subjected to the opposing positions of church and union expressed less interest in the question of Soviet-American relations than other union members.[6]

PUBLIC AND PRIVATE OPINIONS. Related to dropping out of the public is the suppression of doubts and questions about prevalent beliefs and practice. Edwin Paget identified several circumstances that contribute to rather sudden changes in public opinion;[7] we shall mention two. Conventional situations generally evoke formal but relatively meaningless responses. The prevalence of these formal responses, such as patriotic gestures, deference to established authority, and endorsement of values such as academic freedom and scientific objectivity, conveys the impression of overwhelming support. But many people experience private doubts while making their formalized responses. If these doubts accumulate, some event can bring them into the open and lead to abandonment of the formal responses and cause a radical change in public opinion.

Akin to the formal response is the inclination toward acquiescence. When opinions

---

[5] Henry Durant and Ruth Durant, "Lord Haw-Haw of Hamburg: His British Audience," *Public Opinion Quarterly,* 4 (September, 1940), 443–50.

[6] Martin Kriesberg, "Cross-pressures and Attitudes," *Public Opinion Quarterly,* 13 (Spring, 1949), 5–16.

[7] Edwin H. Paget, "Sudden Changes in Group Opinion," *Social Forces,* 7 (March, 1929), 440–44.

are not strongly formed, when the matter does not seem very important, or when friendships are involved, it is easier to say yes than to disagree. Like the formal response, this acquiescence is superficial and can be quickly reversed.

What people are saying or not saying, and the way they are saying it are crucial to the momentary state of public opinion. But the discrepancies between these expressions and the unstated thoughts and feelings become a dynamism leading to opinion change. This thesis has been elaborated by Tom Harrisson on the basis of a distinction between public and private opinion.[8] What a person says only to his wife, himself, or in his sleep constitutes his private opinion. What he will say to a stranger is public opinion. (It should be noted that public opinion is being used here as the opinions people will express as members of a public rather than as the effective opinion of a collectivity.)

Harrisson argues that private opinion is unlikely to become public opinion unless it has social sanction. Such sanction is provided by the support of a single prestigeful person or by the prestige of large numbers of less influential individuals. In the absence of such sanction, private opinion veers away from prevalent public opinion gradually. Then, when sanction is forthcoming, public opinion changes drastically, almost overnight. Those who have listened only to public opinion are shocked at the seeming fickleness of the public. Those who have been paying attention to more indirect and subtle indicators of private opinion will have been able to anticipate the change.

ACCESS AND RECEPTIVENESS. Most publics include fewer people than we might expect. Whether we take as indicator the large percentage of eligible citizenry

[8] Tom Harrisson, "What is Public Opinion?" *Political Quarterly,* 11 (October, 1940), 368–83.

who fail to vote in even the most hotly contested elections in the United States, or the substantial proportions of "no opinion" responses to any opinion poll, we probably overestimate the magnitude of the public. Many of those who vote and who comply with the pollster's request for an opinion have avoided participation in any exchange of opinions and have been quite unaffected by public debate. Every person or group who seeks to stimulate discussion and thought about an issue is confronted by the twin problems of access and receptiveness. These are the indispensable preconditions to the development and enlargement of publics.

All effective influence obviously depends on gaining access to the group to be influenced. Many of the problems in this connection are entirely technical matters, having to do with the coverage of any particular medium of mass communication. Recurrent questions deal with the relative merits of a few major appeals as contrasted to a large number of brief appeals. Will the political candidate, for example, gain a better hearing by having one or two spectacular television rallies or by a large number of brief "spot" announcements? The problem of reaching specialized audiences, and the merits of mass appeal as opposed to selective appeal, confront the advertiser or propagandist. When promoting a school bond election, for example, in which only a minority can be expected to take the trouble to vote, the problem of access is not the number of persons reached but rather the number of parents—the persons directly affected—who can be reached. Or when promoting a measure to benefit the underprivileged, the key problem may be how to get to those who neither read a newspaper nor listen to political discussions but who constitute the potentially strongest body of supporters. The problem of access also includes the question of whether to make a mass appeal or to reach key persons who can then be expected to influence others. In advertising it may sometimes be more important to sell to a recognized fashion leader than to try to sell directly to the masses.

The second condition determining the effectiveness of manipulative efforts is the receptiveness of the mass toward the proposed course of action or thought. In the mass, the receptiveness is that of the individuals, since individuals must decide and act. While the statement that a propagandist can convince people only of what they already believe is too extreme, manipulatory activities must take advantage of at least partial readiness to act in the indicated direction.

Receptiveness is compounded of *interest, motivation,* and *understanding.* Without interest there is no attention to the communications. Without motivation, verbal assent will not be followed by action. Fund drives for various worthy causes are particularly likely to encounter verbal acceptance without being able to dislodge people from a state of normal passivity.

Robert Merton, on the basis of interviews, has shown the importance of guilt feelings in motivating people to buy bonds during the Second World War.[9] Those persons who already felt some guilt over the paltriness of their own contributions to the war effort were led by the appeal to contrast themselves sharply with others who were making very great sacrifices. The intensification of preexisting guilt feelings provided the motivation to make them buy bonds.

Receptiveness toward any proposed course of action or thought also includes the ability to "get the point" of the communication. The recipients must possess the frame of reference necessary for understanding the message. Eunice Cooper and Marie Jahoda have clearly demonstrated how the entire theme of a communication can be completely distorted when the recipient does not share the communicator's frame of reference.[10] For example, a cartoon showing a man in a hospital bed announcing to the doctor that he wants only "sixth generation American blood" for his transfusion is intended to show the ridiculousness of racial and nationalistic prejudices. But one prejudiced man to whom the cartoon was shown questioned whether the cartoon subject was really of the best blood himself and treated the episode as false pretensions by a parvenue, thus missing the point altogether. Deeply prejudiced individuals consistently found other meanings than the one intended or confessed inability to see any point to the cartoon. Psychological defenses protected them from grasping a message that reflected unfavorably on themselves, and more familiar modes of thought guided them in whatever meanings they managed to assign.

DISSIPATION AND TRANSFORMATION OF PUBLICS. Except when issues undergo steady revision and events keep interest alive, the public dwindles rapidly or is transformed into other units. When interests are stabilized, a public often gives way to a number of organized groups with embryonic traditions, engaged simply in bargaining for competitive advantage. When alignments on issues become relatively fixed, conventions against open discussion of controversial questions usually arise. Thus discussion of politics and religion is regarded as poor manners. If each person makes up his mind in private and registers his vote in secret, tempers are not likely to flare and mar social occasions, and hurt feelings are avoided. The resulting behavior exhibits more characteristics of the mass than of the public.

[9] Robert K. Merton et al., *Mass Persuasion* (New York: Harper and Row, Publishers, 1946).

[10] Eunice Cooper and Marie Jahoda, "The Evasion of Propaganda: How Prejudiced People Respond to Anti-propaganda," *Journal of Psychology,* 23 (January, 1947), 15–24.

While enduring issues tend to destroy the public by turning it into organized groups or causing mass behavior, intense issues frequently convert the public into a crowd. On the one hand, intense convictions provoking intolerance transform the public into separate crowds corresponding with each preexisting faction. When one faction refuses to let the other be heard, employs physical violence, or in any way refuses to tolerate other positions, the public has ceased to exist. On the other hand, an event may eliminate the issue as a point of controversy and unite the entire public in a single intolerant group. Such was the consequence of the Japanese attack on Pearl Harbor in 1941. What had been a deeply divided public, concerned with the issue of America's involvement in the war, became a gigantic diffuse crowd intolerant of any who questioned the necessity for active retaliation and defense.

The public is only likely to retain its vitality when one of its factions generates a social movement, which then sustains interest and discussion of the issue. Whenever the original issue is of vital and growing concern, like-minded people who have discovered and formulated their common concerns by participating together in a public will attempt to stabilize and implement their values by forming a social movement. The many conditions that determine whether their effort leads to a fully developed movement will be discussed in later chapters.

Public Opinion as a Normative Phenomenon

The familiar instances of public opinion are more institutionalized and conventionalized than the better-known instances of crowd behavior. We should not understate the importance of the spontaneous development of a public, such as that which debated the future of offshore oil drilling after southern California beaches were polluted and wildlife killed in vast numbers by a massive oil leak in 1969. Nor should we discount the unpredicted swings in public opinion. But even when they are spontaneous and volatile, most publics function within a more conventional and socially accepted pattern than crowds. This is true for at least three reasons.

NORMATIVE FOUNDATION OF PUBLICS. First, the public is founded on trust in a way that crowd behavior is not. There must be trust in the decision makers—that they will listen to public opinion and take it into account. Without this confidence, efforts to form and influence public opinion are futile and some kind of direct action is the normal course. There must also be trust that others will limit themselves to participating in the public and not circumvent the process by employing direct action. Suspicion that one faction plans a *coup d'état* or that ballot boxes will be stuffed destroys the relevance of public discussion and shifts attention toward means of counteraction. And there must be trust in the mutual tolerance of disagreement. Once the adoption of a set of opinions becomes the reason for social ostracism and economic reprisal, as in the case of denying employment because of membership in the Communist party, the possibilities of maintaining a public concerned with related issues are grossly limited.

All of these forms of trust refer to acceptance of a set of understood or stated rules. Trust in the decision makers means that they are believed to be guided by a set of rules that require their attention to public opinion. Without such rules, there can be no such trust, and there is no real occasion for public opinion. Lang and Lang observe that "a public opinion situation exists whenever in a large society, where action requires some implied consent, the decision makers are guided by some assessment of public opinion before they act."[11] The long and important part that public opinion has played in American history reflects a persistent belief in rules and a lasting conviction that leaders do listen. The rising importance of demonstrations, as a way of registering public opinion during the 1960s, indicates continuing confidence that rules can be effective, coupled with a growing conviction that more conspicuous and forceful means are required if the public is to be heard. The rising incidence of direct action during this same period, as in the early 1930s, expresses growing doubts that decision makers are listening to publics, except those they choose to hear.

Trust that others will not circumvent public opinion by direct action depends upon confidence in a moral order. Public opinion in a vital sense only exists in a well-regulated society. It is quickly replaced by a patchwork of crowd actions when anomic conditions set in.

Trust that one will not be penalized for the opinions expressed depends on either or both of two essential conditions. If there are strong enough bonds holding people together, they will develop working accommodations in spite of differences. In a closely knit family the personal bonds and economic interdependency supply incentives for accepting differences. At work and in the community, more impersonal forms of interdependency facilitate mutual tolerance. But public opinion in the vast metropolitan community and the modern nation increasingly involves groups whose need for each other is not readily apparent. Hence publics depend more and more on belief in the tolerance of dissent.

A second reason why publics are more conventionalized than crowds is that they link people and groups who are not in direct interaction. In this respect the public is like the diffuse crowd, operating through various linking groups and through common attention to the mass media. We shall discuss these linkages in greater depth in the next chapter. But communication that goes beyond the range of face-to-face contact depends largely upon the availability of preestablished channels of communication.

Third, there must be some common acknowledgment of a procedure for registering public opinion. The crowd acts directly, and something is tangibly different after it has finished. But the public generates only opinion, and nothing is different unless opinion is registered in a significant manner. Debates over just what public opinion is on any given issue will inevitably continue. But institutionalized procedures for registering public opinion permit some focus of attention as a basis for organizing the public.

A public is necesarily shaped by the manner of registering public opinion toward which it is oriented. If public opinion is to be registered through the secret ballot, the efforts of partisans within the public will be directed toward getting the maximum number of individuals to vote. If it is to be registered through testimony before a congressional committee, the emphasis is more likely to be on securing organizational representation buttressed by convincing evidence of public support. If public opinion is to be registered through informal influence on official decision makers, the inclusion of respected people in the public is crucial.

The existence of a public is dependent upon an awareness that there are effective ways to register public opinion. In a book entitled *The Phantom Public,* Walter Lippmann suggests that "the private citizen today has come to feel rather like a deaf spectator in the back row, who ought to keep his mind on the mystery off there, but cannot quite manage to keep awake...He lives in a world which he cannot see, does

11 Kurt Lang and Gladys Engel Lang, *Collective Dynamics* (New York: Thomas Y. Crowell Company, 1961), p. 385.

not understand and is unable to direct."[12] As the conviction becomes general that nothing can come of public discussion, interest drops, activity subsides, and publics, as we have defined them, disappear. There may be unfocused discussion and random complaining, but there will be few genuine publics entering into discussion with a purpose.

In the analysis of public opinion, avenues of expression other than the ballot have seldom been explored. Herbert Blumer calls our attention to the importance of other modes of expression.[13] Even when questions are supposed to be settled by public election, public opinion occurs during the period when decision makers try to identify the issues upon which public decision hinged. At this point, representatives of organized groups play a major role, and the individual is able to express himself only through organizational membership.

The necessity for a recognized way of registering public opinion and the ease with which unregulated publics turn into crowds suggest that there must be a culturally based conception of the public and of public opinion before it can become a force in the determination of public policy. The image of the public will affect participation in it. Whether union members talk to each other or to their leaders will be affected by their understanding of public opinion. Is it the cumulation of individual opinions or the expressed views of organizational spokesmen?

Conceptions of the public are crucial for judgments regarding the legitimacy of public opinion. Variant conceptions of it are at the heart of arguments over whether periodic demonstrations give legitimate indica-

12 New York: The Macmillan Company 1930, p. 13.
13 Herbert Blumer, "Public Opinion and Public Opinion Polling," *American sociological Review,* 13 (October, 1948), 542–49.

tions of public opinion. The silent majority or silent minority are those who rely chiefly on the ballot and do not participate in demonstrations. Whether demonstrations are accepted as legitimate indications of public opinion depends upon whether the public is conceived of as persons having a stake in decisions or just persons taking part in some activity. Conceptions of public opinion vary with respect to the amount of threat and bargaining that are acceptable. Expressions of public opinion are often rejected when it is suspected that self-interest or fear played a great part. There is undoubtedly much variation by social strata and in different cultures, but these have not been extensively investigated. More knowledge of these conceptions would help us to understand the cultural foundations in the formation of public opinion.

EMERGENT NORMS. We have stressed an established normative structure as the precondition to the development of publics. But publics, like crowds, generate situational norms. The emergent norm approach, which we employed in the analysis of crowd behavior, also applies to publics. We have pointed out that the public operates to define (1) the issue about which people disagree and (2) the alternative positions that people can take with respect to the issue. These definitions are truly normative. Failure to conform by not accepting the defined issue or not identifying with one of the recognized positions is punished by exclusion from discussion and other severe penalties. These definitions are like the rules of the game that players agree upon before the sporting event. Like the emergent norms in crowds, they are related to cultural and organizational factors in the community. The specific issue and alternatives develop in the public and become binding on participants until the public subsides or until a new issue definition displaces the first.

THE PUBLIC AND COMMUNITY STRUCTURE

One could imagine a public resulting from an undifferentiated mass and developing a unique structure simply because of an urgent, universal problem, which requires collective action. But we are unlikely to find a public that has not borrowed its organizational structure from the patterns already present in the society. Therefore a realistic understanding of how public opinion is formed cannot be gained without careful attention to the ways in which the prior organization of the community affects processes in the public. As Herbert Blumer observes, "public opinion gets its form from the social framework in which it moves, and from the social processes in play in that framework; also...the function and role of public opinion is determined by the part it plays in the operation of the society."[1] In this chapter we shall consider four aspects of the way community structure affects processes in the public. First, communication takes place along lines determined by the nature and linkages of preexisting face-to-face groups. Second, the dynamic force behind the formation of public opinion is supplied by interest groups. Third, the mass media of communication are more than simply neutral pathways for the spread of information and opinion. And finally, recurring publics are

[1] Herbert Blumer, "Public Opinion and Public Opinion Polling," *American Sociological Review*, 13 (October, 1948), 543.

conventionalized with the result that they articulate smoothly within the community.

Communication Networks

Because public opinion is formed on a larger scale than collective opinion in compact groups, it cannot be formed without extended interaction chains. These chains are organized into complex communication networks. They do not simply link individuals; they link clusters of individuals who are already organized into families, friendship cliques, work groups, recreational clubs, political cells, and innumerable other groupings. The metaphor of a tangled web is more accurate than the chain, since linkages cross and recross so that there is constant recirculation of information and opinion. One essential step to understanding the formation of public opinion is to explore what happens as information, query, and opinion circulate through these complex and often disorderly networks.

Melvin DeFleur and Otto Larsen report experiments using a simple distinction between *serial* (or chain) diffusion and *radial* diffusion. An eight minute tape-recorded speech on socialism was the initial message. In serial diffusion the solitary listener told a second person about the recording; the second person told a third; and the chain continued until a fifth person gave a final report. In radial diffusion the first person told four other persons separately. It was found that "when oral content is passed through chains, the number of original items tends to *decrease* with each successive retelling; and when the content is successively retold by one person, the number of items tends to increase."[2] The opportunity for the same person to repeat communications in the network (as compared with simple chains) augments the richness of communication. Undoubtedly it also strengthens confidence and facilitates thought about the message. Although the research setting and the use of university students were limited and artificial, other evidence confirms that people are more likely to adopt a new opinion or to act on the basis of new information after receiving interpersonal confirmation.

DIFFUSION THROUGH SOCIAL TIES. Even though it is difficult to trace the development of collective opinions, it has been possible to trace the diffusion of more tangible innovations. Coleman, Katz, and Menzel used prescription records to study diffusion of the use of a new drug, gammanym, among physicians.[3] It was possible to relate the date and the rate at which each physician first prescribed the drug with information about the doctor's professional and friendship associations. Five stages were identified in the diffusion sequence. The first persons to adopt gammanym did so more cautiously than later adopters. The innovators were those doctors most deeply enmeshed in *professional* relationships. Their wide range of exposure led them to hear about the new drug from several authenticating sources, and their close and extensive professional relationship gave them the group support necessary for innovating. The second group

to adopt the new drug was physicians who were less professionally involved but who were linked to several colleagues by friendship ties. Thus interpersonal linkages with other physicians were essential for early adoption of a professional innovation, but professional ties brought earlier adoption than friendship ties. In the next stage the sparse social ties of the more isolated doctors began to take effect. In these cases too, the investigators were able to demonstrate the part played by social ties by comparing the time of adoption within pairs of doctors linked by friendship and professional ties. The fourth stage included those doctors whose adoption of the drug seemed unrelated to the action of associates—persons whose actions reflected independent decisions. The final stage was one in which practically no further adoptions occurred.

It would be foolhardy to generalize this model to other situations prematurely. The situation is simpler than most public opinion settings because all the decisions were made by professionals, because it was possible to secure moderately objective evidence concerning the value of the drug fairly quickly, and because in this case the users seemed uniformly pleased with the results and continued to use the drug. But some parallels to the public opinion process can be hypothesized. (1) A new idea is tried out, and a collective opinion is reached most quickly by those persons who are seriously involved with the area to which the opinion applies. Coworker ties bring about the first diffusion; consequently there is likely to be a first definition of the issue within relevant work and organizational settings. (2) Friendship ties carry the opinion process beyond its original serious nexus. But since the issue has already been formulated and aired, the friendship ties have more to do with lining people up on different sides than with defining the nature of the issue. (3) By the time persons with loose or sparse social ties come into the public, the discussion is likely to be well structured already.

---

2 Melvin L. DeFleur and Otto N. Larsen, *The Flow of Communication: An Experiment in Mass Communication* (New York: Harper and Row, Publishers, 1958), pp. 46–47.

3 James S. Coleman, Elihu Katz, and Herbert Menzel, *Medical Innovation: A Diffusion Study* (Indianapolis, Ind.: The Bobbs-Merrill Co., Inc., 1966).

The foregoing extrapolation is suggested merely for comparison with the sequence in actual publics, when it can be observed. But the analogy is completed by noting that most doctors first heard of the new drug from standard commercial sources, but almost 90 per cent sought or waited for information from other sources before they actually prescribed it. Similarly, an idea, a problem, or an issue is first introduced to most people through the mass communication media. But before they take a firm stand or act on what they have heard, they seek information and confirmation through the direct personal channels at their disposal.

This practice of verifying communication by discussing it with someone else has been demonstrated in a rather different kind of diffusion situation. Project Revere was devised as a study to evaluate methods for communicating with a population in the event of any massive disaster that inactivated telephone, radio, and other media.[4] Leaflets with civil-defense information were dropped over selected communities from airplanes at controlled rates, and interviews were conducted after a suitable time to ascertain the extent and patterns in the diffusion of information. Leaflets were most often picked up by children and brought to adults. The investigators found it useful to distinguish between neutral communicators and others. Neutral communicators—the children—passed on the communication without interpretating or verifying the message. An adult who received the communication from a child was more likely to verify the message by discussing it with another adult than was an adult who first received the message from another adult. Interaction with a neutral communicator did not supply the necessary help and assurance to make an interpretation. Most people sought to discuss the communication with someone who could offer interpretation and confirmation.

Whether the relationships are those of colleagues, friends, or both, the pathways to public opinion consist of preexisting interpersonal relationships. Robert Park observed that "News circulates, it seems, only in a society where there is a certain degree of rapport and a certain degree of tension."[5] But stable interpersonal relationships always tie people into small groups of friends or family members. And it seems to be within these primary groups that the issues, information, and opinions are discussed, and viewpoints are crystallized. As each new item of information or viewpoint is fed into the networks by the mass media, individual members of the public turn to their primary groups for guidance and support in developing a firm conception of the situation and a firm opinion. Baur proposes three stages of increasing social complexity in the public opinion process: "an early stage of mass communication, a middle stage in which voluntary associations become involved, and a final stage in which political institutions are activated. At each stage, however, opinions are relayed through primary groups in which the content is sharpened and clarified."[6]

Baur further suggests that people bring matters into their primary groups for clarification specifically to resolve the ambiguities they feel because of conflicting viewpoints available to them in the community. The internal division of the public into factions creates "the stress of ambivalence...that induces people to seek clarification in primary relationships."[7] Baur believes that persons with firm opinions on the issue are unlikely to shift under the impact of primary group discussion, but that persons who seek relief from ambival-

---

[4] DeFleur and Larsen, *The Flow of Communication*, pp. 166–93.

[5] Robert E. Park, "News as a Form of Knowledge," *American Journal of Sociology*, 45 (March, 1940), 684.
[6] E. Jackson Baur, "Public Opinion and the Primary Group," *American Sociological Review*, 25 (April, 1960), 218–19.
[7] Ibid., p. 210.

ence are candidates for alignment according to the social pressures and supports operative within their primary groups.

OPINION LEADERS. The members of publics are unequal in their effect on the outcome of the opinion process. The general rule that the views of persons whose prestige and reliability are already well established in the community carry more weight than the views of others applies to public opinion. But Lazarsfeld, Berelson, and Gaudet, in a classic study of an election public in Elmira, New York, identified opinion leaders at all levels of the community and in all walks of life.[8] These opinion leaders are people from whom others ask advice. But they are also more interested in the election, seek more information, and consult with more people before forming their own opinions than the nonleaders do. Like the doctors who first used gammanym, they read and listen more to relevant mass media items. Because these opinion leaders pay close attention to the mass media and advise others in forming their opinions, it has become customary to speak of a two-step flow of communication. It goes from the mass media to the ordinary member of a public. As Katz summarizes the two-step flow, "influences stemming from the mass media first reach 'opinion leaders' who in turn, pass on what they read and hear to those of their everyday associates for whom they are influential."[9] Opinion leadership is fairly specific to the matter under consideration, and each opinion leader is especially exposed to those items in the mass media that are appropriate to his sphere of influence. This observation suggests that opinion leaders are persons believed to be more competent regarding the issues at hand than their friends—and in most cases they are knowl-

edgable. Others become opinion leaders because they personify certain values or know a particular person.

Arnold Rose has pointed out that there is another type who has none of these characteristics but who exercises undue influence because his location puts him in contact with people from different integrated groups. Rose calls these people *ecological influentials*.[10] The true opinion leader exercises influence because of his position of respect, but the ecological influential is important because he is the link between various groups. Examples are the bartender, the barber, the small-store clerk, the newspaper vendor, the garage mechanic, and the policeman.

SOCIAL CIRCLES. Groups that are easiest to recognize are those which are either compact or highly organized and institutionalized. But there are other less easily detected groupings that play an important part in forming public opinion. Georg Simmel calls attention to *social circles* as important intermediary units between the individual and the community.[11] The social circle is in many respects similar to the neighborhood and may take its place in serving some needs of city dwellers. Like the neighborhood, its members and leaders are not formally identified, and participation is not institutionalized. Interaction is *dense*—each member has other members as friends, though not all members know or are friends with all other members. Neighborhood membership is based on propinquity, but membership in a social circle is based on some common interests.

Charles Kadushin has rendered Simmel's conception more precise and applied it to a circle he calls Friends of Psychotherapy.[12]

---

[8] Paul F. Lazarsfeld, Bernard Berelson, and Hazel Gaudet, *The People's Choice* (New York: Duell, Sloan and Pearce, Inc., 1944).

[9] Elihu Katz, "The Two-Step Flow of Communication: An Up-to-date Report on an Hypothesis," *Public Opinion Quarterly*, 21 (Spring, 1957), 61.

[10] Arnold M. Rose, "The Ecological Influential: A Leadership Type," *Sociology and Social Research*, 52 (January, 1968), 185–92.

[11] Georg Simmel, *The Web of Group Affiliation*, tr. by Reinhard Bendix (New York: The Free Press, 1955).

[12] Charles Kadushin, "The Friends and Supporters of Psychotherapy: On Social Circles in Urban Life," *American Sociological Review*, 31 (December, 1966), 786–802.

Circle members have three distinguishing characteristics: they have friends outside of their families who have been to psychotherapists; they tell their selected friends that they are applying for psychotherapy, knowing that the response will be sympathetic and understanding; and they ask their selected friends for referrals. The circle consists of a large number of people who believe in psychotherapy and who have friends with similar beliefs. They discuss psychotherapy and trade advice regarding the need for therapy and the choice of a therapist. The circle constitutes a social unit because each member is linked, either directly or indirectly, to every other member by the vast number of friendship pair relationships within the circle.

Kadushin employs data concerning 1452 applicants to ten psychiatric clinics in New York in 1959 and 1960. Employing a statistical procedure known as latent class analysis he estimates that about 56% of the applicants could be identified as belonging to the circle. The most interesting difference between circle members and nonmembers was how they came to apply for psychotherapy. Members had generally received supporting comments, confirming what they already knew and constructively preparing them for psychotherapy. The others had often received unsolicited advice from persons they had annoyed and came to psychotherapy only under great pressure. Kadushin's data also located another circle that overlaps the Friends. About three-fourths of the Friends are culturally sophisticated, as indicated by their frequenting plays, concerts, museums, or art galleries; many of them belong to cultural circles in which such activities serve as the focus in the same manner that psychotherapy supplies the focus for the Friends.

This observation of overlapping circles is important in two respects. First, it suggests that one way to become a member of the psychotherapy circle is to meet members and hear psychotherapy discussed within another circle. And second, it indicates how the views that are developed in one social circle can escape the bounds of that circle and become public opinion.

Although the impact of social circles on issues of public opinion has not been traced in specific instances, it is probably great. Applying for psychotherapy is ultimately an individual act and so is a better example of behavior in a mass than in a public. But within the circle the merits of various kinds of psychotherapy and similar questions are discussed, and collective opinions are undoubtedly formed. If a public develops about an issue of public policy, such as whether to include psychiatric care within the coverage of Medicare, the circle will probably be the locus of intense and informed discussion. Opinions formulated among Friends of Psychotherapy will be widely heard in cultural circles because of the overlap. If no other important circles have specific interest in the issue, opinion may be formed for the entire public in this one circle and diffused through chains of overlapping circles. If there is another circle whose members are especially interested in the question, because of a different type of interest such as reducing taxes, the nature of the issue in the larger public may be established by the contrasting frames of reference between these two circles. The balance of the public may, in effect, be making a choice between the points of view developed in the two circles.

Interest Groups

An essential component has been omitted so long as we think of publics only as complex networks of small primary groups, large and more loosely connected circles, and collegial groups, sifting and interpreting communications from the mass media so as to define issues and align individuals and groups on the various sides of the issues. As Baur observes:

The public is not fully formed until those who believe they will be adversely affected mobilize and take issue with the initial proposal. The diverse interest groups within each faction are unified by alliances, *ad hoc* committees, or new integrating associations. As organizational problems within the interest groups attain solution, more attention is given to the uncommitted outsiders whose support is needed to achieve dominance in the controversy, and they are subjected to persuasion by means of propaganda and personal influence.[13]

Without attention to interest groups, which are normally present before the public develops but are modified and frequently crystallized in the public, we lose sight of the main dynamic force in publics.

In popular usage, *interest group* is a term of invective rather than a term of analysis. To so label a group is to condemn it as having ulterior motives. But everyone has ulterior motives in the sense of having preexisting conceptions in terms of which they view current issues. It is only from the vantage point of one interest group, which regards its own frame of reference as the only justifiable one, that the motives of other interest groups are labeled "ulterior."

In the broadest sense, interest groups are composed of people who consider a standing issue of such general and sustained importance that they assimilate current issues to this issue, rather than treating each question as unique. A group may be so committed to the cause of labor that members subordinate the consideration of any specific issue to the general question of whether their vote is prolabor or antilabor. Members might be inclined to examine an issue on its individual merits, or they may not see the relation of any particular issue to the interests of the group, so spokesmen play an important role in translating particular issues into interest-group terms.

All people belong to interest groups, but certain groups are more conspicuous in their operation than others. Such is the case of minority groups; each issue is frequently translated into its significance for minority-majority relations before a judg-

ment is made. With the tenuousness of the relation between many current issues and minority interests, there is abundant opportunity for minority leaders to manipulate blocs, either in terms of their honest assessment of the issues or in consideration of personal gain.

MOBILIZING INTEREST-GROUP CONSCIOUSNESS. We cannot assume that people will automatically form opinions or even define issues according to the self-interest they share as members of interest groups. This is so partly because most people belong to several interest groups, some of whose relationships to the issue are contradictory. Individuals have ideological commitments that are not easily abandoned merely because they run contrary to perceived group interest. Also, the more personal and particularistic influences in primary groups dilute whatever consistent effect interest-group membership might have. Furthermore, the relationship of an issue to group interest is not always noticed, and when noticed is not always in an obvious direction. For example, is a law to insure public accounting for labor union funds a pro or antiunion measure? Would it protect rank-and-file members from exploitation, or is it a device to harrass unions?

There is an endless trail of evidence against the assumption of a precise connection between interest-group membership and opinion. Exploring voting behavior in nineteenth-century England through the record left in pollbooks, J. R. Vincent is forced "to reject outright...the idea that classes were economically constituted groups acting for economic motives to effect change in the economic order...the belief that it was natural for the rich and poor to be on opposite sides, for economic reasons, was far more widespread than was such behavior in real life."[14] Vincent

---

13 Baur, "Public Opinion," p. 210.

14 J. R. Vincent, *Pollbooks: How Victorians Voted* (Cambridge, Eng.: Cambridge University Press, 1967), p. 30.

turned up some peculiar consistencies—a tendency for grocers to be liberal and butchers conservative—that are difficult to link up with interest-group attitudes. Even with the salience of racial identity and the active definition of racial interests by militant leaders, research indicates that the majority of blacks have not accepted the militant view that they should seek autonomy and separation rather than integration in the American community.[15]

Yet it would be an equal error to overlook altogether the long-range impact of class and racial consciousness. Vincent qualifies his conclusion by observing that "political art cannot undo what is elemental; it can not make a majority of those enjoying authority vote for its diminution, nor a majority of those without it habitually vote for their continued exclusion. Reason and education and other things produced Liberal landowners and Tory craftsmen in numbers: but never a secure majority of either."[16] And the record of three-quarters of a century's Republican voting by blacks, followed by their overwhelming support of the Democratic party after the New Deal period, underlines the potential impact of interest groups. Clearly the interest group that continues to be relevant to issue after issue can be of utmost importance. But members must be taught to identify with their group and to accept some standard definition of the group's interest in connection with any specific issue.

Reference-group theory leads to the presumption that not only the superficial expression of opinion but the genuine convictions of an individual are extensively affected by his group identifications. When a person's opinions are not those of the group, he feels ill at ease to the same extent that he identifies himself with the group.

To the degree that he feels the members of a group are "his kind of people," he will be inclined to accentuate those attitudes within himself that will permit him to hold the group opinion as his own. But the interest group must become a major identification group for the individual if its effect is to be felt.[17]

Problems of making the interest group into a prime identification group can be illustrated with youth. The age group is clearly an important interest group. In a nationwide survey of 718 men and women, aged 18 through 24, they were asked, "With which of the following groups, if any, do you feel a sense of solidarity and identification?" Sixty percent of noncollege youth and from 65 to 68 percent of college youth answered positively for "people of your generation." But 82 percent of noncollege youth and from 65 to 78 percent of college youth answered positively for "your family." Any simple determination of opinion by age-group identification is likely to be diluted by family loyalty. For the noncollege youth there is a conflict of even greater interest. Only 23 percent answered positively for "students" (72 to 75 percent in the case of college students).[18] Students are, however, the interest-group leaders, who define the group interest and mobilize the members. So long as more than half the youth fail to identify with the leaders of their age group, they are unlikely to be effectively mobilized to participate in publics based primarily on their age-interest group.

In the case of persons who fail to approach issues on the basis of an interest-group consciousness, efforts must be devoted to make them receptive before mobilization can be attempted. Efforts may also be necessary to stir people up so that

---

[15] Raymond W. Mack, "The Negro Opposition to Black Extremism," *Saturday Review*, 51 (May 4, 1968), 52–55.
[16] Vincent, *Pollbooks*, p. 32.

[17] Ralph H. Turner, "Role Taking, Role Standpoint, and Reference Group Behavior," *American Journal of Sociology*, 61 (January, 1956), 316–28.
[18] "What They Believe: A Fortune Survey," *Fortune*, 79 (January, 1969), 71.

they will contribute to an effective public. Frequently these efforts to persuade people to listen and become ardent advocates are referred to as *agitation*.

Two important elements of agitation are generally found. First, it is concerned with motivation—the arousal of feelings—more than with the promotion of a particular belief. Propaganda and similar terms connote persuasion to a particular point of view or plan of action, while agitation connotes excitement and arousal. Indeed, agitation may arouse people to a danger, alert their suspicions, or convince them of the necessity for drastic action, even while strengthening quite antithetical programs.

Second, agitation tends to be negative in emphasis, creating, reinforcing, or redirecting discontent. To say that agitation is negative does not mean that it is only negative or destructive in its consequences. It is the sense of discontent that makes the individual receptive to a program of change, that makes him listen to reform programs as more than an intellectual game or a self-righteous broadmindedness. The well-ingrained sentiments in support of the established order override the arguments for reform unless these sentiments are already weakened through dissatisfaction.

Attempts to create a sense of urgency, which is necessary if a public is to appear in support of a program, are likely to fall short because of a pleasant agreement with the speaker—a sort of "Isn't that a fascinating idea!" kind of reaction. There is a considerable market for amusement over our foibles, the inconsistencies in our formal associations, and in-group self-criticism. It is the sense of satisfaction and security with present conditions that allows this acceptance of our own shortcomings without the least thought of taking self-criticism seriously. Programs of change only threaten to disturb the balance within a group that has become narcotized to suffering, and committed to the view that life is hard but one can learn to accept anything.

On the other hand, attempts to promote change may fail because they outrage the sense of loyalty to prevailing institutions. Patriotism and the free-enterprise system are sacred values, which must be preserved even at the cost of suffering for some individuals. As long as confidence in the established order is unshaken, a serious proposal for reform will provoke a sense of outrage which completely obscures any potential positive response to the propagandist.

Herbert Blumer has called attention to the different ways an agitator must function, depending upon the extent of prior development of a public.[19] Where no public or sense of issue exists, any frontal attack on alleged problems will be dismissed or resisted violently However, the agitator, by concealing his purpose and working through indirection, may call attention to faintly sensed sources of discontent. He must maintain the appearance of a member of the in-group, a person whose loyalty to the system is not seriously questioned. He must also be a poised, quiet individual, not given to violent expression or unpredictable outbursts. Thus safely defined as a solid and respectable citizen, he asks the questions that start people wondering why conditions are not as they should be. He points out discrepancies that lead to fairly obvious conclusions about the motives of their present leadership, about the justice of the present system, or about the inevitability of current inequities, without directly suggesting the conclusions himself. As the impact of this agitation develops, the amount of undercover protest talk grows; beneath the cover of overt conformity, widespread ill will develops. Until such covert discontent is widely expressed and discussed so that people are assured that their feeling is widely shared and supported, any frontal attack will still evoke the conventional responses. Indeed, as the discrepancy between overt conformity and covert discontent becomes greater, the

---

19 Herbert Blumer, "Collective Behavior," in *Principles of Sociology*, ed. Alfred M. Lee (New York: Barnes and Noble, Inc., 1953), pp. 203–5.

agitator or propagandist who attacks conditions frontally is more and more likely to be dealt with by indignation and violent repression; the responsive chord he strikes makes people more fearful of unleashing the consequences of such discontent.

However, once this fear has been overcome, the agitator's problem is to push people to the point of acting upon their discontent. No longer is the quiet, poised individual effective—he must now have the enthusiasm that infects others, assurance that makes others forget their doubts, and convictions and feelings extreme enough to make others forget their moderation. The agitator at this stage fits the popular image of the agitator—the daring, contentious individual, the human dynamo.

CONTENDING INTEREST GROUPS. A public in which interest groups are arrayed on two sides because their interests naturally polarize has a very simple structure. This might be the case when campers and conservationists want a redwood forest converted into a public preserve, while lumbermen want the timber for their use.

But in a complex society, interest groups are found aligned on issues for diverse reasons and often involved in alliances that do violence to their positions on other issues. This was the case when the politically conservative isolationists and the pacifistic Socialist party found themselves allied in opposition to American involvement in the Second World War. More recently we have seen the spectacle of a labor union leading the opposition to Negro demands for neighborhood control of schools. The declared values of this labor organization, supporting the aspirations of disadvantaged minorities, were challenged when Negro neighborhood groups sought the power to select the teachers in their schools. To a traditionally powerful teacher's union, this proposal undermined hard-won teacher's rights.

Some of the problems associated with the complex interplay of interest groups in a large metropolis, such as New York City, are examined by Daniel Bell and Virginia Held.

The Community Revolution

Daniel Bell
Virginia Held

One cliché of contemporary political discourse is that "the people have no real voice—or, less and less of a voice—in their political affairs," a view reinforced by a ponderous academic sociology that asserts "a decline or eclipse of the local community" and a change wherein "all groupings based on traditional criteria such as shared ethnic descent and inheritance of status are undermined. . . ."

From *The Public Interest*, No. 16 (Summer, 1969), pp. 142–77. Copyright National Affairs, Inc., 1969. Reprinted in part by permission of the publishers and the authors. Extensive portions dealing in depth with the ideology of participation and with communities and programs in New York City have been omitted, as have most of the footnotes.

We believe both assertions to be quite wrong. In fact, the opposite may be true—that there is more participation than ever before in American society, particularly in the large urban centers such as New York, and more opportunity for the active and interested person to express his political and social concerns. That very state of affairs leads to a paradox because it is the increase in participation which creates a sense of powerlessness and consequent frustration.

A person who is socially conscious wants results, particularly *his* results, and he wants them immediately. But the very fact that there is an increase in the number of claimants leads, inevitably, to lengthier consultation and mediation, and more importantly, to a situation wherein thousands of different organizations, each wanting diverse and contradictory things, simply check each other in their demands. As a Mrs. Gladys Gonzales, vice-president of the Parents Teachers Association of Junior High School 71, is reported as saying at the public hearings of the Board of Education on the school decentralization plan, "You graciously allow us to say what is on our mind and then turn around and do what you want to do anyway." But this is precisely what *every* speaker, whatever his point of view, feels and says at such a meeting; and the result is rancor and a sense of frustration.

Forty years ago, a Tammany political boss could give an order to a mayor. Today, no such simple action is possible. On each political issue—decentralization or community control, the mix of low income and middle income housing, the proportion of blacks in the city colleges, the location of a cross-Manhattan or cross-Brooklyn expressway, etc.—there are dozens of active, vocal, and conflicting organized opinions. The difficulty in governing New York—and many other cities as well—is not the "lack of voice" of individuals in city affairs, or the "eclipse of local community," but the babel of voices and the multiplication of claimants in the widened political arena. In this new participatory democracy the need is for the creation of new political mechanisms that will allow for the establishment of priorities in the city, and for some effective bargaining and tradeoffs between groups; without that the city may end in a shambles.

THE MULTIFARIOUS ASSOCIATIONS

Writing on his trip to the United States in 1904, Max Weber could comment, after Tocqueville, "In the past and up to the present, it has been a characteristic precisely of the specifically American democracy that it did *not* constitute a formless sandheap of individuals, but rather a buzzing complex of strictly exclusive, yet voluntary associations."

No count has ever been made of the number of voluntary associations in the United States or in any major American city. In New York, the *Directory of Social and Health Agencies of New York City* lists 1200 welfare organizations, volun-

tary and public, excluding civic, educational, and religious organizations. Ten years ago, Sayre and Kaufman in *Governing New York City* remarked, "No careful census of these nongovernmental groups in the city has ever been made, but the number seems to run at least to *tens of thousands*. This estimate comprises only those groups sufficiently well organized to have letterheads, telephones, and/or to appear in some published directory." (our italics)

Whatever the total ten years ago, the number of groups, particularly local block associations, tenants organizations, welfare councils—name the issue and a dozen groups spring into being—have since multiplied spectacularly. The chief reason has been the revolution in the political structure of urban life that was initiated by the Kennedy-Johnson administrations, a development obscured and to some extent distorted by the Vietnam war. Just as the Wagner Act of 1935 facilitated—indeed, shaped—the organization of the economic workplace by trade unions, so the community action provisions of the Poverty Act of 1964 established the basis for neighborhood organization by community groups. In so doing, it has created a potential for political bargaining on urban community issues just as there is economic bargaining on issues in the workplace.

There are substantial differences of course. The Wagner Act created a rule-making institution in the National Labor Relations Board with well-defined contestants, specific issues, and real pay-offs. The structure of political bargaining in the community is still inchoate. Whether it will function is moot. The system has been quickly repudiated, in part, by the Johnson and Nixon administrations; the militants, who initially sought to take advantage of the system to gain a place in society, have turned to more radical and direct action tactics; and the established political machines have fought the community action programs and in many places have taken them over. Yet the potential remains, particularly in New York City, for disadvantaged groups—or more specifically their indigenous leaders—to get "a share of the action" or at a minimum to act as veto groups in the system. The full thrust of community organization may have been blunted in these last couple of years, but it would be foolish to ignore what may yet be one of the great structural changes in the political system of American urban society.

THE PATTERNS OF COMMUNAL LIFE

Going back sixty years or more—there has been an extensive network of participation by different kinds of groups in the communal life of New York City, and these have tied into the political system in different ways. For purposes of analysis, one can identify three different kinds of communal systems in the city life.

The first might be called the *civic associations.* These are the old, established, predominantly upper middle class, business, and "good government" organizations. They include such groups as the Citizens Union (established in 1897 growing out of the City Reform Club whose members included Theodore Roosevelt and elected reform mayor William L. Strong), the Citizens Budget Commission (business-supported), the Citizens' Committee for Children (primarily wealthy, liberal Jewish women), the Men's and Women's City Clubs, the Civil Service Reform Association, the Public Education Association, the Citizens Housing and Planning Council, the Commerce and Industry Association, the League of Women Voters, etc. These are all politically-minded, politically active, "clean government," reform movements.

The second is the more numerous and more diffuse *fraternal and service organizations* built, traditionally, around the religious and ethnic groups. These consist of the Protestant Council, the Catholic Charities, the Federation of Jewish Philanthropies, the hospitals, family service centers, old age homes, child care centers, parochial schools, and the like. They are represented in the large, coordinating, research and information agencies, such as the Community Council of Greater New York, and in major service groups, such as the Community Service Society of New York. These agencies, plus the many "old country" associations, particularly among the Jews and the Irish, have provided the means whereby the poor immigrants of an earlier era were helped to settle in New York. These organizations have been the backbone of the communal, self-help structures of New York.

And third, there has been the large network of *neighborhood organizations:* settlement houses, parent-teachers associations, block associations, tenants associations, local churches and synagogues. The center of these activities was often the local political club. City aldermen, state assemblymen, and state senators kept in touch with these organizations which meant grievances or needs were funneled through the elected representatives.

In the past, almost all of these three "communal systems" were private and voluntary. They were sustained by the monies and time of individuals who gained status, political visibility, or simple personal satisfaction through these activities. They were maintained by professional staffs who provided the day-to-day services, as well as structural continuity through time, and who often "recruited" new leaders for these organizations in order to sustain the monies and activities.

In addition, the political system itself was the main "brokerage" agency for patronage, reward, wealth, status, and power. New immigrants could get jobs through "pull" at city hall or through the large number of business concerns whose existence depended in part on political favor; for example, Consolidated Edison, pier stevedore concerns, construction companies, and truckers. The quid pro quo was jobs for votes. The political clubs serviced the new and unorganized poor (on the lower east side before World War I, it was not uncommon for a person who had an appendicitis attack to go to his precinct captain, because he often didn't know where the hospital was, and he certainly did not have a telephone). They told city hall what was needed in the neighborhoods. In the current jargon, the political clubs were the chief modes of communication and control.

Over the past decades, the political machines that were the structure of government in New York have broken down. Under the New Deal, the locus of power and attention shifted to Washington, and the major jobs and finances of the society came under federal control. The rise of middle class liberal reformers within the Democratic Party—reform, previously, had always operated outside the party, usually in some "fusion" slate—cracked the singular power of the old bosses because the reform clubs were oriented more to issues than to jobs. The extension of the merit system in the 1960's, "upward, outward and downward," reduced the role of patronage. More and more frequently, administrators of the top agencies came from career ranks and party background almost became a mark of disqualification. As Theodore Lowi observed, "The triumph of Reform really ends in paradox: *Cities like New York become well-run but ungoverned.*"[1]

In the past thirty years, the influx of Negro and Puerto Rican migrants brought a double problem. They lacked the resources and often the will to build voluntary community structures. They arrived on the scene at a time when the older political mechanisms were in disarray. The blacks did achieve some political power, with the votes of Harlem as a base. When Hulan Jack became borough president in Manhattan in 1953, it became clear that for the foreseeable future this post would be a black prerogative. (And so it has been with his successors, Constance Motley and Percy Sutton.) But the other rewards—political contracts, the protection of rackets, the patronage to the lawyers and professionals—that had gone in the past to the ethnic minorities did not follow this political power: in part, because such rewards were no longer available and, in part, because there were few blacks able to claim them. The chief point here is that the blacks lacked the communal network that could interact with the political base, and thus provide the basis for the kind of advancement that had been made by earlier ethnic groups.

It has always been the case in modern society that the three fundamental hierarchies are power, wealth, and status. In the past, wealth commanded power or power commandeered wealth. But for the ethnic groups in the United States, these two were reinforced through the *communal* structures, which provided status and prestige for the wealthy and powerful, and which also provided a cohesion for the group coming into the society. The communal structures set up a network of full-time professionals who would advance the interests of the ethnic groups and their activities furthered and reinforced the contacts and social ties which aided the lawyer, the businessman, the financier in their business and professional careers.

---

[1] Theodore Lowi, "Machine Politics—Old and New," *The Public Interest,* No. 9 (Fall 1967).

The problem for the blacks, thus, was that at the time they were coming into urban life the political base was restricted and their communal structures were weak. In time, the two weaknesses would doubtless have been corrected. It is only in the last decade, after all, that the blacks have become primarily urban and concentrated in the north. But time is no longer available. What took the Irish three generations, the Italian two, and the Jews one to achieve—the security of middle class status—is something the blacks want immediately. They have been here the longest, and have been held down the most. They no longer want to wait. What they are asking for is power and resources; these have to come through the community.

THE DIREMPTION OF THE CITIES

To this political and sociological crisis is added another crucial fact: the multiplication of social problems arising from the demographic transformation of the country. The population of the country is being concentrated in metropolitan areas, the older sections of the cities are dilapidated, the transportation systems are choked and swollen, and services are lagging. It is easy, and deceptive, to blame this simply on "capitalism," or, more ambiguously on "the system." But this crisis derives in the first instance from one of the most fundamental facts about modern society: *the increase in number and movement of persons, and the increased demand for a level of services and amenities for all which has been hitherto unknown in the society.* Sixty-five years ago, a million persons a year could pour into the country in a steady stream for a decade, and jam together in crowded ghettoes, with little direct impact on the settled middle class lives of the older inhabitants, but that is no longer possible today. Each person wants full access to education and to services; and today each middle class person, sitting in his car, among 80 million others, wants a free and unobstructed highway.

These demands for services underscore what has been evident for a long time: that the administrative structure of the cities, organized as they are in a crazy-quilt pattern of counties, townships, and districts, are out of whack with the times. The United States may have the most modern economy and technology in the world, but its administrative structure, as Samuel Huntington has observed, is a Tudor polity. This is particularly evident in New York. The population of New York *City* (not of the metropolitan region) is *twice* the population of Norway, and is greater than the population of Austria or Sweden. But the city's political structure is wholly incongruent with the social realities. The mayor almost has to keep in touch with every birth, briss, confirmation, wedding, national day, death, and memorial service of the multifarious nationality groups in the city in his ceremonial duties; but in his administrative role, the mayor is unable to be in control of the day-to-day functions of the city or to determine its long-range planning requirements.

In 1947, the Citizens Union proposed the division of New York City into districts "for more orderly planning and decentralization of municipal services and community development." The report recommended the grouping of city services in one location in each district, and proposed that each district would develop its own plan in cooperation with the City Planning Commission. In 1950, the City Planning Commission took up the idea and proposed 66 districts as "logical units for the planning of schools, housing, hospitals, libraries, playgrounds, local street systems and other public facilities as well as for consideration of land use and zoning patterns." As Borough President of Manhattan in 1951, Robert Wagner set up a Community Planning Council, consisting of 15 to 20 members, for each of the 12 Manhattan districts suggested by the City Planning Commission. In part, Wagner did this because the local political clubs that had been the source of information and mediation between the districts and the city had largely ceased to function, and the administrative agencies increasingly were being overwhelmed by the local groups who took their claims and grievances directly to the city heads. Through these Local Planning Boards, Wagner sought to set up a mediating mechanism against the anarchic onslaught of the multiple organizations in the city.

Thus, the idea of decentralization and local community organizations as the basis of new administrative and political functions was underway, slowly, haltingly, and confusedly, in the 1950's.

To this the Kennedy administration added a new ideology, the ideology of "participation." The upsurge of the blacks, the discovery of the poor, the argument that these groups could not help themselves because they were powerless, all led to the conception that in programs fostered by government one should encourage the creation of new communities. In this way, new structures could be built that could provide help and training for the poor through institutions under their control or influence. In these communities, new, indigenous leaderships would emerge who would lead their constituents "into" the society. Thus the groundwork was laid for a change in the structure of American urban life, a transformation fostered by and financed by the federal government. It is a story unique in American history.

THE IDEOLOGY OF PARTICIPATION

The heart of the participation ideology was the Poverty Program, and the section entitled the Community Action Programs (CAP) which provide for participation by the poor in the programs that will affect their lives. The key phrase in the section was "maximum feasible participation," a phrase which for some was rhetoric, for some ideology, and for some an instrumental means whereby the poor would gain a sense of political identity. As Daniel P. Moynihan observes, "Community action with citizen participation was a coherent and powerful idea working its way into national policy, albeit little noticed or understood at the time. . . ."

Whatever the political outcome, the fact remains that a new institutional structure began to be built into the American political system. The question whether local community groups will *control* particular programs—schools, health, housing—is still being fought out. But the *participation* of the community is no longer in doubt. The Johnson administration felt that the Poverty Program had gone too far; but in setting up the Model Cities program it realized that little could be done without community participation, and that act stipulates that local community groups have to be consulted in the drawing up of new neighborhood plans. (Mindful of the experience of the Poverty Program, it provides that the control and final decisions over the plans are to be lodged in the mayor's office and in city hall.) The Nixon admin-istration has chosen to expand the Model Cities program, rather than the Poverty Program, as its instrument for the basis of a coherent urban policy, and the participation of the local community will be further institutionalized under that scheme. How far and how effective the "community revo-lution" will be in American political life, remains to be seen. . . .

THE ACCOMMODATION OF CONFLICT

A number of extraordinary changes are taking place in American life and, in conclusion, we can deal only schematically with these changes and the problems they pose.

There is, first, the increasing "politicalization" of society, particularly in urban affairs. Activities which were once allocated through the market are now subject to political decisions or political controls. Previously, the question of who was to be housed where would be settled through a "rationing by purse." Today, the decisions as to where housing is to be sited, what tax abatements are to be given, what proportion is to be reserved for low income or for municipal housing, etc., are made politically. And this carries over into many other areas as well. The sociological question is whether a society, this society, can carry such an increasing burden. The classical effects of politicali-zation are clear: the decision points are visible, rather than dispersed. The consequences are plain, for people know "whose ox will be gored." There is an overconcentration on law and legisla-tion, and an increasing burden on administration. All of this, inevitably, increases the potential for group conflict. One of the chief reasons why in the last twenty years New York has been deemed to be "ungovernable" is the increasing politicaliza-tion of decision-making.

Second, a group of "new men" have come into the political system, specifically among the blacks. They are angry and they feel deprived. Their goal, in many instances, is not integration or the sharing of power but the control of their "own" institutions and enclaves. Yet two things are remarkable about this movement. The projects in which a large number of the new leaders are employed are federally-funded. And second, other than schools and a few local services such as

health and the like, there is little possibility that the blacks will achieve control of major economic or political resources, for the locus of these resour-ces are not in the neighborhood or community. To this extent, a whole series of unrealistic expecta-tions are being generated in the black communities which may boomerang badly. What the black leadership may be able to achieve is a significant bargaining power, or even a veto in many instances, of city policies, but the talk of the ultramilitants about gaining control of the "major" institutions of society is unreal. The outcome will either be some accommodation or an increase in senseless rage. Despite the ultramilitant talk, the likelihood, still, is of accommodation.

Finally, we have seen the emergence, in a formal way, of the idea of "group rights" as the means whereby disadvantaged groups, particularly the blacks, can establish their claims in the system. The focal point here is education and it lies in the demands of the blacks for control of the schools in black districts, and for a quota or some preferential system in the colleges. This demand has brought the militant blacks squarely into conflict with the teachers union, which has felt its position threatened by the demand. It has raised the ugly spectre of anti-Semitism because a number of the blacks, particularly those in the leadership of the Afro-American Teachers Association, have delib-erately made anti-Semitic statements in order to frighten away Jewish teachers and particularly Jewish principals from schools in the ghetto.

Three issues are involved in the argument for group rights. One is that of merit: the question whether a person should or should not achieve a position on the basis of his demonstrated ability, or whether a proportion of posts should be allotted on the basis of group membership. The second, allied to it, is that of common culture. The argument, made by Rhody McCoy at Ocean Hill, for example, was that any principal from the civil service list would be white, but that a white principal could not understand or guide a black child. Such an argument strikes at the traditional understanding of a common education and raises the question whether, in the future, all education in the major American cities may not be parochial or segmented by class or race. Third is the question of representa-tion. Should there be majority rule or proportional representation; and if the latter, by geography or by group? When the New York State legislature proposed the election of a city Board of Education by boroughs, the Rev. Milton A. Galamison cried that the bill "deprives the blacks and Puerto Rican people of representation . . . Whenever we get into this nose-counting business, it's to the disadvantage of blacks and Puerto Ricans." And the administrator of Harlem's IS 201 district, Charles Wilson, agreed, saying: "The notion that the elected board will democratize the system is not so." What are the appropriate answers?

These divisive questions of political rights and political philosophy conjoin with a different set of problems that arise out of the nature of the size of the polis in a modern society. In a brilliant essay in the *American Political Science Review,* for December 1967, "The City in the Future of Democracy," Robert A. Dahl raised the question, "which is no longer a subject of discussion among political scientists," of what "is the optimum size for a city." And, he remarks, "the evidence seems to me . . . that the all-round optimum size for a contemporary American city is probably somewhere between 50,000 and 200,000, which, even taking the larger figure, may be within the threshold for wide civic participation."

Not only has there been little discussion on the optimum size of a city or a "quarter" of a large city, but there has been little thought as to what is the appropriate size and scope of the appropriate social unit to handle what problems: i.e., what services and functions can be left to a neighborhood or community, what has to be handled on a borough or city level, what has to be conducted in a region, and what has to be federalized? All that we have are shibboleths. We have the traditional decentralizer such as Paul Goodman, or the regionalists, or the federalizers. But nowhere is there a detailed examination of what functions of government are best handled at what levels of government.

A few suggestions may be hazarded, but they must be tentative. They involve ways of separating kinds of decisions in such a way that some are best decided at the periphery by participatory discussion and voluntary agreement, and some are best decided at more central levels, not only in order to arrive at such decisions with dispatch,

but also to be able to bring local interests into line with wider, more regional considerations. An example of such a division of decision-making power is the way the Human Resources Administration divides antipoverty funds between the various poverty areas according to impartial, mathematical calculations of the areas' poverty indexes. But then, once the amounts have thus been centrally fixed on the basis of such formulas, decisions on how to spend these funds are allowed to reflect the ebbs and flows of local sentiment and preference. Another example is the way the central Council Against Poverty decided this year, also on the basis of general and quantifiable criteria, to establish priorities to which all Community Corporations would be expected to allocate 70 percent of their funds. These priorities are "Education Action, Manpower Action, Economic Development and Consumer Education, and Housing." Within the bounds of these general requirements, the localities can then pursue these objectives in ways that satisfy the particular moods, tastes, and nonquantifiable enthusiasms of their members. In the field of housing, central and long-range decisions on appropriate relative proportions of low- and middle-income housing units can be recommended, within which communities can develop the housing projects that seem to them most humane and habitable. And central decisions on the allocation of funds for education according to fairly abstract principles of justice can still make possible neighborhood determination of the particular ways to spend such funds.

Behind the notion of optimum level is not just the question of administrative efficiency. There is the larger question, which is the theme of this essay, of participation. One virtue of participation is a simple one. It not only creates a basis of community, by allowing people to share in decisions that affect their lives, it is also a deeply conservatizing institution for, like property, it gives people a stake in the decision which becomes binding on all.

Participation, however, is not the end of politics, as it seems to be in some of the rhetoric of the new left. It is the beginning, for politics arises in the first instance when one realizes that there is no such thing as *the* people—that no single decision can please all people. There are only *peoples,* with contradictory and conflicting ideas and inter-ests. Suggest a jetport near some builtup area and a committee will arise to save 'our' community; locate an airport on a swamp, and there will be a committee to protect the wildlife; suggest a floating airport and a group will form to keep our lakes and waters clear of pollution.

A rational politics, to the extent there can be one, is bounded by economics, that is the recognition of the principle of relative scarcity and the neces-sity, therefore, of bargaining as a means of alloca-tion and adjudication within some principle of justice. If in a multigroup society, within which there is to be effective participation, social conflict is to be regulated within bounds, then, just as mechanisms for economic bargaining were worked out in the 1940's and 1950's which brought the trade unions into the society, so mechanisms for

political bargaining have to be established which allow for a tradeoff of objectives between groups. This means a more formal recognition of political groups, just as there was recognition of trade unions, and the establishment of rules of the game, within boundaries of defined communities within which the bargaining can take place.

But if economics deals with relative scarcity, politics includes the effort to gain relative advant-age; and this is a never-ending process in human affairs. The political problem is to make sure that the process takes place within bounds and does not tear the society apart. And this possibility can only be realized if one strengthens that most fragile of social relations—the trust that each person has in the other that the rules of the game will be observed and that each will have his chance to participate.

The Mass Media

In spite of the operation of networks, primary groups, circles, and interest groups, the mass media of communication still play a major part in the creation of publics and the formation of public opinion. The fear that people will swallow whatever they read, hear, or see in the mass media leads to the recurring specter of a population parroting mass produced opinions and preferences with the uniformity of a well-disciplined army. But the reassuring evi-dence of Franklin Roosevelt's election and reelections, while the major newspapers of the nation were overwhelmingly arrayed against him, diminishes the credibility of this specter.

The individual is helped to resist the media by at least three circumstances. First, except under totalitarian regimes, a choice is generally available to the audience. One of the strategies employed by such news-papers as the *Los Angeles Times* to main-tain a virtual monopoly in a major metropolitan community has been to in-clude, as regular features, columnists rep-resenting a wide spectrum of political

viewpoints. Neighborhood newspapers fre-quently offset the cosmopolitan outlook of metropolitan dailies, and underground pub-lications thrive in opposition to both. Second, as we have outlined in the earlier portions of this chapter, imagery and opin-ion from the mass media undergo an elaborate sifting process—through commu-nication networks, primary groups, circles, and interest groups, with opinion leaders operating at every level. And third, the imperative under which the media operate to achieve maximum audience size and attention biases the media into telling listeners what they want to hear. W. Lloyd Warner and William Henry suggest that the popular serial dramas on radio (and television) offer listeners an opportunity to indulge phantasies that offset the frustra-tions of everyday life.[20] The programs depict a world that confronts individuals with the same problems the listeners find in real life, but allows them to identify with phantasy figures whose unfaltering

[20] W. Lloyd Warner and William E. Henry, "The Radio Day-time Serial: A Symbolic Analy-sis," *Genetic Psychology Monographs*, 37 (Feb-ruary, 1948), 1–64.

mastery of each crisis allays recurring anxieties.

In order to understand the place of mass media in the formation of public opinion, we must discard the image of putty being molded by newspaper publishers and television producers in favor of a conception of more subtle influences. Six processes merit our attention.

First, the mass media *authenticate* the factual nature of events, which must be taken into account in the formation of public opinion. Information reported through the mass media is frequently assigned an authenticity not accorded word-of-mouth communications. This accounts for the recurring question of whether the accused in any widely publicized criminal case can secure a fair trial, when potential jurors have been exposed to media accounts of the crime. Martin Millspaugh speaks of "trial by mass media" as a phenomenon of contemporary society.[21] The authenticity assigned media reports is also based on their timing. Their versions are presented just at the time when interest is at its peak and when the preoccupation with resolving ambiguities is greatest. The more precise reports of cautious investigations come later, when interest has subsided and ambiguity has been relieved.

Second, the mass media *validate* opinions, preferences, and values. The listener feels more confident of his own opinion when he hears a similar view expressed by a well-known commentator. With this greater confidence he is more likely to express his opinion. And by borrowing the commentator's words he is likely to present his views more effectively. In this case the individual's opinion has not been changed, but the course of public opinion may be changed because this viewpoint is more effectively injected into the filtering process.

Consideration of others, respect for prestigious figures, and social taboos often prohibit the expression of opinions, even when they are felt to be valid. A third effect of the mass media is to *legitimate* tabooed viewpoints and behavior. What one might have said only in private or thought but not said, can be expressed if it has been heard often on television. Impulses that might have been kept under control can be legitimately followed when they become commonplace on television. Research has shown that people express hostility more freely after they have watched television violence than before.[22]

Fourth, the mass media often *symbolize* the diffuse anxieties, discontents, preferences, and prejudices that people experience. In the study of collective behavior we are repeatedly reminded that discontents and preferences are usually vague and ill-defined at first. Until they are specified and labeled, they can only give rise to restlessness and unpredictable feelings. By supplying a plausible identification for these vague feelings, the mass media often facilitate the translation into specific opinions and supporting actions. By supplying symbols —the generation gap, hawks and doves, the sick society, the new morality, hippies— the mass media create a world of objects toward which specific feelings can be directed. Such symbols are influential because of the values they imply and the frames of reference they impose. Herbert Blumer and Philip Hauser, in an early study, show the influence of the movies in providing imagery for the child viewer.[23]

[21] Martin Millspaugh, "Trial by Mass Media," *Public Opinion Quarterly*, 13 (Summer, 1949), 328–29.

[22] Leonard Berkowitz, "The Effects of Observing Violence," *Scientific American*, 210 (February, 1964), 35–41; for a skeptical view, cf. Joseph T. Klapper, "Mass Communication: Effects," *International Encyclopedia of the Social Sciences* (1968), 3, esp. 87–88; for a general treatment of this complex question cf. Otto N. Larsen, ed., *Violence and the Mass Media* (New York: Harper and Row, Publishers, 1968).

[23] Herbert Blumer and Philip Hauser, *Movies, Delinquency, and Crime* (New York: The Macmillan Company, 1933).

Fifth, the mass media *focus* the discontents, preferences, and prejudices into lines of action. By seizing upon certain groups, events, and issues for saturation treatment, they create focuses toward which attitudes are directed and help to establish the nature of the issues and the acceptable alternatives.

Finally, the mass media *hierarchize* persons, objects, activities, and issues. By virtue of the amount of attention they assign and the preferential programming and placement of items, they indicate relative importance and prestige. The effect that frequent playing of a record can have on the popularity of that record has been well documented.[24] Although it is more difficult to document effects on the evaluation of persons and issues, a similar relationship seems probable.

In light of these and other subtle effects, the question of bias becomes a vital one. In addition to deliberate bias, there are inadvertent sources of bias. The very competition for audience produces bias in the direction of majority views. This effect is greatest in media such as television and radio that present a single selection at any given time. The newspaper can diversify its appeal and offer a variety of opinions simultaneously. The television channel either holds or loses its viewers by the attraction of a single program at any period of the day. The effort to maximize the audience at all times requires a consistent appeal to the most widely held preferences.

Each medium conveys its own kind of imagery, with distinctive effects on public opinion. Media coverage of the Vietnam war has been contrasted to the coverage of earlier wars. For the first time there was television coverage of the battlefield, so that audiences saw firsthand the battle casualties, brutality, and fear and hopelessness of civilians whose homes and livelihood were destroyed in combat. It may never be possible to determine the extent that American repudiation of Vietnam involvement resulted from this television image. But probably this war is visualized more as a set of tragic encounters between small groups of people on the battlefield and less as the massive encounter between nations and ideologies than has been true of other wars.

In a classic study, Kurt and Gladys Lang show how the very nature of the television image can create a different impression of an event than did firsthand observation.[25] General Douglas MacArthur was relieved of his command in Korea on April 11, 1951, after challenging the limited war concept being followed by President Harry Truman and the United Nations. When he returned to the United States his supporters organized receptions for him in several major American cities. In Chicago his return was celebrated with a parade, which he rode in. The Langs arranged to have several observers stationed along the parade route record their observations and impressions of the event. They also stationed several observers in front of television sets to make similar records. The two sets of records were then compared. The general effect conveyed by television was more dramatic and exciting, more characterized by continuous activity and interest. Cameras were always focused on points of activity. The on-site viewer witnessed long stretches of dull waiting, broken only briefly by activity. The camera, through its moving perspective, gave the impression of a crowd of enthusiastic hero worshippers, while firsthand observation suggested a crowd of the idle curious, only some of whom were wildly enthusiastic.

Some inevitable bias also enters mass media because of the nature of reporters,

24 Gerhart Wiebe, "The Effect of Radio Plugging on Students' Opinions of Popular Songs," *Journal of Applied Psychology*, 24 (December, 1940), 721–27.

25 Kurt Lang and Gladys Engel Lang, "The Unique Perspective of Television and its Effect: A Pilot Study," *American Sociological Review*, 18 (February, 1953), 3–12.

cameramen, and others who relay the facts *as they see them* to the audience. Because of his own background, the reporter understands some events better than others and interprets the attitudes and motives of some participants better than others. The reporter is not merely an objective observer: he has his own personal encounters with events. In the crowd he may be repulsed by the smell of perspiration; he may be knocked over and his life endangered by rioters or police; he may be feared and resented or welcomed by crowd members. The nature of his encounter with events cannot fail to color his account of the events.

In May, 1968, the Southern Christian Leadership Conference and other black organizations, working with representatives of other impoverished groups, marched into Washington, D.C. and set up a makeshift camp known as Resurrection City. The Poor People's Campaign, as it was known, was supposed to dramatize to a reluctant Congress and an apathetic nation the seriousness and extent of poverty among all racial groups in America. A former newspaper reporter who served as an information officer for the Campaign examines some of the problems that arose in reporting this event.

.The Poor People and the "White Press"

Eric D. Blanchard

Among the headlines in the Washington *Evening Star* when Resurrection City, USA, opened last May was one that said: " 'Oppressed' Adopt Traits of Oppressors." The article beneath was by Mary McGrory, who has excellent credentials as a reporter in the civil rights field, and was about the treatment she got from members of the Poor People's Campaign. Her experience was not pleasant. She quoted an old man who told her bluntly that he had come to Washington to talk to "Lyndon Baines Johnson the President" and "I ain't gonna waste no time talkin' to you." She also described the behavior of some of the young marshals in Resurrection City whose orders were "numerous and arbitrary" and who were apparently determined to prove that the Southern Christian Leadership Conference "can do the strong-arm stuff, too."

Other newsmen ran into the same ill will in the days that followed. The drill of clearing the front gate was uncertain and once a reporter got inside, there was no guarantee of cordiality. A detente developed, but before the campaigners departed at

least one photographer was robbed and two reporters were mauled.

More recently, in early August, the Black United Front, a militant group in Washington, announced plans to bar the press from future meetings because "the press is more interested in playing up fights" than in reporting BUF discussions.

The next day, the National Bar Association, the Negro counterpart of the American Bar Association, complained about the "lack of coverage" of its conference and proposed picketing news offices.

Such episodes of black antagonism toward the news media are not new and not even rare. They have become a commonplace for reporters who regularly cover civil rights affairs. The reason was cited in the report of the Kerner Commission, which observed that, to many Negroes, the news media reflected "the biases, the paternalism, the indifference of white America" and "ironically have failed" to communicate about black life in this country.

Because it affects attitudes, the communications industry ranks alongside—perhaps even ahead—of jobs, education, and housing in responsibility for the condition of American life. Reporting about poor people has become *de rigueur* only relatively re-

From *Columbia Journalism Review,* 7 (Fall, 1968), 61–65. Reprinted by permission.

cently. While many newsmen are trying to meet the new challenge, the bulk of the news machinery has not adjusted yet. Resurrection City (the first time a slum was staged, said the *Village Voice*) and the Poor People's Campaign as a whole are textbook examples of what the Kerner report was talking about. The level of coverage generally was so pedestrian, so police-blotter superficial that *The New Yorker* (June 15, 1968) envisioned newsmen asking Martin Luther King which mountain he had visited and which night it was that he had first started having his dream. Bill Cosby, the comedian, observed on Solidarity Day that had the Washington press been with Columbus, he would have turned around and gone home.

The newspaper and wire treatment (I rarely had a chance to watch television in May and June) of the Poor People's Campaign demonstration at the Supreme Court on May 29 is a case in point.

That day perhaps more than at any other time during the campaign the poor acted as the bloc they wanted to be. Negroes, with their catalog of economic needs, marched in support of Indians. The Indians were seeking "justice" from the Court, which two days before had ruled, in their eyes, against Indians by asserting that the State of Washington had a right to regulate net fishing (not just by Indians, as a matter of fact, but by everyone). Despite a 114-year-old treaty, the Indians are running a distant third to canners and sportsmen in taking fish from the waters of Puget Sound and its tributaries. Interested less in legal niceties than in food, the Indians decided on a direct-action approach to the Supreme Court. Several windows in the building were smashed; a distressed young woman hauled down the American flag.

But almost unanimously newspapers chose to emphasize the disorder almost to the exclusion of background on the Indians' problems. Under the headline, "High Court Stormed in Protest by Poor," *The New York Times* of May 30 ran a 22-inch story with only three sentences of background on the reasons for the demonstration. The ratio was similar (sometimes less background) in *The Chicago Tribune,* the Washington *Star*, the New York *Daily News,* the *Los Angeles Times,* and the *Philadelphia Inquirer.* The terminology in *The Washington Post* was softer (it used the term "besiege" in its headline) and it mentioned the fishing-rights question several times. But the fairest account of the day that I saw was in the Baltimore *Sun,* which subordinated the windows and the flag to the bottom of the front-page matter, while the fishing rights were cited twice on page one.

The net impact of newspaper treatment of the demonstration was almost totally negative (presumably reinforcing the attitudes of those who believe that the poor are criminals and eroding the positions of others who aren't sure yet). Reporters were careful to write only that "windows were broken," but their circumspection was spoiled by "active" headlines. The papers got a good bag from that day. The problem was they were loaded for rabbits, and that's what they got.

Action fascinates the media as news, despite the fact that in our current social upheaval, "events" are so plottable in any newsroom that their occurrence hardly warrants the wide-eyed attention they get. Indian hunger is not new; it is not action. It is old, and it is a first-class news story. Aside from the Indians themselves, officials in the city and state of Washington, Dick Gregory and a few others, nobody knows much about it. If people are ignorant, somebody isn't informing them.

The May 29 story is a good example of what the press does and does not do in reporting the current social upheaval. It was fairly typical of the treatment of the Poor People's Campaign—before, during, and after Resurrection City.

On February 18, for instance—ten weeks before the campaign began, six weeks before Dr. King was murdered—the Washington *Star* ran an AP story that began:

Atty. Gen. Ramsey Clark, the man President Johnson has chosen to direct the federal effort against crime, warns that a growing number of acts of civil disobedience are "irresponsible, intolerable" and cannot be permitted.

Clark made the remarks during an interview centering on Dr. Martin Luther King's plan to bring thousands of impoverished Negroes to Washington in April to demonstrate for jobs.

This law-and-order line, which reflects not only the grab-and-run habits of fact- and quote-gathering but institutional bias, occupied newspapers throughout March. Congressional complaining about the campaign became shrill after the Memphis disorders and the assassination, and the papers covered each squeak faithfully. Even on April 29, the day campaign activity began, *The Washington Post* carried eight sturdy paragraphs on police arrangements to help the press—a housekeeping matter. My notes from the days just before Resurrection City was erected include:

May 3 and 4: The *Star, Post,* and *New York Times* carried substantial stories on the President's concern over "inherent dangers" in the campaign.

May 7: A *Star* editorial began, "The word from Mississippi is that some organizers of the Poor People's Campaign are urging people to pour into Washington and apply immediately for relief."

May 11: The stabbing of a man demonstrating against the campaign caravan in Boston got front-page play in the *Times* and three photographs in the *Post*.

May 12: AP said in the *Star* that the Pentagon had alerted troops "to help deal with any emergency."

The pace did not slacken when the encampment opened. The *Star* bannered: "Some of Poor Want to Go Home," before Resurrection City was 24 hours old. On May 21, the *Times* editorialized that if the campaigners pursued nonviolent methods, "the sympathy that now exists toward the demonstrating groups will prevail." On May 26, the *Star's* main editorial was about violence, and the *Times* contributed an article on "Apprehensive Washington" as a city with "a bad case of nerves."

On May 30, the *Post* played the Supreme Court demonstration out front, adjoining an unrelated story headed: "Street Thugs Fell Doctor on Sick Call." On May 31, a *Post* editorial discussed "Violence Against the Court" but waited until June 3 to say editorially ". . . it is interesting to note what the issues [of the May 29 demonstration] were."

There was a still unexplained escalation of contact between the residents of Resurrection City and the police in the final days of the existence of the A-frame community. The morning it was closed (June 24), the *Post* regretted that because of the "misbehavior" of some of the campers, "accounts of their misdoings reinforce outdated and corrosive racial stereotypes." It deplored a "certain quantity of old-fashioned sinfulness' and "waywardness" now come to the fore." The paper was saddened, finally, because "nine tenths of the comfort and

convenience of urban life arises out of the fortunate circumstance that Negro Americans in overwhelming numbers are honest, industrious, hard-working and dependable."

The next morning, after police in flak jackets cleared the camp grounds, the *Post* said Resurrection City had "become an enemy to the cause." The *Times* concurred, with an editorial blessing, "Go With Dignity."

(Among its posthumous campaign notes, the *Post* of August 12 gave nearly half of a women's page to pictures and text on that very same distressed young woman who had hauled down the flag at the Supreme Court May 29, presumably after discovering she wasn't demented. On August 23, the paper began its account on a social study of the campaigners by discussing the causes of violence in the encampment. Violence isn't mentioned in the study. When the *Post* story was redone in the Washington *Daily News*, it became: " 'Tent City' Leaders Blamed for Violence.")

Clearly, the press was not on a sympathetic frequency with the Poor People's Campaign. There is even some ground for saying that three of the most influential papers in the country are flawed by a bias they both produce and reflect. While such bias does not justify beating reporters, it accounts at least for part of the hostility to the press.

A SCLC leader, Hosea Williams, charged in June that the news media were conspiring "to poison the mind of America." That charge is valid to the extent that the public is either uninformed or misinformed about the causes of domestic upheaval. To the extent he was describing the effect, the impact, of news, he was right. To the extent that he ignored the mechanics of news operations, he was not. The distinction should be made.

Any number of reporters told me during the campaign that they were sympathetic to the cause. Many of them were and are, in spite of sometimes incredible working conditions—hostility, long and uncertain hours, fitful direction by campaign leaders, too much ground to cover, and a campaign information office that often knew less about what was going on than the reporters themselves. On the basis of the "action," the coverage was faithful; I include the "dirty" stories, as being at least good investigative police reportage. The common problem was one white Americans *generally* share about the poor: they don't know very much about their subject. At least one regular reporter during the campaign agrees:

"I think that this story illustrates the total communications gap which now exists between the institutionalized poor and the middle class urban reporter. Most reporters went out there with the understanding that their primary task was to report the 'facts'—who got beat up the night before, how many were in the march, what did Abernathy say. By taking this approach, they lost sight of the significance of the campaign. [There was] very objective, useless reporting. . . . I dont' think many reporters were equipped to deal with it. I don't think any of us were."

The fault with the campaign coverage—and its correction—was in editorial management, not in simple racial bias (although there was reportedly one virulent case) and in a failure in planning the coverage in the first place. On the face of what appeared in print, the campaign was approached like a ball game or a homicide or any of a dozen events, rather than as the manifestation of social unrest. Journalism has no great fraternity of experts in the social-unrest field (black reporters are frequent but not involuntary exceptions to that observation). The body of social legislation is huge, cumbersome, and intricate and requires a background that general assignment reporters by definition do not have. Analysis of relevant legislation, for example, would have enhanced campaign treatment immeasurably.

The *Times*, in one of its articles, did acknowledge the intricacy of such legislation but did not unravel it. To the best of my knowledge, nobody much pursued this avenue. Why specialists such as congressional reporters weren't shifted in greater number to the campaign is not clear. Nor is it clear why the daily coverage of marches and activities wasn't complemented by more articles on the issues of the campaign, since it was a piece of theater designed (if the word can be used) from start to finish to focus attention not on itself but on the injustices being dramatized by the actors. The campaign *could* have been covered as a sidebar, with the main story on substance.

Again, there was no running commentary on how and why injustice—especially hunger—flourishes

in this country. A reporter doesn't have to go to Middle Earth to find out why. True, the press belted Secretary of Agriculture Freeman and Senator Eastland and his cotton subsidy, but I did not see a steady press attack addressed to mis-, mal- or non-feasance of public officials by name (an exception: Drew Pearson's column on subsidies in early June). Nick Kotz did a handsome series on Eastland for the Des Moines *Register* and *Tribune* before the campaign began and Bob Maynard did several stories on Alabama poverty for *The Washington Post*, but these were extraordinary.

A private group asserted in late April that hunger is of crisis proportions in this country. The report was not the work of fly-by-nights but of reputable authorities. Their report got good first-day play, then rapidly deteriorated into charge and countercharge over numbers of starving people. Surely the report must have suggested that there could be as many stories on hunger as there are impacted counties. Hunger gets only perfunctory attention in the press, when it should, as a public health as well as moral matter, be followed as one of the old, continuing, and outstanding stories of American life. Unless we can read in our national press about the violence to the poor that comes from starving for a full stomach, equal treatment, and a reasonably secure future, we will remain ignorant and be frightened of their certain and predictable wrath.

The coverage of the Poor People's Campaign failed because of the absence of imagination in newsrooms. *That* complaint alone should be ample corrective.

I do not slight mechanical factors that curse editors every working day. The Poor People's Campaign was a large story and was not well served by the campaign's information office. Ideally, dozens of reporters from each paper or news agency could have been assigned. Such staffs, of course, do not exist (although there are exceptions even to that rule, certainly among the large papers). Stories—even this one—have to fight for space. There is the just plain loose treatment, such as headlines that do not truly reflect the story. When I discussed the Supreme Court coverage in the Washington *Daily News* of May 29 with the city editor, Stan Felder, some weeks later, he cautioned against being trapped into quibbling over individual words. He said he preferred to concentrate on the "haystack" of a story's overall impact, rather than "straws." The point is well taken, yet unless editors do "quibble" over words, especially when they are in the lead, the cost is reader misinformation. Journalism has lived with these headaches and adjusted to meet the needs of news. Like other parts of the social machinery, journalism is confronted again, this time by a colossal social crisis. It must adjust again.

It has already begun to. Individual reporters who stayed with the Poor People's Campaign were confronted personally by what they saw and heard and felt. They *may* even be converts to the school of thought that there is no such thing as objective reporting, but at least, they will be more sensitive human beings and by definition better journalists. Too, the process of sensitization is not limited to the reporter. It is beginning to filter into the interior of the Establishment, as well; when newsmen got beaten and Maced in Chicago, the Establishment

grumbled. If it was truly affected, there may be real reason for high hopes for the future.

The biggest news of all however, is that the subject of poverty and the poor is getting more news space and time than ever. That fact alone makes the Poor People's Campaign a resounding success. CBS's moving documentary, *Hunger in America,* a variety of programming on that and other networks since then, the cover stories in national newsmagazines, the heavy daily play (UPI's Washington Capital News Service moved more on the campaign than on any other story on many weekdays; Solidarity Day preparations were the only thing on the ticker for a period during the afternoon of June 18) and the more than 700 credentials issued to regular domestic and foreign newsmen and free lancers attest to this.

These are good auguries, for a busy season that finds us, not unconcerned, but unprepared. We must prepare quickly. The police blotter is a useless tablet for the future.

Conventionalized Publics

All forms of collective behavior that recur and have consequences for the group are increasingly conventionalized. The theoretically simplest public is formed because of spontaneous interest that arises from mass preoccupation with events of the day. But the public we know best—the election public—is highly conventionalized. It occurs because a predetermined interval has passed rather than because of heightened mass preoccupation with a problem; the main issue is largely organized and arranged; a set of interest groups known as political parties presides over the deliberations; the manner in which public opinion is to be identified is formally established as the ballot; and the secret ballot and the one-person-one-vote principle diminish the unequal social pressures on individuals at the crucial point of voting.

Conventionalization in this instance arises from two considerations. As with crowd behavior, conventionalization tends to tame the disruptive character of unregu-

lated and unpredicted eruptions, so that it is possible for governments to make plans and carry them out. At the same time, the conventionalized public does not wholly eliminate the spontaneity of unconventionalized publics. Conventionalization also arises from a set of values critical of opinion formation in wholly spontaneous publics.

Social movements of an earlier period found fault with three features of the spontaneous public: the unequal weight of individual opinions, the pressures that some individuals are able to apply to others in order to influence their opinions, and the uncertain and variable assessment of what public opinion is on a given question. Formal election procedures were established as the definitive way of registering public opinion; the one-man-one-vote principle instituted an equality among members of the public; and the secret ballot insulated members from direct social pressure when registering opinion. These procedures cannot, of course, create equality and freedom from social pressure during opinion formation, as our analysis of networks and opinion leadership has clearly indicated. But where such procedures have been strongly conventionalized, they frequently prevent public opinion from becoming a mere expression of the current power structure in the community.

The conventionalizations in the service of democratic values were enacted by deliberate community decision. Most of those that serve stability and continuity have arisen as working adapations without forethought or deliberate community decision. The part played by political parties in election publics is the foremost example of an unplanned outgrowth of continuity between publics and government. Political parties are the superordinate interest groups through which the more specific ones must operate. The parties serve as mechanisms for evaluating several issues simultaneously. By commanding loyalty, they balance many of the opinion fluctuations that would occur from time to time.

We shall not attempt to review here how a party system works to shape the processes in an electoral public except to refer to the careful study of party loyalty by Campbell, Converse, Miller, and Stokes.[26] Although some party organization is probably necessary to prevent the chaos and ultimate nullification of popular influence that is suggested by the Bell and Held paper,[27] the party system can also work to render the election public relatively insensitive to public policy.

The critical initial decision [choice of political party] appears to be taken most frequently under strong social influence early in life, when involvement in politics is at a low ebb, and, presumably, political information is most scanty as well. Thus if involvement and background are preconditions for the establishment of meaningful links between basic values and party preferences, then we must suppose that in the bulk of cases, the individual is committed to a party at a time when he is least

likely to have the wherewithal to bring ideological considerations of this sort into play. Thereafter, the self-reinforcing aspects of a psychological identification progressively reduce the probability of change in partisan allegiance.[28]

Voting, as the means for registering public opinion, establishes one crucial moment for recording what is actually a continually shifting pattern of opinion, and it creates one simplified issue that is supposed to subsume the leading issues defined by more spontaneous publics. As a result, the definiteness of the electoral outcome leaves a great deal of uncertainty about the component issues. "The day after a presidential election a national inquest opens into the causes of the result."[29] After the election the less conventionalized publics come to the fore again in shaping public opinion.

The great danger of the conventionalized electoral public is that the meaning of the outcome will be misread for component issues. On June 2, 1950, a school-bond election was held in Pasadena, California. The election occurred in the course of a vigorous campaign against the newly appointed superintendent of schools and the philosophy of progressive education that he represented. When the bond issue was defeated, the outcome was almost universally interpreted as vote of no confidence in the superintendent, with the result that the school board asked for his resignation. A subsequent survey in the community, however, found a surprising amount of support for the superintendent's policies and led to the conclusion that property owners, many of whom had no children, had turned out in disproportionate numbers to resist the increased financial burden that was to be placed on them. By the time the true meaning of the election became clear, the rift between the superintendent and the community was too deep to be closed.[30]

[26] Angus Campbell et al. *The American Voter* (New York: John Wiley and Sons, Inc., 1964) p. 122.
[27] See p. 207.

[28] Campbell et al., *American Voter,* p. 122.
[29] Ibid., p. 269.
[30] Carey McWilliams, "The Enemy in Pasadena," *The Christian Century,* 68 (January 3, 1951), 10–15.

I2

THE PUBLIC
AND SOCIAL CONFLICT

Publics focused on issues of serious concern often go beyond bargaining and benign coercion to conflict and the use of violence. Graham and Gurr define violence as "behavior designed to inflict physical injury to people or damage to property."[1] Although violence captures attention and creates fear as other behavior does not, it is but one manifestation of conflict. Parties in conflict sometimes employ violence and sometimes do not, depending upon whether it serves their momentary purposes. In this chapter we shall focus on the process of social conflict between groups, as it affects the formation of public opinion.

We shall use the term *conflict,* not in the broad sense that includes all disagreements and all efforts by people or groups to pursue incompatible goals, but in a more restricted sense. Lewis Coser defines conflict as "a struggle over values or claims to status, power, and scarce resources, in which the claims of the conflicting parties are not only to gain the desired values but also to neutralize, injure, or eliminate their rivals."[2] The latter part of the definition should be stressed. Conflict has properties that distinguish it from other processes of

disagreement because there is an autonomous goal of injuring the antagonist— autonomous in the sense that conflict is often continued when it does not promote the ostensible goals of the conflicting party. Conflict exists when the relationship is based on the premise that whatever enhances the well-being of one group lessens the well-being of the other, and that impairing the well-being of the antagonist benefits one's own group.

Four topics will be the principal concern of this chapter. First, every instance of crowd behavior, collective behavior, or conspicuous conflict is observed, evaluated, and interpreted by a public. Often the crowd or social movement gives rise to the public that interprets it. The public mediates between the crowd behavior and its long-term effects on the society. Second, the conflict itself becomes an issue for the outside public, often displacing the initial issues. Third, when conflict becomes the salient process within a public, interaction is governed by a distinctive conflict morality, and the public attaches distinctive meanings to events. And fourth, once a public operates within the conflict pattern of meanings, group differences are often magnified, positions polarized, and agreements that might otherwise have been reached are blocked.

But before we take up these topics, we shall underline the important part that conflict involving disruption and violence has played in the formation of public opin-

[1] Hugh D. Graham and Ted R. Gurr, eds., *The History of Violence in America: Historical and Comparative Perspectives* (New York: Praeger Publishers, Inc., 1969), p. xxxii.
[2] Lewis Coser, "Conflict: Social Aspects," *International Encyclopedia of the Social Sciences* (1968), 3, 232. This usage is in the tradition of Georg Simmel, Leopold von Wiese, Robert Park, and Ernest Burgess.

ion at crucial junctures in American history. Gurr has drawn the following conclusion from an extensive comparative study of violence in the United States and 113 other countries from 1961 to 1965:

The United States unquestionably has experienced strife of greater intensity and pervasiveness in recent years than all but a very few other Western democracies. It is equally certain that violence in America has been less extensive and less disruptive than violence in a substantial number of non-Western nations.[3]

Seymour M. Lipset has effectively challenged the assumption that American history has been governed by consensus politics. Instead, the "politics of conscience" have repeatedly led groups of Americans to ignore the democratic institutions that are supposed to sublimate conflict and to employ violence and illegitimate means to promote their aims.[4]

The Mediating Public

A riot or other intergroup conflict directly affects the destruction of property and life and causes reactions of terror and exhilaration among persons immediately concerned. It also has wider and sometimes more enduring effects in the organization of the larger community and the nature of public policy. Standing between the event and the community is a public that develops a characterization of the event and formulates the issues that the event is believed to have raised.

There is a filtering process between the violent or disruptive encounter and the total community. In the large modern community, most individuals will first hear about an event from the mass media, which will filter the accounts both deliberately

and unintentionally. Paletz has called attention to the response of television broadcasters to criticism that their intensive and instantaneous coverage of riots fanned and extended the rioting. Television stations began exercising deliberate restraint in their coverage of public disorder with the result that black "self-assertion is not fully represented; whites are deceived as to the nature of black discontent, and therefore, of the potential or actual danger their city faces."[5] From the mass media, communication passes into the public, where the meanings and issues are crystallized. Thus filtered a second time, interpretations of the event reach community decision makers, and their actions, in turn, shape the event's effect on the larger community.

CENSURE AND EXONERATION. The most immediate concern of the public is to pass judgment on those who participate in public disturbances. In a confrontation between demonstrators or dissidents and public authorities, the propriety of actions on both sides is a key issue for the public determination. Publics debated whether the disturbances associated with the Democratic national convention in Chicago in 1968 should be called a "police riot,"[6] with the principal blame for violence lodged on the shoulders of police. Public debate aims at identifying and applying the mores regarding legitimate forms of dissent, so as to draw clear lines between proper and improper behavior. In the following selection Marvin Olsen surveys the individual judgments that enter into public discussion of legitimate and illegitimate ways of expressing dissent. His findings call attention to the dilemma of a population, many of whose members approve the aims but disapprove the means employed by racial militants.

---

[3] Ted R. Gurr, "A Comparative Study of Civil Strife," in Graham and Gurr, eds., *The History of Violence in America*, p. 618.
[4] Seymour M. Lipset, "On the Politics of Conscience and Extreme Commitment," *Encounter*, 31 (August, 1968), pp. 66–71.

[5] David L. Paletz, "Press Coverage of Civil Disorders: A Case Study of Winston-Salem, 1967," *Public Opinion Quarterly*, 33 (Fall, 1969), 345.
[6] Daniel Walker, *Rights in Conflict* (New York: The New American Library, Inc., 1968).

Perceived Legitimacy of Social Protest Actions

Marvin E. Olsen

It appears self-evident that a social protest movement must gain fairly widespread public acceptance or legitimacy if it is to be successful.[1] This generalization, however, overlooks the crucial distinction between public acceptance of a movement's goals, and acceptance of the actions it takes to attain these goals. Under what conditions is it possible for a social movement, through the skillful use of established channels of action, to achieve ends which the larger society defines as illegitimate? Conversely, under what conditions is it possible for a protest movement to attain socially approved goals by employing techniques which the society does not perceive as legitimate? Some attention has been given to the first of these questions by political sociologists,[2] but the second problem is almost totally unexplored.

The phenomenon of socially illegitimate means being used to gain legitimate ends, which is the focus of this paper, is particularly evident in the current civil rights movement in the United States. Undoubtedly a large majority of Americans passively accept, if not actively support, the goals of the civil rights movement for social, political, and economic equality of Negroes and whites. It is highly questionable, on the other hand, whether most whites approve of the protest actions—such as mass marches, demonstrations, boycotts, and sit-ins—being used by the major civil rights groups.

This paper reports the results of a limited investigation into two aspects of this problem: (a) the extent of public acceptance of various types of non-violent social protest actions among a sample of highly educated persons in one community; and (b) relationships existing between acceptance or rejection of these protest actions and a number of basic social, economic, political, and demographic variables.

THE RESPONDENTS

Data for these analyses were taken from a survey of political alienation conducted in Ann Arbor, Michigan, in 1965.[3] As part of the research design of this larger study, the respondents were selected entirely from two census tracts within the city. Although these two tracts taken together are fairly typical of Ann Arbor on several social dimensions, they cannot be considered as representative of the entire community, much less the total society. These respondents must therefore be viewed as constituting a population in themselves, and the results of this research cannot validly be generalized beyond this particular population.[4] Nevertheless, the findings obtained here are suggestive for further research on a broader scale.

Two hundred respondents were selected systematically from the current City Directory, and interviews were successfully conducted with 154 of them, for a completion rate of 77 percent. Several overall characteristics of this population are worthy of notice: (a) It is very highly educated; 50 percent are college graduates, and four-fifths of these people also have one or more graduate degrees. (b) It is concentrated near the top of the occupational status hierarchy; 67 percent of the heads of these households hold managerial, executive, or professional jobs (the most common occupation being college professor). (c) As might

---

From *Social Problems,* 15 (Winter, 1968), 297–310. Reprinted in part by permission of the Society for the Study of Social Problems and the author.
[1] C. Wendell King, *Social Movements in the United States,* New York, Random House, 1956, p. 54.
[2] For instance, see Seymour Martin Lipset's analysis of the rise to power of the Nazis in Germany through democratic election procedures: *Political Man,* Garden City, N. Y., Doubleday and Co., 1960, Ch. 5.

[3] Marvin E. Olsen, "Political Assimilation, Social Opportunities, and Political Alienation," unpublished Ph.D. dissertation, Department of Sociology, The University of Michigan, 1965.
[4] Because these respondents were conceived of as a population rather than as a sample, tests of statistical significance were not relevant for these data.

be expected from the previous two items, it is well above the national average in income; 49 percent earn over $10,000 a year. (d) It is almost equally divided between men and women. (e) In age, it is slightly skewed in favor of elderly persons; 28 percent are age 60 or older. (f) Unintentionally, it is almost entirely white, since it includes only three nonwhites. As a consequence, the factor of race is in effect held constant in this research. (g) In terms of political preference, it is predominantly Republican; 46 percent gave this party as their preference, 25 percent chose the Democratic Party, and 29 percent called themselves Independents. The main conclusion to be drawn from these figures, especially those on education and occupation, is that the respondents should be well informed and quite sophisticated concerning the civil rights movement. Consequently, they should be considerably more tolerant of social protest actions than would be the majority of people in this society.

LEGITIMACY OF PROTEST ACTIONS

To what extent do the goals of the civil rights movement enjoy public acceptance? As part of a series of questions on attitudes toward governmental programs, respondents were asked to react to this statement: "If Negroes are not getting fair treatment in jobs and housing, the federal government should see to it that they do." The distribution of responses was as follows: (a) agree strongly, 44 percent; (b) agree mildly, 34 percent; (c) disagree mildly, 9 percent; (d) disagree strongly, 9 percent; (e) don't know, 4 percent. In view of the fact that 78 percent of these people favored the idea of governmental action to promote interracial equality, we may infer that they are overwhelmingly sympathetic with the basic goals of the civil rights movement. But do they look with equal favor upon the tactics currently being used by civil rights protesters as a means of gaining social power and achieving social and political change?

To measure the perceived legitimacy of various types of social protest actions, the following question was asked of all respondents. The percentage of favorable responses to each type of action is given in parentheses.

If a group of people in this country strongly feels that the government is treating them unfairly, what kinds of actions do you think they have a right to take in order to try to change the situation? . . . Which of these actions do you think groups have a right to take in our country?

1. Hold public meetings and rallies. (92%)
2. March quietly and peacefully through town. (70%)
3. Take indirect actions such as economic boycotts or picketing. (60%)
4. Take direct actions such as strikes or sit-ins. (46%)
5. Stage mass protest demonstrations. (41%)

The five responses to this question form a unidimensional scale, using Guttman techniques, with a coefficient of reproducibility of 96.6 percent.[5] Only 31.2 percent of the respondents (48 persons) considered all five of these types of protest actions to be legitimate. The mean scale score was 3.14.

Although the principle of freedom of speech is strongly upheld by these data, it is striking (and perhaps even alarming) that 30 percent of these highly educated and supposedly sophisticated people would deny to dissatisfied groups the right to march quietly and peacefully through town. More relevant for our present concern, though, is the discovery that less than half of the respondents accept the legitimacy of sit-ins, mass demonstrations, and other such protest actions which are widely and effectively being employed in the civil rights movement. Although these findings are only suggestive, we might predict that on a national level the public acceptance of such direct protest actions would be even lower.[6]

In summary, we may tentatively suggest that the goals of the civil rights movement enjoy considerably more social legitimacy than do many of the actions being utilized by protest groups.

RELATED SOCIAL FACTORS

As a first step toward explaining acceptance or rejection of social protest actions, we now focus on patterns of relationships occurring between these attitudes and the variables of education,

---

[5] The highest individual item error rate is 6.3%.
[6] Although well-educated, high socio-economic status people are commonly conservative in domestic economic affairs, repeated studies have shown them to be much more liberal than the rest of the population in all non-economic areas, such as civil rights. See S. M. Lipset, *Political Man, op. cit.,* Ch. 4.

occupation, income, age, sex, race, political preference, and political alienation. Although correlational analysis as performed here cannot demonstrate cause-and-effect relationships, it can be helpful in suggesting theoretical hypotheses and propositions. All analyses reported here were made with the Multiple Classification Analysis computer program, which performs, on non-interval data, statistical computations analogous to partial and multiple correlation.[7] Two summation measures, in addition to eta and beta coefficients, were utilized in this research: (a) mean scores on the protest actions scale, for which the possible range is zero to five, designated as "$\bar{X}$ Score"; and (b) percentage of respondents with scale scores of five, indicating acceptance of all of these types of protest actions, designated as "% Accepting."

On theoretical grounds, we would expect education to be the single factor most highly associated with acceptance of social protest actions. This prediction is borne out by the data in Table 1, in which each of the "explanatory" variables is separately related to the protest actions scale. The higher a person's education, the more likely he is to consider all of these protest actions as legitimate—although a minor inversion does occur between two adjacent category scores. For this correlation, eta = .46 and eta² = .21, but these figures are inflated by the inverted scores.

As we would expect, both occupation (eta = .29, eta² = .09) and income (eta = .31, eta² = .10) are also positively associated with tolerance of social protest actions. Once again, though, inver-

sions occur between adjacent category scores on both variables, which consequently inflate the eta coefficients.

Men tend to be slightly more accepting of these actions than are women (eta = .18, eta² = .03), although the difference is not great. Age is inversely related to tolerance of protest actions, with younger people being the most liberal (eta = .34, eta² = .12). In terms of political party preference, Democrats are the most accepting of protest actions, followed by Independents and Republicans in that order (eta = .13, eta² = .02), but this is a rather weak correlation.

Political alienation is here conceptualized as a set of attitudes of separation or estrangement between oneself and the political system of one's society. Two types of political alienation were investigated and measured: attitudes of political incapability and attitudes of political discontentment. The essential difference between these two phenomena lies in the direction of the alienative process. In the case of political incapability, the person feels incapable of effectively participating in political affairs because of the nature of the political system. Attitudes of estrangement from the political system are involuntarily imposed upon the individual by the nature of that system as he perceives it. This category of political alienation includes such specific attitudes as powerlessness and meaninglessness in relation to politics, and is roughly equivalent to Litt's concept of "political futility."[8] It was measured with a revised version of the political efficacy scale developed by Camp-

---

[7] This program enables one to examine the effects on a designated "dependent" variable of one or more nominally or ordinally scaled "independent" variables, while other related variables are held constant. For each category of each independent variable, the program gives both the "unadjusted" mean of the dependent variable score and an "adjusted" mean which takes into account the effects of all other independent variables (i.e., partials out their effects). The program also determines for each independent variable an eta coefficient which indicates (when squared) the proportion of variance in the dependent variable explained by that "predictor" alone, and a beta coefficient which indicates (when squared) the proportion of variance in the dependent variable explained by the "predictor" holding constant all other variables. Finally, the program gives an "adjusted multiple correlation coefficient," which indicates (when squared) the proportion of variance in the dependent variable explained by all the predictors simultaneously.

[8] Edgar Litt, "Political Cynicism and Political Futility," *The Journal of Politics*, Vol. 25, May 1963, pp. 312–323. Although several writers have attempted to conceptualize and measure powerlessness and meaninglessness as separate dimensions of alienation, this distinction has never been specifically applied to political estrangement. In defense of this position, it can be argued that attitudes of powerlessness and meaninglessness are perhaps inseparably linked in most people's minds. The following articles all distinguish among various dimensions of alienation: Melvin Seeman, "On the Meaning of Alienation," *American Sociological Review*, 24 (December, 1959), pp. 783–791; Dwight G. Dean, "Alienation: Its Meaning and Measurement," *American Sociological Review*, 26 (October, 1961), pp. 753–758; Russell Middleton, "Alienation, Race, and Education," *American Sociological Review*, 28 (December, 1963), pp. 973–977.

TABLE 1   Social Factors Related to Acceptance of Social Protest Actions

Factor	X̄ Score	% Accepting	N
Education			
Over 16 years	4.10	55.2%	58
16-years	3.00	26.3	19
13–15 years	2.42	20.8	24
12 years	2.68	12.0	25
9–11 years	2.36	14.3	14
0–8 years	2.14	7.1	14
Total	3.14	31.2%	154
eta = .46*, eta² = .21*			
Occupation			
High non-manual	3.49	40.2%	97
Low non-manual	2.82	25.0	16
High manual	2.23	7.7	26
Low manual	2.67	20.0	15
Total	3.14	31.2%	154
eta = .29*, eta² = .09*			
Income			
$10,000 or more	3.71	44.0%	75
$6000–$9999	2.66	27.6	29
$4000–$5999	2.72	20.0	25
Less than $4000	2.57	8.7	23
NA	—	—	2
Total	3.14	31.2%	154
eta = .31*, eta² = .10*-			
Sex			
Male	3.47	41.1%	39
Female	2.84	22.2	44
Total	3.14	31.2%	154
eta = .18, eta² = .03			
Age			
21–29	3.88	41.2%	17
30–44	3.71	42.9	42
45–59	3.16	35.3	51
60 or older	2.33	11.6	43
NA	—	—	1
Total	3.14	31.2%	154
eta = .34, eta² = .12			
Political Preference			
Democrat	3.49	38.5%	39
Independent	3.16	36.4	44
Republican	2.93	23.9	71
Total	3.14	31.2%	154
eta = .13, eta² = .02			
Political Incapability			
High (3–4)	2.00	4.0%	25
Above average (2)	2.37	13.3	30
Below average (1)	3.48	37.5	64
Low (0)	3.97	54.3	35
Total	3.14	31.2%	154
eta = .43, eta² = .18			

* Coefficient is somewhat inflated because the relationship is non-monotonic.

Table 1 (cont.)

Factor	X̄ Score	% Accepting	N
Political Discontentment			
High (3–4)	1.88	4.0%	25
Above average (2)	2.82	17.9	28
Below average (1)	3.44	35.4	48
Low (0)	3.71	51.0	49
NA	—	—	4
Total	3.14	31.2%	154
eta = .38, eta² = .14			

bell, et al.,[9] with low efficacy considered to be synonymous with high alienation. In the case of political discontentment, the person feels that the political system is not worth participating in. Attitudes of estrangement from politics are voluntarily chosen by him as his perception of the political system. This second category of political alienation includes such attitudes as dissatisfaction and disillusionment with political affairs, and is similar to Litt's conception of "political cynicism."[10] Political discontentment was measured with a scale specifically designed for this study.[11]

On speculative grounds, we might expect people who score high on either of these political alienation scales to be accepting of social protest actions aimed at effecting social and political change. Persons who feel politically incapable might believe that established political procedures were closed to them, thus forcing them to engage in group protest actions. Persons who feel politically discontented might believe, on the other hand, that direct actions such as these were necessary to bring about the political changes which they desire. Neither of these expectations are supported by the data in Table 1, however. In both cases, the less alienated a person's attitudes toward the political system, the more likely he is to view social protest actions as legitimate. Furthermore, these inverse correlations are moderately strong; for political incapability, eta = .43, eta² = .18; for political discontentment, eta = .38, eta² = .14. Apparently, those individuals who are most accepting of the political system as presently organized are also most tolerant of the rights of others to attempt to change social and political conditions. In contrast, people who feel either incapable or discontented toward the political system are also intolerant of social protest actions. Perhaps the underlying connection here is adherence to democratic political norms which concurrently support the existing political system but also grant individuals and groups the right to try to change that system through non-violent actions. Another possible explanation might be that persons who feel effective toward, or satisfied with, estab-

[9] The original scale is given in Angus Campbell, Gerald Gurin, and Warren E. Miller, *The Voter Decides,* Evanston, Ill., Row, Peterson, and Co., 1954, p. 187. With slight modifications in the wordings of two of the four items, the scale is as follows: (1) I believe public officials don't care much what people like me think. (2) There is no way other than voting that people like me can influence actions of the government. (3) Sometimes politics and government seem so complicated that I can't really understand what's going on. (4) People like me don't have any say about what the government does. Agreement with each of these items indicates attitudes of political incapability. This scale was approximately unidimensional for this population, with a coefficient of reproducibility of 89.3%.

[10] Litt, *loc. cit.*

[11] The scale consists of the following four items: (1) These days the government is trying to do too many things, including some activities which I don't think it has the right to do. (2) For the most part, the government serves the interests of a few organized groups, such as business or labor, and isn't very concerned about the needs of people like myself. (3) It seems to me that the government often fails to take necessary actions on important matters, even when most people favor such actions. (4) As the government is now organized and operated, I think it is hopelessly incapable of dealing with all the crucial problems facing the country today. Agreement with

each of the items was taken as indicative of political discontentment. This scale was also unidimensional for this population, with a coefficient of reproducibility of 91.9%.

lished political processes are accepting of protest actions precisely because they view these actions as a vital functional part of politics in this society.

. . .

[A section reporting multivariate analysis and supplying a more precise basis for the conclusions has been omitted.]

CONCLUSIONS

Although the results of this study must be treated only as suggestions for further research, they do raise a critical theoretical question: What effect does education have on one's willingness to grant legitimacy to the kinds of social protest actions being employed in the current civil rights movement? On the basis of these data, it appears that the relationship is not basically linear or monotonic. Highly educated persons are consistently willing to grant dissatisfied persons the right to engage in protest actions, regardless of their own age, political preference, or political attitudes. Poorly educated persons, in contrast, tend to score rather low on the protest actions scale. We have discovered, though, that if the effects of their strong attitudes of political incapability and discontentment are controlled, then their adjusted protest legitimacy scores are as high as those for college educated persons. Under similar controlled conditions, persons in the middle educational categories have the lowest scores on the protest actions scale. Thus the "true" rela-

tionship between education and acceptance of social protest actions appears to be curvilinear, with persons at the two educational extremes being the most willing to grant legitimacy to such actions.

Regardless of the overall effects of education on perceived legitimacy of protest activities, we have also discovered that two different types of political alienation—attitudes of political incapability and of political discontentment—are also strongly related to one's views toward protest actions. To some extent, these alienated attitudes probably act as intervening variables between the "background" factors of education, age, and political preference, and one's "immediate" response to social protest activities. At the same time, nevertheless, they also appear to have some independent effects of their own upon social protest action scale scores. Taken together, these two attitude scales provide a useful predictor of tolerance for protest actions.

This research has not explored other variables such as race or religion which may also be associated with acceptance or rejection of social protest activities. Nor can the findings obtained here be generalized to any larger sector of the American population. Hopefully, though, this study has opened a few theoretical windows and suggested a number of fruitful hypotheses for more extensive investigations into the types of social protest actions held to be legitimate in this society.

CHARACTERIZING THE EVENT. Passing judgment on demonstrators or rioters leads to a general characterization of what they are doing and the nature of their motives and goals. If their aims are deemed worthy, the rioters are likely to be treated with restraint, even when their tactics are disapproved of. Perhaps the most important determination by publics in recent years has been whether a public disruption or even an assassination is to be construed as an act of social protest, enabling the community to view the instigators and their

problems sympathetically, or their behavior as unredeemed evil. Official commissions' reports play an important part in establishing the meaning of a disturbance. Politically sensitive commisions respond to the play of interest groups; and once their reports are issued, they lend the weight of their official characterizations to one view of the events at the expense of other views. As the following selection indicates, the public creates a meaningful object toward which the community can act.

The Public Perception of Protest

Ralph H. Turner

Starting with Watts, dominant community sentiment and the verdicts of politically sensitive commissions identified mass violence by blacks primarily as acts of social protest. In contrast, gang *rumbles* are seldom viewed as protest, even when Puerto Ricans and other minorities are prominently involved. Three-fourths of an unspecified sample of Los Angeles residents in May, 1969, are reported to have seen disorders in secondary schools as the work of agitators and not as social protest,[1] even though Mexican-Americans and blacks have played leading roles. Events of early 1969 hint at a rising movement to redefine all racial and youthful disturbances in other terms than social protest. The aim of this paper is to suggest several theoretical vantage points from which to predict when a public will and will not view a major disturbance as an act of social protest.

The Meaning of Protest

An act of protest includes the following elements: the action expresses a grievance, a conviction of wrong or injustice; the protestors are unable to correct the condition directly by their own efforts; the action is intended to draw attention to the grievances; the action is further meant to provoke ameliorative steps by some target group; and the protestors depend upon some combination of sympathy and fear to move the target group in their behalf.

When they are identified as social protest, violence and disorder constitute a mode of communication more than a form of direct action. Looting is not primarily a means of acquiring property, as it is normally viewed in disaster situations;[2] breaking store windows and burning buildings is

not merely a perverted form of amusement or immoral vengeance like the usual vandalism and arson; threats of violence and injury to persons are not simply criminal actions. All are ways of expressing outrage against injustice of sufficient magnitude and duration to render the resort to such exceptional means of communication understandable to the observer.

The principal alternatives to protest in identifying the nature of violence and disorder are crime and deviance on the one hand and rebellion and revolution on the other. Defining a disturbance as protest does not preclude disapproving the violence or disorder by which the protest is expressed, nor does it preclude advocating immediate measures to control and suppress the disturbance. The principal indicators of a protest definition are concern with identifying the grievances as the most adequate way of accounting for the disturbance and the belief that the main treatment indicated is to ameliorate the unjust conditions.

Definitions by Publics

The nature of the public definition undoubtedly has consequences for the course and recurrence of the disturbance, and for short- and long-term suppression or facilitation of reform. But the important tasks of specifying and verifying the consequences of protest definition fall beyond the limits of this paper.

The balance of this paper will be devoted to suggesting five theoretical vantage points from which it is possible to formulate hypotheses regarding the conditions under which one group of people will define disturbances by some other group as social protest. First, publics test events for *credibility* in relation to folk-conceptions of social protest and justice. Second, disturbances communicate some combination of *appeal and threat*, and the balance is important in determining whether social protest is the reading given. Third, disturbances instigate conflict with a target group, who may define them as social protest in the course of attempted *conciliation* to avoid full scale conflict. Fourth, defining disturbances as protest is

---

Condensed from "The Public Perception of Protest," *American Sociological Review*, 34 (December, 1969), 815–31.

[1] *Los Angeles Times*, May 19, 1969.

[2] Russell Dynes and Enrico L. Quarantelli, "What Looting in Civil Disturbances Really Means," *Trans-Action*, 5 (May, 1968), 9–14.

an invitation from a third party for the trouble-making group to form a *coalition*. And fifth, acting as if the disturbances were social protest can be a step by public officials in establishing a *bargaining* relationship.

The paper offers theoretical proposals and not tested findings. The proposals are not a complete catalogue of causes for protest interpretation, notably omitting such variables as understanding, empathy, and kindness. The proposals generally assume that there is no well-established tradition of disruptive or violent protest,[3] that the society is not sharply polarized, and that the disturbances emanate from a clearly subordinated segment of the society.

CREDIBILITY AND COMMUNICATION

If a disturbance is to be viewed as social protest, it must somehow look and sound like social protest to the people witnessing it.

Credibility: The Folk Concept

The main outlines of a *folk concept*[4] of social protest appear to be identifiable in contemporary American culture. The folk concept is only partially explicit, and is best identified by examining the arguments people make for viewing events and treating troublemakers in one way or another. Letters to newspapers and editorial and feature columns supply abundant material in which to conduct such a search.

Several components of the folk concept of social protest emerge from examination of relevant materials. To be credible as protestors, trouble-makers must seem to constitute a major part of a group whose grievances are already well documented, who are believed to be individually or collectively powerless to correct their grievances, and who show some signs of moral virtue that render them "deserving." To be credible as protest a disturbance must follow an extended period in which both the powerlessness and the grievances

have already been effectively advertized. Non-violent movements that precede violent disruptions help to establish the credibility of protest. The disturbance itself must be seen either as a spontaneous, unplanned, and naive outburst, or as an openly organized protest of more limited nature that got tragically out of hand. Indications of the use of riots for self-aggrandisement, the settlement of private feuds, or enjoyment of violence and destruction must be subordinated to naive anger and desperation. Finally, some indications of restraint are important clues to interpretation as protest.

If we assume that each group tends to employ its own situation as the point of reference in assessing another group's claims of injustice, we are led to the conclusion that groups who are clearly *advantaged* by comparison with the "protestors" can find the claim of injustice more credible than groups less advantaged. Consequently the great middle segment of American population finds it easier to identify black ghetto disturbances as social protest than to interpret college student demonstrations in this way. Similarly black student demonstrations are less amenable to interpretation as protest than ghetto demonstrations. According to this view, groups who see themselves as even more disadvantaged than the protestors are least likely to grant their claim. Viewed from below, disturbances are most easily comprehended as power plays or as deviance.

Credibility: Crediting Crime, Protest, Rebellion

The credibility of a disturbance as protest also reflects the variable strength of resistances against believing that massive crime, protest, or rebellion is taking place. Rebellion is difficult to credit by all but those whose disaffection with the social order is such that they delight in the threat of its disintegration. When crime and deviance become extensive and blatant, the assumption of a society integrated on the basis of consensus over major values is shaken. When judgments by different socioeconomic strata are compared, the middle strata find it more difficult to credit massive deviance and crime and less difficult to acknowledge protest because of their commitment to society as a system of values.

---

[3] Allan A. Silver, "Official Interpretations of Racial Riots," in Robert H. Connery, ed., *Urban Riots: Violence and Social Change* (New York: Academy of Political Science, 1968), pp. 146–158.

[4] Ralph H. Turner, "The Normative Coherence of Folk Concepts," *Research Studies of the State College of Washington,* 25 (June, 1957), pp. 127–136.

Appeal and Threat Messages

It is a reasonable assumption that most observers could, under appropriate circumstances, see both an *appeal* and a *threat* in a violent disturbance. If this combination of messages is present, reading the disturbance as protest means that the appeal component is more salient to the observer than the threat component. Thus we are led to the proposition that disruptions are interpreted as protest only when the experience of threat is not excessive.

However, a combination of threat and appeal is required to gain attention and to create the sense of urgency necessary to overcome the resistance to acknowledging protest. Hence we are led to suspect that there is an optimal combination of threat and appeal for the probability of seeing disturbance as protest. When the threat component falls below the optimal range, the most likely interpretation is deviance; above the optimal range preoccupation with threat makes rebellion the probable interpretation.

This approach suggests several hypotheses relating interpretation as protest to the nature and bounds of the disorder and to the position of various population segments reacting to the disorders. Intuition suggests that either pitched battles leading to death and injury of any substantial number of whites, or spread of the disorders outside of the boundaries of black neighborhoods and especially into white residence areas would substantially reduce the likelihood of disorders being interpreted as a form of protest and would seriously divert attention away from black grievances.

Differential perception of threat by population segments is affected by a combination of personal involvement and proximity to the events and of ability to perceive the limits and patterns of disorder realistically. On this basis it is easiest for groups who live a safe distance from black neighborhoods and who have no stake in ghetto businesses to turn their attention toward the appeal component of the disturbance message. However, whites closest to the disturbances may be better able to discount inflated reports of violence against the persons of whites, and to see pattern in the properties attacked and protected. Thus persons close enough to fear any spread of disorders but not close enough to correct exaggerated

reports from personal experience may find it most difficult to see the activities as protest.

Finally, according to the assumption of an optimal mixture of threat and appeal it may be difficult to keep the awareness of protest dominant for an extended period of time. Escalation of violence is likely to preclude protest definition because of preoccupation with the threat. But repeated threat that is not followed by tangible injury to the threatened loses its impact.

CONCILIATION OF CONFLICT

A more complex basis for predicting the assignment of meaning to disorders is supplied by viewing the protestors and the interpreters as engaged in a real or potential process of conflict. The aggressive initiative of the moment lies with the protestors. Interpreting the disturbances as protest can then usefully be seen as a *gesture of conciliation,* an action to forestall the incipient conflict or to reduce or conclude the conflict without victory or surrender.

In Coser's definition of conflict as "a struggle over values or claims to status, power, and scarce resources, in which the claims of the conflicting parties are not only to gain the desired values but also to neutralize, injure, or eliminate their rivals,"[5] we underline the latter portion. Conflict has properties that distinguish it from other processes revolving about disagreement because there is an autonomous goal of injuring the antagonist—autonomous in the sense that efforts to injure the antagonist are not fully subjected to the test of effectiveness in promoting the other ostensible goals of the conflicting party.

There is frequently confusion between the steps from disagreement toward agreement and the process of conflict resolution. It is possible to resolve conflict without agreement on substantive issues, but agreement on these issues does not erase the injury that each has done to the other in the course of the conflict. The key to all conflict resolution is the repair of previous injury and protection against future injury

We shall refer to any act whose aim is to avert or

---

[5] Lewis Coser, "Conflict: Social Aspects," *International Encyclopedia of the Social Sciences,* 3 (1968), 232.

discontinue conflict without either asking or offering surrender as conciliation. To be effective, a conciliatory act must incorporate both an offer to discontinue attacks and a tender of help in correcting the harm already done.

Faced with potential conflict, the dominant group has several alternatives, though not all are viable in any given situation. An effort can be made to ignore or depreciate the conflict significance of the disturbances, by interpreting them as deviance. The challenge of conflict can be accepted, in which case the disturbance is defined as rebellion and the appropriate response is retaliatory suppression. This was plainly the dominating white reaction in earlier race riots such as St. Louis in 1917 and Detroit in 1943, when whites not only turned the encounters into massive attacks on Negroes but continued to take punitive action for weeks after the riots were finished and after the evidence of disproportionate injury to Negroes was plain for all to see.[6] It is also common for some individuals to respond by repudiating their own group identification and joining with the dissidents, at least symbolically.

If we omit the possibility of surrender, the remaining alternative is to extend an offer of conciliation. The conciliator offers public acknowledgement that he has done injury to the protestor, promising repentence and corrective actions. By making this acknowledgement he grants that there is some justification for the other's hostility toward him, and he also supplies the basis for believing that the other's antagonism is not unalterable and is not personal to himself or his group.

Interpreting violent and disruptive action as protest is following exactly this pattern. It means assuming that the intent to do injury is secondary in importance to the effort to secure redress, and it means acknowledging that there is some basis in the behavior of one's own group for the antagonism displayed by the protestor.

Individuals and groups seek to avert conflict for four reasons: to avoid the risk of injury (or further injury) to themselves; to avoid the risk of injury or

---

[6] Cf. Alfred M. Lee and Norman D. Humphrey, *Race Riot* (New York: Dryden Press, 1943); Elliott M. Rudwick, *Race Riot in East St. Louis, July 2, 1917* (Carbondale: Southern Illinois University Press, 1964)

further injury to the potential opponent; to protect the relationship between the potential combatants from damage or increased damage; and to avoid the diversion of resources and energy into the conduct of conflict at the expense of other activities. The view of protest interpretation as conciliation and the reasons for conciliation suggest several correlates of protest interpretation.

First, protest interpretation is more likely to occur when there is some apparent danger to the group than when there is none. Second, the stronger the norms, values, or sentiments against doing injury to others, the greater the likelihood of interpreting disorder as protest. Third, the greater the interdependency between groups, the greater the likelihood of protest interpretation.

Fourth, the greater the commitment to activities and resources that may have to be sacrificed in order to carry on the conflict, the greater the readiness to make a protest interpretation. Some groups are flexibly organized so that conflict can be sustained alongside of continuing normal activities. Private industry was long able to avoid treating labor unrest as social protest because private police could be hired to carry on and isolate the conflict while production continued. Universities are not equipped in this fashion, and must therefore face disruption of their normal functions under even mild conflict. Hence universities are relatively quick to interpret internal disturbances as social protest.

Fifth, the less the anticipated costs of conciliation, the greater the tendency to see disturbance as protest. College officials who believe that discontinuing an R. O. T. C. program is sufficient to bring an end to campus conflict find it easy to see student activism as social protest, rather than as rebellious confrontation.

Because of the tendency for moralistic perspectives to be an inseparable part of conflict, an offer of conciliation is typically viewed by the conciliator as an act of generosity, going beyond what could be expected or required of him. Furthermore, the protest interpretation with its clearly implied admission of fault places the conciliator in a precarious position, for his admission of prejudice, militarism, or insensitivity to student needs can be used against him later if the other does not respond in kind. Hence there is a strong tendency for conciliatory gestures to be withdrawn and replaced by active promotion of conflict when there is no discontinuance of insults and threats and no retraction of earlier attacks.

THIRD PARTY POINT OF VIEW

From both the appeal-threat and conflict-conciliation approaches comes the hint that a *third party* may under some circumstances find it easier to interpret disturbance as protest than does the group against whom the disturbance is directed.

Third party protest interpretations indicate either the defense of neutrality against the threat of partisan involvement in conflict or the active acceptance of partisanship on the side of the protestors.

Defining disturbance as protest can be a *defense of neutrality* for the third party for some of the same reasons that it can be a means of conciliation for the target group. Acknowledging valid grievances while condemning improper means is a way of giving something to each side. Protest definition as a defense of neutrality occurs when (1) strong pressures toward partisan involvement play on the third party but (2) partisanship on either side is a costly prospect.

Protest definition as *partisanship* is most likely when circumstances facilitate coalition formation. In the broadest of terms, coalitions are formed when the allies can do better together than they can separately vis-a-vis some other group, and when they can arrange between them an acceptable division of the advantages that accrue from the coalition.[7] On this basis other disadvantaged minority groups might support the efforts of militant blacks, if they could be reasonably sure of gaining a substantial share of whatever concessions militancy wins from the target group. But since the concessions are likely to fall short of meeting black wants, they are unlikely to be divided. On the other hand, forming an alliance with the powerful target group may offer the prospect of

greater rewards than an alliance with blacks. It is clear that contradictory tendencies are at work in this situation but that the problem of distributing limited benefits works against strong coalitions and against interpreting the other minority group's activism as social protest.

Coalitions with disruptive groups are more likely to be favorable for groups of higher standing whose own position is strengthened by adding the threat of disorder from the protesting group to their own established power. Groups and agencies who are in a position to serve as the intermediate link in distributing benefits to protestors may invite the protestors into a coalition by announcing acknowledgement of the latter's grievances.

It is interesting that several principles converge to predict the overwhelming tendency for college and university faculties to view campus disruptions as social protest. First, the credibility-injustice principle is invoked by the faculty position of super-ordination to the students. Through constant contact and intimate familiarity with the circumstances of student life, faculty members readily understand the grievances of students by comparison with their own more favorable position. Second, the earlier student disorders were directed almost wholly against college administrations rather than faculty, making the latter a third party. Structurally the faculty position makes them subject to strong pressures toward partisan involvement, but makes partisanship on either side costly. Organizationally the faculty belong to the same side as the administration, but their contacts with students in the conduct of their work are more frequent and more crucial to the success of their teaching and research activities on the day to day basis. As third parties faculty members sought neutrality by interpreting student disturbances as protest. Third, by virtue of the residue of resentments from their own relationships with administrators, some faculty members were inclined to proffer a coalition to the students. On the basis that the higher status partner in a coalition ultimately gains more if the coalition lasts, this could be an effective tactic in strengthening the faculty position vis-a-vis administration. However, all of these principles operate differently when students take faculty as the target for their disruptions.

---

[7] Theodore Caplow, *Two Against One: Coalitions in Triads* (Englewood Cliffs, N.J.: Prentice-Hall, Inc., 1968).

OFFICIAL ACTIONS

We have spoken of the predisposition by various groups to identify disturbances under varying circumstances as social protest. But we have neglected thus far to assign enough importance to the actions of officials and formal leaders who must react conspicuously. On the basis of well established principles in the study of public opinion, opinion leadership and keynoting by officials should be a substantial determinant of public definitions.[8]

The public definition exhibited by officials is only a simple application of their private views when two conditions are met: the community definitions are overwhelmingly homogeneous; and officials have the resources to be certain their efforts are effective. When Federal Bureau of Investigation officials set out in the 1930's to eradicate gangster leaders, these conditions prevailed and there was no need to explore the possibility that gangsterism was a protest against ethnic discrimination, cultural assimilationism, and poverty. But when these conditions do not prevail, treating disturbances as protest can serve as a hedging tactic. It permits a restrained handling that does not create the expectation of immediate suppression of disturbances, without forestalling a shift toward a harder line after community sentiment and official capability have been tested.

The effect of these official responses is initially to keynote and legitimate the protest interpretation by various community segments. When these responses coincide with substantial prestigious community definitions of the events, the effect is further to establish a situational norm identifying the proper or publically acceptable interpretation. The result is an unstable situation in which temporarily the socially sanctioned view sees disturbance as protest, while dissident views subsist as an audible rumbling in the background.

When the grievance is not so limited and specific that it can be easily and quickly righted, when complete confidence in official capability to supress massive crime or rebellion is lacking, or when community support is uncertain, the standard official approach is to explore the possibilities of resolving the confrontation through bargaining. Accounts of the 1967 racial disorders indicate repeated efforts to identify black representatives who could bargain for the protestors, and numerous instances of tentative bargains that failed because agents on one side or the other could not command the support of the group they were supposed to represent. Official entry into a bargaining relationship serves initially to validate a public definition of the disturbances as social protest, acknowledging the merit of some grievances.

When the potential for disturbances persists, the tendency is to move toward an accommodation through a system of routinized bargaining, such as we practice between management and labor unions or through the sensitive ward organization of machine politics. But the effect of a *routinized* bargaining relationship is to erode the protest meanings. Routinized bargaining and the protest interpretation are incompatible for several reasons. Protest tends to define open-ended commitments: no one can tell how much effort and money will ultimately be required to correct racial inequities in the United States. But bargaining can only occur with respect to specific and delimited demands, permitting concessions to be weighed against costs. The bargainer must view the exchange impersonally, seeing the other's demands as tactics. He cannot afford the sentimentality of viewing them as legitimate grievances. The attributes of spontaneity and naivete that inhere in the folk concept of social protest are no longer met by organized routinized disorders. Quite a different conception of protest is involved in the routinized disorders of the London mobs described by Hobsbaum.[9]

As it becomes evident that the official approach is now the impersonal approach of bargaining, public sanction for the protest interpretation weakens. The result is either to free the suppressed unsympathetic interpretations in the pattern known as "backlash," or to accept the relationship as one of impersonal bargaining. If the former happens there is pressure on public officials to discontinue bargaining. At the time of this writing this is clearly

---

[8] Elihu Katz and Paul Lazarsfeld, *Personal Influence* (Glencoe, Ill.: Free Press, 1955).

[9] Eric J. Hobsbaum, *Social Bandits and Primitive Rebels* (New York: The Free Press, 1959).

happening in connection with the pattern of bargaining by university officials with militant student groups. If the latter happens, minor disturbances come to be accepted as recurring minor annoyances. As in most contemporary labor disputes, public attitude is "what are they asking for this time?" assuming that the aim is competitive betterment rather than grievance correction.

CONCLUSION

A speculative analysis of this sort should be completed by bringing together all of the predictions and indicating where the sets of assumptions are redundant, where they are contradictory, and where they are complementary. But neither the theories nor the variables can be precisely enough designated at the present time to support this type of summation. Three observations will underline the main thrust of the approach we have employed.

First, the analysis exemplifies the assumption that meanings are attached to events as an aspect of intergroup process. The meaning attributed to a public disturbance expresses in large part the current and anticipated interaction between the various relevant groups. Meanings change both currently and retrospectively as the process unfolds and as intergroup relationships change. Second, there are important shades of differences in protest interpretations that correspond with the specific types of intergroup process in which the interpreters are involved. Three kinds of relationship have been reviewed. One group may become *partisans* in conflict with the troublemakers, either because they belong to a group that can usefully make common cause against the target group while maintaining an advantageous position in a coalition with the troublemakers, or because of disaffection from their own group so that they ally with its enemies. Concern of the former with the protestors' grievances is constantly tinged with a comparison of benefits that each group gains from the coalition. For the latter, orientation toward conflict is the salient bond and discomfiture of the target group easily becomes a

more important aim than ameliorating the condition of the troublemakers.

A second group may see themselves as prime target for attack or as neutrals in danger of being drawn into conflict with the troublemakers, and respond with an offer of conciliation. Conciliation involves a generous interpretation of the troublemakers' activities, acknowledging their grievances, admitting fault, and identifying their activity as social protest. Grievances must be identified if conciliation is to proceed. But the salient condition easily becomes protection of the target group, and the protest interpretation is highly vulnerable in the event that conciliation is not reciprocated.

A third group, typically public officials and spokesmen, engages in bargaining by offering some amelioration in return for guarantees against further violence and disorder. But the impersonal and calculating nature of bargaining, especially as it recurs and is routinized, works against seeing the trouble as social protest. The disturbance soon becomes a move in a competitive game, to be met by minimal and calculated concessions. And as the masters of urban political machines have long understood, "buying off" protest leaders directly tends to be a less costly and more immediately effective tactic of bargaining than offering programs for amelioration of underlying grievances.

Our third and final observation is that interpreting public disorders as social protest is an unstable and precarious condition. It requires an optimally balanced set of conditions, and is difficult to maintain over an extended period of time. Insofar as such interpretations are favorable to social reform it appears that they must be capitalized quickly, while conditions are favorable, through programs that can be implemented on a continuing basis by a more routinized and impersonal bargaining. Perhaps a residue of understanding that can be favorable to future reforms may remain in spite of community redefinition. Perhaps also reformers should not overestimate what can be gained by disorderly protest in relation to the many other means for effecting change.

Public Response to Disorder

RESTORATION OF PUBLIC ORDER. Although public disorders and demonstrations often heighten community awareness of an injustice that needs to be corrected, they also create a concern for the maintenance of order. Everyone seems to gain occasional satisfaction from seeing routines disturbed and public officials discomfited. But for most people the satisfaction soon gives way to alarm when lasting damage to public order is anticipated. The issue of public order versus disruption is usually of far wider concern in the community than the injustices at stake. The issue of wages and hours that precipitates a strike by a labor union is of little immediate interest to most people, but the disruption of essential services concerns vast numbers. The problems of black unemployment are of little more than intellectual concern to many people, who nevertheless fear intensely the prospects of spreading violence and a neutralized police force.

When there is considerable public awareness and concern for issues over which conflict occurs, demonstrators' tactics color the perception of these issues. In all publics, abstract principles tend to be converted into questions of relative trust. The police versus the black ghetto-dwellers and the yippies versus the Daly political organization in Chicago are choices for people to make. The tactics reported used by representatives of each group affect the trust that people are willing to place in each group, and thus the position they take on the larger issue. Here lies the danger of "backlash"—the public reaction against a group whose tactics are feared and resented. The strong support for Governor George Wallace's right-wing American Independence party among working-class youth in 1968 and after appears to have

been such a reaction against the disruptive behavior of blacks and college youth.[7]

Often there is little initial awareness and concern for the issues, as the groups in conflict see them, so the threats to public order produce a public that defines issues strictly from the bystander perspective. The *bystander* is one who has no stake in the outcome of the conflict but is in danger of being injured so long as the conflict continues. He is the innocent passer-by who fears stray bullets from either side. To the bystander the issue, as the contestants see it, is of secondary importance; the primary issue is the incidental injury he may suffer.

A housing tract was picketed for a full year because the developer would not sell to blacks. A newspaper reporter interviewed residents, asking them what it was like for a year with pickets marching in front of their homes. Replies described effects on the children, awkwardness when guests were invited, occasional difficulties when essential services were delayed because deliverymen were reluctant to cross a picket line, depressed resale values, and similar results. The residents saw themselves caught in the crossfire between civil-rights activists and the developer, and as having no special stake in the outcome but suffering numerous inconveniences so long as the conflict was not resolved.

The bystander public defines the primary issue as restoration of order and elimination of danger and inconvenience by bringing *any* end to the conflict. The bystander is basically impartial. His slogan is "a plague on both your houses!" The demonstrators are condemned for fomenting trouble, and the authorities are condemned for not maintaining order. The bystander public

[7] Seymour M. Lipset and Earl Raab, "The Wallace Whitelash," *Trans-Action*, 7 (December, 1969), 23–35.

puts pressure on whichever group seems to be the stumbling block to peace at the moment or on whichever group seems capable of restoring peace.

A bystander public frequently first supports established authority against the disrupters. The striking bus-drivers should go back to work and negotiate their grievances without inconveniencing the community. The peace activists should restrict themselves to nondisruptive measures. But if the disorder continues, the bystander public universally shifts attention toward the issue of whether authorities are acting competently and sincerely to bring the conflict to an end. So long as the public does not become an acting crowd, it has better prospects of influencing the conduct of authorities than the behavior of a dissident group. Hence the ultimate stance of a bystander public is usually to undermine confidence in authorities. This shift does not lead to a more favorable view of the disrupters; it simply means increasing preoccupation with the authorities' failure to restore order.

The following letter to The *Los Angeles Times,* published on March 1, 1969, following violence on the Berkeley campus of the University of California, expresses the bystander viewpoint.

I am a university employee of several years standing, and because of the location of my office, have been witness to much of the action between police and demonstrators during the current strike.

At this point, I am forced to realize that the luxury of opining the relative guilt of each faction is no longer relevant. What is relevant is the safety of employees on the south side of campus.

During the increasingly frequent dangerous periods, supervisors have requested permission to send their employees home. The chancellor's memo of February 19, 1969, has stated the employees will not be excused. Windows are broken by flying rocks and glass, in addition to constant bombing and bloody beatings.

Finally on February 20 employees were released in the latter part of the afternoon after police had teargassed the area....

The administration is encouraging continuous escalation of the strike by requesting ever-increasing numbers of police on campus. It is inevitable that people will be seriously injured —possibly by a bomb on a larger scale than we have experienced thus far. The presence of police on campus is not protecting me; rather, it is endangering my safety.

Experienced authorities are well aware of the danger to their own position from continuing disorder. Hence the effect of the bystander public is to press authorities toward hastening the end of disturbances either by vigorous repressive action or by a series of concessions. This promotes gains for the dissidents whenever the alternative of suppression is not employed effectively.

As a general principle, all publics tend to become bystander publics when oppositions remain active over a long period of time. Publics concerned with labor-management strife are almost entirely bystander publics; publics concerned with civil rights and peace actions are taking on the bystander point of view with greater and greater frequency. The restoration of public order is dominant in the later stages of any public controversy.

COERCIVE PROTEST. Because of the dynamics of bystander publics, it is possible to organize protest activities so as to bring great pressure to bear on authorities. When this is done the aim is less persuasion than coercion. David Bayley describes six forms of coercive protest that have become so prevalent as to threaten democratic constitutional government in India. The forms are processions and public meetings; hartals (work stoppages not aimed at employers), boycotts, and strikes; fasts; obstructions; courting of arrest; and riots. Although occasional incidents of this nature are a normal feature of any open society, as a regular way of registering opinion they undermine majority rule. "...a sort of Gresham's law begins to affect the nature of political responses. Direct action and recourse to social violence—either threatened or actual—begin to drive out the orderly, constitutional responses demanded in a democratic state."[8] The well-elaborated tradition of civil disobedience persisted in India after the end of British rule but without the distinctively Ghandian conscience. This tradition, combined with the danger that control efforts will enhance sympathy for the protestors, makes the task of government control without excessive repression an extremely difficult one.[9]

Construction of Reality in Conflict

Whenever conflict becomes the governing process in a public, the combatants visualize reality in a distinctive way. We must recall that in conflict, as distinguished from disagreement, debate, competition, or rivalry, there is an autonomous goal of discrediting or injuring the opponent. Because of this there are certain strategies that require different ethical principles than do other forms of interaction. The aims, strategies, and ethics of conflict all contribute to a distinctive belief system, a way of viewing reality that prevails when conflict is dominant. We shall mention three features of this belief system.

IDENTIFYING THE ANTAGONISTS. For conflict purposes it is essential that all people be classifiable into three categories —friends, foes, and neutrals; that there be quick and dependable ways to tell which category any individual fits; that the relevant characteristics of people who fall into

either the friend or foe category be sufficiently homogeneous so the action directed toward them can be uniform; and that the issues be sufficiently simplified so they neither impede the action nor lead to confusion and doubt over membership. If a certain tension between group and individual identity is a universal feature of interaction, the effect of conflict is to increase the merger of individual identities into group identities and to equate group identities with conflict positions.

Normal tendencies toward invidious characterizations of out-groups are intensified during conflict. The more serious and unrestrained the conflict, the more essential it becomes that the enemy be viewed as wholly devoid of redeeming qualities. Characterizations of the enemy exhibit fairly standard features in all types of conflict. First, the enemy's motivation is simple and not the mixture of sometimes reinforcing and sometimes contradictory impulses we have adopted in social science characterizations. To youth protesting the adult "establishment," college professors conduct research and publish *only* to gain prestige and material rewards. To adults who see events from an embattled position, it is *only* a desire to create disturbances and destroy institutions that lies behind youthful protest.

Second, the enemy's attitudes are not measurable as degrees on a continuum but are polarized. The heating up of racial conflict has substituted the term *racism* for the term *prejudice* with its connotation of an attitude present in varying degrees.

Third, the enemy's normal practice is deception with respect to his real intentions, attitudes, and motives. Hence it is acceptable and even required that the enemy's reasonable actions be discounted and his occasional reprehensible actions taken as indications of his true nature. To provoke the enemy until he finally abandons his reasonable and genteel facade is simply to expose him as he really is.

---

[8] David Bayley, "The Pedagogy of Democracy: Coercive Public Protest in India," *American Political Science Review,* 56 (Sept., 1962), 663–72.

[9] Ibid., passim. Cf. also Myron Weiner, *The Politics of Scarcity: Public Pressure and Political Response in India* (Chicago: University of Chicago Press, 1962).

PREOCCUPATION WITH LOYALTY, VIRTUE, AND LEADERSHIP. The precarious situation of all combatants leads to an anxious preoccupation with the loyalty and virtue of one's fellows, expressed in a volatile mixture of exaggerated loyalty and suspicion. In this atmosphere there is, first, a bending of usual norms to grant each person the right to be suspicious of the loyalty of others on grounds that would not otherwise be acceptable. In particular, to question or criticize the goals, the ideology, and even the capability of the ingroup is sufficient justification for being charged with disloyalty. Similarly, to acknowledge that the opponents' position has any justification is to warrant the assumption of disloyalty.

The obverse of this license to be suspicious is the requirement to demonstrate loyalty publicly. This applies even more strongly to leaders than to followers. Most members have no way to display their loyalty except by lustily and conspicuously attacking the enemy—more often symbolically than physically. In this way leaders and followers develop commitments to a simplified, polarized view of the issues and of the character and motivation of the enemy.

THE UTILITY OF CONFLICT. Although there is often intrinsic enjoyment from participation in conflict, sustention of conflict and its assimilation into the social order require that the conflict be viewed as promoting otherwise valued ends. In order to participate in riots it is therefore essential to believe that conflict is an effective device for making relevant changes in the social order, that the proximate ends attainable in conflict are the keys to larger reforms, and that the tactics most suitable to conflict are effective in changing the attitudes and actions of the enemy.

To the social scientist the effect of conflict, and even of victory in conflict, is neither simple, uniform, nor easily discernible. That even victors in revolution must be so preoccupied with establishing control that they shelve many of their projected reforms has been common knowledge, at least since Sorokin's account.[10] But part of the ideologies of militant groups is a well-developed rationale for believing that conflict is not only a highly effective agent for changing a social order but the only such agent.

The proximate goals in conflict are surrogates for the vaster changes sought. An essential part of the conflict belief system is linking these goals to the changes. Thus the issue of the Vietnam war is fought by opposing military subvention of academic research and ROTC, and the welfare of millions of slum-dwelling blacks is pursued by fighting for the black-studies units in universities and colleges. In both instances highly tentative assumptions become dogma to insure combatants that they are not engaged in a massive diversion of talent and effort away from more direct attack on the main problems.

Unless the aim of conflict is to destroy, expel, or subjugate the enemy by force, it is essential to believe that conflict tactics change the attitudes and behavior of those toward whom they are directed. Three favored tactics are ordering-forbidding, threatening, and evoking guilt. Ordering-forbidding is favored over persuasion and subtle forms of manipulation because it makes the confrontation explicitly normative, it simplifies relationships to compliance and noncompliance, and it maximizes the likelihood that the enemy will lose face when he complies. Similarly, evoking guilt insures discomfort to the enemy while placing the issue on a moral plane. Although behavioral scientists have long expressed doubts concerning the efficacy of these tactics for changing attitudes, the belief system of a typical conflict group assumes

---

[10] Pitirim A. Sorokin, *The Sociology of Revolution* (Philadelphia: J. B. Lippincott Co., 1925).

that the root of the problem is in men's hearts and that reforms can be achieved by use of these methods.

Conflict and Social Reform

As we have reviewed the functioning of publics, we have seen a wide range—from the quiet intellectualizing public to the impersonal bargaining public to the aroused conflict public. When we see how the public can be diverted from the consideration of issues on their merits, we wonder how often public discussion that is not carefully institutionalized and regulated to limit the development of a bystander perspective or the emergence of conflict imagery is an effective vehicle for community decision making. Scholars have sometimes seen the aroused public as an impediment to constructive change rather than its agent.

Crain, Katz, and Rosenthal sought to understand why 316 communities out of 515 in the United States rejected proposals to add fluorides to the water supplies, in the interest of reducing tooth decay. They observe that a majority of Americans favor fluoridation, the medical profession supports it unanimously, and local government officials seldom oppose it. Their investigation indicates that in most cases fluoridation campaigns failed because elected government leaders failed to support fluoridation. The leaders were "simply unwilling to annoy their anti-fluoridation voters, this despite the fact that the anti-fluoridationists are only a 'vocal minority' who are frequently led by persons of low social status, or by the chronic dissenters."[11] The investigators observe that because minorities can seldom be silenced, and because community leaders are accessible and without strong organizational support, the latter find themselves constantly on trial. Community

leaders are therefore unwilling to pay the costs in loss of minority support that go with active support of fluoridation.

. . . . we risk the conclusion that broad popular participation, particularly in the absence of strong executive leadership and an institutional channel for the expression of opposition spells defeat to fluoridation. It does so because fluoridation is a technical issue, the advantages of which are rather small from the citizen's point of view (and even less than that as far as political capital is concerned), and because the opposition can easily implant doubt. Doubt takes root and blossoms the more the issue is discussed. No matter why it is discussed, whether because of a pro-fluoridationist's compulsiveness about "health" education or a tradition of democratic debate in the city's clubs or a tradition of holding referenda, the opposition succeeds in arousing the citizenry.[12]

In his analysis of political violence in contemporary America, H. L. Nieburg sees black militancy as the "most salient precipitant of violence." Black militancy has produced "new norms of political behavior, endowing them with legitimacy, demonstrating their bargaining value to other groups, and eliciting retaliatory behavior."[13] It has also "created an atmosphere of anxiety and incipient terror which is making possible important, but not necessarily positive, social adjustments."[14] Other groups have taken advantage of these effects of black militancy in two ways. First they have sought to exploit black violence for their own purposes. Established groups offer their programs as solutions to black problems. Teachers, welfare recipients, college youth, and others associate their efforts with the aims of black rebellion. Second, the black militant pattern is widely imitated by other groups in promoting their aims. The result is to increase the number and seriousness of

---

11 Robert L. Crain, Elihu Katz, and Donald B. Rosenthal, *The Politics of Community Conflict: The Fluoridation Decision* (Indianapolis, Ind.: The Bobbs-Merrill Co., Inc., 1969), p. 206.

12 Ibid., p. 228.
13 H. L. Nieburg, *Political Violence: The Behavioral Process* (New York: St. Martin's Press, Inc., 1969), p. 139.
14 Ibid., p. 157.

confrontations, polarize the community into extreme positions, stifle communication, and impede the development of viable steps toward solutions.

Some years earlier Robert Park challenged the common view that discussion is a means for reaching agreement in the public.[15] As discussion is intensified, there are two common effects. First, heightened excitement leads to a demand for action. Far from facilitating examination of the issue, this demand strengthens the hands of those who are in a position to act in some conspicuous fashion. Established authorities are most often in this position, and the clever dictator can capitalize on these demands by entrenching himself in power.

Second, intense discussion—especially as it assumes the character of conflict—typically does more to expose hidden disagreements and enlarge known disagreements than to uncover common values. The importance of differences becomes exaggerated through argument, and limited issues become attached to more divisive issues. Issues also become more firmly linked to established group affiliations. All these tendencies combine to conceal the bases for agreement on effective plans for social reform. These conflict publics stimulate a great deal of activity but impede rather than facilitate social change. Park observes that most reform measures are not enacted when public interest and debate are at

their peak. Instead, they are accomplished when the public is at a low ebb.[16]

Park's observation is well illustrated by the action to repeal Oriental exclusion laws in the United States. Between World War I and World War II there were several efforts to expunge these provisions from the law books. But each effort was met by countermovements that stirred up fear and hatred of orientals—perhaps only among a minority but with the same effect as discussion of fluoridation. At the close of World War II a small committee worked quietly behind the scenes and secured the cooperation of enough congressmen to achieve the desired repeal.[17]

It would be foolhardy to translate these observations into an ironclad generalization to the effect that conflict publics impede rather than facilitate change. By altering power relationships in the community they sometimes open the way for change. Through forcing attention to grievances and indicating the desperation and anger that are felt, they probably have a residual effect in the quieter periods after conflict subsides. But it is clear that any simple assumption that widespread and intense participation in public discussion produces solutions to problems and facilitates change cannot be seriously defended.

[15] Robert E. Park, "News as a Form of Knowledge: A Chapter in the Sociology of Knowledge," *American Journal of Sociology*, 45 (March, 1940), pp. 683–84.

[16] Robert E. Park, "Morale and the News," *American Journal of Sociology*, 47 (Nov., 1941), 364–65.

[17] Fred W. Riggs, *Pressures on Congress: A Study of the Repeal of Chinese Exclusion* (New York: Columbia University Press, 1950).

13

SOCIAL MOVEMENTS:
CHARACTER AND PROCESSES

Collective behavior is the study of those phenomena that fall between group behavior, which is organized on the basis of rules and tradition, and disparate individual behavior. The boundaries are vague, shading into the study of organized group behavior and into the dynamics of individual behavior. Perhaps the most ephemeral type of collectivity and that which merges most closely with disparate individual behavior is the momentary panic. The social movement falls toward the other boundary of the area of study, with considerable organization, emergence of rules and tradition, and stability and continuity in time. Indeed, the longer the life of a social movement and the larger and more powerful it is, the more it takes on the characteristics of an association rather than a collectivity.

We have observed that the crowd tends to develop and enforce on its members a uniform course of action. The public determines a course of action that takes account of acknowledged differences of position. If the crowd develops a more enduring sense of group identity and pursues a plan of action requiring more sustained activity than can be maintained through crowd conditions, a social movement is emerging. Or if members of a public who share a common position concerning the issue at hand supplement their informal person-to-person discussion with some organization to promote their convictions more effectively and to insure more sustained activity, a social movement is incipient.

In spite of the relation to other forms of collective behavior, social movements are different in important respects. Popular writers often treat the social movement as an extended crowd made up of people acting under a delusion fostered by the mechanisms of crowd behavior. Because the members are in constant contact with persons who do not adhere to the movement, because sustained activity and enthusiasm over an extended period of time is required, and because some sustained division of labor is required within the movement, the members' activities on behalf of the movement must be disciplined rather than chiefly impulsive. At times the provocation and manipulation of crowd behavior is an effective tactic in making the opposition afraid of the movement, in arousing the enthusiasm of outsiders for the movement, or in strengthening the esprit de corps of the members through crowd experience. At other times the spontaneous resurgence of crowd behavior may lead members of a movement to excesses of behavior that discredit the movement within the public to which it is appealing. In either case, however, the crowd behavior is a phase of the movement rather than the whole of it.

Definition of a Social Movement

A social movement is a collectivity acting with some continuity to promote or resist a change in the society or group of which it is a part. As a collectivity a movement is a group with indefinite and shifting membership and with leadership whose position is determined more by the informal response of the members than by formal procedures for legitimizing authority.

The movement is marked by continuity in several respects. First, the movement's objective must require sustained activity. A movement could hardly develop over so short-range an objective as lynching a kidnapper, though the determination to control kidnapping in general could give rise to a movement. Likewise, there will be some continuity in movement strategy. There will also be continuity in the division of function, with some stability of leader-

ship and other roles. There will be continuity in the sense of group identity, so that even with rapid turnover of membership the sense of group continuity prevails.

In saying that a social movement promotes or resists change we are differentiating it from an informal group whose activities are entirely self-contained in their implications. A group of people who assemble strictly for their own enjoyment or their own betterment without making any demands on the community have not formed a social movement.

Three types of groupings are called quasi movements because they possess some but not all the characteristics of a movement. First, the term *mass movement* is applied to phenomena that fall somewhere between the mass and a true social movement. In a mass migration or a gold rush, for example, there is a certain amount of social contagion and we-feeling, though in the final analysis the behavior remains individual. There may be considerable activity in the common interest, such as combined activity to protect migrants from hostile natives or to promote favorable political measures. But the governing objectives and plans of action remain individual. The numbers involved are likely to be great, and the implications for change in the society considerable. We may learn a good deal about the grass roots, mass support aspects of social movements from the study of this type.

Second, the term *following* is applied to a collectivity that is united in its attention to and admiration of a public individual. The attachment to a hero is the basis for continuity and the subject of interaction among fans. The attachment is to the hero himself rather than to any cause that he represents. Hence, although there may be some organization and a vitally developed we-feeling, the following is short of being a collectivity concerned with promoting some program. However, the following is seldom an altogether neutral force in the larger society, since the members seek to imitate the hero in numerous ways. Hence the difference between a following and a true movement built about an admired leader depends on the degree which admiration for the leader causes the followers to promote a program of social change.

Third, a *cult* is a collectivity that has the continuity of a social movement but that makes demands only on the behavior of its members. A religious cult may demand behavior of its members that is quite different from the established social conventions, while making no effort to promote acceptance of such a program by the society. The cult membership is content to remain withdrawn from the society in general. In many collectivities the members believe that the world can be changed by winning large numbers of people to their way of behaving. Hence they attempt to modify the social order by extensive proselyting—by incorporating more people within their movement and enforcing their behavioral demands upon them. Although this procedure is different from that of the typical movement that attempts to modify society through legislation or influence on policy, it also distinguishes these movements from simple cults. To the degree to which collectivities proselytize as a means toward changing society, they become true social movements.

Grass-Roots Approaches

The questions asked in the study of social movements are (1) When will social movements occur? (2) When will they be successful? and (3) When will they take one course or exhibit one set of characteristics rather than another? Most investigators are chiefly interested in the first two questions. But we shall attempt to look at a wide range of qualitative variations as well.

The commonest approach, and one that has merit as a starting point in any investigation, may be called the grass-roots view of social movements. According to this view, frustration that affects increas-

ing numbers of people, more and more intensely, leads to mushrooming discontent. Identifying their common frustration and agreeing upon a plan to reform the offensive conditions, the discontented band together to promote their objectives. The basic truth in the grass-roots approach can be preserved by making four qualifications: (1) It is not necessarily the most deprived groups who form or support movements; (2) Goals of a movement do not necessarily correspond closely with the source of discontent; (3) The emotion arising from deprivation is seldom as important as effective organization in sustaining a movement; and (4) The rise and decline of a movement often depends more upon the coalitions formed with groups having established power at their disposal than upon the rise and decline of grass-roots discontent. Each of these caveats merits discussion.

Extreme Deprivation and Movement Support. Deprivation often helps to supply the intense motivation necessary for overcoming ordinary obstacles to movement membership. However, frustration by itself is never a guarantee of receptivity to movements. Long-continued frustration characteristically leads to hopelessness and preoccupation with immediate and momentary survival problems, which mitigate against participation in the promotion of any reform. Frustration from recent losses or the experience of improving conditions is more likely than long-continued frustration to make individuals receptive.

The failure of those in greatest need to support movements to better their condition has exasperated many a social reformer. The Social Credit party in Quebec, in 1962, was a new movement whose greatest appeal was among persons who identified themselves as working class. Yet, as Maurice Pinard shows, support was greater among persons of moderate income than among persons in the lowest income category, unless there was some unemployment in the family.[1] Among moderate and higher income respondents, those who said they worried about how they could get along financially in the next year voted for Social Credit more often than did persons who worried "almost none." But among the lowest income respondents, worry was *negatively* related to support for Social Credit.

Recent investigations have turned from the objective deprivations of poverty and discrimination to the subjective states of deprivation reflected in attitudes such as anomie and alienation. It does seem unlikely that persons who feel thoroughly at harmony with the world about them will be avid supporters of movements to change that world. But *anomia,* the attitude of despair and the sense of living in a purposeless and normless world, is more likely to immobilize individuals and undermine the trust essential to collaboration in a movement than it is to promote activism. Similarly, the sense of powerlessness that is one form of alienation discourages commitment to a goal of reforming or transforming society.[2] There are circumstances under which the alienated and the anomic may join in support of an already powerful movement and be the mainstay of cultish groups. But they are unlikely to be in the forefront of activism nor to provide a sufficiently dependable base upon which to build a movement.

GOALS AND THE SOURCE OF DISCONTENT. Theories that attribute the growth of social movements to widespread anomie and alienation and such other attitudes as authoritarianism also relate to the second

[1] Maurice Pinard, "Poverty and Political Movements," *Social Problems,* 15 (Fall, 1967), 250–63.
[2] A generalized psychological state of alienation seems more conducive to immobility than to active protest. However, a relationship of alienation toward a specific object, such as one's work, one's school, or one's church, may predispose an individual toward participation in a movement directed toward reform of that object. Cf. Maurice Zeitlin, "Alienation and Revolution," *Social Forces,* 45 (Dec., 1966), 224–36.

caveat concerning grass-roots approaches: goals of a movement do not necessarily correspond closely with the source of discontent. Even evidence that adherents to a movement exhibit all or some of these attitudes is often deceptive. The sense of powerlessness can serve as an example of the possibilities for misinterpreting research findings. An individual who feels powerless is naturally dissatisfied with his situation. One theory is that, uneasy over his inability to affect the course of events, he is receptive to appeals that promise him a chance to make his influence felt. Hence, the more people feel such a sense of powerlessness, the larger the potential reservoir of support for many kinds of movements. A finding showing that movement adherents more frequently report feelings of powerlessness than do nonadherents seems to confirm the fundamental hypothesis.

But every movement develops an ideology—a view of society, of relevant events, and of the movement and its members—that becomes for loyal adherents the authentic account of what the movement is all about. We shall dwell on the nature of ideology at greater length in Chapter 14. But for the present the important observation is that ideology tells the adherents what attitudes they are supposed to have. Recent American movements centering about civil rights, student protest, and organized opposition to American military involvements in southeast Asia, as well as certain right-wing movements that protest entrenched liberal philosophies, claim to be seeking the return of power to large population segments who have been deprived of a voice in national affairs. From both sides the current unhappy state of affairs is explained on the basis of usurpation and centralization of power. The adherent who pays attention to movement ideology learns that the vague discontent and uneasiness he has felt is the sense of powerlessness.

People who feel restless and discontented do not necessarily understand the causes of their discontent. Normally there are varied and complex causes, only some of which are socially relevant. But in order to do something about such states, the individual must identify the nature of his feeling. This he does by imputing a source. It does not greatly matter whether he identifies the nature and source correctly or not because his actions seldom succeed in eliminating the cause as he identifies it. Unless the imputed source can be successfully eliminated, when it would be possible to see whether the discontent subsides, it is normally impossible to know whether the source has been correctly identified or not. Hence the individual's conviction that he correctly understands his feelings is based on other considerations. Among these considerations are whether his understanding of external conditions and his conception of human motivations make the interpretations plausible, whether he finds social support for his interpretations within his reference groups, and whether these interpretations impel him toward actions that are in themselves gratifying.

In practice, therefore, people identify their social discontents on the basis of conceptions presented to them with authority. It is reasonable to suppose that people feel powerless because they have been exposed to this set of ideas under suitable circumstances rather than because their actual state of powerlessness has led them to feel powerless and therefore discontented. If the ideology of a movement identifies individual discontent as an expression of individual powerlessness, it is hardly suprising that supporters of the movement more often express feelings of powerlessness than do persons not in the movement. It still remains theoretically possible by careful selection of movements with different ideologies to design research that might sort out the predisposing attitudes from the ideological complex, but no such investigation has been satisfactorily carried out. For the present we must treat sceptically any theory of predisposing attitudes when those attitudes correspond closely to the approved

motivations of members according to a well-advertised movement ideology.

As we observed in the earlier discussion of rumor, collective behavior is not only collective action; it is also collaboration in creating an accepted version of reality. Social movements not only respond to the attitudes and motivations of their members; they also create new motivations and attitudes that are attuned to conceptions of the world that they help to create. This is a theme that will receive extended attention in a discussion of the sense of injustice in social movements and throughout the treatment of movements.

Emotion and Movement Continuity. The third caveat applies to the explanations of social movements based on the welling up of emotion and the surging of indignation and anger into a vigorous outflow of action. "If the people become angry enough," goes the observation, "they will do something!" Although there is an important partial truth in this assertion, it applies better to the more ephemeral crowd behavior than to social movements. Aroused emotion is unlikely to supply the staying power for a movement and often interferes with the development of effective organization, goals, and strategy. Emotional arousal demands immediate and dramatic actions rather than considered and effective actions. Emotional arousal also interferes with the accommodations that must be made for the diverse interests and points of view if many people are to work together as a social movement. Such arousal is probably more conducive to abortive actions of a violent nature than to sustained movements. These abortive actions may play a part in the development of a movement when there are more stably based groups that can make use of disorder but do not themselves provide an adequate foundation.

Employing data secured through interviews with a nationwide sample of 913 blacks in late 1964, Gary Marx was able to examine the relationship between anti-white attitudes and activism. If emotional arousal were the simple key to support for a social movement, we could expect to find that blacks with the most intensely anti-white attitudes were also the most active in civil-rights causes. But blacks who belonged to civil-rights organizations less often exhibited strongly antiwhite attitudes than did those who did not belong. And among 184 blacks who belonged to these organizations, those whose style of response to the civil-rights struggle was militant were less likely to report antiwhite attitudes than were blacks whose response was conservative. Noting the more advantaged backgrounds of the activists, Marx suggests that "for many militants their relative tolerance for whites is part of a generally more tolerant world view related to their greater sophistication and greater exposure to official values."[3] The activists also probably combined more hope with their frustration to sustain them in the day-to-day effort toward long-range betterment of the black's position.

In keeping with the dominant emphases in civil-rights movements in 1964, Gary Marx specifically excluded black-nationalist or black-extremist attitudes in identifying militants or activists. In light of changes in the goals of black movements since that time, it would be important to compare inactive with active black nationalists to determine whether the inactives displayed more hatred of whites than did the actives. But if Marx's findings are still valid, the popular supposition that activists have the greatest hatred for whites probably stems from two errors of perception. First, the intense hatred on the part of unaffiliated ghetto-dwellers goes unrecognized by whites except when it is expressed in the sporadic violence of urban riots. Second, black

movements employ a rhetoric of white hatred as part of their strategy for prodding whites into action and for recruiting black support, a rhetoric that does not necessarily indicate more intense feelings than are experienced by less active blacks.

EXTERNAL COALITIONS AND POWER. The fourth caveat, that support of the movement by groups already possessing great power, may have a more important effect than the rise and decline of grass-roots support may be illustrated by referring to McCarthyism, which followed World War II. While still a junior senator, Joseph McCarthy rocketed to national prominence as leader of the fight against alleged communists in government, using hearings of his senate subcommittee to subject the accused to public degradation. He succeeded even without evidence that in most cases would have been needed to secure conviction in a court of law. The movement reached a peak during 1951 and 1952, with the result that thousands of liberals throughout the United States were discredited and blacklisted in government and business. Then quite suddenly McCarthy lost public favor in 1953, and the movement subsided to a small radical-right group. There have been many thoughtful efforts to explain why the movement peaked and declined when it did. Most of these efforts have concentrated on the sources and nature of discontent among large population segments. Postwar economic readjustments, inflation that depressed the position of persons on fixed incomes, the effect of the war in weakening traditional lines of racial separation and subordination, and the changing avenues for upward mobility were among conditions that altered the relative standing of groups in society, creating discontent among those who lost out in these readjustments. These analyses of discontent are important, but they do not explain the sudden decline of the movement. Furthermore, most of the conditions were in the making well before the move-

[3] Gary T. Marx, *Protest and Prejudice: A Study of Belief in the Black Community* (New York: Harper and Row, Publishers, 1969), p. 203; *see also* pp. 198–204.

ment blossomed. Hence it is important to supplement the grass-roots analysis with a different kind of explanation. As a freshman senator, Joseph McCarthy could not have held the subcommittee chairmanship nor received massive publicity for the hearings without the support of powerful persons and groups. McCarthyism arose near the end of a twenty-year period during which the Republican party had been repeatedly frustrated in efforts to unseat the Democratic party nationally. McCarthy injected a new element into the political situation by shaking public confidence in the patriotism of the Democratic establishment. Although responsible Party leaders could not make the kind of unsubstantiated charges and attacks on individuals that Senator McCarthy engaged in, they stood to profit greatly from his efforts. But in 1953 the Republicans came to power, and McCarthy promptly turned his guns on the new administration. It took only a few months for the Republican administration to strip him of the privileges and resources that had enabled him to attract and hold a mass following. In short, the movement prospered when it served the purposes of the Republican party and quickly declined when it no longer did so.

An extreme position in opposition to grass-roots explanations asserts that there is always enough discontent in any society to supply the grass-roots support for a movement if the movement is effectively organized and has at its disposal the power and resources of some established elite group. Hence one looks to power struggles among elites rather than to grass-roots discontents to explain the rise and fall of movements. We shall have more to say about this type of explanation in later chapters. In this bald form it may be as inadequate as the oversimplified grass-roots explanation. The important message is that a simple grass-roots explanation should never be accepted without examining the full situation within which the movement must operate.

Comprehensive Approaches

Theodore Abel's analysis of the rise of Nazism in Germany exemplifies a more adequate framework, recognizing the combination of several kinds of factors.[4] The character of the movement was molded and its success influenced by four general factors:

1. the prevalence of discontent with the existing social order.
2. the particular ideology and program for social transformation adopted by the Nazis.
3. the National Socialist organizational and promotional technique.
4. the presence of charismatic leadership.

Abel does not claim that these same four factors would be equally useful in explaining all movements, though their generality is plain.

An attempt to generalize to a broad class of movements can be illustrated with Michiya Shimbori's interpretation of student movements.[5] Starting with a detailed examination of the Japanese student political movement, Zengakuren, Shimbori looks at similar movements on a worldwide basis and concludes that there are at least six conditions favorable for student movements:

1. a national situation in which a counterelite is almost as powerful as the established political elite.
2. large differences in the ideologies of elite and counterelite.
3. a student status that makes them actual members of the political elite.
4. large numbers of students.
5. geographic concentration of students in a few urban areas.

4 Theodore Abel, *The Nazi Movement* (New York: Atherton Press, Inc., 1966; first published 1938), p. 166.
5 Michiya Shimbori, "Zengakuren: A Japanese Case Study of a Student Political Movement," *Sociology of Education,* 37 (Spring, 1964), 229–53.

6. a philosophy of higher education to train a political or national elite.

A broader generalization is found in Neil Smelser's value-added scheme as he applies it to social movements.[6] In order to predict whether or not a movement will develop, the investigator looks for five essential elements:

1. the condition of the social structure must be *conducive* to formation of a movement.
2. there must be an appropriate type of *strain*.
3. a *generalized belief* must develop that explains the strain and indicates the kind of solution.
4. people must be *mobilized* for action in the name of the generalized belief.
5. the efforts toward *social control* of the movement by authorities must reinforce or at least not undermine the movement.

A theory like this directs the student's attention to five essential components in movement development, though it does not indicate the specific requirement in each case. If the student uses this theory as a guide, he will not overlook the suitability of society for a movement at a given time and place, though the theory will not tell him exactly what conditions are and are not conducive. In this respect Smelser's scheme differs from Shimbori's, which names specific conditions but does not claim that all six conditions are essential nor that they constitute all the essential conditions.

An Approach to Social Movements

The treatment of social movements in this book will not essay a complete theory, such as Smelser's. It will, however, examine movements comprehensively and from several perspectives. Throughout this treatment four emphases will recur. First, movements are in a state of flux, their character

changing from day to day, and the conditions strengthening a movement at one time having an opposite effect at another time. Second, the course and character of a movement are shaped by the constant dynamic of *value orientations, power orientations,* and *participation orientations* within the movement. Third, the course and character are shaped by external relations, including the way it is defined by external publics and the kinds of external support and opposition it encounters. Fourth, social movements mean normative transformations, and the emergent norm theory developed for the analysis of crowd behavior will be extended as a focus for understanding movements.

PROCESSES. To be faithful to the nature of collective behavior, the investigator must generalize about social movements in such a way as to capture the fact of constant change. But this is easier to say than to do. To say that the proliferation of social movements in modern times is associated with cultural confusion, social heterogeneity, widespread individual discontent, and mass communications[7] is to offer important but static generalizations. But to identify regularities in the sequence of development and change so as to predict the next development correctly and to supply a guide for effective intervention in order to change the course of development is the sociologist's most difficult task. Static generalizations are still the bulk of knowledge, but our understanding is increased in sensitivity and power whenever we can identify processes with precision.

One way to describe processes is to identify a typical life cycle, applicable to all or to limited types of social movements. The life cycle consists of an idealized series of stages from the origin to the success or other termination of the movement. Besides providing a process framework, the life

---

[6] Neil Smelser, *Theory of Collective Behavior* (New York: The Free Press, 1963).

[7] C. Wendell King, *Social Movements in the United States* (New York: Random House, Inc., 1956), pp. 11–24.

cycle is a way of organizing our knowledge about movements so as to permit prediction of forthcoming events. The life cycle also offers a framework within which the many aspects of a movement can be seen working together—leadership, ideology, tactics, membership, etc.—rather than each being studied separately. Finally, it provides a framework within which the causes for success can be approached.

A widely used formulation of a typical life cycle for social movements in general contains four stages of development.[8] In the first or *preliminary stage of social unrest* there is unfocused and unorganized restlessness, evidence of increasing disorder, and susceptibility to the appeals of agitators. In the second or *popular stage* unrest is brought into the open and given a positive focus that transforms it into collective excitement. A social myth characterizing the movement and its aims and supplying its justification is fabricated and disseminated. Prophets displace agitators as the principal leaders and are later (in the same stage) displaced by the reformers who attack more specific evils and offer more clearly developed programs of reform. In the *stage of formal organization* the movement is welded into a disciplined organization, capable of securing member commitment to stable goals and strategies and capable of working effectively on community centers of power to promote its aims. Now the reformers and prophets play second fiddle to the statesmen, who are masters of strategy. Finally, the *institutional stage* sees the movement established as an organic part of society, and leadership

devolves on the administrator whose forte is keeping the system working.

This cycle clearly incorporates the assumptions of the grass-roots approach and relies heavily on contagion theory. Perhaps it is a better account of the way movements like to represent their histories than of a true sequence of events. The drama depicting masses of restless and unhappy people, caught up in a collective enthusiasm when the prophet diagnoses their ills and the reformer shows them the way out, accepting organizational discipline to bring about the needed reforms, and then remaining vigilant so that their profound gains are not undermined once the major battle is over is a glorious one. Elements in this cycle are undoubtedly valid and will be examined in greater depth in the ensuing chapters. Other aspects of the cycle are probably myth. But our concern at the moment is less with the merits of *this* formulation than of the life-cycle approach as a way of describing process in social movements.

Interpretation and use of the idealized life cycle in the examination of particular movements and the formulation of generalizations is not a simple matter. Statements of typical life cycles are frequently hedged about with qualifications. Thus we are often told that a movement may change either backward or forward in the cycle and that a movement does not necessarily have to pass through the entire series of stages. But with such qualifications, what is left of the cycle?

The life-cycle approach became popular in the early period of sociology when organismic analogies were in favor. Social forms were thought to have invariant stages of development—from birth to maturity to death—in the same manner as living organisms. With this approach discredited the life cycle is sometimes regarded as merely an empirical sequence of events that has been noted in the examination of several cases.

However, the life cycle acquires signifi-

[8] Herbert Blumer, "Collective Behavior," in Robert E. Park, ed., *An Outline of the Principles of Sociology* (New York: Barnes and Nobel, Inc., 1939), pp. 259ff.; Carl A. Dawson and Warner E. Gettys, *An Introduction to Sociology* (New York: The Ronald Press Company, 1948), pp. 689–709; Rex D. Hopper, "The Revolutionary Process: A Frame of Reference for the Study of Revolutionary Movements," *Social Forces,* 28 (March, 1950), 270–79.

cance in causal analysis when each stage is regarded as containing some of the causal preconditions for the development of the following stage. Without the preceding stage any particular stage cannot occur. However, since each stage includes only a portion of the preconditions of the following stage, the progression to succeeding stages is not inevitable. Frequently there will be not merely one stage but alternative stages that can follow any given one.

Applying the life cycle we have just outlined to a series of revolutionary movements in Latin America, Rex Hopper calls attention to some of the alternative developments that might follow the preliminary stage of social unrest.[9] Often, he notes, incipient movements have been diverted from political objects and turned toward religious pursuits. He suggests that Methodism in England diverted a great deal of the rising working-class discontent into a movement for personal reform. Often a government employs an external war as a device to restrain threatened internal disturbances. Occasionally there is early action that ameliorates conditions sufficiently to dissipate the movement's potential popular support. Since the preliminary stage can be followed by any of these developments as well as by the popular stage, the investigator is led to examine the whole set of contingencies that shapes the course of the movement at a given time.

The special value of the life cycle, then, is to permit us to discover the additional conditions that have to be present if a movement is to proceed from any given stage to the next. The causes that push a movement from the first stage to the second may not be the same as those that push it from the second to the third stage. Thus we can see that the factors contributing to the success of a movement may not be the same in the early and late periods. Through such analysis we can find explanations for movements that make impressive beginnings and then fail and for movements that have weak beginnings and suddenly burst into rapid development. We should also be able to discover the crucial conditions that cause a movement to take one, rather than another, direction when alternatives are present.

Jackson et al. were able to examine and understand why a local movement collapsed after a spectacular beginning by applying this logic.[10] For one month in late 1957 mass meetings in several Los Angeles suburbs attracted thousands of residents who wanted to protest property assessments. During this period individual discontent had clearly been socialized into massive social unrest, unrest had been focused on the County Tax Assessor and his assessment practices, organizations had sprung up in several suburbs, and one man had emerged as publicly acknowledged leader of the entire movement. But the movement lacked several essentials needed to pass from the stage of spontaneous enthusiasm to stages of organization and implementation. As the movement program and ideology crystallized, the powerful commercial-property owners did not lend their support because only residential-property interests were in control. No ready-made communication networks were available to the movement, since suburbs normally communicate by way of the central city rather than directly. The countywide leader was inflexible in his dealings with neighborhood leaders whose motives were seldom pure. And a mass meeting that attracted from 6,000 to 10,000 people gave the appearance of failure because it had been unrealistically scheduled for a coliseum seating 100,000. Problems of coordination, program for-

[9] Rex D. Hopper, "The Revolutionary Process: A Frame of Reference for the Study of Revolutionary Movements," *Social Forces,* 28 (March, 1950), p. 272.

[10] Maurice Jackson, Eleanora Peterson, James Bull, Sverre Monsen, and Patricia Richmond, "The Failure of an Incipient Social Movement," *Pacific Sociological Review,* 3 (Spring, 1960), 35–40.

mulation, and the fostering of an image of sustained growth that were not important during the first stage became crucial to the movement's development in the second stage.

The search for process extends beyond the limits of the single movement. Characteristic sequences of movements have been discerned. The distinctively moralistic theme in the twentieth-century British labor movement can only be understood by recognizing that burgeoning working-class religious movements had preceded the current political movement. Messianic movements have served as training grounds for the more active revolutionary movements in Europe, Indonesia, Africa, and other parts of the world. Minority-group movements seeking fuller integration into a host society are typically followed by separatist movements when aspirations are raised by initial successes and frustrated by limited improvement.

In our analyses of process, however, we shall not rely chiefly on comprehensive and generalized statements of life cycles. Some investigators have argued with considerable justice that the experiences of different movements are much too diverse to make any typical sequence generally valid.[11] Whether their assertion is correct or not, the life-cycle statements in most general use are limited to a very few broad stages, and they quickly lose their generality when efforts are made to refine and increase the stages. Efforts to identify and clarify more limited sequences applicable to a restricted range of situations offer greater promise of augmenting our understanding of movement processes. Thus we suggest the concentrated examination of process and contingencies in such situations as the encounter between authorities and the movement whose objectives are not sufficiently specified to permit systematic bargaining,

the struggle between romantic and pragmatic adherents to a movement, the struggle for unity and persistence in a movement when authorities implement part of but not all its goals, and many others.

Success and Internal Dynamics of a Movement. When speaking of the cycle of a social movement, we have been taking for granted the idea of success. In actual practice, however, the term *success* is likely to have several meanings. Often a movement is regarded as successful so long as the number of its adherents is increasing. However, not all movements depend upon support by large numbers to accomplish their objectives. The labor movement in America, for example, was more successful in collective bargaining and in securing desired legislation when it reduced its membership base for the sake of homogeneity of interest. Success is sometimes viewed as the perpetuation of the movement and its organization. However, a movement may cease to exist because its objectives have largely been achieved, or a movement may persist at the cost of extensive departure from its original goals.

Even measuring success by the degree to which the values the movement promotes are achieved introduces difficulties. Seldom is there a simple, clear-cut value being promoted. A movement to remove a corrupt political administration may succeed in the sense of winning a recall election, but the entrenched power of the old machine may be such that the new officials are never able to gain complete control of the governmental machinery. Or a movement may be unsuccessful in winning its specific goal, such as the adoption of a particular statute, but the strength of the movement may lead to the adoption of other measures that give substantially the same benefits. Or, finally, the very strength of a movement may result in its objectives being stolen by some established party or stronger movement. Thus, the Socialist party in the United States lost a great deal of support

11 William B. Cameron, *Modern Social Movements: A Sociological Outline* (New York: Random House, Inc., 1966), pp. 27–33.

during the 1930s because the Democratic party adopted some of its proposals.

In each instance the decision to describe a movement as successful or unsuccessful depends upon the perspective of the observer. The various criteria of success are found to some degree in every movement and represent essential pursuits. Thus we conclude that among the necessary aspects of a social movement are, first, a program for the reform of society; second, the establishment of power relations favorable to the movement; and third, the promotion of membership gratifications.

If the requirements for each type of success were the same, the tasks of social movements would be greatly simplified. There is a core of mutuality: members usually gain more personal satisfaction from belonging to a powerful movement than to a weak one; a well-formulated program of reform articulated with the values espoused by important groups in the society helps to find a power base for the movement. But at every step in the movement process the discrepant requirements create strains and force choices. In order to gain the support of a powerful established group, the movement must sacrifice parts of programs. In this manner Franklin Roosevelt's New Deal bargained away the promotion of racial democratization in order to maintain support from the South. A movement is often pushed into rash confrontations before it is strong enough to gain by these engagements because adherents lose their enthusiasm when there are no opportunities to join in dramatic activity. On the other hand, some movements become increasingly like social clubs, and members are driven away by efforts to subordinate social activities to study of the goals and ideology of social reform.

We can think of each type of success as possessing its own dynamic. The movement is unrelentingly pushed three different ways from within. An optimum balance involves enough flexibility in the program

to allow for some bargaining in the interests of power and some accommodation to the social and expressive needs of members, without subversion of the main goals. But there is no dynamic principle of equilibrium to protect this balance except for the wisdom of movement leaders and their ability to regulate the divergent tendencies.

We shall speak respectively of the *value orientations,* the *power orientations,* and the *participation orientations* in every movement. Each event in the movement's life is likely to unsettle whatever balance there is among these tendencies. Any major alteration of the balance sets the movement on a new course.

Although the main emphasis should be on the ubiquitous tension among the three orientations in every movement, the relatively extreme cases in which one orientation clearly outweighs the others also supply a basis for classifying movements. In the Nazi movement the power relationship seemed to be the major element, so that ideology and the gratifications of membership fell into place as subordinate to the quest for power. In his analysis of the ideology of the Nazi movement Franz Neumann has concluded that there was no stable ideology but that it was changed from time to time to fit the strategy of power.[12]

Movements of this sort will differ in important respects from those that are closely bound to a particular program for change. Any effort by movements of the latter type to gain power through methods that compromise their program will damage the movement. The achievement of effective power will not be regarded as success unless the program remains intact, and the movement may be judged successful if its program is adopted and carried out by

[12] Franz Neumann, *Behemoth: The Structure and Practice of National Socialism* (New York: Oxford University Press, Inc., 1942).

another group. The crucial, decision-making core of members will be recruited and guided more by the need to promote the ideology and by the need to be consistent with the general scheme of values contained in the ideology than by the effort to establish favorable power relations.

Both the foregoing types of movements will differ from one in which the provision of personal satisfactions to members becomes the orienting feature. In some movements the ideology of societal change and the movement's power situation may have little to do with the continuity of membership, the member's evaluation of the movement's success, and the character of decisions rendered within the movement. Thus a cultish group may depict itself as the ultimate inheritors of society and adhere to an ideology of widespread change. But the hold of the movement on its members may be quite unaffected by the failure to gain any power or to take any effective steps in the direction of modifying society, and the crucial interaction within the movement may be little related to ideology.

The three types can be called value-oriented, power-oriented or control, and participation-oriented movements. It will be fruitful to examine the circumstances that propel a movement toward one of these ideal types. If we understand why value-oriented movements become transformed into power-oriented or participation-oriented movements, we shall know a good deal about why well-intentioned efforts at reform fail to bring about the changes that were initially intended.

EXTERNAL RELATIONS AND DEFINITIONS. In stressing process we underline the constantly changing characteristics of any movement. When noting the tension between value, power, and participation orientations, we call attention to one of several internal sources of this constant change. To complete the picture we must also stress that every movement is engaged in a continuous two-way exchange with the communities and society in which it operates. Each action by the movement provokes a community reaction. The nature of the community reaction is noted within the movement and by potential recruits. Loyalties, goals, and strategies are reassessed on the basis of the community response. For example, the John Birch Society, a right-wing patriotic group, was founded in late 1958 as a secret and highly disciplined organization to counter the "communist conspiracy" by infiltrating and controlling such community groups as the Parent-Teacher Associations. A sudden flurry of newspaper and magazine exposés painted a diabolical picture of the Society and stressed parallels between its structure and the Communist party. The result was a membership crisis, as the ultrarespectable self-conceptions held by most members were contested by the sinister image conveyed in the public media. Some members resigned, and the leaders ultimately replaced secrecy with a positive public-relations program, designed to promote an image of responsibility, respectability, and solid conservatism.[13]

Applying an understanding of the interaction between external views of the movement and the movement's characteristics to a classic distinction between *reform* and *revolutionary* movements adds a dynamic dimension to what are often quite static and doctrinaire concepts. The revolutionary movement is said to challenge the fundamental values of a society, whereas the reform movement seeks modifications within the existing value scheme. The reform movement advocates a change that will implement the existing value scheme more adequately than present conditions, but the revolutionary movement urges replacement of the existing value scheme.

[13] Benjamin R. Epstein and Arnold Forster, *Report on the John Birch Society 1966* (New York: Random House, Inc., 1966).

Taken literally, such a distinction puts the investigator in the position of having to judge the ultimate relation between the movement's program and society's values. No movement advocates total overthrow of existing values. Indeed, ideologists in the most revolutionary movements argue that they seek to reestablish the most fundamental aspects of a current value scheme by doing away with other aspects that adulterate them. Furthermore, it is commonplace that apparently innocuous changes sometimes have revolutionary consequences and that advance predictions concerning the consequences of any movement are highly fallible.

But this distinction, when employed differently, is quite useful. The fact is that every movement is viewed in the society either as generally consistent with, or fundamentally antagonistic to, the established value scheme. How it is viewed will determine the type and tactics of opposition with which it is confronted, the circumstances under which it recruits members, the degree to which it can operate openly through legitimate means, and many other features.

Every movement, through defining and promoting consideration of an issue, creates or fosters a public concerned with both the issue and the movement itself. Part of the function of the public is to define the movement's relations to society's value scheme. The effective definition that emerges from the public will determine the access that the movement has to legitimate means for promoting its program in society. Whether a dispassionate or retrospective evaluation would determine that the movement's objectives were or were not in fact consistent with the basic value structure of society is not the important question. Movements are identified as respectable or revolutionary on the basis of the prevailing public definition. This definition may include considerable awareness of the movement's goals and ideology, or it may principally be based on the bystander

perspective, as we have discussed it in Chapter 12.

Between respectable and revolutionary movements there is an intermediate category. Some movements are regarded as odd, peculiar, or queer. Although they are inconsistent with the basic value structure of society, they are thought to be harmless and consequently can be tolerated and granted considerable access to legitimate means for promoting their objectives. They are opposed largely through ridicule, isolation, and ostracism of their members. Oftentimes the difference between a revolutionary and a peculiar movement is simply one of apparent strength, so that change of a given movement from one to the other type is frequent.

Variations in public definition, character of the opposition evoked, and access to legitimate means of action suggest a further subdivision of the respectable movement into the factional and nonfactional. Certain movements must primarily cope with competing schemes claiming to promote similar ends by superior means. Hence they are concerned not so much with gaining adherence to their general objective as with promoting their own scheme for attaining it. Other movements must primarily overcome lack of interest or enthusiasm rather than factional opposition. Thus movements like Moral Rearmament and the Billy Graham crusade have been respectable and largely nonfactional. They have received widespread lip service from respectable community leaders and no real organized opposition. Their problem has consisted of marshaling effective support rather than of combating active opposition or competition.

In sum, movements fall into four patterns based upon the public definition of the movement's relation to the basic value scheme of the society and upon the consequent general type of opposition evoked and degree of access to legitimate channels of action. The four types are schematized below:

Public Definition	Type of Opposition	Means of Action
1. Respectable-nonfactional	Disinterest and token support	Legitimate means
2. Respectable-factional	Competing movements advocating same general objective	Legitimate means
3. Peculiar	Ridicule and ostracism	Limited access to legitimate means
4. Revolutionary	Violent suppression	Chiefly illegitimate means

Because of the changing circumstances that affect public definitions, movements often change from one to another of these patterns in the course of development.

The Sense of Injustice

Crowd behavior is made possible by the emergence of a special rule or norm that supplies both license and obligation for an unusual course of action in a limited situation. Exchange in the public is made possible by collective imposition and acceptance of a rule that limits the many ways in which the issue for discussion can be viewed. The social movement process likewise generates a new rule, or a revised or reapplied rule, but one that must continue in effect for a longer period and have wider implications for societal reform. Like the other norms, it permits a variety of forms of action, derived from varied motives, to take place under common definition and justification.

A movement is inconceivable apart from a vital sense that some established practice or mode of thought is wrong and ought to be replaced. To the civil-rights movement the practices of racial segregation that had unquestioningly been accepted, or questioned without the urgent sense that they could no longer be tolerated, are viewed as an intolerable evil. To the sectarian religious movement, practices that may have been viewed as anomalous, such as infant baptism or adherence to trinitarian belief, are viewed as positively destructive of religious aims.

Any movement necessarily disrupts many aspects of the social order, and some people and institutions become pawns or suffer as byproducts of the reform. The movement must have a justification that is superior to the hurt that it does. Indeed, if the movement is to proceed at all, there must be little stopping to consider these casual consequences. The promotion of the aim is obligatory; it is conceived as a mission. When it is regarded as the highest form of obligation, adherents can even claim credit for neglecting other obligations. In pursuit of a high obligation to promote the understanding of truth, a devoted truth seeker—such as Socrates—gains credit rather than disapprobation for neglecting his family. The disregard for lesser obligations becomes a mandatory test of true adherence to the higher obligation.

Like the norms in other forms of collective behavior, the movement norm supplies a uniform packaging for diverse kinds of actions. Within the circle of the movement it is a sign of disloyalty to explore the many types of gratifications that can be served by marching on a picket line or to distinguish irrational from rational forms of belief. Like the crowd a social movement depends upon the contributions of many kinds of people, acting in varied ways, for diverse reasons. Also like the crowd it must have some central norm that supplies a ready-made explanation and justification for these diverse elements. The emergent norm underlies the appearance of homogeneity that permits members and society to see the movement as a unit.

SENSE OF INJUSTICE AS THE EMERGENT NORM. The common element in the norms of many, if not most, movements is the conviction that existing conditions are unjust. The rule or norm that gains in importance, that is imposed upon members of the movement, and that the movement seeks to impose on the larger society is a specification that what has heretofore been accepted as a necessary or desirable condition must be viewed as unjust. In the woman-suffrage movement the longstanding differences in the male and female roles are reevaluated as having an unjustifiable imbalance in rights and rewards. To the New Left movement of the 1960s, the traditional pattern in which the university was partially cloistered from the larger community, with limitations on student behavior balanced by compensating immunity from conventional responsibilities, must be reassessed as a basic deprivation of the natural rights of students. To nationalists the accepted idea that there is mutual benefit in a benign colonial system is an insincere dogma used to divert attention from the true injustice of subordinating one nation to another.

The sense of what is just and unjust seems self-evident once it is established in a particular case. The traditional arguments regarding the benefits of colonial status were indeed convincing in an earlier era but have a hollow ring to modern ears. It is difficult for many of us today to understand how the denial of full rights to an individual merely because he was an illegitimate child could complacently be accepted as a necessary device to strengthen the morals of adults. Central to the publics of several social movements today is the issue of whether the unearned advantages and disadvantages that accrue to a child because of the socioeconomic, ethnic, or racial starting point his parentage conveys to him is a fundamental injustice in our society or simply the working of natural law.

It is clear that such historical changes as these involve something more than simply an unimpassioned reexamination of the situation to see clearly the correct application of existing principles of justice. The very circumstances have been re-

defined. For example, the work of missionaries is no longer seen as selfless devotion to bringing spiritual and material opportunity to a retarded people, but it is viewed as a Machiavellian or unwitting effort to impose a foreign system of values upon people and to train them for subjection to the discipline of employment and political passivity under colonial rule. Illustrations to support either view were known from the start and continue to be available. There has never been a careful weighing of evidence to determine which view is the fairest. But there has been a shift in the atmosphere, so that one set of illustrations sounds more representative and convincing than the other.

The complex nature of the sense of justice can be illustrated in another way. Today, throughout most of the United States it is agreed that the denial of equal education or equal employment opportunity for equally qualified persons because of race is unjust. However, if two equally qualified white women apply for a secretarial post, and the position is awarded to the physically more attractive one, there is no organized sense of outrage. People of short stature occasionally complain that there is prejudice against them, that they must offer greater proofs to achieve equal recognition in competition with people who are moderately taller than average. The short man is likely to be introduced with the apologetic observation: "Though he is small, he packs a wallop!" or "Don't be deceived by his size!" If plainlooking people and short people labor against disproportionate obstacles, there is yet no sign of any well-developed sense of injustice concerning their difficulties.

The problem posed for students of collective behavior is why there should be so clear a sense of injustice in the one case and not in the others, and why a set of circumstances that were not seen as unjust should come to be viewed in this fashion at a particular time in history. It is these questions that clarify the meaning of *emergent* norm in connection with social movements.

The emergent norm—the revised sense of justice—matures and crystallizes with the development of the movement; it is implemented through the strategy of the movement and is diffused through the public that is concerned about the movement. The ultimate and most enduring product of a movement is either the repudiation of the revised conception of justice or the establishment in the society of the revised conception. This end-result does not correlate perfectly with the success of the movement as an organization or with the success of the movement in securing the specific programs of reform that it promotes. Through the operation of the public, the conception of injustice may take hold in the society, even though the specific plan of the movement is frustrated and the movement dies as an organization. This was clearly the case of the Townsend Movement, which in the 1930s put forward quite a specific program of old-age pensions on a national scale. Since World War II the movement has been of no political significance, and neither the plan for universal pensions without respect to need nor any other key aspect of it has been implemented. Nevertheless, the popular indifference to the economic plight of the aged clearly came to an end during this era at least partially through the medium of the public that took the Townsend Plan as its primary issue. In the course of debate the earlier view that each person must make diligent preparations for his retirement, and consequently impoverishment in old age is merely the just penalty for lifetime improvidence, was heard less and less frequently. Advocates and opponents of the movement came to accept the view that an impoverished old age following a life of reasonably hard work was fundamentally unjust. The debate accordingly turned more and more to the practical question of what kind of program the economy could support and the workability of the specific scheme advanced by Francis Townsend.

Although our understanding still leaves us far from being able to predict when or how a prevailing sense of justice will be revised, it is possible to identify several conditions that generally seem to be essential for revisions to take place.

MEMBERSHIP IN A SELF-CONSCIOUS GROUP. The most obvious difference between the situation of people whose disadvantages are viewed as injustice and those whose lot is regarded as misfortune is that the former constitute *groups,* but the latter are only categories of people. Although there may be some sociometric separation between more and less attractive women, the separation is neither sharp enough nor comprehensive enough to establish a group with its own internal communication network, sense of group identity, and embryonic subculture. For a disadvantage to be conceived as injustice, it must be shared by a group characterized by all three of these attributes. The sense of collective misfortune is a first step toward ruling out personal inadequacy or the work of fate as explanations.

It is old hat to observe that when a number of people experience shared misfortune, they form a bond because of their common plight and engage in collective action to remedy their grievance. This view treats the injustice as self-evident, as an objective fact in the situation. By contrast the view being advanced is that disadvantage or misfortune is transformed into injustice only when appropriate social definitions take place. The discovery by members of a preexistent self-conscious group that they share the disadvantage is one of the necessary conditions for defining the situation as unjust.

Consequently, revision in the sense of justice frequently follows a social change that separates a category of people from the heterogeneous groups in which they have been members and brings them together into a newly formed social unit. In modern times the loosening of extended family bonds has been an important precipitant for groups that have offered new perpectives on social justice. Separation of the aged from the family unit or segregation of their lives within the family has thrown the aged together. As membership in a multigenerational family unit becomes less salient and fellowship with others of their own generation more central in their daily lives, the many limitations of their condition have come to seem less natural and more unjust. The idea that a division of labor under which male members cast ballots for the family unit was unjust developed after the women's sphere of activity outside the family had been greatly extended on a segregated basis. Women increasingly found themselves brought together in functioning units outside the family.

Modern labor movements did not appear until labor was moved out of the occupationally heterogeneous workshop into factories that were organized into occupationally homogeneous work groups. It is no accident that the first important organized outcries against the economic system in modern times came as peasant revolts rather than as worker uprisings. Peasants worked together in the fields and were integrated into the larger structure solely as a class and not as individuals long before the factory system made the same thing true of industrial laborers. Although urban and village workers were identifiable as a class, their work life occurred in groups that associated them closely with representatives of other classes, and their occupational identity was seldom translated into a vital and comprehensive group identity. The peasants, however, experienced the conjuncture of occupational class, work associates, and living associates that made it possible to view their collective lot as intolerable.

It is useful to search for clues to the emerging sense of injustice in the many investigations dealing with class consciousness. Class consciousness, in its restricted sense, incorporates as a central feature the burning conviction that members of a class suffer from a shared state of injustice. The theory of class consciousness should be viewed as a special case of the more general phenomenon represented by age-group consciousness, national consciousness, racial consciousness, and religious consciousness. In the Marxian analysis it is recognized that classes may exist without class consciousness. The members of an exploited economic class may fail to recognize their situation and consequently not pursue their interests. When, however, they recognize their situation and begin to act collectively to right it, class consciousness has developed. C. Wright Mills observes:

Class consciousness has always been understood as a political consciousness of one's own rational class interests and their opposition to the interests of other classes. Economic potentiality becomes politically realized: a "class in itself" becomes a "class for itself." Thus for class consciousness there must be (1) a rational awareness and identification with one's own class interests; (2) an awareness of and rejection of other class interests as illegitimate; and (3) an awareness of and a readiness to use collective political means to the collective political end of realizing one's interests.[14]

In any such choice of economic class, age group, or race as the focal orientation, the contrasting relationships to in-group and out-group are essential and may have partially distinct roots. David Lockwood comments:

...the development of class consciousness is rooted in two interrelated, yet possibly independent processes. The first is the consciousness of a division of interest between employer

[14] C. Wright Mills, *White Collar: The American Middle Classes* (New York: Oxford University Press, Inc., 1953), p. 325.

and employee, and the second a consciousness of a community of interest among employees. It is only when individual alienation becomes mobilized as collective solidarity that it is appropriate to speak of class consciousness as such.[15]

Recent analyses have suggested that class consciousness of the laborer is on the decline and may have been the consequence of a unique and transitory set of circumstances in Western history. Contemporary research does not reveal a vital class consciousness among industrial workers, and labor unions today limit their activities largely to a bargaining relationship that does not challenge the justice of the underlying relationship between employer and employee. Wilensky, among others, has proposed that class consciousness was a consequence of the correspondence between occupational class and religious, racial, or ethnic identity.[16] This observation illustrates a general proposition, namely, that a state of existence is most likely to be viewed as unjust when it is shared by people who are united into a group by the correspondence between two or more group identities. Where people are already united by membership in a common ethnic group or participation in a common organized religion, their occupational class can readily become the point of reference for a vital sense of injustice over economic arrangements.

PRIDE AND AUTONOMY. To view one's lot as unjust requires some audacity and some confidence in being able to play a more important role than at present. Many disadvantaged groups have been unable to escape from a pattern of accepting their lot as deserved or natural. Two obstacles to

be stressed are lack of pride in group identity and a totally dependent group relationship.

Only when the group identity is one in which members can take some pride is it possible for them to assert that they deserve a better lot than they have and to accept their fellows as common victims of injustice. Pariah groups such as the outcastes of India and the Eta of Japan have been slow to question their lot on a massive scale. So long as they accept the low esteem in which the group as a whole is held in their society, they cannot point to the misfortunes of their fellows as evidence that their own misfortune is undeserved. Wulbert has observed that collective protest is less common in mental institutions than in prisons, and he attributes the difference in part to the fact that there are aspects of being a criminal in which a person can take pride, whereas being a mental patient is almost without prideful aspects.[17] The same principle applies to the problem of conceiving one's situation as unjust.

Individuals and groups who are totally dependent upon a dominant group are those least likely to challenge the propriety of their situation. In total dependence, the very basis for continuing existence is threatened when the terms of the relationship are challenged. Even a state of slavery will be accepted by the majority of its victims without challenge when the slaves are taken out of reach of their homes, denied the skills necessary for independent existence, insulated from the experience of making significant decisions for themselves, and in other respects rendered totally dependent. Under American slavery, the memory of freedom in the recent past, the example of free Negroes in the North, the opportunities for freedom nearby in Spanish Florida, and the identification with successful rebellion in Haiti kept the sense of impotence and dependency from being uni-

15 David Lockwood, *The Blackcoated Worker: A Study in Class Consciousness* (London: George Allen and Unwin, Ltd., 1958), p. 208.
16 Harold Wilensky, "Class, Class Consciousness, and American Workers," in William Haber, ed., *Labor in a Changing America* (New York: Basic Books, Inc., Publishers, 1966), pp. 12–44.

17 Roland Wulbert, "Inmate Pride in Total Institutions," *American Journal of Sociology*, 71 (July, 1956), 1–9.

versal among the slaves. Consequently, there were many local and a few widespread movements of rebellion.[18] The full extent and significance of these movements is currently the subject of debate. But many, if not the majority, of American slaves appear to have been reluctant to accept the interpretation of their situation as injustice rather than great misfortune. Even after slavery was abolished, most Negroes did not seriously challenge their traditional position in the United States until they had been pushed off the plantations and out of paternalistic forms of service. So long as they lived on plantations, which constituted relatively total communities, serious questioning of the legitimacy of the system threatened Negroes' only stable anchorage. Once they found themselves dealing in the open labor market, the dependency was broken, and they could accept the position that racial inequality was fundamentally unjust.

An indigenous nationality group constitutes an ideal medium for protest in this respect, especially when they have largely maintained their group integrity and their traditional mode of life. This is one reason why nationalism is perhaps the most irresistible force in the world today. The traditional culture in its traditional setting provides the assurance that the colonial power is unneeded by the native group. National pride and the evidence of former autonomy are powerful forces conducive to defining subordination as injustice.

EXTERNAL LEGITIMATION AND SUPPORT. A question arises in the examination of specific movements regarding the part played by the disadvantaged group and by the more fortunate outside groups in formulating the conception of injustice. Superficially, at least, the labor movement illustrates the emergence and cultivation of a sense of injustice on the part of the

[18] Herbert Aptheker, *American Negro Slave Revolts,* (New York: Columbia University Press, 1943).

laboring classes themselves. In the United States the success of the American Federation of Labor is sometimes credited to the decision to restrict membership to bona fide laborers. Similarly, modern nationalism, nineteenth-century suffragism, and radical-right movements in the United States appear to have developed when groups defined their own situations as unjust and sought to persuade and coerce others into accepting this view. On the other hand, the American abolition movement was primarily the work of free whites who described the slave's condition as intolerable. There have also been movements to preserve the integrity of traditional American Indian cultures and comparable movements in Latin America, reflecting the white man's sense of distress and his conception of the injustice experienced by the native populations.

The problem of incorporating both these perspectives into an integrated account of the emergence of a normative conception of injustice must be a continuing one. We have begun by looking for origins of the sense of injustice within the victim group. Now we shall offer the hypothesis that a group cannot see its situation as fundamentally unjust without legitimation and support from an outside group whose established status is not problematical. The fact that the American Federation of Labor excluded all but laboring men should not mislead us: the movement consisted of more than the members of the organization and continued to benefit from a great deal of outside support.

One reason why some establishment support is essential is that the claim of a victimized group is not a moral issue so long as it is purely the expression of self-interest. Support and sympathy from those who have nothing at stake let the disadvantaged see their situation as involving a principle wider than their personal plight. The apparent altruism of the outside supporters lends the moral tone to the issue. The bases for believing that there are rights and wrongs in a situation are elusive. But the surest technique for legitimating a moral claim is the "laying on of hands." One who is already legitimated as the arbiter of right and wrong passes that power to another person or himself identifies the rights and wrongs of a situation. Support from prestigious persons or groups outside the disadvantaged group can serve in both these ways. It can identify leaders from within the group as having the moral authority to make authentic declarations on the subject of justice. Recognition by white leaders plays a major part in identifying those blacks to whom other blacks will listen on matters or racial justice. Support from outside prestigious persons also demonstrates that rights and not charity are being demanded.

Support from outside also provides an alternative, so that the group can risk the undermining of their traditional anchorage. As we shall see when we explore power relationships more fully, redefinition of their situation by members of disadvantaged groups is often facilitated by a struggle between established groups. Seeking to bring the disadvantaged group into a coalition so as to strengthen their own position, one or more elite segments call attention to the injustice and promise support in righting the wrongs.

Intellectuals and the Definition of Injustice. Whatever the state of readiness for a new idea of justice, a special kind of person is required to formulate and advertise it. People express discontent, complain, and even engage in impulsive resistance to conditions. But the discovery that their complaints are really expressions of injustice requires that the new terms be formulated and that the people be given the basis for an appeal to authority. For convenience we shall apply the rather inexact term *intellectuals* to the specialists in words and ideas. The talent of the intellectual in formulating discontent as injustice, and the authority of the intellectual in justifying the moral implication appear to be necessary to the complete process.

The idea of an alienated intelligentsia as a revolutionary force comes from the study of Russia in the late nineteenth and early twentieth centuries. From the time of Peter the Great, Russians had gone to western Europe for their learning, bringing back not only the social graces and science from Paris but also many of the prevalent liberal and radical ideas. Steeped in the culture of another land, they could find little either to understand or to admire in indigenous Russian values, and they could make few contributions to the improvement of Russian society within the framework available in national institutions. At the same time Russian economic development was creating a demand for teachers, lawyers, and doctors, so the intelligentsia were exposed to a substantial group of free professionals, western educated and not attached to the government. Other circumstances added to the situation of a group out of touch with their culture, at odds with a repressive political regime, and susceptible to either highly romantic ideas or revolutionary doctrine. Romantic doctrine advocated a pan-slavism in which the evils of Russian society were attributed to the alien Western elements, and the historic culture was to be restored to its proper place in the world through the leadership of the Russian nation. But the revolutionary ideas gradually gained the upper hand. Without this alienated intelligentsia, it is difficult to conceive of the Russian Revolution occurring when and as it did.

There are three separate questions that must be answered in order to establish whether substantial numbers of intellectuals will help to define some aspect of the status quo as unjust and to disseminate and authenticate a new norm of justice. First, we must determine whether there are many intellectuals who are relatively independent of support from classes who have a vested interest in the status quo.

So long as intellectuals are under direct employment or patronage from the ruling classes, whether secular or clerical, their definitions of justice are likely to agree with the existing system. On the other hand, when their patronage comes from a rising class, as was often true of the liberal thinkers of eighteenth-century Europe, or when the idea of academic freedom is institutionalized so as to protect the dissenter from punishment for his views, criticisms of society are likely to form a large part of the intellectual product.

Second, we must inquire whether institutional arrangements lead numerous intellectuals to identify with underdog groups. When circumstances lead to bitterness over the intellectual's role, in the ways we have already described, intellectual identification with the underdog is sometimes a convenient vehicle for attack on the social order at large. Thus the disaffection of the intellectual over his own role can serve the formulation of injustice in other groups.

Finally, we must look for the existence of arrangements that weld the intellectuals into a cohesive public and facilitate the development of a sort of established intellectual catechism. The presence of national centers of intellectual activity and recognized arbiters of intellectual repute contribute to this development. Intellectual history in recent times points to the importance of the salon as a place where intellectual discourse beyond the confines of academic disciplines and free from other professional limitations takes place and where the recognized boundaries of an intellectual community are established. Through such media certain viewpoints come to be the recognized intellectual point of view.

These observations can be summarized by observing that the presence of a body of intellectuals, sufficiently alienated from their own situation to make common cause with an underdog group and sufficiently independent to have protection against repression, is necessary if the situation of a disadvantaged group is to be defined as unjust. The conditions that affect the role of intellectuals may be quite different and independent of those affecting the disadvantaged group. Careful research may show that the strains of the intellectual role and diversity of positions occupied by intellectuals insure that there will be enough intellectuals concerned with uncovering injustice in any society to serve any group that is ready to see its situation in these terms. But it is also quite possible that research will show that changes in the social role of the intellectual have been a major factor in the rise and fall of discontent throughout history.

Selection of a Comparison Group. Two other aspects of a sense of injustice may help to point our attention toward elements in its development. From both exchange and the contract theories we see that a judgment of injustice implies a comparison with a better-situated group of some sort. There is therefore some choice among groups that may serve as a standard of comparison. Second, the idea of justice is a moral notion. Developing a sense of injustice over any particular conditions exhibits the general characteristics of any process of moralization; it is a special case of the formation or application of a rule in a moral code.

Charges of injustice are always based upon unfavorable comparison with the wealth, freedom, power, or other benefit that another group has. Yet people are often aware of groups who have more than they do without making such comparisons the basis for an assessment of the fairness of their own situation. When comparisons are made, the choice of comparison groups can make a situation look fair or unfair. When the middle-class black compares himself with poorer blacks, his situation appears fortunate; when he compares himself with middle-class whites, he has a basis for seeing injustice at work. Part of society's inertia is a fairly general tendency for people to employ only those comparisons that serve to make their own position seem reasonable and fair. Thus the skilled craftsman compares his lot with that of other manual laborers, rather than with workers in semiprofessional and business occupations. The conditions we have already outlined interrupt this tendency. But in addition there are probably some principles governing the selection of comparison groups that provide additional information about a group's discovery that its situation is an unjust one. These principles come from *reference group* theory. A comprehensive examination of the choice of comparison groups as an explanation for feelings of relative deprivation was first presented by Robert Merton and Alice Kitt[19] and has been most carefully applied to class consciousness by W. G. Runciman.[20] We cite four of the principles suggested by Runciman.

The individual normally has a choice between comparing himself with members of his own group or some other group. The former may lead to individual feelings of being victimized, but it prevents the development of any sense of injustice that can be applied to the group as a whole. So long as workers are chiefly jealous of the benefits that come to some of their fellows, they do not formulate a conception of inherent injustice in the worker's position. Cultivation of internal jealousies is a tactic that is often effective in forestalling serious challenge to established intergroup relationships. Catastrophes that strike a class of people indiscriminately, exploitation that does not distinguish between friends and enemies within the group, and categorical repressions are

among experiences that help to divert attention from internal dissension toward other groups that are available for comparison.

Status inconsistency fosters unfavorable comparison with other groups. By status inconsistency we mean a lack of correspondence between attributes, such as educational attainment and income or occupation. The college-educated black who works as a postal clerk compares himself with other college educated persons who are likely to hold better occupational positions. In the case of status inconsistency the individual has two or more membership groups with whom to compare himself. He can legitimately compare himself with others in his own educational category, but he sees racial identity as sharply separating his educational peers into two distinct groups. He compares himself as a black with whites because he might have been united with them on the basis of education.

Sudden disappointment of a stable expectation when shared by members of a group is a third circumstance leading to unfavorable comparisons with another group. Economic depression hits the wage-earner and inflation hits the pensioner. In either case it forces a downward revision in living standards. Such revisions normally cause the victims to look about for other groups that are not similarly affected. There was a widespread conviction in the United States during the depression of the 1930s that the nation's wealth was concentrated in the hands of the well-to-do and that economic problems could be resolved by soaking the rich. Discrepancies between the wealthy and the poor were probably no greater, and perhaps even less, during depression years than in the preceding decade of prosperity. Yet there was a greater tendency for lower-income groups to use the wealthy as comparison groups and more questioning of the fundamental justice of the divisions between the wealthy and other income classes.

[19] Robert K. Merton and Alice S. Kitt, "Contributions to the Theory of Reference Group Behavior," in Merton and Paul F. Lazarsfeld, eds., *Continuities in Social Research* (New York: The Free Press, 1950), pp. 40–105.
[20] W. G. Runciman, *Relative Deprivation and Social Justice* (Berkeley: University of California Press, 1966), pp. 9–35.

Finally, rising expectations may under some circumstances lead to comparison with a group that is better situated than one's own. It is doubtful that the relationship is direct and linear, since it is easy to find situations of steadily improved conditions for a category of people that lead only to increasing self-satisfaction. Most of the widely publicized instances of rising expectations are those in which the sense of injustice has already been developed and conditions do not improve as rapidly as hoped for. Perhaps the significant instances are those in which the improved circumstances permit members of the rising group to assume many of the characteristics of a group above them. When they begin to dress like the higher group, drive similar automobiles, live in similar neighborhoods, speak with similar accents, they then adopt the higher category as a comparison group, which they would not otherwise have thought to do.

RIGHTEOUS INDIGNATION. Even with all the foregoing conditions in effect, it is doubtful that serious and sustained indignation can be aroused except in the course of open conflict between the deprived group and some group that is viewed as the oppressor. A sense of injustice that is vital enough to have consequences seems to require not only a situation that appears unfavorable by comparison with some reference group but also an oppressor, so that the situation can be seen as a product of human will.

It is sufficiently obvious that once the sense of injustice has been aroused and a movement is in operation there will be organized opposition to change from some quarters. From that opposition comes a heightening of indignation and an intensified sense of injustice. But we have reference here to intergroup conflict that precedes the sense of injustice. If this view is correct, events must bring groups into conflict over matters of a more routine and less far-reaching character, leading to organized repressions of some sort. The repressions and the social conflict then provide the combatant mood that leads group members to see their situation from a more jaundiced perspective.

Conclusion

It is doubtful that any list of necessary and sufficient conditions for the occurrence of a social movement can be formulated except in overly general or tautological terms. Rather than essaying such a list we have employed one from among several possible choices as the point of departure in identifying conditions that make a movement more or less likely to occur. The normative transformation that is part of every movement implicates both perceptions or beliefs and actions. Normative revision is not simply an intellectual or emotional exercise that is then followed by action. As the analysis in this chapter has suggested, the emergence of a new normative perspective depends upon the possibilities for action in compliance with the perspective, and the course of the normative revision depends on the course of the action. Hence we are led into a more intensive examination of the processes that shape the course of the movement, stressing the interplay and tension among value orientations, power orientations, and participation orientations.

14

VALUE ORIENTATIONS
OF SOCIAL MOVEMENTS

The first question we normally ask about any social movement concerns its goals. Just what kind of changes does it seek? But the answer is as likely to be a statement of ideology as of specific goals. Every movement promotes both specific changes in people or in social organization and a conception of reality that supports and justifies these changes. At times the goals are clear and the ideology is in process of formulation; at other times a movement— such as the contemporary radical youth group—has a fairly well elaborated ideology without a correspondingly stable set of goals. Men of action are attracted to a movement because of its goals, but more contemplative persons are won by the ideology. Over the long run, goals and ideology are obverse sides of the same coin.

Goals and ideology are the tangible expressions of some value or complex of values. A humanitarian value led to the abolition movement with its goal of eliminating slavery and its conception of slavery as an institution. An equalitarian value led at one time to a goal of racial integration with an ideology linking segregation to inequality and at another time to a goal of minority autonomy and an ideology identifying inequality as an inevitable feature of any gross imbalance of power between interpenetrating groups. The sense of justice that we discussed in the preceding chapter is satisfied when the value is supported in society, and the sense of injustice prevails when society subverts or ignores the value.

A value is any category of objects that is felt to have worth, that ought to be protected and promoted rather than treated with indifference. Objects of value can range from tangible things to broad ideas and activities. People feel good when an object of value is honored; they feel distressed or outraged when it is disregarded or profaned. An object of value is felt to merit the sacrifice of less highly valued objects for the sake of its attainment or preservation. Hence a program to change the values of a society is always a proposal to give up some current gratification for the sake of the newly emphasized value.

The Character of Value Orientations

MOVEMENT IDEOLOGY. Movement ideologies reflect the complexity and indefiniteness that characterize all folk thought. "Political ideologies always combine, more or less felicitously, factual propositions and value judgments. They express an outlook on the world and a will orientated towards the future. They cannot be described as literally true or false, nor do they belong to the same category as taste and colour."[1] Aron's statement is equally true of ide-

1 Raymond Aron, *The Opium of the Intellectuals* (London: Martin Secker and Warburg Ltd., 1957), p. 236.

ologies in religious, educational, and social betterment movements. For intellectual adherents the ideology supplies a foundation from which to evaluate goals and, in part, to select strategies and tactics for promoting the movement goals. For most adherents, ideology supplies a vague but comfortable assurance of the rightness and effectiveness of the movement and a set of resources to employ in promoting the movement among the unpersuaded and in defending the movement from its enemies. These resources range from simple gestures and slogans to complex arguments and images of utopia. We shall identify several more specific functions—not mutually exclusive—that ideologies perform for participants in a movement.

1. Ideologies are prescriptions or maps that tell the individual how to look at events and people, and they provide a simplifying perspective through which the observer can make sense of otherwise overwhelmingly complex phenomena and find definiteness in otherwise vague and uncertain impressions. Ideologies tell the observer how to distinguish figure from ground. The John Birch Society, like its predecessor, McCarthyism, supplies members with a few simple clues by which to tell a Communist or a Communist dupe from a patriotic American. Father Coughlin, the Detroit priest whose depression-era radio following heard his repeated calls to drive the moneychangers out of the temple, disposed of inflation as a bogey invented by bankers to maintain their control of the economy. For black militants any encounter with whites can be reduced to the detection and accusation of racism.

Simplification eliminates the basis for troublesome doubts about whether the attainment of movement goals will actually foster movement values. If all the problems of blacks in the United States are a simple and direct consequence of white racism, the prospect of correcting the situation by militant attacks on racism is much greater than if we accept the hypotheses of the effect of matriarchal family structure or the problem of low skill-levels as the basis of the problem. Simplification also supplies the individual with a manageable formula to cope with a variety of otherwise puzzling and often embarrassing situations.

2. Ideologies place the movement and its goals in a moving time perspective. An account of the past history that led to the present sorry state of affairs is essential to justify the favored approach to a solution. Conventional history is either an ideological creation in support of the existing values or too beset with complexity and contradiction to serve a social movement. Hence every social movement inspires and uses revisionist histories. A view of history as an impersonal historical process calls for direct attempts to alter social structure. An account of widespread moral decline suggests individual regeneration according to the prescriptions of Frank Buchman[2] or Billy Graham. Personal forfeiture of freedom for self-indulgence suggests the "drop out and turn on" formula of Timothy Leary.

Complementing past history, an account of the future depicts the relative or absolute utopia that is to be attained. In any vigorous movement the utopia is treated as inevitable. Collective effort speeds up its attainment, and often participation in the movement insures a personal share in the fruits of the utopia. Joining the movement is riding the wave of the future, helping to usher in a new era.

Movements have sometimes been distinguished according to whether the future they seek is the reinstatement of an idyllic past or the creation of a new and different order. Nativistic movements among people under colonial domination abound with revivalistic themes, with the romanticized historical past restored. But there are probably no movements that lack such

2 Frank Buchman founded a religious movement known as the Oxford Group or Moral Rearmament, which was internationally prominent from the 1930s to the 1950s.

revivalistic elements. Man is generally unable to visualize a future that is not compounded of the familiar. Those images of the future that describe a genuinely novel way of life are frightening and serve mostly as counterutopias or warnings of what might happen if the movement does not succeed. Movements for sexual freedom assume an historical past when man was uninhibited, an idyllic state that was destroyed by the mores that came with civilization but that can be restored by casting off or reforming civilization. Even the sophisticated Marxian ideology brings man full circle to a world in which he will enjoy the primitive pleasures of hunting and fishing at will. In the Indian movement for independence, Ghandi taught his followers to cultivate the traditional crafts, such as spinning, in order to preserve the true Indian culture from the inroads of Western civilization.

3. Ideology translates self-interest into an ideal by identifying group interest with the general welfare. This step is essential if the movement is to have the force of a moral crusade against injustice, a revitalization of the culture. Dr. Townsend's pension plan for the elderly was supposed to bring the United States out of the depression of the 1930s by its massive infusion of purchasing power. An important theme of Jewish and black movements in the United States has been the damaging effect of prejudice and discrimination on the discriminator.

A pattern of puritanism appears in many widely different movements and may be another way in which the movement is established as a moral crusade rather than as an exercise in self-interest. A cargo cult called the Vailala Madness that flourished in New Guinea for a decade after World War I illustrates this feature. Inspired by the prophesied coming of a ship loaded with a cargo that would change their lives, the people abandoned many of their traditional practices, destroyed worldly goods, and discontinued productive labors. Among their rituals was the deliberate violation of some conventional taboos. But this was offset by strict observance of Sunday, cleanliness, hand washing, and adoption of a severe discipline against stealing, adultery, traditional amusements, and personal adornment.[3] A similar puritanism is found among the Black Muslims. Radical movements that promote the abandonment of sexual restraint normally impose other restraints in its place, such as a strict taboo against material wealth and comfort and artificial adornment. Ideological justifications for asceticism in its many forms, such as ritual fasting, depict the movement as a sacrificial endeavor and thus clothe self-interest in a mantle of morality and idealism.

Ideologies always reevaluate the worth of population segments. A rationale is formulated for viewing the constituency in a more positive and elevated light than heretofore. The forgotten man is actually the foundation on which the nation was built. The doctrine that the current generation of young people is the most perceptive, idealistic, and concerned generation in history is inculcated in every adherent to current youth-movements. A doctrine of the superior but unrecognized contribution of women to human well-being is an integral feature of recurring women's movements over the past century.

4. Related to the reevaluation of population segments is the universal creation of villains. Besides devaluing a broad class of people, the ideology identifies a delimited set of individuals who are engaged in a deliberate conspiracy against the general welfare in the service of their own sinister interests. The visible effects of their evil intent are supplemented by imaginary activities, such as the right-wing charge that 16,000 African soldiers were being trained in guerrilla warfare by the United Nations in Georgia, or the black militant charge that the United States government re-

[3] Peter Worsley, *The Trumpet Shall Sound: A Study of 'Cargo' Cults in Melanesia* (London: MacGibbon and Kee, 1957), pp. 75–92.

sponded to the urban riots of 1965 and after by establishing several concentration camps in which blacks would be interned after mass arrests were made. A typical ultrarightist document describes a purported elite group of American traitors, including Senator William Fulbright, former Ambassador George Kennan, and former Defense Secretary Robert McNamara, who were said to communicate in a code language in order to conceal their true intention of bringing the United States under Soviet rule.[4]

Although most movements are less extreme, the villain and conspiracy themes are universal. These themes are often explained on the basis of psychological service to members. Hans Toch describes a category of people whose own personal inadequacy is obvious, or whom the world has clearly passed by, who cannot face reality without experiencing utter self-depreciation. "Conspiracy beliefs correspond to a real need *only* for persons *who cannot preserve their self-esteem unless they conceive of themselves as victims of a plot.*"[5] But the suggestion that movements create villains and conspiracies chiefly to attract the small and marginal group of sick and incompetent adherents is difficult to take seriously. Three other reasons for the universality of villain and conspiracy themes have greater plausibility.

First, belief in villains and conspiracy protects persons from the assumption that evil is inherent or deeply rooted in the situation. Hitler's conspiracy theory of German defeat in World War I saved the Germans from having to face the possibility that they had been outfought. Assumption of a liberal conspiracy in the United States protects the rightist from having to acknowledge that some of the changes he

fears may be an inevitable product of historical forces.

Second, these beliefs simplify a complex situation and indicate how it can be rectified by a simple course of action. Disposing of the villains and unmasking the conspiracy will surely usher in the desired changes.

Third, the identification of villains corresponds with the major approach to social control that society employs. The key to social control is training people to account for evil by identifying the responsible individual. The young child is trained to accept the idea of responsibility. And a satisfactory answer to why some unfortunate event occurred is usually a designation of responsibility. To extend this approach, which works fairly well in bringing much of our immediate daily life under reasonable control, to the larger world of experience is entirely natural.

5. Finally, the ideology identifies the character of the movement. Whether the movement is a religious enterprise or a secular pursuit, whether its members are people of culture or men of the world, whether they represent gentleness or toughness—these and many similar choices form a definite character for the movement. The character is something for the adherent to assimilate into his own self-conception through identification, and it will therefore greatly affect the movement's recruiting. Certain strategies and tactics and certain alliances will be consistent with the movement's character but others will not. The movement's symbolic leaders must personify the movement's character.

THE NATURE OF MOVEMENT GOALS. The goals are the tangible accomplishments sought by the movement, and one criterion by which the movement's success or failure is judged. Goals must be consistent with ideology, and they must also meet several other conditions if they are to sustain a vital movement.

1. Movement goals must be credible to

---

[4] Phyllis Schlafly and Chester Ward, *Strike from Space: A Megadeath Mystery* (Alton, Ill.: Pere Marquette Press, 1965).

[5] Hans Toch, *The Social Psychology of Social Movements* (Indianapolis, Ind.: The Bobbs-Merrill Co., Inc., 1965), p. 69.

the constituency. Romantic goals that appeal to some youthful groups are unlikely to be taken seriously by an older group. Absolute utopias, such as world peace, will find less support than will relative utopias, such as the reduction of warfare, among older people. Medical training and experience limit receptiveness to movements that promise good health and well-being through adherence to simple regimens. The businessman's intimate experience with the complexities and the delicate balance of the economy makes him skeptical of simple schemes for economic reform, be they socialistic planning, the single tax, or schemes to do away with currency exchange.

2. Goals must unite, rather than divide, important constituencies. The Los Angeles County tax-reform movement mentioned in Chapter 13 failed in part because it divided property owners. By representing residential-property interests to the possible detriment of business-property owners, the movement lost the support of the latter group, which was better organized and more powerful.[6] The division of laboring classes into Protestant and Catholic segments has been a continuing problem for labor leaders, who run the risk of selecting goals that will alienate one or the other. An inherent difficulty with any movement for women's rights is locating goals that will unite women of different socioeconomic stations rather than divide them.

3. To achieve sustained effectiveness a movement must present a hierarchy of goals, ranging from some that are almost immediately attainable to others that are virtually unattainable. Movements for the reform of civil government are notably ineffective in the long run because they marshal their forces for a single accomplishment, such as the recall of a corrupt

official or the sensational cleanup of a single corrupt condition. After this is achieved the movement quickly dissipates, and the old conditions are quietly reinstated. Unless the members are convinced before the accomplishment that it is merely an important step toward the ultimate goal, the movement will be difficult to revive. Efforts to revive support will lead to disillusionment rather than to renewed enthusiasm.

On the other hand, movements that can claim no proximate success but only preparation over a long period for an ultimate triumph are unlikely to maintain popular support.[7] Movements like technocracy and Upton Sinclair's "End Poverty in California" (EPIC) movement offered no halfway accomplishments but only finished programs to be established in toto. Each movement had a period of great popular support followed by a fairly rapid falling away of membership and public interest.

Ultimate objectives conceived in fairly general terms permit flexibility in the more specific short-range objectives. Movements that do not subordinate their specific goals to more general goals cannot substitute one scheme for another when conditions demand. The pressure for old-age pensions in the United States, for example, has come from a series of competing and relatively short-lived movements rather than from a single sustained movement. Each movement has been attached to the promotion of a particular plan—The Townsend Plan, "Thirty Dollars Every Thursday," etc. As each plan reached its apex and its program came under attack, the movement declined in spite of its effect in forcing liberalization of existing pension schemes and in causing other improvements.

When the movement does not offer proximate goals to its members, they are likely to create such goals on the spot,

---

[6] Maurice Jackson, Eleanora Peterson, James Bull, Sverre Monsen, and Patricia Richmond, "The Failure of an Incipient Social Movement," *Pacific Sociological Review*, 3 (Spring, 1960), 35–40.

[7] Thomas H. Greer, *American Social Reform Movements: Their Pattern Since 1865* (Englewood Cliffs, N.J.: Prentice-Hall, Inc., 1949), pp. 275ff.

often undermining the long-range goals in process. Cohn points out the intimate relationship between pogroms and the medieval Crusades.[8] The trip to the Holy Land was long and arduous, with no promise of accomplishment and reward until the crusade was complete. Crusaders saw the Jews as the immediate embodiment of the evil they sought to overcome. Hence they attacked the Jews wherever they found them.

4. Movement goals must combine tangible and symbolic gain with goals of general social betterment. The appeal to the self-interest of an established segment of society not only insures vigorous, rather than lip-service, support from that group but it also gives the movement access to the preestablished organization and communication networks of a group with some preexisting homogeneity. By appealing to farmers, laborers, or elderly people, a movement taps the informal communication nets that already link people within these categories, and it may make use of the prestige of recognized leaders.

A movement that has had powerful support may lose it when the tangible benefits come to an end. Seymour M. Lipset points out this difficulty as it has applied to the Canadian Commonwealth Federation, a farmer's movement with a socialistic program and ideology:

Most C. C. F. leaders assume that if farmers are given enough economic security and increased social services they will continue to support the movement in its efforts to socialize the rest of the economy. Experiences in other countries do not lend weight to this assumption. In fact, the contrary seems to be true— farmers tend to become conservative when they achieve their economic goals. The farmer is radical vis-a-vis the larger society when his economic security and land tenure are threatened. He may join other exploited groups, such as the workers, to win his own economic demands. However, once the farmer achieves

these immediate goals and becomes a member of the secure property holders of society, he resents government controls and labor or tax legislation that interferes with the expansion of his business.[9]

A movement whose only value is self-interest can hardly be effective except through sheer power-subjugation of the larger society by a group who is willing to repudiate its identification with that society. Members of the self-interest group will be hesitant to pursue openly so un-idealistic an objective. And all but actively revolutionary movements depend upon a permissive atmosphere in the larger society in which to work. The passive sympathy that contributes to such a permissive atmosphere will be replaced by fear and intolerance when the group's self-interest is not felt to be subordinated to the general welfare. When passive sympathy prevails, overly aggressive opposition to the movement enlarges the sympathetic public. When such sympathy is replaced by fear, aggressive opposition encourages more widespread active opposition.

The self-interest group need not be large if it is crucially related to the legitimate means for realizing the movement's values. W. F. Ogburn has pointed out the rapid success of the movement for safety in industry *after* laws had been enacted making employers liable in case of injury to their employees.[10] The employers, though a relatively small group, possessed the legitimate means to establish and enforce safety procedures and to install safety devices.

SOCIETAL MANIPULATION VS. PERSONAL TRANSFORMATION. Goals and ideology may point in two broad directions. They may point toward changing individuals directly

8 Norman Cohn, *The Pursuit of the Millennium* (New York: Oxford University Press, Inc., 1957), p. 52.

9 Seymour M. Lipset, *Agrarian Socialism* (Berkeley: University of California Press, 1950), p. 229. Reprinted by permission of the Regents of the University of California.

10 William F. Ogburn, "The Psychological Basis for the Economic Interpretation of History," *American Economic Review,* 9, Supplement (March, 1919), 291–308.

or toward changing social institutions. Those ambitious movements that seek to establish the Kingdom of Heaven on earth or to promote international peace by conversion on a mass scale are genuinely value oriented. The major religions of the world, such as Christianity and Buddhism, have sought to promote a new set of values on a societywide basis through attention to the hearts and motives of men.

It is perhaps easier to understand societal manipulation movements, since they act directly to rectify conditions rather than take the indirect route of changing mankind. Whenever an outside object is readily identifiable as the source of injustice and can be practically acted upon, the movement is likely to aim at societal manipulation from the start. Hence we suggest three conditions that are essential if a movement follows the route of personal transformation. First, there must be prevalent in the society a world view that incorporates a basis for believing that widespread self-improvement is possible. The Judaic conception that man was made in the image of God, and Greek and Roman versions of the belief in human perfectibility set the stage for the Christian doctrine, resting upon the divinity of man. Second, the conception of the universe must lead people to assume that the state of the social order will reflect the integrity and character of individual men. The belief in a punishing and rewarding supernatural is one such belief; a view that society is what the sum of its individual members make it is another such belief. Third, the circumstances giving rise to the movement must be such that the people can take some responsibility upon themselves for their present unsatisfactory condition.

For this third reason such movements as the woman suffrage crusade, the abolitionist movement, and the labor movement could only take the direction of societal manipulation. The women could feel no personal responsibility for their position and had to force suffrage upon men. Abolition

was a movement among nonslaveholders, forcing the abandonment of slavery upon slaveholders. And the labor movement explicitly rejected the employers' view that the laboring man deserves his fate for not having initiative enough to get out of the ranks of labor.

Some of these movements begin as quite limited messianic movements or as movements of resignation within subjugated classes. But because of the foregoing conditions they do not take on their full value-oriented character until they become dominated by a better-established membership and subordinate their messianic emphasis. Thus the Christian movement, beginning as a nationalistic messianic movement, only became the movement we know when it centered among the gentile populations of the Roman empire.

Movements of this sort are also not likely to have their main strength in completely depressed classes of people. Such groups are unlikely to have a basis for believing that man's will can transform the world. Consequently these movements are not so much associated with serious deprivation as with loss of a sense of personal purpose and worth in life. In the presence of a certain amount of material comfort, combining a sense of individual capability with an absence of meaningful direction, people are prepared to assume personal responsibility and to feel guilt for the current state of affairs. A movement for social reform that convinces men to adopt a particular set of values is the natural outcome of this widespread feeling of directionlessness coupled with experiences suggesting that man can better himself when he will.

Movements for personal transformation characteristically shift toward a societal manipulation emphasis when they have achieved some success and added persons of influence to their membership. Most Christian codes, for example, have been translated into laws at one time or another. The upsurge of the social gospel in Christendom during the depression of the 1930s suggests that the personal transformation emphasis may also lose ground to societal manipulation when there is pressure for a more immediate solution of social problems than the gradual process of winning men's souls can promise.

REPRESENTATION OF THE VALUES. The logic of a movement's goals and ideology can be communicated in many ways. Formal declarations, speeches of persons thought to represent the movement, dramatic actions, and many other devices serve this purpose. But it would be an error to view goals and ideology primarily as cognitive matters, to be explained in direct language.

The vital element in the ideology and program is a sense of value, a feeling for a certain direction of change. Those who attack particular movements on cognitive grounds constantly point to unworkable details in the programs. Followers are not greatly distressed by a certain amount of this sort of criticism, since their conviction is that practical details can be worked out as the plan goes into operation if people who hold the right kind of values are in control. This is true to a considerable degree of movements that have had an important impact on history as well as of minor crackpot movements.

The official spokesmen of movements necessarily share this sense of value and so subordinate the details of the program. It is not surprising that official representations of a movement's ideology largely depict the movement in terms of values rather than of logical details. Public representations will be more concerned with the arousal of feelings than with rational exposition. This may be the sincere expression of the movement, or it may be simply a tactic to exploit irrational support.

An ideologist for the French Syndicalist movement, Georges Sorel, makes this noncognitive character of movement values the explicit justification for the myth of a general strike. Dedicated to a revolutionary socialism and despising parliamentary socialism as an insincere surrender to capitalist forces, he urges that all socialist energies be devoted to spreading the doctrine of one general strike that will paralyze all society. Sorel's work is of interest here not because of his particular brand of socialism but because of his analysis of the noncognitive character of myth. Only a brief excerpt is included here to suggest the line of thought developed in his book, *Reflections on Violence*.

The Myth of the General Strike

Georges Sorel

. . . Syndicalism endeavours to employ methods of expression which throw a full light on things, which put them exactly in the place assigned to them by their nature, and which bring out the whole value of the forces in play. Oppositions, instead of being glozed over, must be thrown into sharp relief if we desire to obtain a clear idea of the

From Georges Sorel, *Reflections on Violence,* tr. by T. E. Hulme and J. Roth (New York: The Free Press, 1950), pp. 139–40, 142–44, 150–51. Reprinted in part by permission of The Macmillan Company.

Syndicalist movement; the groups which are struggling one against the other must be shown as separate and as compact as possible; in short, the movements of the revolted masses must be represented in such a way that the soul of the revolutionaries may receive a deep and lasting impression.

These results could not be produced in any very certain manner by the use of ordinary language; use must be made of a body of images which, *by intuition alone,* and before any considered analyses are made, is capable of evoking as an undivided whole the mass of sentiments which corresponds to the different manifestations of the war undertaken by Socialism against modern society. The Syndicalists solve this problem perfectly, by concentrating the whole of Socialism in the drama of the general strike; there is thus no longer any place for the reconciliation of contraries in the equivocations of the professors; everything is clearly mapped out, so that only one interpretation of Socialism is possible. This method has all the advantages which "integral" knowledge has over analysis, according to the doctrine of Bergson; and perhaps it would not be possible to cite another example which would so perfectly demonstrate the value of the famous professor's doctrines.

The possibility of the actual realization of the general strike has been much discussed; it has been stated that the Socialist war could not be decided in one single battle. To the people who think themselves cautious, practical, and scientific the difficulty of setting great masses of the proletariat in motion at the same moment seems prodigious; they have analyzed the difficulties of detail which such an enormous struggle would present . . .

. . . There is no process by which the future can be predicted scientifically, nor even one which enables us to discuss whether one hypothesis about it is better than another; it has been proved by too many memorable examples that the greatest men have committed prodigious errors in thus desiring to make predictions about even the least distant future.

And yet without leaving the present, without reasoning about this future, which seems for ever condemned to escape our reason, we should be unable to act at all. Experience shows that the *framing of a future, in some indeterminate time,* may, when it is done in a certain way, be very effective, and have very few inconveniences; this happens when the anticipations of the future take the form of those myths, which enclose with them, all the strongest inclinations of a people, of a party or of a class, inclinations which recur to the mind with the insistence of instincts in all the circumstances of life; and which give an aspect of complete reality to the hopes of imme-

diate action by which, more easily than by an other method, men can reform their desires, passions, and mental activity. We know, moreover, that these social myths in no way prevent a man profiting by the observations which he makes in the course of his life, and form no obstacle to the pursuit of his normal occupations.

The truth of this may be shown by numerous examples.

The first Christians expected the return of Christ and the total ruin of the pagan world, with the inauguration of the kingdom of the saints, at the end of the first generation. The catastrophe did not come to pass, but Christian thought profited so greatly from the apocalyptic myth that certain contemporary scholars maintain that the whole preaching of Christ referred solely to this one point. The hopes which Luther and Calvin had formed of the religious exaltation of Europe were by no means realized; these fathers of the Reformation very soon seemed men of a past era; for present-day Protestants they belong rather to the Middle Ages than to modern times, and the problems which troubled them most occupy very little place in contemporary Protestantism. Must we for that reason deny the immense result which came from their dreams of Christian renovation? It must be admitted that the real developments of the Revolution did not in any way resemble the enchanting pictures which created the enthusiasm at its first adepts; but without those pictures would the Revolution have been victorious? . . .

The myth must be judged as a means of acting on the present; any attempt to discuss how far it can be taken literally as future history is devoid of sense. *It is the myth in its entirety which is alone important:* its parts are only of interest in so far as they bring out the main idea. . . .

The strike throws a new light on all this; it separates the interests and the different ways of thinking of the two groups of wage-earners—the foremen, clerks, engineers, etc., as contrasted with the workmen who alone go on strike—much better than the daily circumstances of life do; it then becomes clear that the administrative group has a natural tendency to become a little aristocracy; for these people, State Socialism would be advantageous, because they would go up one in the social hierarchy.

But all oppositions become extraordinarily clear when conflicts are supposed to be enlarged to the size of the general strike; then all parts of the economicojudical structure, in so far as the latter is looked upon from the point of view of the class war, reach the summit of their perfection; society is plainly divided into two camps, and only into two, on a field of battle. No philosophical explanation of the facts observed in practical affairs could throw such vivid light on the situation as the extremely simple picture called up by the conception of the general strike.

The Sources of Value Orientations

Although our knowledge does not permit us to predict the goals and ideologies that will be selected by movements in the future, retrospective analysis convinces us that value orientations are always understandable against the background of the society from which they emanate. Far from being wholly novel creations, value orientations draw heavily upon themes in the traditional culture, and they rely especially on the world view of the class or other social segment that constitutes the movement's prime constituency. In some respects the movement values may be in contrast to the established values, according to the theory of dialectical process. It is well established that movements come in clusters that share elements of ideology and pursue closely related and mutually supportive goals, leading us to speak of general movements as a major source of value orientations for specific movements. And finally, movement values respond to the focal problems of an era, so that the issues of one generation's movements are not those of the next generation's movements. We shall take up each of these five sources in turn.

THEMES FROM TRADITIONAL CULTURE. Every culture is a storehouse so replete with diverse ideas that to increase the emphasis on some at the expense of others or to examine some in relation to ideas not usually associated with them can supply the justification and direction for restructuring society. Like hundreds of other movements, "Doomsday cult"[11] links the apocalyptic message of the Book of Revelation with the political theme of anticommunism. The Christian final judgment will culminate in a war between democracy and communism, and after democracy wins, God will reveal a new divine system of government to supersede democracy. In eleventh-century Europe Pope Gregory proclaimed the priest Ramirhdus a martyr after the local bishop had him burnt as a heretic for arousing the people against the worldliness of the priests. In the twelfth century Pope Gregory's stand against priestly worldliness was made the justification for indiscriminate violence against priests by the revolutionary followers of Tanchelm.[12] Women's rights and blacks' movements in the United States merely extend traditional goals and their justifications to new populations. Even Carmichael and Hamilton's *Black Power,* offered as a revolutionary challenge to American institutions, contains little that is not already part of the tradition of liberal American thought.[13]

Borrowing from familiar world views is so extensive that Rudolf Heberle finds it useful to make a distinction between constitutive and accidental ideas.

The more important social movements tend to absorb a great deal of the social thought of their time and their ideologies therefore tend to become rather complex aggregates of ideas. Some of these may be regarded as specific

---

[11] This is the pseudonym for a small movement observed in the San Francisco Bay region by John Lofland. Cf. *Doomsday Cult* (Englewood Cliffs, N.J.: Prentice-Hall, Inc., 1966).

[12] Cohn, *Pursuit of the Millennium,* pp. 33–40.

[13] Stokely Carmichael and Charles V. Hamilton, *Black Power: The Politics of Liberation in America* (New York: Random House, Inc., 1967).

and essential to the movement; they are the really integrating ideas. Others may be of mere accidental significance for this particular movement. The former may be called the *constitutive* ideas, since they form the spiritual-intellectual foundation of group cohesion or solidarity.[14]

The major social movements always assimilate several streams of thought already present in the culture and effect a loose and not wholly consistent accommodation among them. Thus traditions of attack on big-city corruption, muckraking, progressivism, city planning, and many other themes coalesced in Franklin Roosevelt's New Deal.[15]

SUBCULTURE WORLD VIEWS. Perhaps the commonest view of the origin of movement values is the class-conflict thesis of Karl Marx. Heberle has put the idea succinctly.

The founders of modern socialism, Karl Marx and Friedrich Engels, as well as the conservative advocate of social reform, Lorenz von Stein, deserve credit for having demonstrated that ideologies are linked with the social situation of certain classes—expressing the socio-political interests or needs of these classes; and that, if they are not linked in this way to the actual social situation of certain classes, the ideas will remain without practical effect.[16]

But this viewpoint is correct or incorrect, depending upon how broad or narrow an interpretation is placed upon it. We must remember that ideologies do not arise spontaneously as the thinking of either masses or classes. Ideologies are produced by specialists—intellectuals and similar types of persons whose special bent includes abstraction and conceptualization. The specialists do not express the point of view of other groups, since the intellectual perspective is in itself a distinctive way of seeing and thinking about events. Very little, even of the constitutive ideas, in Marxism expresses the laboring man's view or would even be acceptable to the laborer if understood or attended to. But what intellectuals do is provide a vehicle to convey the interests or needs of certain classes. The statement must therefore be read as meaning that the ideology is compatible with the sentiments generated by a particular class position in those aspects that the class members attend specifically and critically.

In a classic examination of the labor movement, Selig Perlman explains the unreceptiveness of laboring people to many of the broader social aims that labor ideologists advance.

The manual worker is convinced by experience that he is living in a world of limited opportunity. He sees, to be sure, how others, for instance business men, are finding the same world a storehouse of apparently unlimited opportunity. Yet he decisively discounts that, so far as he is himself concerned.[17]

In a situation of unlimited opportunity it is natural to favor laissez faire, a freedom from restrictive regulations that would prevent each individual from doing the best he can for himself. But when opportunity is thought to be limited, it is important that the group take control of this limited opportunity and apportion it fairly. Unfair competition that leads one man to take what is another's becomes the greatest sin. However, the scarcity viewpoint offers no support for daring and optimistic schemes to reconstruct the entire economic order. The fear of losing the little he has is too real, and his daily experience has given him no basis for identifying with more distant and imaginative goals. Unions have been notably uncooperative with their leaders' efforts to make racial equality and

---

[14] Rudolf Heberle, *Social Movements: An Introduction to Political Sociology* (New York: Appleton-Century-Crofts, 1951), p. 13.

[15] Rexford G. Tugwell, "The Sources of New Deal Reformism," *Ethics*, 64 (July, 1954), 249–76.

[16] Heberle, *Social Movements,* pp. 14–15.

[17] Selig Perlman, *A Theory of the Labor Movement* (New York: Augustus M. Kelley, Publishers, 1949), p. 239.

integration a major goal of unionism. The view of blacks and other minorities as additional competitors for the already limited opportunities is more understandable than the prospect of common cause being used by the oppressed classes to wrest control from capitalist masters. The tremendous solidarity developed in a successful union and the willingness to sacrifice for the collective good through prolonged strikes will only "evoke the response which is desired if the objective of the proposed common undertaking be kept so close to the core substance of union aspiration that Tom, Dick, and Harry could not fail to identify it as such."[18]

Regional and ethnic traditions have played a great or greater part in supplying value orientations to social movements than social class. The constitutive ideas for the abolition movement and the woman suffrage movement in the United States were congenial with the regional culture of the industrial Northeast but antithetical to the Southern plantation view. Nineteenth-century American populist movements incorporated the perspectives of farmers and laborers in the Midwest in opposition to what they regarded as an Eastern establishment. Movements within the developing nations of Africa usually draw their orienting point of view from one of the tribal cultures.

When religious and national identities have been merged for a period of generations, the resulting cultural traditions often supply many of the guiding ideas for social movements. The white Anglo-Saxon Protestant (WASP) traditions have supplied ideologies for many of the nineteenth- and twentieth-century humanitarian movements and for many of the right-wing groups, such as the John Birch Society. Catholic doctrine presented by the Legion of Decency informed the movement to deemphasize sexual themes in motion pictures during the 1930s. And many of today's radical

ideas can be traced back to the Jewish experience.[19]

CONTRACULTURE AND DIALECTIC. Social movements always express dissent from some feature of the established order: it is an easy step to suppose that movement ideas are contrast images to the prevailing culture. Dissatisfaction with the present generates an image of its opposite when life would be as idyllic as it is now tragic. The theme of an upside-down class system recurs from the early Christian declaration that "Many that are first shall be last; and the last first"[20] to contemporary nationalisms that envision small underdeveloped countries transformed into dominant world powers.

But the foregoing illustrations are not truly contrast ideas. The upside-down class system takes the traditional idea of social stratification and merely rearranges the people. Nationalism typically accepts the prevalent image of a world dominated by a few great powers and shifts the nations about. The framework of thought is traditional: the parts are shifted about within the traditional world view. Contrast ideas, such as a wholly new principle of organization or a wholly new way of getting the world's work done, are much rarer. In this sense relatively few movements are truly revitalization movements. Anthony Wallace defines a revitalization movement as "a deliberate, organized, conscious effort by members of a society to construct a more satisfying culture."[21] The basic ideological components of all important movements are familiar ones, and the goals are drawn from experience more than from phantasy.

The concept of a dialectical process affords the most sophisticated use of the assumption that movements formulate their value orientations as contrast conceptions

---

18 Ibid., p. 277.

19 Nathan Glazer, "The Jewish Role in Student Activism," *Fortune,* 79 (January, 1969), 122ff.
20 Mark 10:31.
21 Anthony F.C. Wallace, "Revitalization Movements," *American Anthropologist,* 58 (April, 1956), 265.

to established ideas. Karl Mannheim restricts use of the term *ideology* to world views that support the established system. After the unitary medieval world view was undermined by weakening of the authority of the centralized church, dissidents challenged the ideology and produced counter-ideologies or utopias. Just as ideological thinking made it impossible for the individual to see facts that called the established order into question, so utopian thinking protected the dissident from seeing positive aspects of the established order. But the utopia is more than a cynical perspective on the present order: it is a vision of reality and an image of good that contrast so radically with the perceived social structure that the latter becomes intolerable. The revised sense of justice of which we spoke in the preceding chapter is a key element in the utopia. If we think of any social order as satisfying some human needs and frustrating others, utopias express "in condensed form the unrealized and the unfulfilled tendencies which represent the needs of each age. These intellectual elements then become the explosive material for bursting the limits of the existing order."[22] A utopia may begin as the wish-phantasy of individuals, which then becomes incorporated into the world view of dissidents who are struggling against the current system.

Mannheim's statement remains sufficiently general so that the exact manner in which utopian ideas are generated cannot be specified, except that somehow a population segment starts taking wish-dreams seriously. Most contracultures support systematic deviant behavior that strives for an accommodation within the existing system rather than a movement to change that order. But when the wish-dreams are found to be shared by a whole social class, who also share in a struggle with dominant groups in society, it is pos-sible for them to acquire credibility as a true utopia.

GENERAL MOVEMENTS. Frequently several movements appear at the same time, sharing many similarities in ideology and goals. It is as if one master scheme supplied the common formula that each new movement applies to its special problem. In spite of the failures and successes of individual movements, an increasingly wide acceptance of these common value orientations takes place. Frequently movements are able to form coalitions for strategic purposes because their respective goals are so harmonious. For example, the abolition movement and the woman suffrage movement were closely identified in the pre-Civil War United States because many of their leaders and adherents were moved by a common equalitarian value.

The development of this more general set of value orientations has been called a general movement by Herbert Blumer. The general movement is then the source for the most crucial components of the value orientations of specific movements. A specific movement whose values are inconsistent with the prevalent general movement will have difficulty gaining a hearing. Blumer observes that "a specific social movement can be regarded as the crystallization of much of the motivation of dissatisfaction, hope, and desire awakened by the general social movement and the focusing of this motivation on some specific object."[23]

General movements are not social movements as we have defined them, since they have no organizational identity apart from their component specific movements. The general movement is rather a social trend and a mass preoccupation with certain values, which is both reflected in and facilitated by specific movements. Attributing value orientations to a general move-

22 Karl Mannheim, *Ideology and Utopia* (New York: Harcourt Brace Jovanovich, Inc., 1946), p. 179.

23 Herbert Blumer, "Collective Behavior," in Robert E. Park, ed., *An Outline of the Principles of Sociology* (New York: Barnes and Noble, Inc., 1939), p. 258.

ment does not explain their source, but it does accomplish two things. First, it emphasizes the extensive borrowing of frames of reference among movements that develop in the same era. And second, it redirects the search away from the social developments most closely related to the emergence of the specific movement to the broader changes in the culture and in the social structure. Thus the ideas incorporated in the woman suffrage movement did not have their origin uniquely in the situation of women but in the wider transformation of society that generated a broad value of humanitarianism.

Focal Problems of an Era. General movements are of varying generality. Some, like the liberal-humanitarian movement that provided the main value orientations for the American and French Revolutions and the socialist movement that inspired revolutions all over the world during the first half of the twentieth century, are more pervasive and potent than the movement to replace punishment with therapy in dealing with crime and other forms of deviance, which Sutherland identifies.[24] But if a general movement colors all or many of the specific movements during an historical era, we are led to suppose that there is some corresponding source of strain in the social order of that era. There are, of course, many readjustments and resulting strains that affect different population segments at any given time. Otherwise there would not be the variety of specific movements that are normally in process at any given time. But in order to account for— and eventually to predict—the nature of the general movements in a particular historical era, we look for some social readjustment that creates problems of an unusually fundamental and pervasive sort for a population segment that is relatively pivotal for social stability. If we can understand the broad changes that are occurring in society well enough to identify the focal problems of an era, we shall have taken the first step toward identifying the main value components of the general movement, which in turn, supply the value themes on which many specific-movement values are variations.

One approach to focal problems and resulting value orientations is found in Seymour M. Lipset's distinction between class politics and status politics, which seem to alternate in the course of American history in correspondence with the business cycle.

Class politics refers to political division based on the discord between the traditional left and the right, i.e., between those who favor redistribution of income, and those favoring the preservation of the *status quo*. Status politics, as used here, refers to political movements whose appeal is to the not uncommon resentments of individuals or groups who desire to maintain or improve their social status.[25]

Class politics supplies the major value orientations of movements in periods of economic depression and unemployment, whereas status politics flourishes during prosperity and inflation. During the latter periods poverty and unemployment are not salient problems, but a volatile class structure means that some groups see opportunities for advancement that they do not want jeopardized and others see their relative position threatened by the more rapid advancement of mobile groups or the erosion of fixed incomes through inflation.

In economic conflict the ideology and goals revolve about the inequitable distribution of economic resources and the effort to redistribute wealth and insure economic security. Status politics, on the other hand, glorifies patriotism and the support of

---

[24] Edwin H. Sutherland, "The Diffusion of Sexual Psychopathic Laws," *American Journal of Sociology,* 56 (Sept., 1950), 142–48.

[25] Seymour M. Lipset, "The Sources of the Radical Right," in Daniel Bell, ed., *The New American Right* (New York: Criterion Books, 1955), pp. 167–68; see also pp. 166–233.

traditional cultural values, and it attacks as its villains minority religious and ethnic groups, immigrant groups, and others who seem to threaten the cultural consensus and the prevailing status differentiations. Lipset speaks of status politics as distinctively giving rise to scapegoating; but this judgment undoubtedly reflects the bias of those more accustomed to thinking in terms of class politics. Both systems of thought find their villains in groups who seem to threaten the value that is of paramount concern to them. The effect of cultural minorities in transforming a dominant culture is as real as the effects of the more secure economic classes on the disadvantaged, and economic elites are often as powerless to cope with depression and unemployment as cultural minorities are to nullify their effect on traditional culture. But whereas class politics always sets the oppressed against the wealthy, status politics finds its villains both above and below the movement constituency. Upper working-class and lower middle-class resentment is directed against a prospering and high-living upper middle class, against an intellectual elite who publically questions once sacred values, and against blacks and welfare recipients.

Movements dominated by class politics, such as Franklin Roosevelt's New Deal, are better known, but Lipset also identifies the major waves of social movements dominated by status politics. Just before the Civil War the Know-Nothing or American party expressed a peak of anti-Catholic and anti-immigrant sentiment. The 1880s witnessed the resurgence of anti-Catholic feeling in the American Protective Association. The Progressive Movement of 1900 to 1912 attacked "plutocrat millionaires" and immigrants. The Ku Klux Klan of the 1920s attacked Jews, Catholics, and blacks, but it also capitalized on small-town resentment against urban upper-class cosmopolitanism. The McCarthyism immediately after World War II and the radical-right movements of the 1960s, including the John Birch

Society and the American Independence party of George Wallace, complete the series. All have occurred in periods of prosperity and presumably reflect the problems of such periods.[26]

Evidence bearing on the Lipset thesis is not fully consistent. Father Coughlin's strongly status-oriented movement thrived during the heart of the 1930s depression. And class politics themes were important throughout the period of economic advance during the 1960s.

A more common approach does not distinguish between class and status politics and assumes no regular alternation between fixed types of value orientations. Investigators frequently assume that since the end of the feudal order the focal problems have centered about readjustments of power and control among the social classes. The great liberal-humanitarian general movement that found its most dramatic expression in the American and French revolutions was integrally tied to the rise of the business and industrial middle class. The central value orientation, revolving about a conception of individual rights and freedom from control over thought and enterprise, expressed the major problem of the middle classes in breaking down the residual power of the traditional feudal and land-holding elite. The socialist general movement, ranging from communism to such mild forms as the Roosevelt New Deal, emphasized a theme of material welfare and security that expressed the primary concern of the newly expanded wage-earning classes in an industrial society.

It does not necessarily follow that the focal problems of every era are readjustments among social classes. After a searching examination of collective religious dissent during the early Middle Ages, Jef-

26 Seymour M. Lipset and Earl Raab, *The Politics of Unreason: Right-Wing Extremism in America, 1790–1970* (New York: Harper and Row, Publishers, 1970).

frey Russell concludes that the weight of evidence is against attributing these movements to economic interests.[27] In the contemporary period it is plausible that age-group readjustments may be disturbing the smooth functioning of society more profoundly than readjustments among economic groups. There have been some preliminary stirrings among the elderly, whose numbers and potential influence are increasing. But the more remarkable changes have been in the power and privilege of youth. The postwar reproductive boom has led to an abrupt increase in the proportion of the youthful population. Modern technology has reduced the value of traditional knowledge and of accumulated experience that represent the claims to leadership by the middle aged. Mastery of current technology is easily achieved by youth, increasing their importance in society and weakening the rationale for long periods of deferred gratification. Problems of alienation, of the achievement of self-respect, and of freedom to experiment with unconventional forms of self-indulgence are themes that recur in most of the movements of the current era. These are also some of the problems most closely identified with the effort of youth to implement and extend their new position in society. It is quite possible that the most important general movement of the 1960s and 1970s will turn out to have formed its value orientation about the focal problems of readjusting the social order to the rising power of youth.[28]

The Careers of Value Orientations

Having noted some of the components and sources of value orientations, we must

---

[27] Jeffrey B. Russell, *Dissent and Reform in the Early Middle Ages* (Berkeley: University of California Press, 1965), pp. 230–41.

[28] Ralph H. Turner, "The Theme of Contemporary Social Movements," *British Journal of Sociology,* 20 (Dec., 1969), 390–405.

return to our central emphasis on process. The goals and ideology do not emerge full-blown but develop from limited and tentative beginnings. Nor do they reach a point of full development and remain fixed, but they continue to change. We shall describe first several generally applicable tendencies in the development of movement value orientations and then explore the durability of values in light of the phenomenon of generations.

TRENDS IN DEVELOPMENT. Goals and ideologies are commonly escalated from modest and specific beginnings to bold and comprehensive programs. Initial successes and the discovery of an enthusiastic and like-minded body of coworkers instill confidence and encourage participants to believe that greater things can be done. The movement provides a setting in which grievances are discussed and the initial specific aim is redefined as a limited step in a larger plan rather than as a sufficient accomplishment. Initial success also attracts persons who see the movement as a viable mechanism for promoting their own more extended aims. Publics typically ascribe unannounced broader goals to any movement that attracts attention, and the public definition affects the adherents' conception of their purposes in the movement. For example, early temperance workers merely sought individual pledges of temperance in the use of alcoholic beverages. But as the movement grew, temperance was replaced by abstinence, and the goal of reform by personal transformation gave way to the political aim of enacting prohibition legislation.[29]

A second common trend is the diversification and specification of goals and ideology to suit the varied constituencies attracted to the movement. Hans Toch contrasts the early appeal of Hitler's National Socialism to the elaborate system of appeals in use just before the Party took

---

[29] Donald B. Chidsey, *On and Off the Wagon* (New York: Cowles Book Co., Inc., 1969).

power in Germany.[30] The early theme was a demand for retribution for the humiliation of all Germans in World War I. The appeal was a catchall, corresponding to the general concerns shared by the whole nation. On the eve of taking control of the state, the Party had replaced the catchall with a "cafeteria" of themes. The movement by this time had specific promises for youth, for Prussian landowners, for industrial leaders, for middle-class Germans, for the army, and for other groups. Typically the initial value orientation persists but undergoes change to accommodate the many specialized group value perspectives that the movement absorbs.

A third process is the modification of value orientations through the appropriation of events to the movement. Development of goals and ideology can be likened to the development of a traditional body of legal principles on the basis of judicial decisions in specific cases. The court attempts to formulate a general principle that fits the circumstance of the case that is before it, and the nature of specific cases that happen to have entered litigation then has a profound effect on what kinds of general principles are accumulated. Similarly, any vital movement attempts to interpret and exploit every relevant event of importance as it occurs. A classic example of such an event was the trial and execution of two radicals, Sacco and Vanzetti, in Massachusetts during the 1920s. The usual types of evidence were used to identify these men as two of the four who committed murder in connection with a payroll robbery in South Braintree, Massachusetts. Defense attorneys contended that the defendants were being prosecuted because of their radical activities, but the court found them guilty and a succession of fruitless appeals ended finally with their execution. Current radical movements took up their cause, and then more and more members of liberal movements, including

such famous men as Felix Frankfurter who was to become a Supreme Court justice, made declarations in support of Sacco and Vanzetti.[31] Much of the liberal view that civil courts frequently serve the purpose of suppressing political dissent was evolved and refined during this half decade, and many of the declarations were assimilated into the mainstream of the liberal movements that subsequently coalesced in the New Deal.

Fourth, the movement ideology is constantly formed and reformed in a dialogue with the equally changing ideology of the established order. The theory of a dialectical process assumes a ready-made establishment ideology giving rise to a contrast ideology (utopia). In the struggle between them, what eventually emerges is a synthesis of the two, which then becomes the new establishment ideology and starts a new cycle. The dialectical model is oversimplified in taking ideology as the starting point and a more or less fixed utopia as the opposing component. Ideologies are actually little elaborated upon until they come under attack, and then the nature and direction of their elaboration is determined by the nature of the attacks. For example, the doctrine of the divine right of kings was not evolved until royalty began to come under attack. But once the divine right doctrine was invented and advertised, the ideology of republican movements developed a critique of the divine right doctrine. Similarly, the modern idea of racial differences in the level of inherited intelligence was invented to protect and preserve patterns of minority subordination and segregation after these practices were already under attack. The liberal ideology of identical distributions of inherited intelligence among races and of environmental determination of achieved intelligence was

---

30 Toch, *Social Psychology of Social Movements*, pp. 17–19.

31 An informative, though partisan, account of the case as a political phenomenon is presented by David Felix, *Protest: Sacco-Vanzetti and the Intellectuals* (Bloomington: Indiana University Press, 1965).

then evolved as part of the movement ideology to cope with the inequalitarian doctrine of inherited racial differences.

Fifth, the value orientations of a movement are elaborated and sometimes turned in quite different directions by the extension of some aspects of the ideology in unanticipated directions. For example, schisms develop from time to time within right-wing movements based on the extension of the standard ideas of freedom from governmental regulation to a general doctrine of libertarianism. The popularity of Ayn Rand's writings among college students in the early 1960s seems to have expressed some of these tendencies. In 1969 conservative students broke away from the national conservative organization, Young Americans for Freedom, to form the Free Campus Movement. As declared libertarians, members of this group place "high value on individual freedom, support capitalistic principles, and oppose government meddling in the lives of individuals or affairs of other nations."[32] Carrying the theme of individual freedom to its extreme, they departed from the established conservative position by opposing laws against pornography, abortion, and possession of marijuana and by opposing the United States involvement in Vietnam. Developments of this sort some times result in schisms or suppression of the new viewpoint, but in other instances the new interpretation is effectively promoted and leads to eventual modification of the ideology and goals of the parent movement.

DURABILITY AND THE PHENOMENON OF GENERATIONS. The values that rouse enthusiastic masses at one time fail to do so at another time. The durability of all movement goals and ideologies is limited. Sometimes the very success of the movement removes the problem—slavery was abolished, American independence was attained, and prohibition was repealed. But

more often people lose interest in one battle and turn their attention to another. The most widely applicable explanation for this kind of change is the phenomenon of generations, whose implications have been explored in penetrating fashion by Karl Mannheim.[33]

The nature of human learning is such that "early impressions tend to coalesce into a *natural view* of the world. All later experiences then tend to receive their meaning from this original set, whether they appear as that set's verification and fulfilment or as its negation and antithesis."[34] Whenever a generation of young people share a set of profound and problematic experiences as an integrated group, the community of experience gives rise to a generational natural view of the world, which all later experience is fit into. In America the generation that came to political awareness during the depression of the 1930s found two great problems at the heart of life. One was the problem of economic stability and security, not as a fear of individual poverty but as the prospect of collapse of the total economy. The other problem was the replacement of democratic political structures by totalitarian governments when the former were unable to deal with crises. The two great enterprises of the era were the economic reforms of the New Deal and World War II, the latter viewed as a last-ditch effort to resist the engulfment of democratic governments by totalitarianism. People brought up in this era generally continue to assimilate new problems to these key issues, with American foreign policy in the 1960s the most dramatic example of the persisting preoccupation with the spread of totalitarianism. To the postwar generation the threat of economic collapse is re-

---

[32] *Los Angeles Times,* November 28, 1969.

[33] Karl Mannheim, "The Problem of Generations," in *Essays on the Sociology of Knowledge* (New York: Oxford University Press, Inc., 1952), pp. 276–322.

[34] Ibid., p. 298.

mote and unreal, and the relatively stable system of accommodations between democratic and totalitarian nations makes this difference a minor concern. However, the trauma of being called to fight in a remote war without national mobilization or support and with little foreign sympathy, and the disillusionment with the ineffectiveness of government as a tool for dealing with endemic (rather than epidemic) poverty and discrimination became central.

The persisting social movements, with their leadership drawn from the older generation, treat new problems in the value perspective of their generation. But the young generation spawns a new set of movements and often seeks to capture the older movements. The result is a battle between perspectives, a conflict of value orientations. Time is ultimately on the side of the younger generation, and the only hope for the older value orientations is that they can be reformulated for incorporation into the newer value orientations. When this occurs the continuity of value orientations over generations is possible. When it does not occur the discontinuity means that the important battles won by the older generation are often lost and must be fought again by a later generation.

As Mannheim reminds us, it would be faulty to assume that members of a generation are of one mind regarding the problems of their era. The members of a generation take opposing sides: what they agree on is the identity of the adversaries. The depression split the young generation into supporters and opponents of economic and social reforms in the New Deal pattern. But to the postwar generation the resulting liberals and conservatives seem to be fighting unreal and unimportant battles. A generation is set apart by the division into proponents and opponents of certain key values that are not central to the divisions in another generation.

A strict application of the biological idea of generations quickly leads into difficulties,

since generational replacement is continuous rather than periodic, and a new generation might be said to be formed by each year's cohort of births. The duration of a generation in sociological terms depends on a spurt of change too rapid for the established generation to handle by small and continuous modifications while holding to their main value framework. Thus a generation may last until a rather abrupt change in the social order occurs in a way that directly affects youth; they seek to interpret the change and cope with it in relatively age-homogeneous groups.[35]

Seldom is the generational discontinuity so great that the old value orientations are entirely lost. As Belin-Milleron has demonstrated by the analysis of tracts and other documents from the French revolutions of 1789, 1848, and 1871, many of the same symbolic expressions are employed by the exponents of movements in successive generations.[36] Expressions like "civil liberty," "constitution," "democracy," and "solidarity" persist and give a movement the aura of being deeply rooted in the past. In use, however, the expressions are reinterpreted to suit the new generational value orientations. The result is a mixture in which the older values are both perpetuated and modified by being lodged and reinterpreted in a new context.

It is often impossible to understand the goals and ideology of a movement without knowing the generational values that preceded it. Thus the British labor movement in the early twentieth century exhibited a peculiar evangelistic and even puritanical strain that distinguished it from labor movements in other countries. But this

[35] The special circumstances that give rise to age-homogenous groups in society have been extensively explored by S. N. Eisenstadt, in *From Generation to Generation* (New York: The Free Press, 1956).

[36] Jean Belin-Milleron, "Les Expressions Symboliques dans la Psychologie Collective des Crises Politiques," *Cahiers Internationaux de Sociologie,* 10 (1951), 158–67.

strain can be traced back to the nineteenth-century spread of socialist doctrine through the puritan religious sects made up of working-class adherents.[37] As interest among the British working classes in the twentieth century shifted away from religious movements and turned instead toward radical politics,[38] some of the main value orientations of the religious sects were preserved and transformed to fit into the value complex of the new political labor movement.

[37] Gerhard W. Ditz, "Utopian Symbols in the History of the British Labour Party," *British Journal of Sociology,* 17 (June, 1966), 145–50.

[38] Rodney Stark, "Class, Radicalism, and Religious Involvement in Great Britain," *American Sociological Review,* 29 (Oct., 1964). 698–706.

15

POWER ORIENTATIONS

Whatever the goals and ideology of a movement, influence must be exercised over persons or institutions outside the movement if the values are to be more than the daydreams of a small band of devotees. Hence the cultivation and use of power become central tasks of every movement.

In spite of efforts by scholars such as Bertrand Russell to make power the fundamental concept in social science "in the same sense in which energy is the fundamental concept in physics,"[1] the idea remains elusive. In general the power of a movement—its ability to bring about desired changes—depends on the prestige and other positive evaluations placed on the movement by crucial publics, the size and discipline of the membership, and the value of resources under the movement's control. But power must be exercised. For various reasons movements usually do not make full use of the power at their disposal. Furthermore, power must be converted into influence through the selection of appropriate strategies and tactics. For example, a movement backed by a generous billionaire may attempt to bribe public officials or saturate the community with ill-conceived and offensive literature, generating vigorous opposition when judicious use of the money could have greatly advanced the movement's cause.

Since movement power depends on varied considerations that are discussed in other chapters of this book, we shall not attempt here to expand the brief statement on the determinants of power. But we shall concentrate on the way in which the effort to cultivate and use power affects the course of the movement. First, we shall consider how a movement selects the main power objective and the strategies for the exercise of the power at its disposal. Next we shall examine the special case of nonviolence as a strategy. Then we shall look at tendencies for choosing effective strategy and maximizing movement power to displace value orientations as the guiding principle in a movement. Finally, we shall look at those movements that develop as power-oriented types in which the achievement of control becomes the guiding aim rather than being chiefly the means for changing society in accordance with an advertised set of values.

Main Power Objectives

If a group of people seek a changed way of life, they can work toward that end by using the power at their disposal to get persons in authority to make the desired changes, by seeking to take control of the community or society so that they can institute whatever changes they wish, or by using their power to establish and protect a separate existence free from outside control and interference. We shall call these

---

[1] Bertrand Russell, *Power: A New Social Analysis* (New York: W. W. Norton and Company, Inc., 1938), p. 12.

main power objectives concessions, control, and separation, respectively. The overwhelming majority of movements seek concessions; but occasionally the more extreme directions are taken. Movements often pursue power objectives that are a compromise of two main types. For example, temperance movements in America today often work for local option, which is a compromise between concessions and separation.

In some instances the movement value orientation favors one power objective over the others. Nativistic and nationalistic values naturally incline toward separation, for example, but they still do not preclude the more limited pursuit of concessions, or under the stimulus of remarkable success, the effort to turn the tables on their previous rulers. Thus most values can be pursued under varying circumstances in any of the three directions.

In general the continuum from concessions to control and the continuum from concessions to separation reflect the power ratio between the movement and the people or institutions that must be influenced. When the power is moderate or weak, the normal response is to seek concessions. As the relative strength of the movement increases, the tendency to seek either control or separation is enhanced—unless the value goals have substantially been attained through the concessions won.

It is usually easier to escalate than to deescalate the power orientation along the two lines just identified. Success in gaining concessions, especially when the extent of concessions gained or the ease with which they are gained suggests that there is reserve power at the movement's disposal, encourages the movement to seek either separation or control. However, the effect of an unsuccessful struggle for control or separation impairs normal relationships to such a degree that it is difficult for the movement to settle for the lesser objective of seeking concessions. Failure also demonstrates for the established group the power

ratio in their favor to such an extent that they become less susceptible to the usual strategies for gaining concessions.

Separation can normally be secured and maintained with a less favorable power ratio than can control; although under most circumstances separation requires more power than do concessions. Because of the power ratio differential and the effect of an unsuccessful confrontation for control upon intergroup relationships, separation is commonly sought as a sequel to unsuccessful control efforts. Thus in one characteristic cycle, efforts to secure concessions achieve results that are impressive enough to lead to control efforts that are then frustrated, resulting in a shift toward separatism.

If there is sufficient dedication to the demand for concessions, frustration of efforts toward concessions can lead to renewed efforts, employing new strategies (seeking coalitions, relaxing norms and sensitivities that limit the strategies that can be used, etc.) in which escalation toward control or separation is the consequence. Escalation of this sort depends upon the availability of additional tactics that have not been exploited before or the possibility of strengthening the movement's power base for the next attempt. Advocates of escalation are now willing to exploit their power to the maximum by using some of the more coercive tactics that they formerly eschewed for fear of damaging their relationships in the larger group or community. With these more powerful tactics at their disposal, they can aim for control or separation rather than for concessions.

The choice between the two kinds of escalated power objectives, namely control and separation, as separate lines of development depends upon (1) the degree to which the movement constituency is socially integrated into, and identifies itself in terms of, the larger unit, and (2) the degree to which the movement constituency has resources necessary to maintain a satisfactory existence separate from the established community. When social integration and identification are great and when the constituency lacks resources for self-sufficiency, escalation proceeds in the direction of control. Under reverse conditions escalation goes from the demand for concessions toward separation.

Mixed or alternating goals (between control and separation) are most likely to occur when social integration and identification are low but the constituency lacks the conditions for independent existence. Under these conditions separation is the ideal goal, but realism forces consideration of other goals. This is the typical situation of minority groups such as blacks in America.

Response to frustration of demands for concessions or control by a shift toward separation is most likely when social integration has been high but when the conditions for self-sufficient existence are present. Here the weakening of the social bonds that results from frustration of efforts toward concession and control makes the goal of separation more thinkable, and there are no practical obstacles to interfere. This sequence applies to the American Revolution. Close identification with a common British heritage prevented consideration of separation until requests for concessions had been repeatedly denied.

Principal Strategies

The principal strategies in the exercise of power by social movements can be identified as persuasion, bargaining, and coercion.[2] The types are distinguished by the

manner in which the movement attempts to influence the actions of a target group. The strategies are seldom entirely separate in practice. One strategy is usually foremost in the relationship between movement and target group, but combinations of strategies are usually found. It will be easiest to identify bargaining first and then to identify coercion and persuasion as alternatives to bargaining.

Bargaining takes place when the movement has control over some exchangeable value that the target group wants and offers some of that value in return for compliance with its demands.[3] One of the commonest forms of bargaining in a democratic society is the offer of votes or other support to the target group in return for support of the movement and its objectives. Another form is the offer of one movement to form a coalition with another movement in which each supports the aims of the other, in the manner of the abolition-woman suffrage coalition, or of the attempted labor-civil rights or labor-farmers coalition.

Coercion is the manipulation of the target group's situation in such fashion that the pursuit of any course of action other than that sought by the movement will be met by considerable cost or punishment. The extreme form of coercion is the threat of total destruction when it is in the power of the movement to determine whether the target group will or will not be destroyed. Lesser forms of coercion involve weakening, inconveniencing, or embarrassing the target group. Terrorism is one of the most highly coercive strategies. A less intense form of coercive strategy is organized civil disobedience. Organized authorities are em-

---

2 This section and the next are largely adapted from Ralph H. Turner, "Determinants of Social Movement Strategies," in Tamotsu Shibutani, ed., *Human Nature and Collective Behavior: Papers in Honor of Herbert Blumer* (Englewood Cliffs, N.J.: Prentice-Hall, Inc., 1970). The distinction between coercion, bargaining, and persuasion is an old and widely used one. Among recent uses of this distinction are Amitai W. Etzioni, *A Comparative Analysis of Complex*

Organizations (New York: The Free Press, 1961); and William A. Gamson, *Power and Discontent* (Homewood, Ill.: Dorsey Press, 1968), who speaks of constraints, inducements, and persuasion.

3 For an excellent general discussion of bargaining, *cf.* Peter Blau, *Exchange and Power in Social Life* (New York: John Wiley and Sons, Inc., 1964).

barrassed by having to arrest otherwise law-abiding persons and to give them the dangerous publicity of public trials. Authorities run the alternative risks of arousing public sympathy for the offenders, suffering a loss of confidence for their own ineptness, or weakening the entire authority structure by overlooking the law violations.

Coercion can be viewed as negative bargaining. In the strict sense we employ here, the outcome of successful bargaining is that each party is identifiably better off than it would have been if the bargaining relationship had not commenced. In coercion, the coerced party's best hope is that it will be no worse off than it would have been had the coercive relationship never commenced. The coercing movement offers no value that will improve the target group's position but threatens to worsen their condition unless compliance is granted.

The essence of coercion is usually the threat of harm. Whether actual harm is done or not is a tactical consideration, with the prospect of further or greater harm the coercive element. Actual harm is employed tactically as a way of demonstrating that the movement truly can or will inflict harm or of indicating the extent of harm that is possible. Even if no harm is actually done, the strategy is genuinely coercive to the same extent that the threat is believed.

The threat gives way to actual harm in the extreme or limiting case when the aim is to destroy the target group or so to disrupt its activity as to render it completely powerless. Assassinations may be employed with the intention of frightening surviving members of the target group and strengthening the enthusiasm and resolve of the movement constituency; the threat of further violence is the effective agent of coercion. This differs from the classic *coup d'état* in which the top leaders of government are assassinated, imprisoned, or otherwise disabled so that key movement agents can immediately take over and exercise government power. This bypasses threat and employs coercive force directly to accomplish its ends.

Persuasion is the use of strictly symbolic manipulation, without substantial rewards or punishments under the control of the movement. The basic procedure of persuasion is to identify the proposed course of action with values held by the target group. In a movement to recall a public official, the strategy is to arouse popular indignation by dramatizing how far the conduct of government has drifted from the pattern that is valued by the public. Persuasion always includes calling attention to rewards and penalties that will ensue for the target group on the basis of various courses of action.

There does not appear to be any one-to-one relationship between the objectives and strategies of power as we have identified them, although there are greater and lesser degrees of compatibility between specific pairs. Control is seldom gained without coercion except when bargaining can be employed to form coalitions with other groups out of power in order to assemble enough combined power to take control. Thus, insofar as strategy is directed toward established power and authority, coercive strategy is usually required to secure the goal of control. Insofar as strategy is directed toward other groups whose support is needed to attain control, bargaining characteristically becomes the key strategy, though coercive strategies, such as terrorism, and persuasion may be attempted.

The goal of separation also normally requires stronger strategies than persuasion, and it usually requires coercion to compel the established groups to relinquish the benefits they gain from inclusion of the movement constituency in their orbit. Bargaining with other groups is an important device for gaining enough strength to coerce the established group into granting separation. However, bargaining with the established group may be a means to separation when the movement constituency can offer benefits under separation that would not accrue otherwise.

The goal for which persuasion is likely to be the principal strategy is concession, though even here persuasion is often merely a supplement to bargaining and coercion.

The choice of strategies is determined by two major principles that operate sometimes supportively and sometimes in opposition and by three sets of limiting factors. The two major principles are the strategic and the expressive principles. The first is the rational principle of selecting strategies according to their anticipated effectiveness. The second is the principle of projecting an image through the movement, often an image of power that the movement adherents can assimilate into their own self-conceptions. Before discussing these two major principles we shall review the three sets of limiting factors.

LIMITING FACTORS. First, the values held by the movement constituency affect selection of strategy both directly and indirectly. It should be remembered that the constituency is the larger category of people for whom the movement claims to speak and from whom it recruits most of its adherents. Religious or humanistic values sometimes inhibit the use of coercion as an unacceptable strategy. Extreme democratic idealism may lead to excessive reliance on persuasion and blindness to the possibilities of bargaining. Persuasion, regarded as a high accomplishment among groups who value the skills of verbal manipulation, is downgraded among other groups as unmasculine, an indication of weakness, and self-debasing pleading. Bargaining strategies incur the risk that a movement may be viewed as having sold out, and the sincerity of its adherents may be held in doubt. Coercive strategies, when impressively effective, are likely to evoke admiration and respect. However, they are also conducive to fear. Constituents of social movements differ in the extent to which they are pleased to be viewed with fear or concerned to avoid such a reaction. Likewise they vary in sensitiveness to being thought unscrupulous and unprincipled in their dealings.

The second limiting factor includes the values and interests of publics that may intervene so as to affect the outcome of the movement's efforts.[4] Potentially conflicting interest groups, such as the teachers' union in relation to the black civil-rights group in New York City, are the least important groups in determining selection of strategy because the threat to their interests exists regardless of the strategy employed. Potentially cooptable groups, on the other hand, can have the greatest effect on movement strategy, since the relationship here resembles a coalition in which partners bargain over strategies as well as rewards.

Cooptable groups include those whose interests are different but compatible, so that two movements might benefit by pooling their strength. They also include those who may be expected to give support to the movement on the basis that the movement cause is a tangible expression of their values. Coalitions of the former type have often been attempted, but they have been notably unstable except when the coalition could be achieved through a broadly based, established political party. Coalitions are related to the use of a bargaining strategy, and their stability depends largely on the effectiveness of bargaining efforts. A coalition offers little to enhance persuasion strategy, and the use of coercive strategies tends to create distrust within the coalition.

Adjustment of strategy so as not to affront the values of large, potentially sympathetic groups has been a recurrent factor, limiting the use of coercive strategy and augmenting reliance on persuasive strategy in the movements of various minority interests in the United States. The important thread of charitable and humanitarian values in middle- and upper-class society has supplied a constant flow of support for movements of many sorts. But these supporters are also firmly committed to the established order of things; they are willing

4 The crucial importance of forming coalitions with third parties, for groups who lack stable political resources of their own, is stressed by Michael Lipsky in "Protest as a Political Resource," *American Political Science Review,* 62 (December, 1968), 1144–58.

to lend their support when persuasion is the accepted strategy but are increasingly reluctant when coercion becomes a conspicuous part of the strategy. Although it is true that violence and coercion have been recurring features of social change in America, it is probably also true that coercion and violence have relatively infrequently been adopted and presented as the major strategy of reform movements. The pressure of cooptable humanitarian elements in American society has likely been the major fact accounting for the number of movements that claim to rely on persuasive strategies.

A bystander public often becomes a factor when coercive strategies are employed. A bystander public is one whose concern with the aims of the movement is minimal but that reacts to the disruptions and inconveniences caused by the struggle.[5] Only a sophisticated leadership is likely to be guided by an understanding of this process from the start. But the effect is to reward and encourage the use of coercive strategy over an intermediate span of time.

It is characteristic of small, weak, and inexperienced movements that they are especially fearful of opposition from these publics and hopeful of support from a humanitarian public. Consequently there are strong inhibitions against the use of coercion and a great reliance on persuasion. But there is also a tendency for these restraints to become less effectual as the movement progresses. Similarly, the weaker the tie between movement and constituency, the greater the tendency to rely upon support from other publics and thus to have strategies limited by the conditions imposed from outside.

The third limiting factor is the nature of the relationship between the constituency and the target group. Generally speaking, persuasive strategies are least likely to undermine a positive relationship, whereas coercive efforts are most likely to provoke

5 See Chapter 12.

resentment and consequently damage a relationship. Bargaining is intermediate in its significance, being less threatening and unilateral than coercion but still indicating a manipulative rather than a consensual relationship. The stronger the bonds and the more personal or intimate the relationship between movement constituency and target group, the greater the tendency to favor persuasion and to minimize coercion as a movement strategy.

Just because persuasion signifies a relationship of mutual confidence between constituency and target group, a constituency whose relationship to the target group is pervasively conflictual and marked by severe resentment will eschew persuasion and favor coercion, even when the use of coercion may be strategically unwise. During the 1960s this was frequently the case in the United States civil-rights movement and youth peace movements. Bargaining may be employed when there are independent resources or power, but it may not be a viable device because the angry group sees adherence to the terms of the original bargain as a form of submission to the target group.

The two key variables in the constituency-target group relationship are dependency and interpenetrating relationships. The least restraint against the use of coercive and bargaining strategies applies to movements such as the cargo cults and other nationalistic developments in colonial countries. The presence of a relatively self-sufficient community, able to sustain its members along traditional lines regardless of the presence or absence of colonial rulers and having very few personal dealings with the ruling group, makes any fear of damaging relationships a trivial consideration. The increased use of bargaining and openly coercive strategies in youth movements in the United States is directly related to shifts in both these variables, but especially to the reduction of interpenetration. The rise of the peer group and an elaborated youth society has increased the separation between youth and adults and permitted the growth of an autonomous community of youth. With this community at hand it is less important than formerly if relationships between youth and their parents and other adults are badly strained. In the past, segregation of blacks in American society has not freed them from restraints upon using bargaining and coercion because they remained quite directly dependent upon the favor of specific whites for their employment and many other needs. The decline of special black forms of employment and the dispersion of blacks into the larger impersonal labor force have undermined much of this longstanding sense of dependency.

STRATEGIC AND EXPRESSIVE PRINCIPLES. Within the limits imposed by constituency values, by the pursuit of support from external publics, and by concern for the constituency-target group relationship, selection of strategy is determined by a dynamic interplay between strategic and expressive principles. *Strategic* considerations are those having to do with choosing which strategy is likely to contribute toward the attainment of the movement goals. *Expressive* considerations are those involving the gratifications that come with the exercise and display of power. People gain satisfaction from the act of wielding power, and conspicuous and dramatic displays of power give more personal satisfaction than behind-the-scenes or restrained maneuvering.

Two conditions are foremost in determining the relative strength of these considerations. First, the more sophisticated the leadership, and to a lesser extent the membership, of a social movement, the greater the tendency for the movement's power activities to be directed by strategic considerations rather than by expressive ones. Sophistication is not only a matter of general orientation; it is acquired through experience in social movements. Hence the pursuit and exercise of power in a social movement tends to be less expressive and more strategic as the movement gains

experience. Second, the more effectively disciplined the members, the more the movement will be directed by strategic considerations. The members, who are not closely in touch with the possible consequences of wrong moves and who do not operate under the same sense of responsibility, are more inclined to be governed by expressive considerations than by the leaders. Consequently, an undisciplined grass-roots movement is likely to follow power strategies that are determined largely by expressive considerations. The more a movement can bring its membership under organizational discipline, the greater the chance of subordinating the expressive tendencies to strategic planning.

The major difference between expressive and strategic considerations is found in the tendency to use and display maximum or minimum power. Expressive tendencies mean a preference for coercion rather than for bargaining or persuasion and employment of the more extreme and dramatic forms of power in preference to others. The chief circumstances determining how much of this power display will occur are the sense of confidence and the esprit de corps in the movement. Any apparent successes build up self-confidence and tend to escalate the use of strategies. On the other hand, lack of self-confidence by the constituents, disconcerting setbacks for the movement, and loss of fellow-feeling among members tend to weaken support for strong coercive and bargaining strategies.

The order of preference for strategies under the expressive principle is coercion, then persuasion, with bargaining last. Bargaining comes after persuasion for two reasons. First, in bargaining one must give something in exchange for whatever is gained. To talk the man out of it is more impressive than to buy it! Second, bargaining subjects the bargainer to an agreement that he must honor, an agreement that later becomes a limitation on his own freedom of action. The offer of bargaining, then, tends to come at the lowest ebb of group self-confidence if expressive considerations are paramount.

The first strategic principle is to exercise the minimum power needed to attain the goal at hand. Strategically it is better to win by persuasion rather than to employ bargaining or coercion. With persuasion less must be paid for the results attained, and the resentment often evoked by coercion can be minimized. Furthermore, by not revealing the extent of power at its disposal the movement retains an ambiguity that complicates the target group's efforts to combat the movement. Strategically it is also important not to reveal unmistakable clues to the rise and fall of self-confidence and esprit de corps by corresponding changes of strategy. Coercion may be cheaper than bargaining in the short run, but it is usually more costly in arousing suspicion and resistance in the long run.

The strategy selected is dependent, secondly, upon the resources at the disposal of the movement. The resources vary in both quantity and kind, and the requirements of the three strategies are to some degree qualitatively distinct. Coercion requires resources that will enable the movement to punish the target group; bargaining depends upon resources that the target group desires and that can be exchanged for something of benefit to the movement; persuasion requires little in the way of power in the usual sense, but it does depend upon skills in communication and access to communication media. Strategically, terroristic coercion may be the only potentially effective strategy available to a relatively impoverished, disenfranchised group.

A third strategic consideration is that bargaining and coercion, when applied by movements whose principal strength is in large numbers of supporters, depend upon a well-disciplined membership. Bargaining cannot take place unless agents of the target group are convinced that movement spokesmen can deliver on their promise of block voting. When coercive strategies capitalize on disruptive and violent behavior among members of the constituency, there must be some assurance that disturbances can be turned off by movement spokesmen if the threat of future coercion is to be effective.

Fourth, the exercise of power is a reciprocal phenomenon. The application of power brings forth a response from the group toward which the efforts are directed. The anticipated response initially affects the choice of strategy, and the actual response leads to reinforcement or revision of the strategy. It is important to remember that groups do not normally employ all the power at their disposal. The most fundamental reason for this—apart from the strategic principle of using no more power than necessary to gain the immediate end—is fear of activating stronger retaliatory power on the part of the target group.

The circumstances that inhibit an established target group from exercising all their latent power are: (1) Routines must be disrupted in order to bring unused power into play. The inconvenience of putting aside established routines means that troublesome demands will often be tolerated without retaliation and propitiatory concessions will be made. (2) The costs and risks involved in fairly severe conflict are often great, even when the one-sidedness makes the outcome unquestionable. A large nation that could easily subdue a small one may be unwilling to accept the casualties and property losses involved in even a small war. Similarly, a corporation may prefer to grant concessions to a labor organization rather than to accept an extended strike with the possibilities of violence and property damage. (3) There is danger of alienating groups other than the movement constituency by an excessive display of force and of creating a united opposition where only disparate groups existed before. The uninhibited exercise of power, whether by the state with its monopoly of the legitimate use of violence, by a school or church with its power of expulsion, or by a corporation, is frightening. The resulting reaction may lead to steps that curtail the power of these groups in the future. (4) The established group is often bound by rules and scruples of its own that define only limited exercise of power as legitimate. Thus a modern state is restricted in the exercise of the real power at its disposal by its constitution and legal structure. (5) Finally, an established group is commonly inhibited in the exercise of power by ties to the movement constituency. In the case of youth movements and women's movements that cut across family lines, the interpersonal ties make it difficult to deal with these movements in any but the gentlest of ways. The ties may also arise out of sympathy for the movement cause. Ambivalence concerning the right to national independence inhibited democratic nations from completely ruthless suppression of nationalistic movements in their colonies.

The decision to bargain is principally determined by whether or not the movement has resources with which to bargain. The choice between coercion and persuasion depends upon the effectiveness of the conditions inhibiting a strongly repressive response by the target group and upon the willingness and ability of the movement to undergo such a repressive response. When the inhibiting conditions are strong, and the movement is unwilling or unable to undergo strongly repressive retaliation, coercive procedures will be used tentatively, within the limits that will not provoke a full response. When the inhibiting conditions are weak, the movement will be largely limited to persuasive and bargaining strategies. When the movement is willing to undergo repressions not only will coercive strategies be readily employed but the established group may be provoked into the intemperate exercise of repression, inspiring fear and resentment and uniting other groups in opposition. By acting ruthlessly the established power may arouse indignation and weaken support within its own constituency. Or by exposing an embarrassing disproportion between the massive use of power and its limited effectiveness, the established group may lose the respect and weaken the support from both its own constituency and other groups.

Coercive strategies ranging from harassment to systematic terrorism typically occur under conditions where the movement has very little coercive power in comparison with the target group and would easily be suppressed in an open, frontal, and uninhibited program of repression. A protective cover for the movement is provided by a larger group that the established power is unwilling to punish with full force at their disposal. The group supplying cover may do so out of sympathy for the movement, fear of the movement, or a combination of both. Terrorism as a strategy depends upon just such a combination. Underground resistance movements, such as those that developed in Europe during the German occupation of World War II, depend on popular support and sympathy, but they must still occasionally resort to direct action against the potential informer.

Nonviolence as a Strategy in Social Movements

Among many strategies that are more specific and delimited than the three types we have discussed is nonviolence. Nonviolence as a strategy attracted great attention in the United States during the period just before our direct involvement in World War II, with Gandhi's *Satyagraha* as the model. Interest in nonviolence has been reawakened by the recent civil-rights leadership of Martin Luther King and the efforts to employ nonviolence in the peace and draft-resistance movements.

Nonviolence is a self-conscious and collectively disciplined avoidance of violence when the situation is strongly provocative of violence. Because it is a self-conscious and disciplined strategy, it is inseparable from value orientation: i.e., the strategy of nonviolence is a natural expression of certain kinds of pacifistic and religious values, and the strategy tends to be viewed as intrinsically good and right (apart from its consequences) because it embodies and expresses these values.[6] The use of violence by only a small number of people is enough to make the problem of containing and coping with that violence a central concern of the community and of the opposition. When this happens the movement ceases to be effectively nonviolent, even though the majority of its representatives and even its most widely accepted leaders (accepted by the constituency) remain nonviolent.

Nonviolence always couples persuasive strategy to coercion,[7] and in some respects this combination is its most distinctive feature. The coercion is directed toward the target group (e.g., M. L. King's original bus boycott coerced the bus company and municipal officials); the communication, by exemplifying moral superiority, is aimed primarily at larger publics that the target group must take account of.

Comparing the circumstances that are conducive to nonviolent strategy with those affecting the choice among primary types of strategy leads to the suggestion that nonviolent strategies are most likely to occur when the situation is in some respects in-

hibitive and in other respects conducive to coercive strategy. The situation fosters coercion because of the lack of resources to make persuasive or bargaining strategies effective and because of the social cleavage between the constituency and the target group. However the overwhelming retaliatory power of the target group and/or the symbiotic dependency of the constituency tend to inhibit the use of coercion. Under these circumstances the most common response is withdrawal from the struggle and inability to launch an effective movement. If other conditions are adequate to launch effective movement activity, the alternative tends to be either terrorism or nonviolence. Because of this basic constellation of factors, nonviolence is most commonly found in association with terrorism and not with the more conventional persuasive and bargaining strategies. Both require a well-disciplined group of participants; but nonviolence can prevail only when a large proportion of the constituency accept the general discipline of the movement, whereas terrorism can operate with only a small disciplined group. The two additional ingredients without which a nonviolent movement cannot be sustained are a mobilizable amount of sympathy for the movement's cause within the social circle of the target group (or other considerations that inhibit retaliation in full strength) and the presence in the constituency of an ethos that makes both nonviolence and self-sacrifice admirable experiences.[8]

The black boycott of streetcars between 1900 and 1906 illustrates the fashion in which nonviolence is employed partly because of the values held by business and professional leaders and partly because of the weak and dependent position of the constituency.

[6] For general discussions of nonviolence, cf. Joan V. Bondurant, Conquest of Violence: The Gandhian Philosophy of Conflict (Berkeley: University of California Press, 1967); Leo Kuper, Passive Resistance in South Africa (New Haven: Yale University Press, 1957); William R. Miller, Nonviolence: A Christian Interpretation (New York: Schocken Books, Inc., 1966); and Sociological Inquiry, 38, (Winter, 1968) 1–93.

[7] Clarence M. Case, Nonviolent Coercion (New York: Century, 1923).

[8] Judith Stiehm suggests a distinction between conscientious and pragmatic nonviolence, in "Nonviolence is Two," Sociological Inquiry, 38 (Winter, 1968), 23–29.

The Boycott Movement Against Jim Crow Streetcars in the South, 1900–1906

August Meier
Elliott Rudwick

The prelude to the civil rights revolution of the mid-twentieth century was the dramatic eighteen-month bus boycott in Montgomery, Alabama, led by Martin Luther King, Jr. Unknown at the time was the fact that Montgomery had witnessed a two-year boycott by its Negro citizens over a half century before, when the city council enacted a trolley-car segregation bill. Like the bus boycott of 1955–1956, the streetcar boycott of 1900–1902 was part of a larger regional Negro protest against Jim Crow urban transit. The boycotts in Montgomery, Birmingham, and Tallahassee during the late 1950s had their counterparts in more than twenty-five southern cities between 1900 and 1906. This earlier, forgotten movement was especially remarkable, for, unlike the Montgomery boycott which occurred in a period of rising Negro militance and increasing northern sympathy for the Negroes' cause, the boycotts at the turn of the century came at a time when southern white hostility and northern white indifference were reaching their peak and when, as a result, a philosophy of accommodation had achieved ascendancy in Negro thought and action.

These protests arose in response to the Jim Crow streetcar laws passed at the height of the wave of segregation legislation enacted in southern states two generations ago. Georgia passed the first such law in 1891, but it required segregation only "as much as practicable"; thus, it left implementation to the erratic discretion of the traction companies. Then, beginning about 1900, a number of southern cities passed municipal segregation ordinances. In that year, Atlanta, Rome, and Augusta supplemented the state law with measures requiring segregation. Montgomery in 1900, Jacksonville in 1901, Mobile in 1902,

From *The Journal of American History,* 55 (March, 1969), 756–75. Reprinted in part by permission of the Organization of American Historians and the authors. Footnotes have been deleted.

Columbia, South Carolina, and Houston and San Antonio, Texas, in 1903, all passed such ordinances. Meanwhile, states had begun to enact Jim Crow streetcar laws applicable only in certain localities. Thus a Virginia law of 1902 required segregation in Alexandria and in Fairfax County. An act of Arkansas in 1903 applied only to cities "of the first class," and one in Tennessee of the same year only to counties of 150,000 or more. The latter statute, which affected only Memphis, was never enforced. . . .

Boycotts have been identified in the following cities: Atlanta and Rome, Georgia, 1900; Augusta, Georgia, 1900–1903; Montgomery, Alabama, 1900–1902; Jacksonville, Florida, 1901; Mobile, Alabama, 1902; New Orleans and Shreveport, Louisiana, 1902–1903; Little Rock, Arkansas, and Columbia, South Carolina, 1903; Houston, Texas, 1903–1905; Vicksburg and Natchez, Mississippi, 1904; San Antonio, Texas, and Richmond, Virginia, 1904–1905; Memphis, Chattanooga, and Knoxville, Tennessee, and Pensacola and Jacksonville, Florida, 1905; Nashville, Tennessee, 1905–1906; Danville, Lynchburg, Portsmount, and Norfolk, Virginia, 1906; Newport News, Virginia, and Savannah, Georgia, 1906, 1907.

This listing is probably an underenumeration, for there are serious lacunae in the surviving evidence. The limitations of the sources notwithstanding, it is evident that the boycott movement was an extensive one. Protests occurred in all the states of the former Confederacy. Most of the major cities in Georgia, and every major city in Virginia and Tennessee had one. As the Mobile *Daily Register* observed in 1905: "In every city where it has been found advisable to separate the races in the street cars the experience has been the same. The negroes . . . have invariably declared a boycott."

Negro protests through mass meetings, petitions

to city councils and legislatures, and even an occasional boycott, often began while the segregation bills were being considered. In Savannah, for example, in 1901 a bill before the city council was defeated by the overt opposition of the streetcar company and by the more covertly expressed "conservative feeling of the leading white citizens," whose aid the Negroes had marshalled. Five years later, however, sentiment for segregation was much stronger among whites, and the Savannah Electric Company's president reversed his position. A Negro mass meeting urged defeat of the bill. The mayor, however, termed this protest imflammatory; the city council refused even to hear the Negro delegation and enacted the ordinance unanimously. In San Antonio, where the city council did permit a Negro committee to speak, an ordinance was also passed unanimously. In Jacksonville, after the city council in 1901 had passed a bill over the articulated opposition of the Negro community and its two Negro councilmen, colored people angrily stayed off the cars in an attempt to pressure the mayor into vetoing the bill. This boycotting proved futile, as did a similar step by Pensacola Negroes four years later, when they tried to force the city's streetcar company to lobby against the Avery streetcar-segregation bill, then before the legislature.

Negroes resented these laws as a humiliating disgrace. The Nashville *Clarion* editorially condemned this effort "to humiliate, degrade, and stigmatize the negro." Several Lynchburg Negroes circulated a call for a boycott and termed the law "a gratuitous insult . . . to every one with a drop of Negro blood. . . . Let us touch to the quick the white man's pocket. 'Tis there his conscience often lies." In 1905, after the Avery bill had passed the Florida legislature, Jacksonville Negro ministers urged a boycott of this "unjust, barbaric and . . . cowardly measure" "in order to retain our self-respect." As the Savannah *Tribune* said: "Do not trample on our pride by being 'jim crowed.' Walk!" . . .

Beyond this desire to preserve a status quo that in retrospect appeared to belong to a golden age of "harmonious," if paternalistic, race relations, there was the fear of physical maltreatment at the hands of "poor white trash"—conductors and motormen. The *St. Luke Herald* of Richmond

predicted that "the very dangerous [police] power placed in the hands of hot headed and domineering young white men," already universally hated for their overbearing and insulting conduct, would "certainly provoke trouble." Jacksonville Negroes also vigorously objected to the provision giving police power to conductors as "bound to bring about a strife and possibly bloodshed." In fact, one of the reasons urged for boycotting was the belief that by keeping off the cars Negroes would avoid occasions for friction and disorder.

Although in some cities the white press either ignored or attempted to minimize the extent of the boycott, generally, where the daily newspaper reported the protests, the editors commented upon the boycott's singular effectiveness. Universally the effect was startling to the white population. . . .

The boycotts were easily sustained in their early stages because they were a natural reaction to the humiliation and fears associated with riding the Jim Crow cars. However, informal pressures were also used. In San Antonio, a few days after the movement began, six Negroes were arrested for pulling a youth off a trolley car. In Columbia, the few who rode "were 'guyed' when the cars passed groups of negroes on the streets." In Savannah, those who opposed the boycotts were publicly denounced at mass meetings as "demagogues and hypocrites." The city's police quickly took to arresting Negroes who stood on downtown street corners, heckled riders as they got off, and urged those ready to board the trolleys to take a hack instead.

The traction companies were undeniably hard hit. In April 1908, the president of the Savannah Electric Company informed the city council that the boycott had resulted in a 25 percent decline in business and had cost about $50,000. He estimated that in 1906, when the movement was at its height, the company's loss was over $32,000. The Houston Electric Company, about five months after the boycott began, decided that it was no longer possible to disguise the fact that the protest was "crippling" its receipts.

In three cases, the companies temporarily capitulated to the protesters. Jacksonville city officials, undoubtedly acting at the request of the traction company, ceased enforcing their ordinance after a few months and quietly asked the

Negro ministers to inform their congregations. In Montgomery, after two years, the company was so hard hit that it simply suspended enforcement of the law. The president of the Mobile Light and Railroad Company, in the face of the Negroes' financially ruinous action, decided to test the ordinance in the courts; and he directed employees to permit passengers to sit anywhere. A conductor was convicted in city court for doing this, and the company announced that it would appeal. There was no further mention of the case, however. Apparently, in both Mobile and Montgomery, Jim Crow arrangements were quietly reinstated after a brief period.

In addition to walking, Negroes pressed private carriages, drays, and hacks into service. It is doubtful that the boycotts could have occurred at all except for the Negro hackmen and draymen, who in that period still dominated these two occupations in a number of southern cities. In Jacksonville and Savannah, and undoubtedly elsewhere, the hackmen reduced their fare for boycotters from twenty-five to ten cents. In Savannah, the authorities became so concerned that the police began to look for overworked horses and to arrest unlicensed hackmen. . . .

The step from these arrangements to actual transportation companies was not a long one, particularly in view of the trends in Negro thinking of the period. Because of deteriorating conditions, there had been a shift in emphasis from agitation and politics to economic advancement, self-help, and racial solidarity, often coupled with a philosophy of accommodation. The development of transportation companies, therefore, functioned in three ways: as a means of protesting against discrimination, as a fulfillment of the dream of creating substantial Negro businesses by an appeal to racial solidarity, and—hopefully—as a practical solution to the transportation problems faced by the masses of boycotting Negroes. . . .

The most impressive attempt to develop a Negro-owned alternative to the Jim Crow trolley cars occurred in Nashville. There the boycott began July 5, and by the end of the summer the leaders formed the Union Transportation Company. Its incorporators included the elite of Nashville's business and professional community: the president was Preston Taylor, an undertaker and the

pastor of the Lea Avenue Christian Church; its treasurer was a Fisk University official, George W. Henderson; and its purchasing agent was the Reverend Richard Henry Boyd, general secretary of the National Baptist Publishing Board. For the first few weeks, the company used horses and wagons. By September 21, $7,000 worth of stock had been sold, another $18,000 worth subscribed, and five motor buses purchased. The buses arrived on September 29, and during the day large numbers of race-proud Negroes eagerly inspected them. According to the Nashville *Banner*, "the cars are on the steam wagonette style, and have a large front seat with two long seats running backward, band wagon style. They have a capacity for fifteen persons."

The line began operations early in October. For at least a brief time, it invigorated the boycott, but the buses never fulfilled their expectation. The few vehicles naturally kept infrequent schedules. To remedy this problem, the company's inexperienced officers overpaid for nine more buses. These lacked sufficient power for Nashville's hills. Arrangements for boosting power were made with the local electric company, but either the results were unsatisfactory or the company reneged on its promises; in any event, the bus operations were constantly hampered. Little improvement resulted from a new generator installed at the National Baptist Publishing Board, and battery trouble repeatedly incapacitated the vehicles. Passengers became tired of waiting and increasingly used the Jim Crow streetcars. Two years later, W. E. B. Du Bois described this enterprise as one that cost its shareholders $20,000 for a few months of service.

Legal efforts proved as futile as the transportation companies and, though not entirely eschewed, played a distinctly minor role. In a few cities, Negroes seriously discussed going to court, but only in Florida did they actually undertake a legal attack. This litigation was directed by city councilman and attorney J. Douglas Wetmore, who twice carried test cases to the state supreme court. Arguing that the state law of 1905 was "vague and uncertain," that it violated the equal protection clause of the Fourteenth Amendment, and even that it discriminated among classes of Negroes by providing that Negro nurses accompanying whites could sit in the white section, Wetmore persuaded the court to hold the law unconstitutional. The judges did so, however, on the narrow ground that to allow Negro servants to sit in the white section was class legislation. Negro jubilation over the victory and the temporary end of segregation was short-lived. Jacksonville and Pensacola authorities quickly passed municipal ordinances. This time there was no general boycott. Negroes in both cities again resorted to the courts, but early in 1906 the high court upheld both city laws.

The boycott leaders, where they can be identified, were uniformly an elite group which consisted of prominent business and professional men, with at times a sprinkling of federal employees or a rare politician. Jacksonville, Savannah, Nashville, and Richmond provide the most complete information. In Savannah, the leadership included the outstanding Baptist and African Methodist Episcopal ministers, two physicians, an attorney, an undertaker, a prosperous barber with white patronage, and an insurance executive. The pattern in Jacksonville was similar, except that it was unique in including the city's two Negro councilmen. In Nashville, the prime movers were the Reverend E. W. D. Isaac, editor of the Nashville *Clarion* and the *National Baptist Union,* and the Reverend R. H. Boyd, president of the One Cent Savings Bank, as well as secretary of the Baptist Publishing Board. . . .

The elite leaders who headed the protest were known as impeccably respectable men rather than as radicals or firebrands. Some, indeed, were close friends of the noted accommodator Booker T. Washington, whom contemporaries described as "conservative" in contrast to the "radical" minority of intellectuals that led the opposition to him and his philosophy of accommodation. Moreover, it should be emphasized that this widespread boycott movement occurred in an era when accommodation was in the ascendancy. One wonders, in fact, how it was that this protest movement occurred at all, given the context of race relations in which it took place.

The trolley-car boycotts can best be described as a "conservative protest." First, this movement was conservative in the sense that it was seeking to preserve the status quo—to prevent a change from an older and well-established pattern.

Second, it is also noteworthy that the boycotts avoided a direct confrontation with the laws, such as would have occurred if Negroes had insisted on sitting in the white section. There were instances of Negroes being arrested for occupying seats assigned to whites, but these were rare incidents and, except for the Florida test cases, not part of the organized protest movements.

Third, the statements of the boycott leaders themselves were often remarkably moderate or "conservative." This was true even of the editors, who formed the most militant segment of the movements' spokesmen. . . .

It should be emphasized that, although the boycott was a tactic adopted by many conservative leaders, partly because it avoided confrontation and overt racial friction, it was, nevertheless, a genuine protest weapon. It was so considered by the whites and by those accommodating ministers who opposed its use. But as the least aggressive kind of protest, the least militant variety of what today is called nonviolent direct action, it fitted the conservatism of Negro leaders in southern cities during a period of accommodation. Even in such a time, the boycotts were a natural and spontaneous response, for they sought to preserve dignity in the face of a humiliating social change. . . .

The boycotts ranged in length from a few weeks to as long as two or three years. The Mobile *Daily Register* generalized that it took "about two months" to convince Negroes that they might as well use the cars again. Yet some clearly lasted a good deal longer. The Montgomery boycott was entering its third month when the Atlanta *Constitution* marveled at its "surprising persistency." . . .

In some cities, like Atlanta, Memphis, Natchez, Richmond, and Savannah, leadership cleavages undoubtedly hastened the demise of the protests. But more than anything else, what undoubtedly caused their decline was a feeling of discouragement—a realistic pessimism—that must in time have come over the demonstrators as they saw that their withdrawal of patronage produced no results. Some, like editors Johnson and Mitchell, might continue to walk, but gradually a sense of futility set in.

It is not surprising that, in the end, the boycott movements against Jim Crow trolleys failed in all of the cities where they were initiated. They occurred at a time when southern racism was reaching its crest and when the white South had gained a respectful hearing in the North. With the Supreme Court endorsing the separate-but-equal doctrine and with Negroes in most places virtually disfranchised, the boycotts were the only way of protesting realistically open to them. In retrospect, it is easy to see that their failure was inevitable. The remarkable thing is not that the boycotts failed, but that they happened in so many places and lasted as long as they often did.

The Growth of Power Orientations

Within any movement there is a fairly continuous struggle between value orientations and power orientations. As a consequence many movements that originate with the promotion of a clearly sensed value undergo transformation until the value objectives are extensively subordinated to power objectives. Such a change occurs in three major ways.

First, a strong belief in the unlimited worth of a movement's objectives provokes the attitude that any means are justified by the ends to be gained. The acquisition of power seems to be a much easier way to accomplish the aims of the movement than does the slow process of winning a favorable public and getting constituted authorities to accept the program. To some extent, an extreme dedication to the movement—an inability to understand how anyone could disagree with its aims except through ignorance or willfulness—is a natural product of a highly developed esprit de corps. Such an attitude makes the members and leaders impatient with value-toned discussions of what methods are proper and what are not. Even when leaders are inclined to search their consciences regarding strategy, the demands by members for immediate and tangible accomplishments may force decisions in terms of power, irrespective of their consistency with the movement's values. Such compromise of principle probably occurs in every movement to a degree, but frequently it extends so far that the value orientations sink into the background of movement decisions.

Second, a movement may be taken over or subverted to power considerations by outsiders who see its potential usefulness to themselves. A movement of any considerable strength immediately has to contend with many efforts to capture it for power purposes. Even movements that represent only small minority interests have nuisance value or a potentially crucial influence when major forces are balanced. Consequently opportunists seek to capture the movements and trade concessions of policy for personal gain. Many of the small political movements in the United States have lost their distinctive ideologies in this manner. Starting with a fairly radical viewpoint and commanding a small but vigorous body of supporters, the movement becomes important enough to trouble the leaders of the major parties. As skilled opportunists work themselves into key positions, the sharp edge of the radical doctrine becomes blunted until eventually it becomes almost indistinguishable from that of more established groups.

Third, certain kinds of opposition so narrow the range of tactics available to a movement that it has no alternative other than to adopt effective means irrespective of their consonance with its values. The movement that is regarded as revolutionary by the society in which it operates is in this position, as we have pointed out earlier. If a revolutionary movement is to achieve any appreciable measure of success in the face of restrictive practices, it must develop an extensive strategy and employ tactics that more value-oriented movements avoid. Adherence to a carefully defined strategy must not be weakened by internal division, questions of public acceptability, or matters of sentiment. It is for this reason that some of the clearest and most realistic statements of movement strategy are to be found in revolutionary literature.

The international communist movement, for example, has worked out strategies for organization to their purposes in great detail. The preeminence of power orientations within the movement is evidenced by the fact that some of the major splits among Marxist groups have occurred about the strategy of gaining power rather than about differences in values to be promoted. In connection with the Bolshevik Revolution of 1917, Lenin is said to have commented: "Seizure of power is the point of the uprising. *Its political task will be clarified after the seizure....*"

In many respects the situation of resistance movements is similar. An important component of the French Resistance movement during the years of Nazi occupation in World War II was the maquis, the bands of men who lived in the mountains as guerrillas and systematically inflicted terror on the occupying forces. The manner in which power orientations can become dominant over the value orientations is graphically illustrated by the behavior of some of these bands, especially toward the close of that period. Although the Robin Hood ideal of robbing the evil invaders for the sake of the oppressed Frenchmen prevailed, in practice it was often the property and subsistence of already impoverished Frenchmen that were commandeered and those same people who suffered violence when they did not readily cooperate. Rival bands developed, fought among themselves, and treated the civilians as pawns in their struggles. Indignation and outrage led to vigilante actions in which resistors were often mistaken for collaborators. Thousands were summarily executed, and there is no way to estimate how many of them were genuinely traitors. Most relevant to our concern, many of the bands developed a proprietary attitude toward the territory where they operated. Because they had fought for the village or larger area, they saw it as their own and massively resisted the reimposition of normal authority. Even though the Allies had wisely refused to drop heavy arms for use by units of the Resistance, it was still a major problem to disarm them after the Nazis had been driven out.[9]

The situation here is extreme. The intense risks and sacrifices taken by these bands, the necessity to abandon normal sensitivities and scruples in order to survive, and the poor communication with the larger Resistance organization accentuated normal tendencies for the pursuit and retention of control to become an autonomous goal. But the Resistance also illustrates a principle of general applicability: investment of effort and sacrifice toward any end contributes to a sense of ownership. The hard core of revolutionaries come to feel that they own the revolution and have a right to wield control commensurate with their ownership. The more intense the investment and sacrifice, the more intense is this sense of ownership. Hence the more bitterly fought the battle for a movement's goals, the greater is the tendency for the movement's activists to place the attainment and maintenance of power above the evaluation of their consistency with the value objectives.

Control Movements

Movements in which value orientations are so subordinated to the quest for power that they set no limitations on the strategies employed and in which ideologies and goals are devised and changed chiefly to serve strategic requirements can be called power-oriented or control movements. The processes just reviewed are sometimes carried

9 Blake Ehrlich, *Resistance: France 1940–1945* (Boston: Little, Brown and Company, 1965), esp. pp. 153–200, 265–69.

to the point that a value-oriented move-ment is converted into a control movement, and goals and ideology become window dressing rather than guiding considera-tions. Resistance movements and separatist movements are especially prone to such transformation because the problem of establishing and protecting the group's integrity is so great from the start that what they are resisting *for* or separating *for* receives little attention in comparison to what they are *against*. Nationalistic move-ments also tend in this direction, since the question "Nationhood for what?" is seldom asked in the course of the struggle.

Some of the best-known illustrations of control movements include national dicta-torships, urban movements that culminate in political machines, palace and military revolutions such as those frequent in South America, and recurring factional move-ments for control within established organi-zations. From an examination of these and other examples, it is apparent that such movements operate in two contrasting ways. On the one hand, they may operate like the dictatorships of Mussolini and Hitler on the basis of mass support. Many political machines depend upon their ability to deliver the votes and function quite openly. On the other hand, some control move-ments conceal their activities and even their existence from the mass and achieve control through strategic infiltration and the surprise *coup d'état*.

Control movements of the latter sort, which are not dependent upon mass sup-port, begin within groups that already pos-sess considerable power. Such movements frequently resort to military revolts in which officials use their control of the armed forces to capture the state machin-ery. Military *coups d'état* are often spec-tacular when they finally culminate, but comparable movements in which an eco-nomic elite extend their control to the political sphere or a political elite expand their power or a church elite pursue eco-nomic or political domination may proceed almost unnoticed at the time.

Since elite control movements are the work of those who already hold some legitimate power, their success normally reflects a strongly embedded cultural tradi-tion that provides justification for the ex-tension of power. Societies in which power is conceived of as incorporating a re-sponsibility toward the governed provide less fertile soil for such movements than do those in which power is regarded chiefly as a prize. On the other hand, when the possession of certain types of power is defined in the cultural tradition as evidence of superior worth or supernatural sanc-tion, this circumstance abets the move-ment's extension of such power to other areas. For example, the Western European tradition of noblesse oblige—that nobility implies obligations toward one's inferiors —is an obstacle to the military *coup d'état*. However, the Protestant-Capitalist tradition that the possession of wealth is evidence of superior personal worth facili-tates movements among the economic elite for the control of political and even religi-ous power. This tradition justifies the con-trol movement in its activities and makes the power holders in other spheres receptive to influence from the economic elite.

If such elite control movements are to operate in secrecy, they must also monopo-lize the mass communication. Thus, con-trol of the press by the economic, military, religious, or political elite facilitates the movements. But elite control movements may also operate successfully in fairly open struggle under certain conditions. A mass conviction that shifts in power "up there" make no difference to the life of the ordin-ary man provides the background for a noninterventionist spectator attitude. In-deed, those who resist the *coup d'état* may be viewed as unnecessarily prolonging the crisis and delaying the return to normal activities. Likewise, an aristocratic tradi-tion that keeps the masses from ever realizing that they might wield power leads to a hands off policy when elite power struggles are taking place.

With a tradition of popular control and failure to monopolize the agencies of mass communication, the control movement resorts to mass sanction for its activities and attempts to manipulate mass support as one of its weapons. Mass-control movements range from those inspired by elites seeking to extend their power to those originating among groups that lack legitimate power. Two conditions appear to be essential if control movements dependent upon mass support are to develop and succeed. First, there must be some weakness in the established power, usually produced by a divisive rivalry among the various elites. Second, the masses must lack effective organization through which to determine and register their interests in a continuous manner.

Except when there is no established power, control movements appealing to the masses succeed in large part because of the support they receive from one or more of the established elite groups. In the rivalry among elites one faction sees the budding movement as a weapon that can be used against its rivals. The movement gains access to established power by making bargains with the elite faction. Without such access it would be difficult to overcome the inherent advantage of those already in power. The support of Hitler by the wealthy Junkers, for example, provided resources that made the Nazis more than just one of several competing parties. Political machines often receive surreptitious support from ambitious insiders among the established elite and from business groups who hope to gain more favorable operating conditions from the machine.

The widespread popular support employed by Mussolini, Hitler, Franco, and other dictators in their successful efforts to replace newly formed representative go-

vernments with totalitarian systems led many scholars to seek explanations for mass susceptibility to blatant power appeals. Many variations were developed on a theme presented by Ortega y Gasset in 1930.[10] According to him the indispensable values of shared responsibility for the common good were fostered and protected by the traditional European class system. Although it often led to exploitation and other evils, it did socialize elites to a sense of responsibility and preserved authority in the hands of those who had a stake in a system of positive values. The weakening of traditional class systems without the development of any new stratified order replaced class-man with mass-man. Lacking a sense of responsibility or any understanding of the complex interdependencies of human existence, mass-man indulges himself by supporting any movement that promises to free him from traditional moral codes, to discomfit those who rank above him, and to bring him the good things of life without requiring that he work to earn them.

The idea is given a somewhat more sophisticated interpretation by Emil Lederer who refers to the "Amorphous masses" as the indispensable basis of modern political dictatorship.[11] Large masses of people without respected leadership and stable group affiliation are unable to assess the promises and claims extravagantly made. Unrepresented and unheard by society's legitimate power holders, they are susceptible to movements that pretend some special interest in them. Lacking effective channels of discussion with other groups, they are unable to take note of the contradictory promises made to these other groups.

What y Gasset, Lederer, and Hannah

[10] Jose Ortega y Gasset, *The Revolt of the Masses* (New York: W. W. Norton and Company, Inc., 1932).

[11] Emil Lederer, *State of the Masses: The Threat of a Classless Society* (New York: W. W. Norton and Company, Inc., 1940).

Arendt[12] can agree to is that people who are firmly identified with interest groups, whether the groups are anchored in socio-economic stratification or some other organizing framework, are attracted to movements whose goals and ideologies are congenial with their own interests and world views. But people whose interests and world view have not been articulated through such membership have no frame of reference to apply to the appeals of diverse movements, and they respond to negative appeals and to the display and promise of dramatic power. A society that effectively organizes its population into interest segments produces value-oriented movements; a society that remains amorphous produces power-oriented movements.

The pattern of private dealings with groups in power and public gestures to those lacking all regular channels of influence has been characteristic of political dynasties, such as the Huey Long empire in Louisiana, and of big-city political machines. Through frank bargains with minority interest groups and through a

ward organization that maintains a personal kind of contact with the otherwise unrepresented individuals, the machine incorporates people into an organization that appears interested in their individual needs. Frequently the most intense personal loyalties are evoked.

The control movement is generally a highly centralized, authoritarian organization, making up for its lack of sanctioned respectability by evidence that it can take decisive and drastic action where established authorities appear to act with indecision and compromise. Frequently, elaborate pathological explanations are offered to account for susceptibility to these control movements. However, in the face of a widespread feeling that (1) conditions could not be much worse than they are and (2) there are no real alternatives, nothing is more normal for the unaffiliated and unrepresented than to cast their lot with a movement that appears at least capable of drastic action. A widespread attitude of cynicism toward the stated programs of all organizations obscures ideological differences between power-oriented and value-oriented movements, so that the apparent ability to act becomes the foremost consideration.

12 Hannah Arendt, *The Origins of Totalitarianism* (New York: Harcourt Brace Jovanovich, Inc., 1966).

16

CONFLICT AND SEPARATISM

In discussing conflict and the public we pointed out that a relationship of conflict has its own dynamics that give it a direction independent of the values at issue. There is an affinity between conflict and coercive strategy, the latter almost always leading to the former, and coercion being the only strategy that effectively expresses a conflict point of view. There is also an affinity between conflict and power orientations. Blatant pursuit of power quickly evokes the kind of response that embroils the movement in conflict. And once a movement becomes involved in conflict, for whatever reason, its leaders must increasingly devote their attention to cultivating the movement's power base. In conflict the groups are so intensely valued positively and negatively that advancement of one group and the degradation of another take on the same moral quality as promoting an important reform in society. Conflict, then, is carrying the transition from value orientation to power orientation full circle, reinvesting a value emphasis in the pursuit of power by one group over another.

No movement develops without conflict, but the ways in which a movement copes with and uses conflict have much to do with its growth and adherence to its initial value objectives. In the following discussion we shall examine circumstances that promote extensive conflict and violence and the development of a revolutionary perspective in movement careers. We shall then explore the use and the effects of conflict

on the movement and look separately at countermovements. Finally we shall examine separatism and the wide spectrum of movements that adopt separation as their goal.

Roots of Conflict

SOURCES OF EPIDEMIC CONFLICT. In a comparative study of civil strife in 114 nations between 1961 and 1967, Ted Gurr sought to identify important correlates of the extent and intensity of violence in different countries.[1] Findings vary a little, depending upon whether the extent or intensity of strife is measured and whether all nations or only western nations are included. But the important factors in conflict are persisting deprivation, facilitation, legitimacy of the government, historical levels of strife, and short term deprivation. Persisting deprivation was measured by estimating the intensity and proportion of the population affected by economic and political discrimination, political separatism, dependence on foreign economies, lack of educational opportunity, and religious divisions. Short term deprivation referred to deterioration in the same kinds of conditions, during the 1950s and early 1960s.

[1] Ted R. Gurr, "A Comparative Study of Civil Strife," in Hugh D. Graham and Ted R. Gurr, eds., *The History of Violence in America: Historical and Comparative Perspectives* (New York: Praeger Publishers, Inc., 1969), pp. 572–632.

Facilitation means the availability of physical, organizational, and material support for rebellion as measured by the size and status of Communist parties, the extent of isolated terrain, and the amount of foreign assistance to rebels. It was assumed that a political system had legitimacy in the eyes of the citizenry when it was developed solely by indigenous leaders, rather than imposed from outside, and had endured for many years without substantial structural change. The tradition of strife was indicated by levels of collective violence from 1946 to 1959. The measures are necessarily crude, and there may be contamination between some measures and the level of strife index. But when the inherent difficulties of this kind of investigation are taken into account, this is an exceptionally resourceful study, and the findings are probably the most valid clues to collective violence available to us at present.

Using a somewhat longer period (1948 to 1965) and a smaller number of nations (85), Ivo and Rosalind Feierabend and Betty Nesvold tried to isolate conditions affecting political stability.[2] Nations were scaled from zero to six (six indicating most unstable) by the occurence of events that ranged from holding a regularly scheduled election (most stable) to civil war or mass execution (most unstable). When nations were classified according to level of modernization, the greatest instability characterized those in transition between the least and most modern conditions. This is also the period when discrepancies between expectation and possibility are greatest as measured by such indexes as rapid increase in primary education combined with slow growth of the gross national product. The authors attribute much instability in the United States (scale value = four) to a transitional stage of modernization char-

acterizing specific groups within the society as a whole. The discrepancy between expectation and possibility for such groups as blacks and Mexican-Americans corresponds to the stage of many whole nations in the transitional period, and it differs from the highly modernized condition of middle-class white Americans.

A study of collective violence against whites in Africa from 1944 to 1959 by Robert LeVine supplies another kind of evidence—this relative to the more specific category of nationalistic movements. LeVine found it *not* true that violence was greatest where oppression was greatest or that violence was most likely where Africans were treated most liberally or that the presence of a politically powerful white settler population is conducive to violence. But he did find that inconsistent policies were strongly related to violent outbreaks.

The more the behavior of the European-run government arouses in the African population conflicting expectations regarding their political autonomy, the greater the probability of an outbreak of African violence directed at European lives and property. . . . In a territory where the government has pursued a relatively consistent policy favoring African self-government, there will be little anti-European violence; where the government has pursued a consistently repressive policy toward African self-rule, there will also be little anti-European violence.[3]

Bringing these observations together, we observe that the enduring deprivation isolated by Gurr coupled with the experience and prospect of something better contribute to intense feelings. Linking these feelings with the idea of facilitation suggests what Wildavesky calls the anger plus opportunity theory in explaining the massive outbreaks of violence in the black movement. The anger had been recorded by such observers

2 Ivo K. Feierabend, Rosalind L. Feierabend, and Betty A. Nesvold, "Social Change and Political Violence: Cross-national Patterns," in Graham and Gurr, eds., *History of Violence,* pp. 632–87.

3 Robert A. LeVine, "Anti-European Violence in Africa: A Comparative Analysis, "*Journal of Conflict Resolution,* 3 (December, 1959), 422, *See also* 420–29, copyright 1959 by the University of Michigan.

as Frazier[4] and Powdermaker[5] much earlier, but then it was suicide for the black to express his rage directly. "Just as soon as Negro strength increased sufficiently in Northern cities and whites became troubled about brutal retaliation, it became safer for Negroes to act on violent feelings."[6] Paradoxically, it is when the community is ambivalent about the movement and restrains its agents that the chance of fully developed conflict is increased. This is also the situation leading to inconsistent policies, alternately encouraging and enraging the movement people. The police, army, or other agents of the authorities are placed in a relatively untenable position where their lives are in danger, yet they are uncertain of community backing when they act according to established policy. Periodic instances of overreaction are certain to occur under these circumstances.

Closely related to the factor of legitimacy of the government is the generalization that violence is most common when a movement has no alliance with a major political party or other channel for acting directly on the community decision centers. An accessible order is more likely to be accorded legitimacy than an inaccessible order. The problem of legitimacy is further compounded when movement people can deal only only with intermediaries who have no real discretion or power to influence policies at a higher level. The frustration of the client who cannot get past the receptionist in the waiting room or the minor bureaucrat in a government agency is matched by the fury of workers who can express their grievances to no one beyond the foreman or the colonial people who can

only gain the ear of a minor colonial functionary or the Mexican-American who can only vent his anger on the policeman who "just does what he is told."

A legitimate order is one vested with authority and not merely power, as Robert Nisbet distinguishes them. Authority is the principal restraint on the use of naked force either by movements of the disadvantaged or by agents of established power. When authority weakens, power enters to fill the vacuum.

Authority has no reality save in the memberships and allegiances of the members of an organization, be this the family, a political association, the church or the university. Authority, function, membership: these form a seamless web in traditional society. The authority of the family follows from its indispensable function. So does that of the church, the guild, the local community, and the school. When the function has become displaced or weakened, when allegiances have been transferred to other entities, there can be no other consequence but a decline of authority.[7]

Thus our examination of circumstances that accentuate tendencies toward conflict in the relationship between movement and community agents brings us to a set of conditions resembling in many respects those that contribute to the rise of movements in which value aims are subordinated to power orientations.

STRATEGY OF CONFRONTION. Once conflict has been accepted as the main relationship between movement and community, a wholly new strategy is called for. Abandoned is the hope of winning support by evoking sympathy and understanding from the enemy. Bargaining is out of the question because no offers by the enemy can be trusted and because any compromise of movement objectives can only be understood as selling out. As black movements

4 E. Franklin Frazier, *Negro Youth at the Crossways* (Washington, D.C.: American Council on Education, 1940).
5 Hortense Powdermaker, *After Freedom* (New York: The Viking Press, Inc., 1939).
6 Aaron Wildavesky, "The Empty-headed Blues: Black Rebellion and White Reaction," *The Public Interest,* 11 (Spring, 1968), 8, *see also* 3–16.

7 Robert A. Nisbet, "The Twilight of Authority," *The Public Interest,* 15 (Spring, 1969), 5, *see also* 3–9.

had begun to recognize in 1957, "by the creation of a crisis, social change could be effected in spite of popular opposition and official apathy."[8] Tactics on both sides are now guided by a strategy of confrontation in which the aims are to create fear, disorder, and injury. The conflict belief system described in Chapter 12 supplies the dominant orientation to events as they occur.

Efforts at direct and violent injury typically create unfavorable publics. As Taft and Ross have concluded from their historical review of American labor violence, "The effect of labor violence was almost always harmful to the union. . . . A community might be sympathetic to the demands of strikers, but as soon as violent confrontation took place, the possibility was high that interest would shift from concern for the acceptance of union demands to the stopping of the violence."[9] Hence confrontation strategies stress a more restrained kind of harassment and especially a systematic program of provocation and immobilization. By provoking the enemy into rash and improper actions, the movement can win a series of encounters in spite of limited power and resources.

The use of provocation tactics depends on the special ethics of conflict, involving revised lines of division between ethical and unethical actions and the assumption that since the true but hidden nature of the enemy is evil, any action that provokes an evil response from him is justified as serving to expose his true character. An example of special ethics is supplied by a letter in the UCLA *Daily Bruin* by students who employed physical coercion to prevent the university from holding a

course on "The Control and Guidance of Tactical Missiles" for engineers.

We would like to correct an error in your article on the Coalition's demonstration against the tactical missile course. The Bruin reported that "Coalition members attempted to rush the classroom where the course on the guidance and control of tactical missiles was being conducted." This is absolutely false. No one ever tried to "rush the classroom."

The Coalition's tactic was to block the door of the classroom and thus prevent the engineers from entering. We didn't fight with the engineers. In fact, we handed out literature to them and attempted to strike up conversations. When the Unicops tried to get the engineers in through another door, we linked arms, formed a line, and blocked off that entrance, too. The only violence occurred when Unicops used their nightsticks against us and when a couple of engineers slugged us.

We were, incidentally, successful in keeping most of the engineers from entering the classroom.[10]

Symbols can be employed as devices for harassment and provocation rather than for communication of viewpoints with the aim of persuasion. Use of symbols to generate anger and fear is often a highly refined tactic in the strategy of confrontation. This use of symbols for confrontation is a step further removed from persuasion than is even coercion. Symbols used in coercion are designed to instill fear, but they must also convey some promise or hope that compliance will bring relief from further terror. The most effective coercive symbols evoke more fear than anger. But confrontation symbols are often designed to educe more anger than fear—rage so intense as to overcome fear and propel the enemy into rash actions. By offering no hope that compliance will bring relief from terror, they contribute toward acts of desperation. Two features of confrontation symbols warrant emphasis.

First, the symbols are selected largely for

8 Lewis M. Killian, *The Impossible Revolution? Black Power and the American Dream* (New York: Random House, Inc., 1968), p. 58.
9 Philip Taft and Philip Ross, "American Labor Violence: Its Causes, Character, and Outcome," in Graham and Gurr, eds., *History of Violence*, pp. 383–83.

10 UCLA *Daily Bruin*, July 31, 1969.

their potency in affronting the target group. For example, profanity will be used where it serves no other purpose than effrontery; modes of dress such as hippie outfits will be worn because they offend; grievances and issues at hand will be merged with subjects such as obscenity and other unrelated matters that serve to arouse disgust and antipathy. When symbols are used for persuasion the aim is to select symbols that are as free of complicating side issues as possible and that arouse little initial antipathy. Symbols used in confrontation are chosen with exactly opposite criteria in mind.

Second, the confrontation group insists on rejecting overtly (though not always covertly) the conventional meanings of the symbols they employ. While adopting clothes modeled after the hippie pattern, many radicals will forcibly deny that wearing the clothing means accepting hippie values. The Castro-style beard first became popular among American youth soon after Castro won control of Cuba. Yet many young people berated persons who interpreted the wearing of such a beard as indicating the advocacy of a Communist form of social order. The assault on standard meanings of symbols impairs communication, lessening the chance of persuasion, bargaining, or conciliation from either side. In this way the prospect of a pure confrontation of force is enhanced.

Perhaps the greatest danger to confrontation strategy is the temptation to respond affirmatively to conciliatory gestures. Hence confrontation strategy includes ways of handling conciliatory initiatives from the enemy. The demand is for unconditional surrender. The offer of less is treated as an affront and the tender of any offer as a sign of weakness and defeat. The conciliator is stripped of all dignity, and the enemy is accused of even greater infamy and deceit by virtue of his initiative. By handling conciliation in this way the movement leaders insulate themselves and their members

against taking peace initiatives seriously, and they increase the likelihood that the initiatives will be quickly withdrawn.

THE TREND OF CONFLICT. Unlike competition and accommodation, escalated conflict tends to be of limited duration, intermittent rather than continuous.[11] As radicals have frequently observed, agents of a viable order constantly devise new ways to counter the tactics they employ, so that once effective provocations and harassment no longer work. Movement adherents tire of confrontations, and an impatient bystander public intensifies pressure for an end to violence and disruption. In general, a strategy of conflict must achieve concessions or unseat some established power group in a fairly brief period of time or fail.

The continued reliance on conflict is also self-defeating because it effects a transformation in the nature of the movement. Vigilante movements have fallen into this trap. The South Carolina Regulators were organized in 1767 to protect settlers from the outlaw bands remaining from the Cherokee Indian War. The movement succeeded in its main object, but its practitioners became increasingly "arbitrary, extreme, and brutal." An opposition movement called the Moderators then countered violence with violence until, in 1769, the Regulators disbanded. Again in San Francisco, in 1856, the antivigilante Law and Order group harnessed the fears of citizens against the vigilantes whose successes were now leading them to excesses. Richard Brown concludes that in the majority of instances, vigilante movements had the support of the community and voluntarily disbanded when their goals were attained, typically within a year or two of their beginning. But sadists invariably found vigilante movements attractive and were

11 Robert E. Park and Ernest W. Burgess, *Introduction to the Science of Sociology* (Chicago: University of Chicago Press, 1924), p. 574.

sometimes able to take control of the movement or force it in the direction of tyranny. When this happened the vigilante movement posed as great a threat to order as the criminals they initially sought to suppress.[12]

When conflict and violence are effective in bringing about change, it is either because results are achieved rather quickly or because violence is brought under movement discipline, to be used sparingly on strategically crucial occasions. The strategy of terror avoids open and massive confrontations, substituting focused engagements at times and places of the movement' choosing.

Revolutionary Movements

A movement is revolutionary when it is viewed as a threat to the society and consequently is denied access to legitimate means for promoting its aims (See Chapter 13). Movements become revolutionary in the eyes of the community and relinquish efforts to employ legitimate means at the culmination of periods of conflict during which (1) the movement fails to make substantial progress toward its major aims but retains the loyalty of a determined core of members and wins widespread applause in the constituency and (2) the community is unable to find a basis for seeking accommodation with the movement through bargaining.

REVOLUTIONARY IDEOLOGY. Revolutionary doctrine (or ideology) is simply the conflict world view, as described under conflict publics (Chapter 12), integrated with a pervasive value orientation. The values espoused by the movement—freedom, equality, rule of the superman, universal love, or whatever they may be—are applied so as to find the existing state of affairs absolutely intolerable. The logic of conflict

[12] Richard M. Brown, "The American Vigilante Tradition," Graham and Gurr, eds., *History of Violence*, pp. 154–226.

world views is embodied in polarization between a utopian condition in which the values are fully realized and the current abominable situation and between that oppressed group of people that is deprived of those values through no fault of their own and the oppressors who act from pure self-interest or delight in doing evil. As in any true conflict situation, the evil characteristics of the present state of things and of the oppressor class are more precisely documented than are the deserving qualities of the beneficiary class or is the nature of the forthcoming utopia. The more intolerable the present conditions, the less frequently movement spokesmen will be called on to specify the utopia they offer in its place. If conditions are bad enough, any change must be for the better! The more evil the oppressors, the less demand there is to show that the oppressed are truly deserving.

Since man is so highly adaptable a creature, he manages to find satisfactions in almost any form of existence; rarely does a large mass of people view its situation as absolutely intolerable or its oppressors as unmitigatedly evil. Hence a revolutionary perspective is difficult to maintain throughout a movement. The most effective way to do so is to engage in occasional excesses that frighten or provoke the oppressors into overreactions that confirm the polarized images. The more sophisticated ideologists of revolutionary movements employ the conflict conception, that the enemy's true nature is hidden and only revealed under exceptional conditions to protect the polarized imagery. Because the oppressors know they are evil, they seek to hide their true motives. Only in the crisis for which he is unprepared does the white man expose his true racism, the capitalist his exploitative attitudes toward workers, the male his contempt for the female. Only in the napalm bombing of Vietnamese children is the true nature of American government revealed: charitable acts toward

Biafran children and efforts to promote popular self-government in other countries are not to be taken at face value, according to revolutionary perspective.

The constant threat to revolutionary ideologies is the prospect of ameliorative steps that soften the polarized conflict relationship and lead to accommodation. Hence revolutionary ideologies always include the definition of ameliorative conditions as disguised efforts to prevent change. Some of the most violent epithets used by revolutionary socialists were saved for the moderate socialists who sought to achieve change gradually and through constitutional procedures. Sociologically sophisticated revolutionaries in the United States are able to discount efforts to come to terms with them as cooptation. In his classic call to revolution in the "Third World" Frantz Fanon writes,

...the more brutal manifestations of the presence of the occupying power may perfectly well disappear. Indeed, such a spectacular disappearance turns out to be both a saving of expense to the colonial power and a positive way of preventing its forces being spread out over a wide area. But such a disappearance will be paid for at a high price: the price of a much stricter control of the country's future destiny.[13]

Because the revolutionary movement seeks to prevent amelioration of the condition of the oppressed and because it anticipates a violent struggle in which many will suffer and die, the ideology contains some basis for glorifying self-sacrifice for a cause. We shall defer consideration of the ways in which movements prepare their members to endure suffering until Chapter 17, except to observe that the positive value of self-sacrifice holds a prominent place in revolutionary ideologies. And in case the potential

revolutionary is deterred by conventional attitudes toward violence, Fanon reminds us that, "At the level of individuals, violence is a cleansing force. It frees the native from his inferiority complex and from his despair and inaction; it makes him fearless and restores his self-respect."[14]

REVOLUTIONARY DEVELOPMENT. In spite of revolutionary doctrines carefully nurtured by a determined core of adherents, no movement is absolutely revolutionary, and there are few movements that could not under appropriate circumstances become revolutionary. Strong commitment to revolutionary strategy is usually the culmination of a long period of nonrevolutionary activity with limited progress toward movement goals. Intensified efforts to hasten progress have a disturbing effect on the community. When the community fails to define these disturbances as the expression of social protest (see Chapter 12) because of fear or lack of understanding, they brand them as revolutionary and call for repressive measures that leave only illegitimate tactics at the movement's disposal.

The accusation of revolutionary aims and values is a common tactic of groups threatened by a movement. Those who fight segregation or demand collective bargaining are said to be "threatening our whole way of life." In the United States during World War I the International Workers of the World (the Wobblies) concentrated their efforts on organizing migratory laborers in the West. Employers' organizations were able to stimulate government repression of these efforts by branding the I.W.W. as revolutionary. Publics readily acceded to this definition because of the normal tendency to translate every lesser issue into an aspect of the larger preoccupation with the war. Strikes were viewed as treason—actions against wartime national interest—and people readily believed that the I.W.W was receiving money from

---

[13] Frantz Fanon, *The Wretched of the Earth,* tr. by Constance Farrington (New York: Grove Press, Inc., 1963), p. 113; copyright 1963 by *Présence Africaine.*

[14] Ibid., p. 73.

Germany to undermine American participation in the war.[15]

Although revolutionary themes are far from dominant in today's black movements, they have markedly increased in importance over the past few decades. Whites did not initially view black movements as revolutionary, except in the South. The appeal was to traditional values of equality, freedom, and respect for law. Opinion polls today show majority support for black objectives but growing opposition to the means they employ.

Much of white support for Negro rights appears to be lip service, an approval of rights without a corresponding commitment to do anything to grant them. But the strategy that Negroes have found to be effective in moving the society to effective action also threatens the secure, orderly world of white America. As white people feel threatened, pushed, and even overpowered by demands for rapid change, they come closer to defining the movement, whatever its goals may be, as dangerous and truly revolutionary. In turn, their preference for moderation and gradualism convinces Negroes that a lessening of protest would mean the end of progress. Thus the cycle that leads a social movement into increasing reliance upon aggressive displays of power is set in motion.[16]

The very fact of objective improvement in the position of a class of people makes traditional limitations more frustrating. For example, to the poor black who cannot afford to dine out, a segregated restaurant is only a minor irritant. But when blacks can pay the price, their arbitrary exclusion from the better restaurants becomes an intense irritant. George S. Pettee suggests the term *revolutionary cramp* to identify the resulting feeling. "The cramped individual is one who not only finds that his basic impulses are interfered with, or that he is threatened

by various ills, this is to say, who is deprived of liberty and security, but who also feels that this repression is unnecessary and avoidable, and therefore unjustifiable."[17]

Blacks experience ideological, social, economic, and political cramp. The ideological cramp is the discrepancy between the promise of desegregation and the reality of tokenism. Social cramp comes from the persistence of social barriers while legal and economic limitations are falling away. Economic cramp is expressed in the growing bitterness and frustration of unskilled and undereducated blacks who find jobs that they could fill growing scarcer as the society becomes more affluent. Political cramp grows from the inability of the government machinery to adjust quickly and decisively enough to satisfy the demands of the discontented classes.[18]

It is neither accidental nor unusual that revolutionary cramp should become intense after a period of improving conditions. As James Davies has stated the J-curve hypothesis: "revolution is most likely to take place when a prolonged period of rising expectations and rising gratifications is followed by a short period of sharp reversal, during which the gap quickly widens and becomes intolerable."[19] Davies documents the hypothesis on the basis of the French Revolution, conditions in the American South before the Civil War, the German prelude to Nazism, and the status of American blacks prior to the violence of the 1960s. The J-curve hypothesis is offered as a necessary but not sufficient condition for revolution. Thus Davies asserts that revolution will not break out without

---

[15] Michael R. Johnson, "The I.W.W. and Wilsonian Democracy," *Science and Society,* 28 (Summer, 1964), 257–74.

[16] Killian, *The Impossible Revolution?*, p. 88.

[17] George S. Pettee, *The Process of Revolution* (New York: Harper and Row, Publishers, 1938) p. 33.

[18] Killian, *The Impossible Revolution?*, pp. 58–64.

[19] James C. Davies, "The J-curve of Rising and Declining Satisfactions as a Cause of Some Great Revolutions and a Contained Rebellion," in Graham and Gurr, eds., *History of Violence,* 690, *see also* 690–730.

such a pattern of change but that other conditions are necessary to insure the outbreak.

REVOLUTION AND AFTERMATH. The revolutionary movement rejects the folk prescriptions for bringing about change and openly repudiates, or is forced to repudiate, claims to respectability within the established order. As we have pointed out earlier, however, the degree of change advocated may not indicate the degree of change that a movement actually brings about. An apparently conservative movement may set in motion a series of changes with extensive ramifications. Or what appears to be a demand for major changes may turn out to alter nothing but superficial forms or the occupants of established positions. It has even been argued that the very natures of the revolutionary movement and of the process of successful revolt undercut any program of change, so that no thoroughgoing change can be effected.[20] Without endorsing the contention in so strong a form we can, however, note some of the influences in this direction.

Because it is not respectable, the revolutionary movement is denied access to the conventional techniques for winning adherents, for appealing to a public, for gaining support of key persons, etc. Consequently, as we have suggested earlier, the revolutionary movement must resort to the use of more blatant power techniques. But the greater the degree to which such techniques are used, the more the chance is that the values of the movement will be compromised in the process. A revolutionary movement that aims to improve the position of minorities, for example, is forced to block palliative programs that reduce protest and to disregard the stated desires of those minority members who do not realize that fundamental change is required to eliminate inequality. Thus constant disregard of the

[20] Pitirim A. Sorokin, *The Sociology of Revolution* (Philadelphia: J. B. Lippincott Co., 1925).

minority's immediate interests and the view that the movement knows better what is good for the minority than they do themselves may develop into an actual hostility toward the minority. Eventually, the interests of that group are served only as a reward for supporting the movement.

Denied access to influence through the legitimate structure, the revolutionary movement must eventually establish its own government to bring about desired reforms. Movements that are not revolutionary usually accomplish their desired reforms through existing machinery. But the successful revolution follows a period of attacking the legitimacy of the existing order and of encouraging people to disobey its dictates. Often law and order themselves have been defined as obstacles to progress. When the revolutionary movement has overcome the existing order, it encounters the new problem of restoring respect for the legitimacy of an order—the new order. There is considerable urgency, since the underlying economic structure and communications system will have been disrupted in revolution. Not only must these functions be restored quickly but attempts at counterrevolution or further revolt from competing movements must be blocked. Under these circumstances a revolution is likely to be followed by a period when the revolutionary regime resorts to techniques reminiscent of the old regime to maintain its control and restore minimum order.

During this period the problem of power predominates over the problem of societal reform in the preoccupations of the revolutionaries. From their standpoint the ultimate possibilities of accomplishing long-range reform depend on successfully maintaining control and civil order in the short run. But the reforms may also be stifled in the long range. The movement may lose popular support because it appears to have repudiated all its former idealism, and the loss of popular support will force even more exclusive concern with the retention of power. Internal control of the movement shifts to those who have the skills most needed at the moment, including the human insensitivities necessary to subjugate the populace. Once these leaders are in control, the reformers may never again have crucial influence. Furthermore, the practical difficulties of instituting reforms and of gaining popular support for reforms believed to be in the people's interests and the increasing preoccupation with the details of administering reforms rather than with the broad outlines of the reforms themselves cause the reformers to think in terms of an ever longer time span for successful achievement.

One striking feature during this period of consolidation of power is internal dissension within the victorious movement. Minor internal dissension in a movement not yet in power becomes serious when the movement acquires power. In the precarious state of initial control, any internal dissent makes the movement vulnerable to attack and suggests the possibility of defection to one of the competing groups or to the counterrevolution. Consequently, more severe efforts are likely to be made within the movement to suppress dissenting elements. The more repressive policy toward internal disagreement in turn breeds fear and mutual suspicion among the movement leadership.

The power-consolidation period is one that introduces new points of disagreement within the movement. Persons who have agreed on the broad outlines of movement objectives disagree on the immediate techniques of implementation. Especially crucial as a source of dissension are the compromises of program that are made to establish control. And finally, now that the movement has recognized prestige and effective power to bestow on individuals, personal rivalries are likely to come to a head.

These problems of consolidating power over the society and of suppressing internal dissension give rise to a period known dramatically as the reign of terror. The bloodshed of these periods has been extensively depicted in the popular accounts of the French and Russian Revolutions. The succession of leaders, each deposed and guillotined, is a well-known feature of the French Revolution.

Recent discussions place less emphasis on the outcome of the struggle by any particular movement and relate the ultimate outcome of revolutionary transformations to shifts in the class system. One aspect of social change is the shifting concentration of society's wealth and informal power among the classes. While these shifts are taking place legitimate power resists change, so that there develops a discrepancy between formalized power and the functioning of the social and economic order. Ultimately, revolution may be the means whereby the artificially maintained formal authority is deposed and the class that economic and social conditions have made ascendant acquires formal control commensurate with its functioning ascendancy. Thus the end-result of a revolutionary movement will depend upon the degree to which the changes it demands serve to bring the formal prestige and power structure into close coordination with actual societal functioning.

Countermovements

Movements evoke varying kinds and degrees of opposition. Probably most unsuccessful movements arouse no organized or active opposition of any kind. Unopposed movements die through simply being unnoticed or from disillusionment or internal dissension among their members. On the other hand a movement may die from the unanimity of lip service given its program, with the result that no group attaches the program to its primary interests.

Under some circumstances, however, opposition will be focused in a movement with some organization, program, recognized leadership, and membership. The presence of any vested interest group whose prerogatives seem to be threatened by the initial movement is a primary source of countermovements. The likelihood that opposition from vested interests or other groups will be organized into a countermovement depends on the supposed strength of the initial movement itself. The judgment that a movement is potentially strong may come from a belief that its grievances are real. A countermovement is more likely to develop against an initial movement combating widely recognized grievances than against a movement reflecting superficial dissatisfactions.

The public appearance of an initial movement also affects the strength imputed to it. An official interpretation of the successful drive to enact woman suffrage in the Illinois state legislature attributes the success in part to an underestimate of the strength of the drive, with the result that no effective countermovement was organized. Regarding Mrs. Sherman Booth, who did the work of contacting legislators, it was remarked that "she was so obviously helpless that even the bitterest antis did not worry about her."[21]

It is characteristic of countermovements that the effort to defeat or wrest power from the initial movement begins to transcend the original program and ideology in shaping the opposition movement's course. The most important determinant of changes in the ideology of a countermovement is the increasing success or failure of the initial movement. When the latter is weak, the countermovement ideology is likely to describe its personnel as traitors, heretics, conspirators—terms that completely outgroup the members and evoke intolerant suppressive activity. When the initial movement is strong, however, the countermovement cannot afford to attack its members in this manner but must treat them with some respect and depict them as well-meaning but misguided, misled by an

insidious minority, victims of propaganda, and the like.

A more fundamental change in countermovement ideology also takes place with the increasing success of the initial movement. The countermovement begins to adopt popular elements of the initial movement's ideology as its own, attempting thereby to satisfy some of the discontent and also to get the opposed movement identified with only the most extreme portions of its whole program. Where movement and countermovement are of long standing, it is not infrequent for the countermovement eventually to promote everything that the early adherents of the initial movement sought. At times a movement and countermovement become ideologically indistinguishable.

This adoption of the initial movement's ideology by the countermovement can be illustrated in some degree by the anti-socialized medicine movement. From an early tendency to include many types of health insurance and prepayment medical plans within the despised category of socialized medicine, there has been increasing espousal of these same programs as the free enterprise answer to socialized medicine. The definition of the opposed object has been altered, and the countermovement now champions some of the opposed movement's earlier accomplishments. Similar tendencies can be observed in the anti-New Deal movement and the antiprohibition movement. It was a far cry from the 1936 campaign of "repeal social security" to the Eisenhower program to expand social security coverage, for example. Likewise, the antiprohibitionists' claim to be the true advocates of effective liquor control, assuring the public that they would never allow the pre-Prohibition saloon to return to America, represents ideological absorption from the prohibition movement.

The ideology of a countermovement also has certain distinctive characteristics merely because it is more preoccupied with opposing than with promoting a particular pro-

---

[21] The National Woman Suffrage Association, *Victory: How Women Won It* (Bronx, N.Y.: H. W. Wilson Co., 1940), p. 86.

gram. Suggestive in this regard is an interesting study by Elizabeth Herzog comparing the kinds of arguments used by the pros and the cons in response to questions dealing with several issues of interest to the United States government. The most important difference lay in the relative emphasis upon means or ends:

It was found repeatedly that those who reported in favor of a program or policy tended to speak in terms of the objective: the ends to be served, the needs to be met. The opposition, on the other hand, tended to voice objections to the means proposed, insisting either that these would not achieve the objective or that their concomitants and results would be so bad as to offset any possible gains—or both.[22]

Whether a similar difference applies to the ideologies of pro- and countermovements and whether the results apply generally or merely to the rather moderate kinds of proposals included in the study constitute questions for further investigation.

The significant long-range effects of the conflict of movement and countermovement may be not so much in the ultimate victory of one or the other in the power struggle but in the effect on societal myth. We speak of myth in a sense similar to that defined by Malinowski, not as a sort of primitive science or recreational speculation but as a statement of supposed reality which serves "to strengthen tradition and endow it with a greater value...."[23] While

myth for Malinowski always refers to the supernatural, we use it more broadly, as dealing with *beliefs concerning fundamental reality that justify prevailing institutions.* Countermovements depend chiefly on evoking the established myths of the society to oppose change. However, as a countermovement absorbs elements from the new movement's ideology it must reinterpret the societal mythology into consistency with these additions. It is thus through the agency of the countermovement that far-reaching changes are incorporated into the society's values without loss of continuity. Thus today the ideas of free enterprise, civil rights, and the republican form of government persist as strongly as ever, but they have been extensively modified from their earlier meanings by the very activities of their staunchest defenders.

We have been speaking of countermovements led and supported by members of the leading interest groups in the community, whose prerogatives are threatened. These are the countermovements with which the initial movement is most likely to achieve some accommodation. But there are at least two other important constituencies for those countermovements that are generally subsumed under the name of *backlash.* The first are groups who thrive on conflict and often play a deviant role in the community until they find an unpopular enemy. Opposing an unpopular movement gives them license to fight and to transform their troublemaking into an admirable cause. One such group that developed in reaction to youthful rebellion in 1969 is the British skinheads, described briefly by Robert Toth.

22 Elizabeth Herzog, "Patterns of Controversy," *Public Opinion Quarterly,* 13 (Spring, 1949), 42.
23 Bronislaw Malinowski, *Magic, Science, and Religion* (Garden City: Doubleday and Company, Inc., 1954; first published 1925), p. 146.

Battling Skinheads of London Plague Police

Robert C. Toth

LONDON—The latest mutation in far-out youth, the skinheads, have come down from the trees and begun to give English police "some cause for concern."

With closely cropped hair and with steel-toed boots, they are the antithesis of the beatniks, the hippies and the flower people. They are, in fact, the backlash to the unwashed longhairs who speak of love and peace when not attacking the American Embassy.

Skinheads would love nothing better than to kick in a few hippie heads, and while that has not happened on a large scale yet, the possibilities have made Scotland Yard anxious.

"Skinheads refer to hippies as hairies and hate them," said a Scotland Yard official, "or they call them those lazy louts around Eros," a statue in Picadilly Circus around which hippies gather.

"And they believe the Hell's Angels were hired as stewards at the pop concert in Hyde Park last July to keep them, the skinheads, suppressed," the official added.

DAMAGE HELD DOWN

More than 250,000 people, by police estimate, attended the free, open-air concert July 6 given by the Rolling Stones. The only casualties seem to have been a silver birch sapling and whatever the 3,600 released butterflies were able to eat.

This astonishingly low damage was probably due in large part to the Angels, who stood with Nazi helmets and arms akimbo around the bandstand and even supervised the garbage cleanup later.

English Angels are rather staid compared to their California forebears, but how any leather-jacket

_____

From the *Los Angeles Times*, Sept. 8, 1969. Copyright, 1969, *Los Angeles Times*. Reprinted by permission.

types could get into peacekeeping work must be classed as mysterious. Police insist that neither they nor the park police asked Angels' help. The Communist Party newspaper, Morning Star, claims the program's organizers hired them, but this could not be confirmed.

The Angels' role in July would be enough to explain skinhead enmity. But it goes back at least to Easter when several hundred skinheads attacked a lesser number of Angels whom they call "greasers" because Angels, too, are less than tidy and clean.

Skinheads are agreeably neat, much as were their direct ancestors here, the Mods, a decade ago with smart Italian-style suits and neat shirts and ties. Normal dress for skinheads is conventional— tailored jackets but never flaired trousers, for example.

NOT ASHAMED

Only when skinheads are on their way to an "agro," short for aggravation, do they change into the Huckleberry Finn cutdown jeans held up by suspenders of shocking red, collarless T-shirts and commando boots. The boys are from working class families, school dropouts who are neither proud nor ashamed of their lack of education but generally dissatisfied with their poor jobs and the poverty of their lives.

"It's the boredom really," one skinhead named Chris explained. "We go down and have a fight and it relieves the monotony."

Scotland Yard had feared some kind of violence at the Isle of Wight gathering last weekend of over 100,000 hippies and Bob Dylan fans. Skinheads and Hell's Angels were there, but neither group was very obvious or in great number, presumably because of the distance and cost of getting there.

Of more significance than groups like the skinheads are the less spectacular but more widely supported backlash movements. The movement that nominated George Wallace for United States president in 1968 combined resentments against black movements, peace movements, youth movements, and others. As a repository for a wide assortment of resentments, it linked the many "little people" who felt they were being pushed around. A large component was derived from the bystander publics produced by each conflict engagement. A movement of this sort is not merely the last gasp of a passing generation crying out against change. Rather, the movement displays its vitality by its substantial recruitment of Southern and working-class youth.[24] Unlike the elite countermovements that are prone to adjust their values by making practical accommodations to the success of the intial movement or the borderline deviant countermovements that are likely to be of brief duration and significance, this type of backlash moves in the direction of polarizing the entire society by reinforcing regional and class differences with polarization about the values at issue in the main controversy.

Separatism

Separatism usually results from sustained and ineffectual conflict involving many members of a constituency as individuals or as a movement initially seeking concessions or control. Separatist movements include movements for national independence, such as the American Revolution and the Confederacy, religious sects that set themselves apart from and in opposition to established religion, minority ethnic and racial movements whose aim is to preserve a vanishing national identity and culture or to return the people to their historic homeland, political parties formed by splintering from major parties, and dissenting schools of thought and art.

Unless the separatist movement is able, like the nineteenth-century Mormon Church, to migrate to an uninhabited area to create their own society in isolation, the problems of insulating the movement from the parent society become central to the group's career. The hippie movement of the 1960s exemplifies the difficulties that one type of separatist group had in seeking coexistence with the larger society.

[24] Seymour M. Lipset and Earl Raab, "The Wallace Whitelash," *Trans-Action,* 7 (December, 1969), 23–35. For a fuller discussion see, by the same authors, *The Politics of Unreason: Right-wing Extremism in America, 1790–1970* (New York: Harper and Row, Publishers, 1970).

The Flowering of the Hippie Movement

John Robert Howard

The greatest fool in history was Christ. This great fool was crucified by the commercial pharisees, by the authority of the respectable, and by the mediocre official culture of the philistines. And has not the church crucified Christ more deeply and subtly by its hypocrisy than any pagan? This Divine Fool, whose immortal compassion and holy folly placed a light in the dark hands of the world.*
The Vision of the Fool, Cecil Collins

This article is written for people who, in future years, may want to understand something of the hippie movement. To that end, I have (1) described

From *The Annals of the American Academy of Political and Social Science,* 382 (March, 1969), 43–55. Reprinted by permission.

* Cecil Collins, *The Vision of the Fool* (London: Grey Walls Press, n.d.).

the hippie scene as an anthropologist might describe the culture of a South Sea island tribe, (2) reviewed some of the more prominent "explanations" for the movement, and (3) advanced what seems to me to be a useful theory of the hippie phenomenon.

The data for this article were drawn from literature by and about hippies and other Bohemians in American society, and from extensive informal participation in the hippie movement.

THE HIPPIE SCENE

I first heard the term "hippie" in the Fall of 1966. I had gone to the Fillmore Auditorium in San Francisco to hear a rock musical group, one of a number which had formed as a result of the smashing impact of the Beatles upon youth culture. The Fillmore previously had presented mostly black performers, but, increasingly, white rock groups were being featured.

A new cultural style was evolving and was on display that evening. The rock group blasted its sound out through multiple amplifiers, the decibels beating in on the room like angry waves. Above and behind them, a melange of colors and images played upon a huge movie screen. Muted reds and somber blues spilled across the screen, shifting and blending, suddenly exploding like a burst of sunlight let into a dark room, then receding slowly like a gentle tide. Bright images and jagged shapes leaped out from the screen, only to be washed away by the colors before appearing again. Image and color fused and swirled, then melted apart. Film-clips of old serials played on two smaller screens suspended high on the walls of either side of the hall, while shifting multicolored lights illuminated the dancers, the shafts of yellow and blue and red seeming to leap and bounce off the frenetic dance floor. The total effect was that sought by the Dadaists in the early 1920's, a breaking up of traditional linear habits of thought, a disconnection of the sensory apparatus from traditional categories of perception.

Late in the evening, I fell into conversation with a gaily dressed couple, and, in the course of an exchange of remarks, the girl referred to the persons at the dance as "hippies." I had not heard the term before and asked them of its derivation but they had no idea how it had originated.[1] As we parted, neither they nor I realized that within nine months, there would be no hamlet or haven in the United States that would not have heard of hippies. Within a year, young people by the thousands were to stream to San Francisco—hippie heaven—while little old ladies in Des Moines trembled at this new evidence that the foundations of the Republic were crumbling.

THE LIFE AND DEATH OF HAIGHT-ASHBURY

Before the rise of Haight-Ashbury, the aspiring writer or artist from the Midwest fled to Greenwich Village. By the summer of 1967, Haight-Ashbury had replaced the Village as the place to go, and, indeed, people were leaving the Village to move to San Francisco. The words of Horace Greeley, "Go west, young man," had rarely been so diligently heeded.

The Haight-Ashbury area was for many years an upper-middle-class neighborhood. Haight Street was named for Henry Haight, a conservative former governor of California, who would be appalled could he have foreseen that his name was to be associated with the "love generation."

As the city grew and the residents of the area prospered, they moved out and rented their property. Eventually, the expanding black population began to move in and, in the late 1950's and early 1960's, were joined by beatnik refugees from the North Beach area of the city. Eventually, in this relatively tolerant community, a small homosexual colony formed. Even before the hippies appeared, then, Haight-Ashbury had become a kind of quiet Bohemia.

---

[1] During the 1950's the term "hipster" was used by beatniks and those familiar with the beat scene. It had several meanings. The hipster was an individual whose attitude toward the square world (a steady job, material acquisitions, and the like) was one of contempt. He shared with beats an appreciation of jazz-cum-poetry, drugs, and casual sex. The hipster might also be a kind of confidence man, sustaining his participation in the beat scene by some hustle practiced on squares. The word "hip" identified these orientations. "Hip" and "hep" were common words in the jive-talk of the 1940's; both indicated familiarity with the world of jazz musicians, hustlers, and other colorful but often disreputable types. I suspect that the word "hippie" derives from "hipster" which, in turn, probably derived from "hip" or "hep."

"Hippie" is a generic term. It refers to a general orientation of which there are a number of somewhat different manifestations. In the following section, I shall discuss four character types commonly found on the hippie scene: (1) the visionaries, (2) the freaks and heads, (3) the midnight hippies, and (4) the plastic hippies.

The Visionaries

The visionaries gave birth to the movement. It lived and died with them in Haight-Ashbury. Let us attempt here to understand what happened.

The hippies offered, in 1966 and 1967, a serious, though not well-articulated, alternative to the conventional social system. To the extent that there was theory of change implicit in their actions, it might be summed up by the phrase "transformation by example."[2] Unlike political revolutionaries, they attempted no seizure of power. Rather, they asked for the freedom to "do their thing," that is, to create their own social system. They assumed, implicitly, that what they created would be so joyous, so dazzling, so "groovy" that the "straight"[3] would abandon his own "uptight" life and come over to their side. A kind of anti-intellectualism pervades hippie thinking; thus, their theory of change was never made explicit.

The essential elements in the hippie ethic are based on some very old notions—the mind-body dichotomy, condemnation of the worship of "things," the estrangement of people from each other, and so on. Drastically collapsed, the hippie critique of society runs roughly as follows:

---

[2] Interestingly, Martin Buber, in *Paths in Utopia*, suggested that the example of the *kibbutz* might transform the rest of society. The values of the *kibbutzim* and those of the hippie movement are not dissimilar.

[3] We shall have occasion to speak frequently of "straights." The derivation of the word is even more obscure than that of "hippie." At one time, it had positive connotations, meaning a person who was honest or forthright. "He's straight, man" meant that the referent was a person to be trusted. As used in the hippie world, "straight" has a variety of mildly to strongly negative connotations. In its mildest form, it simply means an individual who does not partake of the behavior of a given subculture (such as that of homosexuals or marijuana users). In its strongest form, it refers to the individual who does not participate and who is also very hostile to the subculture.

Success in this society is defined largely in terms of having money and a certain standard of living. The work roles which yield the income and the standard of living are, for the most part, either meaningless or intrinsically demeaning. Paul Goodman, a favored writer among the young estranged, has caught the essence of this indictment.

Consider the men and women in TV advertisements demonstrating the product and singing the jingle. They are clowns and mannequins, in grimace, speech, and action. . . . What I want to call to attention in this advertising is not the economic problem of synthetic demand . . . but the human problem that these are human beings working as clowns; and the writers and designers of it are human beings thinking like idiots. . . .

> "Juicily glubbily
> Blubber is dubbily
> delicious and nutritious
> —eat it, kitty, it's good.[4]"

Further, the rewards of the system, the accouterments of the standard of living, are not intrinsically satisfying. Once one has the split-level ranch-type house, the swimming pool, the barbecue, and the color-television set—then what? Does one, then, measure his progress in life by moving from a twenty-one-inch set to a twenty-four-inch set? The American tragedy, according to the hippies, is that the "normal" American evaluates himself and others in terms of these dehumanizing standards.

The hippies, in a sense, invert traditional values. Rather than making "good" use of their time, they "waste" it; rather than striving for upward mobility, they live in voluntary poverty.

The dimensions of the experiment first came to public attention in terms of a number of hippie actions which ran directly counter to some of the most cherished values of the society. A group called the Diggers came into existence and began to feed people free in Golden Gate Park in San Francisco and in Constitution Park in Berkeley. They themselves begged for the food that they prepared. They repudiated the notion that the

---

[4] Paul Goodman, *Growing Up Absurd* (New York: Vintage Books, 1960), pp. 25–26.

right of people to satisfy their basic needs must be mediated by money. If they had food, one could share it with them, no questions asked. Unlike the Salvation Army, they did not require prayers as a condition of being fed; unlike the Welfare Department, they did not demand proof of being without means. If a person needed lodgings, they attempted to make space available. They repudiated the cash nexus and sought to relate to people in terms of their needs.

Free stores were opened in Berkeley and San Francisco, stores where a person could come and take what he needed. Rock groups such as Country Joe and the Fish gave free concerts in the park.

On the personal level, a rejection of the conventional social system involved dropping out. Given the logic of the hippie ethic, dropping out made sense. The school system prepares a person for an occupational role. The occupational role yields money and allows the person to buy the things which society says are necessary for the "good life." If society's definition of the good life is rejected, then dropping out becomes a sensible action, in that one does not want the money with which to purchase such a life. By dropping out, a person can "do his own thing." And that might entail making beads or sandals, or exploring various levels of consciousness, or working in the soil to raise the food that he eats.

They had a vision of people grooving together, and they attempted to remove those things which posed barriers—property, prejudice, and preconceptions about what is moral and immoral.

By the summer of 1968, it was generally felt by those who remained that Haight-Ashbury was no longer a good place. "It's pretty heavy out there on the street," a former methedrine addict remarked to me as we talked of changes in the community, and his sentiments were echoed in one of the underground newspapers, *The San Francisco Express Times:* "For at least a year now . . . the community as a common commitment of its parts, has deteriorated steadily. Most of the old crowd is gone. Some say they haven't actually left but are staying away from the street because of bad vibrations."

In those streets, in the summer of 1968, one sensed despair. Significantly, the agencies and facilities dealing with problems and disasters were still very much in evidence, while those which had expressed the *élan* and hope of the community either no longer existed, or were difficult to find. The Free Clinic was still there, as was the shelter for runaways, and the refuge for persons on bad trips; but free food was no longer served in the parks, and I looked for several days before finding the Diggers.

Both external pressures (coercion from the police and various agencies of city government) and internal contradictions brought about the disintegration of the experiment. Toward the end of this paper, I shall discuss external pressures and why they were mounted. At this point, I am analyzing only the internal contradictions of the hippie ethic.

Stated simply, the argument is as follows. The hippies assumed that voluntarism (every man doing his thing) was compatible with satisfying essential group and individual needs and with the maintenance of a social system in which there was an absence of power differentials and invidious distinctions based on, for example, wealth, sex, or race. That assumption is open to question. Voluntarism can work only where the participants in a social system have a sufficient understanding of the needs of the system to be willing to do things which they do not want to do in order for the system to persist. Put somewhat differently, every system has its own needs, and where voluntarism prevails, one must assume that the participants will both understand what needs to be done and be willing to do it.

Let me clarify by way of illustration. I asked one of the Diggers why they were no longer distributing food in the park.

Well, man, it took a lot of organization to get that done. We had to scuffle to get the food. Then the chicks or somebody had to prepare it. Then we got to serve it. A lot of people got to do a lot of things at the right time or it doesn't come off. Well, it got so that people weren't doing it. I mean a cat wouldn't let us have his truck when we needed it or some chick is grooving somewhere and can't help out. Now you hate to get into a power bag and start telling people what to do but without that, man, well.

By refusing to introduce explicit rules designed to prevent invidious power distinctions from arising, such distinctions inevitably began to appear. Don

S., a former student of mine who had moved to Haight-Ashbury, commented on the decline of the communal house in which he had lived.

We had all kinds of people there at first and anybody could stay if there was room. Anybody could crash out there. Some of the motorcycle types began to congregate in the kitchen. That became *their* room, and if you wanted to get something to eat or a beer you had to step over them. Pretty soon, in a way, people were cut off from the food. I don't mean that they wouldn't give it to you, but you had to go on their "turf" to get it. It was like they had begun, in some very quiet and subtle way, to run things.

In the absence of external pressures, the internal contradictions of the hippie ethic would probably have led to a splintering of the experiment. Significantly, many of the visionaries are trying it again outside the city. There are rural communes throughout California. In at least some of them, allocation of task and responsibility is fairly specific. There is the attempt within the framework of their core values—freedom from hang-ups about property, status, sex, race, and the other furies which pursue the normal American—to establish the degree of order necessary to ensure the persistence of the system within which these values are expressed.

The visionaries used drugs, but that was not at the core of their behavior. For that reason, a distinction between them and more heavily drug-oriented hippies is legitimate. The public stereotype of the hippie is actually a composite of these two somewhat different types.

Let us now discuss the heavy drug users.

Freaks and heads

Drugs are a common element on the hip scene. The most frequently used are marijuana and hashish, which are derived from plants, and Lysergic Acid Diethylamine (LSD) and methedrine, which are chemical derivatives. Much less commonly used are opium and heroin. The plant derivatives are smoked, while the chemicals are taken orally, "mainlined" (shot into a vein), or "skin-popped" (injected under the skin). To account for the use of drugs among hippies, one must understand something of the mythology and ideology surrounding their use.

Marijuana is almost universally used by the hip

and by hippies.[5] For some, it is simply a matter of being "in"; others find it a mild euphoriant. A subgroup places the use of drugs within a religious or ideological context.

Both freaks and heads are frequent users of one or more psychedelic agents; the term "freak," however, has negative connotations, suggesting either that the user is compulsive in his drug-taking, and therefore in a "bag," or that his behavior has become odd and vaguely objectionable as a result of sustained drug use. The mild nature of marijuana is suggested by the fact that, among drug users, one hears frequent mention of "pot heads" but never of "pot freaks." LSD and methedrine, on the other hand, seem to have the capacity to induce freakiness, the "acid freak" and the "speed freak" being frequently mentioned.

In 1966 and 1967 in Haight-Ashbury, the drug of choice for those who wanted to go beyond marijuana was LSD. An elaborate ideology surrounded its use, and something of a cult developed around the figure of Dr. Timothy Leary, the former Harvard professor who advocated it as the answer to the world's problems.

The LSD ideology

The major tenets of the ideology may be summed up as follows.

(1) LSD introduces the user to levels of reality which are ordinarily not perceived.

The straight might speak of "hallucinations," suggesting that the "acid" user is seeing things which are not real. The user admits that part of his trip consists of images and visions, but insists that part also consists of an appreciation of new and more basic levels of reality. To make the straight understand, some users argue that if a microscope had been placed under the eyes of a person during the Middle Ages, that person would

---

[5]Marijuana, also known as "weed," "pot," "grass," "maryjane," and "reefers," has not been proven to be physically addictive. It is one of a number of "natural" hallucinogens, some of which are found growing around any home: Jimson weed, Hawaiian wood roses, common sage and nutmeg, and morning-glory seeds. There are claims in Haight-Ashbury that the dried seeds of the bluebonnet, the state flower of Texas, have the same property. In California, the bluebonnet is called "Lupin" and grows wild along the highways, as does the Scotch broom, another highly praised drug source.

have seen a level of reality for which there was no accounting within the framework of his belief system. He possibly would have spoken of "hallu-cinations" and demanded that microscopes be banned as dangerous.

Some users speak of being able, while on a trip, to feel the rhythm and pulse of the earth and to see the life within a tree. They contend that the trip leaves them with a capacity to experience reality with greater intensity and greater subtlety even when not high.

(2) LSD develops a certain sense of fusion with all living things.

The tripper speaks of the "collapse of ego," by which he means a breakdown of the fears, anxieties, rationalizations, and phobias which have kept him from relating to others in a human way. He also speaks of sensing the life process in leaves, in flowers, in the earth, in himself. This process links all things, makes all things one.

The ideology can be expanded, but these are some of its essential elements.

Three things account for the decline of "acid" use in Haight-Ashbury :(1) personal disillusionment on the part of many people with Timothy Leary, (2) a rise in the frequency of "acid burns" (the sale of fake LSD), and (3) the rise of methedrine use.

Let us deal with the decline and fall of Timothy Leary. Leary was, in a sense, the Johnny Appleseed of LSD. He was hailed by some as a new Christ. When the unbelievers began to persecute him, however, he had need of money to fight various charges of violation of drug laws which carried the possibility of up to thirty years in jail. Possibly for that reason, he embarked upon what was, in essence, a theatrical tour. His show (billed as a religious celebration) was intended to simulate the LSD experience. It was bad theater, however, and consisted mostly of Leary sitting cross-legged on the stage in front of candles and imploring his audience, which might have had to pay up to $4.00 apiece, to commune with the billion-year-old wisdom in their cells. Leary's tour coincided in time with the beginning of his decline among hippies, and probably contributed to it. Addi-tionally, the increased demand for LSD brought on traffic in fake "acid," the unsuspecting would-be tripper possibly getting only baking soda or pow-dered milk for his money.

In 1967 methedrine replaced LSD as the major drug in Haight-Ashbury. There is no evidence that marijuana is physically harmful. The evidence on LSD is open to either interpretation. Methedrine, on the other hand, is a dangerous drug. It is a type of amphetamine or "pep" pill and is most com-monly referred to as "speed." Taken orally, it has the effect of a very powerful amphetamine. "It uses up body energy as a furnace does wood. ... When it is shot [taken in the blood stream] it is said to produce an effect of watching the sun come up from one hundred miles away. And the user is bursting with energy." In an interview which I counducted in July 1968, a former "speed freak" discussed the effects of the drug.

You're really going. You know you can do anything when you're high on speed. You seem to be able to think clearer and really understand things. You feel powerful. And the more you drop the stuff the more you feel like that. It kills the appetite so, over time, malnutrition sets in. You're in a weakened state and become susceptible to all kinds of diseases. I caught pneumonia when I was on speed. But I couldn't stop. I was falling apart, but it was like I was running so fast I couldn't hit the ground. It was a kind of dynamic collapse.

The use of methedrine seemed to have leveled off in mid-1968 and was even possibly in decline.

From 1966 through 1968, there was a discernible pattern in drug use in Haight-Ashbury, a pattern which has relevance in terms of the effectiveness of drug laws. I would advance as a proposition that the volume of use of a drug is determined not by the laws, but by the effects of the drug. If a drug is relatively harmless (as with marijuana), its use will spread, irrespective of severe laws. If it is harm-ful, its use will be limited, despite more lenient laws (as with methedrine). That heroin, cocaine, and the like have not penetrated Haight-Ashbury can probably be explained in terms of the fact that their deleterious effects are well known. Methedrine was an unknown, was tried, and was found to be dangerous; thus, one frequently hears in Haight-Ashbury the admonition that "speed kills."

In summary, then, the pattern of use probably reflects the effects of each drug. Marijuana, being relatively mild, is widely used. LSD is much more powerful; a person may have a good trip or a very bad one; thus, its pattern of use is checkered. Methedrine is dangerous; consequently, powerful sentiment against it has begun to form. Hippies, then, are very much predisposed to go beyond tobacco and alcohol in terms of drug use, and if what has been said here is correct, the pattern of use should be seen as a realistic response to the effects of the drugs available to them.

The plastic hippie

Everybody is familiar with the story of King Midas who turned whatever he touched into gold. Ironically, this faculty eventually brings tragedy to his life and, with it, some insight into the nature of love. In a strange kind of way, the story of Midas is relevant in terms of the hippie movement. The hippies repudiate the values of conventional society, particularly as these relate to work and commerce. They decry the consumption mania— the ethic and passion which compels people to buy more and more. They grieve that so many people are locked into the system, making or selling things which other people do not need, and buying from them equally useless things. The system is such that every man is both victim and victimizer.

Their repudiation of conventional society brought notoriety to the hippies, and, ironically, they themselves became a marketable item, another product to be hawked in the market place. And the more they defamed the commercial process, the more they became a "hot" commercial item.

Those who used the hippie phenomenon to make money appealed in part to an audience which wanted to be titillated and outraged by revelations about sex orgies and drug parties, and in part to adolescents and young people were were not inclined to drop out, but who viewed wearing the paraphernalia of the hippie—love beads, head-bands, Benjamin Franklin eyeglasses, leather shirts, and the like—as daring and exciting. These were the plastic hippies.

Any movement runs the risk of becoming merely a fad, of being divested of substance and becoming mostly style. Symbols which might at one time have powerfully expressed outrage at society's oppression and absurdity become merely fashionable and decadent. By the spring of 1968, the plastic hippie was common in the land, and leather shirts and trousers sold in Haight-Ashbury shops for

more than S100. Some of the suits at Brooks Brothers did not cost as much.

In April of 1968, I interviewed Deans of Students at four Bay Area colleges—San José State College, Stanford University, Foothill Junior College, and the College of San Mateo. The research, financed by the United States Office of Education, focused on students who dropped out of school to live the hippie life. Uniformly, the deans indicated that, despite appearances, there were very few hippies on campus. Despite long hair and beads, most of their students were as career-oriented and grade-conscious as ever. They wore the paraphernalia of the outsider, but were not themselves outsiders.

The plastic hippies have, unintentionally, had an impact on the hippie movement. First, in one important respect, their behavior overlaps with the core behavior of the true hippie—many are users of marijuana. By the summer of 1968, the demand for "grass" had become so great that there was a severe shortage in the Haight-Ashbury area. Beyond the obvious consideration of price, the shortage had two consequences. The number of "burns" increased, a "burn" being the sale of some fraudulent substance—alfalfa, oregano, ordinary tobacco, and the like—as genuine marijuana. And a synthetic marijuana was put on the market.

The "pot squeeze" and the resulting burns, along with persistent but unsubstantiated rumors that "the Mob" (organized crime) had moved in and taken over the lucrative trade, contributed to what was, by the summer of 1968, an accelerating sense of demoralization in the Haight-Asnbury community.

The midnight hippie

Most hippies are in their teens or early twenties. There are a significant number of people, however, who share a whole complex of values with hippies, but who are integrated into the straight world to the extent of having families and careers. Most of these people are in their thirties. They were in college during the 1950's and were nonconformists by the standards of the time. Journalists and commentators of the 1950's decried the apathy of youth and spoke of a "silent generation." These people were part of that minority of youth who were not silent. They were involved, even then, in civil rights and peace and the other issues which were to engage the passions of youth in the 1960's.

There was no hippie scene into which these people could move. They could have dropped out of school, but there was no Haight-Ashbury for them to drop into. Consequently, they finished school and moved on into the job world. Significantly, many are in professions which can accommodate a certain amount of Bohemianism. They teach in colleges and universities and thus avoid working the conventional nine-to-five day, or work as book salesmen on the college and university circuit. Relatively few are in straight occupations such as engineering or insurance or banking. They are in jobs in which there is some tolerance for new ideas and which facilitate trying out various styles of life.

The midnight hippie provides an important link between straight society and the hippie world. The straight finds hippies strange, weird, or disgusting. Therefore, he views any action taken against them as justified. The midnight hippie, on the other hand, looks straight. He has a straight job, and does not evoke the same immediate hostility from the straight that the hippie does. The midnight hippie's relative social acceptance allows him to articulate and justify the hippie point of view with at least some possibility of being listened to and believed.

HIPPIES, BEATS, AND THE "LOST GENERATION"

How may we account for the hippie phenomenon? Is it simply the traditional rebellion of youth against parental authority, or does it have more profound implications for the society and greater consequences for those who take part in it?

I am inclined to view it as more significant than previous youth movements. Hippies differ in important ways from the beats of the 1950's or the "lost generation" of the 1920's, two groups with whom they have often been compared. In attempting to account for the movement, I have developed a theory of social deviance which identifies its unique features and yields certain predictions with regard to its future.

VERTICAL AND LATERAL DEVIANCE

The literature of sociology is rich in theories of deviance. Some focus on "cause," as, for example, the delinquency theories of Cloward and Ohlin

which suggest that lower-class boys, in the face of inadequate opportunities to realize middle-class goals, resort to various forms of unlawful behavior. Others deal with the process whereby a person learns to be a deviant, Howard Becker's paper "Becoming a Marijuana User" being a major example.

In the approach taken here, neither cause nor process is the focus. Rather, I identify two types of deviance: vertical and lateral. The dimensions of each type seem to be useful in differentiating the hippies from earlier Bohemians, and in reaching conclusions about their future.

Vertical and lateral deviance occur in the context of social systems in which differentiations according to rank exist, that is, officer-recruit, teacher-student, adult-child, boss-employee, or guard-convict. Inevitably, certain privileges and prerogatives attach to the superior ranks. That is one of the things which makes them superior. Adults can smoke, consume alcoholic beverages, obtain drivers' licenses, vote, and do a host of other things which are denied to children or teen-agers.

Vertical deviance occurs when persons in a subordinate rank attempt to enjoy the privileges and prerogatives of those in a superior rank. Thus, the ten-year-old who sneaks behind the garage to smoke is engaging in a form of vertical deviance, as is the fourteen-year-old who drives a car despite being too young to get a license and the sixteen-year-old who bribes a twenty-two-year-old to buy him a six-pack of beer. They are attempting to indulge themselves in ways deemed not appropriate for persons of their rank.

Lateral deviance occurs when persons in a subordinate rank develop their own standards and norms apart from and opposed to those of persons in a superior rank. Thus, the teen-ager who smokes pot rather than tobacco is engaging in lateral deviance, as is the seventeen-year-old girl who runs away to live in a commune, rather than eloping with the boy next door. Lateral deviance occurs in a context in which the values of the non-deviant are rejected. The pot-smoking seventeen-year-old, wearing Benjamin Franklin eye-glasses and an earring, does not share his parents' definition of the good life. Whereas value consensus characterizes vertical deviance, there is a certain kind of value dissensus involved in lateral deviance.

Let us explore the implications of these two types of deviance.

Where vertical deviance occurs, power ultimately remains with the privileged. The rule-breaker wants what they have. They can control him by gradually extending prerogatives to him in return for conforming behavior. They have the power to offer conditional rewards and, in that way, can control and shape the deviant's behavior. The sixteen-year-old is told that he can take the car if he behaves himself at home. Where lateral deviance occurs, the possibility of conditional rewards being used to induce conformity disappears. The deviant does not want what the privileged have; therefore, they cannot control him by promising to let him "have a little taste." From the standpoint of the privileged, the situation becomes an extremely difficult one to handle. Value dissensus removes a powerful lever for inducing conformity. The impotent, incoherent rage so often expressed by adults towards hippies possibly derives from this source. A letter to the Editor of the *Portland Oregonian* exemplifies this barely controlled anger.

Why condone this rot and filth that is "hippie" in this beautiful city of ours? Those who desecrate our flag, refuse to work, flaunt their sexual freedom, spread their filthy diseases and their garbage in public parks are due no charitable consideration. The already overloaded taxpayer picks up the bill.

If every city so afflicted would give them a bum's rush out of town, eventually with no place to light, they might just wake up to find how stupid and disgusting they are. Their feeling of being so clever and original might fade into reality. They might wake up and change their tactics.[6]

The second implication follows from the first. Being unable to maintain control via conditional rewards, the parent, adult or other representative of authority is forced to adopt more coercive tactics. This, of course, has the consequence of further estranging the deviant. What constitutes coercion varies with the situation, and can range all the way from locking a teen-age girl in her room to setting the police on anyone with long hair and love beads. Lateral deviance has a certain potential for polarization built into it. To the

extent that polarization takes place, the deviant becomes more committed to his deviance.

The third implication follows from the first two and allows us to differentiate hippies from earlier Bohemians. Bennett Berger, the sociologist, contends that the Bohemians of the 1920's and the hippies of the 1960's are similar as regards ideology. Borrowing from Malcolm Cowley's *Exile's Return*, he identifies a number of seemingly common elements in the thinking of the two groups, and, following Cowley, suggests that Bohemians since the mid-nineteenth century have tended to subscribe to the same set of ideas. The ideology of Bohemianism includes: the idea of salvation by the child, an emphasis on self-expression, the notion that the body is a temple where there is nothing unclean, a belief in living for the moment, in female equality, in liberty, and in the possibility of perceiving new levels of reality. There is also a love of the people and places presumably still unspoiled by the corrupt values of society. The noble savages may be Negroes or Indians or Mexicans. The exotic places may be Paris or Tangier or Tahiti or Big Sur.[7]

I would dispute Bennet Berger's analysis and contend that the differences between the hippies and the lost generation are quite profound. The deviant youth of the 1920's simply lived out what many "squares" of the time considered the exciting life—the life of the "swinger." Theirs was a kind of deviance which largely accepted society's definitions of the bad and the beautiful. Lawrence Lipton contrasted values of the lost generation with those of the beatniks, but his remarks are even more appropriate in terms of the differences between the lost generation and the hippies.

Ours was not the dedicated poverty of the present-day beat. We coveted expensive illustrated editions and bought them when we had the ready cash, even if it meant going without other things. We wanted to attend operas and symphony concerts, even if it meant a seat up under the roof in the last gallery or ushering the rich to their seats in the "diamond horseshoe." . . . We had disaffiliated ourselves from the rat race . . . but we had not rejected the rewards of the rat race. We had expensive tastes and we meant to indulge

---

[6] Letter to the Editor, *Portland Oregonian*, July 31, 1968, p. 22

[7] Bennett Berger, "Hippie Morality—More Old Than New," *Trans-Action*, Vol. 5, No. 2 (December 1967), 19–20.

them, even if we had to steal books from the bookstores where we worked, or shoplift, or run up bills on charge accounts that we never intended to pay, or borrow money from banks and leave our co-signers to pay it back with interest. We were no sandal and sweatshirt set. We liked to dress well, if unconventionally, and sometimes exotically, especially the girls. We lived perforce on crackers and cheese most of the time but we talked like gourmets, and if we had a windfall we spent the money in the best restaurants in town, treating our friends in a show of princely largess.[8]

Could they have been more unlike the hippies? The lost generation was engaging in vertical deviance. They wanted the perquisites of the good life but did not want to do the things necessary to get them. They were a generation which had seen its ranks severely decimated in World War I and, having some sense of the temporal nature of existence, possibly did not want to wait their turn to live the beautiful life. Their deviance was at least comprehensible to their elders. They wanted what any "normal" person would want.

From 1957 through 1960, the beat movement flourished, its major centers being the North Beach section of San Francisco and Greenwich Village in New York. The beat movement and the hippie movement are sufficiently close in time for the same individual to have participated in both. Ned Polsky, writing about the Greenwich Village beat scene in 1960, indicated that "the attitudes of beats in their thirties have spread rapidly downward all the way to the very young teen-agers (13–15)."[9] It is not unlikely, then, that some hippies began as beats. There are several reasons for suggesting beat influence on the hippie movement. The beat indictment of society is very much like that of the hippies. Lipton recounted Kenneth Rexroth's observations on the social system and its values:

As Kenneth Rexroth has put it, you can't fill the heads of young lovers with "buy me the new five-hundred-dollar deep-freeze and I'll love you" advertising propaganda without poisoning the very act of love itself; you can't hop up your young people with sadism in the movies and television and train them to commando tactics in the army camps, to say nothing of brutalizing them in wars, and then expect to "untense" them with

Coca Cola and Y.M.C.A. hymn sings. Because underneath . . . the New Capitalism . . . and Prosperity Unlimited—lies the ugly fact of an economy geared to war production, a design, not for living, but for death.[10]

Like the hippie a decade later, the beat dropped out. He disaffiliated himself, disaffiliation being "a voluntary self-alienation from the family cult, from moneytheism and all its works and ways." He spoke of a New Poverty as the answer to the New Prosperity, indicating that "it is important to make a living but it is even more important to make a life."

Both the hippie and the beat engage in lateral deviance. Their behavior is incomprehensible to the square. Why would anyone want to live in poverty? Given the nature of their deviance, they cannot be seduced back into squareness. Lipton recounts the remarks of a beat writer to the square who offered him an advertising job: "I'll scrub your floors and carry your slops to make a living, but I will not lie for you, pimp for you, stool for you, or rat for you."[11]

The values of beats and hippies are virtually identical: the two movements differ principally with regard to social organization. Hippies have attempted to form a community. There were beat enclaves in San Francisco and New York, but no beat community. The difference between a ghetto and a community is relevant in terms of understanding the difference between the two movements. In a ghetto, there is rarely any sense of common purpose or common identity. Every man is prey to every other man. In a community, certain shared goals and values generate personal involvement for the common good. Haight-Ashbury was a community in the beginning but degenerated into a ghetto. Significantly, however, more viable rural communities have been established by hippies in response to the failure of urban experiment. The beats had neither any concept of community nor any dream of transforming society.

Given their attempt to establish a viable community, the hippies will probably survive longer than the beats, and should have a more profound impact upon the society. As has been indicated, if a society fails to seduce the lateral deviant away from his deviance it may move to cruder methods (police

[8] Lawrence Lipton, *The Holy Barbarians* (New York: Grove Press, 1959), p. 284.

[9] Ned Polsky, "The Village Beat Scene: Summer 1960," *Dissent,* Vol. 3, No. 3 (Summer 1960), 341.

[10] Lipton, *op. cit.,* p. 150.

[11] *Ibid.*

harassment, barely veiled incitements to hoodlums to attack the deviants, and the like). A functioning community can both render assistance to the deviant in the face of these assaults and sustain his commitment to the values which justify and explain his deviance.

The beats, then, have influenced the hippies. Their beliefs are very similar, and there is probably an overlap in membership. The hippies' efforts to establish self-supporting communities suggest, however, that their movement will survive longer than did that of the beats.

In summary, the hippies have commented powerfully on some of the absurdities and irrationalities of the society. It is unlikely that the straight will throw away his credit cards and move to a rural commune, but it is equally unlikely that he will very soon again wear the emblems of his straightness with quite so much self-satisfaction.

SOURCES OF SEPARATISM. In locating the sources of separatism we see that sectarian movements have more in common with nationalistic and nativistic movements that is immediately apparent. Behind the issues of theology, faith, and practice about which controversies have raged, many investigators have noted the dissent of a disadvantaged minority. Several decades ago John L. Gillin pointed out that religious sects have their origin in social rather than in religious antagonisms. Social heterogeneity and the breakdown of insularity bring diverse groups into contact. Power is unequally distributed, and sects arise in the disadvantaged groups. The religious sects are but part of the effort of those groups who do not possess legitimate power to "...organize themselves so as to be able to deal as classes with the upper classes."

Almost every sect of Protestant Christendom has originated in the lower classes as a protest against what they felt was oppressive by the superior classes. That their griefs were largely social is shown by their leanings toward apocalyptic hopes of a kingdom in which their wrongs would be righted; and the seriousness of their oppressions is indicated by the fact that they expected it to come suddenly. Their doctrines apart from this are mostly negative, another indication that they arose out of class consciousness.[25]

[25] John L. Gillin, "A Contribution to the Sociology of Sects," *American Journal of Sociology*, 16 (September, 1910), 245.

In accounting for separatist movements the crux of the matter is not discovering the sources of divergent interests but finding out why a sufficient number of persons should organize for separation rather than for some other manner of handling their differences. Longstanding dissent and persisting minorities are characteristic of any organization. Reform and control movements that take place entirely within an established group are the source of continuing adaptation by the organization to social and cultural change. The struggles may be bitter and chronic without splintering the group.

Three broad types of conditions will determine whether such internal movements become splinter groups. These are (1) the extent of integration of the dissenting group into the parent body; (2) the power of the parent body to enforce its legitimate actions and suppress dissent; and (3) the ability of the parent body to absorb dissent either through changing in response to growing pressures or by encompassing internal variability.

Merely expressing dissent within an established body is different from the more serious step of relinquishing the privileges and self-identification of membership. Consequently, only those who have been consistently deprived of the normal privileges of membership or who have failed to attain an emotionalized self-identification with the group are likely to band together in a separatist movement. This observation sheds light on the economic foundations of religious sectarianism. Questions of faith and practice are constantly raised and disputed within established churches by persons who participate with full equality in church activities, who have a great deal in common with fellow members in spite of points of disagreement, and who are accepted within the group so long as they do not press their dissent too far. But when the disputants feel that they are not accepted as first-class members of the church and experience no deep emotional response to the ceremony and ritual of the organization, it is relatively easy for them to break away from the parent group. The movement for church reform in England that subsequently became the sectarian movement known as Methodism was built around working-class people who constantly found conceptions of white-collar respectability held against them in the church and who experienced only frustration in the reserved expressiveness of the established church ceremony.

V. O. Key, Jr., suggests what may be a special application of this principle in generalizing about the minor political parties, which serve as a form of dissent against the two major parties in the United States.

The distribution of minor-party strength suggests a hypothesis about the conditions that permit and discourage minor-party activity. The strength of these parties has been greatest in those western states without strong traditions governing political behavior, with a social system in a state of flux, and with comparatively weak and unstable governing groups. Third-party strength over the entire period of 1864–1936 was at its weakest in the South. Social stratification, political tradition, and the pressure to conform exerted by the governing groups have been very different in the South than in the West. One kind of condition may facilitate the operation of dissenting groups; the other definitely discourages such movements.[26]

[26] V. O. Key, Jr., *Politics, Parties, and Pressure Groups* (New York: Thomas Y. Crowell Company, 1953), p. 302.

Integration into the established body is weakened by the availability of a well-established substitute group with which the dissenters may continue to identify while relinquishing identification with the parent body. This principle may be one of the reasons for the sectional basis of many third-party movements. John D. Hicks has observed that the two major parties must try to command support in every section of the United States. "Let a whole section begin to feel that its interests are being permanently discriminated against by both old parties, and the time for a plain-spoken third party, organized mainly along sectional lines, is about ripe."[27] Thus the loyalty due one's region can provide a rallying point that offsets the loss of identification with an established political party.

Many organizations undergo a progressive departure from the interests of rank and file members. Organizations often lose sight of other issues in their preoccupation with strategy, procedural matters, and legalities. Fred E. Haynes regards this tendency in political parties as a source of third-party movements:

The two great political parties have had for their principal interests political and constitutional reforms, while the group of lesser parties—beginning with the Anti-Monopoly and Reform parties of the seventies, continuing with the Greenback and Labor parties of the eighties, and ending with the Populist party of the nineties—have voiced the protests of people who felt keenly the need of economic and social change.[28]

The power of a parent body to suppress dissent depends upon its possession of values that the members are unwilling to dispense with. Widely divergent elements are maintained within the confines of each major political party in the United States

[27] John D. Hicks, "The Third Party Tradition in American Politics," *Mississippi Valley Historical Review,* 20 (June, 1933), 27–28.
[28] Fred E. Haynes, *Third Party Movements Since the Civil War* (Iowa City: The State Historical Society of Iowa, 1916), p. 470.

because a dissenting group can hardly hope to duplicate the entrenched and elaborate political machinery nor to overcome traditional party loyalty in the majority of voters. The Catholic Church has been able to make the fear of excommunication and other penalties more effective against separatism than have most of the Protestant churches.

Absence of a strong nationalistic tradition and the dominance of democratic traditions among the controlling elements facilitate the toleration of minorities within the confines of the state. Frequently the confidence of the parent body in its own principles allows toleration of divergent elements within its membership. In spite of. the strict insistence on certain core beliefs and practices, the Roman Catholic Church has exceeded the Protestant denominations in its ability to permit divergent forms of religious practice, as represented by the various orders, within the church.

REASSIMILATION OF SEPARATIST MOVEMENTS. In spite of conflicts of interest, the values held by members of most separatist movements are extensively identified with those of the parent body. Even a subject people borrows much from the dominant group's culture. Often revivalistic values are essential to differentiate the separatists from the parent body. Gandhi had to *teach* the Indians to value their traditional culture, such as their primitive methods of spinning cloth, which they were fast relinquishing. Trivial issues are magnified to justify separatism. Because of the underlying value identity and because of the sacrifices demanded by sustained separatism, separatist values are usually short-lived.

The observation by William B. Hesseltine that all successful new political parties in the United States have achieved success very quickly is relevant to the foregoing generalization.[29] One unsuccessful election often is sufficient to convince people that their vote is being wasted or to raise doubts about the social acceptability of their political alignment.

On the other hand the values of separatism may gradually be displaced by a return to conventionality within the movement itself. Bringing some people who have been relatively isolated from meaningful group ties into a satisfying group relationship is a socializing experience. And the personal dedication to a set of values arouses a desire for respectability where little had existed before. After a classic examination of the successive waves of new Christian sects that developed in Europe and America after the Protestant Reformation, H. Richard Niebuhr reached the following conclusion:

...one phase of the history of denominationalism reveals itself as the story of the religiously neglected poor, who fashion a new type of Christianity which corresponds to their distinctive needs, who rise in the economic scales under the influence of religious discipline, and who, in the midst of a freshly acquired cultural respectability, neglect the new poor succeeding them on the lower plane. This pattern recurs with remarkable regularity in the history of Christianity. Anabaptists, Quakers, Methodists, Salvation Army, and more recent sects of like type illustrate this rise and progress of the churches of the disinherited.[30]

[29] William B. Hesseltine, *The Rise and Fall of Third Parties: From Anti-masonry to Wallace* (Washington, D.C.: Public Affairs Press, 1948).

[30] H. Richard Niebuhr, *The Social Sources of Denominationalism* (New York: World Publishing Company, Meridian Books, 1957; first published 1929), p. 28.

17

MEMBER COMMITMENT AND CONTROL

Values and power refer to external effects of a social movement. Values identify the changes sought in the social order, whether by direct overhaul of the system or by reform of individual ideals. Power is the ability to control men and events on behalf of the movement. Conflict is a relationship into which movements are frequently precipitated during efforts to exercise power. But successful contention and the implementation of value and power goals require a movement of sufficient size and suitable internal organization. A substantial and committed body of adherents is the fundamental resource of a movement. Hence in the next two chapters we shall consider the ways in which movements secure commitment and maintain control over their members and the forms of gratification that make participation in the movement a source of intrinsic satisfaction. The latter topic brings us to the third main direction of movement functioning, and we can see how participation orientations support and subvert value and power orientations under various circumstances.

If we are to think effectively about membership, we must leave behind the idea of membership derived from a stable and formalized organization. A movement is a collectivity engaged in sustained collective action to facilitate or impede some change in society. A first criterion of membership is therefore action from time to time in support of the movement. We thus eliminate two categories of persons: first, those who believe in the movement but prefer to take no supporting action and second, those who are willing and anxious to support the movement but are in situations that provide no opportunity to do so.

When we recall that a movement exists through *collective* action, then we must add criteria of group participation to action. A movement member can, therefore, be defined as a person who from time to time acts so as to advance the movement and whose action is oriented to the facts that (1) he identifies himself as a member of a group, pursuing its common goal, (2) he looks to this group (movement) for direction and support in his action, and (3) he is in communication with others of this group in connection with his own action and in defining the goals and strategies of the movement.

Membership can mean widely varied things in different movements. The most important distinction is between respectable movements in contrast to peculiar and revolutionary movements. Membership in the former can be scheduled into a normal life pattern. Hence securing commitment and maintaining control over members of a respectable movement centers about coordinating roles inside and outside the movement. Membership in peculiar and revolutionary movements normally requires a choice between the movement and a normal life style. Hence commitment and control center about facilitating a clear-cut choice and making the choice irrevocable.

In the following pages we begin with discussion of some of the methods used to achieve commitment to a movement. In some cases commitment means an emotional transfer of loyalty and total acceptance of a new belief system, which we know in the religious case as conversion. Next we consider the problems of maintaining member loyalty, especially in those situations that offer crucial challenges to continuing adherence. Finally we examine some of the circumstances under which defections occur in spite of initial commitment and organization control.

Commitment

Commitment to a movement is achieved through esprit de corps; by the provision of secondary rewards for participation; by devices that anchor the individual identity in the movement, often through conversion; and in case of movements strongly at odds with society, by burning the bridges back to conventional life.

ESPRIT DE CORPS. A social movement must weld its members into a group with a strong in-group sense and enthusiasm for the fellowship or comradeship of the movement and give them determination to continue in the face of obstacles. Herbert Blumer makes a distinction between esprit de corps and morale which corresponds in part to the difference between adherence because of the gratification of participation and adherence because of a belief in the program and ideology of the movement. Whereas morale gives "persistency and determination to a movement," esprit de corps gives "life, enthusiasm, and vigor to a movement." Esprit de corps is "the sense which people have of being identified with one another in a common undertaking." In making the distinction Blumer also points out the limitations of a movement too preponderantly built about mere participation orientations, with too little devotion to the values the movement promotes. Except for such infrequent motivations as the desire

for martyrdom, apparent failures may stop new recruitment and lower the enthusiasm of members. Esprit de corps feeds on success, but the test of morale is "whether solidarity can be maintained in the face of adversity."[1]

Blumer suggests three principal techniques through which esprit de corps is developed. These techniques are "the development of an ingroup-outgroup relation, the formation of an informal fellowship association, and the participation in formal ceremonial behavior."[2] Each technique will be considered briefly.

Rosabeth Kanter compares 9 utopian communities that survived for 25 years or longer with 21 that did not survive, in order to identify the commitment mechanisms that contributed to the success of this kind of movement.[3] All communities were founded in the United States between 1780 and 1860. One set of mechanisms found more frequently in successful than in unsuccessful communities she calls renunciation and communion. Renunciation means the disparagement and repudiation of ties that are inconsistent with community ties. Because of the comprehensive demands that a utopian community made on its members, practically all outside ties were to be severed. Besides renouncing loyalties the members learned to think of all other groups as inferior. The successful communities employed a variety of devices to insulate members from the outside world, such as physical separation, distinguishing dress, prohibition of newspapers and books from outside, regulation of visitor arrangements, and ceremonial cleansing after contact with outsiders.

[1] Herbert Blumer, "Collective Behavior," in Alfred M. Lee, ed., *New Outline of the Principles of Sociology* (New York: Barnes and Noble, Inc., 1953), p. 208.
[2] Ibid., p. 206.
[3] Rosabeth M. Kanter, "Commitment and Social Organization: A Study of Commitment Mechanisms in Utopian Communities," *American Sociological Review*, 33 (August, 1968), 499–517.

Kanter's *communion* corresponds with Blumer's informal fellowship. "The emphasis in communion mechanisms is on group participation, with members as homogeneous, equal parts of a whole, rather than as differentiated individuals."[4] Communistic labor, communistic sharing, and regularized group contact contribute to communion.

Whereas these relatively small and compact utopian communities attempted to replace separate cliques and family units with a primary group fellowship of the whole, the typical movement depends largely on the development of a network of primary groups to achieve cohesion. The classic study of the German army in World War II by Shils and Janowitz demonstrates that the key to cohesion lay in the intimate ties of affection and trust that were cultivated in the small groups of soldiers who fought together on the battlefield.[5] A movement places its members in a similarly precarious position in case the movement should fail, and in most cases it depends on the development of cliques consisting of close personal friends to generate enthusiasm and loyalty for the larger unit. The most tangible sense of the movement is the set of interpersonal feelings generated in these primary groups whose members demonstrate together, work together, take risks together, and sometimes dwell together.

Collective ritual is of central importance in welding the movement into a whole. Each movement celebrates special occasions, such as the birthdays of their heroes and the anniversaries of their heroes' great trials. Difficult rituals are memorized and practiced together. Special signs and gestures serve to identify members to one another and to provide a means for jointly renewing the pledge to the cause. And even the most casual and segmental movements develop their own songs. There is a strik-

ing similarity in the songs of movements that serve quite different objectives, as documented by Roland Warren in a comparison between National Socialist songs in Germany and traditional Christian hymns.[6] To the extent that the shared musical experience contributes to interpersonal cohesion more than to a system of values, the similarity is to be expected. The singing of "We Shall Overcome" has given courage and the assurance of group support to civil-rights activists in many situations of fear and disappointment. Songs of protest that once welded together groups of laboring men as they challenged their employers have become a large part of American folk music.

We are anticipating the later discussion of control over members once they are committed to a movement, since esprit de corps is both part of the committing process and a continuing element of cohesion. Studies of religious and other forms of conversion show the importance of social support during the crucial period of changing loyalties. In the study of a movement whose prediction of world catastrophe was disconfirmed by events, those members who were able to reassess the situation in close association with their intimates from the movement lost none of their conviction, but those who underwent the experience alone abandoned their commitment.[7]

REWARDS FOR PARTICIPATION. Under limited circumstances it is possible to reward a faithful adherent to a movement by supplying opportunities for prestige in the larger institutional structure. Ordinarily there are severe limitations in this respect because a movement seeks change that undermines some aspect of the established order, and institutional prestige depends

---

4 Ibid., p. 510.
5 Edward A. Shils and Morris Janowitz, "Cohesion and Disintegration in the Wehrmacht in World War II," *Public Opinion Quarterly,* 12 (Summer, 1948), 280–315.

6 Roland L. Warren, "*German Parteilieder* and Christian Hymns as Instruments of Social Control," *Journal of Abnormal and Social Psychology,* 38 (January, 1943), 96–100.
7 Leon Festinger, Henry W. Riecken, Jr., and Stanley Schacter, *When Prophecy Fails* (Minneapolis: University of Minnesota Press, 1956).

upon support for the conventional order. However, there are at least two principal circumstances in which such rewards can be offered. First, the activist may be sought as a curiosity. Advocates of bizarre ideas are widely sought as highly paid lecturers in American society. And whether the motive be guilt, ennui, or a genuine concern with problems, leaders of minority protest groups find many doors open to them. Second, and more commonly, movements are useful in the continuing struggles between established groups in society. One group then rewards active adherents to the movement as a way of strengthening its position vis-à-vis the adversary. During the nineteenth-century struggle between the rising class of industralists and the traditional landowning class in America, the abolition movement was a useful weapon in the hands of the industrialists. The effective campaigner could count on their support and prestige. In universities there is commonly a degree of tension between academic and administrative personnel. A faculty member's stature among his peers is instantly enhanced if he appears able to "stand up to the administration," as indicated by his participation in a movement that is troublesome to the officials. The easiest way for faculty members to become popular with students is to take advantage of the normal youthful tensions against the establishment.

In movements which are less able to appeal for support to major segments of the institutional structure, rewards are sometimes in the nature of special license for members. Whenever the members of a movement claim a special moral, ethical, intellectual, or aesthetic superiority over others, the superiority tends to become an accomplished fact that is unimpaired by actual behavior. In some of the small Christian sects today, a member who has been "saved" feels free to gamble and do other things against the religious code occasionally because being saved makes him thenceforth incapable of sinning. The pattern here is an old one, going back at least as far as the Medieval "Free Spirit" movements.

The core of the heresy of the Free Spirit lay in the adept's attitude towards himself: he believed that he had attained a perfection so absolute that he was incapable of sin.... The "perfect man" could always draw the conclusion that it was permissible for him, even incumbent on him, to do whatever was commonly regarded as forbidden. In a Christian civilization, which attached particular value to chastity and regarded sexual intercourse outside marriage as particularly sinful, such antinomianism most commonly took the form of promiscuity on principle.... What emerges then is an entirely convincing picture of an eroticism which, far from springing from a carefree sensuality, possessed above all a symbolic value as a sign of spiritual emancipation —which incidentally is the value which "free love" has often possessed in our own times.[8]

ANCHORING THE SELF-CONCEPTION TO THE MOVEMENT. Every group that commands loyalty from its members must facilitate the incorporation of membership into the self-conception. The more that an individual identifies himself with a movement—thinking of himself first as a civil-rights worker, as a minuteman, as an ecumenicist, as a conservationist—the more dependable his loyalty is likely to be.

Essien-Udom describes a portion of the procedure by which new members are initiated into the Nation of Islam, popularly known as the Black Muslims:

Initiation of new members is aimed at facilitating their withdrawal from society, reorienting their values, and maintaining discipline, cohesion, loyalty, and enthusiasm in the movement. The first step at withdrawal and emotional detachment from the "normal" society and the individual's beliefs about his past is the neophyte's negation of his "Negroness," i.e., all the stereotypes associated with

8 Norman Cohn, *The Pursuit of the Millennium* (New York: Oxford University Press, 1957), p. 152.

Negroes. He is taught to believe that his nationality is "Muslim" or "Asiatic." He is made to change his name—a process of dissociating himself from the manipulated image of the Negro. He is taught to submit himself totally to the will of Allah and Muhammad. Withdrawal is facilitated by lessons which are intended to give him new perspectives and values. This continues long after the individual has become a registered Muslim.[9]

The symbolic mechanism of changing names is supplemented by such devices as imposing special dietary rules regarding food, demanding modesty of dress that sets them apart, and requiring the support of "Brothers" and "Sisters" when they are in trouble.

The self-conception reflects commitments and investments. When the individual goes on record in public in support of a movement, he becomes committed because persons around him are inclined to treat him as an adherent and to expect continued adherence from him. The public ritual of accepting the religious obligation before a large congregation that includes both the faithful and curious outsiders is a standard practice of evangelistic movements. Investment refers to the personal sacrifices that a person makes for the movement. As he foregoes the comforts and security he would otherwise like to have in order to participate in the movement, his investment increases. If he does not withdraw early, it becomes increasingly more difficult for him to avoid a strong personal identification with the movement.

Activity in the movement contributes toward anchoring the self-conception when it gives the individual a part to play in a drama that highlights the movement's goals and when it supplies successful experience that builds self-confidence. Merrill Proudfoot's *Diary of a Sit-in* is a valuable document because it reports the transformation

of a white Protestant minister from an anxious but sympathetic bystander to a confident and determined activist through the medium of participation.[10] The lunch counter sit-in nicely simplifies the plot of civil rights, for it shows how irrational are the practices of segregation, how simple it would be to set them aside, and how clear is the moral issue. Proudfoot reports surprise at seeing himself step forward to confront the system and its spokesmen, and he experiences elation as he discovers a new dimension within himself—the capability of some heroism in a worthy cause.

Kanter found processes of mortification and surrender present in her sample of successful utopian communities. Mortification procedures include confession and mutual criticism; rigid social stratification according to spiritual attainments but negation of stratification by skill, intelligence, or expertise; formal probationary periods; and deindividualizing devices such as a uniform style of dress and communal dwellings that minimize opportunities for privacy. Mortification emphasizes the individual's smallness before the greatness of organization, helps to strip away all anchorages for the identity apart from the movement, and leaves no way to achieve a sense of worth except by adhering to movement norms. Surrender is a fusing of personal identity with the group identity, based on a personal experience of great power and meaning from participation in the movement. The institutionalized awe depends upon both an ideology with vast and pervasive implications and minute regulations of behavior. A decision-making process characterized by distance and mystery contributes to this awe. The devices of mortification and surrender strip away non-movement identities and merge the individual with the group in movements that require a radical rejection of normal life as a condition of membership.

In cases where a fundamental and whole-

---

9 E. U. Essien-Udom, *Black Nationalism: A Search for an Identity in America* (Chicago: University of Chicago Press, 1962), pp. 201–2.

10 Merrill Proudfoot, *Diary of a Sit-in* (New Haven, Conn.: College and University Press, 1962).

hearted reversal of former values, attitudes, and beliefs is required for commitment to the movement, we can speak of conversion. While the religious experience is best known, there are many kinds of secular conversion. Most so-called religious conversion is not truly conversion to a new value system but regeneration in the values and organization where loyalty has been lodged since early childhood. There is typically an awakening in adolescence when contact with the wider world of reality brings an awareness of the significance of religious beliefs that have heretofore been given only lip service.[11] But students of those true conversions in which change is from irreligion to deep involvement in a religious movement, from religion to the promotion of secularism, or from individualism to activity in a socialist cause generally find more continuity between the old and new commitments than appears on the surface. In a study of conversion to a small and esoteric millenarian movement in California, Lofland and Stark note three circumstances that universally preceded contact with the movement in the case of subsequent converts.[12] All suffered tensions from frustrated aspirations; all had long been accustomed to attach religious rather than political or psychiatric interpretations to events; and all had passed through a period of searching, during which they either tried out several religious groups or explored occult conceptions of reality, mixing conventional religious elements with the esoteric. Toch reports that converts have typically been trained in childhood to a set of absolute values and beliefs that are not supportable in reality. Maturation and fuller contact with the real world brings disillusionment. But the need for absolutes persists, and in

a frenzy of panic the convert adopts a new set of absolutes or a new way of life that promises attainment of the old absolutes.[13]

The drastic repudiation of conventional patterns of speech, dress, living arrangements, and occupations among youthful adherents to beat movements, hip movements, New Left, and other protest movements indicates a widespread conversion experience. But conversion to these movements is often seen as an attempt to attain values that parents teach their children but do not follow themselves. In a Harvard University commencement address, enunciating the perspective of youthful protesters in 1969, Meldon Levine said, "We are *not*—as we have been accused— conspiring to destroy America. We are attempting to do precisely the reverse: we are affirming the values which you have instilled in us and which you have taught us to respect."

It is possible to understand these conversions and many others as disturbance of the customary balance among a variety of values. A person who is fully integrated into society achieves a set of compromises among the values he espouses and much compartmentalization of values into different spheres of life. Values of generalized human compassion or equalitarianism are consigned to the charitable sphere; values of personal intimacy and trust may be prominent in family life but irrelevant to the work life. The longer and more completely a young person is insulated from workaday situations in which he would have been forced by necessity to compromise and rewarded systematically for doing so, the greater the likelihood that he will become disproportionately committed to some values at the expense of others. The resulting disillusionment is culminated by conversion to the world view of a movement that promises a way of life in which the favored values are not compromised. In

---

11 Kurt and Gladys Lang, *Collective Dynamics* (New York: Thomas Y. Crowell Company, 1961), pp. 157–58.
12 John Lofland and Rodney Stark, "Becoming a World-saver: A Theory of Conversion to a Deviant Perspective," *American Sociological Review*, 30 (December, 1965), 862–75.

13 Hans Toch, *The Psychology of Social Movements* (Indianapolis, Ind.: The Bobbs-Merrill Co., Inc., 1965), pp. 111–20.

these cases conversion is not the substitution of one value for another but is the radical decision to accept some of the conventional values without adopting the full complex of values in which they are customarily embedded.

Accounts of conversion experiences indicate one or a few crucial precipitating experiences that allow the accumulating but only dimly recognized disillusionment to be brought dramatically to the forefront of attention, so as to prepare the individual for the radical break with his past. Lofland and Stark note that each of their converts had reached a natural turning point in his life—a second failure in college, failure in business, or career disruption because of a long illness. The precipitating experience or turning point makes the individual unusually receptive, and conversion occurs if the individual finds social support in a movement promoting appropriate values. The instant conversion becomes real and lasting if the message of the movement is buttressed by intense and gratifying social ties and the external ties are severed.

Methods used by Communist Chinese to win the adherence of noncommunists call for a radical conversion, for the repudiation of old identities and the substitution of new ones that are lodged in the Communist movement. At the close of the Korean War a small team of social scientists attempted through intensive interviews with Chinese prisoners to reconstruct the process by which the Communist Chinese government sought to convert recently conquered and recruited Nationalist Chinese soldiers to communism and to incorporate them as dependable members of their organization. Investigators found no indication of the use of primary groups and buddy relationships. But they found a highly rationalized and consistent set of procedures that were highly effective so long as the military organization remained intact.

Three learning situations were central to the process. (1) A regular feature of the period of induction into the Communist army was airing-of-grievances or "speak bitterness" meetings, devoted to airing criticisms against the Nationalist army and its officials. Every man was required to join in the criticism, and it was made clear that his standing in the Communist army depended upon the public evidence he gave of correct thinking. (2) Lectures expounding Communist values, followed by discussion groups, were a part of the daily schedule. (3) Meetings for self-and mutual-criticism were a keystone in the continuing program to establish and maintain correct thinking and correct speaking. As in airing-of-grievances and lecture-discussion sessions, aggressive participation was required. Failure to confess personal derelictions with sufficient ardor insured that the individual would be subject to vigorous attack himself. Failure to join ardently in exposing the faults of one's associates brought the individual under attack for insufficient diligence in the cause. After the men passed through the painful shock of the first few sessions of criticism, they found themselves embedded in a highly effective system of control by peers, not unlike some contemporary forms of encounter group therapy.[14]

BURNING THE BRIDGES. In movements that demand complete and exclusive dedication and in those that are adjudged revolutionary or peculiar, adherence is reinforced by requiring the member to burn his bridges behind him at the time of entry. When a movement is viewed as seriously threatening, the community applies pressures that are supposed to break up the movement and frustrate its operation. Often they succeed to a considerable degree. But in the process they brand the known members or make former membership a stigma that can still be applied to the individual many years later. By taking this step the community, in effect, burns the

[14] William C. Bradbury, *Mass Behavior in Battle and Captivity*, Samuel M. Meyers and Albert D. Biderman, eds. (Chicago: University of Chicago Press, 1968), pp. 179–86.

bridges and makes it difficult for an adherent ever to be fully accepted again into the community. He may be officially welcomed and even gain prestige as one who knows what the dreaded group is really like from firsthand experience. Like many ex-Communists in the United States during the 1950s, he may be valued as an informer. But he is likely to be shunned in more intimate relations and not fully trusted. There is a continuing suspicion that the bad judgment that first led him to embrace the movement will lead to other mistakes that may endanger his friends and associates.

The movements that most consistently force their members to sever ties with the outside world are the millennial groups. Cohn's history of millennial movements during the later Middle Ages in Europe is replete with such instances. The heresy of the "free spirit" flourished for several centuries, commencing with the eleventh. Central to its value system was the cult of poverty. At a time of increasing wealth, adherents abandoned their possessions for the sake of extreme destitution. Priests and minor clerks frequently relinquished their careers. By violent attacks upon the regular clergy and the church, they made return more difficult.[15] During the sixteenth century, Anabaptism flourished, and in common with many such groups proclaimed the importance of common ownership of property. In those instances when the doctrine was implemented, a great practical incentive to remain in the movement was created.[16]

The pattern of common ownership has often acted as a bond among movement members. In the several communistic societies in nineteenth-century United States, so meticulously described by Charles Nordhoff, the common ownership of property restrained the member who felt dis-

illusionment over the movement.[17] More recently the Kingdom of Father Divine, which flourished in Harlem and spread in black communities throughout the United States during the 1930s and 1940s, established communal living. Although members worked for pay on the outside, their wages belonged to Father Divine, who took care of all their needs. Even further, husbands and wives were separated within the kingdom so that there could be no conflict of loyalty, and children were abandoned when their parents entered the Kingdom.[18]

In the great rash of millennial movements in the East Indies, Africa, and many other underdeveloped areas under colonial rule, the bases for traditional living have often been almost irrevocably undermined by actions required of adherents.

Expecting, and hoping for, the millennium, people have destroyed their cattle, their crops, their means of livelihood. Southern Bantu died in the thousands in the nineteenth century by killing off their cattle and destroying their crops in response to a prophet's appeal; in this century, Eskimos in Greenland became so convinced of the imminence of the millennium that they stopped hunting and ate into their stores of food.[19]

Although the aftermath was often disillusionment, the people were seldom able to return to the way of life they had left. They were separated permanently from the comfortable acceptance of traditional life, and they possessed a new perspective and a new sense of group identity that enhanced their receptiveness to later movements of a more activist nature.

The return to normal life can also be

---

15 Cohn, *Pursuit of the Millennium,* pp. 149–94.
16 Ibid., pp. 272–83.

17 Charles Nordhoff, *The Communistic Societies of the United States* (New York: Schocken Books, Inc., 1965; first published 1875).
18 Hadley Cantril, *The Psychology of Social Movements* (New York: John Wiley and Sons, Inc., 1941), pp. 123–43.
19 Peter Worsley, *The Trumpet Shall Sound: A Study of 'Cargo' Cults in Melanesia* (London: MacGibbon and Kee, 1957), p. 225.

blocked by a systematic indoctrination regarding the nature of conventional life and the motives of persons who do not support the movement. An essential element in puritanical movements is a well-developed ideology that finds sinister purposes and evil consequences in the forbidden types of behavior. The temperance movement of recent decades has principally been directed against socially accepted practices in the consumption of alcoholic beverages rather than against the disorganized patterns of the period before Prohibition.[20] Because the consumption of alcohol has become a routine and ceremonial part of respectable social life at the higher socioeconomic levels, the abstainer is constantly subjected to pressure to accept a drink in a conventional situation, to the detriment of the movement. Exaggerated accounts of the effects of small doses of alcohol and lurid tales of personal deterioration and corruption, which are supposed to have been concealed from public view by members of the degenerate's family, are accepted as fact within the movement. Such beliefs tend to isolate the adherent from the social circles in which drinking is acceptable.

A dogma regarding the hypocrisy and shallowness of conventional adult life is inculcated in the cluster of contemporary movements prevalent among youth and sometimes called the New Left. Deeply enough internalized, these beliefs block any sincere effort to establish a conventional life and insure an interpretation of events that increases the chances that such an effort will fail. Although the temperance supporter or the New Leftist may withdraw from active adherence to the movement, there is no bridge that will move him fully into the nonmovement round of life. He is likely, then, to remain in limbo, experiencing ambivalence and limited personal effec-

20 Joseph R. Gusfield, *Symbolic Crusade: Status Politics and the American Temperance Movement* (Urbana: University of Illinois Press, 1963).

tiveness for a considerable period thereafter.

Member Control

CONTROL IN CRISIS SITUATIONS. Securing an initial commitment to a movement and maintaining control over adherents who are already committed shade into each other. As the foregoing discussion has demonstrated, commitment is not the sudden and decisive transformation so often envisioned in the popular imagery of conversion. No matter how effective are the initial commitments, a movement requires a continuing system for control over the members.

Extraordinary control is required when circumstances create tests of member loyalty that exceed those for which the ordinary commitment process has prepared them. Such tests originate both from within and without the movement. The movement may demand unusual sacrifice from a member or require that he violate his own moral convictions or personal loyalties in its cause. A demand for him to perform violence or sabotage or to break with family and friends will tax a member's loyalty. From outside the movement comes persecution that can be escaped or at least mitigated by repudiating the movement or assuming a less active role. The adherent is then forced to make an irrevocable choice between the movement and the outside world. Commitment techniques that lead to repudiation of the outer world in advance of the test or create disillusionment and partial withdrawal from the outer world prepare the individual for the ultimate test. But added support and discipline are required on such occasions.

The start of the eighteenth century in France saw heightened intolerance and repression of Protestantism. Because of persecution many Calvinists publicly converted to Catholicism and others fled to England and Holland. Among those who remained, the prophetic trance became an increasingly important aspect of religious observance. For the Camisards of the Cévennes region the experience of ecstacy included four stages: the warning, the whisper of inspiration, the prophecy, and the gift. The trance was manifested by behavior characteristic of a pathological seizure and by glossolalia (speaking with tongues). Rosen observes that "such experiences were undoubtedly needed to encourage the Camisards in the unequal contest in which they were involved."[21] The trance supplied them with assurance that they were indeed under divine guidance and had protection that was sufficient to offset the unfavorable odds against which they labored.

[21] George Rosen, *Madness in Society: Chapters in the Historical Sociology of Mental Illness* (New York: Harper and Row, Publishers, 1968), p. 211; see also pp. 209–12.

Perhaps the extreme test of control is martyrdom. While some members make their way into persecuted movements because they find martyrdom congenial, a movement under consistent persecution cannot depend upon such exceptional motivations to maintain its strength. It must develop a systematic program to prepare its members for the imminent possibility of martyrdom. In the following reading Donald Riddle has shown how the Christians, under persecution by Rome, developed such an elaborate program. In the early stages of Christianity, when persecution was sporadic and frequently more a matter of spontaneous mob action than of institutionalized legal process, there was little opportunity to prepare members systematically for the test. But in later periods the procedures described were consistently practiced.

The Martyrs

Donald W. Riddle

PERSECUTION AND SOCIAL CONTROL

The aspect of the behavior of the martyrs as the result of social control has not yet received adequate attention, though it is of the highest significance. It is obvious that control is a major factor of religion, and the experiences of the martyrs constitute an example of control which is most instructive. Clearly the fate which was suffered by not a few of them was one against which ordinary impulses vehemently rebel. Nevertheless, for certain reasons, and in spite of the usually held points of view, it was not unwillingly accepted. The willingness to undergo suffering is a social attitude which was present as the result of control. It follows that the behavior of the martyrs offers a field for investigation in

From Donald W. Riddle, *The Martyrs: A Study in Social Control* (Chicago: University of Chicago Press, 1931), Chapters 1–4, passim. Reprinted in part by permission of the University of Chicago Press and the author.

which much may be learned of the technique of control as it is applied in the religious life, and the sources reflecting their experiences become a veritable laboratory of research. . . .

The elements of the situations which obtained in the best-known cases of Christian martyrdom were simple. The demand on the part of the state in the persecution of Decius, for example, made any subject liable to examination in court. Upon presenting himself, he was faced by a simple alternative: he might confess that he was a Christian, and be remanded for further discipline; or he might deny that he was a Christian, and, upon offering evidence to substantiate his denial, be set at liberty. This procedure reduced the situation to the barest simplicity for both the persecuting and the persecuted groups. . . .

. . . In situations of widespread persecution, or in local situations where one person or a small group was subjected to coercion, the task of the group to which the victims belonged was clearly recognized. So fully was it perceived, indeed, that the terminology which was used to meet it became quite technical. In brief, the task of the Christian group was to secure from those of its adherents who were being tried a confession; while, on the other hand, it was the object of the state to induce them to deny the accusation that they were Christians. . . .

As shall be shown, the Christian groups bent serious effort to assist in the resolution of the doubtful elements in the dilemmas before prospective martyrs. They undertook to prepare such persons as were likely to be examined, so that these would be ready to offer the answer desired by the religious fellowship, hoping thus to inhibit the tendency toward the opposite response. They exerted control even during the conduct of the examination; and after a confession had been made, they frequently found it possible and valuable to keep in touch with the martyr-designate.

The Christian groups accomplished their task by following a specific method. The process was essentially as follows: to secure from its adherents the behavior which was necessary if the movement were to survive, rewards of a sufficiently compelling nature were held forth, so that in the person being examined, or likely to be examined, there would be generated a wish to maintain his present relation. Negative sanction was secured by threatening punishment for failure to do so. The desired goal was repeatedly called to attention by careful visualization. Its realization by others was frequently pictured as a glorious fact. Encouragement was given by the thought of the participation of others in similar experiences, and it was pointed out that failure or success would be witnessed by one's fellows. In specific detail proper attitudes were suggested, stock answers to the prospective questions were taught, and stereotyped arguments were supplied, together with persuasive evaluations and heroic imagery. The attempt was made to induce in the candidate an emotion of overpowering character, so that he might be carried, if he had been sufficiently prepared, through the harrowing experience with a minimum of exception to the type of behavior which had been found to be desirable.

The facts demonstrate that the method followed by the Christian groups was successful to the point that not a few Christians accepted a fate

against which the most basic impulses normally rebel. . . .

THE PREPARATION OF THE MARTYR

The preparation of the martyrs was a process which ranged from extreme informality to specific organization. Of course in the earlier situations technique and method of control had not been acquired, so that it was only in the persecutions proper that the fully worked-out process of control may be seen in operation. The earlier periods are instructive for their evidence of the development of technique.

It was first necessary to induce in the prospective martyr a willingness to undertake the experience, even though he knew it to be unpleasant. The wish for the experience was reinforced by such sanctions as were found to be effective. Rewards for success were suggested with definite imagery, and punishments for failure were pictured with no less specificity. The effect of group contacts was utilized, and from such social influences proper attitudes were engendered and crystallized by powerful indoctrination. All such steps in the process may be seen in the sources which reflect situations of persecution. . . .

It must be understood that not merely a hope of reward was offered but that rewards were assured with exact specification. What the rewards were may readily be discovered. For one thing, it was important to some of the early Christians that death by martyrdom guaranteed resurrection from among the dead, or, as the Greek rather than Jewish thought-patterns of life after death became current, the immediate and personal immortality of the martyr. . . .

Another value which it was alleged was guaranteed by martyrdom was the forgiveness of sins. Since sin is an ever present problem to the religious person and the religious group, it is no accident that the early Christians saw in martyrdom a means of securing the satisfactory solution of a troublesome question and used this as a sanction to induce the martyr attitude. . . .

Still other values were alleged to be secured by martyrdom. One of these, of much greater significance in the ancient world than in the modern scientific world-view, was the triumph over those demonic powers which were so real to the early Christians. Another was the ability to intercede for one's earthly companions, while others were the authority to judge one's judges and the position of coregent with Christ. . . .

It is also clear that the willingness to undergo punishment for the crime of being a Christian was largely induced by the fear of the consequences of failing to confess. The threat of punishment in the afterworld was urged with co-operative force with the rewards which were at the same time promised. In this matter, again, the sanctions were various, ranging from the exclusion from the religious group to alleged fates of a cosmic consequence. The thought that denial not only would entail the loss of fellowship with the church group but would result in eternal punishment in the afterworld appears to have been of considerable influence in inducing the attitude of willingness to suffer as the result of confession. At any rate, the literature of martyrdom repeatedly suggests the fact. . . .

. . . Specific misfortunes immediately following denial were alleged. Cyprian, for example, related a series of such (Treatise iii, 24–26). One denier was forthwith stricken dumb. Another was seized by an evil spirit and made to bite out her own tongue, death quickly followed. . . .

Beside the skillful utilization of the sanctions of reward and punishment, the willingness to undergo martyrdom was induced by a second factor, namely, by indoctrination through the use of sacred scriptures. Evidently it was a source of satisfaction to the martyr to reflect that his fate was so fully under the control of God that it had long ago been foretold. The thought that he was one of a noble company was tremendously effective, and he was conscious of his heroic status largely because he found himself to be in a situation similar to those celebrated in sacred story. In the same source were to be found many comforting exhortations, which, if known and heeded, would greatly assist him by pointing out the position gained by exemplary characters of the past, and promising him a like fame. . . .

Indoctrination was effected not only through the use of Scripture but also by the discipline of church customs. It cannot be too forcibly stressed that the conflict of church and state was a conflict of loyalty to groups. The churches were religious societies, exactly as was the state in its attempt to secure religious conformity to approved patterns. To which society should the Christian affirm loyalty? Membership in the Christian group had appealed to him sufficiently to cause him to join it and to remain in fellowship up to the moment of this crisis. Presumably it had not only brought him satisfactions but had also left its mark upon him in teaching him certain manners and habits. Such factors, when perceived in connection with his as yet unbroken fellowship, strongly influenced him. Common worship, the association of the liturgy, particularly of the common liturgical meal, the practical benevolence practiced by the several societies, and all such social features, operated to unite the members into well-knit groups.

The force of such a relation is apparent in the crises through which the churches passed. It is apparent as fellowship was lost through denial. Much distress followed. The sources suggest that many of those who lacked the courage to confess nevertheless, immediately after defection, returned to their group beseeching restoration to fellowship. Many deniers resorted to the confessors in prison to beg "peace" from them. . . .

The effect of the discipline of custom is seen also in the operation of ritual. The withdrawal of the Eucharist, where most particularly dramatic communion was secured, was a serious matter to deniers. Doubtless in this central sacramental feature of the common worship there was considerable magical value for the devotee. But whatever may have been the motive in ascribing value to the rite, the social effect of its customary celebration is undoubted. It is equally obvious that it operated powerfully in the process of control. . . .

. . . There is abundant evidence that willingness to undergo martyrdom depended largely upon the strength of the social contact of the confessor with his church. This appears indubitably from the fact that martyrdom away from the home associations was held by Christian leaders to be less desirable than the public death of a martyr in the sight of his fellows. . . .

THE PRODUCTION OF ATTITUDES

The goal of the church groups, as general practice became typical, was to anticipate whatever event might ensue in the relations between the state and Christians. Uniformity of behavior was desirable; if each witness might be taught to do exactly what his predecessors had done, the possibility of failure to confess would be much reduced. Failure, when it occurred, came when the witness was unprepared, had not undergone the discipline of normative custom, or was faced by some unforeseen circumstance which impaired the uniformity of the course of events. . . .

In the first place, the answers to the question of guilt were centrally important. The witness must admit that he was a Christian. Consequently, as the acts of the martyrs were published, one sees the skillful use which was made of the court dialogue. By circulating representations of the cases of successful witness, and in then citing the questions asked by the court and the answers given by the confessor, the first necessity, namely, that of suggesting the proper answer to the question of guilt, was met. . . .

There is a hint that a certain posture during the examination was thought to be especially effective. Thus Tertullian: "Then, too, in using such words as these, it (i.e., the soul) looks not to the Capitol, but to the heavens. It knows that there is the throne of the living God, as from him and from thence itself came down" (*Apology* 17).

Certainly it was believed that to make the sign of the cross was efficacious. Tertullian affirms, "We trace upon the forehead the sign" (*On the Crown* 3), and in another place says, "We have faith for our defense, if we are not smitten with distrust also, in immediately making the sign of the cross and adjuring" (*Scorpiace* 1). . . .

The definiteness of these attitudes and the specificity of their functioning were secured by maintaining a degree of fixity of attention upon the end so ardently desired. This prevented the intrusion of unprepared-for eventualities. Control, as is well known, is obtained largely by the focus of attention being fixed upon a given point. The Christian groups maintained, with a high degree of success, such a fixation of attention upon the values which it was thought would lead to the behavior deemed proper. . . .

The discussion of the attitudes which controlled the martyrs necessitates the recognition that in part, at any rate, they were of a psychopathic character. It hardly needs to be said that the experience of martyrdom was one against which ordinary judgment recoils. It will occasion no surprise, then, to find that in cases of martyrdom certain symptoms of a psychosis appear. One finds, for example, a morbid desire for the experience of martyrdom. Even though it may be rationalized that the desire was so keen because of the rewards which were expected to materialize, the affirmation may be offered that the desire was morbid. In the phenomena there appear, too, evidences that there was a morbid pleasure derived from the pains which were endured. Indeed, it seems that martyrdom in the later church occupied the place which in the earlier church was filled by such ecstatic experiences as trance and speaking in tongues. There is a definitely discoverable basis for such phenomena. . . .

THE INFLUENCE OF THE GROUP

. . . True as it was that the readiness with which martyrs endured their bitter experience was the result of preparation, of the production of attitudes, and of the fixation of attention, it is equally true that the crucial moment was that moment when the witness was at the very tribunal. . . . It is easy to suppose that however well prepared one might be, or however strong may have been his resolution to confess, the terror of that moment might, without proper encouragement, undo all that had previously been taught.

Consequently, it is not surprising to find that the Christian groups carried their control to the dramatic point when the witness must confess or deny. Doubtless their practice was learned from bitter experience, for it was early learned that defection had evil influence upon those yet to be examined.

In the first place, Christians who were being examined found that they were not left alone. It was usual for a number of their fellows to be present during the legal process. Naturally this was a factor of importance in the determination of the suspect's conduct. Doubtless it lent encouragement for him to be conscious that friends were present. Of still greater force was the perception that the candidate's own standing was importantly affected by their judgment of his conduct; presently he would be a hero to be praised or an apostate to be reviled. It has been shown that the approval or disapproval of one group or the other would control. The church group took care to exercise all possible influence to impress the candidate that eternal destiny weighted the scale of values in favor of confession, and saw to it that the witness would feel its influence at the critical time. Too, the fact that the general public saw the outcome was of great effect. Not infrequently a denier was greeted by the jeers of the bystanders. . . .

Another aspect of the influence of the group is apparent in the lesson learned by the Christian leaders that successful examples of martyrdom were salutary only when accomplished in the martyr's home surroundings. It was found that when death occurred elsewhere, the loss of effect upon the candidate and upon other Christians was serious. . . .

But the group influence controlling the witness was not alone that of those fellow-Christians who were actually present with him or awaiting him in his familiar surroundings. Fully as powerful in control were the groups whose fellowship was in the realm of the imagination. The martyr was frequently controlled by so intangible a value as this type of imagery. Fellowship with God was a factor. It was made more definite by the thought of fellowship with Christ, especially in view of the fact that Christ was the great protomartyr. Fellowship with other martyrs who had preceded him in suffering furnished comfort. Altogether the force of such imagined relations possessed influence quite comparable to that of one's immediate friends. The fact was turned to account by the Christian leaders in developing their processes of control in persecution. . . .

It was thus most fortunate for the persecuted Christian that he need not feel himself to be alone in the moment of his crises. Experience in other similar cases proves that resolution flags lowest when the sense of loneliness is the strongest. But the candidate for martyrdom had a large roster of fellows. Standing by were some of the associates of his church group. The officials who were his ecclesiastical superiors were aware of his status. And as his imagination lent itself to flights of comforting fancy, there were the whole line of heroes who before him, through suffering, had been victorious. Scripture taught him of many famed

ones, and the rapidly growing Christian tradition was constantly adding to their number. He was persuaded that, if his courage did not fail, he was ever drawing nearer the apostles. Most dazzling in the whole prospect was the thought that God and Christ were supremely careful of his fate—more so, indeed, than were his earthly friends. Truly, beside the circle of present associates there was indeed a "crowd of heavenly witnesses."

Great as was the force of the influence of the group before and during the martyr's examination, it is of the utmost significance that it was not allowed to end as that crucial moment passed. It was found to be of the highest importance that fully as potent influence was exerted after the legal process was concluded. If the candidate had denied, effort was made to induce him to change his mind and alter his testimony. On the other hand, if he had affirmed his faith and accepted condemnation, the influence of the group was useful after the confession had been made. Attention followed the martyrs-designate while they were languishing in prison. It was a comforting assurance to the confessor that he would enjoy many favors while he possessed that rank. Charity operated in his behalf, so that his physical wants were not neglected. Of even greater importance was the prestige which he enjoyed as a confessor and a prospective martyr. But the matter did not end here; the candidate for martyrdom was assured of still more favorable position after his death. These were considerations which had tremendous influence over candidates. . . .

It became a part of the process of control in persecution to assure those who were liable to martyrdom that after their death they would be made the central figures of cults of veneration which verged upon worship. This assurance appears to have done much to make numbers of candidates the more willing to undergo an otherwise calamitous fate.

Just why the prospect of becoming the center of a cult should assist in building up the attitude of willingness to undertake martyrdom is less easy for the modern than for the ancient to see. But it must be remembered that the early Christians shared the pre-scientific world-view. It may not be amiss to point out that the similarity of the cult of the martyr to the familiar Graeco-Roman hero cults is not without significance. The older conceptions of heroic behavior resulting in apotheosis doubtless paved the way for the rise and ready popularity of the martyr cult of the Christians, who naturally shared common conceptions of the same milieu. . . .

. . . It is not to be thought that martyrs in any significant number could have undergone their fate if they had been abandoned in it by their fellow-Christians. They were able to meet their crisis only because they were members of societies which kept effective the influence of their social bonds. That such influence was operative before and during the time of confession, and even after the confession had been secured, while the confessor lay in prison, or actually, as he fondly supposed, after his faithfulness unto death, accounts for the maintenance of the martyr's courage. In other words, he was enabled to emerge through the painful course of punishment because he was one of a number. He was such a person as he proved to be because of group influences, of which, for this purpose, his Christian fellowship was the most effective. It was because of his integration as one of a group that he was thus controllable. The essential factor in control was the influence, variously applied, of the group.

MAINTENANCE OF STRATEGY. Social control in a movement is more than winning and holding adherents and insuring that they make sacrifices even to the point of death. It must also direct the behavior of its adherents in support of the movement. The problem is to discourage courses of action that undermine the strategy, or that damage the image of the movement. It is frequently necessary to restrain the enthusiasm of adherents for quick and ill-conceived actions. Often a special problem arises—insuring that adherents follow just one strategy rather than weakening the movement by following several alternative paths. Most adherents are not in a position to understand the general strategic situation affecting the movement and must therefore be induced to accept direction rather than to follow their own judgment. This requirement becomes especially onerous when the adherents see the movement as a blow for personal freedom and as a vehicle for challenging what they see as an authority- and convention-ridden society.

Sometimes a manual is developed that specifies procedures. On the basis of experience in the Congress of Racial Equality (CORE) and the Friends Peace Committee, Martin Oppenheimer and George Lakey prepared such a handbook for the use of civil disobedience participants.[22] During the movement phase in which CORE, SNCC (Student Nonviolent Coordinating Committee) and similar groups were primarily concerned with provoking tests of local laws that ran counter to federal rulings against racial segregation and unequal treatment, it was important for activists to tread a narrow path of legality. It was essential for them to understand and be prepared to deal with the strategies that would be employed against them. When appealing to a relatively well educated body of high school and college students, the movement could achieve considerable coordination by the use of such a manual.

But seldom do movements rely on so literate a body of workers that a manual of this sort can be effective. And circumstances and strategies change—as they did for SNCC soon after the manual appeared.

Of more general and enduring use is the sacred text. This is a volume that contains many prescriptions regarding movement strategy but is read more with awe and reverence than with discriminating perception. The text is vague and often so contradictory that it can be read to support

22 Martin Oppenheimer and George Lakey, *A Manual for Direct Action* (Chicago: Quadrangle Books, Inc., 1964).

different strategies in the same situation. The text may indicate a general type of strategy, but it does not offer the simple and direct advice that is found in the manual. How, then, does it work as a control mechanism?

The secret of the sacred text is that the rank-and-file adherent does not read it himself, or when he dutifully reads passages he does not presume to interpret them. He does, however, firmly believe that answers are to be found within the text. Consequently, he looks for direction to those specially qualified persons who can give authentic interpretations. In this way, functionaries at the intermediate level in the movement can give instructions with the authority of the sacred text behind them.

There have been many works of this character. Adolf Hitler's *Mein Kampf* follows an autobiographic format to present both objectives and strategy.[23] Upton Sinclair's *How I Ended Poverty in California* was a less effective sacred text for the short-lived EPIC movement of 1934.[24] The *Red Guard's Handbook* of quotations from Mao Tse-tung was used by the youthful Red Guard movement in China during the late 1960s.[25]

Many of the more effective movements, and particularly those of a revolutionary character, emulate military organization. When the movement is authoritarian in its ideology, organization by cadre is natural. But it is less difficult than might be supposed to establish such organization in movements whose value orientations run against authoritarianism. First, the military model is a natural guide to groups that feel themselves outnumbered or persecuted.

Subordination of the individual and subjection to group discipline are the unavoidable costs of preserving the movement under such circumstances. Second, a peculiar affinity exists between a doctrine of altruism or self-sacrifice and acceptance of authority. The giving up of self-assertion and self-interest to higher authority is not easily distinguished from self-relinquishment in the interests of others or for the sake of a great ideal.

A device that strengthens military discipline is the trial engagement. Here the movement takes on a limited objective in which the group can expect to encounter some adversity. The consequences of poor coordination and discipline are made plain by the chaotic outcome, and members are more willing to drill and to accept orders without question. Hitler's Beer Hall Putsch was not intended to be a mere trial engagement, but its humiliating failure helped to convince early adherents to Nazism of the necessity for a well-disciplined organization.

When there is a charismatic leader he can employ such techniques as a threat to leave the movement, do penance for the sins of his followers, or other shaming devices to impress conformity to approved strategy upon the adherents. This approach is probably applicable only in a movement heavily imbued with a religious motif. Gandhi's autobiography tells how he suspended the *Satyagraha* when his followers began to employ violence.[26] He entered into a period of fasting and called upon his followers to purify themselves before another effort could be launched.

It is the nature of a movement that anyone who claims to be a member and can convince some important public that he is a member has the effect of being one. Hence control over strategy and public image requires that the movement take conspicuous steps to claim as members those

23 Adolf Hitler, *Mein Kampf* (Munchen: F. Eher Nachf., 1934).
24 Upton B. Sinclair, *I, Governor of California and How I Ended Poverty: A True Story of the Future* (New York: Farrar, Straus and Giroux, Inc., 1933).
25 *Mao Tse-tung's Quotations: The Red Guard's Handbook* (Nashville, Tenn.: George Peabody College for Teachers, 1967).

26 Mohandas K. Gandhi, *Gandhi's Autobiography: The Story of My Experiments with Truth* (Washington, D.C.: Public Affairs Press, 1948).

persons who represent the desired image and to repudiate those whose presence is likely to besmirch it. Many a candidate for public office has been forced to repudiate support offered publicly by groups that are considered dangerous. When a movement lacks either a strongly entrenched charismatic leader or core group who can identify representatives of the movement authoritatively, newcomers who are not fully steeped in the movement's current strategy often foment a conflict among internal factions for control. In some instances —especially in the case of countermovements—the personnel of the movement also hold key positions in the institutional structure. When this is the case they are able to employ institutional procedures to discredit an unwanted member. Killian describes how Southern segregationist leaders in Florida used legislative committee hearings to discredit the ultramilitant segregationist, John Kasper in 1957.[27] The segregationist countermovement at that time favored a strategy of resistance by peaceful and legalistic moves, a strategy that would have been undermined by the violence and disorder associated with Kasper. Student activists have recognized a category of people whom they call crazies, who join in any disorder, although they have not been part of the movement and are not subject to its discipline. An important aspect of member control is the neutralization and guard against the provocative influence of the crazies in any critical situation.

The Failure of Control

In spite of conversions and enthusiasm for the cause and irrespective of the organization of the movement to maintain control over its adherents, there will be failures of control. Once-loyal supporters will defect, often publicly, and other supporters will fall away less dramatically. Groups will splinter off and compete with the original movement as a consequence of internal struggle.

DEFECTION AS PREORDAINED. One common explanation of defection from movements holds that the defector was not entirely in tune with the movement from the start; joining was a mistake that is corrected by leaving. This viewpoint permits us to interpret defection without assuming that the individual changed his values at a deep level. Toch supplies an excellent example of this attack on the problem.[28]

Toch's four stages in defection begin with qualified joining. The new adherent feels that he is thoroughly committed, that his loyalty is without qualification. But he has misconceptions about the movement or about his own values that will not become apparent until his experience with the movement has increased. Qualifications are of many sorts. The joiner may not have realized the extent to which the movement will demand that he repudiate other aspects of his daily life; he may have formed a distorted or incomplete picture of the movement because of his vantage point; he may even expect a more intense devotion to the cause than the movement is oriented toward making.

The next period may be brief or of many years duration. The period is marked by "symptomatic manifestation of latent reservation." When looking back on this stage the individual is likely to recognize that various annoyances, resentments, and disagreements were recurrent and cumulative, although he did not appreciate their importance at the time. During this period the adherent has no explicit doubt that he is still loyal and committed.

The latent reservations are translated into open disaffection by precipitating events during the third stage. These events are varied in nature. Sometimes they are happenings that make dramatically clear

27 Lewis M. Killian, "The Purge of an Agitator," *Social Problems*, 7 (Fall, 1959), 152–56.

28 Toch, *Psychology of Social Movements*, pp. 157–81.

some characteristic of the movement that the member had never accepted. Defections from Communist groups followed such events as Stalin's nonaggression pact with Hitler in 1939, the armed suppression of the Hungarian uprising of 1956, and the invasion of Czechoslovakia in 1968. In his important study on the nature of Communist appeals, Almond points out that defections often occur when members of a tightly disciplined movement are allowed to spend an extended period of time observing and reflecting, away from the close exchange and support of their fellows in the movement.[29]

It should be added that one way individuals deal with the growing burden of reservations about a cause is by building up a more and more elaborate system of belief to justify their commitment and to overcome their reservations. But the more elaborate the system of rationalization, the more points there are at which the scheme can be discredited. The more assumptions of fact and the more absolute commitments to values there are, the more indefensible the whole system becomes. In this respect Biderman has observed the remarkable imperviousness to Chinese Communist brainwashing on the part of US Air Force personnel during the Korean War.[30] Generally Americans made poor showings when called upon to describe and defend the American conceptions of democracy, and they were unable to make effective attacks on the Communist doctrine being presented to them. Many came back to the United States urgently demanding that there be more effort to train citizens in the rationale for our system. But Biderman proposes that the very lack of dependence upon elaborated ideology helped to make captives unreceptive to the ideological arguments with which they were bombarded. Americans had lived in a setting where commitment to the system was seldom fundamentally challenged and had therefore evolved a nonideological faith that was less vulnerable to direct atack than a highly rationalized belief system would have been.

In Toch's scheme the crisis precipitated by key events may be sudden or may be extended over a period of time. It may lead to immediate withdrawal from the movement, but the defection is never complete until there has been an extended period of cognitive reorganization. Old beliefs and sympathies keep cropping up. The defector must create for himself a new identity to take the place of the old; he must find new social milieus within which he can feel at home and that can afford him personal support. This is often a long and painful process, one that is sometimes never satisfactorily completed.

The foregoing scheme for interpreting defection helps the investigator to maintain a healthy scepticism about sensational reports of total personal transformation. But the scheme must be applied with two important caveats. First, sensational defectors are much less frequent than persons who drop quietly into inactivity in nearly all movements. The steps described by Toch may apply less to the latter group. Second, it is not clear that the scheme meets the criterion of disprovability. It is difficult to conceive of anyone joining any movement without some attitudes or beliefs that could later be identified as incomplete acceptance of the movement, its goals, or its strategy. Every movement has within it sufficient contradiction and undergoes sufficient change, so that it is impossible to conceive of a member being in total agreement at any moment in time and even more difficult when the passage of time is considered. Thus all adherents are qualified joiners in Toch's sense. Only if an empirical comparison of defectors and nondefectors showed that the initial differences and

29 Gabriel Almond, *The Appeals of Communism* (Princeton, N.J.: Princeton University Press, 1954).

30 Albert D. Biderman, "Effects of Communist Indoctrination Attempts: Some Comments Based on an Air Force Prisoner-of-war Study," *Social Problems*, 6 (Spring, 1959), 304–13.

reservations about the movement were identifiably different in magnitude at the time of joining would the scheme be useful for prediction.

The description of the manner in which the defector retrospectively redefines his own experience in order to reestablish his self-esteem is useful. As he turns against the movement and views its aims, its procedures, or its members as reprehensible, he confronts a disfiguring scar across his own self-conception by virtue of having accepted and promoted what he now despises. But now he can discover a series of clues that show that his true self was never anchored in the movement. His true self never really accepted the movement—at least as the movement actually was or became. In defecting he is merely abandoning a false and superficial self to allow the true self to regain its proper supremacy. The more public his defection, the greater will be the necessity to convince himself and others that the sequence was truly as Toch has described it.

THE PROTEST ADHERENT. There is a whole category of movement support that is liable to weaken just at the time of important test. This support comes from people who have never taken seriously the goals or ideology of the movement but who see the movement as a way to protest against the established order. Such adherents are not likely to participate in an active way or to carry out any task that involves sacrifice or dedication. They are likely to support the movement only in the undemanding, yet often crucial, activity of voting. The Communist movement in many countries receives a substantial amount of support of this kind.

Hadley Cantril quotes a French white-collar worker who describes the protest voter in his own country.

The workers won't go out of their way to do anything for the Communists, but they will vote for the Communist Party or for the CGT (Confederation Generale des Travailleurs) in shop elections or national elections. They say,

"I don't care; I don't own anything. I'll take a chance. Voting Communist doesn't hurt me. It may help me. Nothing like putting a big scare in the patron.[31]

This is essentially the same kind of voting as we observed earlier, which facilitates the predominance of power orientations in a movement and helps to bring men like Adolph Hitler to power.

Cantril describes protest voters as those who lack faith that any type of political and economic system can be attuned to their wants. Sustained and intense personal frustrations have convinced them that the present system is hopelessly devoid of concern for them. Their experience of partisan politics has led them to view the claims of Communist officials with cynical disbelief also. But for the present the Communists are no threat because they are not in power. Voting for them is not an expression of belief in communism but a protest against established power.

Support of this kind is unstable and undependable. If the movement comes to power it cannot count on continued support from this group except while its activities are negative. If strategic considerations call for coalitions with "respectables" or for the toning down of free-swinging attacks on the establishment, the movement becomes less attractive to protest voters. As a movement becomes more familiar and provokes less consternation among established groups, it is less attractive as a protest vehicle.

EXTERNAL PRESSURE. Among adherents who genuinely favor the goals of a movement but who, nevertheless, fall short of supporting the movement by appropriate action in a test situation and follow up this failure with passive withdrawal, external pressures are commonly at work. The student fails to strike or sit-in at the university because of fear for his academic career; the

31 Hadley Cantril, *The Politics of Despair* (New York: Basic Books, Inc., Publishers, 1958), p. 71.

employee fails to man the picket line because of fear for his job or his promotions; the conservative in a politically liberal neighborhood fails to show his colors lest he isolate himself and his family.

The participation of Christian ministers in civil-rights activities, ranging from civil disobedience and courting arrest and physical danger to maintenance of a studied silence, often reflects such pressures. The religious presence has increasingly become an aspect of demonstrations in behalf of civil rights and economic opportunity. As Eugene Carson Blake, top official of the United Presbyterian Church at the time, explained when he sought arrest with a group of ministers protesting a segregated recreation facility outside of Baltimore, Maryland, in July 1963, ministers have wanted to demonstrate that their convictions are real. It is too easy to mouth convictions from the pulpit with the protection of ministerial license and a guaranteed annual salary. The ministerial presence sometimes gives moral legitimacy to protest, which forces the community and its leaders to treat the protest as a serious moral confrontation. So concerned have ministers been over the religious "presence" that several who participated in a 1967 demonstration against the California governor's threatened closing of a poverty area service center in Venice bought or borrowed clerical collars for the occasion, although they did not usually wear them.

Jeffrey Hadden and Raymond Rymph were able to compare participants and nonparticipants in a Chicago civil-rights demonstration, in June, 1966 to show how the minister's institutional affiliation permits or discourages such activity. Forty eight ministers from seven Protestant denominations were participating in an intensive study program at the Urban Training Center for Christian Missions in Chicago. All were sympathetic toward the effort to get away from de facto school segregation. The day before the first protest march directed against the Chicago school board,

the trainees were given extensive briefing on the school situation. Thursday classes at the Center were dismissed so that all could participate in the first day's march. The protest activities continued for three days, with the police arresting demonstrators who refused to disperse or accept police direction on Friday and Saturday. Forty of the forty-eight ministers marched on the first day, and ultimately twenty-five of those who continued to demonstrate were arrested on either Friday or Saturday or on both days.

When the twenty-five ministers who were arrested were compared with the twenty-three who were not, there were conspicuous differences in the likelihood that they would be subject to parish pressures against engaging in civil disobedience. All four ministers from integrated metropolitan parishes, all six from nonmetropolitan parishes, and seven of the nine from nonparish posts were arrested. The first of these groups could expect parish support for their activity, and the last had only denominational boards and officials to account to. The nonmetropolitan group is not subject to so clear an explanation, but several of them saw the training course as a step toward reassignment in a metropolitan post and therefore felt relatively little concern over possible disapproval from the local parish. By contrast, seven out of nineteen ministers in nonintegrated inner-city churches and only one of ten from white suburban parishes were arrested. Community organization and pressure are greatest in the suburbs, and the minister there is most likely to be held accountable for behaving in a manner which his parishoners disapprove of.[32]

The number of cases here is small, and ministers may select the kind of assignment that suits their personal predispositions. But there is suggestive evidence that external

[32] Jeffrey K. Hadden and Raymond C. Rymph, "The Marching Ministers," *Trans-Action*, 3 (September, 1966), 38–41.

pressure determines the extent of activism in a social movement.

COMBAT FATIGUE. Every movement loses members and loses control over the actions of other members from the wear and tear of participating in a continuing struggle. First, neither the accomplishment of a movement nor the satisfaction of participating live up to the heroic and romantic expectations that play some part in the initial motivations of most active adherents. Second, a movement brings people together in new and often strange relationships, placing adherents in unfamiliar roles and creating novel problems of interpersonal relationships.

A frequent instance of the latter difficulty is the union of traditionally dominant and subordinated classes in a movement for the underdog. Within the classic charitable movement, roles and standing mirror those in the society. Thus a white man's movement to save the souls or the cultures or the material well being of the Indians in America has typically incorporated Indians only as flunkies. In the early phases of such a movement, the Indians—or blacks, or aged poor, or day laborers—may be pleased by such arrangements. But soon the sense of being suppressed and "used" by the dominant group leads to disappointment and resentment, and the movement is abandoned or its leadership challenged. When the normal inequalities and segregation are avoided within the movement, members of both groups are confronted with endless situations in which they do not know how to behave, and there is a growing strain from constantly acting in a contrived and unnatural fashion.

Charles Levy describes in vivid terms the sequence experienced by many whites who seek to work with blacks in movements to advance the blacks' cause. Central to these relationships is the mistrust of whites by Negroes, a mistrust from which the white civil rights worker is not exempt. In return for repudiating the white world, the white civil-rights activist requires such intense trust from blacks that he does not at first recognize that trust is being withheld. The initial contentment of participation in a truly biracial world is broken as the white begins to sense that the blacks maintain formality in dealing with him long after the barriers should have been dissolved through familiarity. The stage of contentment then gives way to indignation, as the white rejects utterly the assumption that there is any legitimate basis for withholding complete trust in his case. As full realization that the mistrust is real and deeply rooted dawns on the white, he moves into a third stage, awkwardness, during which he unfailingly seeks to act in such a way as to exempt himself from the mistrust normally directed against whites. The strategy is aimed at proving to blacks that he too is really one of them. In the process the white becomes hypersensitive to his whiteness, as he sees every action from the point of view of the mistrustful black. Increasingly he discovers that only by downgrading himself can he avoid acting like a white, but as he does so he brings into even sharper focus the separateness of white and black. In the final stage, dismay, the hopelessness of his efforts becomes clear. "When the White discovers that he cannot withdraw from his Whiteness by converting to Blackness, he withdraws from Negroes." Having learned to "think black," the white can now see his own work only as undermining rather than as aiding the movement.[33]

The pattern of "weariness in the cause" is described from a psychiatric perspective by Robert Coles, drawing upon experience in the civil-rights movement in the United States.

[33] Charles J. Levy, *Voluntary Servitude: Whites in the Negro Movement* (New York: Appleton-Century-Crofts, 1968), p. 123 passim.

Social Struggle and Weariness

*Robert Coles**

Struggle to make our world a better one for more people demands effort and commitment, and these are sometimes repaid with exhaustion and despair. I am writing this paper to describe the onset of weariness in veteran activists of the civil rights movement in America and to indicate that there are ways to help diminish its paralyzing effect upon those who suffer from it.

I speak as a white psychiatrist, a New Englander who first came upon the South—upon Mississippi, in fact—during a tour of military duty. After a brief return North, I went back—this time to Georgia—in order to observe further how individual Negroes and whites manage the social changes obviously afoot throughout the region.

In my work, much of which has been done in association with the student civil rights movement, I have tried to carry psychiatric study into an active social struggle. The method of observation employed may be described as just short of participant observation. That is, though I have never taken part in a "sit-in," picketed, or accompanied a Negro trying to register or vote, I have watched

demonstrations of all kinds all over the South for four years, I have lived with the students staging these demonstrations, followed them about, interviewed them at great length, visited them in jail and even treated some of them there, in consultation with prison doctors, for temporary episodes of anxiety, borderline psychosis, and severe depression; in addition, I have attended their meetings and conducted "groups" at their request, groups where they could talk about their feelings and problems. The Student Non-Violent Coordinating Committee (SNCC) called me their "staff psychiatrist"; and the real heart of the work, besides leading many discussion groups, consisted of my prolonged interviews with—relationship with—23 students, white and Negro, men and women, over a span of four years and under the various conditions mentioned above.

Young men and women in the American South have been staging nonviolent protest demonstrations against segregationist laws and customs for several years. How they manage the various inner stresses and outer trials of their lives, engaged as they are in full-fledged social struggle, is the question that I am considering here. Some understanding of this question can perhaps be gained, I propose, by looking at how an increasing number of them *don't* manage; how they grow weary and lose interest in themselves and their cause. Since I have worked with these young Southerners and studied them for a long time indeed, I feel that I have some sense of what ails many of them and how they can be helped.[1] My observations,

From *Psychiatry,* 27 (November, 1964), 305–15. Copyright The William Alanson White Psychiatric Foundation. Reprinted by special permission of the Foundation and the author.

* A. B. Harvard College 50; M. D. Columbia Univ. 54; Intern, Univ. of Chicago Clinics 54–55; Res. in Psychiatry, Mass. General Hosp. 55–56; Res. in Psychiatry, McLean Hosp., Belmont, Mass. 56–57; Res. in Child Psychiatry, Judge Baker Guidance Center (Children's Hosp.) 57–58; Teaching Fellow in Psychiatry, Harvard Med. School 55–58; Staff Member and Chief of Girls' Section, Children's Unit, Metropol. State Hosp. 57–58; Staff Member, Alcoholism Clinic, Mass. General Hosp. 57–58; Chief of Neuro-Psychiatric Service and Wards, USAF, Keesler Hosp., Biloxi, Miss. 58–60; Fellow in Child Psychiatry, Judge Baker Guidance Center (Children's Hosp.) 60–61; Psychiatric Consultant, Lancaster Industrial School for Girls 61; Clin. Asst. in Psychiatry, Harvard Med. School, and Member of Psychiatric Staff, Mass. General Hosp. 60–62; Rsc. Psychiatrist and Consultant on "Psychiatric Aspects of Desegregation in the South," Southern Regional Council 61–; Rsc. Psychiatrist, Harvard Univ. Health Service 63–.

[1] I have given my general impressions of many of these youths in a chapter called "Serpents and Doves: Non-Violent Youth in the South" in *Youth: Change and Challenge,* edited by Erik Erikson; New York, Basic Books, 1963. Also, in studying children going through initial desegregation in Southern schools, I have come to know young Negro students as they slowly become involved in more general protest activities in contrast to their court-sanctioned admission and attendance at formerly all-white schools—a stress enough despite its "legality." See "Southern Children Under Desegregation" in *Amer. J. Psychiatry* (1963) 120: 332–344.

therefore, may be useful to others. It is with this hope that I am reporting them.

SOCIAL PROTEST IN THE SOUTHERN SETTING

Sit-ins are not as new as they seem to many of us. A number of them were staged spontaneously in the earlier years of this century, isolated, ineffective expressions of resentment by Negroes at their peculiarly hard lot in this country.[2] The fact that such efforts in our time have emerged as a "movement" illustrates the intersection of private struggles with the historical enablement of them. That is, events in the life of our nation have transformed random discontent into a highly complicated, organized social and political phenomenon. This development contrasts with other kinds of social protest which have from the start been more deliberate and planned, or with those which have been taken up by groups already firmly in existence.[3]

The demonstrations have had several purposes: To call attention to the exclusion of Negroes from hotels, restaurants, movie houses, even voting booths; to try to end this practice by entering such places in the hope of being served or accepted; to exert moral, social, and economic pressure on private businesses or on public institutions such as schools and libraries so that they will reconsider their policies; or to prepare the basis for litigation by testing customs clearly illegal constitutionally. The persons taking part in the demonstrations may not all have these aims precisely in mind. Many of them think of their goal in terms of abstractions like "justice," and rely much more heavily on feelings, such as their sense of being denied and scorned.

In the South this kind of social struggle has been chosen by a relative handful in the face of strong resistance, open and devious. Indeed, any discus-

sion of nonviolent protest in that region must somehow establish the psychological quality of the Southern Negro's life and, reciprocally, that of his white neighbors, grounded as they both are in history, customs, and hard legal, economic, and political realities. The Negro's daily life is determined by his terrible past and his present condition of relative poverty, powerlessness, restriction, and isolation from his fellow countrymen. There may be no reason to repeat such obvious facts; they have been fully established by historians, political scientists, economists, and sociologists.[4] Yet, there is every reason for a psychiatrist studying the adjustment of students involved in social protest to keep constantly in mind what it means to grow up as a Negro; how it feels; how the world is seen and engaged; what is lacking for these people and what they expect, and how much of either is grounded in fantasy and how much in reality. The reality of the Southern Negro's life is unrelentingly menial in its public and private relationship to the white world; to appreciate this fact fully, perhaps, one must have had some residence in the South.

COMPOSITION OF THE PROTEST MOVEMENT

No convenient generalizations quite do justice to the astonishing number of ways in which the mind can handle an unpleasant or curbed fate. The rationalizations, denials, projections, and reaction-formations developed under such circum-

---

[2] See, for example, E. Franklin Frazier, *The Negro in the United States;* New York, Macmillan, 1957.

[3] The labor movement in the 30's in this country resembles the civil rights movement in certain ways, but it drew upon a long history of protest that had become increasingly organized and institutionalized. There are a number of organizations whose stated purposes are various kinds of reform, and, of course, our two national parties differ in their goals and actions with respect to social changes.

---

[4] A very suggestive book which combines a historical, sociological and psychological approach is Stanley Elkins' book, *Slavery;* Chicago, Univ. of Chicago Press, 1959. Gunnar Myrdal's *An American Dilemma* is indispensable. It has recently been revised: New York, Harper and Row, 1962. C. Vann Woodward's various historical works are stimulating and filled with the artist's keen sense of irony and paradox. For example, *The Strange Career of Jim Crow;* New York, Oxford Univ. Press, 1955. Wilber J. Cash's *Mind of the South* (New York, Knopf, 1941) is still the moving classic on the general background of the South's pride and agony. Another classic from a sociological viewpoint is Allison Davis and John Dollard, *Children of Bondage;* Washington, D. C., Amer. Council on Educ., 1940. And Lillian Smith's *Killers of the Dream* (New York, Norton, 1961) is for me the most sensitive and acute psychological study written on how whites have come to get along with Negroes and see one another in the South.

stances will easily be imagined by psychiatrists, as conscious as we are now of "ego psychology"; and they have been set forth.[5] Such information, in fact, cautions us against any supposition that *all* Negroes feel alike, respond to their situation in like fashion, or are prepared to take similar arms against their "sea of troubles."

On the contrary, we are presented with the question of who *does* join these demonstrations, or who, given what kind of personality and background, *would.*

Many reasons indeed have caused Negroes, and for that matter whites, to join the several protest movements. They may generally be stated as combinations of private experiences or emotions engaging with public events in the context of a summoning historical time. I have seen the most diverse kinds of youths join sit-ins for a wide variety of personal reasons, and participate in them in highly individual ways, briefly and fearfully, steadfastly, defiantly, quietly, exhibitionistically.

Those who bulk largest in the Southern movement and are most influential in it are Negro college students or recent graduates from college. Several reasons explain this fact. This is their generation's time. Their parents could scarcely have envisaged, let alone help bring about, what has happened in race relations in the past fifteen years. This is also their *own*, their personal time, when they are grown enough to leave home and develop their own attitudes, yet still largely young enough to be spared the heavy social and economic responsibilities of parenthood, while granted the flexibility and mobility of studenthood. Many are only fresh out of college and their condition has been best described by Erikson.[6] They are trying to figure out who they are, what they believe, how to live their lives, and with what ideals to guide them; or they are a bit older and have been storing their energies for a ripe kind of exertion of them.[7]

There are, of course, much older men and women in the movement too, persons who have found their professions in social work, the ministry, teaching, or law, but have found also that their "work" is impossible without prior dedication to the achievement of their dignity as human beings. For the most part they are the well-known leaders, particularly so in the more established Negro civil rights organizations. Yet a good deal of the most earnest social struggle, in the hardest, most unyielding counties of the "deepest" South, is today carried on by youths, and indeed is organized and directed by them. These are the ones who rode the freedom buses, and the same ones who are often called by newsmen "the shock troops" of the movement; long hours a day over months of time their work demands almost impossible sacrifices of living conditions and freedom in towns whose existence and character in this nation are perhaps unbelievable if not seen and confronted in some depth of experience.

The work of these students is not totally the action caught by cameras or reported in the news. The brunt of it is taking actual residence in towns where their goals are considered illegal at best and often seditious; considered so by local police and judges, by state police and judges, by business and political leaders. Their very presence in these towns, in fact, is regarded as a violation of law and order. Most significantly, they are also feared, and resented too, by their own kind, by Negroes as well as whites. The job of organizing Southern Negroes into effective groups for sustained assertion of their rights is a hard one, and one not suitably described by a rhetoric which denounces segregation and fails to consider what such a system does to those segregated, or, for that matter, to those born to enforce segregation, believe in it, and often profit from it.

Negroes in Southern towns are heavily apathetic, widely illiterate, predominantly anxious, and afraid of any protest in their own behalf; let alone

---

[5] See, for example, A. Kardiner and L. Ovesey, *The Mark of Oppression;* New York, Norton, 1951, and New York, Meridian, 1962.

[6] Erikson's well-known discussion of identity formation in young people, and, for that matter, of identity problems in Negroes, is continually helpful in research of this kind. More than that, his ideas have now become what Auden called, referring to Freud and his works, "a whole climate of opinion." See his *Childhood and Society;* New York, Norton, 1963, *Young Man Luther;* New York, Norton, 1958, and "Identity and the Life Cycle" in *Psychological Issues;* New York, Internat. Univ. Press, 1959.

[7] Erikson's discussion of "moratorium," for example, in his study of Luther's life is helpful in looking at these students in the midst of a similar kind of struggle; that is, inward as well as outward, in their growing up as well as their demonstrating on streets.

joining such protests, they are stubbornly reluctant to believe those who advocate them. At the same time, they are largely poor, menially worked, constantly susceptible to unemployment, and subject to laws often hardly sensitive to their civil rights though acutely sensitive to their history and their customary position in society. These are grim psychological realities for those youths who take up the struggle against them. They are the facts of the oppressor's disposition, of the victim's submission, of the fear they both share for different reasons. Every tape I have from every student tells these facts, and they help explain the development of some of the psychiatric symptoms this paper aims to describe.

CLINICAL SYMPTOMS OF WEARINESS IN THE CAUSE

What unites all of these students is the development in each of them of certain specific clinical symptoms. These symptoms emerge in youths of different classes and ages and with different reasons for participating in such struggles; they crop up in people whose character structures vary, whose choice of defense mechanisms encompasses the entire range of the ego's possibilities. To develop they take time and certain kinds of experiences; but given both, they occur, in my experience, almost universally. They are clinical signs of depression. They constitute "battle fatigue." They indicate exhaustion, weariness, despair, frustration, and rage. They mark a crisis in the lives of those youths who experience them, and also one in the cities which may experience the results, translated into action, of such symptoms.

Because of these symptoms students may depart the movement, go "back to the world" of schools, jobs, pursuit of career, to be replaced by younger or fresher cadres. Or they may linger on, disabled. Or they may stay on but become troublesome, bitter, and a source of worry, of unpredictable action, of potential danger to themselves and their "cause." The development of these symptoms, these depressive episodes, is a problem for civil rights organizations, and for the country too. Leaders of the civil rights organizations well know that their struggle is a long one, not to be resolved in a year or two. In a sense they

are more than leaders of organizations; they are generals worried about "war-neuroses" in their front-line troops. The rest of the country is the scene of the battle, and thus has good reason for regarding closely the state of mind that develops in many of these young men and women.

Briefly the symptoms reveal fear, anxiety, and anger no longer "controlled" or "managed." Depressions occur, characterized by loss of hope for victory, loss of a sense of purpose, and acceptance of the power of the enemy where before such power was challenged with apparent fearlessness. The youth affected may take to heavy drinking or become silent, sulky, and uncooperative. Frequently one sees real gloom, loss of appetite, withdrawal from social contacts as well as from useful daily work in the movement. Sometimes withdrawal from the movement becomes a precursor of the abandonment of a commitment to nonviolence, the advocacy of total, disruptive assault upon the society, or complete, hateful disengagement from it. In such cases the nonviolent movement itself may be attacked instead of the segregated society formerly felt to be the enemy. One very bright and exceptionally intuitive young man summarized his feelings very concisely:

I feel I've lost those years. They've come to nothing, really. No real change. So I feel betrayed by the movement, and I guess it's easier to get angry at it than at the white world. I just want to *pull out* of the white world. I mean you can't hate it the way I do and live with it . . . . That's it, my hate for the movement is a release or something . . . . I can hate it and do something about it. You know, attack them or undermine them. But what can a Negro do to the white world without getting destroyed eventually?

There are warning signs, and they are increasingly spotted these days by certain leaders. But full-fledged depressions still appear without being anticipated, and I have treated several of them. They are difficult to treat because they seem to have developed over a long period of time and in people resourceful at concealing them. Once they make their appearance, they seem refractory to anything but the strongest of medical and psychiatric measures—medication, psychotherapy, a change of environment, even temporary hospitalization. On the other hand, increasing sophistication has enabled certain key "officers" to recognize the beginning of weariness, the first stages foreshadowing collapse, with their signs of anxiety and fretfulness and with their subtle changes in thinking and feeling.

For example, minor complaints of insomnia or headaches may herald depression. So also may comments like, "What's the use?" or "Why fight them, they're too strong?" Such remarks may be quickly denied even by those making them, but experience in the movement has shown that it is wise not to ignore their significance. Somatic complaints are also significant: stomach pains, or menstrual cramps newly bothersome and disabling, or vague skin itching and nondescript and self-ascribed "allergies." Then there are the "accidents," with bikes, with cars; and the injuries, due to drinking, or to "friendly" fighting, or "horsing around," or suffered in athletic games. They are often the result of rising tensions deflected by consciences not easily prone to acknowledge their presence, let alone their strength and pervasive influence.

The forms of despair and exhaustion are really only limited by the ingenuity of the human mind. We have seen pregnancy serve as an "escape," not only for women who must leave to have a baby, but for men who must leave for marriage. We have seen parental disapproval of protest activity suddenly accepted and embraced as a means of dodging one's own depression and guilty wish to leave the struggle. We have seen reckless, defiant behavior adopted to deal with the guilt over the wish to leave, as if severe punishment at the hands of the segregationists would satisfy the demands—often quite unconscious—of the student's conscience. It is as if a voice tells them, "For wanting to leave you must seek and get punishment, and from the very people you were up to this point managing so well through your controlled, nonviolent behavior." Two young men showed bursts of dedication, a kind of outlandish zeal quickly seen for its compulsive and strange quality by others; the denial of other feelings, of inertia and apathy based on depression, explained their actions. And I have seen exhaustion attributed to others; or young people become exquisitely sensitive to the weakness of others as they struggle with their own budding feelings of dejection.

The very institutional development of the sit-in movement parallels such individual psychological developments. At first there were simply youths—vigorous, unfatigued, keen to protest, indifferent to organizational concerns, and inexperienced in just how to sustain their momentum—that is, how to raise social, political, and economic support for themselves. But as it became clear that sit-ins were "working," more participants became available, and organizational developments began: The students formed committees, they met, elected leaders, opened up offices, bought equipment for them, appealed for money, became conscious of publicity. The makings of a bureaucracy were thus established, and within time came the tensions, the rivalries, rigidities, and inertia associated with such developments. One student—a political science major—put it quite bluntly:

I'm tired, but so is the whole movement. We're busy worrying about our position or our finances, so we don't *do* anything any more . . . . We're becoming lifeless, just like all revolutions when they lose their first momentum and become more interested in preserving what they've won than going on to new challenges . . . . Only with us we haven't won that much, and we're either holding to the little we have as an organization, or we get bitter, and want to create a new revolution . . . . You know, one like the Muslims want, which is the opposite of what we say we're for. It's as if we completely reverse ourselves because we can't get what we want.

Both bitterness and organizational preoccupations can be a refuge or outlet for anxious, depressed veterans of active protest, and often these two developments occur together. For example, a 24-year-old veteran of numerous sit-ins came to see me because he knew he had been depressed for several weeks, and more recently had become aware of his reluctance to join any active demonstration. Even the "softest" demonstrations in the more northerly South bothered him. He was afraid, hence unwilling to do anything but work in the regional headquarters of the organization. The thought of going to jail, once regarded as a laughing matter and almost welcomed as a means of earning pride in himself and esteem from others, terrified him now.

He had trouble sleeping, and nightmares afflicted him:

I dream I'm going to be hurt, you know, kicked and manhandled by those jailers. [There had always been reason for him to fear such possibilities as probabilities; but until now he had been able to "dismiss" or make light of such "reality."] Sometimes I wake up in a cold sweat, and I remember that I've actually dreamed that the whole movement was arrested .... I mean all of us were taken in custody, and then I escape and a few of us get a boat and go to Africa, or we take refuge in one of the African embassies .... I mean to get away from whites, all of them, that's what the dream says; the reverse of integration, you might call it.

This young man was actually quite agitated when he came to see me, and he was "furloughed" for "rest and rehabilitation." (The language of the students is commonly "war language.") He became a member of a small group I was asked to lead as a means of dealing with such "casualties." . . .

18

PARTICIPATION ORIENTATIONS

The ostensible reason for the existence of any social movement is found in its value orientations. The means for promoting the changes sought by the movement inevitably acquire some independent momentum, as power orientations. But the movement is ultimately made up of people, and they must experience gratification from participating in the movement if they are to continue their support. Not all the gratifications are directly connected with the movement's values. Involvement can be partially or entirely an end in itself. The presence in every movement of members who are not attracted and held chiefly because of the movement's distinctive goals and ideology gives rise to an independent momentum that we call participation orientations. Every movement is shaped in part by the demand for gratifications unrelated to the movement's stated objectives.

We begin the discussion of participation orientations by asking whether there are participation prone types of people. Are there distinctive personality types whose needs are especially likely to be satisfied by joining social movements? Second, we shall observe that participation gratifications give rise to an expressive component in all movements. Goals and strategies are modified so that the movement can serve as a vehicle through which the experience of membership in a cohesive group and the personal problems and preoccupations of members are acted out and resolved symbolically. Third, we look at that vast group

of movements in which the participation orientations are paramount in shaping the movement's course and character. Many of these movements operate in a relationship of accommodation to society. But our fourth topic is those movements—chiefly built around millennial myths—that initially offer a wish-fulfillment substitute for the current world but have a potentiality for spawning violently active movements under appropriate conditions.

The Participation Prone

The convergence approach to collective behavior leads some investigators to treat identification of the dimensions of participation proneness as the central task in understanding social movements. As we have abundantly seen, programs and ideologies that attack established orders and accepted values have deeper roots than this, and neither the actual dislocations in the social order nor the processes by which movements develop can be underestimated in an adequate approach to social movements. But the convergence approach is still important in focusing on one among several variables causing and shaping social movements. And the cautious assumption, that some kinds of people are more susceptible to the appeals of any type of movement than others, is worthy of careful consideration.

Unfortunately, many characterizations of the participation prone personality are deficient in various respects. Often analyses of membership types are ill-disguised efforts to discredit certain kinds of movements by "proving" that neurotics, incompetents, and the unscrupulous constitute the bulk of their members. The investigator's biases then make his findings inevitable. Analyses also frequently begin with some preconceived theory of personality rather than with observation of the movement to "explain" the social movements. Statements are many times based upon a few types of movements, and it is seldom clear how extensively they may be generalized. Finally, the same error repeatedly creeps in, as we noted in discussing the crowd. Apparent homogeneity of membership may actually conceal a variety of types of persons who interact to make the movement work.

Catton was able to question some of the people who attended meetings held by a man who announced himself as the reincarnation of Christ, in Seattle, Washington, during 1952. Catton distinguished seekers from observers by noticing that seekers returned for several meetings more often and became more favorable rather than more skeptical of the movement's leader. He found that:

...seekers were less likely to be church members, attended church less often than did observers, more frequently read the Bible, were more inclined to believe in the possibility of a second coming, devoted somewhat more of their idle thoughts to questions of where and how they would spend eternity, were lonelier, were slightly more apprehensive about war and depression. In short, seekers tended to be those who had strong religious interests that were not being satisfied through normal institutional channels.[1]

These findings are typical of what emerges from investigations of attraction to a wide variety of movements. First, the seekers have selected the kind of movement that embodies values they emphasize in their own persons. These Bible-reading seekers may be susceptible to appeals from many different religious movements, but they are not likely to be in the forefront of those who respond to more secular appeals. They respond to a movement that promises to take seriously a set of values that conventional institutions support in a carefully moderated fashion. Second, the loneliness and apprehensiveness of the seekers suggest problems of a more pervasive nature in their relationships to the community. These qualities might be generally applicable components of a participation proneness. But we must be wary of generalizing widely from a movement of this character.

Eric Hoffer proposed that "all movements, however different in doctrine and aspiration, draw their early adherents from the same types of humanity." Foremost among these early adherents is the true believer, "the man of fanatical faith who is ready to sacrifice his life for a holy cause." The key to the true believer is a deep personal frustration that can be relieved by finding the source of his troubles outside himself, by engaging in a drastic self-renunciation coupled with acquisition of a sense of unlimited power and hope that comes from identifying with the movement. "The ideal potential convert is the individual who stands alone, who has no collective body he can blend with and lose himself in and so mask the pettiness, meaninglessness and shabbiness of his individual existence."[2]

Hoffer's is but one trenchant statement of a widely shared view that the impetus for mass movements comes chiefly from people whose emotional needs make them candidates for psychiatric attention. The cautious observation from Catton's research that seekers tend to be lonely and apprehensive is grossly magnified and generalized

[1] William R. Catton, Jr., "What Kind of People Does a Religious Cult Attract?" *American Sociological Review*, 22 (October, 1957), 563.

[2] Eric Hoffer, *The True Believer: Thoughts on the Nature of Mass Movements* (New York: Harper and Row, Publishers, 1951), pp. xi, xii, 34.

here. Hoffer has borrowed from an important tradition that sees a combination of personal inadequacy and authoritarianism as predisposing the individual to the appeals of those movements that offer great public displays of power. The best known statement of this theme is Erich Fromm's treatment of the circumstances of modern society that encourage receptivity to movements such as Nazism. Out of the isolation and sense of powerlessness experienced by many men in modern industry there develops a "sado-masochistic" character structure, one which takes delight in being punished by and subservient to those above and in turn gains pleasure from mistreating those beneath him. Through yielding up his independence in subservience to an authoritarian movement, the individual "escapes from freedom" that he lacks the resources to use and gains a sense of overwhelming power through identification with the powerful movement and its dictator leader.[3]

Authoritarian types of people are found among the adherents of almost any movement with a program of societal reform. These people are dissatisfied unless they can impose their wills on others. In the classic study by Theodore Adorno and his associates, an effort was made to show that there are several authoritarian personality syndromes that incline people to accept fascist types of ideology.[4] But the opportunity to dominate masses of people may also be provided in the most democratic movements. Even in movements dedicated to strengthening popular control there are authoritarian satisfactions in forcing the masses to "accept their responsibilities" and in manipulating the intolerance of the masses to bring dissident individuals into conformity.

These and other bold characterizations of

movement proneness largely indicate the motivations that *the investigator* thinks would have to distinguish anyone who participated in some group of movements. Documenting these motivations empirically is a much more difficult matter, and little evidence has been produced that would warrant any but cautious and provisional generalization. A scholarly review of evidence dealing with the motivation of radicals, published in 1950, produced more evidence of the shifting fashions of personality analysis than of a clearly delineated radical personality.[5] Recent student movements have produced an exceptional increment of evidence on this question because of the accessibility and receptivity of their members to scholarly investigation.

Borrowing the Oedipal conflict theme from psychoanalysis, many writers attribute youthful movements of protest to unresolved conflicts between father and son. Accordingly, activists in such movements should be drawn disproportionately from young men (1) on bad terms with their fathers and (2) in violent political disagreement with their fathers. But available evidence fails to support these hypotheses. Although the presence of some generation gap has been widely documented, it does not appear to be more characteristic of activists than of other youth. Characteristic findings come from Richard Flacks' comparison of two small samples of student activists in Chicago with control groups.[6] The activists came disproportionately from homes in which liberal values prevailed and where the home atmosphere was democratic and attitude toward the children was permissive. In another investigation Braungart compared leftist Students for a Democratic Society (SDS) members with the

[3] Erich Fromm, *Escape From Freedom* (New York: Farrar and Rinehart, 1941).

[4] Theodore W. Adorno et al., *The Authoritarian Personality* (New York: Harper and Row, Publishers, 1950).

[5] Thelma H. McCormack, "The Motivation of Radicals," *American Journal of Sociology*, 56 (July, 1950), 17–24.

[6] Richard Flacks, "The Liberated Generation: Exploration of the Roots of Student Protest," *Journal of Social Issues*, 23 (July, 1967), 52–75.

rightist Young Americans for Freedom (YAF).[7] The former came largely from high status Protestant backgrounds and homes where secular and liberal values prevailed. YAF members came from strongly religious and conservative homes in lower middle-class and working-class settings. Lipset summarizes these and other studies by observing that "students are more 'idealistic' and 'committed' than their parents —but generally in the same direction."[8]

Like Catton's religious seekers, the student activists are chiefly distinctive by seriously pursuing selected values that they have learned in conventional institutional settings but that they are not willing to see compromised or interpreted in the usual balanced relationship with other prevalent values. Further efforts to infer a distinctive personality complex make use of the finding that leftist activists are likely to have experienced permissive child rearing in families dominated by a strong mother. But since these experiences are especially characteristic of upper middle-class Jewish families, and the liberal Jewish home contributes far more than its share to activism, there is no reason to lay special weight on child rearing.[9] Strong socialization to a particular value tradition continues to offer a more convincing explanation for the activist than any qualities of personality yet identified.

If there is a movement prone configuration, the most promising clue to follow may be the tendency to adopt values in a more literalistic fashion than most people do. Promoting a value in which others believe but without the usual concern for its interaction with other values or for one's own social standing can usefully be seen as an instance of high risk taking. When a movement is factional, and even more when it is not respectable, the adherent risks his own prestige and propriety. One who is highly sensitive concerning his standing in the community assumes a greater risk by joining a movement than one who cares little about community position. It is not surprising, then, that Surace and Seeman found white civil-rights activists, as compared with inactives, inclined to place little emphasis on the conforming and status-conferring character of their behavior.[10]

The risk in activism for a movement with a generally favorable public is different, for such a movement, as we noted in the previous chapter, can often confer prestige. A prestige isolation overtakes any individual who sets himself apart from his fellows by assuming a leadership role or an active role with respect to values that his fellows accept passively. His fellows can no longer joke about their political convictions or make light of their candidate's foibles in the presence of an individual who is committed to serious and unequivocal support of a reform program. The adherent's serious preoccupation makes his fellows fear that their small talk will not be of interest to him. Ordinary, informal communication is thus inhibited, and relations become stilted. Furthermore, the activist is the recipient of friendly kidding for going overboard or of a certain amount of awe and admiration for having more courage and conscientiousness than his fellows, all of which sets him apart from ordinary primary group relations. A certain kind of social insensitivity or indifference to intimate and informal relations may therefore facilitate membership in this type of movement.

Before we are tempted to use the civil-rights activist's lesser concern with prestige or the seeker's loneliness and apprehensiveness to construct an image of the movement prone individual, we must observe contradictory evidence. First, in the Surace-Seeman study black civil-rights activists did not exhibit the same characteristics as white

[7] Richard G. Braungart, "SDS and YAF: Backgrounds of Student Political Activists," mimeographed, 1966.

[8] Seymour M. Lipset, "The Activists: A Profile," *The Public Interest*, 13 (Fall, 1968), 46.

[9] Ibid., pp. 49–50.

[10] Samuel J. Surace and Melvin Seeman, "Some Correlates of Civil Rights Activism," *Social Forces*, 46 (Dec., 1967), 197–207.

activists. The black's situation is sufficiently different from the white's situation that the social meanings of activism are different and hence motivations are not the same. Second, we do well to compare the loneliness and apprehensiveness of the seekers with Searles' and Williams' finding that black college students who participated in sit-ins were distinguished by their optimism regarding civil rights and the extent of their communication with whites.[11]

Four observations will summarize the tentative conclusions about movement proneness. First, we are probably on safer ground to assume that different kinds of motivations draw people to different kinds of movements than to search further for a generalized movement prone configuration. Second, we must reiterate the point made earlier, that each movement modifies the attitudes and motivations of its members, so that distinctive attitudes reflect experience in the movement as much as predispositions. Disparagement of prestige and conformism are emphasized in the ideology of civil-rights movements, and training to deemphasize these traits is part of the commitment and control program in such movements. Since the small religious sects play upon fear more than religious denominations do, a period of seekership in such movements may well augment apprehensiveness. Third, whatever movement a person joins may serve as a vehicle for the expression of preexisting personal needs, without these needs having been crucial in bringing him to the movement. This feature of movements will be the subject for the ensuing discussion of expressive components in social movements.

Finally, while it is only possible to speak of generalized movement proneness in weak and cautious terms, there are undoubtedly personality types who are attracted to any movement without ever constituting more than a small fraction of its members. Hoffer's true believer may well be veri-

fied in later research as a small but important component in every mass movement. Persons who crave martyrdom also find their way into a variety of movements. Although they are few in numbers, their rash actions often have disproportionate consequences for the movement. Hazel Wolf has demonstrated the anticipation of martyrdom shown by many of the prominent figures in the American abolition movement.[12] From letters and public statements she has shown that many not only expected to be martyred but expressed morbid satisfaction in looking forward to their ultimate demise. In less active form, rank-and-file members sometimes pride themselves on belonging to a despised minority. As a way of life the martyrdom attitude takes care of certain adjustments that the individual might otherwise have to make. The fact that he is persecuted explains in advance any personal failures and protects him from the necessity of making effective long-range plans for himself. As a recipient of unfair treatment from society at large the individual feels himself morally freed from the obligations that society might otherwise impose upon him.

The Expressive Component in Social Movements

Behavior in the expressive crowd is more symbolic than effective and more consummatory than instrumental. Similarly, the gratifications that come from participation in a movement contribute an expressive component to every such enterprise. Every movement is constantly pressed to choose between a strategy based on a careful weighing of the consequences of each course of action and a strategy whereby the members are given the opportunity to participate in dramatic gestures of support for its goals. The adherent clamors for a chance to put himself on record for the cause, to strike a blow for freedom now!

---

[11] Ruth Searles and J. Allen Williams, Jr., "Negro College Students' Participation in Sit-ins," *Social Forces*, 40 (March, 1962), 215–20.

[12] Hazel Wolf, *On Freedom's Alter* (Madison: University of Wisconsin Press, 1952).

The demonstration, the march, the ringing declaration of principle, the act of collective self-sacrifice that demonstrates commitment—all are powerful means for expressing dedication to a cause even when they offer no hope of hastening attainment of the movement's goals. No movement can survive without these concessions to the morale of its members. But every movement is confronted by the constant danger that expressive actions will undermine the movement's principal strategies and that expressiveness will supplant objective progress in a cause as the movement's overriding aim.

The extent to which expressive elements abound in popular advocacy can be sensed from the frequency with which persons who have been heralded as popular heroes have in fact been utter failures in promoting the reforms they sought. Many Old Testament prophets were famous for forecasting the calamities that were to befall the Hebrew people. Their own efforts to get the people to mend their ways and thus avert the vengeance of God were ineffectual and usually ill-conceived. Napoleon, who brought the French nation to the brink of catastrophe, is enshrined as a national hero in consideration of the temporary greatness he brought to France with his ultimately disastrous military exploits. Like Robin Hood, who did little good for the peasants and managed to bring destructive retaliatory raids down upon them, the symbolic leader does not depend upon effectiveness in bringing about desired reforms for his popular adulation.

Besides the clamor for actions that will symbolize and dramatize the movement's values, members seek to express their sense of the movement as a cohesive group and their unique and shared identity problems. These sources of expressiveness further diffuse the goals and constrain the internal structure of the movement.

THE EXPERIENCE OF SOCIAL COHESION. A nearly universal feature of social movements is that the ecstatic experience of membership in a cohesive, committed, like-minded group becomes an independent source of satisfaction for many of the members. As this happens, the demands that members make upon their movement change in harmony with their use of it to recapitulate the exhilarating experience. When a movement lifts its members out of the ordinary humdrum, enables them to cast aside conventional restraints, and creates consternation among outsiders, there are at least three gratifying components. The feeling of new-found spontaneity, the sense of power, and the vision of enthusiastic consensus rather than of reluctant compromise and concession abound in the reports by members both in the early stages and on occasions of vital confrontation between the movement and its enemies. Together these components produce a sense of vitality, of being real persons having real experiences rather than being puppets manipulated in accordance with a script.

Something of the flavor of this new-found sense of vitality is conveyed in a participant's report on the 1968 student rebellion at the University of Paris.

When the great Sorbonne was overrun on June 16 by police units of the C. R. S., you half expected the cry to go up, "Babylon is fallen, Babylon is fallen!" For a mad mixture of a world had sprung up inside the huge building and overflowed throughout the Latin Quarter and along the left bank in Paris. The streets were no longer populated by automatons going to and from work, by automatons buying bread and cheese and daily newspapers. They were filled with human beings, with people.[13]

As this sense of cohesiveness becomes intense, the movement becomes a surrogate for reality to the members. Because events outside the movement seem unreal, artifi-

---

[13] Roy Walford, "Paris: Faces Dull and Hard Become Tender and Beautiful," *Los Angeles Free Press,* July 5, 1968, p. 3. The *Compagnies Republicaines de Securite* (CRS) is the French National Guard.

cial, and contrived, they are discounted and underestimated. The only credible image of the outside world is a projection of the movement experience. Thus it is that in 1966 ardent pacifists could disregard the evidence from opinion polls and misinterpret electoral outcomes to retain a deep conviction that they indeed represented the will of the American people.[14] Many movements have foundered because of ill-conceived actions that were taken on the basis of a similar misconception of their active or latent community support.

When the movement is a surrogate for reality, experience within it demonstrates the attainability of utopian goals in the community at large. Spontaneity within the movement proves that extrinsic and artificial incentives are unneeded in the larger world. Decision by apparent consensus shows that laws, police, and courts are but pernicious impediments to true agreement in the community. Equality and fraternity among "brothers and sisters" in the movement afford a model for the society. Cohesiveness in this fashion contributes to an escalation of goals from modest to comprehensive schemes of reform and away from qualification by practical considerations.

Means are often transformed into ends through this process. The movement begins

[14] Seymour M. Lipset, "The President, the Polls, and Vietnam," *Trans-Action,* 3 (Sept., 1966), 19–24.

as an instrument—to bring an end to a war, to protect minority voting rights, to reform a corrupt government. But as the movement becomes the model for reality, extension to the community of the movement's pattern of organization and decision making becomes an independent goal. Thus participatory democracy evolved as the normative pattern for decision making in New Left movements, and then the spread of this pattern to the community became a more lasting goal than many of the specifics of university reform, voting drives, draft repeal, and associated objectives. For many adherents the conviction developed that these and other specific problems existed largely because of the nature of contemporary decision-making patterns. If only these patterns were replaced by participatory democracy on the larger scene, the problems of the university, or political representation, and of world peace would be well on the way to resolution. The replacement of the structure of the community by the structure of the movement emerges as the primary goal.

The following brief statement by a participant in the Berkeley Free Speech Movement of 1964 and after illustrates the reassessment of means as ends and the elevation of the spontaneity of relationships within the movement to a model for the entire society. Direct action "reduces the issues to the magnitude of the individual man."

Generational Revolt and the Free Speech Movement

Gerald Rosenfeld

. . . Those who said they agreed with the ends of the Free Speech Movement but took offense at the means it used claiming it should have sought judicial rulings through the courts or statutory

From *Liberation,* 10 (Jan., 1966), 18–19. Reprinted in part by permission.

changes by the legislature to achieve its ends, failed to understand what the ends of the movement were, for the means the students used *were* the ends of the movement. What the students were fighting for was the right to participate directly in the world they live in, for the right to confront other men and not catalogs and regulations, forms and procedures, an amplified voice and a televised face. To resort either to legal processes, in which other men, lawyers, argue the merits of the case while the protagonist sits and watches, or to electoral tactics, in which one chooses other men or brings pressure to bear on other men to act on one's behalf, would have been to surrender the life of the movement.

What enlivened the Free Speech Movement was the exhilaration of feeling that you were, for once, really acting, that you were dealing directly with the things that affect your life, and with each other. You were for once free of the whole sticky cobweb that kept you apart from each other and from the roots of your existence, and you knew you were alive and what your life was all about. "For a moment all the hypocrisy was swept away and we saw the world with a greater clarity than we had before." (Savio) It was the tactics of direct action, the sense of immediate personal involvement, that made this possible.

The value of direct action is that it reduces the issues to the magnitude of the individual man. As Rossman told *Look* magazine, "We're making changes in society with our own two hands; that's a new feeling for my generation." The trouble with trying to understand politics and society as they are taught in the university is that everything seems so complex, so subject to a multitude of seemingly unrelated or contradictory constructions and interpretations. It is only when one can confront it himself, only when it is reduced to its ultimate terms of what it means to the lives of individual men, that "society" can really be known and understood.

The style of the Free Speech Movement made possible the vitality and spirit and the genuine feeling of camaraderie among its participants. There was something more in this style, too; there was a good-natured humor, an informality, a looseness—a relaxed acceptance of themselves that goes back, I think, to the Beat's rejection of

the taboos of society and his attempt to attune himself to the needs of his own body. The frank acceptance of one's sexual nature, the openness to new experiences, the appreciation of the rhythms of jazz in the Beat, the Hip, the Negro elements of this generation's development have contributed to its character. The F.S.M. was a swinging movement.

The F.S.M., with its open mass meetings, its guitars and songs, its beards, and its long-haired chicks, made the aloofness and reserve of the administrators, the turgid style of the pronouncements emanating from the University Information Office, the formality of the coat and tie world, seem lifeless and dull in comparison. And when the administration once managed to muster its dignity to produce the Extraordinary All University Convocation at the Greek Theatre, throwing every bit of gravity, every sacred symbol of classical education into the presentation, with President Kerr pronouncing the final solution worked out between himself and the Committee of Departmental Chairmen in the sonorous tones of the liberal rhetoric ("This community is divided not so much on ends as on means . . ."), the whole thing collapsed in confusion when Mario Savio walked up to microphone with the intention of announcing an F.S.M. rally.

Whatever beauty, grace, love, or joy was shown in the course of the struggle came from the students, and this was made possible by the sense of integrity they had gained; by the essential unity of their ideals with their actions, of their ends with their means, and, underlying this, the unity of their ideals with what it was necessary for them to do in order to be men.

The Free Speech Movement was the culmination of a reaction against life in Post-Modern America that had been building for some fifteen years. The accumulated experience of those years was articulated by the F.S.M. in the course of the unfolding of events at Berkeley, and the statement articulated was the manifesto of a New Radicalism. . . .

In this respect current movements are similar to movements of the 1920s and 1930s in the United States. During the incubation period of World War II, a theme

commonly expressed in the Progressive Education movement was that the method of cooperation supplied the answer to all social problems, including war. A faith in the inevitable goodness and rightness of solutions achieved through cooperative methods led to deemphasizing the specific nature of different social problems.

At the same time that members are seeking to impose the movement pattern on the outside world, they often confront the danger that the internal organization of the movement will deviate from the valued pattern. As the organization enlarges, as the voice of practical members is heard, as issues recur and activities are routinized, more conventional forms of organization appear. Although these organizational procedures may facilitate quick decisions, draw more effectively upon expert and experienced advice, and free more of the members' time for carrying out the movement's program, they are threatening to those who have learned to find deep satisfaction in the experience of cohesiveness. The experience we have described can best be attained either through some kind of participatory decision process or through a highly authoritarian organization. Either the dilution of participation by some degree of bureaucracy or the weakening of hierarchy by questioning and discussion of authoritarian edicts threatens the sense of spontaneity, power, and consensus. Resistance to compromises of this character renders a movement inflexible and threatens its continuance. For lack of compromise the authoritarian movement often breaks down by splintering into competing authoritarian groups. The participatory group likewise splinters as segments seek to reinstate the original utopian organization they have seen compromised.

Besides promoting utopian goals and rendering the internal organization inflexible, the gratifications derived from the experience of movement cohesiveness also have a continuing effect on strategy. There is a strong tendency to direct the movement into actions that reinforce the cohesiveness experience as a substitute for actions that promote the formulated objectives of the movement. The massive confrontation is much more effective in arousing the sense

of vitality in members than are the less spectacular methods that produce more results in some situations. Writing individual letters to congressmen, speaking individually to friends and neighbors, conducting meticulous research to clarify the nature of a problem cannot compare with the mass demonstration as a means of enacting solidarity and inducing the ecstatic sense of identification with a powerful legion of the like-minded.

Symbols, Ritual, and Identity. Self and world are inextricably bound together. When the outer world seems bland, uninteresting, and unreal, no vital sense of self develops. Without a clear sense of personal identity, the world fails to come into sharp focus. Social movements serve at the same time as vehicles for the objectification of a personal search for identity and as means for the creation of values in the surrounding world.

Sometimes the individual identity crises and the requirements of a movement's value orientations are in perfect harmony. This seems to have been the case at one point for the young black whose participation in southern lunch counter sit-ins supplied the concrete means by which he could cast off an unwanted identity and replace it with a more satisfying self. John grew up in a border city where the completely segregated school system puzzled him and preyed on his mind. His father belonged to the NAACP and expressed occasional strong feelings about discrimination, but he was not an activist. As early as age thirteen, John made modest attempts to test the segregated system; later he was greatly influenced by reading of Gandhi and hearing Martin Luther King speak. John was well behaved and making good grades in college in Greensboro, N. C., when he formed a close friendship with three other boys who felt as he did. Together they shared and reinforced their attitudes of shame and anger over the way they embodied a stereotype of the subservient black with strong back and weak mind. At the peak of one of their emotional bull sessions the four decided to sit-in at a lunch counter where they knew blacks were not served. After the sit-ins John remarked that he felt entirely different about himself, not guilty as before, feeling that at last he had *done* something and not just talked about it.[15]

In other instances the movement becomes a vehicle for acting out personal problems without respect to the effect in promoting either the values or the power of the movement. Illustrations of this point are endlessly varied. But a frequent effect is to add to any movement for reform a theme of antiestablishmentarianism. The movement against slavery became for many a vehicle for a total attack on Southern values and customs. The movements for withdrawal of American troops from Vietnam often seems more like a vehicle for attack on the entire American concept of government and economy than a simple call for peace. When this happens the movement acquires a collection of symbolic trappings that serve as expressions of the secondary goals attached to it. It is notable that young people supporting Senator Eugene McCarthy as peace candidate in 1968 found it necessary to shave and tidy up so as to make their message effective. But a year later several students reporting their observations of a UCLA campus demonstration against ROTC independently remarked that the organizing group could be distinguished from the mass of sympathizers by their "outlandish" appearance and dress.

Within most movements there is a continuing struggle between those who see the secondary goals as diversionary and those to whom the secondary goals give the movement an important larger meaning. When the latter gain strength, the movement attracts more new adherents because of the secondary goals rather than because of the earlier central aim.

Gusfield has shown that the American temperance movement underwent changes that transformed it into primarily a movement of protest against the upper middle class and their way of life.[16] As the consumption of alcohol became a more openly accepted part of upper middle-class living after the repeal of Prohibition in 1933, the Women's Christian Temperance Union attracted lower middle-class women who were frustrated in their own life situations and felt a mixture of resentment and envy against the upper middle class. The consumption of alcohol was not only a concern in its own right but more and more a symbol of the upper middle class. Thus the temperance movement became the medium for acting out resentments born of the frustrating life situations of lower middle-class women.

Although social movements have always supplied a vehicle for resolving identity crises—from the medieval crusades to the Protestant reformation, modern nationalism, and the Women's Liberation Front— the search for identity has become a more explicit theme in the latter half of the twentieth century. Nearly every contemporary movement has been affected by this theme but none more clearly than the black civil-rights movement. It became increasingly clear during the 1960s that improvement of the blacks' economic situation and the elimination of barriers to free choice in residence, education, and play was subordinate to the black's effort to be proud of himself. The repudiation of integration by militant blacks—so difficult for liberal whites to comprehend—expresses this concern with black dignity. By voluntary separation the black declares that he does not

15 Frederic Solomon and Jacob R. Fishman, "Youth and Social Action: II. Action and Identity Formation in the First Student Sit-in Demonstration," *Journal of Social Issues,* (April, 1964), pp. 36–45.

16 Joseph R. Gusfield, *Symbolic Crusade: Status Politics and the American Temperance Movement* (Urbana: University of Illinois Press, 1963).

seek or need the association of white men, and that blackness is a quality to promote rather than to hide.[17]

Orrin Klapp sees the collective search for identity as the central preoccupation of modern society, expressed in faddism, cults, mass followings, and the contemporary crusade.[18] The lack of clear-cut identities relates to the failure of society to generate meaningful symbols, which in turn are produced and maintained through meaningful rituals. In his search for identity man can try to change himself by following peer group fashions or hero worship; he can seek interactive confrontations in which to discover a new image of himself, as in the sensitivity training pattern adopted by many contemporary movements; or he can seek deep feelings or "kicks." All of these avenues are to be found in various kinds of social movements. And contemporary social movements are disproportionately attuned to providing these opportunities for self-rectification, whatever their manifest goals.

If many movements supply vehicles for acting out the personal problems of their adherents, it is likely that they inadvertently provide a form of psychotherapy. Ari Kiev compares the religious ritual in pentacostal sects that attracts West Indian immigrants in England to psychotherapeutic procedures, and he notes striking parallels. The repetitive themes of salvation and reward for the religious life contribute to the reduction of anxieties.

During services a reduction of self-awareness and a sense of merging with the group is increased by the dogmatic preaching and testi-monies in an emotionally aroused atmosphere, with the group singing and clapping in unison to the ministrations of the preacher. Losing one's self-awareness and self-consciousness in this spirited assembly would seem to contribute to an increase of positive good feelings, elation and sometimes exaltation which may contribute to the psychotherapeutic efficacy of the meetings.[19]

Klapp observes that if the cult often proves more successful than group or individual therapy in changing people, it is because:

...it is better organized in such things as group fellowship and support, ritual for dramatizing identity change, cultic formula, the role of the devotee as a life pattern (rather than just a temporary therapy), and deeper centering by faith and feeling about ultimate values.[20]

Nowhere has the idea of social movements as instruments for acting out personal problems been more fully exemplified than in Lewis Feuer's wide-ranging examination of the place of youth in political movements. The psychoanalytic interpretation he chooses to place on his findings has appropriately been the subject of much controversy. Other interpretations fit the data equally well or better. But the historical documentation of similar patterns in participation by youth at diverse times and places is impressive. Any movement that relies significantly on a youthful constituency will surely be affected by the ways in which youth employ the movement as a vehicle for acting out the identity problems common to their age group.

---

[17] Sidney M. Wilhelm and Edwin H. Powell, "Who Needs the Negro?" *Trans-Action,* 1 (September, 1964), 3–6.
[18] Orrin E. Klapp, *Collective Search for Identity* (New York: Holt, Rinehart and Winston, Inc., 1969).

[19] Ari Kiev, "Psychotherapeutic Aspects of Pentacostal Sects among West Indian Immigrants to England," *British Journal of Sociology,* 15 (June, 1964), 136, *see also* 129–38.
[20] Klapp, *Collective Search for Indentity,* p. 208.

The Conflict of Generations

Lewis S. Feuer

The distinctive character of student movements arises from the union in them of motives of youthful love, on the one hand, and those springing from the conflict of generations on the other. We shall thus be inquiring into the complex psychological origins of human idealism, for we cannot understand the destructive pole of student movements until we have brought to light the obscure unconscious workings of generational conflict. Then perhaps we shall know why student movements have been fated to tragedy.

To their own consciousness, students in student movements have been the bearers of a higher ethic than the surrounding society. Certainly in their essential character student movements are historical forces which are at odds with the "social system." A society is never altogether a social system precisely because such contra-systemic "unsocialized" agencies such as student movements arise. As Walter Weyl said: "Adolescence is the true day for revolt, the day when obscure forces, as mysterious as growth, push us, trembling, out of our narrow lives into the wide throbbing life beyond self." No society ever altogether succeeds in molding the various psychological types which comprise it to conform to its material, economic requirements. If there were a genuine correspondence between the material, economic base and the psychological superstructure, then societies would be static social systems, and basic social change would not take place. In every society, however, those psychological types and motivations which the society suppresses become the searching agents of social change. Thus psychoethical motives, which are not only independent of the socio-economic base but actually contrary to the economic ethics that the social system requires, become primary historical forces.

The Russian revolutionary student movement is

From *The Conflict of Generations: The Character and Significance of Student Movements*, by Lewis S. Feuer (New York: Basic Books, 1969, copyright Lewis S. Feuer). Reprinted in part by permission of the author. Footnotes have been omitted.

the classic case of the historic workings of the ethical consciousness. When in the 1860s and 1870s several thousand student youth, inspired by feelings of guilt and responsibility for the backward people, embarked on their "back-to-the-people" movement, it was an unparalleled collective act of selfless idealism. . . .

The students' ethical consciousness was utterly independent of class interests and class position. The largest single group among those who were arrested in the back-to-the-people movement from 1873 to 1877 were children of the nobility. They could have availed themselves of the ample openings in the governmental bureaucracy. Instead, many of them chose a path of self-sacrifice and suffering. Rebuffed by the peasants, the revolutionary student youth later gave themselves to the most extreme self-immolation of individual terrorism. And when terrorism failed to produce the desired social change, circles of student intellectuals provided the first nuclei of the Social Democratic party. Lenin aptly said that the intellectuals brought a socialist consciousness to the workers, who by themselves would not have gone beyond trade union aspirations. The intellectuals Lenin referred to were indeed largely the self-sacrificing revolutionary students.

The ethic of the Russian student generations was not shaped by the institutional requirements of the society. The universal theme of generational revolt, which cuts across all societies, produced in Russia a "conflict of generations" of unparalleled intensity because of special social circumstances. The Russian students lived their external lives in a social reality which was absolutist, politically tyrannical, and culturally backward; internally, on the other hand, they lived in a milieu imbued with Western cultural values. Their philosophical and idealistic aims transcended the social system, and were out of keeping with it; the philosophical culture and the social system were at odds with each other, in "contradiction." The revolutionists, we might say, were historical transcendentalists, not historical materialists. The government opened universities to provide recruits for its bureaucracy. Some students followed the appointed path, but the universities became the centers not only for bureaucratic education but for revolutionary dedication. The idealistic student as a psychological type was recalcitrant to the specifications of the social system.

The civil rights movement in the United States has likewise owed much to students as the bearers of an ethical vocation in history. A wave of sit-ins which spread through Negro college towns began on February 1, 1960, when four freshmen from the all-Negro Agricultural and Technical College at Greensboro, North Carolina, sat down at the lunch counter of the local Woolworth dime store. The surrounding community was puzzled that it was precisely "the best educated, the most disciplined and cultured—and essentially middle class—Negro students" who took the self-sacrificing initiative. Moreover, it was recognized generally, to use one writer's words, that "for the time being it is the students who have given a lift to the established civil rights organizations rather than the other way around." Then in the next years came movements which resembled even more the "back-to-the-people" movement of the Russian studentry. The Freedom Riders of 1961, the several hundred white students in the Mississippi Summer Project of 1964 risking their lives to establish Freedom Schools among the Negroes, were descendants in spirit of the Russian students of the preceding century.

Nonetheless, the duality of motivation which has spurred student movements has always borne its duality of consequence. On the one hand, student movements during the past hundred and fifty years have been the bearers of a higher ethic for social reconstruction, of altruism, and of generous emotion. On the other hand, with all the uniformity of a sociological law, they have imposed on the political process a choice of means destructive both of self and of the goals which presumably were sought. Suicidalism and terrorism have both been invariably present in student movements. A youth-weighted rate of suicide is indeed characteristic of all countries in which large-scale revolutionary student movements are found. In what we might call a "normal" country, or one in which there is a "generational equilibrium," "suicide," as

Louis Dublin said, "is much more prevalent in advanced years than during youth." But a "normal" country is one without a revolutionary student movement. Where such movements have existed, where countries are thus characterized by a severe conflict of generations, the rate of suicide has been highest precisely for the youthful group. Nihilism has tended to become the philosophy of student movements not only because it constitutes a negative critique of society; it is also a self-critique that is moved by an impulse toward self-annihilation. . . .

. . . Every student movement tries to attach itself to a "carrier" movement of more major proportions —such as a peasant, labor, nationalist, racial, or anti-colonial movement. We may call the latter the "carrier" movements by way of analogy with the harmonic waves superimposed on the carrier wave in physics. But the superimposition of waves of social movements differs in one basic respect from that of physical movements. The student movement gives a new qualitative character and direction to social change. It imparts to the carrier movement a quality of emotion, dualities of feeling, which would otherwise have been lacking. Emotions issuing from the students' unconscious, and deriving from the conflict of generations, impose or attach themselves to the underlying political carrier movement, and deflect it in irrational directions. Given a set of alternative paths— rational or irrational—for realizing a social goal— the influence of a student movement will be toward the use of the most irrational means to achieve the end. Student movements are thus what one would least expect—among the most irrationalist in history. . . .

In the case of the Russian student movement, it was the opinion of the most distinguished anarchist, Peter Kropotkin, that "the promulgation of a constitution was extremely near at hand during the last few months of the life of Alexander II." Kropotkin greatly admired the idealism of the Russian students, yet he felt their intervention had been part of an almost accidental chain of circumstances that had defeated Russia's hopes. Bernard Pares, the historian, who also witnessed the masochist-terrorist characteristics of the Russian students at first hand, wrote, "The bomb that killed Alexander II put an end to the faint beginnings of Russian constitutionalism." A half-hour before the Czar set out on his last journey on March 1, 1881, he approved the text of a decree announcing the establishment of a commission likely to lead to the writing of a constitution. "I have consented to this measure," said Alexander II, "although I do not conceal from myself the fact that this is the first step toward a constitution." Instead, the students' acts of Czar-killing and self-killing brought into Russian politics all the psychological overtones of sons destroying their fathers; their dramatic idealism projected on a national political scale the emotional pattern of "totem and taboo," the revolt and guilt of the primal sons Freud described. People turned in shock from the sick, self-destructive students; the liberals felt as if they had had the ground pulled out from under them. . . .

The history of civilization bears witness to certain universal themes. They assert themselves in every era, and they issue from the deepest universals in human nature. Every age sees its class struggles and imperialistic drives, just as every age sees its ethical aspirations transcend economic interest. Every society has among its members examples of all the varieties of motivation and temperament; it has its scientists and warriors, its entrepreneurs and withdrawers. Thus, too, generational conflict, generational struggle, has been a universal theme of history.

Unlike class struggle, however, the struggle of generations has been little studied and little understood. Class conflicts are easy to document. Labor movements have a continuous and intelligible history. Student movements, by contrast, have a fitful and transient character, and even seem lacking in the substantial dignity which a subject for political sociology should have. Indeed the student status, to begin with, unlike that of the workingman, is temporary; a few brief years, and the quantum-like experience in the student movement is over. Nevertheless, the history of our contemporary world has been basically affected by student movements. Social revolutions in Russia, China, and Burma sprang from student movements, while governments in Korea, Japan, and the Sudan have fallen in recent years largely because of massive student protest. Here, then, is a recurrent phenomenon of modern times which challenges our understanding.

Generational struggle demands categories of understanding unlike those which enable us to understand the class struggle. Student movements, unlike those of workingmen, are born of vague, undefined emotions which seek for some issue, some cause, to which to attach themselves. A complex of urges—altruism, idealism, revolt, self-sacrifice and self-destruction—searches the social order for a strategic avenue of expression. Labor movements have never had to search for issues in the way in which student movements do. A trade union, for instance, calls a strike because the workingmen want higher wages, better conditions of labor, shorter hours, more safety measures, more security. A trade union is a rational organization in the sense that its conscious aims are based on grievances which are well understood and on ambitions which are clearly defined. The wage demands and the specific grievances of working-men are born directly of their conditions of life. Their existence determines their consciousness, and in this sense the historical materialism of Karl Marx is indeed the best theoretical framework for explaining the labor movement. The conflict of generations, on the other hand, derives from deep, unconscious sources, and the outlook and philosophy of student movements are rarely materialistic. If labor seeks to better its living conditions as directly as possible, student movements sacrifice their own economic interests for the sake of a vision of a nobler life for the lowliest. If historical materialism is the ideology of the working class, then historical idealism is the ideology of student movements. If "exploitation" is the master term for defining class conflict, then "alienation" does similar service for the conflict of generations. . . .

. . . We may define a student movement as a combination of students inspired by aims which they try to explicate in a political ideology, and moved by an emotional rebellion in which there is always present a disillusionment with and rejection of the values of the older generation; moreover, the members of a student movement have the conviction that their generation has a special historical mission to fulfill where the older generation, other elites, and other classes have failed. . . .

A student movement thus is founded upon a coalescence of several themes and conditions. It tends to arise in societies which are geron-tocratic—that is, where the older generation possesses a disproportionate amount of economic and political power and social status. Where the influences of religion, ideology, and the family are especially designed to strengthen the rule of the old, there a student movement, as an uprising of the young, will be most apt to occur. As against the gerontocracy, a student movement in protest is moved by a spirit of what we may call *juvenocracy*. If an element of patriarchy prevails in most governments, the student movement by contrast is inspired by a will to *filiarchy*. Gerontocratic societies, however, have often existed without experiencing a revolt of the younger generation. A gerontocratic order is not a sufficient condition for the rise of a student movement. Among other factors, there must also be present a feeling that the older generation has failed. We may call this experience the process of the "de-authoritization" of the old. A student movement will not arise unless there is a sense that the older generation has discredited itself and lost its moral standing. The Chinese student movement which was born in May 1919 thus issued from a tremendous disillusionment with the elder statesmen who, in the students' eyes, had capitulated with shameful unmanliness to the Japanese demands at Versailles. The Japanese student movement which arose after the Second World War was based on the emotional trauma which the young students had experienced in the defeat of their country. Traditional authority was de-authoritized as it never had been before; their fathers, elders, teachers, and rulers were revealed as having deceived and misled them. Japan in 1960 was far more technologically advanced than it had been in the twenties, and also far more democratic. Yet because in 1960 the psychological hegemony of the older generation was undermined, there arose a large student movement, whereas there had been little unrest among students in earlier and more difficult years.

A student movement, moreover, tends to arise where political apathy or a sense of helplessness prevails among the people. Especially where the people are illiterate will the feeling exist among the young that the political initiative is theirs. The educated man has an inordinate prestige in a society of illiterates. He is a master of the arts of reading and writing, and a whole world of knowledge and the powers of expression are at his command. Throughout human history, whenever people of a society have been overwhelmingly illiterate and voiceless, the intellectual elite has been the sole rival for political power with the military elite. . . .

From the combination of youth, intellectuality, and altruistic emotion, there arise certain further basic traits of student movements. In the first place, a student movement, unlike a labor movement, has at its inception only a vague sense of its immediate goals; indeed, its "ultimate aims" are usually equally inchoate. A trade union, as we have mentioned, comes into being because a group of workers have certain specific grievances relating to wages, hours and conditions of work, seniority rights, safety precautions. It is only with difficulty that political propagandists can get workers to think in generic terms of opposing the "system." A student movement, on the other hand, arises from a diffused feeling of opposition to things as they are. It is revolutionary in emotion to begin with, and because its driving energy stems largely from unconscious sources, it has trouble defining what it wants. It tries to go from the general to the particular, and to find a justifying bill of grievances; what moves it at the outset, however, is less an idea than an emotion, vague, restless, ill-defined, stemming from the unconscious. A Japanese student leader of many years' standing, Shigeo Shima, remarked, "One cannot understand the student movement if one tries to understand it in terms of the labor movement. The strength of the student movement lies in its energy of consciousness trying to determine existence, instead of the other way around." An intellectual has been defined as a person whose consciousness determines his existence, in the case of the young intellectuals of a student movement we might add further that their ideological consciousness is founded on the emotional unconscious of generational revolt. . . .

A student movement thus tends to take its stand as the pure conscience of the society; it is concerned with ideal issues, not, like an economic movement, with the material, bread-and-butter ones. Every student movement, however, also has a populist ingredient. A student movement always looks for some lowly oppressed class with which it can psychologically identify itself. Whether it be to the peasantry, the proletariat, or the Negro, the students have a tremendous need to offer themselves in a self-sacrificial way, to seek out an exploited group on whose behalf their sacrifices will be made. Conceiving of themselves as deceived, exploited sons, they feel a kinship with the deceived and exploited of society as a whole. The back-to-the-people spirit is at once the most distinctive, noblest, and most self-destructive trait within student movements. The populist ingredient separates the student movement sharply from what we might call student syndicalism. . . .

The populist and elitist moods in student movements can merge into a morbid self-destructive masochism, as they did, for instance, among the Russian students. The burden of guilt which a generation in revolt takes upon itself is immense, and it issues in perverse and grotesque ways. Nevertheless, something would be lost in our understanding of student movements if we were to see in them solely a chapter of history written on an abnormal theme. For student movements, let us remember, are the most sincerely selfless and altruistic which the world has seen. A student is a person who, midway between childhood and maturity, is imbibing the highest ideals and hopes of the human cultural heritage; moreover, he lives in comradeship with his fellow-students. The comradeship of students is usually the last communal fellowship he will experience. The student feels that he will then enter into a maelstrom of competitive and bureaucratic pseudo-existence; he has a foreboding that he will become alienated from the self he now is. Articulate by education, he voices his protest. No edict in the world can control a classroom. It is everywhere the last free forum of mankind. Students meet together necessarily, think together, laugh together, and share a common animus against the authorities. The conditions of student existence remain optimal for spontaneous rebellion. When the absolutism of the Czar stifled the nascent democratic strivings in a culturally backward people, the universities stood as isolated fortresses of relatively free expression. As Lenin wrote in 1903, "The actual conditions of social life in Russia render (soon we shall have to be saying: rendered) extremely difficult any manifestation of political discontent except through the universities." . . .

The more backward a people is with respect to its culture and intellect, the greater is the likelihood that it will have a student movement of an elitist and revolutionary character. Where the "cultural distance" between the students and the surrounding population is great, the chances for the rise of a student movement are increased. One whole class of student movements is born of "uneven development," from the unbalanced situation in which advanced ideas are combined with material backwardness. In such cases the "cultural strain," the cultural alienation, which arises between the students and the masses, is most poignant and intense, for it involves a de-authoritization of the elder generation as cultural inferiors, as persons of whom one is ashamed. The students then are in part motivated to overcome the cultural distance between their people and themselves, and in part by an acceptance of the elitist status which their cultural superiority confers. What is most important to bear in mind is that the culture of the student movements, of the intellectual elite, is the one genuinely international culture. Students at any given time throughout the world tend to read the same books. We might call this the law of the universality of ideas, or the law of universal intellectual fashions, or the maximum rate of diffusion for intellectual culture. At any rate, the Chinese students of 1917, like their counterparts in America and Britain, were reading Bertrand Russell, John Dewey, and later Lenin and Marx; earlier they had read Ibsen, Tolstoy, and Spencer. Kwame Nkrumah as a university student in America and Britain studied Marx and logical positivism, Jomo Kenyatta sank himself in the writings of Marx and Malinowski. Today in Africa the young students, like their fellows in France, the United States, and Japan, read Marx, Camus, and the existentialist writers. In the Soviet Union young university students try to find copies of Camus and Freud, and overcoming the obstacles interposed by the government against the free flow of books and ideas, succeed in maintaining a bond with the world intellectual community. . . .

. . . A generation in the sociological sense consists of persons in a common age group who in their formative years have known the same historical experiences, shared the same hopes and disappointments, and experienced a common disillusionment with respect to the elder age groups, toward whom their sense of opposition is defined.

Often a generation's consciousness is shaped by the experience of what we might call the "generational event." To the Chinese Communist students of the early thirties, for instance, it was the "Long March" with Mao Tse-tung; that was what one writer called their "unifying event." More than class origin, such an historical experience impresses itself on the consciousness of a student movement. The depression, the struggle against fascism, the ordeals of the civil rights agitation—all these were generational events; they demarcated a generation in its coming of age. . . .

What keeps generational consciousness most intense is the sense of generational martyrdom, the actual experience of one's fellow-students assaulted, killed, imprisoned, by armed deputies of the elder generation. Whether in Russian, Chinese, or Latin American universities, or at Berkeley, the actual physical clash made students frenzied with indignation. The youthful adolescent resents the elders' violence especially for its assault upon his new manhood. Student movements make of their martyrs the high symbols of a common identity. The Iranian Students' Association, for example, published a leaflet in their exile to commemorate "Student Day" for three of their comrades. Its language was that of the martyrology of generational consciousness:

STUDENTS MASSACRED

On December 7th, 1953, the armed forces of the post-coup d'etat government invaded the Tehran University. Some soldiers entered a classroom and threatened to kill the professor . . . As the terrified students started to run away the soldiers opened fire with their machine guns in the hallway and wounded many students and killed three.

. . . The students were going to demonstrate against the government on December 9th, 1953, the day that Vice-President Richard M. Nixon was going to visit Iran and its "free" people. . . .

The three students, Chandchi, Bozorgnia and Shariatrazavi, died, but their memory and their heroic sacrifice will forever remain with us to guide the student movement of Iran. To honor their memories and to rededicate ourselves to the cause for which they gave their lives, this day will always be honored. . . .

Every student movement has cherished similar memories of brothers whom their fathers destroyed. . . .

We have tried to unravel the nature of political idealism, the complex of emotions of love, destruction, self-sacrifice, and nihilism on which it is founded. The unconscious ingredient of generational revolt in the students' idealism has tended to shape decisively their political expression. We have tried to bring to consciousness what otherwise are unconscious processes of history. That has been the whole purpose in our use of the psycho-historical method—to help defeat the cunning of history which has so often misused the idealistic emotions. With a melancholy uniformity, the historical record shows plainly how time and again the students' most idealistic movement has converted itself into a blind, irrational power hostile to liberal democratic values. Yet we refuse to accept a sociological determinism which would make this pattern into the fatality of all student idealism. Our working hypothesis is that knowledge can contribute to wisdom. When students perceive the historical defeat which has dogged their youthful hubris, they may perhaps be the more enabled to cope with irrational demonry; they may then make their political idealism into an even nobler historical force.

For student movements have thus far been too largely an example of what we might call *projective politics,* in the sense that they have been largely dominated by unconscious drives; the will to revolt against the de-authorized father has evolved into a variety of patterns of political action. This hegemony of the unconscious has differentiated student movements from the more familiar ones of class and interest groups. The latter are usually conscious of their psychological sources and aims, whether they be material economic interests or enhanced prestige and power. Student movements, on the other hand, manifest a deep resistance to the psychological analysis of their emotional mainspring; they wish to keep unconscious the origins of their generational revolt. A politics of the unconscious carries with it untold dangers for the future of civilization. We have seen the students Karl Sand and Gavrilo Princip adding their irrational vector to deflect the peaceful evolution of a liberal Europe; we have seen the Russian students helping to stifle the first possibilities of a liberal constitution; we have seen the American student movement in its blind alley of the Oxford Pledge and its later pro-Soviet immolation. All these were fruits of the politics of the unconscious. It is only by persisting in the understanding of these unconscious determinants that we can hope to see a higher wisdom in human affairs.

Guilt feelings fused with altruistic emotions have led students to seek a "back to the people" identification. In Joseph Conrad's novel, the guilt-tormented Lord Jim could conquer his guilt only by merging his self in the most romantic dedication to an alien, impoverished, exploited people. The aged ex-revolutionist Stein saw Jim's salvation rendered possible only by his immersing himself in the "destructive element"; thereby, guilt was assuaged. And since it is guilt which assails the sense of one's existence with the reproaches of one's conscience, it is by the conquest of guilt in a higher self-sacrifice that one recovers the conviction of one's existence. In a sense, every student seeking to merge himself with peasant, proletarian, the Negro, the poor, the alien race has had something of the Lord Jim psychology. His guilt is that of his generational revolt, his would-be parricide. He can conquer this guilt only with the demonstration that he is selfless and by winning the comforting maternal love of the oppressed; they bring him the assurance of his needed place in the universe. To reduce this determinism of unconscious guilt has been one purpose of this study. For only thus can we isolate and counteract the ingredient of self-destruction.

When generational struggle grows most intense, it gives rise to generational theories of truth. Protagorean relativism is translated into generational terms; only youth, uncorrupted, is held to perceive the truth, and the generation becomes the measure of all things. This generational relativism in the sixties is the counterpart of the class relativism which flourished in the thirties; where once it was said that only the proletariat had an instinctive grasp of sociological truth, now it is said that only those under thirty, or twenty-five, or twenty, are thus privileged. It would be pointless to repeat the philosophical criticisms of relativist ideology. This generational doctrine is

an ideology insofar as it expresses a "false consciousness"; it issues from unconscious motives of generational uprising, projects its youthful longings onto the nature of the cosmos, sociological reality, and sociological knowledge, but represses precisely those facts of self-destruction and self-defeat which we have documented. Moreover, the majority of studentries have usually been at odds with the student activists, whose emotional compulsions to generational revolt they do not share. The engineering and working-class students, who so often have been immune to the revolt-ardor of middle-class humanistic students, stand as dissenters to the doctrine of generational privilege. They have held more fast their sense of reality, whereas the literary-minded have seen reality through a mist of fantasy and wish-fulfillment.

The reactionary is also a generational relativist, for he believes that the old have a privileged perspective upon reality, that only the old have learned in experience the recalcitrance of facts to human desire. But the philosophical truth is that no generation has a privileged access to reality; each has its projective unconscious, its inner resentments, its repressions and exaggerations. Each generation will have to learn to look at itself with the same sincerity it demands of the other. The alternative is generational conflict, with its searing, sick emotions, and an unconscious which is a subterranean house of hatred.

The substance of history is psychological—the way human beings have felt, thought, and acted in varying circumstances—and the concept of generational struggle which we have used is a psychological one. There are those who see the dangers of "reductionism" in our psycho-historical method; they feel that the genesis of student movements in generational conflict has no bearing on the validity of their programs, goals, objectives. Of what import, they ask, is the psychology of student movements so long as they work for freedom, for liberating workers and peasants and colored races, for university reform, and the end of alienation? To such critics we reply that the psychological origin of student movements puts its impress on both their choice of political means and underlying ends. Wherever a set of alternative possible routes toward achieving a given end presents itself, a student movement will usually tend to choose the one which involves a higher measure of violence or humiliation directed against the older generation. The latent aim of generational revolt never surrenders its paramountcy to the avowed patent aims. The assassination of an archduke, for instance, may be justified by an appeal to nationalistic ideals which are said to have a sanctity overriding all other consequences; actually the sacred cause, the nationalistic ideal, becomes too easily a pseudo-end, a rationalization, a "cause" which affords the chance to express in a more socially admired way one's desire to murder an authority figure.

When all our analysis is done, however, what endures is the promise and hope of a purified idealism. I recall one evening in 1963 when I met with a secret circle of Russian students at Moscow University. There were twelve or thirteen of them drawn from various fields but moved by a common aspiration toward freedom. Among them were young physicists, philosophers, economists, students of languages. Their teachers had been apologists for the Stalinist repression, and the students were groping for truthful ideas, for an honest philosophy rather than an official ideology. Clandestine papers and books circulated among them—a copy of Boris Pasternak's *Dr. Zhivago*, of George Orwell's *1984*—reprints of Western articles on Soviet literature, a revelation of the fate of the poet Osip Mandelstamm. The social system had failed to "socialize" them, had failed to stifle their longing for freedom. The elder generation was de-authorized in their eyes for its pusillanimous involvement in the "cult of personality." Here on a cold March night in a Moscow academic office I was encountering what gave hope to the future of the Soviet Union. The conflict of generations, disenthralled of its demonry, becomes a drama of sustenance and renewal which remains the historical bearer of humanity's highest hopes.

Participation-oriented Movements in Accommodation with Society

A great many movements come close to being mere cults in which the expressive component altogether subordinates any value and power goals. These movements usually claim dedication to the improvement of society and relief of human ills, often through personal reform. But unlike personal transformation movements, they offer the member something and neglect to concern themselves with how the member then serves the outside world. Participation-oriented movements are those in which dedication to the reform of society does not go beyond tokenism, and the activities and organization of the movement are overwhelmingly geared to supplying the adherents with concrete or symbolic gratifications.

PERSONAL STATUS MOVEMENTS. The personal status movement alters crucial frustrating aspects of the individual's life in one of two broad ways. It may redefine the individual's value scheme, supplanting his old reference groups with new ones representing new values. Or it may reorient its members by assisting them to attain the types of success already recognized in the society.

The first pattern is commonly found among minority groups, in religious movements, and in various political, aesthetic, and intellectual movements that remain out of touch with practical considerations for implementing their schemes. Anton Boisen observes the vast increase of membership in "Holy Roller" or "pentacostal" sects in the United States during the depression years of the 1930s and the preponderance of the poor among the members.[21] In the doctrines of sin and salvation these people

[21] Anton T. Boisen, *The Exploration of the Inner World: A Study of Mental Disorder and Religious Experience* (New York: Harper and Row, Publishers, 1936).

can accept guilt for their personal inadequacies in the supportive setting of Christian fellowship and through mystical experience come to grips with some of the problems of values in their lives. The effect is not to direct them toward reform of the institutions that have made their situation unjust but to discover a new frame of reference within which their misfortunes become tolerable.

Hadley Cantril has formulated a set of principles similar to Boisen's but more comprehensive and systematic. His theory appears most clearly as he examines the Kingdom of Father Divine, a black cult centered in New York's Harlem and built on the conviction that a black man known as Reverend Divine is God. Membership in the movement is attributed to three kinds of needs that are satisfied for the participants. (1) Members are assured an *escape from material hardships* through the provision of "food, shelter, peace, security." Belief in miracle cures for physical ailments helps to substantiate the conviction that Father Divine's world is the kingdom of heaven on earth at present. (2) The movement provides *meaning*:

...an escape from a tortuous mental confusion caused by complex, conflicting circumstances. He gives meaning to the individual life and to the world. It is perhaps largely for this reason that one finds in the movement so many "joiners"—people, many of them whites, who have been Baptists, Holy Rollers, Christian Scientists, and Theosophists before coming to Father. Their search for a solution to the meaning of life leads them from one formula to another.[22]

(3) Finally, the movement *raises the members' status*. Father Divine speaks out against all discrimination; he encourages the self-respect of his followers and builds the impression of membership in a huge and universally recognized movement.

In the present world the acculturation of rural populations to patterns of urban industrial life is a source of much status disorientation. In an interpretation that is not inconsistent with Boisen's, John B. Holt attributes the rise of "holiness religion" in the southeast United States to this phenomenon.[23] The Assemblies of God, Nazarenes, various Church of God groups, the Pentacostal and Holiness churches flourished in the decades between World Wars I and II among lower-class whites affected by urbanization. The destruction of old rural values and life-ways, the disruption of social ties, and isolation from durable personal ties constitute what Holt calls culture shock. This in turn leads to a vigorous religious revivalism, an extreme orthodoxy and rejection of liberal trends in the established churches.

Improvement of personal status may also be gained by cultivating a more satisfactory personal status within the existing scheme. When material success and prestige are linked with religion, movements flourish that offer shortcuts to success through religion and in particular through somewhat less personally exacting forms of religion. When the relation of physical well-being to mental health and personal success is being stressed by legitimate medical authorities, food-faddism thrives in dozens of movements. As psychiatry has achieved respectability and public recognition, some movements promise success by way of techniques patterned after the popular conceptions of psychiatry.

Typical of these movements was the New Thought cult of the early twentieth century.[24] For the unpleasant, conventional route to success via hard work, it substituted success by "right thinking." But at the same time it drew its ideology out of the

22 Hadley Cantril, *The Psychology of Social Movements* (New York: John Wiley and Sons, Inc., 1941), p. 141.

23 John B. Holt, "Holiness Religion: Cultural Shock and Social Reorganization," *American Sociological Review*, 5 (October, 1940), 740–47.
24 Alfred W. Griswold, "New Thought: A Cult of Success," *American Journal of Sociology*, 40 (Nov., 1934), 309–18.

culturally sanctioned traditions of American society, wearing the dress of a religious movement and supporting the doctrine that economic success reflects personal moral worth. The Dianetics movement of the 1950s drew upon the currently popular view that success reflects one's psychic adjustment. Through a set of procedures vulgarized from psychoanalysis, the member sought to become "clear," and thus able to deal with life's problems more masterfully. Contemporary Scientology revives many features of Dianetics.

These two movements are manifestations of a general movement in American history that Donald Meyer dubs *mind cure*.[25] He relates the general movement to a peculiar nervousness or neurosis ascribed to the American character by numerous observers since the post-Civil War era. This is a condition of anxiety and passivity that appears as a reaction to the more salient success ethic. Movements such as Christian Science, which taught "how the weak might feel strong while remaining weak," first appealed largely to women. The nineteenth century was an era of expanding opportunity for men but of declining usefulness for women. But as the twentieth century opened and the creation of industrial society gave way to the maintenance of routines for most men, the same passive themes spread into the new movements that promoted business success by right thinking. Although the general movement has increasingly found expression in secular movements, the followers attracted to Norman Vincent Peale's "power of positive thinking" still accepted his words as a religious message in the period after World War II.[26] As late as 1970 the International Society for Krishna Consciousness, a new movement of purported Indian origin, began attracting many ordinary people in California by its promise that repetitive chanting of certain phrases would insure attainment of the heart's desire.

When there is a general movement spawning personal status movements in this way, there are usually parallel value-oriented movements. Thus the women's suffrage movement and the mind cure movements were alternative responses to the women's plight during the last two decades of the nineteenth century. Similarly, the beatnik movement and its successor, the hippie movement, have been paralleled by the growth of the New Left since World War II. Many of the symbols are shared, though how much actual exchange of personnel takes place between the value- and participation-oriented streams is not well known.

Millennial Movements: Crucible for Activism

Especially prominent in recent times, but also of great antiquity, are the millenerian or millennial movements that center on the prophecy of a total and apocalyptic transformation of an evil world into a utopian state within the near future. These movements employ a religious ideology and are usually inspired by the leadership of a contemporary prophet. The prophet experiences a vision that reveals the evil nature of present arrangements, the outlines of the imminent new world, and the steps required of the faithful who would prepare themselves for the millennium. The prophet attracts a following of people who often identify him as their traditional deity or the reincarnation of a superhuman folk hero, although Wallace observes that most of these prophets have viewed themselves as emissaries and not as God or the folk hero personified.[27]

[25] Donald Meyer, *The Positive Thinkers: A Study of the American Quest for Health, Wealth and Personal Power from Mary Baker Eddy to Norman Vincent Peale* (Garden City, N. Y.: Doubleday and Company, Inc. 1965), p. 121.
[26] Norman Vincent Peale, *The Power of Positive Thinking* (Englewood Cliffs, N.J.: Prentice-Hall, Inc., 1952).
[27] Anthony F. C. Wallace, "Revitalization Movements," *American Anthropologist*, 58 (April, 1956), 272.

Wherever Europeans have colonized more primitive peoples and missionaries have endeavored to convert them to Christianity, movements combining apocalyptic themes with a traditional native world view have sprung up outside the conventional religious structures. Always they depict the white rulers as the cause of their misfortunes. With the coming of the messiah, or another apocalyptic event, whites will be driven out or permanently enslaved, and the people will live in a paradise patterned after a romantic image of their own past enriched by the material goods and comforts they have learned to appreciate from European cultures. In Melanesia these movements have often taken the form of cargo cults. Here the belief is that some great cargo of goods sent to the native people by their deity has been diverted by white men. The prophesied rescue of the cargo and punishment of the whites will insure plentifulness and peace thereafter. In Africa the blacks typically identify themselves with the Hebrews in their struggle to regain the promised land and use such Christian rituals as baptism to ward off sorcery and other local evils. In Latin America the projected savior is often a Catholic saint. In each area the movement takes a form that reflects unique features of

the contact between Europeans and natives.[28]

Millenarian movements also flourished in Europe under feudalism, suggesting parallels between feudal and colonial subjugation. They are distinctive in their commitment to revolutionary change that will come about not through their own attacks on the unjust order but through the intervention of external and usually supernatural force. In this respect they are initially passive, alerting their people to prepare for the coming event rather than to precipitate it. The passiveness undoubtedly derives from a combination of (1) so great an imbalance of power as to make effective use of bargaining or coercive methods inconceivable and (2) so great a cultural discrepancy that the millenarian constituency cannot form any understandable and coherent conception of the dominant culture. The applicability of these conditions to American Indians who participated in the ghost dance movements during the latter half of the nineteenth century is clear from the following account.

[28] Vittorio Lanternari, *The Religions of the Oppressed: A Study of Modern Messianic Cults* (London: MacGibbon and Kee Ltd., 1963).

Acculturation and Messianic Movements

Bernard Barber

Robert H. Lowie has recently called our attention again to the problem of messianic movements among the American aborigines. Among the North American Indians, one of the fundamental myths was the belief that a culture-hero would one day appear and lead them to a terrestrial paradise. Under certain conditions, which this paper will describe and analyze, these myths have become the

From the *American Sociological Review*, 6 (Oct., 1941), 663–69. Reprinted by permission of the American Sociological Association and the author.

ideological basis for messianic movements. In the messianic movement, the ushering in of the "golden age" by the messiah is announced for the *immediate* future. Twenty such movements had been recorded in the United States alone prior to 1890.

The messianic doctrine is essentially a statement of hope. Through the intervention of the Great Spirit or of his emissary, the earth will shortly be transformed into a paradise, enjoyed by both the living and the resurrected dead. In anticipation of the happy return to the golden age, believers must immediately return to the aboriginal mode of life. Traits and customs which are symbolic of foreign influence must be put aside. All members of the community—men, women and children—must participate. Besides reverting to the early folkways, believers must adopt special ritual practices until the millennium arrives. Thus, in the American Ghost Dance movements ceremonial bathing and an elaborate dance were the chief ritual innovations. The doctrine always envisages a restoration of earthly values. These values will be enjoyed, however, in a transcendental setting, for in the age which is foretold there will be no sickness or death; there will be only eternal happiness. The messianic doctrine is peaceful. The exclusion of the whites from the golden age is not so much a reflection of hostility toward them as a symbolization of the fulfillment of the former way of life. The millennium is to be established through divine agency; believers need only watch and pray.

The general sociocultural situation that precipitates a messianic movement has been loosely described as one of "harsh times." Its specific characteristic is the widespread experience of "deprivation"—the despair caused by inability to obtain what the culture has defined as the ordinary satisfactions of life. The fantasy situation pictured in the messianic doctrine attracts adherents chiefly because it includes those things which formerly provided pleasure in life, the loss of which constitutes deprivation. The pervasiveness of the precipitating cultural crises may be inferred from the broad range of sociocultural items to be restored in the golden age. For example, one of the Sioux participants in the Ghost Dance experienced a vision of an old-fashioned buffalo hunt, genuine in all details. He said that he had beheld the scouts dashing back to proclaim the sighting of a herd. Now, the killing off of the buffalo was probably the greatest blow to the Plains Indians. Another bitter grievance was the expropriation of the Indian lands and the segregation of the tribes on reservations; removal to a new geographical setting had more or less direct repercussions on every phase of the culture. For example, the prophet Smohalla promised, among other things, the restoration of the original tribal lands.

Deprivation may arise from the destruction not only of physical objects but also of sociocultural activities. In the aboriginal Sioux culture, millions of buffalo furnished an unlimited supply of food. Buffaloes and their by-products were perhaps the most important commodity in the Sioux economy, being employed as articles of exchange, as material for tepees, bedding, war shields, and the like. In addition, the buffalo was the focal point of many ritual and social activities of the Sioux. When the buffaloes were destroyed, therefore, the Sioux were deprived not only of food, but also of culturally significant activities. The tribal societies concerned with war and hunting lost their function and atrophied. The arts and techniques surrounding the buffalo hunt, arts and techniques which had once been sources of social status and of pride in "workmanship," were now rendered useless.

The impact of the white culture, besides depriving the Indians of their customary satisfactions, adds to their suffering by introducing the effects of new diseases and intoxicating liquor. In 1889, the Sioux suffered decimating epidemics of measles, grippe, and whooping cough. It is significant that Tenskwatawa prophesied that there would be no smallpox in the golden age. Complaints about the evil influences of firewater were expressed by "Open Door"; by "Handsome Lake," the Iroquois Prophet; by the Delaware Prophet; and by Kanakuk, among others.

The messianic movement served to "articulate the spiritual depression" of the Indians. Those groups which faced a cultural impasse were predisposed to accept a doctrine of hope. Correlatively, the tribes that rejected the doctrine were in a state in which the values of their old life still functioned. In a condition of anomie, where there is a disorganization of the "controlling normative structure," most of the members of the group are thrown out of adjustment with significant features of their social environment. The old set of social and cultural norms is undermined by the civilized culture. Expectations are frustrated, there is a "sense of confusion, a loss of orientation," there is no longer a foundation for security. At such a time, messianic prophecies are most likely to be accepted and made the basis of action. Messiahs preach the return to the old order, or rather, to a new order in which the old will be revived. Essentially, their function is to proclaim a *subtle order*, one which will define the ends of action. Their doctrines describe men's former life, meaningful and satisfactory.

The stabilizing function of the messianic movement may be illustrated in specific cases. Investigation of the 1870 and 1890 North American Ghost Dance movements shows that they are correlated with widespread deprivation. The two movements, though they originated in the same tribe, the North Paiute of Nevada, spread over different areas, depending upon the presence or absence of a deprivation situation. A comparison of the two movements makes the relationship clear-cut. The Ghost Dance of 1870 spread only through northern California; the tribes in that area had "suffered as great a disintegration by 1870 . . . as the average tribe of the central United States had undergone by 1890." In 1890, the Ghost Dance once again spread from the North Paiute, but this time not to California. By 1875, the movement there had exhausted itself and was abandoned. All the dancing and adherence to the rules of conduct had failed to bring the golden age. Disillusionment supervened upon the discovery that the movement was an inadequate response. The alternative response seems to have been a despondent and relatively amorphous adaptation. The Indians "had long since given up all hope and wish of the old life and adapted themselves as best they might to the new civilization that engulfed them." The 1890 movement did spread to the Plains tribes because by 1890 their old life had virtually disappeared, and the doctrine of the Ghost Dance was eagerly adopted for the hope that it offered. The radical changes among the Plains tribes in the twenty-year period, 1870–90, may best be traced by examining the history of the Teton Sioux. Up to 1868, they were the least affected by white contact of all the tribes of the Plains area. By 1890, however, they were experiencing an intense deprivation situation, the climax of a trend which had begun twenty years before. Especially severe were the years between 1885–90, when crops failed, many cattle died of disease, and a large part of the population was carried off by epidemics.

Further corroboration of the positive correlation of the messianic movement with extended deprivation has been presented by Nash. In 1870, the Ghost Dance doctrine was presented to three tribes which had been brought together on the Klamath reservation six years before, the Klamath, the Modoc, and the Paviotso. Of the three tribes, the Modoc, who had experienced the greatest amount of deprivation, participated most intensely. The Paviotso, who had experienced minimal cultural changes, participated least of all. Moreover, Nash found that within the tribes the members participated differentially, in rough proportion to the deprivation experienced.

A case study of the Navaho furnishes still further support for our thesis. Until quite recently, the Navaho territory was relatively isolated; few roads crossed it and there were not more than two thousand white inhabitants. The Navaho had managed to maintain the essentials of their own culture; their economic life had remained favorable; and, from 1869 to 1931, they increased in numbers from less than 10,000 to 45,000. In 1864, in retaliation for their marauding, the United States Government rounded up the Navaho and banished them to the Bosque Redondo on the Pecos River. This exile was an exception to the fact that in general they had not suffered deprivation. They could not adapt to the agricultural life imposed on them and begged for permission to go home. Many died during epidemics of smallpox, whooping cough, chicken pox, and pneumonia. After four years, they were given sheep, goats, and clothing by the Government and allowed to return to their own country.

The equilibrium of the Navaho culture was quickly restored. The tribe grew rich in herds and silver. The old way of life was resumed in its essentials despite the greater emphasis on a pastoral economy. The deprivation situation of 1864–68 was left behind; life was integrated around a stable culture pattern. In the winter of 1889–90, when Paiute runners tried to spread the belief in the coming of the Ghost Dance Messiah, their mission was fruitless. "They preached and prophesied for a considerable time, but the Navaho were skeptical, laughed at the prophets, and paid but little attention to their prophecies." There was no social need of a redeemer.

Within the last fifteen years, however, the entire situation of the Navaho tribe has changed. There has been constantly increasing contact with the white culture. Automobiles and railroads have brought tourists. The number of trading stores has increased. The discovery of oil on the reservation has produced rapid changes. Children have been sent to Government schools, far from their homes. Since 1929, the depression has reduced the income from the sale of blankets and silver jewelry. By far the most important difficulty now confronting the Navaho is the problem of overgrazing and soil erosion. To avert disaster, a basic reorganization of the economic activities of the tribe is necessary. Therefore, the Government to meet this *objective* condition, has introduced a soil-erosion and stock-reduction program but it has been completely unsatisfactory to the Navaho. Stock-reduction not only threatens their economic interests, *as they see them,* but undermines the basis of important sentiments and activities in the Navaho society. To destroy in a wanton fashion the focus of so many of their day-to-day interests cuts the cultural ground from under them.

Thus at present the Navaho are experiencing widespread deprivation. Significantly enough, within the past few years there has been a marked emergence of anti-white sentiment. Revivalistic cults have appeared. There has also been a great increase in recourse to aboriginal ceremonials on all occasions. Long reports of Navaho revivalistic activities were carried recently in *The Farmington Times Hustler*, a weekly published in Farmington, New Mexico. These activities bear a detailed similarity to the Ghost Dance and other American Indian messianic doctrines.

Despite the positive correlation of the messianic movement and deprivation, there is no one-to-one relation between these variables. It is here suggested that the messianic movement is *only one of several alternative responses*. In the other direction, the relationship is more determinate; the messianic movement is comprehensible only as a response to widespread deprivation. The alternative response of armed rebellion and physical violence has already been suggested. The depopulation among the natives of the South Pacific Islands may be viewed as still another response. The moral depression which, it often has been held, is one of the "causes" of the decline of the native races may be construed as a mode of reaction to the loss of an overwhelming number of satisfactions.

The theory of alternative responses may be tentatively checked against another set of data. The Ghost Dance among the Plains tribes lasted little more than a year or two, coming to a sharp end as a result of the suppression of the so-called "Sioux outbreak" with which it adventitiously had become connected in the minds of the whites. The Government agents on the Indian reservations successfully complied with their instructions to exterminate the movement. However, the deprivation of the tribes remained as acute as ever. It is in this context that the Peyote cult emerged and spread among the Indians *as an alternative respose.* It became the focus of a marked increase of attention and activity after 1890, thus coming in approximate temporal succession to the Ghost Dance. Completely nonviolent and nonthreatening to the White culture, the Peyote cult has been able to survive in an environment which was radically opposed to the messianic movements.

The general and specific sociocultural matrices of the Peyote cult are the same as those of the messianic movements. The Indians

Fifty years ago, when Peyote first became known to them . . . were experiencing . . . despair and hopelessness over their vanishing culture, over their defeats, over the past grandeur that could not be regained. They were facing a spiritual crisis . . . Some turned to Peyotism, and as time has but intensified the antagonistic forces, more and more have become converted to the new religion which offers a means of escape . . .

The Peyote cult, like the messianic movement, was an "autistic" response, in Lasswell's terms, but the essential element of its doctrine was different. Whereas the Ghost Dance doctrine had graphically described a revision to the aboriginal state, the Peyote cult crystallized around passive acceptance and resignation in the face of the existing deprivation. It is an alternative response which seems to be better adapted to the existing phase of acculturation.

Thus we have tested the hypotheses that the primitive messianic movement is correlated with the occurrence of widespread deprivation and that it is only one of several alternative responses. There is a need for further studies, especially in regard to the specific sociocultural conditions which produce each of the possible responses.

Although the inescapability of American domination made the ghost dance little more than a temporary diversion, millennial movements elsewhere have had more notable consequences. They have often supplied a vehicle through which a traditional culture threatened with obliteration could be revitalized and protected. The Christianization of native peoples has usually been a shallow reinterpretation of Christian ideas being fit into native frames of reference, with many primitive beliefs and practices continuing sub rosa. As native culture is undermined in the colonial situation, the millennial movement promises a coherent and complete way of life that integrates the threatened religious practices with the whole of life. In religion the people can find a freedom to practice their traditional values that is difficult to find in other spheres of life. "Religious autonomy resolves the conflict between an outside power striving to destroy native culture and the culture's own power to resist and survive, between willful opposition to an alien culture and supine acquiescence in the demands of an alien ruling minority."[29]

In practice, many of these movements go far beyond waiting passively for the apocalypse. When making explicit the evil view of their current situation, millennial movements reinforce and sanction negative views of the established order. In combination with the radical world view the movement supplies a new perspective from which the native people can transform discontent into a sense of injustice. It provides ritual procedures through which to express collective resentment. Frequently under this stimulation some of the members become impatient and violence breaks out against the rulers.

The main ostensible program of a millennial movement is to prepare members for the millennium. This is done through acts of ritual purification and disidentification with established conditions. These range from keeping aloof, being noncooperative, destroying their own property, and discontinuing their regular work, to breaking hallowed taboos and desecrating established religious symbols. Even when there are no attacks on people or property outside the movement, bizarre and unpredictable acts on a mass basis and the prospect of economic routines being interrupted concern the authorities. Worsley's accounts of Melanesian cargo cults repeatedly demonstrate how government efforts to control the movement because of its disruptive potential gave people their first experience of mass confrontation for a cause.[30]

Cohn identifies the supporters of those medieval European millennial movements that frequently became violent as:

...the surplus population living on the margin of society—peasants without land or with too little land even for subsistence; journeymen and unskilled workers living under the continuous threat of unemployment; beggars and vagabonds—in fact from that amorphous mass of people who were not simply poor but who could find no assured and recognized place in society at all.[31]

Waves of chiliastic excitement—as the more active manifestations of millenarianism in Europe were called—occurred after such great disasters as the plague, famine, and the Black Death. These marginal people required the authority of the medieval church for stability and security, yet found no place for themselves in that church. The unconventional religious movements were substitutes for the church. Detached from conventional authority, driven by the desperation of the adherents, and oriented to a forthcoming apocalypse that made the here and now irrelevant, these movements

[29] Laternari, *Religions of the Oppressed*, p. 320.

[30] Peter Worsley, *The Trumpet Shall Sound: A Study of "Cargo" Cults in Melanesia* (London: MacGibbon and Kee, 1957).
[31] Norman Cohn, *The Pursuit of the Millennium* (New York: Oxford Press, 1957), p. 314.

often became ruthless totalitarian forces. As one movement succeeded another, borrowing and adding to earlier ideologies, there developed a powerful ideological tradition in which Cohn sees the roots for the fanatical and totalitarian themes of modern Fascist and Communist movements.[32]

Although Cohn's argument rests more on resemblance than on demonstrated influence, the progression from cargo cults in Melanesia and messianic prophet movements in Africa to the powerful nationalist movements in both areas can be documented convincingly.[33] Millennial movements crossed over tribal boundaries and supplied the basis for a new unity in collective action. It brought forth and apprenticed leaders for the larger unity. Although discouragement caused an initial setback when forecasted millennia failed to materialize or when the "infallible" prophet leader was killed or imprisoned or bought off by the government, the prevailing accommodation to colonial rule had been destroyed. Restlessness soon developed. Wiser from the experience and less fearful after once confronting the white man, leaders turned in a more secular direction. Talmon speaks of millenarianism as "a *connecting link* between pre-political and political movements. It lubricates the passage from pre-modern religious revolt to a full-fledged revolutionary movement."[34]

The case of millennial movements that change from psychological escape to active attack on a repressive order can also be illustrated from the history of the Black Muslims in the United States. In 1938 Beynon wrote about a group known in the Detroit community as the "voodoo cult," because of their supposedly outlandish and primitive rituals.[35] They revered a leader who spoke for Allah, adopted Arabic names, and followed what they imagined to be the Moslem religion. Initially the movement offered little beyond the participation gratifications of a group-supported perspective, enabling adherents to deny the inferior status objectively assigned them in America. But popular fear of the group with the attendant revolutionary definition and militant leadership helped to turn the movement increasingly toward the active part it came to play as the contemporary Black Muslims.

[32] Ibid., pp. 307–19.

[33] Worsley, *The Trumpet Shall Sound*; Thomas Hodgkin, *Nationalism in Colonial Africa* (New York: New York University Press, 1957).

[34] Yonina Talmon, "Pursuit of the Millennium: The Relation between Religious and Social Change," *Archives Europeennes de Sociologie*, (No. 1, 1962), p. 143, see also pp. 125–48.

[35] Erdmann D. Beynon, "The Voodoo Cult among Negro Migrants in Detroit," *American Journal of Sociology*, 43 (May, 1938), 894–907.

19

MOVEMENT ORGANIZATION AND LEADERSHIP

We have chosen to arrange our examination of social movements about the *functioning* of movements—generating and implementing values, cultivating and exercising power, and supplying membership gratifications. From time to time we have pointed out how patterns of *organization* in movements affect performance of the functions. There is no need to repeat all of these scattered observations in a comprehensive review of the principles of movement organization. But there are a few organizational variables that warrant separate treatment. We shall deal with two questions in this chapter. (1) How does the unusually prominent part played by individual leadership in social movements affect their functioning? (2) What influences affect the type of organizational pattern adopted by a movement?

Leader-dominated Movements

The continuity in some forms of collective behavior depends almost entirely on conspicuous leadership. The effects that this principle of organization has on collective behavior can be seen most clearly in the case of *followings,* which lack the full development and societal impact of true movements. Many of the same effects are visible in the *charismatic* movement, a true movement centered about a leader to whom unusual or supernatural qualities are attributed.

THE FOLLOWING. The following is a collectivity made up of persons interacting to express their adoration for a public personage. Since they are too preoccupied with worshipping their hero to promote social reforms, the following—like the cult—is a *quasi-movement.* Indeed, cults are often followings and followings are sometimes cults. The preoccupation with gratifications derived from worshipping the idol makes the following an almost purely participation-oriented form of collective behavior.

The most obvious followings are the fans who worship a star in the entertainment or sports world. Because adolescents frequently appear prominently in these followings and because of bizarre behavior such as swooning, screaming, and weeping in the presence of the idol, pathological interpretations of the behavior of fans are often made. Undoubtedly such interpretations are justified in the case of more extreme participants. But, as we have noted for crowd behavior, an atmosphere of permissiveness and sanction among normal people is at least a minimum condition for such extravagant expression. Furthermore, a comparison with more conventional followings reveals widespread similarities. Many characteristics of followings of political leaders or even leaders in the world of scholarship resemble those of the fan clubs for movie stars.

In listing some common characteristics of followings, we shall offer examples from two contrasting followings. E. J. Kahn's account of the original Sinatra following, which needs little revision to describe followers of Elvis Presley, Chubby Checker, the Beatles, and more recent adolescent idols, supplies one set of illustrations.[1] The more sedate followings composed of adult professionals or business people and centered on prominent scholars or business leaders provide a companion set of examples.

1. The followers develop a definite group sense, communicate extensively among themselves, and develop symbols and norms whereby the ingroup can be distinguished from the outgroup. The special slang that fans adopt, often taking the favorite phrases of their idols, is approximated by the professional jargon whereby the followers in particular schools of thought can be identified. The ingroup sense not only distinguishes the outgroup but also the less acceptable followers. The unduly boisterous admirers of Sinatra were known as fiends to be distinguished from fans, and schools of thought differentiate the naive from the sophisticated adherents.

2. The followers develop a prestige hierarchy among themselves based upon proximity to the leader and recognition extended by him. Sinatra's fans gained prestige by seeing him, touching him, or acquiring intimate souvenirs, and they feared to offend his chief lieutenants. Training under a thought leader, or receiving his attention, or even teaching in the same school, confers prestige in an academic following.

3. Members of a following define their relations to other followings as opposition and rivalry. Sinatra's followers actually enjoyed opportunities to defend their idol against imagined or real slurs, and they constantly attempted to detract from other bobby-sox idols and popular singers. Ardent academic followers devote great pains to proving that the ideas of their leader can-

---

[1] E. J. Kahn, Jr., *The Voice* (New York: Harper and Row, Publishers, 1947).

---

not coexist with other contemporary schools of thought and concentrate on discovering the underlying fallacies in other viewpoints.

4. The members of a following are preoccupied with accumulating every conceivable item of information about their hero, seeking to identify and interpret his opinions on various subjects. The singer's fans want to know what he eats for breakfast and thinks about the world situation; academic followers are often more concerned with correctly interpreting the master's opinion on a subject than they are with the subject itself.

5. The followers identify with the leader, gloating in his success and suffering personally under his setbacks. Sinatra's fans wrote letters to newspapers and producers to promote his interests and they suffered during his illnesses. Academic followers experience reflected prestige when their leader is recognized and devote much personal energy to assuring that he is properly recognized by all.

6. To the followers, the prestige of their leader translates the commonplace into the profound and resolves uncertainties by providing a position they can adopt. Many of Sinatra's followers attributed omniscience to him and wrote for personal advice. Academic or business followers quote commonplace opinions of their leader as profound contributions and substitute his authority for arguments in resolving moot issues. The academic or business leader, like the popular entertainer, constantly finds remarks that he has made lightly or "off the cuff" taken unduly seriously by his followers.

THE CHARISMATIC MOVEMENT. The idea of charismatic leadership was introduced into sociological thinking by Max Weber, and the term has since come into widespread popular use. "The term 'charisma' will be applied to a certain quality of an individual personality by virtue of which he is set apart from ordinary men and treated as endowed with supernatural, super-human, or at least specifically exceptional powers or qualities."[2] These are qualities deemed inaccessible to ordinary people, of divine origin or at least in the nature of "gifts" rather than achievements. Belief in his gift of superhuman wisdom, strength, or goodness encourages uncritical support of the charismatic leader's commands.

The full range of qualities and capabilities ascribed to the charismatic leader is clearly more image than reality, and much of the reality is in the nature of self-fulfilling prophecies. No leader is so wise or infallible as the most ardent followers of Franklin Roosevelt, Dwight Eisenhower, or John Kennedy supposed them to be. Fear of provoking the wrath of their loyal followings led many public figures to comply with their requests, thus contributing to the image of omnipotence. On the other hand, there are undoubtedly some personal qualities without which charisma will not be ascribed to an individual. Until we examine this question later in the chapter, we shall assume that few *people* are potential charismatic leaders but that most charismatic *qualities* are more image than reality.

The leaders of popular followings who are not also leaders of charismatic movements lack two important characteristics of the latter. First, their spheres of competence are compartmentalized, whereas the charismatic leader's capabilities are wide range. The popular entertainer or athlete does enter the race for political office with an initial advantage, but he must also prove his acceptability in the new sphere of activity, and he usually loses some of his earlier following by this effort to extend his leadership beyond his original sphere. Second, the leadership of most popular idols is not taken seriously by persons who make the decisions about important events. When the President of the United States appears to consult evangelist Billy Graham on ques-

tions of public policy, he gives evidence that Graham is a charismatic leader and not merely the leader of a specialized following.

A movement takes on certain characteristics by virtue of being built around a charismatic leader. The nature and basis of adherence will affect the "texture" of the movement.[3] The personal following of the charismatic leader provides a highly flexible body of adherents who will give enthusiastic support without questioning unexplained changes or ideological inconsistencies in the movement program. The confidence in the exceptional personal qualities of the leader also contributes an intense and unwavering quality of support that may be lacking in movements without a charismatic leader.

In a strictly value-oriented movement uncomplicated by a charismatic leader the recurring problems of maintaining active support within the movement are likely to revolve about varied interpretations of the movement's values and the necessary value compromises to power considerations. While these problems are lessened when there is strong devotion to the leader, the specific problem of maintaining the charisma of the leader becomes crucial in this type of movement. A movement with a well-worked-out program of reform may suffer an irremediable setback because the popular image of the leader is discredited. It may not even be essential that he is discredited as a person; it may be sufficient merely to demonstrate that he is no more than a capable and conscientious mortal.

The decision-making process in the charismatic movement has an effect upon the stability of the movement objective. The concentration of decision in the person of the charismatic leader frees the movement from the inconsistencies of program due to shifting power structure within the movement. But the decision process is also freed from the stabilizing effect of internal

2 Max Weber, *The Theory of Social and Economic Organization,* tr. by A. M. Henderson and Talcott Parsons, Talcott Parsons, ed. (New York: Oxford University Press, 1947), p. 358.

3 The word "texture" is borrowed from Rudolph Heberle, in *Social Movements* (New York: Appleton-Century-Crofts, 1951), pp. 128ff.

criticism and discussion, so that personal inconsistencies and idiosyncrasies enter disproportionately into program determination.

There is a major tendency in every movement for the leader, by virtue of his elevated position, to be protectively isolated from normal criticism. A man can seldom maintain a balanced perspective regarding himself when his exposure to evaluations by others is highly selective. The public worship and the expressed admiration of those close to him generate in the leader an exaggerated conception of his own capabilities. Such an exaggerated conception leads to arrogance, dependence on his own hunches rather than a careful weighing of viewpoints, and intolerance of all opposition. Thus the personal and impulsive element in decision-making increases, the disproportionate influence of personal favorites becomes greater, and the probability of strategic blunders that will wreck the movement is magnified.

Hans Gerth has demonstrated in the case of the Nazi movement how charismatic dominance led to a certain kind of internal organization. Crucial to the entire organization was the "inner circle," consisting of top officials who were personally favored by Hitler. There was no defined route nor any set of prescribed qualifications for gaining or losing membership in the inner circle. Members were not assigned to specific offices with defined responsibilities and authority. Instead each member received a vague commission from the Fuhrer and sought to extend his power at the expense of others among the inner circle. "Purges" resulted when individuals or factions within the inner circle fell from favor. Exaggerated attention to such expressions of homage as the "Heil Hitler" salute and fantastic praise of the leader were constant means of attempting to insure the member's continuing position. Thus key control of the movement was based not on qualifications to lead but upon, "the changing personality preferences of the leader and...the power which the individual member may secure through institutional entrenchment and factional support by powerful 'friends' "[4]

Leader Roles

Up to this point we have been discussing the single conspicuous leader in a movement and treating him as if all the leadership functions were vested in a single person. However, there are many leaders in every movement, some of whom are conspicuous and some of whom are completely unknown to the bulk of the adherents. Furthermore, the term *leadership* implies several different kinds of roles that are essential to a movement but that are often vested in specialized personalities.

These leadership functions can be initially divided into two: namely, symbol and decision maker. The leader as symbol is one whose own activities are of less significance to the course of a movement than the image of him that the members hold. As a symbol he represents to them some important aspect of the movement—its ideology, its struggle, its assurance of success, or the kind of people who constitute the ingroup. In contrast, the leader as decision maker is one who actually helps to determine the course of the movement by his own preferences and activities and by the effectiveness with which he promotes his own inclinations. In this section we shall discuss the leader as symbol, and in the following we shall consider his position as a decision maker.

THE LEADER AS SYMBOL. The leader may serve as a very general symbol to the movement, or he may symbolize only one specialized feature. The charismatic leader has the former quality of symbolizing the entire character and objectives of the movement and the struggle from which it emerges. For this reason the charismatic

4 Hans Gerth, "The Nazi Party: Its Leadership and Composition," *American Journal of Sociology*, 45 (January, 1940), 521, see also 517–41.

movement normally demands a leader who is somewhat apart from the conventional authority. Authorities who are known to be capable, who are widely respected and unquestioningly entrusted with major institutional decisions, may be abandoned in favor of unproven leaders when a movement begins to develop. The leader who symbolizes the revolt against convention by his uncultured manner, who symbolizes personal struggle in his own life, who symbolizes the personal independence and power of impulsive action, will strike a more responsive chord than the competent conventional leader among those who have become dissatisfied with the established order.

In an even more specific way the charismatic leaders of different movements in different eras symbolize the prevalent personal struggles of the group to whom a particular movement appeals, or the predominant struggles of an era. Erik H. Erikson has offered an interesting set of speculations concerning the imagery surrounding Adolf Hitler and its relation to the struggles of German youth within a highly patriarchal family system.[5] John M. Mecklin has examined the saint as a leader of charismatic movements specific to certain historical eras.[6] He attempted to show that the saint rose to prominence in the Middle Ages because he symbolized one of the basic conflicts of that era and was replaced by a different kind of charismatic leader when an era with new preoccupations succeeded the Middle Ages. The symbol of the saint won devotion in a way that leaders symbolizing nationalistic striving or class striving have done in more recent times.

The symbol embodied by a leader is partly a reflection of his own personal characteristics, partly a creation of the promoters of the movement, and largely a projection by the followers. The appeal of the symbol and the desire to discover the successful resolution of their own struggles exemplified in a person of high prestige create a potential following of persons who are ready to supply the gaps in the leader image and to overlook contradictions. Some apparent success, recognition, or personal strength is a necessary condition for such large-scale projection to take place. Many outstanding charismatic leaders have failed miserably and been mere objects of ridicule in their first efforts at leadership. At a time when they had not yet validated their claim to charisma, the process of imputing the qualities of the symbol to them did not automatically take place. But once sufficiently startling success or personal power can be demonstrated, the symbol-imputation process snowballs.

Besides the danger of revealing personal weakness or lack of self-confidence and unwavering decision, the chief danger to the leader symbol is its defilement because of the practical demands imposed by the movement. The prophet who only preaches and is never faced with the practical necessity for implementing his ideas encounters less danger here than the leader with a genuine program to carry out. The latter will be faced with the advantages of compromise, of deals with vested interests and established conventional leaders, and the dangers from conspicuous errors of judgment and programs that do not work as they are intended to. But even the sheer prophet must cope with jealousy and power struggles within high movement echelons, and heresy and schism within the following.

Two mechanisms help to protect the inviolability of the leader symbol from these dangers. One is the self-protecting character of the symbolizing process itself, which makes for selective perception and a special valuation on the actions of the symbolized person. The followers do not see the faults of the leader, they refuse to believe them and attribute the accounts to the malice of others. And the very actions that are de-

[5] Erik H. Erikson, *Childhood and Society* (New York: W. W. Norton and Company, Inc., 1950), 284–315.
[6] John M. Mecklin, *The Passing of the Saint* (Chicago: University of Chicago Press, 1941).

spised in the unsuccessful are admired in charismatic leaders. Intolerance in a lesser person becomes resolute action in the leader; inconsistency and wavering in the lesser person become inspired leadership.

The other mechanism is the delegation to subordinates of the more practical tasks and the assignment to them of responsibility for actions that might compromise the leader symbol. It has even been suggested that every great leader has to have someone to do his dirty work for him so that his own image remains unbesmirched. As the movement gains by tactics or compromises that violate the purity of its value orientations, the leader is conceived as succeeding in spite of these defections and as suffering for the frailties of his followers. In extreme cases the lieutenant can be sacrificed as a scapegoat to an unpopular decision or notorious failure.

In addition to the generalized-symbol leaders there are the many types of specialized symbols that play important but segmental roles in the success of a movement. These specialized images are crucial at certain stages in the development of a movement or in dealing with special groups of adherents. There is probably an unlimited number of different symbol types that play parts in maintaining the support and strength of a movement. But unlike the charismatic leader who symbolizes the movement in general, these specialized symbols are only effective at certain junctures. At the wrong time in movement development, or in dealing with the wrong population, they are ineffectual, if not damaging, to the movement. We shall discuss only one of these specialized symbols, the *martyr*.

The function of the martyr symbol is chiefly to strengthen the determination of persons who are already adherents and to marshal active support from those who are giving passive support or are ambivalent about the movement. This function of winning persons on the borderline and reinforcing those within the movement is accomplished by two effects of the martyr symbol. First, the image of the martyr arouses indignation against the opponents of the movement. The suspicion that the movement concerns a disagreement among reasonable men is dissipated if it can be shown that the opponents will stop at nothing to resist the movement. The martyr should be outnumbered, never given a chance, betrayed, and killed in an unnecessarily brutal way. Indignation, demand for retributive justice, and the conviction that the movement's opponents are persons outside the moral order help to win support.

Second, the image of the martyr symbolizes true and unwavering devotion to the cause and thereby evokes guilt and shame in the half-hearted adherents. The member is reminded of his own delinquent support by contrast to the martyr and may even feel that the martyr would not have died except for his and other people's indifference.

While the martyr is sometimes personally worthy of the badge, he is often merely a fool who has been a constant embarrassment to movement leaders and whose demise takes place in a foolhardy and profitless undertaking. Sometimes he is merely a chance victim. In either case, his image is quickly translated into that of the true martyr. The martyr is more likely to be created in the early than the late phases of a movement. Extreme sacrifice and posing irreconcilable oppositions are more in keeping with the melodrama and enthusiasm of a movement's early stages than with the more practical and either self-confident or defeatist spirit of the later stages.

THE LEADER AS DECISION MAKER. There are many kinds of decisions that must be made within a movement, and to varying degrees they are vested in different leaders. Many different classifications of these types of leaders have been attempted. Crane Brinton, for example, suggests four:

I suggest very tentatively that the entrepreneurship of revolution or other radical change requires at least four kinds of skills not often possessed by one man. First, there is the discovery, the invention, of basic ideas, or better yet, theories. Second, there is the devising of suitable methods of spreading these ideas, getting them accepted, influencing men to act upon them—in short, the task of the propagandist and advertiser. These two functions, that of the theorist and that of the propagandist, are usually in real life very closely interwined—a classical example is Karl Marx —but I hope you will agree with me that we ought to make an effort to distinguish them in analysis. . . . Third, there is the task of creating and holding the personal loyalty of the followers. This is the function for which the terms orator, symbol, priest, hero are not quite adequate. It is in fact a very complex function, and one which we do not understand very well, though we can recognize success at it in men like Robespierre and Hitler. Fourth, there is the manipulator in the narrow sense, the man in the smoke-filled room, the man who deals not with the masses, but personally and directly with the few important men at the top.[7]

Rex D. Hopper has called our attention to a popular classification of leader types according to their predominance at successive stages in development of the movement.[8] Beginning with the agitator, the succession is to the prophet and reformer, then to the statesman, and finally to the administrator-executive. The succession reflects a steady increase in preoccupation with administering the movement and with tactics for implementing objectives, and an increasing separation between the functions of symbol and decision maker.

From studying the history of the Women's Christian Temperance Union, Gusfield was impressed by the inability of one leader to perform equally effectively the

tasks of articulator and mobilizer. Articulation means establishing favorable relationships with the community, and mobilization means stimulating and inspiring the movement's adherents.

As an articulator of the movement in the total society the leader must learn the limits and possibility of actions in the light of the power ideologies of influential persons and organizations outside of the movement. He must attempt to sway these to the uses of the movement as best as may be done. . . . In its function of mobilization, the movement develops an elan for the ideas it espouses and for the work or sacrifice that the mission of the movement entails. Because membership must be "counted on" in moments of crises, the mobilization function entails the development of the separate identity of the movement and the forging of strong ties between membership and staff.[9]

Because the articulator tries to make the movement acceptable to outsiders, he strikes much of the excitement and sense of unique mission from the movement. The mobilizer strengthens these features but frightens and offends outsiders. The mobilizer is more important during early stages of movement growth and the articulator during later stages. Movements of long duration achieve a solution to the contradiction between these roles in two ways. First, they alternate leadership types. Gusfield found a consistent alternation during the history of the W. C. T. U. But movements also minimize contradiction by selecting colorless leaders who perform both functions in a mediocre fashion but pursue neither task aggressively enough to undermine the other.

The popular identification of a movement with the conspicuous leader tends to obscure questions concerning the consonance between decisions by leaders and the

7 Crane Brinton, "The Manipulation of Economic Unrest," *The Tasks of Economic History,* Supplement VIII (1948), pp. 25–26, by permission of the Economic History Association.

8 Rex D. Hopper, "The Revolutionary Process: A Frame of Reference for the Study of Revolutionary Movements," *Social Forces,* 28 (March, 1950), 270–79.

9 Joseph R. Gusfield, "Functional Areas of Leadership in Social Movements," *Sociological Quarterly,* 7 (Summer, 1966), 140, see also 137–56.

decisions that in fact guide the movement. And yet in many different ways the actual course of a movement will not correspond to the personal decisions of any of its leaders. We illustrate this observation with three prominent kinds of discrepancy.

First, there is usually a continuous conflict between leaders who are more value oriented and those more concerned with the power and organization of the movement itself. At different stages the decisions run more in the direction of one group than of the other, but the conflict and compromise between points of view are continuous and give rise to de facto decisions that do not correspond precisely to the personal inclinations of either type of leader.

Second, a movement is frequently precipitated into an extreme position that its more moderate leaders then find themselves committed to defend and promote. Extreme declarations or actions by minor leaders and others publicly identified with the movement operate in two ways to render moderate positions untenable. On the one hand they anger the opposition and make them less receptive to negotiation and compromise. And on the other hand, as symbols to the adherents, they become rallying points within the movement for extreme action. An incident symbolized as martyrdom likewise precipitates more extreme positions. Many famous leaders have been like George Washington, who at first favored compromise within the framework of the British Empire and reluctantly moved into leadership of the revolutionary movement that had been precipitated by the actions of others. Lucretia Mott and Susan B. Anthony, who became major leaders in the American woman suffrage movement, were among those not originally in sympathy with women's unseemly departure from their historic status. Changes in the temper of black movements since World War II have caused the rapid obsolescence of leaders who did not shift to an ever more militant stance. The massive urban violence of 1965 and 1967 created a severe problem for most black leaders.

The established Negro leaders, whether of the old elite or of the newest, most militant generation, had to react to the riots even though they did not desire them. It was their response to the violence of the crowd that brought illegal rioting into the mainstream of the revolution and made it part of the strategy of protest. This response was essentially one of using the riots as a weapon of protest even while deploring them. There was little else that the leaders could do if they were to preserve even a semblance of leadership.[10]

Third, the ideologist or prophet who formulates the ideals of the movement frequently suffers disillusionment over the translation of his ideas into the less visionary frames of reference of the movement personnel. Such distortion occurs through the necessary mixing of ideal- and self-interest within the movement. Labor ideologists, for example, frequently hold the broader conception of labor movement objectives as including promotion of general community welfare in contrast to membership who apply the more immediate self-interest criteria to policy statements. Within the C.I.O. the leadership have encountered reluctance and occasionally open revolt in their efforts to make equalitarian race relations an objective on a par with improved wages and working conditions.

John Milton provides an instructive example of an ideologist whose absolute ideals led him to reject movement after movement, shifting his own position from that of a moderate reformist to more and more extreme positions as he became disillusioned with all attempts to implement moderate ideas.[11] The end result was to

10 Lewis M. Killian, *The Impossible Revolution? Black Power and the American Dream* (New York: Random House, Inc., 1968), p. 106.

11 Dora N. Raymond, *Oliver's Secretary: John Milton in an Era of Revolt* (New York: Minton, Balch and Co., 1932).

alienate him from all the independence movements of his time and to create a personal disillusionment that led him to adopt essentially aristocratic patterns of thought that contradicted his lifelong dedication to equality and freedom.

THE PERSON AND SCOPE OF THE LEADER. After examining the characteristics of the following, the creation of the charismatic image, and the functions of leaders as symbols and decision makers, we return to the question of who the person is that steps into one of these roles. The most general answer that can be given to this question is to suggest that each occasion makes its own demands of the leader, and these demands are seldom identical from one situation to another. This conception is neatly summarized by Clarence Marsh Case in what he refers to as the "conjuncture" theory of leadership.[12]

Leadership, Case suggests, results from the conjuncture of certain personality traits, a unique social situation, and an event. An event is an intrusive change that "disrupts the smooth flow of routinary change, of static, recurrent social process" in a specific situation. The event creates the occasion for leadership, and the situation determines the tasks of leadership. The personality traits suited to leadership in one situation are inappropriate to another situation. A man or woman is boosted into a position of leadership not because he possesses any generalized qualities of leadership but because he happens to be in the appropriate place when an event occurs and is able to exhibit the qualities and employ the skills that are demanded by the specific situation.

The conjuncture theory is surely more nearly correct than any theory that singles out potential leaders on the basis of universally applicable qualities of personality. And yet we cannot escape the observation that some people turn up as leaders in a

variety of situations. The study of leadership traits is difficult because institutional leadership positions protect and support the authority of persons who do not possess qualities of spontaneous leadership. The leaders of social movements are less well protected and their own effectiveness should therefore play a larger part. On the other hand, the leader of a movement is in a situation unlike that of the leader in a small face-to-face group. His direct personal contacts are with but a few persons in key positions and his relations with the bulk of membership personnel are through intermediaries and his public personality. The effective primary group leader may lack a public personality, and a person who is unimpressive and even disliked in primary relations may become a tremendously effective charismatic leader.

But the leader personality is more than just what he brings to the situation; it includes the personal transformations he undergoes after he begins carrying out the leader role. The image that the following creates demands his conformity. The selective communication that he receives modifies his perspective. The sense of his role and the routine imposed upon him require extensive adjustment. J. E. Hulett, Jr. has supplied an instructive account of the manner in which Elizabeth Kenny evolved from the Australian bush nurse putting forward a novel technique for treating paralyzed victims of poliomyelitis to the "Sister Kenny" who was the charismatic leader of a worldwide movement against the asserted blindness and selfishness of the established medical profession. For example, Hulett notes that:

One of the ways in which a cult leader responds to the leadership situation is to undergo an evolution of ideas regarding the theoretical basis for the movement. This leader's conception of her role has evolved from that of a simple pragmatist to that of the astute hypothesist. Whereas at first she merely applied a pragmatic discovery to the treatment of the disease, she now has developed

12 Clarence M. Case, "Leadership and Conjuncture: A Sociological Hypothesis," *Sociology and Social Research*, 17 (July, 1933), 510–13.

a whole "new concept" of the disease which she describes as "the direct opposite" of the concept previously held by medical world.[13]

The characteristics, then, that distinguish the leader of a movement are not fully apparent in the individual before he assumes leadership but exist largely in the capacity to respond to his role and his public image in an effective way.

A final question that arises from the preceding discussion concerns the scope of the leader's effectiveness. If the leader is precipitated into a leadership position by a unique historical conjuncture and his effective retention of leadership depends upon supporting the image that his followers create and upon making decisions in keeping with trends in the movement, it may appear that the leader is merely a puppet. Perhaps he is nothing but the passive agent through which the determinism of history takes place.

While the issue of such total determinism is not ultimately resolvable by historical evidence, one of the clearest and most considered statements on the issue has been made by Sidney Hook.[14] Although events normally allow the leader little real discretion, there are certain moments in history in which real alternatives do exist, so that the decision of a person in power determines which of these alternatives will be followed. Decisions at these junctures are often made by persons who merely happen to be in power and have little conception of the significance of their decision. But occasionally decisions are made in such situations by true heroes or event-making men who understand the significance of the situation confronting them and act accordingly. Sidney Hook argues that the events in Russia in 1917 created such a situation and that

Lenin, as an event-making man, took command and made and effectively implemented the decisions that determined that world history should follow one path rather than another. Because there were truly several courses of action opened up by an historically determined crisis, Lenin's decisions made a real difference. Because the consequence of choosing one course of action rather than another became more rather than less significant with time, the decisions shaped history. And because Lenin understood the principal consequences of making one choice rather than another, he was an authentic event maker and not a mere pawn of historical determinism.

Patterns of Movement Organization

The nature of the leadership role and relationships between leader and followers are central features of movement organization. But the separation between leader and followers is only one instance of the differentiation among member roles. Some movements assign members to highly specialized tasks, but others make few distinctions among their members. Some movements practice highly centralized decision making, but others are loose clusters of relatively autonomous units. Movements are hierarchical or egalitarian, secretive or open, regulation-ridden or inspirational, bureaucratic or sentimental. The choice of organizational forms is to be explained on the basis of (1) the unique mission and setting of a particular movement and (2) the stage in movement development from sect to institution.

MISSION AND SETTING. Organizational forms are nearly always familiar. Movements borrow from the reservoir of patterns already exemplified in the institutions about them. The most likely form of organization is that which members are accustomed to. Movements originating among academic people have commonly employed the pattern of standing committees and member

[13] J. E. Hulett, Jr., "The Kenny Healing Cult: Preliminary Analysis of Leadership and Patterns of Interaction," *American Sociological Review*, 10 (June, 1945), 366.

[14] Sidney Hook, *The Hero in History: A Study in Limitation and Possibility* (New York: The John Day Company, Inc., 1943).

ratification of policy decisions characteristic of the universities' academic senates. The Methodist Church retained the hierarchical system of bishops and other organizational forms from the Church of England, which had in turn kept most of the structure of the Catholic Church at an earlier date. Some of the participatory and volatile decision patterns in youth-based movements reproduce characteristics of the youth culture as it was described a decade or two earlier, which in turn correspond with theories of decision making imported into high schools by the progressive education movement.

But the forms borrowed from the prevailing culture are chosen because they exemplify the mission as members in the movement's formative period conceive it. Sometimes this involves taking an organizational form copied from an institution with which members are not intimately familiar. The salience of various aspects of the mission has a profound effect on choice of organizational form.

When a prominent aspect of the movement's value orientation is the proper organization of decision making in the larger society, the exemplification of that form of organization in the movement becomes crucial. It may be, as we have suggested earlier, that the form of movement organization has as much influence on movement values as values have on the organization. But the strain is toward consistency in either case. Liberal political movements such as Americans for Democratic Action seek to embody the familiar procedures of republican government. The antibureaucratic and antiestablishmentarian New Left favors a participatory democratic organization. The "hang-loose" ethic of the hippies finds nonorganization the only acceptable form of organization.

Movements that promise to improve the relationships of man to man, to restore love to human relationships, have universally represented themselves as a great family. The members become brothers and sisters; leaders become benevolent parents.

When conflict is salient in the movement conception of mission, there is a strong tendency to adopt a form of organization from an established conflict group, a form that has already demonstrated its effectiveness in conflict. Besides the family, the commonest organizational pattern in social movements is the army. The strict discipline, the centralized decision making, the precisely defined hierarchy and lines of command and responsibility, all are suited to combat with a dangerous enemy. Like other embattled movements, the Black Panthers use a military model of organization. Personification of evil as the "legions of the devil" has made the military model appropriate for many religious movements in their more aggressive stages. The Salvation Army in its early years sought to overcome comfortable tolerance and substitute an aggressive attack upon evil, and the military model of organization seemed the most suitable.

A countermovement often copies the organizational form of the movement it opposes. People who believe in a powerful and insidious conspiracy see a counterconspiracy as the most effective strategy of opposition. The tremendous success they ascribe to the original conspiracy recommends their form of organization as the most efficient model for the counterconspiracy. The John Birch Society supplies a recent example.

The Birchers are organized into small units designed to operate as isolated islands, impervious to penetration by outsiders. The Communists call these units "cells"; the Birchers call them chapters.

The Birch membership is supervised and directed by paid professional organizers, set up on an area, state and local basis. These professionals are called "organizers" by the Communists; the Birchers call them "coordinators."

Like the Communists, the Birchers get their official "line" from a central headquarters.

The Communists got their "line" from Moscow, via National Party headquarters; the Birchers get their line from Founder Welch via Birch headquarters in Belmont.[15]

A movement whose mission is to assume authority of which their constituency has been unjustly deprived seeks an organiza-

[15] Benjamin R. Epstein and Arnold Forster, *Report on the John Birch Society 1966* (New York: Random House, Inc., 1966), p. 3, by permission of the Anti-Defamation League of B'nai B'rith.

tional form that will represent the legitimacy of their claim. Revivalistic nativistic movements commonly adopt traditional tribal forms of organization. An interesting example of claiming legitimacy by representing the movement as the reestablishment of a traditional legal institution is found in Africa. The New Anlu is interesting both for the modification of a traditional form to fit the purposes of the movement and for the unusual fact that women's power was its goal.

Anlu: A Women's Uprising in the British Cameroons

Robert E. Ritzenthaler *

On November 22, 1958, 2,000 women of the Kom tribe, bedecked with vines, entered the government station at Bamenda after a 38 mile march of a day and a half, in protest at the summoning for interrogation of four of their leaders.

This was one of the more dramatic aspects of an uprising of some 7,000 women in Bamenda Province which began in April, 1958, and has lasted for a year with no end in sight. Its interest is that here is an example of an old institution called *Anlu* (pronounced ah-loo, with "a" nasalized), which traditionally operated to punish offenders of certain "moral" rules, being converted (with the aid of two male instigators) into an organization of political pressure, the major objective of which was to unseat the party in power, and vote in the opposition party in the January, 1959, elections. The change in form and function of *Anlu* will be the primary concern of this paper.[1]

Anlu traditionally referred to a disciplinary technique employed by the women for particular

From *African Studies*, 19, No. 3 (1960), 151–56. Reprinted with the permission of the Witwatersrand University Press, Johannesburg.
* Dr. Ritzenthaler is Curator of Anthropology in the Milwaukee Public Museum.
[1] The research for this paper was financed by the Wenner-Gren Foundation for Anthropological Research.

offences. These included the beating or insulting (by uttering such obscenities as "Your vagina is rotten") of a parent; beating of a pregnant woman; incest; seizing of a person's sex organs during a fight; the pregnancy of a nursing mother within two years after the birth of the child; and the abusing of old women. A woman thus offended would summon women to her aid by sounding a war-cry made by beating the lips with the fingers while uttering a high-pitched sound. A man could present his complaint to the head woman of his compound. She would discuss the matter with older women of the quarter and they would then decide on a course of action. The women could summon the offender, hear the case, and decide to accept the apologies and payment of goat and fowls. This would settle the case. An intermediary could also plead the case of the offender. If the offender failed to appear, or if he was an habitual offender, more drastic action was taken. In the early stages of the persecution, however, the women had to clear their action with the Fon's (the paramount chief's) representative, the **tabek-witfon**, the man serving as priest, chief executor of the Fon's orders, and head of the once-powerful secret society known as **kwitfon**. The **tabek-witfon** could bring an immediate halt to the proceeding if he thought it unjustified. His agreement was symbolized by his turning over his drum to the women who now had official sanction to continue.

The women of the quarter and sometimes the neighbouring quarters then were enlisted. On a set day they dressed in leafy vines, articles of men's clothing, and paraded to the culprit's compound around five o'clock in the morning. There they danced, sang mocking and usually obscene songs composed for the occasion, and defiled the compound by defecation or by urinating in the water storage vessels. If the culprit was seen he could be pelted with stones or a type of wild fruit called "garden eggs". Then the women shed their vines and garden eggs in the compound, leaving some of each hanging on the threshold as the *Anlu* sign that its use has been banned. In some cases they would prohibit the offender from visiting other compounds and instruct the people that no one should visit him. Sometimes the culprit fled to another compound or even another village, but *Anlu* was continued. At the next weekly market the women voluntarily attended, dressed in their vines, and publicly ridiculed the culprit by dancing and singing mocking songs.

A person thus persecuted rarely could hold out for as long as two months. When his endurance was at an end, he put the *Anlu* vines around his neck as a sign of capitulation and went to the women to plead for pardon. If his pleas and indemnity goods were accepted, they took him naked to the stream and bathed him (the whole body had to be immersed), a ritualistic act which removed the guilt. If they had contaminated his cooking pots with the garden eggs, contact with which caused one to become thin and sick, these were washed in the stream. Then they led him back to his compound, rubbed him with powdered camwood and palm oil and gave him food. The important act, however, was the bathing. After this the incident was never mentioned again.

The invoking of *Anlu* was a serious affair and used sparingly. One informant, about 35 years of age, said he had seen it used only four times in his lifetime.

Such then was *Anlu*, an institution probably brought with them when the Kom migrated into their present area from the north-east some 300 years ago. Among the other tribes of this Tikar

migration *Anlu*, or its counterpart, seems absent.

Anlu persisted in its traditional role until the latter part of 1957. Then began its conversion into a highly organized and powerful political organization that was to seize control of tribal affairs from the men, control the tribal vote in the 1959 election, and by its persecution and sometimes terroristic treatment of non-members create disturbances that caused considerable concern to the local authorities. Men who attempted to interfere with *Anlu* were chastized by their wives who might refuse to feed them (the women supply most of the food as well as prepare it) until they capitulated, and there were stories of women hiding all the clothing of their husbands so they were restricted by modesty to their compounds.

The conversion of *Anlu* into a political organization was the work of two politically ambitious Kom men. They held out to the women the hope of a solution of their real and imaginary problems. Some of the latter were introduced for the occasion, for example, the rumour that the government was selling their land; that the Fon was selling it to the Premier who was selling it to the Ibo. The hatred of the Ibo, although there are none in the Kom area, is almost a neurosis and one shared by most people in Bamenda. Since the Kom women are the farmers and their lands are regarded as almost sacred this was a serious threat, and this fear that their land was being sold was by far the most important reason for the uprisings. The fact that perhaps 99% plus of these women are illiterate made the introduction of such falsehoods relatively easy. On the other hand the two men made good use of actual, though minor, grievances such as the government's negligence in expediting their claims of crop damage against the Fulani, whose unfenced cattle strayed into Kom farms and ruined their crops. Actually there are few Fulani in the Kom area. It was, however, a fairly serious problem in the Bafut and Nsaw areas where women took it upon themselves to kill a number of Fulani cattle in retribution. The premature enforcement of a relatively new contour-farming regulation did nothing to help matters. This regulation, passed in August, 1955, ruled that the women must orient their linear garden beds horizontally to the slopes rather than the traditional vertical arrangement, to prevent soil erosion in this mountainous terrain. The Kom women believed that this ruling was a proof of the fact that their land was being sold, and the fact that some of the women were fined for infraction of this rule was a further source of dissatisfaction. The uprooting of "wrongly" planted beds by an injudicious Agricultural assistant (he was later discharged) in an attempt to enforce the rule heaped more coals on the fire.

By the use of demagoguery, sincere promises, the exploitation of dissatisfactions, intimidations, and the clever mingling of Kom and European ideas, the women were welded into an effective organization whose membership at its height was estimated at 99% of the Kom women. Traditional *Anlu* was a disciplinary technique, not an organization. New *Anlu* was efficiently organized with officers, local chapters, weekly meetings, and a treasury kept solvent by weekly dues. Elements of old *Anlu* that were retained included : the name, the concept of the right of women to band together for the purpose of punishing an offender, the use of the "war-whoop" as a signal, demonstrations by dancing and singing of mocking songs, bedecking the person with vines and garden eggs when demonstrating, and the use of the garden egg plant as a sign of stigma.

The organization of new *Anlu* is based on local chapters or "cells" located in every quarter. The division of tribal areas into quarters (or wards) is the old Tikar pattern of political and social organization. Each *Anlu* chapter has a "quarter head" (náŋlu), a leader who conducts the quarter meetings and transmits orders from central headquarters.

At the top of the organization is the Queen (nafónanlu), who determines policy and "law" with the aid of ex-officio male counsellors and issues the orders for its execution. She rarely attends quarter meetings, but is informed of their wishes and needs by the Spies. Beneath her dress she wears bells around her waist and on official appearances she dons a monkey skin hat and a red bandolier. The idea of a Queen chosen by the women to represent them is an ancient one in the Kom area. In former times such a woman had considerable authority and even her own stool (symbolic of chiefly rank), but the previous Fon had suppressed this office.

Second in command is the Spokesman,

(ánkumtɛ), who makes the announcements and most of the speeches and acts as the official spokesman for *Anlu*. When the District Officer comes for investigations, for example, she will represent the group as spokesman. During the demonstration she wears a man's shirt, shorts and hat, puts soot on her face, but does not wear the vines. She is referred to in pidgin as the "D.O."

Third in importance are the Quarterheads, followed by the Spies (gwézɛ). This is an adaptation from the warring days when men called gwézɛ spied upon the enemy. Today Spies vary in number with the size of the quarter, the smallest having five Spies; the largest, eight. Their function is to meet with the Queen and take information and instructions back to their quarters. If it is decided that a non-member should be prohibited from working her farm, a Spy from that quarter will place the vines and garden egg plant on the farm to mark it taboo.

Below the Spies are the Messengers(lɛ̀lɛ ntum), from three to six for each quarter, who, besides carrying messages, summon people for an interview or meeting. On duty they wear red caps, men's shirts and shorts, sometimes shoes, and carry staffs.

Perhaps the most unusual adaptation is that of the Scribes (kínulua), usually referred to as "Sanitaries," for Sanitary Officer. Each quarter has one or two of these whose duty it is to stand at meetings with pencil and exercise book and pretend to record any orders or rules passed. There are said to be several who can actually read and write. They copy the form and costume, if not the function, of the male Sanitary Inspector found in every market. They wear men's clothing, like that of the Sanitary Officer, consisting of a shirt, belt, trousers and a pith helmet.

At the bottom of the ladder are the deliberately humorous Jesters or clowns (níkoŋ).They wear white paint over their entire bodies and often wear huge feathered headdresses. They perform only at large, central meetings of *Anlu* and their duty is to entertain the crowd. Male clowns are in evidence at many Tikari ceremonies, particularly funerals and the annual dances, but this is the only instance in which women have used the clown.

This is the structure of the society which by the

summer of 1958 had seized the power from the men rendering the Fon and his executive council ineffectual, a breakdown of traditional authority which persists as this is being written in May, 1959. By the middle of 1958 this tightly organized and well-disciplined group was strong enough to take the political initiative and begin a series of mass actions.

On July 3, 1958, at a huge meeting at Njinikom, where the two male advisors and the two female leaders reside, it was decided to march to the neighbouring village of Belo to show that *Anlu* had taken over authority in the whole Kom area. This first mass demonstration took place on July 8, when some 2,000 women dressed in men's clothing, vines, and carrying wooden staffs seven feet long, marched from Njinikom to the weekly market at Belo village, eight miles away. Upon arrival they crowded the market so that business came to a halt. Even when the **tabekwifon**, the Fon's representative, tried to announce the news in the marketplace as is the custom, the women seized his staff of authority and would not permit him to speak. The staff has not been returned to this day. The zinc roofs of the market were pounded with their staffs, parts of them being dented and otherwise damaged, and one part was torn off. When it was discovered that the nearby mission school was still in operation (they thought it had been closed), they rushed up the hill to close it and sealed it with the taboo plant of garden eggs. After trying to keep the school open, the two mission groups in the area decided that the low attendance warranted closing three weeks early, and, except for a few schools in the bush areas, all were re-opened in September at the end of the summer vacation. The attendance in September, however, was sharply reduced, in some instances to one-third of normal, but when the second session started in February it was back to about 90% of normal in most schools.

Back in the market the women leaders laid down the following ultimatum, including:

1. From now on *Anlu* would be in control.

2. That any people who did not follow *Anlu* would be exiled.

3. That any woman who did not follow *Anlu* would not be allowed to farm.

4. That there would be no more use of courts, schools, churches or hospitals, and that any woman who sent her child to school would be exiled.

5. That the Fon and *ju-ju* men were no longer in authority.

6. That no strangers would be allowed to stay in the Kom area; all Hausa, Fulani and Europeans should leave. (To illustrate this, they tore off part of the thatching of a nearby house owned by a man from another tribe, Bafut.)

7. That four mission teachers at Njinikom must leave the Kom area.

On July 11, 1958, the Premier made his scheduled visit to the Kom region, despite inhospitable warnings. His caravan, escorted by the District Officer, encountered a number of road blocks in the form of stones piled as high as three feet across the only road leading in and out of Kom. The party cleared paths wide enough to allow passage of the vehicles and met with no other form of resistance. The women, however, had been instructed to boycott his speeches, and only a few men were present.

As a result of these threats and machinations the District Officer together with the Fon went to a mass meeting of *Anlu* at Njinikom on July 14, 1958. There were an estimated 5,000 to 6,000 women present, all dressed in men's clothing, covered with vines, and holding their formidable-looking staffs. The District Officer stated that "it looked more like a forest than anything else." The women were quiet and orderly during the meeting in which they presented their grievances. They were told that their complaints would be heard and considered, but that law and order must and would be maintained, that further demonstrations, particularly assaults, damage to markets, and the blocking of roads would not be tolerated. They were assured by the District Officer, and the fact was confirmed by the Fon, that stories about their land being sold were nonsense. They were told that the rule enforcing contour-farming would be held in abeyance and that where fines had been paid to the court because of the rule, the cases would be reviewed to determine whether or not they were justified. They were informed that the requested transfer of the four teachers from the mission school was not within the jurisdiction of the government, that while they were at liberty to keep their own children from attending school they must, under no circumstances, molest or interfere with any other children whose parents wished them to continue. The meeting broke up with the women apparently satisfied. *Anlu* activity continued, however, but there were no more overt outbreaks or demonstrations for some time.

Although *Anlu* is not a nativistic movement, it is apparent that there are a number of nativistic elements in it. The rejection of modern institutions such as schools and courts in favour of the old ways is a case in point. A Belo missionary was told, "In five years you will see no more zinc roofs in Kom." There was some difference of opinion, however, with some of the more radical members wanting to eliminate all European things, and others wishing to retain such European-introduced institutions as the public corn-mill and the maternity hospital. There is also a xenophobic element in *Anlu*, although no foreigner actually has been expelled from the area. Besides the partial destruction of the Bafut man's roof there was some talk of driving out the Fulani and Hausa, but no action was taken except for the killing of ten Fulani cattle at Babanki because of crop destruction. Little antagonism has been shown Europeans. The one example of a European who attempted to drive through a mass of *Anlu* women on the road and had his Land Rover pounded with their sticks until he stopped, apparently was a case of mistaken identity. They thought he might be one of the Premier's party, but when he got out and identified himself he was allowed to pass through.

The most important element of the movement, however, appears to be a political one. They seem to have been united more by what they are against (government as embodied in the K.N.C.[2] party) than sure of what they are for. This anti-K.N.C. feeling, at times fanatical, did not stop with the K.N.D.P.[3] victory in the January election of 1959. Most European observers were of the opinion that *Anlu* would subside after this victory, that they would let bygones be bygones, but such was not the case. Persecution of the K.N.C. sympathizers continued and even accelerated. There was still no

neutrality—a person not for *Anlu* was considered to be against it. Non-*Anlu* persons were still prohibited from attending any public function or ceremony, even a funeral, although they were allowed to attend the weekly market. Their crops were uprooted and the garden beds levelled. Some farms were confiscated. The uprooting of crops is a particularly serious affair, and the old *Anlu* never would have sanctioned it. Similarly, one case of *Anlu* women beating a non-*Anlu* pregnant woman was an offence specifically prohibited by old *Anlu*.

The problem of crop destruction was brought to a head by a man who took the matter to court when the fields of his wives were scattered. The destruction had been witnessed and photographed by a party of travellers passing through from Nigeria. As a result some 35 women were brought to the Bamenda court and fined £170 plus £186 for the lawyer's fees. This was a bewildering experience to the women who believed that since "their" party had won the election, the government, police and the courts were theirs. Since then crop destruction apparently ceased.

As the women began to realize that they had been used for a political purpose they began dropping out of *Anlu*. One woman said, "This is not the old *Anlu*, this is white man's *Anlu*." From nearly 100% membership, it has dropped off to about 60%, but *Anlu* still is a force to be reckoned with.

Various solutions to the problem have been suggested by the Kom men, who, along with a sizeable minority of the women, are quite weary of the whole affair. "*Anlu* should be outlawed and all further meetings prohibited." "The leaders should receive heavy fines if further activity is discovered." An educated man from a neighbouring tribe suggests that the "present Fon, who is old, be retired in favour of a younger man."

Whatever the solution, it is apparent that the techniques of political persecution such as beatings, sabotage, ostracism, and above all intimidation, do not make for a contented society. One police offical defined *Anlu* as "mass intimidation." The fact that unrest among the women is present in several neighbouring tribes is also a source of some concern. Whether deliberately spread or merely contagious, *Anlu* or something similar,

---

[2] Kameruns National Congress.
[3] Kameruns National Democratic Party.

has become an agency or clearing house for women's dissatisfactions in a widening area. Among one tribe the reason for an uprising is resentment of new farming techniques, another tribe protests the education levy of the local authority, a third demands retribution for crop damage. Whether all such "disturbances," as they are officially called, should be termed *Anlu* is debatable. It is apparent, however, that the same pattern of mass demonstration recurs with each tribe utilizing such elements as the donning of vines, the carrying of the long staff, the use of the rather eerie "war-cry," and the mocking song. That a good part of the women's complaints are legitimate, or that a women's emancipation movement might be justified, is not to be denied. It is rather the almost desperate methods employed that cause the concern.

The statement of one young man is fairly representative of the more sober-minded men in Kom. "New *Anlu* has been a bad thing for Kom people, for it has caused too much suffering, and a serious loss of school time for many children. Even families have been split by this movement, with some sisters being estranged from one another because of their difference in opinions. We know that old *Anlu* is dead and will never be revived, but new *Anlu*, even if it is put down now, will leave scars that will be with us for a long time."

INSTITUTIONALIZATION. The very success of a movement, in the sense of increased membership and power, leads to a transformation. Increased size threatens to remove control of the movement from any set group and render control and policies entirely capricious. Consequently those in control will seek to regularize procedures to support their own power and policies, and those on the periphery will demand responsibility and predictability. The very fact of continuing existence will translate earlier spontaneous patterns into embryonic traditions governing behavior within the movement. Hence out of the demands of both leadership and membership and from the mere fact of repeated association, any movement tends to become rigid with time.

Some movements tend not merely toward stability but also toward institutionalization. A movement is institutionalized when it has reached a high degree of stability internally and been accorded a recognized position within the larger society. Institutionalization occurs when the movement is viewed as having some continuing function to perform in the larger society, as it is accepted as a desirable or unavoidable adjunct to the existing institutional arrangements.

Through institutionalization the environing society imposes additional stability upon the movement. A key aspect of institutionalization is the establishment of patterns by which the community can deal with the movement. An indispensable condition for such dealings is responsibility, the assurance that authentic decisions will not be negated by unpredictable shifts in leadership or in the loyalties of members. The bargains that recognized agencies of the larger society have struck with the movement accord prestige to those representatives of the movement with whom they choose to deal. Thus the prestige structure built up within the movement is modified so as to fit better the prestige structure of the society and the requirements of stable, responsible commitments.

A particularly important aspect of institutionalization is the recognition of certain areas of competence and of certain functions as constituting the legitimate scope of the movement. Thus, by calling in labor leaders to testify in public hearings or to participate in conferences as spokesmen for the interests of labor, the society grants the labor union this special area of competence. By the same action institutionalization restricts the scope of a movement that has tended toward a self-definition of universalized competence. Religious movements that have pretended to judicial and economic functions relinquish these as they become institutionalized within a society whose governmental and economic institutions are already well established.

Institutionalization is imposed not only in the process of dealing with the environing society but also through the acquisition of a stabilized body of adherents with stabilized expectations. Members become dependent upon participation in the movement for certain gratifications. Not only does the movement satisfy preexisting needs of its members, but participation creates needs that can only be satisfied through continuing predictable participation. The institution fills a fixed space in the life scheme of people.

As it becomes institutionalized, the movement tends to diversify the gratifications of participation. It multiplies and diversifies activities so as to provide gratifications for all kinds of people. The church establishes the young people's social and sponsors various recreational groups. The political machine organizes boys' clubs and charity programs.

Particularly important in this multiplication of gratifications is the addition of societal prestige. Participation and prominence in the movement now become a recognized route to prestige in the larger society. So long as the movement is not accorded institutional status, active members gain prestige only in the eyes of persons who look favorably upon the movement. But when the entire organization is respected in the society, prestige within the group is translated into prestige in society.

As diversification of participation-gratifications takes place and as persons are increasingly attracted to the movement in order to attain society-wide prestige, conventional motivations and patterns of behavior displace the distinctive and deviant in the movement. Ideologies are toned down so as to be acceptable to a wider range of people and so as not to undercut the prestige that participants gain.

Any type of movement can take on this institutionalized character. A value-oriented movement may become a national safety organization, a national health organization, a women's organization, etc. Religious sects tend in the same direction, as was indicated earlier in a quotation from H. Richard Niebuhr. Religious groups that have passed to the stage of institutionalization are referred to as denominations or churches. Earl Brewer suggests four sets of criteria for differentiating the two extreme types and shows that the Methodist movement shifted between 1780 and 1940 from an intensely sectarian body to a predominantly church–type organization. The four sets of criteria are (1) The sect renounces established religious institutions and presents utopian ideals to a select few; the church seeks to conserve a developed religious pattern and accommodates its ideals to gain widespread adherence. (2) The sect is a "personal fellowship of small, voluntary, select, and exclusive groups"; the church is inclusive and heterogeneous in membership, and large, impersonal, and hierarchical in organization. (3) The sect rejects mores and folkways of the larger community and substitutes its own much stricter norms and austere patterns; the church largely accepts community norms and its rites become "elaborate, professional, colorful." (4) Poverty and communal sharing on a primary group basis characterize the sect; wealth and formally organized philanthropy mark the church.[16]

[16] Earl D. C. Brewer, "Church and Sect in Methodism," *Social Forces,* 30 (May, 1952), 400–408.

part five

SOCIAL FUNCTIONS
OF COLLECTIVE BEHAVIOR

20

COLLECTIVE BEHAVIOR, SOCIAL CHANGE, AND SOCIAL STABILITY

Collective behavior can be studied from several vantage points. It is possible to focus upon individual motivations as they find expression through crowds, publics, and social movements. This approach, which is properly the psychological study of group phenomena, has been de-emphasized throughout our discussion. Instead, we have examined collectivities as groups, characterized by structure and process. Thus we have explored the composition of collectivities, the changes that take place within them, their internal organization, their expansion and contraction and their success and failure. It is also appropriate to examine collective behavior from a third standpoint. Collectivities can be studied from the vantage point of the society in which they exist. We can ask what their effects are upon the larger society of which they are a part. We have already, for example, traced the development, the denouement, and the quiescence of a crowd. There remains the question of what lasting effect this crowd has had upon the course of events in the larger society.

Looking first at the ongoing social order, we observe that it has many parts. Each of these parts is geared in with the other parts so that it contributes in some way to the operation of the whole society. The contributions that any part makes to the whole are known as its functions. Since collectivities are parts of the whole social order, we shall ask whether they serve any functions. In particular, we shall ask whether collective behavior plays any part in the maintenance of stability or the promotion of change in society.

Most of the answers have been supplied in the preceding discussions. The chief purpose here will be to bring together the scattered observations that describe the effect of collective behavior on society. Although the entire subject matter of collective behavior is deficient in precise empirical demonstration, the analysis of the long-term effects lacks even more. Our discussion should be regarded as a series of considered speculations in which we present conclusions for which there is some justification in theory or circumstantial evidence, and that appear to be worthy of further study and empirical test.

Effectiveness of Collective Behavior

Has collective behavior any real effect on the course of events, or is it merely the shadow of significant events? Perhaps the causes for change are deeply embedded in history, and the eruptions of crowd behavior and the mobilizations of social movements are but diversionary antics. From this viewpoint collective behavior often hampers the orderly process of change and makes change more costly in lives and human happiness than need be, but it does not materially alter long-term trends.

The view of collective behavior as pathology—a sort of collective mental illness—suggests efforts to reduce it's incidence. If social change follows predetermined lines, then any lessening of the violence and disruption, of the diversion of energy into futile quests, of the feelings of guilt and anxiety, of the sacrifice of human comfort, is a worthy contribution to human welfare. One prescription is to reinforce authority, to strengthen the rule of law and order. The justification for this prescription is trenchantly depicted in the terrifying novel, *Lord of the Flies*.[1] Culture is a thin veneer that disguises the primordial savage whose base impulses find expresssion in collective behavior. The pathology of public disorder is inevitable whenever the discipline of centralized authority over the masses is relaxed.

Another prescription calls for education and mass psychotherapy. To writers such as Everett D. Martin and Eric Hoffer, participants in these disturbances are misguided, or they are acting out their unresolved mental conflicts.[2]

These views cannot be entirely disregarded. The experience of ungoverned and weakly governed frontier communities offers much illustrative support for the *Lord of the Flies* conception. And the significant impact of at least a minority of disturbed and uninformed participants on the course of collective behavior is incontestable. But even without crediting either of these views, one can be led to the conclusion that collective behavior makes no lasting difference for long-term trends on the basis of a tendency toward conservatization that eventually infects any movement.

Although a movement finds fault with contemporary conditions in society, the criticism is justified by reference to accepted values, and the movement borrows from the cultural reservoir of folk techniques for its concrete proposals. A movement always demands that one value be assigned increased importance at the expense of another value. The movement for fair employment practices, for example, urged that the value of freedom from interference for the owner in running his business should be subordinated to the value of equal opportunity irrespective of race or nationality. Every culture contains a set of folk-prescriptions for dealing with recognized problems. Since few values elicit complete conformity, society must constantly cope with the problems arising from value failures. Hence each culture includes prescriptions covering almost any kind of value failure. These folk prescriptions, however, are palliatives that keep problems under control,

---

[1] William Golding, *Lord of the Flies* (New York: G. P. Putnam's Sons, 1959).

[2] Everett D. Martin, *The Conflict of the Individual and the Mass in the Modern World* (New York: Holt, Rinehart and Winston, Inc., 1932); Eric Hoffer, *The True Believer* (New York: Harper and Row, Publishers, 1951).

quarantine disorders to prevent their spread, or conceal instances of successful deviation. Such palliatives depend, for their effectiveness, upon the fact that the problems are of limited incidence in the society and that the normal operation of the society keeps the problems at a minimum. They depend also on the fact that they are relatively seldom used. For example, imprisonment undoubtedly is of some value in controlling crime so long as the normal operations of society promote law-abiding behavior most of the time and only a small minority of the population are ever imprisoned.

Most social movements advocate a program that consists of making more extensive and vigorous use of the folk-prescriptions for dealing with a given problem. Most popular movements for the reduction of crime, for example, advocate better law enforcement, improved crime detection, and stiffer penalties. Movements also call for extension of the folk-prescription into new areas of application. Thus the standard means of controlling crime are advocated for dealing with heretical or unpatriotic thinking, the weakening of traditional morals, or racial discrimination.

Movements of this sort may work when an aroused public can make important contributions to the problem's solution. But when more fundamental changes are essential, such movements actually block change. They channel off much of the protest and potential reform activity into ineffectual work. They postpone the day of reckoning by controlling or concealing some of the symptoms without touching underlying conditions. Because of their unrealized linkage with conventional folk-prescriptions, they help to resist change while appearing to be the vanguard demanding change. Kingsley Davis contends that the mental hygiene movement at one time illustrated this conservatization through the retention of traditional folk-prescriptions for dealing with a problem that had ac-

quired new forms and new dimensions.[3]

In stressing the conservatizing tendencies within a key movement such as mental hygiene, we should not overlook the fact that the movement itself is subject to constant influence from other movements. A pattern such as the following is not infrequent: A movement depending upon traditional folk-prescriptions gains ascendance and partial institutionalization. Among competing movements it acquires a privileged position because its very restriction to folk-prescriptions makes it respectable and acceptable to persons of established prestige. Because of its key position, the movement becomes the focal point of efforts by other movements concerned with the same problem. By "infiltration," by attempted control, or by the influence of continued discussion, the more radical movements gradually modify the program of the key movement. As the key movement is won over, its established respectability enables it to promote the programs of the more radical movements more effectively than they could do by acting directly upon the established organizations of society. Thus, an essentially conservative movement becomes a vehicle for change in the same way that a countermovement, by successive strategic revisions of program, actually promotes the changes it officially opposes.

Movements are also conservatized by transformation into participation-oriented groups, no longer concerned with actively promoting their stated objectives. Sheldon Messinger has described how the Townsend Movement in California underwent conversion to a federation of social clubs after it began to lose out in competition with the McLain old age pension movement.[4] By the

[3] Kingsley Davis, "Mental Hygiene and the Class Structure," *Psychiatry*, 1 (Feb., 1938), 55–65.
[4] Sheldon L. Messinger, "Organizational Transformation: A Case Study of a Declining Social Movement," *American Sociological Review*, 20 (Jan., 1955), 3–10.

1950s, club meetings usually consisted of abbreviated business meetings, followed by the main activity of the evening—card playing and other recreation. Financial requirements of the movement were met, not by aggressive solicitations for help in a great cause but by the sale of "Dr. Townsend's Vitamins and Minerals" and royalties for the use of Dr. Townsend's name on other products.

Whereas some may discount the idea of change through collective behavior for reasons we have just reviewed, many people hold an opposite fear—that crowds and social movements have momentums of their own. Far-reaching changes in the social order, neither warranted nor predictable from underlying conditions, are foreseen when collective behavior abounds. Rabble-rousers are blamed for stirring up a heretofore contented populace, who then force changes that eradicate both good and bad features of the existing order indiscriminately. Once collective behavior has reached sufficient proportions, it can no longer be controlled or even guided constructively.

If we are to make an intelligent judgment of how much independent effect collective behavior has on social trends, we must ascertain when in the course of change collective behavior occurs on a large scale. After we look at some of the major theories of change, we shall return to the main question, the effectiveness of collective behavior in change and stability.

Sources of Widespread Collective Behavior

THEORIES OF INHERENT CHANGE. Theories of large-scale change in society fall into two categories, those which find the impulse and direction of change to inhere in the cultural sequence itself and those which attribute change to external events. In the first category are the theories of continuous cycles. Among the best known theories of continuous cyclical change is that of Pitirim

Sorokin.[5] Sorokin holds that there is an inherent tendency for culture to oscillate between sensate and ideational saturation. A sensate culture is one dominated by naturalism, reliance on reason and mechanical contrivance, and realism. An ideational culture is one marked by mysticism, dependence on sentiment and religion, and symbolism. Each type bears within itself the seeds of its own destruction. As it approaches complete dominance by sensate forms or by ideational forms the culture runs out of opportunities for further development in the same direction, so change can only reverse itself. The most recent peak of ideational culture occurred during the Middle Ages. Twentieth century United States has already witnessed the peak of sensate dominance and countertrends are now well in evidence.

Accompanying the cycle of sensate and ideational dominance is another cycle of increasing and declining societal integration. The peaks of integration occur slightly before the peaks of sensate and ideational dominance, society functioning most smoothly while there is still opportunity for development and elaboration of the dominant tendency. As complete saturation of either sensate or ideational tendencies approaches, integration in the society declines, discontent and disorder increase, and widespread collective behavior supplants much of the established institutional behavior. Thus the general conditions of dissatisfaction with the established culture that are the breeding ground for collective behavior occur as the opportunities for creative activity become limited by the exhaustion of one of the major cultural themes. Collective behavior expresses itself in the exploratory behavior through which the swing toward the opposite cultural pole is established.

5 Pitirim A. Sorokin, *Social and Cultural Dynamics* (New York: American Book Company, 1937–41).

According to this viewpoint collective behavior is an important agency of change. However, it is the mechanism through which predetermined change takes place rather than the originator of change. The content of collective behavior, i.e., the kinds of values that will be expressed, are predetermined by the imminent cultural change.

Whether Sorokin's complete theory of change is accepted or not, certain portions of it may have merit in themselves. The suggestion that any given cultural emphasis has within it only certain limited possibilities for development offers one generalized explanation for cultural change. As these possibilities are exhausted, activity within the traditional cultural framework becomes less rewarding, so that discontent develops. Out of the discontent comes collective behavior, collective exploratory activity through which a variety of directions are tested. Out of this testing process emerges a new dominant cultural direction, whereupon the collective behavior subsides in part and is conventionalized and institutionalized in part to make up a considerable portion of the new cultural machinery.

Another type of theory that makes change inherent in the nature of sociocultural process proposes a dialectic in place of cyclical change. In the various versions of dialectical theory the culture is first dominated by one scheme of values, one kind of socioeconomic system, etc. The dominant system gives rise to its opposite, and there then ensues a struggle between the two. Out of the struggle both systems are destroyed but there arises a new system which reconciles the crucial elements from the original pair of opposites. Expressed in terms of ideologies, the process has been described as a *thesis* giving rise to its *antithesis,* and the struggle between the two producing the *synthesis.* In the inexorable historical process the synthesis becomes the new thesis which generates its antithesis as a new dialectical sequence takes place. The philosopher Hegel is identified with the fullest formulation of historical process in terms of a dialectic of ideologies. But the application of dialectical theory by Karl Marx is of greatest interest in the discussion of collective behavior.[6] Marx proposes a sequence of continuing, self-inducing change, centering about the distribution of social power as derived from economic processes. All history is a record of struggle between those who have power and those who do not have power. Each class is supplanted by a class over which it formerly exercised control. Each new ruling class produces a new suppressed class which develops under domination of the former. The suppressed class eventually overthrows the ruling class and a new dialectic begins.

The dialectical pattern is not entirely uniform throughout history, however. During past turns of the sequence, subordinate classes have gradually risen to power and displaced the dominant group. The bourgeoisie who are the present ruling class differ from earlier ruling classes in having dispossessed those below them. Consequently, the current or capitalistic era has been marked by a new tendency in history, a tendency toward greater and greater extremes of difference between the rulers and the ruled. As this discrepancy becomes greater, the bourgeoisie become fewer and fewer in number with corporations larger and monopolies more general, and the consciousness of being an oppressed class becomes stronger and more widespread in the rest of the society. The developing sense of class solidarity leads to varied forms of collective behavior, which will culminate in revolution and overthrow of the ruling class.

In Marxian theory the place of collective behavior is clearest for the contemporary period. Collective behavior accompanies the development of class consciousness and is its expression. It results from the extreme

6 Karl Marx, *Capital* (New York: Modern Library, Inc., 1936).

inequity arising out of the prevailing economic system. To what extent collective behavior is a part of the more gradual process through which a ruling class is dispossessed is not so clearly indicated. It is clear, however, that in Marxian theory collective behavior on a widespread scale is an expression of the opposition between the rulers and the ruled (as determined by their economic position) and its extensiveness and intensity are functions of the degree of discrepancy in economic condition between the two classes.

We have neither presented an adequate account of Marxian thought regarding social change nor shall we attempt its thorough evaluation. Events have not supported well the application to capitalism, though it is still possible to interpret changes which are taking place as an application of the dialectical principle. Many historical periods of extensive collective behavior can be plausibly interpreted as the process of working out a new order from the conflict between ruling classes and ruled. Contrary to the Marxian supposition, there is evidence that leads us to believe that large-scale and concerted collective behavior directed toward overthrow of the ruling group are more likely to develop under improving conditions and when the distribution of economic goods is not extremely inequitable than under opposite conditions. Extremely inequitable conditions appear in history to be more generally associated with apathy and resignation in the submerged classes. However, the experience of steadily losing advantages that a class has formerly had is likely to bring about vigorous protest activity.

BREAKDOWN OF CULTURE AND SOCIAL ORGANIZATION. There are many hypotheses of a less ambitious sort than the cyclical and dialectical theories, hypotheses that merely specify the conditions that characteristically give rise to change and associated collective behavior. Earlier (Chapter 4) we have discussed certain conditions likely to set the stage for collective behavior. These include the breakdown of a system of formal or informal social control, value conflicts, frustration, and the failure of communication. Theories that place collective behavior in the context of social change go one step behind these conditions. They indicate the broad kinds of circumstances that are likely to create on a society-wide scale such conditions as control failure or weakening of communication, which latter will in turn give rise to widespread collective behavior. In the context of social change we look at the conditions specified earlier as the intervening variables between the broad instigating conditions of change in a society and the development of widespread collective behavior. The breakdown of normal communication patterns, for example, is an intervening cause between the events that set change in motion and the emergence of collective behavior.

If we describe the immediate conditions giving rise to collective behavior as states of culture and of social organization, our problem is defined as locating the general conditions that initiate change in the culture or the social organization. Widespread collective behavior arises out of the inadequacy of culture on the one hand and out of the failure of the social organization to operate on the other hand.

Culture, as a set of established ways of acting and thinking, ceases to provide directives through which people can express their impulses. Conditions of life create problems or give rise to impulses for which culture cannot provide avenues of solution or modes of expression. The social organization, as the established pattern of interactions among people, ceases to operate in such a way as to get the group's business done. Communication breaks down at essential points. Confidence in the basis for the established division of labor weakens. The control agencies of the society cease to function adequately.

Organization and culture are but two sides of the same phenomena. The going social system may be described in terms of its established behaviors and values as culture or in terms of the system of relations among people and groups through which the culture is expressed. Any event that seriously disrupts the one must necessarily also unbalance the other. If established cultural values are seriously challenged, then the system of social relations cannot endure without change. If events alter the power among groups in society or change communication networks, a change in the culture must follow to bring the established ways of thinking and feeling into harmony with the organization.

Let us consider first the sources of change in the culture, the basis for questioning the established values and ways of looking at things. The best documented source of challenges to the existing culture is extensive and intimate culture contact. The kind of contact that gives people an opportunity to view a different culture at least partially from the inside gives them a new perspective from which they observe their own culture. The outside culture is like an observation post from which, for the first time, they can look at their own culture in other ways than through the eyes of their culture itself. Culture contact means in part some borrowing of perspectives from the other culture. Such borrowing, however, may not be as important as is sometimes supposed. When individual traits are adopted from another culture, they are likely to be modified in the process into consistency with the borrower's culture.

More important than borrowing is the discovery that there is a vantage point from which one's own values no longer appear unquestionable axioms but as merely one among alternative systems of value. Thus it is not so much the particular culture with which culture contact takes place as it is the attitude toward one's own culture that is induced by any serious culture contact. The new attitude creates a receptiveness toward ideas from the other culture and permits the development of new ideas and values from an examination of the adequacy of one's own culture. Culture contact gives rise not only to borrowing but to new ideas concerning the necessity for change in the established order and the directions in which such change should go.

In addition to this external source of cultural change, there are also probably internal sources. We have already noted Sorokin's view and the dialectical theories. These latter theories must remain hypothetical since the evidence to support them is tenuous and verification difficult. Somewhat more convincing is the thesis that culture, under favorable conditions, develops in the direction of increasing man's control and understanding of both his natural and social environment. To a considerable degree man's cultural values and ideas are a function of the kind of understanding he has of the world around him and the kinds of control he is able to exercise over it. For example, a set of values attuned to a world of semi-isolated small communities becomes untenable in a world that has developed the technical means for rapid transportation and communication on a worldwide basis. Man's conception of himself is built upon what he believes he can and cannot do. As his powers increase his self-conception changes. And the values that he espouses reflect his self-conception. A change in self-conception leads to the discovery of new kinds of values that seem natural and obvious under the altered self-conception. Developments in technology and in the natural and social sciences seem to have this quality of opening up new self-conceptions and accordingly creating new value perspectives.

The historical phenomenon of generations is a further internal source of cultural change. Culture is never transmitted intact, nor is it acquired passively. Culture is like a picture presented in outline, for the individual to paint in the details and to determine the emphasis among its various features. Crucial experiences that occur while the culture is being learned supply these details and emphases. When an entire generation of youth share an experience such as the Vietnam War, World War II, or the Great Depression, a distinctive stamp is placed on the common culture they later share as adults. Because the pressing problems and preoccupations change every few years, there is a succession of adult cohorts in every society, each with a somewhat different generational culture.

The most important kind of change in social organization for instigating collective behavior is a redistribution of power among major population segments, whether classes, age groups, ethnic groups, sex groups, or occupational groups. The customary patterns of rights and obligations must be in harmony with the distribution of power. But customs become embedded in an institutional complex that resists change. The incongruities between the growing resources and power of a group and the traditional rights and duties assigned them is a prime cause for the discontent that sets collective behavior in motion.

Redistributions of power and other disturbances in the social order are brought about in many ways. Any drastic change in population or population trends will alter the power structure in abundant ways. Increase and decrease in rates of population growth change the rates of upward mobility within the class system. They force adjustments in economic activity. They alter the balance between supply and demand. The established organization ceases to serve people's wants in the manner to which they are accustomed.

Widespread and lasting catastrophe taxes a social order. Studies of disasters that are limited in their scope show that, while much of the established order remains in abeyance immediately after the catastrophe, it tends to be restored and in full operation soon after. Spontaneous forms of social organization that arise immediately do not contradict or change the established order but merely fill the gap until it can be set in full operation again. Furthermore, catastrophe may be envisioned within the existing social order so that the populace are prepared to accept its inconveniences without doubting the basic adequacy of the established system. Such is generally the case in modern wars. Each nation prepares its populace to accept and deal with a considerable amount of bombing, and results indicate that intensive bombing over an extended period of time does not necessarily break confidence in the existing order. Hope by some that concentrated bombing of civilian populations would lead the enemy to revolt against their own leadership turned out to be unfounded.

But when catastrophe is of long duration, widespread, and contradictory of the assumptions of the established order, pressures multiply for a change in the system. Thus, when bombing can no longer be accepted as a necessary condition to be tolerated while the armies are steadily moving toward victory, collective opposition to the established order may develop. The epidemics of the plague that scourged entire areas of Europe during the Middle Ages left the social order completely ineffectual in many instances and gave rise to the dancing manias, pogroms, and other types of collective behavior.

Extensive movements of population have often resulted in disruption and challenge to the established order and a period of widespread collective behavior. The two periods when race riots against blacks were most widespread in the United States during the current century were associated with the wartime migration of blacks to the North and their movement into new areas of industrial employment. The tolerance of blacks that had prevailed was based upon their limited numbers and the maintenance of distance. The order of interracial relations broke down as the implicit premises upon which it had operated were violated. Frontier communities that have grown rapidly generally lacked a clearly defined order with effective means for exercising social control and bases for agreement on the working system of social stratification.

Population movement need not disrupt the social order, however. In the first instance cited above the population movement altered the social composition of the populace and caused redistribution of privileges and alteration of social distance patterns. In the second instance the problem was establishing a social order where none existed and where many people saw no immediate gain in a stable social system. A nomadic people, on the other hand, carry their social order with them and possess a social order that is adapted to movement. Population movements such as the migration of the Pilgrims to America also brought their own social orders with them. Having an organization from the start, migrating by families rather than by detached individuals, and moving into a sparsely settled area, they were able to cope in an orderly fashion with problems that developed. Nineteenth and twentieth century immigrants to the large cities of the United States taxed the social order in certain respects, but the development of collective behavior was limited. The expansion of industry in the United States provided places for the immigrants in the social system. The conflict between old and new social systems for the immigrants created considerable disorganization in the immigrant communities and weakened in some respects the systems of communication and control in the American community. But the control systems in the larger community were strong enough to prevent the eruption of discontent into collective behavior except sporadically.

The social order is dependent upon the functioning of the subsistence or economic system. Although no simple economic determinism can be justified, minimum effectiveness of the economic system is essential if the entire social order is to continue to operate. Hence, any disturbance in the economic realm is likely to be reflected in

challenge to the social order. Periods of economic depression in modern society witness the rise of social movements and crowd activity and heightened activity in publics. Drought or other conditions that reduce the food supply may have such an effect in primitive societies if the events are not defined as a punishment requiring even closer conformity in the future.

Over a more extended period, changes in the mode of subsistence or developments in technology and other conditions that alter the economic system have the effect of changing the established distribution of power in society. The traditional order tends to perpetuate the old distribution of power after its economic supports have weakened and the bases for transfer of power to a different class have been established. A struggle then develops between the old and the new, until the traditional order has been destroyed, its defenders have given up attempts to restore it, and the new distribution of power has become recognized. A traditional ruling class may hold onto power that has lost its economic supports because theirs is the only power that is recognized as legitimate by the general populace. The class with newly achieved power must turn its economic control into social power by acquiring popular recognition. Its attempts, resistance by the ruling group, and the entry of other interests that can take advantage of the breakdown of traditional controls give rise to widespread collective behavior.

Finally, a social order may become rigidified so that it ceases to adjust to ordinary changes and to cope adequately with ordinary discontent. Among various writers who have stressed this tendency in social organization is Vilfredo Pareto, in his theory of the circulation of the elite.[7] He proposes that in a normally functioning social order the elites, or those who exercise the legitimate power, constantly replenish their numbers by bringing in outstanding

---

[7] Vilfredo Pareto, *The Mind and Society* (New York: Harcourt Brace Jovanovich, Inc., 1935).

individuals from the lower classes. In this manner new ideas are being constantly brought into the elites, the quality of the elites is kept high, and potential leadership for the lower classes is removed. Sometimes, however, this circulation process is interrupted, the elites merely perpetuate themselves from within, and upward movement from the lower classes is blocked. When this happens not only do the elite become decadent but individuals who might otherwise have been absorbed into the elite now become the leaders of the subordinate classes. They help to focus discontent and eventually to lead movements for the overthrow of the traditional elite. Thus a period of heightened collective behavior develops when the normal circulation of elites is interrupted.

The Function of Collective Behavior in Change

NEW PERSPECTIVES AND SOCIAL CHANGE. Whatever the combination of sources of change, a period of heightened collective behavior depends upon the widespread arousal of both discontent and a sense of expanding horizons. The latter is particularly the product of cultural contact or rapid growth of technology. Most collective behavior depends as fully upon the striking awareness of new possibilities as upon dissatisfaction. The expanding horizons supply the ideas in terms of which publics may conceive issues and social movements may formulate ideologies.

There appear to have been periods in history when increasing discontent occurred without exposure to new ideas, leading to limited development of certain kinds of collective behavior. A sort of hypersensitiveness may prevail that increases susceptibility to crowd behavior without providing ideological rallying points to sustain collective behavior and give it continuity. Tendencies to panic are heightened, expressive crowd behavior readily develops beyond the boundaries of conventional behavior,

and acting crowds develop to the point of violence with a minimum of provocation. Power struggles based upon the changing distribution of effective power take place, but the resulting control movements operate from an elite rather than a mass base. The only types of movements with any mass appeal are participation-oriented movements, often providing a type of security by revivalist emphases.

When developments imminent within the culture or the new perspectives brought in from the contact between cultures are added to discontent, however, people begin to see the current situation in light of possible directions of change. The awareness of better conditions as a concrete possibility develops. Familiar conditions within the society can now be reconceptualized in the terms supplied by a new or different cultural framework. Discontent, instead of being vague and unfocused, is now identified, usually in a variety of ways. And as it is identified various courses of action are suggested for coping with the supposed sources of discontent.

THE FUNCTION OF SPECIFIC FORMS OF COLLECTIVE BEHAVIOR. It is under these conditions—widespread discontent *and* the availability of new cultural perspectives that suggest new possibilities for coping with discontent—that collective behavior ramifies and becomes crucial to the life of the society. Out of the unrest there begin to spring up loosely conceived publics, made possible by the definitions of issues. The publics at this point are extremely volatile, short-lived, and small in size. The publics are many, corresponding with a prevalent variety of ways of defining issues. If collective behavior is sustained, the number of publics declines, their size increases as publics combine, and a few of the ways of defining issues survive while the rest disappear.

At times situations arise that can be quickly defined in the terms established in the prevalent publics, and which are felt to embody most critically and urgently the essence of the issue. These incidents give rise to acting crowd behavior. The crowd action may come from either direction, in support of traditional culture values and patterns of social organization against dangerous new ideas or in support of one of the newer viewpoints. The pattern of lynchings in the United States represented crystallization of the viewpoint of those who resisted the changes that had been occurring in the interracial social organization. The incidents bringing about lynchings most frequently were depicted as such ultimate breakdown of the caste system as sexual attack on a white woman by a black man. Epitomizing the feared condition in its ultimate form, the incident conveyed a sense of urgency that combined with a lack of confidence in legal procedures to demand drastic and extreme action. Crowd actions *against* the traditional social order often arise when repressive action is taken against the newer ideas and attacks on the existing order. The repression of discussion or of efforts to change the traditional structure epitomize to the discontented the ultimate evils of the traditional order. Thus a sense of urgency provokes the demand for immediate and drastic action.

When there are no new perspectives during an era of widespread discontent, acting crowds protest grievances of limited and localized significance, and expressive crowds, affording temporary respite from conventional behavior, abound. Thus, religious expressive crowds, such as the frontier revivals, very quickly become dominated by overtones of revelry contrasting with the somber quality of frontier life and with license to violate the prevalent mores in symbolic or actual sexual excitement and other unconventional behavior. Or the pogroms—mob violence against Jewish communities—of certain periods in Europe were episodes of mass brutality unconnected with any broad definition of issues and conception of long-range changes to be brought about.

But when new cultural perspectives have been applied to contemporary discontents in the formation of publics, crowd activity gets defined in the terms provided by some prevalent public. Not only is the crowd activity the expression derived from a pre-existing public, but the crowd action itself becomes a focal point for subsequent consideration by publics. On the one hand the crowd may go sufficiently far in its behavior—further than its particular faction of the public is prepared to defend—that there is a revulsion and opposing factions of the public are strengthened. Thus in the United States when labor strikes turn into crowd violence, the prolabor factions in publics usually lose support. And lynchings became progressively more embarrassing to those who sought to preserve the interracial caste patterns. On the other hand, crowd action may unify the members of public factions and supply them with leaders and heroes. The crowd action itself may become an important symbol, serving as a continuing rallying point to bring about more vigorous support. The unpredictable events in the course of the crowd action may change the emphasis in the public or modify the definition of the issue. But most of all, the crowd action, by precipitating an issue that is only being discussed in the public, tends to draw more sharply the lines between opposing factions in the public, to restructure the issues in more irreconcilable terms.

Thus it is hardly possible to speak of the consequence of crowd behavior taken by itself. Its significance depends first upon whether it springs out of a well-established public, and second upon how the publics conceive the crowd after it has subsided.

Against this background LeBon's suggestion that crowds serve to destroy the old order in preparation for the emergence of a new one may be considered. As we have seen, crowds may be directed toward preserving the status quo ante as well as toward destroying it. These efforts may boomerang, but in other instances they may help to preserve the existing structure. The importance of LeBon's observation is perhaps clearest in the periods when discontent is not complemented by novel perspectives. During such periods the activities of crowds are generally feared by officials of the established order, since they represent behavior outside conventional controls. While the crowds are in operation spontaneous leadership takes over and outcomes are unpredictable. In such activity the populace discovers the possibilities and pleasures of escaping the controls of the established social order. People realize that they are conforming largely because they have to rather than because they spontaneously desire to do so. The excitement of following new, though temporary, leaders helps to disenchant them concerning the established leaders. By contrast to the even slightly charismatic crowd leaders, the established leaders are made to appear both prosaic and remote.

The net result of this development is to weaken spontaneous and willing adherence to the established order. The established order itself is not likely to be destroyed from below on this basis alone, since no new ideas and values are present to direct and sustain collective behavior. But people will be readier to hear new ideas and readier to apply them if they become available.

From the publics in a period of heightened collective behavior there emerge not only crowds but social movements. Whereas power-oriented movements with an elite base and participation-oriented movements are found in unsettled periods, the value-oriented movements come into prominence when culture contact or cultural development has brought new perspectives into play. Value-oriented movements are the more stable groupings that develop from the interaction within publics and the attempt to define discontent. The emerging movements partly reflect the definitions of issues that already prevail and partly sup-

ply their own modified definitions to the publics. Idiosyncrasies of a charismatic leader, tactical considerations, and response to heterogeneous membership are among the many influences leading a social movement to establish its own somewhat unique definition of the issue.

THE TENTATIVE PROCESS. This entire development in which crowds and social movements operate within the context of changing publics may be regarded as the tentative process within which new directions of culture and social organization are worked out. The process of working out a dominant major direction of change or of settling on a limited number of contending positions whose dialectic will be a continuing feature of change involves two major groups of developments.

First are the processes centering about the defining of issues and values. To a certain degree accepted statements of values and issues emerge through discussion, as affected by crowd activity and promotion by value-oriented movements. But more generally shifts in values occur obliquely. Changes in the prevalent definitions of issues permit realignments without complete reversals in values among individuals. Similarly, change occurs only partially through clear-cut victories by particular movements. Of more consequence for long-term change is the absorption by contending movements of important parts of the most successful movements' values. Victories of particular movements may be ephemeral. Reactions against overly successful movements set in for a variety of reasons, often creating apparent swings between rival viewpoints. For these reasons the interplay of contending movements might have little consequence for long-range directions of change except that the value-orientations of each of the movements undergoes change. Thus certain issues come to be settled, not by admitted agreement but by moving on to new issues. The value of state support for the aged was established in the United States through acceptance of this principle by the countermovements which effectively defeated the major old-age pension movements of the 1930s. The value of social security became firmly established when the movement that had unsuccessfully opposed it began concentrating its opposition on other matters.

But second, the emerging directions of change may be equally shaped by struggles and alignments to which value questions are secondary. Some movements arise almost exclusively about the efforts of groups to gain control for its own sake. Control movements also develop when the commitment of value-oriented movements to their own persistence and power becomes stronger than their dedication to the values they originally promoted. And movements committed to their own existence may remain after issues to which their values apply have been relegated to the past. Certain value-oriented movements may lose out or gain more than others in the struggle with control movements. Certain values may gain or be discredited by being adopted for tactical purposes by control movements. Separatist movements may draw support away from major value orientation.

In part these two directions represent the mechanisms of change in culture and social organization respectively. Value orientations are direct proposals for alteration of the culture. Issues within publics constitute questions of the relative emphasis or the nature of application of values in the culture. Power orientations, on the other hand, concern social organization. Successful redistribution of power leads to reorganization, with implications for modification of the cultural values bound to accompany the changes.

From the preceding discussion we may summarize the relation of collective behavior to change in the following manner. (1) A certain amount of isolated and sporadic collective behavior characterizes the most stable society and has no important implications for change. It is simply a response to events that fall outside the limits with which the established order and culture are prepared to cope. (2) Widespread collective behavior over a period of time is probably not a sufficient condition to bring about social and cultural change, though it probably always makes the social order more susceptible to change when the necessary ideas and values can be supplied. (3) Widespread collective behavior becomes the major vehicle of change when contact between diverse cultures or developments within the culture supply novel values about which collective behavior can become focused. (4) Collective behavior then becomes the medium through which tentative directions of change are tested until one major direction prevails. (5) Thus collective behavior is an integral part of the process of social and cultural change. It appears probable that broad potential directions of change are predetermined in the very developments of culture and society that originally give rise to the collective behavior, so that the latter is more a process of discovery than of determination. But it is also plausible that details of change and selection among limited alternatives are actually determined in the collective behavior processes, within a range of broadly predetermined directions.

LASTING OR TEMPORARY CHANGE. If collective behavior sometimes produces dramatic effects in the short run—the passage of new laws, the replacement of public officials, popular endorsement of new values—will there be lasting effects? Fletcher Bowron, elected mayor of Los Angeles at the culmination of a broadly based movement to recall the former mayor, complained that he could not carry through many of his intended reforms because the movement dissolved once the recall was successfully completed. The powerful abolition movement was no longer on hand when new patterns were being instituted to maintain white supremacy in the absence of slavery. A great idea is not enough. The power of any idea to mobilize human energy on a massive scale is of limited duration. Nothing is so ineffectual as yesterday's warmed over ideas.

We shall answer the question of lasting effects with four considerations: the relevance of the ideas to social structure, the involvement of vested interests, the prospect of a stable bargaining relationship, and the outcome of the autonomous process of conflict. In each case we assume that collective behavior has been crystallized into an effective social movement whose effects can be either short- or long-lived.

E. J. Hobsbaum presents an account of what he calls *primitive* forms of protest that do not actually bring about changes in the organization of society but merely exact concessions within the existing structure.[8] Robin Hood figures appear in several countries, symbolizing the peasants' frustrations and providing vicarious gratification for them through the troubles their hero causes the ruling class. The Italian Mafia was a sort of countergovernment established outside the law, counterbalancing the power of official agencies; it has parallels in some modern political machines and in the contemporary ghetto organizations that monitor police activities. The city mobs of London in the 1700s were used to exact tribute and periodic concessions from the city fathers. But none of these forms of protest activity was guided by an ideology that included the possibility of changing the organization of authority. Each depended upon continuation of the existing structure as the source of whatever benefits it could gain. So long as a movement's ideas are of this character, its achievements are limited to the immediate gain from a particular encounter.

Tilly observes that these primitive forms of protest, in contrast to modern protest, activate one local communal group against another.[9] Only when protest groups are linked beyond the boundaries of local communities into classes, ethnic groups, age groups, and other broad constituencies are they able to generate a conception of changing the structure of things. Reactionary protest developed historically during the transition from primitive to modern protest. As traditional society was undermined in Europe with the passing of the Middle Ages, protest groups were often organized beyond the bounds of the local community, but their members chiefly demanded a return to their previous condition. Reactionary protest continues today, as segregationists seek a return to the early twentieth-century pattern of race relations and hippies seek restoration of a scheme of life copied from tribal patterns suited to sparsely populated lands. Because reactionary protest refuses to take account of the changed underlying conditions of life, its short-range accomplishments cannot persist,

If a movement's ideas must be neither primitive nor reactionary but attuned to the nature of social structure, it is also true that the movement must have the support of a strong vested interest if its effects are to last. Movements for governmental reform usually have only short-run success because everyone is against corruption, but there is no one class or other segment of the community whose peculiar interests are served by keeping government honest. For this reason the movements with the most lasting effects on society have been those whose constituencies were rising classes and where the connection between the movement's aims and the constituency's self-in-

[8] Eric J. Hobsbaum, *Social Bandits and Primitive Rebels* (New York: The Free Press, 1959).

[9] Charles Tilly, "Collective Violence in European Perspective," in Hugh D. Graham and Ted R. Gurr, eds., *The History of Violence in America: Historical and Comparative Perspectives* (New York: Frederick A. Praeger, Inc., 1969), pp. 4–44.

terest was clearly identified. In 1934 Robert C. Binkley asked whether the new perspective on governmental responsibility ushered in by the New Deal would last.[10] He answered that it could only survive by creating powerful vested interests committed to its maintenance, or legitimating the powers of some existing interests. Subsequent events show that the perspective did last. New Deal legislation legitimated the labor movement and supplied it with the legal basis for stable power. The labor organizations in turn became the most solid constituency for the persisting liberal movement in American politics.

It is still possible for a movement to count on the support of an interest group with considerable disruptive power and yet have no lasting effect on the organization of society because it has nothing to offer in a sustained bargaining exchange. Management representatives had to come to terms with labor and to revise their conception of the rights and duties of management because they needed the work of laborers. Hence, whenever the labor movement could mobilize sufficient power, they could force management to bargain with them, and a pattern for continuing relationships between management and labor was established. But the difficulty that constantly besets black movements is that they have nothing to offer whites in a bargaining exchange to match their disruptive potential. Minority groups that have held a monopoly in some essential occupation have been able to bargain with the community. But the end of the plantation economy and the elimination by automation of many of the "brute" occupations in industry that only blacks could be induced to accept makes it difficult for the white man to see why he needs the black. If enough whites were convinced that society needs the infusion of that quality known as soul, and that only blacks have it, the prospect of a bargain-

ing relationship in which the structure of society is modified to give the black a special place would be brighter.

Finally, most movements that pursue far-reaching change necessarily become embroiled in conflict. The side effects that stem from conflict have much to do with the enduring effect of the movement. We shall not recapitulate the many observations made earlier about the effects of conflict, except to underline once more that distinctive conceptions of reality are generated in the process of confrontation. When conflict is pervasive, enduring, and intense, a strong polarization of positions develops. Each polar position is reinforced by the invention of a complex set of ideas to support it. Thus the genetic concept of racial inferiority was developed as a defense for the white supremacist position. A deep emotional and moral aversion to persons whose opinions identify them with the opposing pole is a barrier to revising and softening extreme opinions. Because conflict evokes deeply moralistic sentiments and because victory is achieved by coercive force, the losers do not view the reforms as legitimate and feel justified in undermining them in whatever ways they can.

The American abolition movement is a striking example of the polarization of views through conflict until the aims of the movement could only be achieved through a bitter civil war. From the time of the Revolution until the mid 1820s, opinion on slavery was divided within the South. Many Southerners believed that slavery was fundamentally wrong and favored its eventual abolition. The invention of the cotton gin made slavery profitable in cotton cultivation, so the defense of slavery became more assertive about the turn of the century. But as the abolition crusade grew, slaveholders were treated as all one kind, and Southerners were not distinguished from slaveholders.

The abolitionist attack finally drove Southerners toward adopting a stern uniformity in

---

10 Robert C. Binkley, "An Anatomy of Revolution," *The Virginia Quarterly Review,* 10 (Oct., 1934), 502–14.

outlook and a program of repressing liberal thought. But their stand was neither passive nor defensive. Beset by hostile criticism and bitter ridicule, they struck back with what were often telling arguments in justification and rebuttal.[11]

It would be difficult to assess how much of the polarized and uniformized opinion in the South was caused by the new profitability of slavery and how much by the conflict with aggressive abolitionists. But history makes it clear that Southerners never accepted the legitimacy of abolition and worked for a whole generation after the Civil War to insure an even deeper entrenchment of white supremacy than there was before. The intense conflict may have been the only way to dislodge the institution of slavery because of the powerful interests it served. But the harvest of conflict was a far more sophisticated set of beliefs and institutions in support of white supremacy than had existed before.

With the ultimate betrayal of the magnificent ideals of the French Revolution under Napoleon, of the Russian Revolution under Stalin, of the Spanish Revolution under Franco, and many similar examples, it is frequently asked why the American Revolution was followed by a stable regime that made a good beginning toward instituting many of the liberties that were unsuccessfully sought in other revolutions. Many scholars believed that the American Revolution was better disciplined and that its constructive outcome was made possible by the absence of unruly mobs so characteristic of Paris. But Gordon Wood shows that mobs in France were not so unruly as formerly supposed and that mobs played a greater part in the American Revolution than is generally advertised. He suggests that the difference lay not in the nature of the mob actions but in the re-

sponse by constituted authority. Popular authority in America was too weak to oppose the mobs effectively and consequently made repeated concessions rather than enter into a fully reciprocal conflict relationship. The constant temporizing of state legislatures in the face of threats to law and order during the years of the confederacy made a mockery of any conception that the state existed to protect the natural rights of individuals. But it did avert the eruption of serious violence on the scale found in many other revolutions. And because the new nation was not bathed in blood and not polarized, a more radical and lasting transformation of the society was possible.

Perhaps the American Revolution was as moderate as it seems, so lacking in the violence and ferocity of the French Revolution, not because it was inherently conservative and unrevolutionary, led by law-abiding men with limited objectives, but rather because it was so unrestrained, so lacking in strong resistance from counterrevolutionary and authoritarian elements, and consequently so successfully revolutionary. Unchecked by any internal opposition, unrestrained by any solid institutional bulwarks, the American Revolutionaries may have ultimately carried themselves further in the transformation of their society, although without the bloodshed or the terror, than even the French Revolutionaries were able to do. For if the American mob was no less a mob because of the absence of effective resistance, was the Revolution any less a revolution?[12]

The Function of Collective Behavior in Stability

As we observe collective behavior in change, we are forced to note that what are the new ideas of one period become the conservative values in a stable era that follows. The change from a new and radical

---

[11] Louis Filler, *The Crusade Against Slavery: 1830–1860* (New York: Harper and Row, Publishers, 1960), pp. 7–8.

[12] Gordon S. Wood, "A Note on Mobs in the American Revolution," *William and Mary Quarterly*, 23, 3rd series (Oct., 1966), 642, see also 635–42.

value to an accepted value that exemplifies the respectable base for a stable order is a gradual one. And the accompanying reduction in the incidence of widespread collective behavior is similarly gradual. But the change is only in part a reduction of collective behavior. It is equally the preservation and transformation of a certain amount of collective behavior, turned now to the purpose of preserving what are coming to be the established patterns. Thus a certain amount of collective behavior is institutionalized, so that it is evoked under conventionalized situations and proceeds within conventionally understood bounds. The processes of the conventionalized crowd, the conventionalized public, and the institutionalized movement, as already discussed, come into play in support of the existing order.

Culturally allowable issues—matters on which there can be disagreement without challenging the fundamental consensus of culture—are resolved through publics under varying degrees of conventionalization. Some follow the highly formalized procedures of an election. Others, less formalized, are constrained to approximate the procedures of an election. Despite varying degrees of formalization, these conventionalized publics are alike in preventing differences of opinion from unduly disrupting the stable order.

The particular services of conventionalized crowds are two. First, the acting crowd may arise within a conventionalized framework to maintain a major value in the culture when the social order is temporarily failing to do so. Vigilante committees that have operated in California and elsewhere have frequently maintained a highly conventionalized pattern, carefully imitating the procedures of an institutionalized court of law. In California the vigilante committee arose in the mid-nineteenth century when the *forms* of standard American legal procedure had been extended to the new state, but the

system itself had not begun to operate properly. The work of the committee hastened the translation of the forms of government into a functioning government.

The acting crowd within a conventional framework is perhaps the exception. But the conventional expressive crowd appears to be a constant accompaniment of any stable social order. The service of the conventional crowd is to revivify the social order, to combat the tendency of the social order to degenerate into an uninspired enactment of daily routines without imagination or sense of purpose. Frequently the established order demands of individuals a marshalling of energy and enthusiasm or courage not required in performance of routine responsibilities. The conventionalized expressive crowd is employed to arouse the necessary enthusiasm or courage. The disregard of personal safety demanded of the Iroquois warrior entering battle is cultivated through an expressive crowd experience that is part of the ritual preceding battle. Through this experience the individual warrior acquires a vital sense of group support and group pressure which permits him to enter battle. The same principle is employed in preparing an athletic team for exceptional effort, in a political rally to make people overcome their conventional reserve about knocking on doors to campaign for a favorite candidate, or in the religious service to prepare people to overcome normal cautiousness in giving their money to a worthy cause.

But even in the performance of more routine tasks, people require a vigorous sense of group identity or morale and a conviction that imbues key values with a religious quality. Conventional expressive crowds are used to establish moods and reinforce convictions that are likely to be lost in daily routine. Thus a sense of purpose and worth in routine activities and a basis for aspiration are supplied.

In a stable order social movements tend to be absorbed into established institutions, to be transformed into independent institutions such as churches and political parties, or to disappear. Power struggles with a limited elite base produce small movements of which the majority of the populace are unaware and whose success will make little difference to the course of the society. Participation-oriented movements offer special satisfactions to minority elements in the society, thus serving as palliatives against the inequities that might otherwise focus discontent against the social order itself. Within conventional bounds, these limited control movements and participation-oriented movements permit occasional redistributions of power and provide substitute satisfactions for frustrated elements, thus assisting in maintaining the social order.

Constant change, discontent, and conflict are characteristic of the most stable order. Hence there will always be new injustices discovered that form the basis for value-oriented movements. But movements will generally concentrate on specific reforms rather than attack the social order in general. In large part this will be the case because a stable order can be more tolerant of dissent and is less likely to define movements as dangerous and revolutionary. Most of the value-oriented movements will be fairly quickly conventionalized within established institutions. There will be movements dealing with religious values, but these will develop and contend within the institutionalized denominations rather than outside of them. Instead of making mass appeals, they will pursue their unique interpretation of faith by trying to convince key elements within the denomination. Similarly, political movements will exist, but they will operate primarily within established political parties. Insofar as movements accept these institutional boundaries to their actions and limit their tactics to those that are acceptable to the established institutions, they operate as conventionalized movements supporting the general social structure and the culture.

Institutionalization may be an effort to maintain certain useful features of a social movement without retaining the movement as a whole. Max Weber's classic discussion of the "routinization of charisma" deals with this type of process.[13] The true charismatic leader is a product of his following: he only acquires charisma as he acquires a vigorous following who then create and give social support to a superhuman image of their leader. The tremendous trust and devotion toward the charismatic leader is an asset to any social order. Consequently there is an attempt to invest various offices of authority with charisma. Through ritual and myth the king acquires, in the eyes of his subjects, some of the superhuman qualities of a genuine charismatic leader with a following devoted to his person rather than to his office. The order can command devotion and spontaneous conformity from the populace to the same degree as such charisma can be carried over from the leader crucial in bringing about change to his successors who maintain the changed order through their institutionalized office. Thus, from Jesus Christ, charisma is passed to his hand-picked disciples, from whom charisma is further passed through the institutional office to the entire line of Roman Catholic Popes. Or the personal charisma of the revolutionary leader, Lenin, is transmitted via his office to his successor, Josef Stalin.

A final feature of all types of collective behavior during periods of stability is their alleged safety valve function. According to this often expressed view, collective behavior is a means of releasing accumulated tensions, letting people express their discontents so as to rid themselves of them. Frequently a stable social order is characterized by occasional or even regular incidents of crowd activity that either attack the established order or contradict the established values. These episodes are followed by acquies-

[13] Max Weber, *The Theory of Social and Economic Organization*, tr. A. M. Henderson and Talcott Parsons, Talcott Parsons, ed. (New York: Oxford University Press, Inc., 1947), pp. 363ff.

cence, as if the steam of rebellion had indeed been expended.

In a classic essay, Max Gluckman calls attention to the widespread existence of "rituals of rebellion" in primitive societies.[14] These are ceremonies, held infrequently, that require the open expression of social tensions that are normally covert in the society. In one example the women, who are normally quite subordinated, assume men's clothing, perform men's tasks, and violate taboos such as obscenity rules. In another example the people enact rebellion and express hatred against their king, who in turn humiliates himself before them. These rituals end with reassertion of the traditional relationships of authority and subordination. By bringing the inevitable tensions in relationships of authority out into the open, giving free rein to their expression, and finally reaffirming the traditional order, rituals of rebellion are thought to renew the unity of the tribe. Gluckman believes that the rituals can serve this purpose only in societies where there is no serious challenge to the system. In Swaziland there are rebels who sometimes challenge the individual occupants of positions of authority but no revolutionaries to challenge the *system* of authority. In Britain, ritual rejection of the queen would not integrate the system because too many Britons resent the entire institution of monarchy. Only where devotion to the system sets limits to the rebellion can the rituals contribute more to unity than to disunity.

Gluckman is cautious about asserting the exact nature of the mechanism through which the rituals foster unity. But the commonest explanation makes use of the idea of catharsis. By the periodic release of stored up resentments, the potential for disruptive conflict is dispelled. There is, however, another way of viewing these episodes and other forms of ritual taboo

violation. Man cannot fully evaluate his own thoughts until he has expressed them in words. He cannot see his own potential actions in perspective until he has overtly engaged in them. During these episodic manifestations of collective behavior, people say openly those things they have vaguely felt and behave in ways they have only expressed in private fantasy. Just as a man may discover when he writes it down that his "great idea" is commonplace, so words and actions often turn out to be quite disappointing when compared with unspoken fantasy. Or a person who is more strongly committed to a particular social system or set of values than he realizes suddenly discovers the strength of his commitment when he witnesses or participates in an attack on them.

From this standpoint such episodic collective behavior is not a process of dispelling tensions by expressing them or of achieving catharsis. It is rather a process of *testing* the group's commitment to their value system by discovering what it is like to have them attacked. The enactment of the role of attacker of values evokes the responsive role of defending the values. In the process of becoming involved in both types of roles the actors discover where their more profound identification lies. By this occasional testing of loyalties and convictions, conventionalized crowd behavior might contribute to stability of the social order.

Thus, in summary, collective behavior has a place both in change and in stability. In stability it helps to maintain a certain fluidity that resists tendencies toward total inflexibility in the social structure. And it helps to maintain some of the vitality and vigor and religious devotion to values that characterize periods of change. Institutional behavior is associated with man's submission to essential routines, but collective behavior is associated with his ideals. The institutionalization of collective behavior helps to weld these two aspects of life together.

[14] Max Gluckman, *Order and Rebellion in Tribal Africa* (New York: The Free Press, 1963), pp. 110–36.

NAME INDEX

SUBJECT INDEX